report topic #5
due Saturday
2012

Action Meets Word

Gropen et. al   Apr 1

skim bkg
- ?'s on general
- co

Monday
topic #4
Naigles+Hoff ans
Fisher+Song

no report
#7

M000316065

For 3113,
Fisher+Song

Action Meets Word

How Children Learn Verbs

EDITED BY
Kathy Hirsh-Pasek
Roberta Michnick Golinkoff

OXFORD
UNIVERSITY PRESS

OXFORD
UNIVERSITY PRESS

Oxford University Press, Inc., publishes works that further
Oxford University's objective of excellence
in research, scholarship, and education.

Oxford   New York
Auckland   Cape Town   Dar es Salaam   Hong Kong   Karachi
Kuala Lumpur   Madrid   Melbourne   Mexico City   Nairobi
New Delhi   Shanghai   Taipei   Toronto

With offices in
Argentina   Austria   Brazil   Chile   Czech Republic   France   Greece
Guatemala   Hungary   Italy   Japan   Poland   Portugal   Singapore
South Korea   Switzerland   Thailand   Turkey   Ukraine   Vietnam

Copyright © 2006 by Oxford University Press, Inc.

Published by Oxford University Press, Inc.
198 Madison Avenue, New York, New York 10016

www.oup.com

First issued as an Oxford University Press paperback, 2010

Oxford is a registered trademark of Oxford University Press

Library of Congress Cataloging-in-Publication Data
Action meets word : how children learn verbs / edited by Kathy Hirsh-Pasek
and Roberta Michnick Golinkoff.
p.   cm.
Includes bibliographical references and index.

ISBN 978-0-19-975371-0
1. Language acquisition.   2. Grammar, Comparative and general—Verb.
I. Hirsh-Pasek, Kathy.   II. Golinkoff, Roberta M.
P118.A174   2005
401'.93—dc22   2005008496

9 8 7 6 5 4 3 2 1

Printed in the United States of America
on acid-free paper

We dedicate this volume to our mothers, Anne and Joan, whose Actions and Words have always been supportive of our endeavors,

to our families (Jeffrey, Josh, Benj, and Mikey; Larry, Jordan, and Allison), who are there for us in many ways . . .

and to all the families and children who dedicated their time to our research so that children could teach adults.

Preface

Word learning has come of age. And just as children take risks at adolescence, the field of word learning has taken a risk by moving into the area of verb acquisition. Adolescents who learn to take careful, socially acceptable risks do so because they have been lucky enough to experience good parenting. Along the way, we have had guidance from some of the best, people whose work and perspective infuses the chapters of this book. Their work has become the backdrop for the field, sometimes in ways that now seem so obvious that their contributions are taken for granted. Of course, we refer to ovarial work by Lila Gleitman, Lois Bloom, Steven Pinker, and Michael Tomasello, who knew that the field of word learning would never mature if it did not move beyond the study of nouns. Ten years ago the field took its first tentative steps with an influential volume on verb learning edited by Michael Tomasello and William Merriman, appropriately called, *Beyond Names for Things*. Look how we've grown!

This volume represents a proliferation of research on this exciting new frontier and expands greatly on what we knew about verb learning a decade ago. Just as Chomsky once said that "language is a window on the mind," verbs provide a window on the relational thinking that makes us human.

There are many to thank for this volume. We thank the authors of these chapters, a wonderfully professional and responsive group. We feel fortunate to be in such company. Readers should recognize, however, that this volume does not represent the full force of the field; as our chapters became finalized, other stimulating research emerged that might well have been included. Thanks also go to our superb laboratory coordinators (Amanda Brandone and Meredith Jones), who allowed us to focus on assembling the volume, and to our graduate students (Shannon Pruden, Rachel Pulverman, Sara Salkind, Julia Parrish, and Weiyi Ma) who read the chapters with us and served as apprentice editors. Undoubtedly, students like these will take the ideas in this volume to the next level, becoming the editors of such a volume ten years hence. Roberta's secretary, Maryanne Bowers, was, as always, invaluable in helping us with every aspect of the book and keeping our lives on track.

Oxford University Press has been a friend to us, welcoming our new projects even in their most incipient, inchoate stages. For this we thank Catharine Carlin, wine connoisseur and editor extraordinaire, and Jennifer Rappaport. Since much of the research appearing in this volume was supported by federal agencies, we collectively thank the National Science Foundation, the National Institutes of Mental Health, and the National Institutes of Child Health and Human Development.

Children and families are at the core of everything we do. Their participation in the studies reported here affords the progress of basic science. Basic science continues to provide us with the foundation for understanding how children learn. It fuels the development of applications that help children reach their linguistic potential. It provides the source for dissemination of scientific knowledge to the families, teachers, and policy makers who have children's best interests at heart. Basic research like that found in this volume illustrates how a phenomenon like language acquisition is complex and multidetermined.

We saved the best for last. Our action-packed families, a source of enduring support, have taught us about the necessity of multitasking. Thank you, Jeff Pasek, for always being there and for being such a great husband to both of us. Your newly acquired expertise in literary contracts gives us a sense of security and the price is right. Larry Ballen, who arrived midstream, is just starting to understand that "bootstrapping" does not refer to something that happens in a shoe store. Life often turns on relational actions.

Mikey, Benj, and Josh Pasek and Allison and Jordan Golinkoff have grown into editors themselves (well, we helped a little). We thank them for teaching us how action meets words.

Contents

Part III When Action Meets Word: Children Learn Their First Verbs

topic #4 — april 1

Part IV How Language Influences Verb Learning: Cross-Linguistic Evidence

Contributors

Dare Baldwin
Department of Psychology
1227 University of Oregon
Eugene, OR 97405

Douglas A. Behrend
Department of Psychology
University of Arkansas
Fayetteville, AR 72701

Jui Bhagwat
Department of Human
   Development
G38 MVR Hall
Cornell University
Ithaca, NY 14853

Camille W. Brune
Department of Psychiatry
University of Chicago
5841 S. Maryland Avenue, MC3077
Chicago, IL 60637

Jennifer Sootsman Buresh
Department of Psychology
University of Chicago

5848 S. University Avenue
Chicago, IL 60637

Marianella Casasola
Department of Human Development
G38 MVR Hall
Cornell University
Ithaca, NY 14853

Jane B. Childers
Department of Psychology
One Trinity Place
Trinity University
San Antonio, TX 78212-7200

Soonja Choi
Department of Linguistics and Oriental
   Languages
San Diego State University
5500 Campanile Drive
San Diego, CA 92182

Morten H. Christiansen
Department of Psychology
Cornell University
Ithaca, NY 14853

Kim T. Ferguson
Department of Human
  Development
G38 MVR Hall
Cornell University
Ithaca, NY 14853

Cynthia Fisher
Department of Psychology
University of Illinois
Champaign, IL 61820

James N. Forbes
Department of Psychology and
  Sociology
Angelo State University
ASU Station #10907
San Angelo, TX 76909

Dedre Gentner
Department of Psychology
Northwestern University
633 Clark Street
Evanston, IL 60208

Roberta Michnick Golinkoff
School of Education
University of Delaware
Newark, DE 19716

D. Geoffrey Hall
Department of Psychology
University of British Columbia
2136 West Mall
Vancouver, BC V6T 1Z4
Canada

Etsuko Haryu
Graduate School of Education
University of Tokyo
7-3-1, Hongo, Bunkyo-ku
Tokyo 113-0033
Japan

Kathy Hirsh-Pasek
Department of Psychology
1801 N. Broad Street
Temple University
Philadelphia, PA 19122

Erika Hoff
Department of Psychology
Florida Atlantic University
2912 College Avenue
Davie, FL 33314

Derek Houston
Department of Otolaryngology—
  Head and Neck Surgery
Indiana University School of Medicine
699 West Drive/RR 044
Indianapolis, IN 46202

Mutsumi Imai
Keio University at Shonan-Fujisawa
5322 Endo, Fujisawa
Kanagawa 252-8520
Japan

Alan W. Kersten
Department of Psychology
Florida Atlantic University
Boca Raton, FL 33431-0991

Tracy A. Lavin
Department of Psychology
Northwestern University
2029 Sheridan Rd.
Evanston, IL 60208

Li Lianjing
International Office
Renmin University of China
No. 59, Zhongguancun Street
Haidian DIST
Beijing 100872
P. R. China

Jeffrey Lidz
Department of Linguistics
University of Maryland
College Park, MD 20742

Jeffery T. Loucks
Department of Psychology
1227 University of Oregon
Eugene, OR 97405

Mandy J. Maguire
School of Behavioral and Brain
    Sciences
University of Texas—Dallas/Callier
    Center
1966 Inwood Road
Dallas, TX 75235

Jean M. Mandler
Department of Cognitive
    Science—0515
University of California
    San Diego
9500 Gilman Drive
La Jolla, CA 92093-0515

Toben H. Mintz
Department of Psychology
SGM 501, MC-1061
University of Southern California
Los Angeles, CA 90089-1061

Padraic Monaghan
Department of Psychology
University of York
York YO10 5DD
UK

Letitia R. Naigles
Department of Psychology
University of Connecticut
406 Babbidge Road, U-20
Storrs, CT 06269-1020

Thierry Nazzi
Laboratoire Cognition et
    Développement
CNRS—Université René Descartes
71 Avenue Edouard Vaillant
92100 Boulogne Billancourt
France

Hiroyuki Okada
Tokai University, School of Science
1117, Kitakaname, Hiratsuka-shi
Kanagawa-ken 259-1292
Japan

Diane Poulin-Dubois
Centre for Research in Human
    Development
Department of Psychology (PY-170)
Concordia University
7141 Sherbrooke Street West
Montréal, Québec H4B 1R6
Canada

Shannon Pruden
Temple University Infant Laboratory
580 Meetinghouse Road
Ambler, PA 19002

Rachel Pulverman
Department of Psychology
University of Michigan
530 Church Street
Ann Arbor, MI 48109

Sara J. Salkind
School of Education
University of Delaware
Newark, DE 19716

Jason Scofield
College of Human Environmental
    Sciences
University of Alabama
Tuscaloosa, AL 35487

Jun Shigematsu
Keio University at Shonan-Fujisawa
5322, Endo, Fujisawa-shi
Kanagawa-ken 252-0816
Japan

Linda B. Smith
Department of Psychology
Indiana University
1101 E. Tenth Street
Bloomington, IN 47405

Hyun-joo Song
Department of Psychology
University of Illinois
Champaign, IL 61820

Twila Tardif
Department of Psychology and
    Center for Human Growth
    and Development
University of Michigan
300 North Ingalls, 10th Floor
Ann Arbor, MI 48109-0406

Michael Tomasello
MPI EVAN
Deutscher Platz 6
04103 Leipzig
Germany

Sandra R. Waxman
Department of Psychology
Northwestern University
2029 Sheridan Road
Evanston, IL 60208

Amanda Woodward
Department of Psychology
University of Chicago
5848 S. University
    Avenue
Chicago, IL 60637

Hanako Yoshida
Department of Psychology
Indiana University
1101 E. Tenth Street
Bloomington, IN 47405

Action Meets Word

Introduction: Progress on the Verb Learning Front

Roberta Michnick Golinkoff and
Kathy Hirsh-Pasek

The time for *action* is now. It's never too late to do something.
—Antoine de Saint-Exupery

This is a world of *action*, and not for moping and droning in.
—Charles Dickens

When I was kidnapped, my parents snapped into *action*. They rented out my room.
—Woody Allen

As the quotations above suggest, action is central to life—and central to language. It is through action that we carry out our thoughts and plans. But we don't just *act*; we talk about action, too, from the toddler commenting on his own actions (e.g., "Me run!") to the adult commenting sarcastically on the unseen actions of others (e.g., "She said she went to Brazil but she really went to Brooklyn"). While not all verbs capture action per se, some events elicit many more verbs of action than others, as when we watch a football game or a tennis match. Verbs allow us to talk about the relationships that exist between the objects and individuals in our lives. Without verbs, we would be unable to specify just what took place between Sally, the brick, and John. At the critical juncture between words and grammar lies the frontier of verb learning. Until recently, however, the study of how young children learn how to talk about action has taken a back seat to how they talk about the objects found in their world. Arguably, the study of verb learning is the study of language learning. This volume signals the progress we have made in entering this frontier and appropriately elevating the expression of action to its central position in language learning.

3

What Is a Verb?

Verbs are the architectural centerpiece of the grammar, determining the argument structure of a sentence. Verbs can be defined syntactically or semantically. Syntactically, a verb is a word that takes a subject (or agent) or an object or both. Verbs, for example, can take different morphological forms based on gender, person, number, animacy, and indefiniteness, and they can be passivized or dativized in many languages. Semantically, verbs are words that "encode events: A cover term for states or conditions of existence . . . processes or unfoldings . . . and actions or executive processes" (Frawley, 1992, p. 141). A verb is a description of a relation that occurs over time. However, verbs are not the only syntactic categories that express action and events, and this surely complicates the child's verb learning task! As Lidz points out in chapter 16, one can comment on events by using a noun, as in "The race was exciting," or an adjective, as in "The birds are noisy today." In general, however, the first relational terms are verbs and the first verbs are motion verbs. If verbs exist in the vocabulary of young children from the outset,[1] why has noun acquisition has been the dominant focus for the field? Why did the study of verbs fail to capture most researchers' interests (but see Bloom, Lightbown, & Hood, 1975; Gleitman, 1990) while the study of nouns took center stage?

For early researchers in language acquisition, nouns offered a good foundation for studying word learning for a number of reasons. First, nouns appeared to be more predominant in the child's first 50 words (Fenson et al., 1994; Goldin-Meadow, Seligman, & Gelman, 1976). (Some might argue that even that claim was ethnocentric or limited to Western Indo-European languages; e.g., Tardif, 1996.) Second, and importantly, nouns are learned quickly and easily compared to other types of words (e.g., chapters 12 and 17). Thus, for both researchers and children, nouns offered a convenient and tractable toehold into the word-learning system.

Although the literature on nouns shaped theories of word learning, some heralded the importance of studying verbs (Bloom, Lifter, & Hafitz, 1980; Landau & Gleitman, 1985). Further, two influential articles appeared that jolted the field and moved it forward, chastising researchers in early word learning for their myopic attention to nouns (Bloom, Tinker, & Margulies, 1993; Nelson, 1988). Both articles pointed out that the field was studying word learning qua noun learning, despite the fact that children's early vocabularies included diverse word types. In response, researchers started to branch out and investigate other form classes including adjectives (Waxman & Klibanoff, 2000) and verbs (Tomasello & Merriman, 1995). Importantly, the initial focus on nouns and the call to include verbs set us on a trajectory that focused on word learning as it developed within particular syntactic categories. This lens often obscured our study of lexical acquisition in general. Thus, as the field progressed, we attempted to understand the development of nouns or of verbs or of adjectives, rather than finding a more global and comprehensive theory of word learning.

Are Verbs Really Harder to Learn Than Nouns?

A classic and influential article by Gentner (1982) makes this point. Gentner posits that verbs pose special challenges for word learners. Verbs label events that are comprised of components like manner (*walk* vs. *swagger*), instrument (*hammer, shovel*), path (*ascend, descend*), and result (*open, break*)—any of which can be the dominant focus for the label (Talmy, 1985). Further, across languages, different components are highlighted such that *manner* is often conflated in English verbs (e.g., *skip*), while *path* is often an integral part of Spanish verbs (e.g., *ascendere*; see Slobin, 2001, or Talmy, 2000, for reviews).

Verbs also describe events in the world and events are by nature more ephemeral than the objects that nouns tend to label (Langacker, 1987; Slobin, 2001). Furthermore, in speech to children, verbs often label these events even *before* the action has taken place (Tomasello & Kruger, 1992), while nouns tend to label enduring entities available for prolonged inspection. Another difference between nouns and verbs is that nouns have a tendency to have more restricted meanings than do verbs. For example, the average dictionary entry for the noun *ball* has only two definitions, while the verb *run* has a dramatic 53 entries, all under the verb classification (Pickett et al., 2000). Finally, verbs are inherently relational; the use of a verb implies the presence of an actor to carry out that action. These factors (and more—see Golinkoff, Jacquet, Hirsh-Pasek, & Nandakumar, 1996) suggest that verbs are harder to learn than nouns.

Indeed, in the last 10 years both word count studies and experimental studies of language acquisition support the claim that nouns and verbs are learned and processed quite differently. Overall, this work has largely affirmed the noun bias in early word learning and has supported the claim that verbs seem more difficult to learn than nouns.

Are Verbs Really Harder to Learn Than Nouns? The Evidence

Goldin-Meadow, Seligman, and Gelman (1976) were the first to note that children's productive vocabularies were overwhelmingly composed of nouns. Gentner's 1982 article spawned even more work in this area as a flurry of studies literally counted the number of nouns and verbs in children's vocabularies. Gentner's original work collected data from six languages (English, German, Japanese, Kaluli, Mandarin Chinese, and Turkish) and concluded that nouns were the largest and earliest class of words to be acquired, with verbs lagging behind. Other studies in Spanish (Jackson-Maldonado, Thal, Marchman, Bates, & Gutierrez-Clellen, 1993), Italian (Caselli et al., 1995), and French (Bassano, 2000; Parisse & Le Normand, 2000; Poulin-Dubois, Graham, & Sippola, 1995), among other languages, affirmed this finding. The most recent large-scale study that counted nouns and verbs looked at the relative prevalence of word classes across comparable 20-month-old children from seven countries (Bornstein et al., 2004). Using the Early Language Inventory (a precursor of the CDI), 269 families participated in research that controlled for a number of factors including family income, birth order, and whether they lived in an urban or a rural area. Results suggest that the early vocabularies of children evidence more nouns than verbs in Spanish, Dutch, French, Hebrew, Italian, Korean, and American English. Thus, even when the method of data collection was controlled and the sample sizes were large, there seems to be a substantial noun bias. Though most of the comparison of noun and verb acquisition has occurred in the word-counting studies, experimental studies also show the relative difficulty in learning verbs as opposed to nouns. One particularly interesting example comes from what Gleitman and her colleagues refer to as the "human simulation" project (Gillette, Gleitman, Gleitman, & Lederer, 1999; Snedeker & Gleitman, 2004). In these studies, adults viewed a series of video clips of a mother and child playing. A beep occurred coincident with either the missing noun or verb. Participants guessed what word the speaker might have used at that point. The findings in these studies were dramatic. Adults, who presumably had no conceptual difficulties with the objects and events represented on the tapes, correctly guessed the missing nouns in 45% of the cases. Their proportion correct for guessing the verbs, however, was a paltry 15%. In fact, if one looked solely at responses for the verbs representing mental actions, the proportion of correct verb guesses dropped to zero! These results demonstrate that mapping from word to action is considerably more challenging than from word to object. There is a lesson in these studies on the difficulty of verb learning given that the participants were adults and the task was one of simply mapping known verbs to events.

For children learning a novel verb, the verb disadvantage appears to be even more pronounced. A number of investigators have found that verbs are harder to learn than nouns for a variety of reasons, including a preference to attach a new word to an unknown object rather than to its unknown action (chapters 12 and 19; Childers & Tomasello, 2002; Kersten & Smith, 2002), a preference for labeling simple actions over complex actions (chapter 14), and a preference for labeling actions of the self over the actions of others (Huttenlocher, Smiley, & Charney, 1983). Importantly, this noun advantage is not limited to English, where verbs appear in a disadvantaged position in the middle of the sentence, but also holds true for languages such as Japanese and Chinese, where verbs can appear in isolation or at the end of the sentence (chapter 18; Tardif, 1996). Cross-linguistic experimental research in both Japanese and Chinese supports the claim that children are worse at mapping and extending labels to verbs than nouns (chapter 17; Imai, Haryu, & Okada, 2005) even at the age of five and later! Thus, even in those languages that are thought to have a verb advantage, children struggle with verbs for years after they have mastered noun learning in seemingly identical situations.

Interestingly, there is a convergence in the neurological evidence. Studies have described a dissociation between the processing of nouns and verbs (Caramazza

& Hillis, 1991; Goodglass & Kaplan, 1983; Hillis & Caramazza, 1995; McCarthy & Warrington, 1985; Miceli, Silveri, Nocentini, & Caramazza, 1988; Miceli, Silveri, Villa, & Caramazza, 1984; Saffran, Berndt, & Schwartz, 1989; Thompson, Lange, Schneider, & Schapiro, 1997). However, while it may be the case that nouns and verbs are processed differently in the adult brain, in early acquisition the distinction between nouns and verbs may not be that clear. There may be a better way to explain these data other than appeal to form class.

Is It Really Nouns Versus Verbs?

The data seem clear. Nouns are easier to process than verbs. But is the distinction really between these syntactic form classes, or do the differences in learning across form classes represent a more general division in the types of concepts that words represent? That is, the relevant distinction may not be between nouns and verbs per se but rather between concepts that are more or less abstract and relational. Gentner and Boroditsky (2001) and Snedeker and Gleitman (2004) first mentioned this alternative, and Maguire et al. (in press) have developed the argument even further. Nouns and verbs might be better thought of as falling on a continuum defined by the concreteness (or imageability or individuability or shape; see Maguire et al., in press) of the named concept. At the "easy" end of the continuum are the words that children learn early—nouns like *shoe* and *car* and verbs like *kiss* and *eat*. At the "difficult" end, however, are words for concepts that are less perceptually tied and less bound to context. So nouns like *uncle* (part of the kinship system) and *passenger* (a relation an individual has with respect to a vehicle) and verbs like *imagine* and *believe* (that require an understanding of theory of mind) will both be learned late.

The prediction this view makes is that children should first learn the names of concrete objects and of actions that are visible and part of routines. It also predicts that because verbs in general are inherently relational and capture ephemeral events, they are further along that continuum and should be on the whole learned somewhat later than nouns. This prediction also suggests that, as Gleitman (1990) and Gentner and Boroditsky (2001) pointed out, when verb meanings are dependent on the linguistic system in which they are embedded for their meanings, they will be harder to learn. Second, when young children are said to have verbs in their vocabularies, the meanings of these verbs might be somewhat impoverished. They might not rise to the relational level that they do in adults (Gallivan, 1988; Theakston, Lieven, Pine, & Rowland, 2002).

Whether this view is correct or not, the important point is this: The very fact that a debate has emerged about whether there is a distinction between nouns and verbs or between concrete and abstract words is a sign of progress made in the area of verb learning. In the last ten years, aspects of verb learning not previously considered have come to the fore.

Verb Learning Is on the Move

Another way to gauge progress in the area of verb learning (or word learning in general) is to compare this volume with its precursor. In 1995, Tomasello and Merriman (hereafter referred to as TM) edited the first compendium on verb learning, *Beyond Names for Things: Young Children's Acquisition of Verbs*. That volume was a capstone for the burgeoning interest in verb learning. The TM volume had three sections: "Early Words for Action," "Basic Principles of Verb Learning," and "The Role of Argument Structure." In "Early Words for Action," there were three chapters, each using observational data to study verb learning. The last ten years have added to that database, yielding many studies that probe verb learning in the laboratory. Although there is no substitute for good observational data, moving the study of verb learning to the lab also has its advantages. First among these advantages is that laboratory research permits manipulation of the factors putatively involved in verb learning, allowing us to gain insight into the *process* of verb learning. Furthermore, laboratory studies allow us to uncover the meanings of the verbs children use by systematically studying their extension.

In the second section of TM's work, "Basic Principles of Word Learning," five chapters discussed either the fast mapping of verb meanings, building on related work with nouns or the social and discourse contexts in which verbs are learned. In 1995, inclusion of the effects of social context and discourse represented an advance. By 2005, the fact that multiple factors play a role in verb learning seems commonplace. Indeed, there have been many calls for a multifactor theory of word learning (Karmiloff-Smith, 1992; Woodward & Markman, 1998; etc.). For example, the emergentist coalition model (ECM; Hollich et al., 2000; Maguire et al., in press; Poulin-Dubois & Forbes, in press) posits a word learner who is influenced by perceptual, social, and linguistic cues in establishing reference for a new term. Furthermore, these factors are weighted in development such that word learning is first influenced by the perceptual salience of the concepts words encode, then by the social factors that help establish a referent and refine word meaning, and finally by linguistic information that children were not able to use earlier in the process, such as the frames surrounding the verb. The recognition that verb learning (and word learning in general) is a product of numerous factors is pervasive in this book.

Finally, research continues apace on the topic of the third section of the TM volume, "The Role of Argument Structure" (see chapters 13, 15). New research is teasing apart the elements in the sentence surrounding a verb that children exploit to extract the verb's meaning. For example, young children seem to be sensitive to argument number as a clue to meaning (chapters 15 and 16; Hirsh-Pasek, Golinkoff, & Naigles, 1996) as well as to the noun phrase position (e.g., Fisher, Hall, Rakowitz, & Gleitman, 1994).

The volume edited by TM filled a significant gap in language acquisition research at the time. Furthermore, by its inclusion of appealing and pioneering work, it implicitly invited new researchers to contribute to the area. Work described in that volume continues, and some of the same researchers appear in this one. However, our new understanding of the process of verb learning allows us to divide this book into four different sections, three of which could not have been included 10 years ago. Although we are just breaking through the verb learning frontier, we can now talk about four preliminary tasks (Golinkoff, Chung, et al., 2002) that children must conquer to master the verb system in any language. These tasks mirror the sections that appear in this volume. First, children must be able to locate the verb in the stream of speech. Second, infants must attend to, individuate, and form categories of actions in their environment. In other words, they must find ways to conceptualize actions and events. Third, children must be able to *map* words to actions and action categories. And fourth, they must map verbs to actions in language specific ways, as languages differ in the kinds of meanings they conflate in their verbs (Talmy, 1985). Next we discuss the organization of the volume and why these four sections fall out of the work currently being conducted in the field.

Organization of This Volume

Our goal for *Action Meets Word: How Children Learn Verbs* was to provide readers with a volume that might impact the field, serving as a heuristic and spurring researchers on to grapple with questions raised in its pages. The four parts of the volume contain chapters that focus on key issues in verb learning.

Part I. Prerequisites to Verb Learning: Finding the Verb

The first task children face in learning verbs is to locate the verb in the stream of speech. Since 1995 when TM's book was published, the field has exploded with studies of how infants find units in the speech stream, through the use of metrical information such as word stress (Jusczyk, 1997), statistical and distributional computations (Saffran, Aslin, & Newport, 1996), and even the phonological properties of frequently heard names (Bortfeld, Morgan, Golinkoff, & Rathbun, 2005). Finding the verb in the stream of speech does not mean that infants label it as such, or that, at first, they even recognize that the verb refers to an event. Yet, without this discovery, verb learning could not proceed.

How do children find the verb? Christiansen and Monaghan in chapter 3 make a useful distinction between the kinds of cues children might use to find verbs in sentences, a distinction that seems to be adopted implicitly by all the chapters in this section. *Language-internal* cues include "aspects of phonological, prosodic, and distributional information that indicate the relation of various parts of language to each other," while *language-external* cues refer to the correlations between language and the world. Clearly, as pointed out by Gleitman (1990), language-external cues cannot be sufficient for locating the verb or discerning its meaning. This leaves us to determine which language-internal cues (prosodic, distributional, or phonological) children rely on to find the verbs in sentences.

Of the three chapters in this section, each takes a slightly different tack in their attempt to uncover how babies find the verb. In chapter 1, Mintz discusses distributional evidence in the form of what he calls "frames" for finding the verb. In Mintz's words, "the general hypothesis is that words of the same grammatical form-class category (e.g., noun, verb, adjective, etc.) occur in similar distributional patterns across utterances, and that this information could be a basis for learners to identify verbs as well as other categories." To see whether frames could help babies find verbs, Mintz reports a frequent frame analysis of six corpora of child-directed speech conducted computationally and shows that these frames yield a high degree of predictability for a word's form class. For example, a large number of verbs occur in the frame "you . . . it," suggesting that if babies could exploit these regularities, they would be on their way to verb identification. Mintz finds that by 12 months—an age not far from the 13.5 months Nazzi and Huston suggested—babies are able to extract the category of verb from the input. Babies seem to expect verbs to appear in certain frames. Although Mintz is cautious about interpreting his findings as strictly supporting infants' use of frames, his analysis of how infants use nonadjacent dependencies to categorize elements (although not how to label those elements as "verb") is provocative. Mintz fully recognizes, however, that there are often correlated cues available in the input (such as bigram frequency and phonological information) and that it is too soon to know what babies actually rely on to find the verbs in the stream of speech.

Chapter 2, by Nazzi and Houston, is an excellent review of how babies segment speech into nouns using prosodic and phonological cues, with a frank admission that the work on verbs is just beginning. These authors trace infants' transformation from language generalist to language specialist as infants discover the properties of their native language. In particular, they discuss research on how infants might zero in on the acoustic correlates of the word classes of noun and verb. They describe how verbs are at a disadvantage (at least in English) from the start because of their "shorter durations, lower frequency of appearing in syntactic/prosodic constituent-final positions, and predominant stress pattern being the opposite of that of the majority of English words." Nazzi and Huston report that verbs are isolated from the speech stream by 13.5 months, about 6 months later than when babies isolate nouns.

Finally, Christiansen and Monaghan embrace a multiple-cues approach and try to evaluate the usefulness of one family of cues over others. They perform computational analyses on two sets of child-directed corpora and come to the conclusion that the set of cues a child might use to identify nouns is different than the set of cues used to identify verbs. For verbs, phonological cues might be required to draw together a coherent lexical category. For nouns, distributional cues rather than phonological cues may prove sufficient. However, nothing is simple. The authors identify 16 different types of phonological cues that operate at the word level as well as at the syllable and phoneme level. Whether children rely mainly on distributional cues, as Mintz argues, or acoustic correlates of form class, as Nazzi and Houston and Christiansen and Monaghan suggest, or both, is clearly an issue that must be resolved empirically. Furthermore, as predicted by a model like the ECM (Hollich et al., 2000), the extraction of form classes from the speech stream may be a moving target in that cues that are useful for verb segmentation in the first year of life may yield to other cues in the second year of life once the child has some language. At that point, language-external cues may become useful as well.

Part II. Prerequisites to Verb Learning: Finding Actions in Events

The second task that children must solve to learn a verb is finding individual actions in events. Verbs are about events and infants must attend to and individuate actions in their environment. Research suggests that infants are keenly aware of movement and use movement to individuate objects (e.g., Mandler, 1992a, 1998, 2004) and actions (Sharon & Wynn, 1998; Wynn, 1996) and even to predict action outcomes (Wagner & Carey, 2005). However, just as finding a verb is not enough, finding the action is not enough: infants must also be able to form categories of action without language. The action of jumping, for example, refers to a decontextualized category of jumping motions that include different kinds of jumps made by the same actor (e.g., Elmo jumping off tables and chairs), and the same action performed by different actors (e.g., Elmo jumping off the chair and Lala jumping off the chair). Language's efficiency in communication is rooted in the fact that we do not need a new label for each nonidentical instance of an action. Importantly, finding actions is itself only a beginning as verbs label relations that go well beyond attention to only action or movement.

The seven chapters in this section of the volume could not have been written in 1995 when the first volume on verb learning was published. At that time, there was a large amount of work on infants' categorization of objects in the world (e.g., Oakes & Rakison, 2003, for a review) that dovetailed well with the field's focus on noun learning. However, other than work on object permanence that involved dynamic events and some studies on support (e.g., Keil, 1994), causation (e.g., Cohen & Oakes, 1993), and discrimination of action roles in events (Golinkoff, 1975; Golinkoff & Kerr, 1978), studies on concepts foundational to verb use were few and far between. Only Choi and her colleagues (e.g., Choi & Bowerman, 1991; Choi, McDonough, Bowerman, & Mandler, 1999) conducted research on how infants conceptualized dynamic spatial events encoded in verbs in Korean.

Mandler's (1992a, 1992b) work stimulated researchers to consider using the framework of the cognitive linguists (Langacker, 1987; Talmy, 1985) to conceptualize how infants viewed events and how that knowledge interfaced with language learning. In chapter 4, Mandler takes the position that "actions are central in organizing the beginning conceptual system" and that a list of prelinguistic primitives (or for Mandler, "image-schemas") is needed to understand how infants acquire their first verbs. Since, depending on the language, either verbs or prepositions are used to encode dynamic relations, she prefers to use the term *relational words*. Her review of the research from her own lab and others leads her to the conclusion that children are in possession of the foundations for verb learning by the end of the first year of life. By Mandler's reading of the research, for example, infants know about the fact that actions are goal directed and related to other actions when actions are causal. Furthermore, actions can result in many spatial outcomes such as fitting *tightly* or *loosely*.

The chapters that follow by Pulverman, Hirsh-Pasek, Golinkoff, Pruden, and Salkind; Casasola, Bhagwat, and Ferguson; and Choi fit beautifully with Mandler's chapter as they investigate questions about children's conceptual base prior to verb learning. The relationship between language and thought is a fundamental issue that runs through these chapters and one that will require a good deal more research to sort out. The Pulverman et al. chapter evaluates whether difficulty in analyzing and conceptualizing nonlinguistic events contributes to the documented difficulty in verb learning (see also chapters 14 and 21; Imai et al., 2005). In particular, research is reported from our labs on two semantic components of nonlinguistic events: *path*, or the trajectory of an action with respect to a ground (e.g., above or under a ball), and *manner*, or how the action is performed (e.g., jumping and running are different manners) (e.g., Pulverman, Sootsman, Golinkoff, & Hirsh-Pasek, 2003; Pruden, Hirsh-Pasek, Maguire, & Meyer, 2004; Salkind, Golinkoff, & Brandone, 2005). Their findings suggest not only that infants discriminate between events based on these components but that they are capable of forming some *categories* of events along these lines. Furthermore, there is a relationship between infants' ability to see certain distinctions in nonlinguistic events and their level of language development. They conclude, much as Mandler did, that infants can look *within* motion events to find the primitives that form the basis for verb learning and can even form categories based on these primitives.

Chapter 6, by Casasola, Bhagwat, and Ferguson, also has as its focus infants' understanding of motion events and, in particular, how language shapes organization and understanding of these events in the manner required for linguistic expression. They, too, explore events in which manner and path are varied and find sensitivity to these distinctions before much language is acquired. In addition, they report on research (similar to Choi & Bowerman, 1991; Hespos & Spelke, 2004) in which infants are familiarized with the spatial relation of containment. Both 10- and 18-month-old infants reared in English-speaking environments are capable of forming this category. However, not all categories relevant to language may be formed early and/or without language. Casasola et al. provide evidence that the superimposition of language itself may play a pivotal role in highlighting categories for infants that will be relevant to the learning of relational words (see Casasola, 2005; Waxman & Markow, 1995; Yoshida & Smith, 2005). The mechanism by which this effect occurs begs for more research.

Chapter 7, by Choi, addresses several key questions about the relationship between category formation and language in the domain of the same spatial concepts Mandler and Casasola et al. discuss in chapters 4 and 6. Choi's work is directed at understanding the kinds of spatial categories that are formed preverbally and how these interact with the language-specific semantic categories that will later be expressed as either verbs (in Korean) or prepositions (in English). Choi's data bear on the question of whether there is a universal conceptual core. To address these fundamental issues, Choi used the intermodal preferential looking paradigm (Golinkoff, Hirsh-Pasek, Cauley, & Gordon, 1987; Hirsh-Pasek & Golinkoff, 1996) with Korean- and English-reared babies of various ages. Since Korean cuts up the categories of *in* and *on* differently than English, these two languages make excellent test cases. Choi's results fit with those of Casasola et al. and Hespos and Spelke (2004), who report that containment relations seem to be understood at an early age while support relations, possibly because they are more heterogenous, are more difficult for children to learn.

The rest of the chapters in this section are concerned with how children find the action in an event and when and whether they use the actor or speaker's intention as a cue to locating and identifying an action. In chapter 8, Buresh, Woodward, and Brune ask whether children analyze events for their meanings or whether they focus on more superficial perceptual aspects of events. In addition, they probe whether infants are aware of what other people attend to in the environment. They report that infants do not begin their action analysis with the general expectation that human actions are goal directed. However, by the end of the first year, babies are capable of flexible action analysis in situations with highly familiar actions like grasping. The authors then examine the way children use action words in situ and conclude that the emergence of well-organized action representations precedes their expression in verbs by about a year. They point out that "having an organized idea does not automatically provide a word meaning," a conclusion similar to that reached by the authors of chapter 9, Loucks and Baldwin. Loucks and Baldwin are concerned with the same question that Buresh et al. pose. Do infants focus on superficial, perceptual aspect of events, or do they analyze what they see in conceptual ways? They review their work on how infants (and adults) find units in the stream of action in the world, units that will have relevance for the learning of verbs. For example, consider a scene of someone working in her kitchen and picking up a fallen dish towel. How should this scene be divided into units? Loucks and Baldwin raise the possibility that action analysis can actually be hierarchical, analogous to the organization of language. Thus, it can occur at a number of levels, from noting rapid changes in movement or what they call *featural information* (e.g., a unit might occur when the woman bends to pick up the towel), to analyzing the inferred intentions of the actors or what they call *configural information*, or global relations among motion elements (e.g., she wanted to rehang the towel). They go on to consider how infants form categories of action, relying on the established literature on face processing as a guide to the questions research might consider. Although more questions are raised than Loucks and Baldwin can answer, their findings and speculations are relevant to the way in which language influences event segmentation because different languages seem to parse events at different levels of generality.

The final chapters in this section, chapter 10 by Poulin-Dubois and Forbes and chapter 11 by Behrend and Scofield, increase the grain size of our analysis by asking how children's cognitive, social, and linguistic abilities interact to enable them to analyze action in events and learn novel verbs. Both chapters focus on the role that understanding the intention of the actor and speaker plays in learning verbs. Poulin-Dubois and Forbes conclude that "infants not only are competent in discriminating human actions and object motion but also understand that many different agents are capable of performing the same actions by the beginning of the second year." However, these achievements are insufficient for verb learning and extension because toddlers must become aware of the intentions of the actor. Borrowing from the ECM (Hollich et al., 2000), Poulin-Dubois and Forbes conclude that verb learning and extension first occur based on a superficial perceptual analysis of how the action looks, followed by learning and extension based more on what the actor intends to do.

Chapter 11 is also concerned with how children interpret the intentions of others and how that effects their judgment about which action is the referent of a novel verb label. Behrend and Scofield turn the sensitivity to actor and speaker intent on its head, studying the effects of whether labeling an action influences whether children interpret the action as either accidental or intentional. By the time children are learning verbs, they need to be sensitive to whether, for example, an intended action was completed or failed. And children must learn the distinction between intended action (as in the verb *pour*) versus accidental action (as in *spill*). The authors conclude that information about an actor's stated intentions helps children learn novel verbs at least by three years of age. They reach the interesting conclusion that a recursive relation exists between understanding intention and learning verbs. They write, "children can bootstrap their way into the verb lexicon as a result of their early understanding of language and intentions, and then they can use their growing competencies with verbs to help them further refine their understanding of actors' intentions."

Part III. When Action Meets Word: Children Learn Their First Verbs

The first two sections of the volume are primarily concerned with the underpinnings implicated in verb learning. This section addresses how children map words to actions and action categories. The fact that infants have action words among their first words is testimony to the fact that they can successfully form some word-action mappings (e.g., Bloom, 1993; Smith & Sachs, 1990). Since the TM volume appeared in 1995, there is much more work on the fast mapping of verbs and the factors that influence verb learning and extension. It is still unclear, however, what specific parameters guide the extension of action labels to action categories. Furthermore, the chapters in this section harken back to the chapters in part II. Even if nonlinguistic studies suggest that children are able to form categories of action, we still need to explain why children have such difficulty learning and extending new verbs. Several of the chapters in this section attempt to do just that.

This part of the book has four chapters that address a range of questions on the factors that influence first verb learning. Chapter 12, by Childers and Tomasello, addresses the way in which novel verbs are presented and how factors like number of exposures, time between exposures, and number of models influences verb learning. The authors also enter the debate about whether nouns are easier to learn than verbs by controlling a number of variables neglected in prior studies. For example, they controlled for the frames in which nouns and verbs were presented, created stimuli where both objects (labeled with nouns) and actions (labeled with verbs) were both moving, and where self or other was the actor of the action. Under a range of manipulations, verbs were indeed harder to learn than nouns. Indeed, children who had no trouble in a nonverbal condition remembering and understanding an action still had trouble learning a name for it! Their findings in this study support the view that "noun learning is more robust and less vulnerable to variations in presentations than is verb learning."

Naigles and Hoff in chapter 13 are concerned with these "variations in presentations" presented in chapter 12. However, they construe these variations in terms of the nature of the linguistic input to the child as opposed to the number of times and over what days children hear a verb linguistically instantiated. They are interested not just in learning but in what factors allow children to extend a verb meaning to a new situation. While limits to extendability have been well documented, the reasons for young children's conservativism are not clear (see also Bloom, 2000; Dromi, 1987; Golinkoff, Mervis, & Hirsh-Pasek, 1994). As a result of their research, Naigles and Hoff believe that the verbs 1-year-olds know may be highly idiosyncratic and that differences in input may be responsible. They conclude that "rather than examine verb knowledge cross-sectionally and at a single point in time, we believe that what is needed are intensive studies of individual children, who are studied longitudinally from their first use of their first verb." In other words, Naigles and Hoff believe that we could explain much about both early verb learning and extension in individual children if we knew what input they had received.

Maguire, Hirsh-Pasek, and Golinkoff in chapter 14 accept the findings of studies like Childers and Tomasello's in chapter 12 as a starting point, in that they accept the conclusion that verbs are more difficult to learn and extend than nouns. Similar to Childers and Tomasello's findings on the ease with which children can

remember actions without labels, they provide a unique example of the verb learning problem. They describe a study in which infants from 9 to 12 months form a
nonlinguistic category of an action (Salkind, Sootsman, Golinkoff, Hirsch-Pasek,
& Maguire, 2002) that they prove unable to map a verb to a full year later (Maguire
et al., 2002). These data are relevant to what they called the verb-learning paradox:
Verbs are difficult to learn but appear in children's earliest vocabularies. Inspired by
Gentner and Boroditsky (2001) and Snedeker and Gleitman (2004), Maguire et al.
posit that the problem in verb learning is not a problem with the form class of
verbs per se but with relational words, which include verbs and some nouns, for example, *uncle* or *passenger* (see Hall & Waxman, 1993; Keil & Batterman, 1984).
They argue that "to learn any word—noun or verb—children must coordinate perceptual, social, and linguistic inputs to uncover more precise word meanings." By
viewing word learning through the lens of the ECM (Hollich et al., 2000), a theory
blind to word class, they conclude that the ECM offers a unified account of word
learning.

Chapter 15, by Fisher and Song, specifically focuses on children's use of linguistic cues to verb meaning in the context of syntactic bootstrapping, or the theory that children can glean information about verb meaning from the syntax
surrounding a verb (Fisher, 1996; Gleitman, 1990; Hirsh-Pasek, Golinkoff, &
Naigles, 1996; Landau & Gleitman, 1985; Naigles, 1990). As such, Fisher and Song
do not focus on the verb per se but on a key element in the sentence that offers
information about the verb: the sentence subject. Two broad questions motivate
Fisher and Song: "What aspects of sentence structures are informative to young
children, and what semantic information is conveyed to young children by the
structure of sentences?" The authors, in three experiments, asked what information learners can gain if they identify the noun phrase serving as a sentence's
grammatical subject. This then leads to the question of how children find the
grammatical subject to begin with. Fisher and Song suggest that there are a number of cues to sentence subject (such as agency, animacy, and first or second person), which provide probabilistic links between form and meaning. Just as these
patterns show up "as powerful tendencies" in English, other, related patterns may
show up in other languages. In sum, the identification of sentence subject by
whatever means may influence verb interpretation in important ways.

Part IV. How Language Influences Verb Learning: Cross-Linguistic Evidence

In 1995, TM's work had only a single chapter on verb learning in a language other
than English (Choi & Gopnik, 1995). There has been tremendous progress in
studying verb learning in languages other than English, and the six chapters here
are testament to that assertion. Such data are crucial for understanding verb learning because languages partition the meanings of verbs in different ways. More
interestingly, cross-linguistic research is going beyond the description of verb

learning in other languages to use other languages as a laboratory for asking questions about process.

In chapter 16, Lidz eloquently describes the problem of verb learning in general and how constraints from linguistic theory might impact on the child's verb learning. Then he asks how cross-linguistic regularities in children's verb learning inform us about what linguistic universals likely exist. Given that linguistic universals are arguably based in principled constraints on what a human language is, Lidz examines verb learning to see what generalizations seem to be operating. He notes that causation is universally expressed with transitive sentences, although transitive sentences are not necessarily causal. In experiments on syntactic bootstrapping, children seem to use transitivity as a cue to causation (e.g., Hirsh-Pasek, Golinkoff, & Naigles, 1996; Naigles, 1990; Naigles, Gleitman, & Gleitman, 1992). But does sentential transitivity signal causation to children because they interpret input that way or because they expect transitivity and causation to be linked across languages? To disentangle this issue, Lidz focused on the language Kannada, spoken in India. Kannada provides an excellent test case because it has a reliable morphemic marker that indicates causation. Using an experimental, "act-out" method (Naigles, Gleitman, & Gleitman, 1992), Lidz reported that 3-year-olds uniformly relied on argument number (i.e., transitivity) and not on the morphology that signaled causation more reliability than the syntax! Lidz concludes that some aspects of syntax to semantic mappings need not be learned. From this and another study, Lidz concludes that "children are constrained to hypothesize verb meanings for novel verbs in just the ways that those verbs are represented in adult languages."

Four of the five remaining chapters focus on Asian languages. It has been argued that Chinese, Japanese, and Korean present a test case for the early claim—mostly based on data from English—that nouns are easier to learn than verbs. If nouns are truly easier to learn than verbs, then the particular language learned should be irrelevant. But if the nature of the language has an impact on verb learning, then children learning one of these three languages should find verb learning easier given the presence of prodrop and SOV sentence structure, which places the verb in the privileged sentence-final position.

Tardif in chapter 18 (and see Tardif, 1996) reports that the vocabularies of children learning Chinese contain roughly equal numbers of nouns and verbs. Tardif's chapter examines the factors that may give Chinese children their advantage in verb learning and answers a question posed to her by the late Liz Bates, "But are they really verbs?" Tardif answers with a resounding "yes" and goes on to describe the data sources of the verb advantage as well as a study with adults using the "human simulation" paradigm of Gillette, Gleitman, Gleitman, and Lederer (1999). Both English-speaking and Chinese-speaking adults who are asked to guess missing verbs when they observe scenes of a Chinese mother and child at play also show a verb advantage (Snedeker, Li, & Yuan, 2003). Why should Chinese verbs be easier for children to learn and for adults to guess? Tardif suggests that the factors responsible include a combination of frequency in the input as well as the specificity of Chinese verb meanings compared to English verb meanings. In fact, recent research by Ma and colleagues (2006) provides confirmatory data: Chinese verbs learned early by young children are more imageable than the verbs English children learn early.

Chapter 17, however, questions the assumption that verbs in languages like Chinese, Korean, and Japanese are easy to learn and extend, despite the comparable ratio of nouns and verbs in these children's early vocabularies. Imai, Haryu, Okada, Lianjing, and Shigematsu criticize the data used to support the early verb claims. In particular, they criticize the use of checklist and production data, especially on the grounds that the use of a word does not mean that its meaning is fully mastered. In contrast to Tardif's work, Imai et al. report on experimental research using a dynamic action event to examine how verbs are fast mapped in Japanese and Chinese as well as in English (Meyer et al., 2003). In their studies, they show children a novel action being performed with a novel object as they label the scene in various ways. The question they ask is whether children will map a new verb to the new action and then extend it to an exemplar involving a new object. In a noun condition, they ask whether children can fast map a new noun to the novel object. Their results are startling: While children in all languages readily learn and extend the novel noun by 3 years of age, even 5-year-olds were not at ceiling in the verb condition. English-speaking American children could in fact only fast map a verb at age 5 if they had a sentence with full syntax, as in "The girl miffed it!" More striking yet is the data from Chinese children. It was not until the age of 9 that they could reliably map the novel verb to the novel action. Imai et al. conclude that their data overwhelmingly support a noun advantage for fast mapping—even in Chinese and Japanese—and that it is the structure of the verb lexicon that is to blame. That is, verbs do not all extend in the same way because languages (and verbs within languages) differ in their conflation patterns (e.g., manner vs. ground vs. cause). Imai et al. endorse Tomasello's (1995) view that verbs are learned, therefore, one verb at a time, with rules for extension extracted only slowly and with considerable language experience.

Kersten, Smith, and Yoshida in chapter 19 study English, a language that conflates manner of motion into its verbs, and Japanese, a language that tends to conflate path into its verbs. They begin from the assumption that the meanings of verbs in general are more flexible and changeable across different semantic contexts than the meanings of nouns, having the effect that verbs take longer to learn than nouns. They also argue that the meanings of verbs are more dependent on the objects with which they are involved. For example, we understand that the meaning of say, *run*, implies that its actor has legs. If it is true that knowledge about the object involved in an event is important to learning a new verb, then verb learning should occur more readily in the presence of a known rather than a novel object. Earlier work by Kersten and Smith (2002) demonstrated this was in fact the case. Recall, however, that Japanese has many path verbs. Would it still be true that verbs are more likely to be learned in the presence of a known object when path rather than manner of motion is conflated into the verb's meaning? The answer surprisingly, was yes: even Japanese children learning more "extrinsic" path than "intrinsic" manner verbs were sensitive to the object used in the sentence. Whether the lack of difference between peformance of English and Japanese children is due to a general need for object information in verb learning or whether attention to the object is a generalization from noun learning is unclear. However, the link between Kersten et al.'s chapter and Imai et al.'s chapter is striking. Object knowledge may be key to learning new verbs.

Lavin, Hall, and Waxman in chapter 20 endorse a multifactor view of word learning, opting for a social explanation based in cultural factors. Using a modification of Gillette and Gleitman's human simulation paradigm, Lavin et al. asked adult subjects (Western students, Japanese students, and second-generation Japanese students) to guess the words an American mother was saying to her child in the play scenes. They did not specify the form class of the word to be supplied. The general prediction was that Japanese students would focus on actions more than nouns and vice versa for the Western students. They found that all three groups identified more nouns than verbs but that this effect was more pronounced with the Western students. However, there were no differences in the number of correct matches for nouns between the three groups or for the accuracy of the verbs guessed. Reasoning from these data gathered with adults, Lavin et al. conclude that cultural factors may indeed influence the English-speaking child to learn more nouns than verbs. The contrast between Lavin et al.'s findings and Tardif's report (see also Snedeker et al., 2003) needs to be reconciled. In future studies, it will be important to disentangle cultural effects from the effects of input.

It is appropriate for Gentner to have the last chapter in this section because she has been a major theorist in discussions of noun and verb learning, as witnessed by the citation of her work in virtually every other chapter of this book. She first reviews her earlier work and points out the two predictions that the natural partitions/relational relativity hypotheses make for language acquisition. First, her prediction of a universal early noun advantage seems to be supported by chapters 12, 14, and 17, although Gentner evaluates conflicting claims on this prediction and offers some additional evidence for it. Second, she predicts that knowing many nouns assists in learning relational terms like verbs and prepositions. She goes on to evaluate more predictions that flow from her theorizing and to review four possible reasons why verbs seem to universally lag behind nouns. The thrust of her chapter is that verbs are more difficult to learn than nouns because of issues with mapping; that is, because verbs do not map transparently to events, children seem to be very conservative in their learning of verbs.

As is very clear from our review of the chapters in this volume, substantial progress has been made in the study of verb learning. Indeed, it can be argued that collectively we have conceptualized the study of verb learning in a far more diverse and empirically grounded way than in 1995 when TM's work was published.

Given the wealth of current research we are finally in a position to offer a more coherent—although preliminary—treatment of the field. In examining the chapters here, there appear to be four new trends worthy of discussion.

The Mapping Problem With Verbs (Is It Unique to Verbs?)

In comparison to 1995, there appears to be a recognition that the problem with verb learning has to do with mapping. New research suggests that the conceptual underpinnings for many (but not all) verb concepts are present early (see chapters 4, 5, and 6). Furthermore, nouns are readily mapped to novel objects while children appear reluctant to map and extend verbs to novel actions (chapters 8, 11, 12, 13, 14, 17, 19, 21). A parallel set of studies shows that in the same experimental design where children mapped nouns to novel objects, children are a full year older before they can map verbs to novel actions (Golinkoff, Hirsh-Pasek, Bailey, & Wenger, 1992; Golinkoff et al., 1996). Candidate factors responsible for the problem with mapping verbs to actions are suggested in this volume. In fact, researchers may be starting to gain some purchase on the factors that facilitate mapping in young children. For example, when verbs labeling visible actions (chapter 14), occur with high frequency in the input (chapter 13), and are performed by known objects (chapter 19), they are more likely to be learned than when these factors are not present.

Interestingly, there is also a dawning recognition that the mapping problem may not be unique to verbs but may also extend to abstract nouns as well as words from other more abstract word classes such as prepositions (chapters 14 and 21). When words are abstract (also discussed by various authors as less imageable, less likely to share a common shape, or less individuable) they appear to be harder to learn. This is not a surprise. Consider struggling as a second language learner with a noun like *politics* compared to a word like *pen*. More instances of use, more surrounding linguistic context, and more computation of speaker and actor intentions would be necessary to learn the former than the latter term. Recent work also suggests that language itself may contribute to solving the mapping problem. When perceptually diverse objects and scenes are labeled with the same word, toddlers appear to interpret this as a cue that the items labeled are equivalent in some way as well (chapter 6; Balaban & Waxman, 1977; Waxman & Markow, 1995).

The Search for Multiple Factors

Once we grant that multiple factors influence the mapping process, we are beyond naive theories of verb learning. The recognition that learning verbs is difficult because, as Slobin (2003, p. 159) pointed out, "utterances are not verbal film clips of events," and because verbs encode relations (Gentner, 1982) requires a more complex theory of verb learning. Gleitman and Bloom and their colleagues led the way here, pointing out early and often that verb learning, while central to grammar, must be explained by complex theories. Gleitman captured this insight well in one of her article titles, "A Picture Is Worth a Thousand Words But That's the Problem" (Gleitman & Gleitman, 1992). The basic point was that any theory of verb learning that claimed that children could read the meanings of verbs directly from their observation of events could never succeed.

While the insight came early that relying on event perception was insufficient for verb learning, researchers have more recently begun to search for multiple interacting factors in the verb learning process. Lidz, for example, includes observation of events, sentence structure, and morphology in his work. An emphasis on multiple factors was not as prominent in 1995 but today there is an attempt in the field to meet the challenge raised by Hollich et al. (2000, p. 109) "of creating a model that considers the impact of multiple sources of information in solving the complex task of word learning." The field has begun to move beyond "smoking gun" theories that account for verb learning with one particular process or type of input. This change is also responsive to calls for multifactored approaches to language learning (e.g., Gelman & Williams, 1998; Karmiloff-Smith, 1992; Nelson, 1996; Siegler, 1996; Thelen & Smith, 1994; Woodward & Markman, 1998). Maguire et al. and Poulin-Dubois and Forbes attempt to expand the ECM (Hollich et al., 2000) initially posited for noun learning to cover verb acquisition. That model describes the role of perceptual, linguistic, and social cues and how their weightings change over the course of word learning and development. Many other chapters grant that multiple factors matter for verb learning. Other examples come from chapter 20, by Lavin et al., who point to cultural factors in verb learning, and chapter 8, by Buresh et al., who suggest the importance of social processes for learning verbs.

The Importance of Social Cues

Even in 1995 in the TM volume, two chapters discussed the role of linguistic cues in verb learning (Gillette et al., 1999; Naigles, Fowler, & Helm, 1992). Yet few researchers (other than perhaps Tomasello and his colleagues and Nelson, 1996) considered the role that social factors might play in verb learning. In this volume, there are numerous examples of the impact of social cues on verb learning and some of them are stunning. For example, Imai et al. found that 9-year-old Chinese children in their study interpreted a novel verb as a noun. When Imai et al. examined their videos to try to understand this phenomenon, they noted that the actor held the object for a second before the action began. Children apparently noted this subtle extralinguistic and interpreted object holding as a signal that the object, and not the action, was being named. When this extra second was removed, Chinese children were significantly more likely to map the verb to the action!

Another example of the impact of social cues in verb learning comes from Poulin-Dubois and Forbes. They created actions that were only distinct by whether they appeared to be accidental or on purpose. Children noted this distinction in their verb learning (see also chapters 8 and 11). Furthermore, to learn verbs like *think, believe,* and *promise* and use them as adults do, children must have a theory of mind, or the computation of these verbs' meanings would not hit the mark. In addition, many verbs turn on intention for their meanings. Verbs such as *spill* and *pour,* and *slide* and *slip,* label actions that look remarkably similar but are distinguished mainly by whether they were performed with or without intention. To learn these verbs, children must discern an actor's intention.

The Search for the Underpinnings of Verb Learning

In 1995, some chapters in the TM volume focused on the perceptual and conceptual groundwork of verb learning (Choi & Gopnik, 1995; Golinkoff, Hirsh-Pasek, Mervis, Frawley, & Parillo, 1995; Smiley & Huttenlocher, 1995). However, the laboratory research on these underpinnings was just beginning. This volume contains two sections that could not have been included in 1995. The first section on finding verbs addresses the fundamental question of how children isolate verbs in the stream of speech. The second is the section on finding the actions in events. To learn verbs, children must be able to view an event and find its components. Until recently, there has been very little work on how adults, let alone children, parse events (but see Zacks & Tversky, 2001). This will soon be remedied with an edited collection on event perception (Shipley & Sacks, in press), as well as the present collection of chapters that probe infants' understandings of the events that verbs label. Various approaches (e.g., intention analysis, statistical units, image-schemas, and finding nonlinguistic analogues to linguistic constructs) have been proposed in this volume (e.g., chapters 4, 5, 9, and 10). Research is yielding exciting new findings about how infants find actions (chapters 4, 6, and 9), note their language relevant components (chapters 5 and 14), categorize them (chapters 5, 6, and 8), focus on their intentional underpinnings (chapters 8, 9, and 10), and use their native language to shape their nonlinguistic concepts (chapter 7).

Conclusion

What does it take to learn a verb? This is the fundamental question this volume considers. By investigating this question, we enhance our understanding of the building blocks of language and develop new ways to assess key aspects of language growth. The chapters in this volume provide preliminary answers from a number of different perspectives and involving a number of different causal factors in interaction. Despite the fact that Shakespeare wrote in Hamlet, "suit the action to the word, the word to the action," the chapters in this volume show us that that is no simple task! Given the nuances of verb meaning, there are many verbs that can be used to describe the same action. Part of the task that children face is to uncover the meanings of the verbs they hear, even when different verbs are used in exactly the same setting. Furthermore, as these chapters have detailed, children must first find the verbs in the input before they can make conjectures about their meanings. And they must perceive events in the world in ways that align with the concepts encoded in verbs. As the chapters in the volume indicate, none of these steps in the verb learning process are straightforward—for the child or the researcher—to crack.

How shall we evaluate our efforts to gain some purchase on the verb learning problem? Hemingway reminds us that we must "never mistake motion for action." Ten years hence when this volume is evaluated by its successor, we hope that its chapters will be taken to represent action forward on the verb learning front and not just motion.

Acknowledgments We thank Amanda Brandone for her helpful comments.

Note

1. There exists a debate on whether children have the syntactic category of *verb* (see Pinker, 1984) or whether they simply have the category of *action word* (see Olguin & Tomasello, 1993).

References

Balaban, M. T., & Waxman, S. R. (1977). Do word labels facilitate object categorization in 9-month-old infants? *Journal of Experimental Child Psychology, 64,* 3–26.

Bassano, D. (2000). Early development of nouns and verbs in French: Exploring the interface between lexicon and grammar. *Journal of Child Language, 27,* 521–559.

Bloom, L. (1993). *The transition from infancy to language: Acquiring the power of expression.* New York: Cambridge University Press.

Bloom, L. (2000). The intentionality model of word learning: How to learn a word, any word. In R. Golinkoff, K. Hirsh-Pasek, L. Bloom, L. Smith, A. Woodward, N. Akhtar, M. Tomasello, & G. Hollich (Eds.), *Becoming a word learner: A debate on lexical acquisition* (pp. 3–17). New York: Oxford University Press.

Bloom, L., Lifter, K., & Hafitz, J. (1980). The semantics of verbs and the development of verb inflections in child language. *Language, 56,* 386–412.

Bloom, L., Lightbown, P., & Hood, L. (1975). Structure and variation in child language. *Monographs of the Society for Research in Child Development, 40* (2, Serial No. 160).

Bloom, L., Tinker, E., & Margulis, C. (1993). The words children learn: Evidence against a noun bias in early vocabularies. *Cognitive Development 8,* 431–450.

Bornstein, M., Cole, L., Maital, S., K., Park, S. Y., Pascual, L., et al. (2004). Cross-linguistic analysis of vocabulary in young children: Spanish, Dutch, French, Hebrew, Italian, Korean and American English. *Child Development, 75,* 1115–1140.

Bortfeld, H., Morgan, J. L., Golinkoff, R. M., & Rathbun, K. (2005). Mommy and me: Familiar names help launch babies into speech stream segmentation. *Psychological Science, 16*(4), 298–305.

Caramazza, A., & Hillis, A. E. (1991). Lexical organization of nouns and verbs in the brain. *Nature, 349,* 788–790.

Casasola, M. (2005). Can language do the driving? The effect of linguistic input on infants' categorization of support spatial relations. *Developmental Psychology, 41,* 183–192.

Caselli, M. C., Bates, E., Casadio, P., Fenson, L., Sanderl, L., et al. (1995). A cross-linguistic study of early lexical development. *Cognitive Development, 10,* 159–199.

Childers, J. B., & Tomasello, M. (2002). Two-year-olds learn novel nouns, verbs, and conventional actions from massed or distributed exposures. *Developmental Psychology, 38,* 967–978.

Choi, S., & Bowerman, M. (1991). Learning to express motion events in English and Korean: The influence of language-specific lexicalization patterns. *Cognition, 41,* 83–121.

Choi, S., & Gopnik, A. (1995). Names, relational words, and cognitive development in English and Korean speakers: Nouns are not always learned before verbs. In M. Tomasello & W. E. Merriman (Eds.), *Beyond names for things: Young children's acquisition of verbs* (pp. 63–80). Hillsdale, NJ: Lawrence Erlbaum.

Choi, S., McDonough, L., Bowerman, M., & Mandler, J. M. (1999). Early sensitivity to language-specific spatial categories in English and Korean. *Cognitive Development, 14,* 241–268.

Cohen, L. B., & Oakes, L. M. (1993). How infants perceive a simple causal event. *Developmental Psychology, 29,* 421–433.

Dromi, E. (1987). *Early lexical development.* Cambridge: Cambridge University Press.

Fenson, L., Dale, P. S., Reznick, J. S., Bates, E., Thal, D., & Pethick, S. J. (1994). Variability in early communicative development. *Monographs of the Society for Research in Child Development, 59* (5, Serial No. 242).

Fisher, C. (1996). Structural limits on verb mapping: The role of analogy in children's interpretations of sentences. *Cognitive Psychology, 31,* 41–81.

Fisher, C., Hall, D. G., Rakowitz, S., & Gleitman, L. (1994). When is it better to receive than to give: Syntactic and conceptual constraints on vocabulary growth. *Lingua, 92,* 333–375.

Frawley, W. (1992). *Linguistic semantics.* Hillsdale, NJ: Lawrence Erlbaum.

Gallivan, J. (1988). Motion verb acquisition: Development of definitions. *Perceptual and Motor Skills, 66,* 979–986.

Gelman, R., & Williams, E. M. (1998). Enabling constraints for cognitive development and learning: Domain specificity and epigenesist. In W. Damon (Series Ed.), D. Kuhn & R. S. Siegler (Vol. Eds.), *Handbook of child psychology: Vol. 2. Cognition, perception, and language* (5th ed., pp. 575–630). New York: Wiley.

Gentner, D. (1982). Why nouns are learned before verbs: Linguistic relativity versus natural partitioning. In S. A. Kuczaj II (Ed.), *Language development: Vol. 2. Language, thought, and culture* (pp. 301–334). Hillsdale, NJ: Lawrence Erlbaum.

Gentner, D., & Boroditsky, L. (2001). Individuation, relativity and early word learning. In M. Bowerman & S. C. Levinson (Eds.), *Language, culture, and cognition: Vol. 3. Language acquisition and conceptual development* (pp. 215–256). New York: Cambridge University Press.

Gillette, J., Gleitman, H., Gleitman, L., & Lederer, A. (1999). Human simulations of vocabulary learning. *Cognition, 73*, 135–176.

Gleitman, L. (1990). Structural sources of verb meaning. *Language Acquisition, 1*, 3–55.

Gleitman, L., & Gleitman, H. (1992). A picture is worth a thousand words, but that's the problem: The role of syntax in vocabulary acquisition. *Current Directions in Psychological Science 1*, 31–35.

Goldin-Meadow, S., Seligman, M. E. P., & Gelman, R. (1976). Language in the two-year-old: Receptive and productive stages. *Cognition, 4*, 189–202.

Golinkoff, R. M. (1975). Semantic development in infants: The concepts of agent and recipient. *Merrill-Palmer Quarterly, 21*, 181–193.

Golinkoff, R. M., Chung, H. L., Hirsh-Pasek, K., Liu, J., Bertenthal, B. I., Brand, R., et al. (2002). Young children can extend motion verbs to point-light displays. *Developmental Psychology, 38*, 604–615.

Golinkoff, R. M., Hirsh-Pasek, K., Bailey, L., & Wenger, N. (1992). Young children and adults use lexical principles to learn new nouns. *Developmental Psychology, 28*, 99–108.

Golinkoff, R. M., Hirsh-Pasek, K., Cauley, K. M., & Gordon, L. (1987). The eyes have it: Lexical and syntactic comprehension in a new paradigm. *Journal of Child Language, 14*, 23–45.

Golinkoff, R. M., Hirsh-Pasek, K., Mervis, C. B., Frawley, W. B., & Parillo, M. (1995). Lexical principles can be extended to the acquisition of verbs. In M. Tomasello & W. E. Merriman (Eds.), *Beyond names for things: Young children's acquisition of verbs* (pp. 185–222). Hillsdale, NJ: Lawrence Erlbaum.

Golinkoff, R. M., Jacquet, R., Hirsh-Pasek, K., & Nandakumar, R. (1996). Lexical principles may underlie the learning of verbs. *Child Development, 67*, 3101–3119.

Golinkoff, R. M., & Kerr, J. L. (1978). Infants' perceptions of semantically defined action role changes in filmed events. *Merrill-Palmer Quarterly, 24*, 53–61.

Golinkoff, R. M., Mervis, C. V., & Hirsh-Pasek, K. (1994). Early object labels: The case for a developmental lexical principles framework. *Journal of Child Language, 21*, 125–155.

Goodglass, H., & Kaplan, E. (1983). *The assessment of aphasia and related disorders.* (2nd ed.). Philadelphia: Lea & Febiger.

Hall, D. G., & Waxman, S. R. (1993). Assumptions about word meaning: Individual and basic-level kinds. *Child Development, 64*, 1550–1570.

Hespos, S. J., & Spelke, E. S. (2004). Precursors to spatial language. *Nature, 430*, 453–456.

Hillis, A. E., & Caramazza, A. (1995). Representation of grammatical categories of words in the brain. *Journal of Cognitive Neuroscience, 7*, 396–407.

Hirsh-Pasek, K., & Golinkoff, R. (1996). The preferential looking paradigm reveals emerging language comprehension. In D. McDaniel, C. McKee, & H. Caims (Eds.), *Advances in infancy research, Vol. 8*. Norwood, NJ: Ablex.

Hirsh-Pasek, K., Golinkoff, R. M., & Naigles, L. (1996). Young children's use of syntactic frames to derive meaning. In K. Hirsh-Pasek & R. M. Golinkoff (Eds.), *The origins of grammar: Evidence from early language comprehension* (pp. 123–158). Cambridge, MA: MIT Press.

Hollich, G. J., Hirsh-Pasek, K., Golinkoff, R., Brand, R., Brown, E., Chung, H. L., et al. (2000). Breaking the language barrier: An emergentist coalition model for the origins of word learning. *Monographs of the Society for Research in Child Development, 65(3)*.

Huttenlocher, J., Smiley, P., & Charney, R. (1983). Emergence of action categories in the child: Evidence from verb meanings. *Psychological Review, 90*, 72–93.

Imai, M., Haryu, E., & Okada, H. (2005). Mapping novel nouns and verbs onto dynamic action events: Are verb meanings easier to learn than noun meanings for Japanese children? *Child Development, 76*(2), 340–356.

Jackson-Maldonado, D., Thal, D., Marchman, V., Bates, E., & Gutierrez-Clellen, V. (1993). Early lexical development in Spanish-speaking infants and toddlers. *Journal of Child Language, 20*, 523–549.

Jusczyk, P. (1997). *The discovery of spoken language.* Cambridge, MA: MIT Press.

Karmiloff-Smith, A. (1992). *Beyond modularity: A developmental perspective on cognitive science.* Cambridge, MA: MIT Press.

Keil, F. C., & Batterman, N. (1984). A characteristic-to-defining shift in the development of word meaning. *Journal of Verbal learning and Verbal Behavior, 23*, 221–236.

Kersten, A. W., & Smith, L. B. (2002). Attention to novel objects during verb learning. *Child Development, 73*, 93–109.

Landau, B., & Gleitman, L. R. (1985). *Language and experience: Evidence from the blind child.* Cambridge, MA: Harvard University Press.

Langacker, R. W. (1987). *Foundations of cognitive grammar: Vol. 1. Theoretical prerequisites.* Stanford, CA: Stanford University Press.

Ma., W., McDonough, C., Lannon, R., Golinkoff, R. M., Hirsh-Pasek, K., & Tardif, T. (2006). A mental image is worth a thousand verbs: Imageability predicts verb learning. Manuscript in preparation.

Maguire, M. J., Hennon, E. A., Hirsh-Pasek, K., Golinkoff, R. M., Slutzky, C. B., & Sootsman, J. (2002). Mapping words to actions and events: How do 18-month-olds learn a verb? In B. Skarabela, S. Fish, & A. H. J. Do (Eds.), *Proceedings of the Boston University Annual Conference on Language Development* (pp. 371–382). Somerville, MA: Cascadilla Press.

Mandler, J. M. (1992a). The foundations of conceptual thought in infancy. *Cognitive Development, 7*, 273–285.

Mandler, J. M. (1992b). How to build a baby II: Conceptual primitives. *Psychological Review, 99*, 587–604.

Mandler, J. M. (1998). Representation. In D. Kuhn & R. S. Siegler (Eds.), *Handbook of child psychology: Vol. 2, Cognition, perception, and language* (pp. 255–308). New York: John Wiley & Sons.

Mandler, J. (2004). *The foundations of mind: Origins of conceptual thought.* New York: Oxford University Press.

McCarthy, R., & Warrington, E. K. (1985). Category specificity in an agrammatic patient: The relative impairment of verb retrieval and comprehension. *Neuropsychologia, 23*, 709–727.

Meyer, M., Leonard, S., Hirsh-Pasek, K., Golinkoff, R. M., Imai, M., Haryu, R., et al. (2003). *Making a convincing argument: A cross-linguistic comparison of noun and verb learning in Japanese and English.* Poster presented at the Boston University Conference on Language Development, Boston, MA.

Miceli, G., Silveri, M. C., Nocentini, U., & Caramazza, A. (1988). Patterns of dissociation in comprehension and production of nouns and verbs. *Aphasiology, 2*, 351–358.

Miceli, G., Silveri, M. C., Villa, G., & Caramazza, A. (1984). On the basis for agrammatic's difficulty in producing main verbs. *Cortex, 20*, 207–220.

Naigles, L. (1990). Children use syntax to learn verb meanings. *Journal of Child Language, 17*, 357–374.

Naigles, L., Fowler, A., & Helm, A. (1992). Developmental changes in the construction of verb meanings. *Cognitive Development, 7*, 403–427.

Naigles, L., Gleitman, H., & Gleitman, L. R. (1992). Children acquire word meaning components from syntactic evidence. In E. Dromi (Ed.), *Language and cognition: A developmental perspective* (pp. 104–140). Norwood, NJ: Ablex.

Nelson, K. (1988). Where do taxonomic categories come from? *Human Development, 31,* 3–10.

Nelson, K. (1996). *Language in cognitive development.* New York: Cambridge University Press.

Oakes, L. M., & Rakison, D. H. (2003). Issues in the early development of concepts and categories: An introduction. In D. H. Rakison & L. M. Oakes (Eds.), *Early category and concept development: Making sense of the blooming, buzzing confusion* (pp. 3–23). New York: Oxford University Press.

Olguin, R., & Tomasello, M. (1993). Twenty-five-month-old children do not have a grammatical category of verbs. *Cognitive Development, 8,* 245–272.

Parisse, C., & Le Normand, M. (2000). How children build their morphosyntax: The case of French. *Journal of Child Language, 27,* 267–292.

Pickett, J. P., et al. (Eds.). (2000). *The American Heritage Dictionary of the English Language* (4th ed.). Boston: Houghton Mifflin.

Poulin-Dubois, D., Graham, S., & Sippola, L. (1995). Early lexical development: The contribution of parental labeling and infants' categorization abilities. *Journal of Child Language, 22,* 325–343.

Pruden, S. M., Hirsh-Pasek, K., Maguire, M. J., & Meyer, M. A. (2004). Foundations of verb learning: Infants form categories of path and manner in motion events. In A. Burgos, L. Micciulla, & C. E. Smith (Eds.), *Proceedings of the 28th Annual Boston University Conference on Language Development* (pp. 461–472). Somerville, MA: Cascadilla Press.

Pulverman, R., Sootsman, J. L., Golinkoff, R. M., & Hirsh-Pasek, K. (2003). The role of lexical knowledge in nonlinguistic event processing: English-speaking infants' attention to manner and path. *Proceedings of the 27th Annual Boston University Conference of Language Development* (pp. 662–673). Somerville, MA: Casadilla Press.

Saffran, E. M., Berndt, R. S., & Schwartz, M. F. (1989). A quantitative analysis of agrammatic production: Procedure and data. *Brain and Language, 37,* 440–479.

Saffran, J. R., Aslin, R. N., & Newport, E. L. (1996). Statistical learning by 8-month-old infants. *Science, 274,* 1926–1928.

Salkind, S. J., Golinkoff, R. M., & Brandone, A. (2005, April). *Infants' attention to novel actions in relation to the conflation patterns of motion verbs.* Society for Research in Child Development. Atlanta, GA.

Salkind, S., Sootsman, J., Golinkoff, R. M., Hirsh-Pasek, K., & Maguire, M. J. (2002, April). *Lights, camera, action! Infants and toddlers create action categories.* International Conference on Infant Studies. Toronto, Canada.

Sharon, T., & Wynn, K. (1998). Individuation of actions from continuous motion. *Psychological Science, 9,* 357–362.

Shipley, T. F., & Sacks, J. (in press). *An invitation to an event: A cognitive science approach to the psychology of event perception, representation, and action.* New York: Oxford University Press.

Siegler, R. S. (1996). *Emerging minds.* New York: Oxford University Press.

Slobin, D. I. (2001). Form-function relations: How do children find out what they are? In M. Bowerman & S. C. Levinson (Eds.), *Language acquisition and conceptual development* (pp. 406–449). Cambridge: Cambridge University Press.

Slobin, D. I. (2003). Language and thought online: Cognitive consequences of linguistic relativity. In D. Gentner & S. Goldin-Meadow (Eds.), *Advances in the investigation of language and thought* (pp. 157–191). Cambridge, MA: MIT Press.

Smiley, P., & Huttenlocher, J. (1995). Conceptual development and the child's early words for events, objects, and persons. In M. Tomasello & W. E. Merriman (Eds.), *Beyond names for things: Young children's acquisition of verbs* (pp. 21–62). Hillsdale, NJ: Lawrence Erlbaum.

Smith, L. B., & Sachs, J. (1990). Cognition and the verb lexicon in early lexical development. *Applied Psycholinguistics, 11,* 409–424.

Snedeker, J., & Gleitman, L. (2004). Why is it hard to label our concepts. In G. Hall & S. Waxman (Eds.), *Weaving a lexicon* (pp. 603–636). Cambridge, MA: MIT Press.

Snedeker, J., Li, P., & Yuan, S. (2003). Cross-cultural differences in the input to early word learning. *Proceedings of the 25th Annual Conference of the Cognitive Science Society.* Mahwah, NJ: Lawrence Erlbaum.

Talmy, L. (1985). Lexicalization patterns: Semantic structure in lexical forms. In T. Shopen (Ed.), *Language typology and the lexicon, Vol. III: Grammatical categories and the lexicon* (pp. 57–149). Cambridge: Cambridge University Press.

Talmy, L. (2000). *Toward a cognitive semantics: Vol. I. Conceptual structuring systems.* Cambridge, MA: MIT Press.

Tardif, T. (1996). Nouns are not always learned before verbs: Evidence from Mandarin speakers' early vocabularies. *Developmental Psychology, 32,* 492–504.

Theakston, A. L., Lieven, E. V. M., Pine, J. M., & Rowland, C. F. (2002). Going, going, gone: The acquisition of the verb "go." *Journal of Child Language, 29,* 783–811.

Thelen, E., & Smith, L. B. (1994). *A dynamic systems approach to the development of cognition and action.* Cambridge, MA: MIT Press.

Thompson, C. K., Lange, K. L., Schneider, S. L., & Shapiro, L. P. (1997). Agrammatic and non-brain-damaged subjects' verb and verb argument structure production. *Aphasiology, 11,* 473–490.

Tomasello, M. (1995). Pragmatic contexts for early verb learning. In M. Tomasello & W. E. Merriman (Eds.), *Beyond the names for things: Young children's acquisition of verbs* (pp. 115–146). Hillsdale, NJ: Lawrence Erlbaum.

Tomasello, M., & Kruger, A. C. (1992). Acquiring verbs in ostensive and nonostensive contexts. *Journal of Child Language, 19,* 311–333.

Tomasello, M., & Merriman, W. E. (1995). *Beyond names for things: Young children's acquisition of verbs.* Hillsdale, NJ: Lawrence Erlbaum.

Wagner, L., & Carey, S. (2005). Twelve-month-old infants represent probable endings of motion events. *Infancy, 7,* 73–84.

Waxman, S. R., & Klibanoff, R. S. (2000). The role of comparison in the extension of novel adjectives, *Developmental Psychology, 36,* 571–581.

Waxman, S., & Markow, D. (1995). Words as invitations to form categories: Evidence from 12- to 13-month-old infants. *Cognitive Psychology, 29,* 257–302.

Woodward, A. L., & Markman, E. M. (1998). Early word learning. In D. Kuhn & R. S. Siegler (Eds.), *Handbook of child psychology: Vol. 2. Cognition, perception, and language* (pp. 371–420). New York: John Wiley & Sons.

Wynn, K. (1996). Infants' individuation and enumeration of actions. *Psychological Science, 7,* 164–169.

Yoshida, H., & Smith, L. B. (2005). Linguistic cues enhance the learning of perceptual cues. *Psychological Science, 16,* 90–95.

Zacks, J. M., & Tversky, B. (2001). Event structure in perception and conception. *Psychological Bulletin, 127,* 3–21.

Part I

Prerequisites to Verb Learning: Finding the Verb

1 Finding the Verbs: Distributional Cues to Categories Available to Young Learners

Toben H. Mintz

Introduction

Before language learners can start to learn the meanings of verbs, they must first determine what words in their language are verbs. In this chapter I will discuss a kind of information inherent in the structure of children's linguistic input that they could use to categorize verbs together. The information is a type of *distributional information* involving the patterning of words in sentences. The general hypothesis is that words of the same grammatical form-class category (e.g., noun, verb, adjective, etc.) occur in similar distributional patterns across utterances, and that this information could be a basis for learners to identify verbs as well as other categories. The specific distributional patterns considered are those arising from *frequent frames* (Mintz, 2003). For the purposes of this chapter, a *frame* is defined as any two words that occur in a corpus with exactly one word intervening. For example, in the sentence, "Who wants some ice cream?" *who _____ some* is a frame containing the word *wants*. The hypothesis explored here is that the words that are contained by a given frequent frame—a frame that occurs above some frequency threshold in a learner's input—belong to the same grammatical category, and hence that frequent frames could provide a *bootstrap*, or initial basis, for categorizing and identifying verbs.

The focus of this chapter is a two-part examination of the degree to which the category of words can accurately be derived from distributional information. The first part motivates and discusses in detail a recent approach I have carried out involving frequent frames as a distributional context (Mintz, 2003), and along the way provides a comparison to other recent distributional approaches. The second part presents preliminary behavioral evidence that infants, indeed, categorize novel words based on distributional information, and perhaps based on frequent frames.

Deriving Categories From Distributional Information

In a classic study, Roger Brown (1957) showed that given a scene and a novel word, 3- to 5-year-old children's interpretation of how the word relates to the scene changed depending on the word's morphosyntactic environment. When shown an image of a pair of hands kneading a confetti-like material in a bowl, children who heard the scene described using the word *sib* as a verb, as in *to sib*, or *sibbing*, thought that *sib* referred to the kneading action; whereas if they heard *a sib*, they thought *sib* referred to the bowl. In short, the assumptions children made about word meaning depended on the grammatical category of the word.

Brown's study showed, among other things, that children pay attention to the syntactic privileges of words in determining their meanings. From a linguistic point of view, they appeared to categorize the novel word based on the morphosyntactic environment, as either a verb or a noun, and inferred a meaning for the word that depended on this categorization. One way the children could have determined the category of the unknown word was to note what words surrounded it, and to note its morphological marking. For instance, children could identify as verbs, words that occurred after *to* or affixed with *-ing*.

The process by which a word's environment—the words that surround it, its morphological marking, its relative position in a sentence—is used to determine its category is called *distributional analysis*. Maratsos and Chalkley (1980) advanced a theory that children perform distributional analyses on their input to identify grammatical form classes. On their proposal, children tracked the range of environments in which words occurred—including co-occurrence with other words and affixes—and grouped words together that occurred in overlapping environments. Semantic information played a role as well, in that an affix such as *-s* would be treated as a different element when it designates plurality than when it designates present tense. However, for Maratsos and Chalkley, a primary source of information was distributional information.

The possibility that children use distributional information to classify words is appealing. After all, linguists rely on distributional analyses to discover what words belong together as a class in newly studied languages (Harris, 1951). If distributional information is useful for linguists in constructing a grammar of a language, couldn't it also be informative for children learning their first language? Despite the appeal of this possibility, it is not without problems. Some problems have been thought to be so serious that the approach was not widely considered viable (see especially Pinker, 1984, 1987).

One potential problem concerns how a learner is to identify the appropriate distributional contexts on which to base an analysis. To take an extreme example, the absolute position of a word in a sentence (e.g., third word, first word, etc.), while a perfectly coherent distributional attribute, is clearly not an adequate basis for categorizing words (Pinker, 1987). Clearly, then, distributional environments appropriate for categorization must be defined relative to other words (and morphemes) in an utterance. The problem then becomes, to which environment should one attend? On the surface, this is a difficult question, since the "right" context might vary from utterance to utterance. Consider the target word *monkey*:

1. *The monkey* is climbing up a tree.
2. *The* furry black and very funny *monkey* is climbing up a tree.

Perhaps *adjacent-to-the-left* is an informative distributional environment. In (1), a distributional analysis procedure that categorized words based on this environment would categorize *monkey* with all the other words immediately preceded by the determiner *the* in other utterances, which, one can easily imagine, will include a number of other nouns. But in (2), while the same informative determiner is present, it is not immediately adjacent to the target word; in fact, there is no constraint on the number of words that can intercede. *Monkey* would not be correctly categorized in this case, and *furry* would be incorrectly grouped with other nouns. The problem is that informative contexts are not necessarily in the same relative positions to target words from utterance to utterance (or even within an utterance). How is a learner to know which contexts to pay attention to in any given situation? (For additional problems of this type, see Pinker, 1984, 1987.)

Arguments against distributional analyses as a means of *initially* categorizing words were not blanket arguments against the importance of distributional analyses at later points in language acquisition. Rather, the idea was that learners would already have to have a considerable amount of linguistic knowledge in order to know how to treat the distributional information in a linguistically meaningful way. It was only once a considerable amount of structure was already fixed in the child's developing grammar (and, crucially, that categories had already been assigned to many words and affixes by nondistributional means) that distributional information could play a role in determining the category of an unknown word. Indeed, Pinker describes the concept of *structure-dependent distributional learning* (Pinker, 1984, pp. 40–42) to refer to distributional analyses that are guided by some knowledge of phrase structure and knowledge of the category membership of some other words or inflections in a sentence. In other words, although a relatively advanced language user (e.g., those in Brown's study) could use distributional information to categorize a novel word, it was argued that the earliest categorization of words had to be based on other sources.

Deriving Categories From Semantic Information

Given the link between grammatical form and meaning, some researchers proposed that learners initially determine the grammatical category of a new word by observing what kind of entity it refers to. If it refers to an object, or a substance, then it is a noun; if it refers to an action, then it is a verb. Such a proposal forms part of Pinker's (1984) semantic bootstrapping hypothesis (see also

Grimshaw, 1981; Macnamara, 1972). According to Pinker, aspects of the meaning of an utterance—who and what are being talked about—are transparent to learners even before they have acquired much knowledge of the vocabulary and structure particular to their language. This allows learners to identify the *semantic* category of a word (e.g., action word) by observing the referential contingency of the word's use (e.g., that it is used to refer to an action). Innate linking rules then allow the child to classify the word syntactically (e.g., as a verb). The newly categorized word can then be fit into the developing grammar, and at early stages might be used as a source of information for determining certain language-specific aspects of the grammar (e.g., head branching direction, case marking, etc.).

One problematic aspect of semantic bootstrapping that has been discussed extensively in the literature has to do with the difficulty of identifying the meaning, and thus the semantic category, of unknown words, especially verbs (for example, see Gillette, Gleitman, Gleitman, & Lederer, 1999; Gleitman, 1990). For verbs, the problem is not that the meanings cannot be recovered; clearly they can, since children eventually learn verbs. Rather, because of ambiguities inherent in verb-to-world mappings, learners apparently rely on structural information in the carrier utterance to focus them on the relevant aspects of the world. For example, when confronted with scenes in which a causative and a noncausative action simultaneously occur (e.g., one character feeds another character, and the latter eats what is fed to him), 2-year-olds interpret novel verbs in transitive constructions as referring to causative actions (feeding), and novel verbs in intransitive constructions as referring to noncausative actions (eating) (Fisher, Hall, Rakowitz, & Gleitman, 1994; Naigles, 1990; Naigles & Kako, 1993). But on a semantic bootstrapping account, that structural information (transitive or intransitive) would not yet be available in early stages of verb learning, as that is precisely what is hypothesized to be ultimately deduced once the category of the word is identified. Thus, this crucial information would not be available to cue the learner as to the intended referent of the verb.

To overcome the kind of ambiguity present in the example above, when syntactic cues are unavailable, semantic bootstrapping accounts assume that a learner can deduce the referent of a novel word by observing many situations in which the same unknown word is used to describe different scenes. The learner then abstracts away the elements that are common across all uses to arrive at the correct interpretation. For example, the child may hear the word *feed* used in situations in which there is no eating (e.g., one can feed a dog without the dog eating), and may hear the word *eat* used in situation where there is no feeding (e.g., when the dog finally comes to eat the food). However, compelling arguments have been made that cross-situational comparison cannot solve some of the logical problems in identifying a word's referent, without recourse to syntax (Fisher et al., 1994; Gillette et al., 1999; Gleitman, 1990; Gleitman & Gleitman, 1997; Landau & Gleitman, 1985). A classic example involves the events of chasing and fleeing. In any situation in which there is a chasing event there is also a fleeing event, and vice versa, so that no amount of exposure to chase/flee events in which the word *glip*, say, is uttered could resolve this mapping ambiguity (Fisher et al., 1994; Gleitman, 1990; Gleitman & Gleitman, 1997; but see also Pinker, 1994). To be sure, the problem faced by a learner in categorizing a word as a verb is less complex than determining its meaning; nevertheless, studies with adults have shown that cross-situational observation alone is not even suitable for determining weather an unknown word is a noun or a verb (Snedeker, Brent, & Gleitman, 2005; Snedeker, Gleitman, & Brent, 1999). In sum, procedures for identifying verbs that rely initially on identifying a word's semantic type might not be feasible.

Another problem for semantically driven categorization is that, even if the learner could reliably recover the semantic type of a word, the links between semantic and grammatical categories are not one-to-one, but many-to-many. One aspect of the problem is that that there are words for which the semantic antecedent conditions (e.g., action implies verb) do not come into play. For example, *know* and *love* are not actions, so linking rules would not be relevant for identifying them as verbs. This state of affairs (i.e., many semantic types mapping to the verb category) is not fatal for semantic bootstrapping: structure-dependent distributional learning was proposed to solve exactly this kind of problem. A more serious difficulty is that, as Maratsos and Chalkley (1980) discuss in detail, semantic-to-syntactic linking rules are subject to one-to-many mappings as well; that is, one semantic type can be associated with several syntactic types. For example, the words *action* and *noisy* are not verbs, but, Maratsos and Chalkley argue, they have action-like semantics and thus would be mapped to the verb category given the linking rules that would categorize words like *throw* and *kick* as verbs. In other words, nouns and adjectives can have action semantics as well, so young learners could apply action word–to-verb linking rules to words that are not verbs. Thus, even if mapping the to-be-categorized word to the correct semantic type could be reliably achieved, many incorrect grammatical assignments would be made by purely semantic-to-grammatical linking rules. Of course, distributional analyses do not run into these problems: since the initial categorization is not dependent on accessing word meanings, the problems associated with finding a word's referent in the world do not come up, and the unreliability of semantic linking rules is not a factor.

Frequent Frame Approach to Distributional Bootstrapping

Recently, investigators have started to reexamine the usefulness of distributional methods in providing an initial classification of words in child directed speech (Cartwright & Brent, 1997; Mintz, 2003; Mintz, Newport, & Bever, 1995, 2002; Redington & Chater, 1998; Redington, Chater, & Finch, 1998). By analyzing transcripts of input children actually receive, researchers have endeavored to understand whether the arguments raised against distributional approaches in principle are indeed problematic in practice. In different ways, the learning algorithms employed in these recent approaches take into account frequency when grouping words with other words in the input, essentially combining statistical and distributional approaches to categorizing words. The consideration of frequency is potentially relevant because if the problematic aspects of distributional information are relatively rare—for example, if sentences like (1), above, are the norm, and (2) are infrequent—it may be possible to filter out the problematic cases via a sensitivity to frequency.[1] Frequency plays an important role in the present research in that the distributional environments that are analyzed in the service of categorization are only the environments that occur frequently.

While considering frequency might increase the informativeness of analyzing a given distributional context (e.g., adjacent-to-the-right) by filtering out deviant or misleading cases, the antecedent question of which distributional patterns should be analyzed remains. Distributional analyses can cover many (indeed, infinitely many) types of patterns and relationships among a variety of linguistic units (e.g., phonemes, syllables, morphemes, words). A challenge in developing an account of grammatical learning that incorporates distributional analyses at an early stage is discovering which distributional patterns might be particularly informative and determining whether learners are sensitive to these patterns. One way to approach this challenge is to look to the behavioral literature for reasonable conjectures about the types of distributional environments very young learners are likely to attend to, and then determine whether those environments embody grammatically relevant properties. For instance, could they be used to group verbs with other verbs, nouns with other nouns, and so on? The logical problem of which distributional context to attend to can be circumvented if one can demonstrate that the distributional contexts that learners do attend to can support categorization. Part of the motivation for studying the distributional properties of frequent frames (Mintz, 2003) arose from such a consideration. Another motivation is a logical analysis of how frequent frames could provide an informative categorizing context. These points will be addressed in turn.

Sensitivity to Frames in Processing

There is a growing body of evidence that infants are sensitive to patterns of regularity in their linguistic input. For example, infants notice patterns in syllable sequences and make conjectures about the words in their language based on sequences that are highly predictable (Saffran, 2001). Patterns of this type involve computing relations between adjacent elements, however languages also give rise to patterns of regularity that involve nonadjacent elements. For example, present progressive sentences in English involve some form of the copula (e.g., *is*) followed by the affix *-ing*, with a variable amount of intervening material, as in the sentence "She *is* wash*ing* the car, or "She *is* slowly wash*ing* the car." Eighteen-month-olds are apparently sensitive to these nonadjacent dependencies, as they notice when an ungrammatical auxiliary verb (e.g., *can*) occurs in place of the copula in the examples above (Santelmann & Jusczyk, 1998). In other words, infants store information about elements that co-occur at a distance and surround other material, which is just the type of pattern that constitutes frames, as defined here.

Further evidence that infants track framelike co-occurrence patterns comes from artificial language learning studies with 18-month-olds. In one study, Gómez (2002) tested 18-month-olds' sensitivity to the contingency between two nonadjacent words separated by exactly one intervening word. She exposed learners to multiple sequences of nonsense words that each followed the pattern *aXb*, where *a* and *b* stand for particular words and the word in the *X* position varies across sequences. She found that infants noticed the nonadjacent dependency between words *a* and *b* when the *X* word alternated between 24 different words (but not when it alternated between 3 or 12 different words). That is, a high degree of variability in *X* caused infants to noticed the relationship between *a* and *b*. Taken together, the Gómez (2002) and Santelmann and Jusczyk (1998) studies demonstrate that 18-month-olds attend to just the kind of nonadjacent dependencies that define frames.

Additional evidence comes from work by Childers and Tomasello (2001) in which 2.5-year-olds were instructed to produce novel action-verbs in transitive frames. Experimenters modeled the task using English verbs in transitive frames. Children performed better when the task was modeled with verbs that were embedded in the frequently occurring pronoun frames (e.g., "He's pulling it," which creates the frame *he* _____ *it*) versus the less frequent frames created as a consequence of common noun arguments (e.g., "The cow's pulling the chair"). In other words, the verb category was more strongly activated when the verbs fell within frequent frames.

Of course, frames more broadly construed have been shown to play an important role in verb learning (Fisher, Gleitman, & Gleitman, 1991; Fisher et al., 1994; Gillette et al., 1999; Gleitman, 1990; Landau & Gleitman, 1985; Naigles & Hoff-Ginsberg, 1998). Finally, research from my own lab (Mintz, 2002) has shown that adults categorize nonsense words based on the words' distribution within frames.

In sum, a number of different studies from different lines of research support the notion that infants attend to framelike nonadjacent co-occurrences of words (and morphemes), and that for children and adults, the frame influences how an intervening word is processed.[2] Together, these independent lines of research converge in support of the notion that frames are a salient distributional environment for young language learners. I now consider why frequent frames might logically be thought to provide informative contexts for categorizing words, and in particular verbs.

Frequent Frames as an Informative Context

To understand the specific benefits frequent frames might provide, it is instructive to overview an alternative type of distributional information that has recently been studied—information from *bigrams* (Mintz et al., 1995, 2002; Redington et al., 1998). A bigram is any two-word sequence in an utterance, and, typically, one word provides the distributional context for the other. Two of the many differences of the frequent frames approach are worth mentioning because they demonstrate potential advantages of using frequent frames: (1) the use of more restricted contexts and (2) the use of the frequency of the distributional context as opposed to the frequency of the target word to select which target words to categorize.

Comparing Frame and Bigram Contexts

The difference between bigrams and frames is illustrated by comparing how the context of the target word is represented under each type of system. Recall that a frame is defined here as the two end elements of a three-word sequence. Thus, the target word, W, in the sequence "$X W Y$" occurs in the frame X _____ Y. In other words, it "jointly follows X and precedes Y." In contrast, bigram contexts would record two independent co-occurrence patterns, namely, "follows X," and "precedes Y." To understand the potential consequences of such a distinction, consider the three word sequence "to put it" that might occur in a child-directed utterance. Under the current approach, the word *put* would be recorded as falling within the frame *to* _____ *it*, and it would be classified with other words that fall within that frame throughout the corpus. When this frame was analyzed in six corpora of child-directed English (see below), the resulting category contained exclusively verbs. In contrast, in a bigram analysis, the representation of the word *put*'s distribution would overlap somewhat with the representation of all words that are immediately preceded by *to*, and all those that are immediately followed by *it*. For example, sequences like "to the store" and "know about it" would give rise to representations of *the* and *about* that overlap somewhat with the representation of *put*. *Put* would not necessarily be categorized with *the* and *about*—its category would depend on details of the specific computational model and corpus—but the possibility is greater than in a case in which distributional information comes from frames.

This example demonstrates that frame contexts are structurally more restrictive than bigrams because they involve a relationship between the context elements themselves (the framing words), in addition to the relationship between context and target word. Moreover, the frames used for categorization are required to be *frequent*, which imposes an additional constraint on the context (the frame). It is reasonable to assume, a priori, that if a given frame occurs frequently in a corpus of natural language, the co-occurrence of the frame words (i.e., the existence of the frame) is likely to be caused by some systematic aspect of the language, rather than by accident. Therefore, words that, throughout a corpus of speech, occur inside instances of a frequent frame are likely to have some linguistically pertinent relationship, such as grammatical category membership. This is not a necessary outcome, but arguably a likely consequence of using frequent frames as contexts. Thus, the added restrictive nature of frame contexts versus bigrams, while not specifically linguistic, plausibly provides a more linguistically relevant context.

Verbs, in particular, might benefit from framelike contexts, because in most simple transitive sentences, the verb's arguments form a frame around it. Given the relatively high frequencies of pronouns compared to full nouns, frequently occurring framing elements in subject and object position are likely to be the very small and frequent set of pronouns (and perhaps determiners in the object noun phrase). Hence, frames consisting of pronouns are likely to be very frequent and informative verb environments. With this in mind, recall that Childers and Tomasello (2001) reported that learning novel verbs is facilitated by pronoun-frame contexts.

Determining Which Words to Categorize

Another important difference between the present approach and prior distributional approaches concerns the criteria used to select which words are categorized. Although the selection criteria are logically independent of the categorization contexts (i.e., frame, bigram, etc.), in the bigram studies by Mintz et al. (2002) and Redington et al. (1998), the most frequent words in the corpus were categorized, regardless of the frequency of the contexts in which they occurred. A potential drawback to such "target-centered" selection criteria is that the contexts of the most frequent words may not be among the most informative. For example, the word *and* is very frequent, but it occurs in a variety of contexts because it is relatively free in the kinds of words and phrases it can conjoin (nouns, noun phrases, relative clauses, etc.). As a result, its immediate contexts are extremely varied and overlap with the distributional patterns of words from different grammatical categories. In contrast, in the present approach, only words occurring in frequent contexts (the frequent frames) are categorized. This imposes a frequency criterion on the context itself, rather than on the target words. Under the assumption that frames that occur frequently are governed by linguistically relevant phenomena, this selection criterion is potentially advantageous because it selects target words that have linguistically informative contexts. Again, the issue of target word selection is logically independent of the distributional contexts used for categorization; it just so happens that the recent bigram approaches used target-centered selection criterion, and the frequent frames approach uses a context-based criterion (but see chapter 3, this volume, for a different approach).

In summary, frames provide a more restricted distributional context than bigrams, and frequent frames might provide a way of constraining distributional analyses to contexts that are likely to be determined by structure in the grammar, and hence to be linguistically informative. This kind of restriction could be beneficial for filtering out accidental and potentially misleading co-occurrence patterns (Pinker, 1984, 1987) by providing a means of capturing relevant contexts before learning the grammatical details of a language. Finally, frequent frames might be especially well suited for identifying verbs in English, as frames might occur around transitive verbs more reliably than around other categories.

Frequent Frame Analysis of Six Corpora

Analyses reported in Mintz (2003) evaluated the usefulness of frequent frames in categorizing words by analyzing transcriptions of speech to six different children, taken from the CHILDES database (MacWhinney, 2000): Eve (Brown, 1973), Peter (Bloom, Hood, & Lightbown, 1974; Bloom, Lightbown, & Hood, 1975), Naomi (Sachs, 1983), Nina (Suppes, 1974), Anne (Theakston, Lieven, Pine, & Rowland, 2001), and Aran (Theakston et al., 2001). The frequent frames in each corpus were used to classify the words contained therein, and the resulting categories were compared to the target grammatical categories by visual inspection and by quantitative measures. Only sessions of each corpus in which the target child was 2 years, 6 months or younger were analyzed, and only utterances of the adults were analyzed. For a more complete description of the input corpora, see Mintz (2003).

Distributional Analysis Procedure

The following procedure was carried out separately on each corpus. First, an exhaustive tally was made of all the frames—where a frame is the first and third word of a three-word sequence—and the number of times each frame occurred in the corpus. Sequences that spanned two utterances could not contribute to a frame. Although utterance boundaries were explicitly marked in the corpora, there is evidence that infants perceive utterance boundaries from prosodic cues (Hirsh-Pasek et al., 1987), so restricting frames within utterances is not unreasonable. Next, a subset of these frames was selected as the set of frequent frames. The principles guiding inclusion in the set of frequent frames were that frames should occur frequently enough to be noticeable, and that they should also occur enough to include a variety of intervening words. Recall that variability within a frame was a crucial aspect of what made frames salient in Gómez's (2002) study. Several versions of the analysis were performed using different frequency criteria—one using an absolute frequency threshold, and another using a threshold that was relative to the total number of frames in the corpus. The outcomes varied little, so the results using only the relative threshold are discussed here. In that version, the set of frequent frames was selected to include all frames whose frequency in proportion to the total number of frames in the corpus surpassed a predetermined threshold. (Complete details can be found in Mintz, 2003.) This resulted in fewer than 50 frequent frames for each corpus (out of on average 2×10^4 unique frames). From the set of frequent frames that satisfied the frequency criterion, frames that had only one or two intervening word types were removed,[3] to ensure that there was some variability within the frames (Gómez, 2002). On average, only four frequent frames per corpus failed to satisfy this variability criterion.

Next, each instance of a given frequent frame was located in the corpus, and the intervening word was recorded and grouped together with the other intervening words for that frame, creating a frame-based category. The number of times each word occurred in a frame was also recorded. One can therefore distinguish between the number of word types that occur in a frequent frame, and the number of word tokens.

Quantitative Evaluation Measures

To obtain a standard measure of categorization success, comparable across corpora and to a control condition (described below), a quantitative measure of categorization called *accuracy* was calculated for each corpus. Accuracy was calculated by taking all the possible pairs of the words that were categorized together, and computing the proportion of pairs in which the items belonged to the same category. For example, if a frame-based category contained 30 words, there were 435 possible word pairs (30 × 29 / 2). If all words were verbs but one, all but 29 possible word pairings would result in pairs of the same category (since the one non-verb could pair with 29 verbs), so the accuracy would be 406 / 435, or .93.

Linguistic category membership was determined by hand using one of two different labeling protocols. In standard labeling, each categorized token was labeled as noun (nouns and pronouns), verb (verbs, auxiliaries, and copula forms), adjective, preposition, adverb, determiner, *wh*-word, "not," conjunction, or interjection. In expanded labeling, nouns and pronouns were labeled as distinct categories, as were verbs, auxiliaries, and the copula. In situations where the grammatical category of the word was ambiguous (for example, if it was unclear whether *walk* was used as a noun or a verb) the corpus was consulted to disambiguate and appropriately label the word.

Accuracy was the primary outcome measure. A second measure, completeness, assessed the degree to which the analysis grouped in the same frame-based category words that belong to the same grammatical category. High completeness scores result when words that belong to the same linguistic category are concentrated in one distributional category. For example, completeness would be higher if all the verbs in an analysis occurred in just one frame rather than two or three, regardless of how accurate the groupings were. A complete description of the evaluation metrics are given in Mintz (2003).

Computing Chance Categorization

Chance-categories were created for each corpus as a baseline control against which to compare the accuracy of the frame-based categories. For a given corpus, a chance-category was generated for each frame-based category such that it contained the same number of tokens as the corresponding frame-based category. The content of the chance-categories was determined by selecting the word tokens from all the frame-based categories at random and randomly assigning them to chance-categories. Token and type accuracy and completeness were computed (for both standard and expanded labeling) on the chance-categories to yield baseline measures.[4] The baseline essentially indicates the accuracy and completeness that could be achieved by randomly assigning the words in a manner that superficially matches the actual analysis (in the number and size of resulting categories) but ignores the distributional structure of the corpus.

Results of Frequent Frame Analysis

The frequent frames contained, on average, 450 different word types per corpus, comprising approximately 4,000 word tokens per corpus.[5] The number of tokens categorized in a given corpus was only about 5% of the total number of tokens in that corpus, but the types constituted approximately half of all the tokens in each corpus. In other words, for each instance a word occurred in a frequent frame, it occurred about nine times in a position that was not within a frequent frame. This means that a large portion of word types in a corpus pass through the most frequent frames, even if only a relatively small portion of tokens of each type do, allowing robust categorization with minimal analysis. But how well did frequent frames categorize words? And, in particular, how well did they categorize verbs?

Tables 1.1 and 1.2 provide representative examples of the several of the frame-based categories computed from two of the corpora. Frequent frames contained words from a range of categories, including nouns, verbs, adjectives, pronouns, adverbs, and auxiliaries. As the tables show, the words contained in each frame-based category were almost exclusively from one grammatical category, and many of these categories were verb categories. In fact, for all corpora, the plurality of frames contained verbs (and nearly only verbs).

Quantitative accuracy measures for frequent frame analyses were also very good, averaging .98 for tokens and .94 for types (significantly higher than chance baseline scores of .49 and .50, respectively), reflecting the fact that words within a given frame-based category were almost exclusively members of the same grammatical category. Completeness scores (.08 for token and type), although significantly higher than in the baseline analyses (.04 for token and type), were relatively low, reflecting the fact that although the derived categories were accurate, it was not the case that there was a single noun category, a single verb category, and so on. Rather, words from a given grammatical category often occurred

Table 1.1 Several frame-categories derived from the Peter corpus, including frequency counts

Peter					
you _____ it			*I _____ it*		*the _____ one*
put (52)	move (3)	squeeze (1)	see (18)	knock (1)	other (21)
see (28)	hold (3)	showing (1)	put (12)	knew (1)	red (11)
do (27)	give (3)	show (1)	think (9)	get (1)	yellow (8)
did (25)	fixing (3)	said (1)	got (8)	fixed (1)	green (8)
want (23)	drive (3)	rip (1)	thought (5)	finished (1)	orange (6)
fix (13)	close (3)	read (1)	have (5)	close (1)	big (6)
turned (12)	catch (3)	reach (1)	found (5)	build (1)	blue (5)
get (12)	threw (2)	pushed (1)	do (4)	bet (1)	right (4)
got (11)	taking (2)	push (1)	take (3)		small (3)
turn (10)	screw (2)	play (1)	open (3)		little (3)
throw (10)	say (2)	pick (1)	fix (3)		wrong (1)
closed (10)	ride (2)	parking (1)	did (3)		top (1)
think (9)	pushing (2)	made (1)	closed (3)		round (1)
leave (9)	hit (2)	love (1)	use (2)		only (1)
take (8)	hiding (2)	left (1)	tie (2)		light (1)
open (8)	had (2)	knock (1)	tear (2)		empty (1)
find (8)	eat (2)	knew (1)	need (2)		black (1)
bring (8)	carry (2)	hid (1)	know (2)		
took (7)	build (2)	flush (1)	hear (2)		
like (6)	brought (2)	finished (1)	guess (2)		
knocked (6)	write (1)	expected (1)	give (2)		
putting (5)	wiping (1)	dropped (1)	doubt (2)		
pull (5)	wipe (1)	drop (1)	wear (1)		
found (5)	wind (1)	draw (1)	took (1)		
make (4)	unzipped (1)	covered (1)	throw (1)		
have (4)	underneath (1)	closing (1)	threw (1)		
fixed (4)	turning (1)	call (1)	saw (1)		
finish (4)	touching (1)	broke (1)	read (1)		
try (3)	tore (1)	blow (1)	pushed 1)		
swallow (3)	tie (1)		pick (1)		
opened (3)	tear (1)		move (1)		
need (3)	swallowed (1)		leave (1)		

in several frames. This was especially true for verbs because, as previously mentioned, the plurality of frequent frames contained verbs. This issue will be taken up in a later section of this chapter.

Not only did frequent frames produce very accurate categories, but there was a considerable amount of consistency across the six corpora in the frequent frames that occurred. On average, 45% of the frequent frames that occurred in any given corpus occurred in at least three of the five additional corpora. Depending on the specific threshold criterion for frequent frames, approximately 20–30% of the

Table 1.2 Several frame-categories derived from the Aran corpus, including frequency counts

Aran					
you _____ *it*			*the* _____ *and*		*put* _____ *in*
put (28)	gave (2)	move (1)	tractor (5)	ignition (1)	it (49)
want (15)	found (2)	manage (1)	horse (4)	hut (1)	them (14)
do (10)	fit (2)	make (1)	shark (3)	holes (1)	him (11)
see (7)	enjoy (2)	load (1)	back (3)	hippo (1)	things (6)
take (6)	eat (2)	liked (1)	zoo (2)	hens (1)	that (5)
turn (5)	chose (2)	lift (1)	top (2)	ham (1)(1)	those (4)
taking (5)	catch (2)	licking (1)	tiger (2)	floor (1)	teddy (2)
said (5)	with (1)	let (1)	roof (2)	fire + engine (1)	dolly (2)
sure (4)	wind (1)	left (1)	leg (2)	eye (1)	yourself (1)
lost (4)	wear (1)	hit (1)	grass (2)	entrance (1)	you (1)
like (4)	use (1)	hear (1)	garage (2)	elephant (1)	what (1)
leave (4)	took (1)	give (1)	window (1)	dolly (1)	this (1)
got (4)	told (1)	flapped (1)	wellingtons (1)	doctor (1)	these (1)
find (4)	throwing (1)	fix (1)	water (1)	cups (1)	some (1)
throw (3)	stick (1)	finished (1)	video (1)	cows (1)	panda (1)
threw (3)	share (1)	drop (1)	train (1)	controls (1)	her (1)
think (3)	sang (1)	driving (1)	sun (1)	carts (1)	Pingu (1)
sing (3)	roll (1)	done (1)	station (1)	carpark (1)	
reach (3)	ride (1)	did (1)	stars (1)	cake (1)	
picked (3)	recognise (1)	cut (1)	shop (1)	bus (1)	
get (3)	reading (1)	crashed (1)	shirt (1)	bull (1)	
dropped (3)	ran (1)	change (1)	sand (1)	brush (1)	
seen (2)	pulled (1)	calling (1)	round (1)	box (1)	
lose (2)	pull (1)	bring (1)	rain (1)	bottom (1)	
know (2)	press (1)	break (1)	pussycat (1)	book (1)	
knocked (2)	pouring (1)	because (1)	postbox (1)	blue (1)	
hold (2)	pick (1)	banged (1)	panda (1)	bits (1)	
help (2)	on (1)		nuts (1)	bank (1)	
had (2)	need (1)		mother (1)	bananas (1)	
			monkey (1)	animals (1)	
			lion (1)	air (1)	
			kite (1)		

frequent frames for a given corpus occurred in all six corpora; for verbs, these included frames like *you* _____ *it, you* _____ *the*, and *to* _____ *it*. The consistency is appealing because it indicates that informative contexts are not idiosyncratic in the input to any particular child; this, in turn, means that a learner would not have to adjust his or her frame-based processing from one speaker to another. Whatever factors determine the structure of frames in a sample of speech apparently have broad similarity across corpora, as would be the case for reflexes of the grammar, as opposed to influences from idiosyncrasies of the speaker and situation.

Further Consolidation of Frame-Based Categories

These findings suggest that frequent frames could provide an extremely informative context for categorizing words. However, several issues need to be addressed to further understand how frames could provide a basis for finding the verbs. One issue has to do with how comprehensive the frame-based categories are: As noted above, while it is clearly the case that the groupings that the frame-based analyses produces are very accurate, there are multiple frame-based categories that correspond to a given linguistic category. The learner would need a way of consolidating a number of frame-based categories to come up with a uniform class that corresponds to a linguistic category. Fortunately, there is at least one plausible way that further consolidation can be achieved using information inherent in the frame categories themselves.

Not surprisingly, there is considerable overlap in the words contained in many of the frame-based categories. For example, the verb categories defined by frames *you _____ to, she _____ to, you _____ the*, and so on, will generally have a number of member words in common because many of the same verbs can appear in each environment. Hence, multiple frame-based categories could be unified if they surpass a threshold of lexical overlap, and the resulting *consolidated* category might be a much more comprehensive collection of, say, all the categorized verbs in a corpus. This procedure was tested on the results from the six analyzed corpora, using a criterion of 20% token overlap. Specifically, each frame-based category was exhaustively compared to all the others; for a comparison between any frame-based categories A and B, if 20% of the tokens in category A were also in category B, and 20% of the tokens in category B were also in category A, then A and B were tagged to be joined into one consolidated category. All such comparisons between categories were performed only once, before any consolidation was carried out, and consolidation was transitive: if A and B were tagged to be joined, and B and C were tagged to be joined, then the consolidation process would place tokens in A, B, and C, in the same consolidated category.

The results produced consolidated categories that were as accurate as the categories defined by the individual frequent frames. In addition, the procedure came considerably closer to comprehensively including all the analyzed words of a given grammatical category. Interestingly, the largest consolidated category for each corpus (in tokens, and in types in all but one case) contained predominantly verbs. For example, in the Peter corpus, 24 frame-based categories containing primarily verbs were consolidated into one category containing 2,904 tokens (254 types) that were main verbs, auxiliaries, or copulas, out of a total of 3,191 tokens (283 types). These high proportions were actually the lowest out of all of the corpora. Table 1.3 gives descriptive information for the largest consolidated category for each corpus (always verbs) resulting from the initial frame-based categories. The table includes the number of frame categories that were joined, and the number and proportion of verbs (including modals, auxiliaries, and copula forms) in tokens

Table 1.3 Number of frequent frames underlying the largest consolidated category, by corpus

Corpus	Number of Frames Consolidated Into Largest (Verb) Category	Verb Token Proportions	Verb Type Proportions
Peter	24	2904 / 3191 (91%)	254 / 283 (90%)
Eve	16	1449 / 1468 (99%)	180 / 194 (93%)
Nina	10	1316 / 1333 (99%)	155 / 167 (93%)
Naomi	18	690 / 700 (99%)	135 / 144 (94%)
Anne	13	1445 / 1474 (98%)	169 / 182 (93%)
Aran	9	1721 / 1760 (98%)	199 / 224 (89%)
Mean	15	Total tokens (97%)	Total types (92%)

Proportions represent the number of verbs (tokens and types) in the largest consolidated category out of the total number of words in that category (percentages in parentheses).

and in types. As the table shows, on average, across all corpora, 97% of the tokens in the largest consolidated category were verbs. Tables 1.4 and 1.5 list the largest category for two of the corpora: the Peter corpus, which yields the poorest verb category, and the Eve corpus, which yields one of the best and is representative of the other corpora.

In sum, these findings suggest that frequent frames could provide a robust cue for categorizing words and could be particularly informative for categorizing verbs. But so far the discussion has been focused on how the distribution of words in frequent frames could be used as grouping cue, one that would group nouns with other nouns, verbs with other verbs, and so on. But grouping is only a part of true linguistic categorization: The learner must also identify which of the frame-based categories are the verbs, which are the nouns, and so on. It was not enough that the children in Brown's (1957) study knew that *sib* was a different kind of word in the environments *to sib* and *sibbing* compared to *a sib* or *any sib*. They had to know what the specific linguistic consequences were; essentially, they had to know that *sib* was a verb in one case and a noun in the other. How could children identify the verbs in categories derived from frequent frames?

Linking Frame-Based Categories to Syntactic Categories

One solution assumes that part of children's innate linguistic knowledge is that there are categories such as noun, verb, and adjective. The problem then becomes one of labeling or associating distributionally derived categories with the innately specified system. Although it is questionable whether verb referents can be identified by learners without access to sentential structural information (Gleitman, 1990), the referents of concrete nouns have been argued to be recoverable from observations of the circumstances in which they are used (see also discussions in

Table 1.4 Largest consolidated category for the Peter corpus

put (307)	pull (24)	tear (9)	learn (5)	smell (3)	throwing (2)	wish (1)	singing (1)	misunderstood (1)	finding (1)
want (262)	read (21)	know (9)	fixing (5)	said (3)	talk (2)	wiping (1)	shut (1)	missed (1)	feed (1)
have (182)	hit (21)	knocked (9)	*down (5)	rip (3)	start (2)	*who (1)	sharpening (1)	mess (1)	fasten (1)
see (143)	do (21)	help (9)	carry (5)	pushing (3)	showing (2)	*what (1)	set (1)	marked (1)	expected (1)
*in (131)	push (20)	catch (9)	bet (5)	pushed (3)	shaking (2)	wear (1)	scared (1)	love (1)	erase (1)
think (96)	going (19)	unscrew (8)	wipe (4)	patting (3)	saw (2)	waving (1)	scare (1)	lost (1)	emptying (1)
like (92)	find (19)	made (8)	were (4)	opened (3)	repeat (2)	watching (1)	saying (1)	losing (1)	emptied (1)
get (83)	use (16)	guess (8)	unwind (4)	left (3)	remember (2)	watch (1)	s(u)pposed (1)	lock (1)	dropped (1)
take (76)	turned (15)	*about (8)	told (4)	kick (3)	lose (2)	walk (1)	run (1)	listening (1)	drop (1)
need (75)	try (15)	write (7)	tie (4)	*into (3)	learned (2)	using (1)	referring (1)	lifted (1)	drawing (1)
fix (73)	took (15)	screw (7)	swallow (4)	*how (3)	knew (2)	unzipped (1)	*ready (1)	lick (1)	decorate (1)
*on (72)	finish (15)	knock (7)	roll (4)	hiding (3)	*inside (2)	untie (1)	reach (1)	kissed (1)	covered (1)
open (70)	closed (15)	fixed (7)	riding (4)	*for (3)	hurt (2)	understood (1)	promise (1)	juggle (1)	cover (1)
do (66)	move (14)	cut (7)	pour (4)	feel (3)	heard (2)	underneath (1)	practiced (1)	hug (1)	cook (1)
is (64)	hear (13)	say (6)	*from (4)	dump (3)	hand (2)	under (1)	poured (1)	hole (1)	come (1)
turn (56)	found (13)	making (6)	eating (4)	drink (3)	goin(g) (2)	tying (1)	pointing (1)	hid (1)	closing (1)
make (40)	eat (13)	keep (6)	changed (4)	brought (3)	go (2)	tryin(g) (1)	persuade (1)	having (1)	clicking (1)
throw (38)	wind (12)	drive (6)	break (4)	bringing (3)	giving (2)	tried (1)	pay (1)	havin(g) (1)	chew (1)
got (38)	trying (12)	doing (6)	*at (4)	bite (3)	finished (2)	touching (1)	passed (1)	has (1)	*by (1)
close (35)	show (12)	does (6)	writing (3)	*behind (3)	empty (2)	tore (1)	parking (1)	*happy (1)	buy (1)
leave (31)	putting (12)	change (6)	was (3)	*all (3)	drew (2)	tip (1)	pack (1)	grabbed (1)	bouncing (1)
hold (30)	play (12)	build (6)	turning (3)	*with (2)	doubt (2)	thougt (1)	*over (1)	goes (1)	blow (1)
did (30)	draw (12)	bang (6)	*through (3)	were (2)	call (2)	taught (1)	opening (1)	getting (1)	bend (1)
thought (29)	touch (11)	*under (5)	threw (3)	wearing (2)	broke (2)	taping (1)	*off (1)	gave (1)	be (1)
ride (28)	wanted (10)	talking (5)	stir (3)	wash (2)	bought (2)	swallowed (1)	*of (1)	forgot (1)	*back (1)
give (28)	tell (10)	pick (5)	stick (3)	used (2)	are (2)	supposed (1)	*not (1)	fold (1)	attach (1)
bring (25)	tape (10)	mean (5)	squeeze (3)	unwrap (2)	answer (2)	stuff (1)	*near (1)	flush (1)	ask (1)
*to (24)	taking (10)	let (5)	spill (3)	understand (2)	work (1)	spread (1)	moving (1)	fitting (1)	*and (1)
	had 10					sit (1)			Pat (1)

Words are ranked by frequency in the contributing frames (listed in parentheses), and asterisks indicate words that did not adhere to the predominant verb tendency of the category.

Table 1.5 Largest consolidated category for the Eve corpus

want (143)	fold (8)	turned (3)	buy (2)	shake (1)
have (118)	did (8)	stir (3)	bed (2)	scratch (1)
put (91)	thought (7)	spill (3)	ask (2)	rocking (1)
like (91)	finish (7)	sing (3)	are (2)	reading (1)
get (63)	dropped (7)	shoot (3)	wrote (1)	reach (1)
going (54)	crack (7)	putting (3)	wiped (1)	ran (1)
see (52)	be (7)	jump (3)	wear (1)	push (1)
do (52)	wipe (6)	hit (3)	washed (1)	pour (1)
take (35)	spilled (6)	had (3)	wanted (1)	poke (1)
eat (34)	need (6)	goin(g) (3)	wan(t) (1)	pointing (1)
know (30)	move (6)	drop (3)	use (1)	playing (1)
say (26)	help (6)	catch (3)	untied (1)	ought (1)
play (25)	do (6)	bit (3)	twist (1)	must (1)
think (24)	cook (6)	watch (2)	turning (1)	loving (1)
read (24)	were (5)	wash (2)	trying (1)	look (1)
write (21)	taste (5)	untie (2)	try (1)	liked (1)
turn (16)	peel (5)	tie (2)	top (1)	lick (1)
make (16)	open (5)	swim (2)	throwing (1)	left (1)
find (15)	cut (5)	standing (2)	talk (1)	learn (1)
tell (14)	chew (5)	saying (2)	swallow (1)	kiss (1)
go (14)	blow (5)	riding (2)	suck (1)	*just (1)
doing (14)	bite (5)	*on (2)	stick (1)	*it (1)
throw (13)	*with (4)	made (2)	step (1)	*how (1)
bring (13)	went (4)	leave (2)	stay (1)	hope (1)
sit (12)	took (4)	knit (2)	stand (1)	heard (1)
give (12)	shut (4)	keep (2)	spit (1)	*head (1)
drink (12)	said (4)	fixed (2)	*some (1)	having (1)
hear (11)	pull (4)	fall (2)	snap (1)	guess (1)
fix (11)	pee + pee (4)	eating (2)	slipped (1)	*glad (1)
show (10)	*in (4)	cracking (2)	slept (1)	gave (1)
hold (10)	hurt (4)	cool (2)	sleep (1)	found (1)
touch (9)	draw (4)	come (2)	sitting (1)	*for (1)
had (8)	climb (4)	color (2)	shook (1)	fly (1)
got (8)	wish (3)	close (2)	sharing (1)	fixed (1)
forgot (8)	wind (3)	carry (2)	share (1)	finished (1)
				drinking (1)
				drew (1)

Words are ranked by frequency (listed in parentheses), and asterisks indicate words that did not adhere to the predominant verb tendency of the category.

Fisher et al., 1994; Gillette et al., 1999). If this is so, then the distributional category that contains nouns could be readily identified based on the concrete nouns that are its members. Note that using a semantic-to-syntactic generalization to label an independently derived category avoids the one-to-many mapping problem encountered when attempting to derive syntactic categories from semantic ones because the semantic information is simply used to determine a general tendency of a group of words that is independently categorized. (Indeed, this combined use of distributional and semantic information approaches more closely Maratsos & Chalkley's 1980 proposal.)

Once the noun category (or categories) is labeled, identifying the distributional class which contains verbs becomes much more straightforward and is perhaps achievable without recourse to additional semantic information. A cross-linguistically viable procedure would be to label as verb the frame-based category whose members satisfy one of a predetermined set of possible relationships with already identified nouns, specifically, the category whose members take the nouns as arguments. A coarse representation of the argument structure of a set of utterances—the position of the nouns and a limited set of possible verb positions—might be sufficient to determine which distributionally defined word class is the verb category. Thus, initially words would be clustered distributionally. Next, the cluster containing nouns would be identified from the semantic tendencies of its members. The location of nouns in utterances would then be used by syntactically constrained mechanisms to guide the labeling of the verb category.

The procedure just outlined for labeling the verb category requires some notion of predicate-argument structure. Interestingly, an effective procedure for labeling verbs exists for the corpora analyzed here that does not require such knowledge. In these corpora, verbs are the largest categories after nouns. If the noun categories are labeled following the manner above, the next largest category could be identified as the verbs. Such an approach would be successful if applied to the consolidated categories as well. Of course, such a simplistic procedure for identifying the verb categories might not turn out to be viable cross-linguistically, or even in other English corpora. Nevertheless, the results from the present analyses leave open the intriguing possibility that identifying the frequent frames that contain verbs is possible without calling upon knowledge of predicate-argument relations.

There is an alternative to the view that the distributionally defined categories must be linked to syntactic labels and that infants have innate knowledge of syntactic categories. According to Tomasello (2000a, 2000b), children's early lexical categories are not abstract adult categories, like "verb." Rather, initial categories are "item based" and organized around the specific environments in which words occur. The present findings might appear to mesh well with this view: Children's early grammar could be constructed around individual (or consolidated) frame-based categories, and only later would these categories take on the more abstract status as in the adult grammar. In that case, perhaps one need not posit that children have an innate verb category that must be associated with the relevant frequent frames. But, eventually, children would have to assign words to the adult category, and something akin to the labeling procedures outlined above would be required. Thus, even if children's initial categories turn out to be more restricted than adults, the issue of how they are eventually integrated into an adult grammar remains.

The previous discussion provided a practical demonstration that a distributional analysis using frequent frames as contexts could successfully group words in accordance with their grammatical category. Approximately half the words in a corpus were categorized by analyzing the distributional contexts of only 5% of the tokens, so frequent frames are efficient categorizing contexts as well. Together with research suggesting that infants attend to frame-like context, these findings suggest that infants may well be carrying out the kinds of analyses necessary to categorize words using frequent frames. I will now present preliminary findings that show that 12-month-old infants categorize novel words based on the words' distribution within frequent frames, and that they may be especially sensitive to frames that contain verbs.

Evidence That Children Use Distributional Information to Categorize Novel Words

This experiment used a version of the headturn preference procedure (HPP; Hirsh-Pasek et al., 1987; Kemler Nelson et al., 1995), similar to the one described by Jusczyk and Aslin (1995). First, infants heard a set of sentences that each contained a nonsense word; they were then tested on whether they categorized the nonsense words based on the frames in which the words occurred. In half the sentences, the nonsense word occurred in a noun frame (henceforth, *nonce nouns*), and in the other half, the nonsense word occurred in a verb frame (henceforth, *nonce verbs*). For example, in "She wants you to deeg it," the nonce word occurred in the *to* _____ *it* verb frame; in "I see the bist in the room," the nonce word occurred in the *the* _____ *in* noun frame. After familiarizing an infant with sentences like these, categorization was assessed by testing for a difference in the infant's listening preference to novel grammatical sentences, in which the occurrence of the nonce word was supported by the distributional information (e.g., "I deeg you now!"), versus novel ungrammatical sentences (e.g., "I bist you now!"). The ungrammatical and grammatical sentences differed only in the nonce word. A difference in infants' preference for grammatical versus ungrammatical sentences indicated that they could discriminate the two sentence types. The simplest explanation of such a discrimination was that infants categorized the novel words based on the distributional information in the familiarization sentences and noticed whether the nonce word occurred in a position that was consistent with that categorization. Counterbalancing procedures (see below) further ensured that infants' listening behavior was not due simply to an idiosyncratic preference for a specific sentence or sentences but rather reflected the relation between test and familiarization sentences.

Twenty-four infants averaging 12 months, 2 days (range 11 months, 15 days, to 12 months, 14 days) participated in the study, and were randomly assigned to two groups, A and B, with equal numbers of subjects in each group. Group assignment determined which of two counterbalanced sets of familiarization materials an infant heard.

Familiarization Stimuli

The full set of materials for groups A and B is given in table 1.6. Each infant heard two nonce verbs and two nonce nouns in a total of 12 familiarization sentences: 6 containing verbs and 6 containing nouns. The 6 verb sentences were comprised of two sets of "pair-sentences" and two singleton sentences. Paired sentences were identical except they differed in the particular nonce word; for example, one pair in group A was "She wants you to deeg it," and the other was "She wants you to lonk it." The four pair-sentences provided the distributional basis for categorizing the two verbs together. The two singleton sentences each contained

Table 1.6 Familiarization sentences, group A & B, and test sentences, both groups

GROUP A	
Verb Frame Familiarization Sentences	*Noun Frame Familiarization Sentences*
She wants to *deeg* it.	I see *the gorp in* the room.
She wants *to lonk* it.	I see *the bist in* the room.
You *can deeg*.	That's *your gorp*.
You *can lonk*.	That's *your bist*.
Can *you deeg the* room?	I put *his gorp on* the box.
I *lonk you* now!	Here's *a bist of* a dog.

GROUP B	
Verb Frame Familiarization Sentences	*Noun Frame Familiarization Sentences*
She wants *to gorp* it.	I see *the deeg in* the room.
She wants *to bist* it.	I see *the lonk in* the room.
You *can gorp*.	That's *your deeg*.
You *can bist*.	That *your lonk*.
Can *you gorp the* room?	I put *his deeg on* the box.
I *bist you* now!	Here's *a lonk of* a dog.

TEST ITEMS	
Grammatical-A, Ungrammatical-B	*Ungrammatical-A, Grammatical-B*
Can *you lonk the* room?	Can *you bist the* room?
I *deeg you* now!	I *gorp you* now!
I put *his bist on* the box.	I put *his lonk on* the box
Here's *a gorp of* a dog.	Here's *a deeg of* a dog.

a different one of the two nonce verbs. The singletons provided a basis for later testing categorization because the missing pair corresponded to one of the novel grammatical test items (e.g., the singleton "I lonk you now!" has the test sentence counterpart "I deeg you now!"). Nonce-noun sentences followed the same structure.

An attempt was made to select frames that were found in the prior distributional analyses to be frequent frames across the six analyzed corpora. The prevalence of a given frame across all corpora was taken to be an indicator of its general ubiquity in speech to children and of the likelihood that it would be recognized by infants in our study. An additional selection criterion was that none of the frames shared the same initial word or the same final word. That is, selection of the frame *you _____ the* precluded selection of the frame *you _____ it.*[6] Because of this constraint, it was not possible to select only frames that occurred in all six corpora because the most frequent and consistent frames overlapped considerably in the framing elements. Nevertheless, two of the verb frames were frequent frames in all six corpora, and one (occurring in a singleton sentence) was a frequent frame in four of the six corpora; one noun frame was a frequent frame in all six corpora, and one (occurring in a singleton sentence) was so in five. The frame surrounding the nonce noun in the remaining singleton noun sentence, "I put his _____ on the box," was not a frequent frame in any corpus because no other frequent frames satisfied the restriction on shared elements. However, that sentence followed the general structure of existing frequent frames in that it there was a determiner to the left and a preposition, *on*, to the right.

Finally, in one of the noun frames and one of the verb frames, the frame context was modified to allow the nonce word to be the last word in the sentence. This was done in order to heighten the salience of these novel word forms and increase the likelihood that infants would successfully segment them when they were sentence-internal. Thus, nonce words in those sentences were not strictly in frames. Nevertheless, the majority of occurrences of a given nonce word in the familiarization materials was within a frequent frame.

Although both nonce nouns and nonce verbs occurred in frequent frames, the frequency of the noun frames and verb frames differed in the six corpora. Pooling the corpora, the verb frames in this study occurred with an overall frequency of approximately 2,200, whereas the noun frames occurred approximately 820 times. Hence, the relative difference in frequency between frames types is close to a factor of three. Inasmuch as these differences are indicative of relative differences in frame frequency in the input to a given child, one might predict that the frame environments for nouns and verbs in this study would be differently effective in mediating categorization. Thus, we might expect categorization to be stronger in this study for verbs than for nouns, on the assumption that the more frequent environments might more readily foster categorization.

As can be seen by comparing materials for the two groups, in table 1.6, the nonce words were counterbalanced across groups A and B, such that nonce nouns for group A were nonce verbs for group B, and vice versa.

Test Stimuli

The four singleton frames (two for nouns, two for verbs) provided environments to test category generalization. Table 1.6 shows the eight test items that were presented to both familiarization groups after the familiarization phase. Each singleton familiarization sentence provided the basis for one novel grammatical and one novel ungrammatical test sentence. The grammatical sentence was created by replacing the nonce word with the one from the same category that did not occur in that frame during familiarization. The ungrammatical sentence was created by replacing the nonce word with one of the nonce words from the other category. Thus, group A's familiarization sentence, "Can you deeg the room?," formed the basis for creating the novel grammatical test sentence "Can you lonk the room?" and the novel ungrammatical test sentence, "Can you bist the room?" Both groups of infants received the same test items. Due to the counterbalanced design, grammatical test sentences for group A infants were ungrammatical for group B infants, and vice versa. This ensured that grammaticality was not confounded with particular test sentences.

The familiarization and test sentences were recorded by a trained female native English speaker who was blind to the predictions of the experiment. The speaker was trained to produce the sentences with normal prosody, appropriate for a simple declarative sentence or a question. The spoken materials were then digitized onto the computer that controlled the experiment.

Procedure

The infant sat on the caretaker's lap in a sound-attenuated booth, and the experimenter sat in a separate control room. On each wall to the right and left of the infant, approximately at the infant's eye level, a yellow light was mounted, and beneath each light was a loudspeaker. On the wall in front of the infant a red light was mounted, and beneath the light was a small video camera through which the experimenter could view the infant. The presentation of stimuli through the loudspeakers and the activation of the lights were controlled by a computer. The computer also measured and recorded the infant's orientation times to each test stimulus, as indicated by the experimenter. During the experiment, the parent listened to masking music through tightly fitting headphones.

To initiate the experiment, the center light flashed until the infant looked center, at which point the center light was extinguished and the familiarization sentences were played through both loudspeakers. While the familiarization sentences played, the lights functioned as in the test phase to help keep the infant alert (see below), however the familiarization materials were played continuously and independently of the infant's head turn behavior and the light activity. The familiarization sentences were presented in six randomized blocks, for a total duration of approximately 90 seconds. Group A subjects heard familiarization sentences from List A, Group B subjects heard sentences from counterbalanced List B.

Following the familiarization phase was a brief contingency training phase. The center light was activated until the infant oriented to it for 2 seconds. The light was then extinguished and a randomly selected side light was activated. When the infant looked towards the side light, a 500-Hz pure tone with a duration of one second was repeated through the associated loudspeaker with a 100-ms pause between repetitions. The tone repeated until the infant looked away for two consecutive seconds or until the completion of 15 repetitions. At that point the light was extinguished, the sound stopped, and the center light commenced flashing to initiate a new trial. There were two trials of this type to provide the infant with a demonstration of the contingency between the lights, the auditory stimulus presentation, and the infant's behavior.

Test trials were identical to contingency training trials except that test sentences replaced the pure tone and the duration of the pause between repetitions of a test item within a trial was approximately 300 ms. On a given trial, infants heard one of the eight test sentences (four grammatical, four ungrammatical). Trials were presented in two blocks, with trial order randomized within each block. Group A and Group B subjects heard the same test items; but the grammatical sentences for Group A subjects were the ungrammatical sentences for Group B subjects, and vice versa.

Selection of the stimulus presentation side on a given trial was random but constrained such that the same side would not be selected in more than three consecutive trials.

Results and Discussion

Overall, infants listened longer to ungrammatical over grammatical strings. Infants' mean listening time to grammatical and ungrammatical sentences was 7.5 seconds (SE = .35) and 8.2 (SE = .33) seconds, respectively. The difference was significant by a two-tailed t-test, $t(23) = -3.38$, $p < .005$, and by a Wilcoxon matched-pairs signed-ranks test ($p < .005$). Eighteen out of 24 infants showed longer looking times to ungrammatical sentences. Since the only systematic difference between the two sentence types was the distributional category of nonce words, infants' sensitivity to the difference strongly suggests that they categorized the nonce words based on distributional information.

Next, the grammaticality effect was tested separately for noun frame and verb frame sentences. Recall that the corpus frequencies of the noun frames and verb frames differed such that the verb frames were nearly three times as frequent as the noun frames. It was of interest, then, to see if there was a correlated difference in the degree to which the noun and verb frame contexts revealed the grammaticality effect. Separate analyses of listening times to test sentences in which the nonce word was in a verb frame and those in which the nonce word was in a noun frame revealed that the grammaticality effect was due entirely to verb-frame sentences. For noun-frame sentences, listening times to grammatical and ungrammatical items were not significantly different (7.5 s, SE = .42, and 7.8 s, SE = .46, respectively; $t(23) = -.581$, n.s.), whereas listening times to grammatical and ungrammatical verb-frame items were (7.5 s, SE = .41, and 8.6 s, SE = .26, respectively; $t(23) = -4.32$, $p < .001$, two-tailed). Figure 1.1 graphs mean listening times to grammatical and ungrammatical sentences for each frame type individually.

The grammaticality effect provides support for the hypothesis that 12-month-olds categorized novel verbs based on distributional information in the familiarization sentences. Thus, at an age when infants are just starting to produce their first words, they apparently are using sequential information to group words into classes. The failure to find this effect in the noun frame items could have been due to a variety of factors, and should be interpreted with caution. However, an intriguing possibility is that the difference in the effect for noun frames and verb frames is related to their different relative frequencies in children's input. As previously mentioned, the noun frames were, overall, less frequent in the corpus analyses than the verb frames. These and other factors could have resulted in the verb frames being noticed more, or used more effectively for categorization.

It is interesting to note that in a study with older, 15-month-old learners of German, Hohle, Weissenborn, Kiefer, Schulz, and Schmitz (2004) found evidence that infants use distributional information to categorize novel nouns, but not novel verbs. Using bigram contexts, they showed that novel words following a

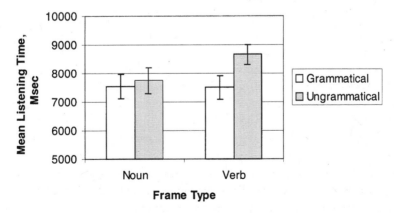

Figure 1.1. Mean listening times to grammatical and ungrammatical sentences, by frame type.

determiner were categorized as nouns but novel words following a subject pronoun were not categorized as verbs. They attributed this difference to the fact that determiners are more predictive of nouns than pronouns are of verbs in child-directed German. In other words, they, too, linked categorization to distributional properties in the input. There are other differences between Hohle et al.'s study and this study that could account for differences in the results. But in a broader sense, the findings are similar: both studies suggest that categorization is driven by the informativeness of distributional contexts.

An additional point is that in this study, detecting categorization of the nonce words depended on different environments than initially categorizing them did. Infants may have categorized the nonce nouns together based on the familiarization pair-sentences (e.g., "I see the gorp in the room!" and "I see the bist in the room!"), but the test sentences may not have provided a sufficient cue to trigger recognition of the category. To address these issues, we are carrying out further studies in our lab to replicate the finding with verbs and to explore conditions under which categorization of noun frames might also be obtained.

Whatever the explanation for the advantage for verb categorization turns out to be, the verb/noun discrepancy suggests further that infants' categorization of verbs was not solely due to the distributional information contained within the familiarization material itself. If a grammaticality effect had resulted for both verb frames and noun frames, one could not with certainty conclude that categorization was due to the frames being frames of English. That is, the patterning of the nonce words in the set of familiarization sentences could provide evidence to a distributional learner who lacked experience with English that certain words "belonged together" (Mintz, 2002). Although evidence of strictly experiment-internal distributional learning would certainly be interesting, the present pattern of results suggests that this is not the critical process at work. The immediate distributional environments of the nonce nouns and nonce verbs are, formally, equally informative. But they differ is in the range of situations in which a given infant has heard those words and environments prior to the study. Infants apparently brought their experience with English to bear on how they analyzed the nonce words in this study.

A final note of caution is warranted in interpreting the results as evidence of infants' categorization from frames as such. Although the frequent frames were carefully selected for the experimental materials, in accord with the corpus analyses presented earlier, there is no guarantee that the categorization cues infants used were the frames themselves. There could be other informative distributional cues that infants exploited, including bigram information from the word preceding (or following) the nonce word. However, much research that I am aware of on bigram contexts suggests that bigram cues aid categorization only when correlated cues are provided from other sources, for example, phonological cues, semantic cues, or other types of distributional cues (Braine, 1987; Frigo & McDonald, 1998; Gerken, Gómez, & Nurmsoo, 1999; Gómez & Lakusta, 2004; Mintz, 2002; Smith,

1966; Wilson, 2000; Wilson, Gerken, & Nicol, 2000). In normal circumstances, correlated cues certainly are available (see chapter 3, this volume), and it is reasonable to suppose that learners will recruit converging sources of information in acquisition. However, in this study it is unlikely that any other source of information was available apart from distributional patterns.[7] Future work can make use of this experimental method to elucidate what specific distributional cues infants respond to. For example, by manipulating the distributional contexts such that frame-based accounts would predict degraded categorization performance but other accounts (e.g., bigram models) would not predict a change, one can see whether infants' behavior follows one or the other prediction in a consistent manner.

General Discussion

The first part of this chapter propounded, on logical and empirical grounds, the benefits of frequent frames in providing distributional information from which learners could determine the category membership of novel words. The second part of the chapter presented a preliminary step in investigating whether very young children indeed categorize a novel word based on its distribution within frames. The initial results suggest that, as early as 12 months of age, infants categorize novel words based on some type of distributional information, and, tentatively that infants might be especially sensitive to the distributional information relevant to verbs. Although the results of the study with infants are consistent with the interpretation that infants categorized based on frames, many details remain to be worked out as to precisely which distributional patterns were and are the relevant ones. Nevertheless, the fact that infants used distributional information to categorize words after very little exposure and that categorization is measurable with this experimental technique suggest that further research will shed light on these remaining questions.

Cross-Linguistic Viability

The distributional analyses explored here rely on word order patterns to form categories. As noted above, the patterns corresponding to simple transitive sentences might make frequent frames especially useful for categorizing many verbs. Given the fact that word order patterns differ cross-linguistically and that in many languages word order is much freer than in English, it is important to consider whether this approach to categorization is universally viable. Two points about this issue are worth noting. First, in a language in which word order is relatively free—grammatical relations being marked by inflectional morphology—it may turn out that there is nevertheless enough consistency in word orders that informative frequent frames would result. This is clearly an empirical question, however

Slobin and Bever (1982) have shown that both children and adults prefer canonical patterns for sequencing nouns and verbs, even in free word order languages (e.g., Turkish). Perhaps these canonical patterns will turn out to yield informative frequent frames. Second, even if canonical patterns are not informative, the essential properties of frequent frames might nevertheless be relevant for categorization in heavily inflected, free word order languages. A fundamental property of a frequent frame is that it is a relatively local context defined by frequently co-occurring units. In the procedures explored here, the units were words and the frame contexts were defined by words that frequently co-occur. In heavily inflectional languages, frequently co-occurring units are likely to be the inflectional morphemes, which are limited in number and are extremely frequent (much like the pronouns and other closed-class words in the frames here). Hence, if the learning mechanisms that notice nonadjacent dependencies (Gómez, 2002) are flexible as to the level of granularity of the entities involved (i.e., words or affixes), such mechanisms would potentially identify frames in which the framing elements are inflections.[8] Indeed, the morphosyntactic dependencies that infants in Santelmann and Jusczyk's (1998) study represented involved the affix -*ing*. It is an empirical question whether morphological frames would provide useful category information for the relevant languages or whether other types of distributional information is best suited for analysis at this level; what type of information is relevant for infant learners of these languages is yet another empirical question. Clearly, further research into typologically different languages is necessary to determine whether a frame-based approach is universal applicability. Of course, cross-linguistic issues equally impact other types of distributional information. With additional flexibility of the type just described, frequent frames are amenable, in principle, to categorization in typologically different languages.

Summary and Conclusion

In summary, as with other recent studies, the frequent frames analyses described here demonstrate that many of the hypothesized problems for bootstrapping into word categories from distributional information turn out not to be relevant when actual corpora are analyzed. Furthermore, the nonadjacent dependencies involved in frequent frames form distributional patterns to which infants and young children have been shown to be sensitive. The distributional analyses presented here show that these patterns would be especially useful for categorizing verbs: frames containing verbs constituted the plurality of frequent frames, and when overlapping frame-based categories were joined together, the largest category contained the verbs. An account was provided as to how distributionally defined categories could become syntactic. The proposal was that the distributional information provides a bootstrap into a preexisting linguistic system in which grammatical form-class categories—e.g., noun, verb, adjective—are distinguished:[9] Frequent frames provide a means of initially categorizing words; then the distributional category that contains the nouns can be identified by the tendency of its members to refer to concrete objects. Several possible procedures for identifying the distributional category containing the verbs were then discussed: either by simple descriptive properties (e.g., the largest category that is not the nouns) or more linguistically informed procedures that involve structural notions. Just as cross-linguistic research is necessary to empirically test the viability of frequent frames as a universal approach to initial word classification, cross-linguistic research is also necessary to determine what kinds of mechanisms might be universally appropriate for labeling the verb category, but several plausible options are available.

Finally, the accompanying behavioral study was an initial investigation into infants' use of frames in categorizing novel words. The results demonstrate that infants as young as 12 months of age categorize novel words based on distributional information. After hearing novel words used in very limited contexts, infants categorized the words on distributional grounds. Moreover, there is some indication, although preliminary, that 12-month-olds might be selectively attentive to frames containing verbs.

One might wonder whether this advantage for verbs puts in question the proposal outline above, in which labeling verb categories depends on first labeling nouns. How would this work if infants are first sensitive to verb distributions? Recall that categorization and labeling are separable processes, and the infant study reported here concerned only categorization. It is conceivable that the order in which words are grouped together differs from the order in which the resulting groups are associated with syntactic categories (i.e., labeled).

The research on frames and framelike contexts in early syntax acquisition is just beginning, and many questions remain open. Nevertheless, the computational and behavioral studies presented here provide converging evidence that young learners initially use distributional information to find the verbs.

Acknowledgments This research was supported in part by a grant from the National Institutes of Health (HD40368).

Notes

1. One might question the practice of ignoring or discounting evidence because it is rare. For example, in some areas of syntax acquisition, rare constructions can provide crucial information (e.g., Gibson & Wexler, 1994; Wexler & Culicover, 1980). But there is no reason that the same considerations must hold throughout all domains and all stages of acquisition. It is reasonable to posit a system that builds an initial categorization of words in which relative frequency of occurrence matters, and later stages in which importance is placed on different aspects of the input.

2. For further research on the properties of human and nonhuman primates' sensitivity to nonadjacent linguistic dependencies, see Newport and Aslin (2004), and Newport, Hauser, Spaepen, and Aslin (2004).

3. A *word type* is a particular word form: for example, *dog* and *cat* are different word types. A *word token* refers to a specific instance of the type: for example, each instance the word *dog* in a corpus is an individual token of the type *dog*.

4. See note 3.

5. This section presents the results in summary form; for details, and for results of related analyses, refer to Mintz (2003).

6. A full explanation of the reasons for this restriction would be lengthy and of minimal theoretical interest. Briefly, the restriction eliminates alternative explanations of the predicted results that do not involve categorization.

7. The results also leave open the possibility that infants employed structure-dependent distributional learning, as outlined by Pinker (1984). That is, infants could have used knowledge of English phrase structure, as opposed to frequent frames, to guide their distributional analyses. Again, further study is needed to address the plausibility of this and other alternative distributional explanations. However, since these infants were only a year old, it is not clear whether the representations necessary for structure-dependent learning would be in place.

8. Concerns about the perceptibility of affixes, and therefore their reliability in early acquisition are mitigated when one considers that for languages for which this level of analysis would be most fruitful, the affixes are phonologically more prominent (Gleitman & Wanner, 1982).

9. See Pinker (1984, p. 43) for an excellent discussion of what this means.

References

Bloom, L., Hood, L., & Lightbown, P. (1974). Imitation in language development: If, when, and why. *Cognitive Psychology, 6*(3), 380–420.

Bloom, L., Lightbown, P., & Hood, L. (1975). Structure and variation in child language. *Monographs of the Society for Research in Child Development, 40*(2, Mono), 1–97.

Braine, M. D. S. (1987). What is learned in acquiring word classes—A step toward an acquisition theory. In B. MacWhinney (Ed.), *Mechanisms of language acquisition* (pp. 65–87). Hillsdale, NJ: Erlbaum.

Brown, R. (1957). Linguistic determinism and the part of speech. *Journal of Abnormal and Social Psychology, 55*, 1–5.

Brown, R. (1973). *A first language: The early stages*. Cambridge: Harvard University Press.

Cartwright, T. A., & Brent, M. R. (1997). Syntactic categorization in early language acquisition: Formalizing the role of distributional analysis. *Cognition, 63*(2), 121–170.

Childers, J. B., & Tomasello, M. (2001). The role of pronouns in young children's acquisition of the English transitive construction. *Developmental Psychology, 37*(6), 739–748.

Fisher, C., Gleitman, H., & Gleitman, L. R. (1991). On the semantic content of subcategorization frames. *Cognitive Psychology, 23*(3), 331–392.

Fisher, C., Hall, D. G., Rakowitz, S., & Gleitman, L. R. (1994). When it is better to receive than to give—Syntactic and conceptual constraints on vocabulary growth. *Lingua, 92*(1–4), 333–375.

Frigo, L., & McDonald, J. L. (1998). Properties of phonological markers that affect the acquisition of gender-like subclasses. *Journal of Memory and Language, 39*(2), 218–245.

Gerken, L. A., Gómez, R. L., & Nurmsoo, E. (1999, April). *The role of meaning and form in the formation of syntactic categories.* Paper presented at the Society for Research in Child Development, Albuquerque.

Gibson, E., & Wexler, K. (1994). Triggers. *Linguistic Inquiry, 25*(3), 407–454.

Gillette, J., Gleitman, H., Gleitman, L. R., & Lederer, A. (1999). Human simulations of vocabulary learning. *Cognition, 73*(2), 135–176.

Gleitman, L. R. (1990). The structural sources of verb meanings. *Language Acquisition: A Journal of Developmental Linguistics, 1*(1), 3–55.

Gleitman, L. R., & Gleitman, H. (1997). What is a language made out of? *Lingua, 100*(1–4), 29–55.

Gleitman, L. R., & Wanner, E. (1982). Language acquisition: The state of the art. In E. Wanner & L. R. Gleitman (Eds.), *Language acquisition: The state of the art* (pp. 3–48). Cambridge: Cambridge University Press.

Gómez, R. L. (2002). Variability and detection of invariant structure. *Psychological Science, 13*(5), 431–436.

Gómez, R. L., & Lakusta, L. (2004). A first step in form-based category abstraction by 12-month-old infants. *Developmental Science, 7*(5), 567–580.

Grimshaw, J. (1981). Form, function, and the language acquisition device. In C. L. Baker & J. J. McCarthy (Eds.), *The logical problem of language acquisition* (pp. 165–182). Cambridge, MA: MIT Press.

Harris, Z. S. (1951). *Structural linguistics.* Chicago: University of Chicago Press.

Hirsh-Pasek, K., Nelson, D. G. K., Jusczyk, P. W., Cassidy, K. W., Druss, B., & Kennedy, L. (1987). Clauses are perceptual units for young infants. *Cognition, 26*(3), 269–286.

Hohle, B., Weissenborn, E., Kiefer, D., Schulz, A., & Schmitz, M. (2004). Functional elements in infants' speech processing: The role of determiners in the syntactic categorization of lexical elements. *Infancy, 5*(3), 341–353.

Jusczyk, P. W., & Aslin, R. N. (1995). Infants' detection of the sound patterns of words in fluent speech. *Cognitive Psychology, 29*(1), 1–23.

Kemler Nelson, D. G., Jusczyk, P. W., Mandel, D. R., Myers, J., Turk, A., & Gerken, L. (1995). The head-turn preference procedure for testing auditory perception. *Infant Behavior and Development, 18*(1), 111–116.

Landau, B., & Gleitman, L. R. (1985). *Language and experience: Evidence from the blind child.* Cambridge, MA: Harvard University Press.

Macnamara, J. (1972). Cognitive basis of language learning in infants. *Psychological Review, 79*, 1–13.

MacWhinney, B. (2000). *The CHILDES project: Tools for analyzing talk* (3rd ed.). Mahwah, NJ: Lawrence Erlbaum.

Maratsos, M. P., & Chalkley, M. A. (1980). The internal language of children's syntax: The ontogenesis and representation of syntactic categories. In K. E. Nelson (Ed.), *Children's language, Vol. 2* (pp. 127–214). New York: Gardner.

Mintz, T. H. (2002). Category induction from distributional cues in an artificial language. *Memory and Cognition, 30*(5), 678–686.

Mintz, T. H. (2003). Frequent frames as a cue for grammatical categories in child directed speech. *Cognition, 90*(1), 91–117.

Mintz, T. H., Newport, E. L., & Bever, T. G. (1995). Distributional regularities of grammatical categories in speech to infants. In J. Beckman (Ed.), *Proceedings of the 25th annual meeting of the North Eastern Linguistics Society* (Vol. 2, pp. 43–54). Amherst, MA: GLSA.

Mintz, T. H., Newport, E. L., & Bever, T. G. (2002). The distributional structure of grammatical categories in speech to young children. *Cognitive Science, 26*(4), 393–424.

Naigles, L. R. (1990). Children use syntax to learn verb meanings. *Journal of Child Language, 17*(2), 357–374.

Naigles, L. R., & Hoff-Ginsberg, E. (1998). Why are some verbs learned before other verbs? Effects of input frequency and structure on children's early verb use. *Journal of Child Language, 25*(1), 95–120.

Naigles, L. R., & Kako, E. T. (1993). 1st contact in verb acquisition—Defining a role for syntax. *Child Development, 64*(6), 1665–1687.

Newport, E. L., & Aslin, R. N. (2004). Learning at a distance I. Statistical learning of non-adjacent dependencies. *Cognitive Psychology, 48*(2), 127–162.

Newport, E. L., Hauser, M. D., Spaepen, G., & Aslin, R. N. (2004). Learning at a distance—II. Statistical learning of non-adjacent dependencies in a non-human primate. *Cognitive Psychology, 49*(2), 85–117.

Pinker, S. (1984). *Language learnability and language development.* Cambridge, MA: Harvard University Press.

Pinker, S. (1987). The bootstrapping problem in language acquisition. In B. MacWhinney (Ed.), *Mechanisms of language acquisition* (pp. 339–441). Hillsdale, NJ: Lawrence Erlbaum.

Pinker, S. (1994). How could a child use verb syntax to learn verb semantics? *Lingua, 92*(1–4), 377–410.

Redington, M., & Chater, N. (1998). Connectionist and statistical approaches to language acquisition: A distributional perspective. *Language and Cognitive Processes, 13*(2–3), 129–191.

Redington, M., Chater, N., & Finch, S. (1998). Distributional information: A powerful cue for acquiring syntactic categories. *Cognitive Science, 22*(4), 425–469.

Sachs, J. (1983). Talking about the there and then: The emergence of displaced reference in parent-child discourse. In K. E. Nelson (Ed.), *Children's language* (Vol. 4, pp. 1–28). Hillsdale, NJ: Lawrence Erlbaum.

Saffran, J. R. (2001). Words in a sea of sounds: The output of infant statistical learning. *Cognition, 81*(2), 149–169.

Santelmann, L. M., & Jusczyk, P. W. (1998). Sensitivity to discontinuous dependencies in language learners: Evidence for limitations in processing space. *Cognition, 69*(2), 105–134.

Slobin, D. I., & Bever, T. G. (1982). Children use canonical sentence schemas—A crosslinguistic study of word order and inflections. *Cognition, 12*(3), 229–265.

Smith, K. H. (1966). Grammatical intrusions in the recall of structured letter pairs: Mediated transfer or position learning? *Journal of Experimental Psychology, 72*(4), 580–588.

Snedeker, J., Brent, M. R., & Gleitman, L. R. (2005). *The changing character of the mental lexicon: An information-based account of early word learning.* Manuscript submitted for publication.

Snedeker, J., Gleitman, L. R., & Brent, M. R. (1999). The successes and failures of word-to-world mapping. In A. Greenhill, H. Littlefield, & C. Tano (Eds.), *Proceedings of the 23rd annual Boston University Conference on Language Development* (pp. 654–665). Somerville, MA: Cascadilla.

Suppes, P. (1974). The semantics of children's language. *American Psychologist, 29*, 103–114.

Theakston, A. L., Lieven, E. V. M., Pine, J. M., & Rowland, C. F. (2001). The role of performance limitations in the acquisition of verb-argument structure: An alternative account. *Journal of Child Language, 28*(1), 127–152.

Tomasello, M. (2000a). Do young children have adult syntactic competence? *Cognition, 74*(3), 209–253.

Tomasello, M. (2000b). The item-based nature of children's early syntactic development. *Trends in Cognitive Sciences, 4*(4), 156–163.

Wexler, K., & Culicover, P. W. (1980). *Formal principles of language acquisition.* Cambridge, MA: MIT Press.

Wilson, R. (2000). *Category learning in second language acquisition: What artificial grammars can tell us.* Unpublished master's thesis, University of Arizona.

Wilson, R., Gerken, L. A., & Nicol, J. (2000, November). *Artificial grammar research extends to natural language: Implicit learning of categories.* Paper presented at the annual meeting of the Psychonomic Society, New Orleans.

2 Finding Verb Forms Within the Continuous Speech Stream

Thierry Nazzi and Derek Houston

Introduction: Why Study Word Segmentation?

The central issue of the present chapter is infants' segmentation of verbs from fluent speech. This issue is part of a larger domain of research pertaining to infants' perception and representation of linguistic sounds and more specifically, their representation of the sound patterns of words. Over the last 35 years, developmental scientists have learned much about the development of the perceptual and cognitive abilities that allow infants to transform the acoustic input into a representation of linguistic sounds that becomes specific of their native language (see, e.g., Jusczyk, 1997), although probably at least as much has yet to be explored and specified. We focus on one level of language (word forms) and one specific cognitive operation (their segmentation from fluent speech). Although the chapter's ultimate goal is to present what is known about how infants segment verbs from fluent speech, it will become apparent that this issue has just started to be explored. Therefore, we devote some of this chapter to a review of findings on infants' segmentation of nouns from fluent speech; this will allow us to draw a sketch of the development of word segmentation abilities in the first year of life, which will constitute a reference point for the findings on verb segmentation. Before entering into these details, let us discuss the importance of the word segmentation issue that has recently given rise to intensive research.

Learning the sound patterns of isolated words is, obviously, a requirement for the acquisition of a lexicon in which these sound patterns are associated to their meanings. However, access to isolated word forms is also a crucial, though often unstated, requirement for the acquisition of syntax: Theories of syntax acquisition take for granted that infants process sentences as sequences of individuated words, and the distributional approach developed by T. Mintz (chapter 1, this volume) relies on full, correct (adultlike) segmentation of the speech stream into words. Thus, a crucial question is whether infants have means of accessing the isolated forms of the words they hear. This issue would be trivial if the words presented to infants were clearly delimited; that is, if words were (often) presented in isolation or if word boundaries were clearly marked in fluent speech.

The presence of isolated word forms in speech directed to infants has been recently evaluated for infants acquiring English (Aslin, 1993; Brent & Siskind, 2001), and for a Dutch-German bilingual infant (van de Weijer, 1998). The results from these studies differ somewhat; however, they all suggest that most speech to infants consists of multiword utterances but that some words are spoken in isolation. In spontaneous speech, isolated word types seem to account for about 10% of all the words present in the analyzed samples (Brent & Siskind, 2001; van de Weijer, 1998). These isolated forms might help infants' acquisition of these words, which is supported by the finding that the frequency with which a word was presented in isolation (rather than the total frequency of that word) partly predicts whether a given word will be produced several months later (Brent & Siskind, 2001). However, not every type of word appears in isolation (e.g., grammatical words, and verbs unless in imperative forms), and many of the words that appear in isolation correspond to fillers (*yes*, *hmm*), vocatives ("baby's name"), and social expressions (*hi*) (van de Weijer, 1998). Moreover, Aslin (1993) has shown that in a situation in which mothers are specifically asked to teach new words to their infants, the new words were presented in isolation only about 25% of the time, ranging from 0 to 70% of the times across mother-infant dyads. This study, however, identified two factors that could help the infants retrieve the target words from their sentential context, namely the great variety of words preceding the target word, and its presentation in utterance-final position (90% of the time, sometimes even resulting in ungrammatical sentences).

In summary, although it appears that some words are presented in isolation, a phenomenon that possibly enhances their acquisition, the majority of words occur only in the context of connected speech. Thus, it appears that infants need to acquire mechanisms for correctly parsing the continuous stream of speech into discrete lexical units. The task of extracting the sound pattern of words is not trivial, as the acoustic marking of word boundaries in the speech signal is not systematic (Cole & Jakimik, 1978, 1980; Klatt, 1979, 1989): There are no obvious pauses between words equivalent to the spaces that separate the words written on this page (but see below for a discussion of more subtle cues partly correlating with word boundaries). In the following section, we review 10 years of research exploring how infants start segmenting sound patterns of words (mainly nouns or pseudowords) from fluent speech.

Literature Review: Early Segmentation of Nouns

After presenting evidence for the segmentation of monosyllabic words, this review outlines two lines of research that have studied the segmentation of multisyllabic words in order to uncover the mechanisms on which word segmentation is based. One line investigated infants' use of possibly general computational mechanisms. These tools include statistical/distributional mechanisms calculating transitional probabilities between syllables, information that is subsequently used to segment incoming utterances at points of low transitional probabilities (Saffran, Aslin, & Newport, 1996), memory mechanisms based either on the extraction of previously stored units from incoming utterances (Brent & Cartwright, 1996), and mechanisms of gradual reinforcement of units being repeatedly spliced out (Perruchet & Vinter, 1998). The second line of research follows a phonological bootstrapping perspective, according to which prosodic/phonological information (i.e., intonation, segmental durations, pauses) provides cues to higher levels of linguistic organization, such as the lexicon and syntax. Therefore, it explores how knowledge about the phonology of the ambient language, and in particular knowledge of the partial correlations between some phonological cues and word boundaries, is used by infants to segment words from fluent speech.

Segmentation of Monosyllabic Nouns

Most words in English are monosyllabic. In a seminal study, Jusczyk and Aslin (1995) investigated English-learning infants' segmentation of this most common word form from fluent speech. They tested 6- and 7.5-month-olds' segmentation using a modified version of the headturn preference procedure (HPP; Kemler Nelson et al., 1995). During the *familiarization phase*, the infant was presented with recorded repetitions of two words (*cup* and *dog* or *bike* and *feet*), one at a time, produced in citation form by a female talker speaking in a lively voice. After familiarization with the words, the infant was presented with four passages recorded by the same female talker during the *test phase.* Each passage contained repetitions of one of the four target words. It was predicted that infants would orient longer to the passages containing the familiarized target words (familiar passages) than to the passages containing the unfamiliar words (control passages) if they were able to segment the target words from fluent speech and recognize them.

Jusczyk and Aslin (1995) found that 7.5-month-olds looked significantly longer to the familiar passages than to the control passages but 6-month-olds did not, suggesting that by 7.5 months of age infants are able to segment monosyllabic words from fluent speech. In order to further test 7.5-month-olds' segmentation skills, they presented a second group of 7.5-month-olds with two of the passages during the familiarization phase and then presented them with all four of the words produced in citation form during the test phase. The results were equivalent to those of the initial experiment. In both conditions, infants looked longer to the familiarized items that to the control items, suggesting that they were able to segment words from fluent speech and match them to the words presented in citation form.

Infants' ability to match the words presented in isolation to those presented in the context of fluent speech is impressive, especially considering that the words presented in citation form were not spliced out from the target words in the passages. Instead, they were naturally produced words that were acoustically different than the same words produced in the context of the passages, suggesting that infants were able to deal with a degree of acoustic variability in recognizing words. Jusczyk and Aslin (1995) further explored what information infants used to match the words in citation to those in the passages by presenting another group of 7.5-month-olds with pseudowords during familiarization that differed by one or two phonetic features from the original words (e.g., *zeet*). Infants were then presented with the same passages as before, which contained the real target words. In contrast to the first experiment, infants in this experiment did not look longer to the familiar passages, suggesting that infants' representations of words, while generalizable enough to recognize phonologically equivalent words in different contexts, were at the same time detailed enough not to cause false alarms for near matches. In a follow-up study, Tincoff and Jusczyk (1996) conducted a similar experiment with pseudowords that differed by the final phoneme from the target words (e.g., *feek*). They also found that infants did not have false alarms for the near matches, supporting the possibility that infants form detailed representations of the sound patterns of words that they segment from fluent speech.

Recognizing words in fluent speech based on detailed phonetic information is critical for language comprehension. However, there is also an enormous amount of information in fluent speech that conveys nonlinguistic or *indexical* information, such as the affect, sex, and identification of the talker. Do infants also include this indexical information in their representations of the sound patterns of words that they segment from fluent speech? And if so, how might indexical information affect infants' recognition of words in fluent speech?

To investigate this issue, Houston and Jusczyk (2000) tested 7.5-month-olds' ability to segment and recognize monosyllabic words from fluent speech that were produced by a different talker from the one who produced the words during the familiarization phase. The authors found that when the talker who produced the words during familiarization and the talker who produced the passages during testing were of the same sex, infants demonstrated recognition of the words. However, when the familiarization and test talkers were of the opposite sex, 7.5-month-olds failed to recognize the familiarized words in the passages. Acoustic analyses of the stimuli revealed that the mean F_0 of the words and passages was more similar when produced by the talkers of the same sex than when produced by the talkers of the opposite sex. These findings suggest that young infants include indexical information in their representations of the sound patterns of words and that this information affects their ability to recognize familiar words in fluent speech.

In contrast to the findings with 7.5-month-olds, Houston and Jusczyk (2000) found that 10.5-month-olds were able to recognize words in passages that were produced during familiarization by a talker of the opposite sex. What might be the consequences of infants' emerging ability to cope with talker variability in recognizing words in fluent speech? Houston (1999) hypothesized that exposure to words by multiple talkers over time enables infants to form representations of the sound patterns of words that are more robust to talker variability. To test this possibility, Houston familiarized infants with words produced by four different talkers and then tested their recognition of the words in passages produced by a fifth talker. He found that infants were better able to recognize words in passages produced by a novel talker when the familiarization talkers were perceptually dissimilar to each other than when they were perceptually similar to each other, suggesting that exposure to variability when hearing words helps infants form robust representations.

Taken together, these findings suggest that English-learning infants can segment monosyllabic words from fluent speech and can form detailed representations of their sound patterns. It is possible that infants' representations of words become more robust as they are exposed to more variations of words, and that the word representations that are encoded into long-term memory become available for the recognition processes. There is some evidence that infants do indeed encode the sound patterns of words and voices in long-term memory (Houston & Jusczyk, 2003) and can recognize familiarized words 2 weeks after intensive exposure to the words (Jusczyk & Hohne, 1997). However, there are several other issues to consider in our attempt to understand what information in fluent speech infants encode in memory and how their ability to segment words from fluent speech changes over development. We have seen that infants can segment some monosyllabic words from fluent speech, but what about other types of words? Are infants able to segment all syllables from fluent speech and encode them into memory or do they only encode syllables that are acoustically salient, such as stressed syllables, into memory? And with words having different numbers of syllables in natural speech, how might infants determine where one word ends and the next begins? In other words, what are the mechanisms infants use to segment words, and what information do they rely on? To address these questions, it is important to consider what types of multisyllabic utterances infants segment from fluent speech.

Segmentation of Syllable Sequences: Statistical Information and Memory

Segmenting multisyllabic sequences from connected speech involves determining not only where the word boundaries are but also what sequences of syllables form cohesive units. If infants are able to notice co-occurring syllables in fluent speech, then they may use this information to identify cohesive units. For example, if an infant frequently and consistently hears *doc* followed by *tor*, the infant may infer that *doctor* forms a cohesive unit. And by contrast, if a syllable, such as *nurse*, occurs in many different contexts, the infant may infer that that syllable is independent. Goodsitt, Morgan, and Kuhl (1993) discovered that infants are sensitive to such properties. They reported that 7-month-olds were more likely to treat bisyllables as cohesive if they were previously presented in a variable context than if the context was fixed. In an influential study demonstrating what has become known as statistical learning, Saffran, Aslin, and Newport (1996) presented 8-month-olds with sequences of 12 synthesized consonant-vowel (CV) syllables. The ordering of the syllables was controlled such that four three-syllable sequences/pseudowords were constructed, which appeared in random order in the artificial language. For example in one condition, *da* was always followed by *ro*, which was always followed by *pi* (1.00 probability). However, *da* was preceded by three different syllables and *pi* was followed by three different syllables (.33 probability). After a 2-minute exposure to the sequence of syllables, 8-month-olds showed a significant looking time difference between the 1.00 probability sequences and the .33 probability sequences, suggesting that they treated the 1.00 probability sequences as cohesive. These results are consistent with the hypothesis that infants use transitional probabilities to segment fluent speech, a mechanism that does not seem to be specific to linguistic sequences (Saffran, Johnson, Aslin, & Newport, 1999) nor to humans (Hauser, Newport, & Aslin, 2001).

Similarly, two other general mechanisms have been proposed as potential tools for early segmentation. The first one, PARSER (Perruchet & Vinter, 1998), offers an alternative interpretation to Saffran et al.'s (1996) findings. According to this model, the speech signal is segmented randomly into short disjunctive strings made of one to three syllables. These units, some of which correspond to a real word, are memorized and given a weight. The processing of each incoming unit increases the unit's weight (if that unit was already present in the lexicon) and the weight of the syllables that comprise it. On the other hand, it decreases the weight of all other stored units in which the syllables of the incoming unit are embedded (retroactive interference). Together with a mechanism of forgetting (gradual decrease of the weight of every unit with time), this mechanism ensures that the sequences of syllables that will receive significant increases in weight are those that always appear together (i.e., sequences corresponding to words). This computational model was found to replicate Saffran et al.'s results. However, there is not yet any experimental evidence that infants might use such a mechanism to segment fluent speech, although there is some emerging evidence that adults might use such a mechanism in related domains (Perruchet & Peereman, 2004). The second mechanism proposed, INCDROP (Brent & Cartwright, 1996), relies on the use of previously memorized sequences to segment incoming sequences. If an incoming sequence does not contain sequences already memorized, it will be stored as a whole (thus leading to long sequences of words stored in memory, which is not predicted by PARSER). If it contains stored sequences, it will then be segmented, in a way that will optimize the number of word types and tokens in the segmentation and the total length (in phonemes) of the words in the segmentation. Computational simulations established that this model segments fluent speech with a high degree of accuracy. But again, experimental evidence for the use of this mechanism exists only for adults (Dahan & Brent, 1999).

General computational mechanisms may be important for speech segmentation by infants. However, much more work is needed to understand how those mechanisms may contribute. For example, in order to understand in what way infants may make use of transitional probabilities of syllables to segment words from natural speech, it is important to explore what infants extract and encode from fluent speech. For example, what effect does syllable stress have on infants' perception and encoding of syllables from fluent speech? More generally, it is possible that phonological properties affect infants' perception of speech, which could have consequences on how the transitional probabilities are computed. For example, infants are likely to have difficulty computing transitional probabilities of syllables that are difficult to perceive and represent from the input. Because phonological properties are language specific, we now turn to infants' sensitivity to language-specific properties and how it may affect their segmentation of words from fluent speech.

Sensitivity to Language-Specific Properties

Soon after the first 6 months of life, infants begin to display sensitivities to the organization of sounds in the ambient language. The first evidence of this came from studies showing that infants' discrimination of segmental contrasts is affected by the language that they are exposed to. For example, Werker and Tees (1984) found that English-learning infants' ability to discriminate Hindi and Nthlakapmx (A Northwestern Native American language) contrasts declined between 8 and 10 months of age. These findings and others suggest that infants' sensitivity to pairs of phones that are not linguistically contrastive in their language changes as they gain experience with their native language (see Houston, 2005, for review).

At around the same time in development that infants display a decline in the ability to discriminate some nonnative segmental contrasts, infants also show preferences for speech that contains segments from their native language. For example, Jusczyk, Friederici, et al. (1993) found that Dutch- and English-learning 9-month-olds (but not 6-month-olds) showed a preference for lists of words in their native language over lists in the other language. Because the rhythmic properties of Dutch and English words are similar, the findings suggest that infants were sensitive to the differences in segmental information between the two languages. By 9 months of age, infants not only are sensitive to which phonemes comprise their native language, they are also sensitive to their phonotactics (rules on phoneme orderings within words). Phonotactics can inform the listener about word boundaries in fluent speech. For example, the phoneme sequences /mt/ is more likely to occur between words than within a word. Friederici and Wessels (1993) found that Dutch 9-month-olds preferred lists of pseudowords that contained sequences that are phonotactically permissible in Dutch over impermissible sequences. In a similar investigation, Jusczyk, Luce, and Charles-Luce (1994) showed that English-learning 9-month-olds preferred pseudowords containing frequent phoneme sequences to those containing rare sequences, even though both were phonotactically permissible in English. These findings suggest that before the end of the first year of life, infants become sensitive to the organization of phonemes in the ambient language.

Infants are not only sensitive to segmental information in their native language but are also highly sensitive to its prosodic patterns. For example, infants as young as 2 days of age can discriminate native and nonnative sentences, even when the segmental information was reduced using low-pass filtering (Dehaene-Lambertz & Houston, 1998; Mehler et al., 1988). In addition, Nazzi, Bertoncini, and Mehler (1998) presented French newborns with low-pass filtered sentences from pairs of nonnative languages. They found that the newborns could discriminate nonnative languages, but only when the languages had different rhythmic properties.

Infants are also sensitive in the first months of life to prosodic differences at the word and syllabic levels, be it amplitude (Bull et al., 1984), duration (Eilers et al., 1984), or pitch (Bull et al., 1985; Karzon & Nicholas, 1989; Nazzi, Floccia, & Bertoncini, 1998). Moreover, they begin to show sensitivity to the rhythmic properties of the words of their native language during the second 6 months of life. Jusczyk, Friederici, et al. (1993) presented English-learning 6-month-olds with Norwegian and English words, which differ in their prosodic characteristics. Even when the stimuli were low-pass filtered, the English-learning infants looked longer to the English than to the Norwegian word lists. Jusczyk, Cutler, and Redanz (1993) found that English-learning 9-month-olds, but not 6-month-olds, listened longer to words that follow the predominant strong-weak stress pattern of English (e.g., *pliant, donor*) than to words that follow a weak-strong stress pattern (e.g., *abut, condone*). Taken together, these findings suggest that infants are sensitive to prosody at a very young age and then become sensitive to the rhythmic properties of words around the middle of the first year of life.

Segmentation of Multisyllabic Nouns

Infants' sensitivities to phonological regularities in their language may help bootstrap them into segmenting multisyllabic words from fluent speech. For example, Echols, Crowhurst, and Childers (1997) found that English-learning 9-month-olds were better able to recognize strong-weak than weak-strong bisyllables contained within weak-strong-weak and four-syllable sequences. In a series of experiments using the HPP, Jusczyk, Houston, and Newsome (1999) discovered that English-learning 7.5-month-olds demonstrated the ability to segment strong-weak words (e.g., *doctor*). Moreover, they did not show evidence of recognizing strong-weak words in passages after being familiarized with only the strong syllable (e.g., *dock*), suggesting that they segmented the strong-weak words from fluent speech as cohesive units.

Jusczyk, Houston, and Newsome (1999) found a different pattern of results with infants' segmentation of weak-strong words (e.g., *guitar*). When familiarized with the whole words, infants did not show recognition of the words in the passages. But when familiarized with only the final strong syllable (e.g., *tar*), infants did display recognition of the whole words in the passages. These findings suggest that English-learning infants may initially follow a metrical segmentation strategy (Cutler, 1990) by which they treat stressed syllables as onsets and then pay attention to what follows. If a stressed syllable is consistently followed by another syllable, then the two may form a cohesive unit.

As a further test of this hypothesis, Jusczyk, Houston, and Newsome (1999) familiarized 7.5-month-olds with passages in which weak-strong target words were always followed by the same function word (e.g., *guitar is*). This time, 7.5-month-olds did not evidence segmentation of only the strong syllable from the weak-strong words. Instead, they displayed segmentation of the strong-weak nonwords (e.g., *tar_is*) from fluent speech, strongly supporting the idea that sensitivity to the rhythmic properties of words influences English-learning infants' segmentation of words from fluent speech. Moreover, in a cross-linguistic investigation of two rhythmically similar languages, English and Dutch, Houston et al. (2000) found that 9-month-old Dutch-learning and English-learning infants segmented strong-weak Dutch words from Dutch fluent speech, suggesting that infants can segment words that follow the predominant stress pattern of their native language from fluent speech even when the words and passages are in a foreign language.

In a further investigation of the role of syllable stress in infant speech segmentation, Houston, Santelmann, and Jusczyk (2004) tested 7.5-month-old English-learning infants' segmentation of three-syllable strong-weak-strong words from fluent speech. They found that when familiarized with words in which the initial syllable carried the primary stress (e.g., *cantaloupe*), infants displayed recognition of the familiarized words in the passages. However, infants did not recognize words in passages in which the final syllable carried the primary stress (e.g., *jamboree*) after familiarization with the whole word or after familiarization with only the initial strong-weak unit (e.g., *jamba*). Instead, infants recognized the words in the passages, only after familiarization with the final syllable (*ree*), suggesting that degree of stress plays a role in infants' segmentation of syllables from fluent speech.

While rhythmic properties of words appear to play a crucial role in 7.5-month-olds' segmentation of words from fluent speech, older infants seem to be able to segment words that follow different stress patterns. Jusczyk, Houston, and Newsome (1999) tested 10.5-month-olds' segmentation of weak-strong words from fluent speech. They found that unlike the 7.5-month-olds, 10.5-month-olds were able to segment weak-strong words from fluent speech. Moreover, 10.5-month-olds did not display evidence of segmenting strong-weak units that crossed word boundaries (e.g., *tar_is*) from fluent speech.

It is possible, that by 10.5 months, infants use information in addition to rhythm to segment words from fluent speech. Possibly infants at this point give more weight to distributional information. Moreover, recent work suggests that older infants may be able to use phonotactic and allophonic information (rules on the specific phonetic realization of phonemes within words) to segment words from fluent speech. For example, Mattys, Jusczyk, Luce, and Morgan (1999) found that phonotactic properties influenced 9-month-old English-learning infants' perception of cohesiveness of bisyllables (see also Mattys & Jusczyk, 2001b). Also, Jusczyk, Hohne, and Bauman (1999) found that 10.5-month-old but not 9-month-old English-learning infants treat two-syllable sequences as "nitrates" or as "night rates" depending on which allophonic variant of /t/ they hear word medially. These findings in combination with Mattys et al.'s suggest that sensitivity to phonemes, their variants, and their typical orderings may influence how infants segment words from fluent speech.

In summary, many studies on infants' segmentation abilities have been conducted with English-learning infants. The findings suggest that infants' sensitivity to phonological properties of their native language may bootstrap their word segmentation skills. In particular, infants are sensitive to the rhythmic properties of their native language at a very early age and several studies have shown that rhythmic properties of words play an important role in English-learning infants' segmentation of words from fluent speech. Jusczyk (1997) has proposed that initial, stress-based segmentation strategy may allow infants to break fluent speech into smaller, more analyzable units, allowing them to then extract information about phonotactic and allophonic cues to segmentation. Infants may then integrate suprasegmental and segmental phonological information in addition to transitional probabilities of syllables in acquiring a more sophisticated strategy for segmenting words from fluent speech. Given that phonological properties are language-specific, future research will have to evaluate how word segmentation emerges in different languages. So far, only a couple of studies have explored segmentation in two other languages with rhythmic properties similar to English (Dutch: Houston et al., 2000; German: Höhle & Weissenborn, 2003), and a couple of studies have explored segmentation in French (Parisian French: Gout, 2001; Nazzi, Iakimova, Bertoncini, Frédonie, & Alcantara, in press; Canadian French: Polka & Sundara, 2003). The studies on Parisian French show that segmentation in this language develops differently than in English, as a reflection of phonological/rhythmic differences between the two languages.

Phonological Markers of Lexical Classes: Nouns and Verbs

So far, the studies presented have focused on English-learning infants' segmentation of either nouns or sequences of pseudowords constituting an artificial language.

However, all grammatical classes are not learned simultaneously. Most importantly for our present purpose, in many languages including English (Dromi, 1987; Gentner, 1983; Goldin-Meadow, Seligman, & Gelman, 1976; Golinkoff, Jacquet, Hirsh-Pasek, & Nandakumar, 1996; but see Bloom, Tinker, & Margulis, 1993), though not in Japanese and Korean (Au, Dapretto, & Song, 1994; Gopnik & Choi, 1995), infants initially learn more nouns than words from any other lexical categories, including verbs. Hence, reviewed findings of infants' early segmentation of nouns might not generalize to other lexical categories, or at least the onset of the segmentation of different lexical categories might vary, and infants might begin segmenting nouns at an earlier age. Other than the verb segmentation study that we present in the next section, only one study has explored the segmentation of words from another lexical class (grammatical words). Höhle and Weissenborn (2003) investigated German-learning infants' segmentation of grammatical words. However, because this study was conducted in German, these findings of grammatical word segmentation cannot be directly compared to the English noun segmentation data, especially if one is trying to evaluate whether acoustic and phonological properties of lexical classes have an impact on segmentation. In the following, we present data regarding acoustic and phonological differences between nouns and verbs and discuss how these differences might affect the ease of segmentation of both categories of words.

Although studies exploring the kinds of information that specify and distinguish lexical classes have mainly focused on semantic and syntactic information, there is some evidence supporting the existence of acoustic and phonological correlates of lexical classes (see Kelly, 1992, or Black & Chiat, 2003, for proposals in favor of an interrelated definition of lexical classes based on phonological, semantic and syntactic properties). The emerging picture is that there are cues distinguishing words from different lexical classes, but these cues are not necessarily systematic. There can be a substantial overlap in the distribution of two classes for a given cue. Thus, the differences between lexical classes are often probabilistic rather than categorical. However, there is also evidence that the combined use of multiple cues can provide a more powerful tool to assign individual items to their appropriate class.

The best illustration of this comes from a study looking not at the noun/verb distinction, but at the distinction between lexical and grammatical words (Morgan, Shi, & Allopenna, 1996). These authors examined the acoustic correlates of these two classes of words by analyzing the production of mothers talking to their infants, in three languages: English, Mandarin Chinese, and Turkish. Their analyses revealed that overall, lexical words are made up of more syllables than grammatical words (the latter being mainly monosyllabic), that the syllables of the lexical words tend to be more complex (contain more consonants), and finally that the vowels of the lexical words have longer durations and higher amplitude. Having identified these differences, the authors trained neural networks to perform classifications of the words based on these cues. Performance turned out to be rather poor when each cue was used in isolation (about 60% at best); however, when all of the cues were used together, correct performance was between 80% and 90%. These findings suggest that there are multiple acoustic and phonological cues that contribute to distinguishing lexical and grammatical words and may help to explain why newborns demonstrate the ability to discriminate lists of lexical and grammatical words (Shi, Werker, & Morgan, 1999).

Concerning nouns and verbs, a few studies have explored some acoustic and phonological properties that could differentially mark these two lexical categories. The factors that have been identified as potential contributors to the noun-verb distinction are listed in table 2.1.

Let us start with the two phonological factors that are likely to have a differential impact on the segmentation of nouns and verbs and that both belong to the prosodic domain. The first of these prosodic elements is stress pattern. Several corpus analyses of English have established that the predominant stress pattern of English words corresponds to the strong-weak pattern of a stressed syllable followed by an unstressed syllable (Cassidy & Kelly, 1991; Cutler & Carter, 1987; Kelly & Bock, 1988). However, not all lexical classes follow this predominant stress pattern. Although both nouns and verbs can have either the predominant strong-weak stress pattern or the less common weak-strong pattern, it turns out that the distribution of nouns and verbs for the two patterns is highly asymmetrical. Out of a representative sample of English words (3,000 nouns and 1,000 verbs), Kelly and Bock (1988) found that 94% of the nouns had a strong-weak pattern, while 69% of the verbs had a weak-strong pattern; conversely, and maybe more relevant to the infants' acquisition task, 90% of strong-weak words were nouns, while 85% of weak-strong words were verbs. How could this difference impact infants' segmentation of bisyllabic words? Given Jusczyk, Houston, and Newsome's (1999) findings that infants show evidence of segmenting strong-weak nouns from fluent speech by 7.5 months of age but do not demonstrate segmentation of weak-strong nouns until 10.5 months, one might expect that infants would be able to segment most bisyllabic verbs at a later age than they would be able to segment most bisyllabic nouns. Note that this prediction relies on the assumption that the segmentation bias in favor of strong-weak nouns extends to all lexical

Table 2.1 Phonological cues to the noun/verb distinction

Likely to influence segmentation
- Stress pattern — N 1st   V 2nd
- Duration
- Syntactic position within sentence
- Number of phonemes per syllable

Less Likely to influence segmentation
- Number of syllables
- Vowel quality
- Consonant quality

classes, even to those in which the strong-weak pattern is not predominant. In other words, the strong-weak segmentation procedure would be "applied" to all speech.[1]

The second prosodic factor that distinguishes nouns and verbs is duration. It appears that nouns tend to have longer durations than verbs in connected speech. This was first shown in a study by Sorensen, Cooper, and Paccia (1978) in which they instructed subjects to produce noun-verb homophones such as /coach/, embedded in similar phonetic and stress pattern environments. The investigators found that the durations for the nouns were longer than for the verbs in typical sentences. However, the same study showed that if nouns and verbs are both placed in phrase-final or clause-final positions, their duration is equivalent. Hence, the longer duration of nouns compared to verbs possibly reflects syntactic differences; more specifically, it may reflect the fact that nouns in English are more likely to appear in constituent-final positions than verbs.[2] Given that words in final positions tend to be lengthened, nouns would be lengthened more often than verbs. Note that the increased duration of nouns and their more frequent presence in constituent-final positions potentially make nouns clearer speech units than verbs, which may contribute, overall, to making nouns easier to segment than verbs. Thus, even if the bias in favor of strong-weak words applied to all lexical classes, strong-weak verbs could still be more difficult to segment from fluent speech than strong-weak nouns.

Finally, a few other factors distinguishing nouns and verbs have been identified, although it is less clear how they could impact on segmentation. First, it has been found that nouns and verbs differ in terms of number of syllables; nouns typically having more syllables than verbs (Kelly, 1992). Listeners seem to be sensitive to this difference: when children or adults are presented with new pseudowords and asked to use them in sentences, the likeliness that they will use them as nouns increases with the number of syllables of the word, while the likeliness that they will use them as verbs decreases in parallel (Cassidy & Kelly, 1991). However, it is not clear how this factor could impact on early segmentation. Although more nouns should be affected than verbs if memory constraints make the segmentation of longer words more difficult, the predominance of monosyllabic and bisyllabic words in English should leave little room for this effect to express itself. Second, there are differences in the quality of some phonemes constituting nouns and verbs. Kelly (1996) reports that nouns tend to have more low vowels while verbs tend to have more high vowels; moreover, nouns tend to have more nasal consonants than verbs. Again, it is not clear how this factor could introduce an asymmetry in how easily nouns and verbs are segmented.

In summary, we have reviewed the existence of several phonological factors that distinguish nouns and verbs. As we have seen, two of these factors, stress pattern and duration (due to constituent-final position or to number of constituting phonemes) may result in easier segmentation of nouns than verbs. Determining the ages at which infants are able to segment verbs from fluent speech is a crucial next step for understanding how these phonological factors influence segmentation and for further delineating the emergence of word segmentation.

First Evidence Regarding Verb Segmentation

In this final section, we report the results of a study investigating whether and when young American infants growing up in an English-speaking environment segment verbs from fluent speech (Nazzi, 2002; Nazzi, Dilley, Jusczyk, Shattuck-Hunagel, & Jusczyk, 2005). Briefly, this study was doubly motivated. First, as already mentioned, nouns and verbs are not acquired at the same pace, and a noun advantage has been reported for English. Second, we reviewed evidence suggesting that there are acoustic and phonological differences between nouns and verbs that might make nouns more salient than verbs. Accordingly, evidence regarding the segmentation of verbs should provide useful information on the development of segmentation abilities and the acquisition of the different lexical classes.

Nazzi et al. (2005) evaluated four questions. The first one is whether, and if so when, infants can segment verbs from fluent speech. The second question has to do with timing: Does the segmentation of verbs start at the same time, or later than that of nouns? As discussed in the literature review above, some differences between nouns and verbs (duration, presence of a syntactic or prosodic boundary after the word) might make verbs more difficult to segment. Third, as discussed earlier, the predominant stress pattern of bisyllabic verbs is the opposite of that of nouns: bisyllabic verbs are predominantly iambic (weak-strong) while bisyllabic nouns are predominantly trochaic (strong-weak). This raises the question of whether the bias for strong-weak words found in the segmentation of nouns extends to verbs or not; data on this issue should inform us on infants' sensitivity to the noun-verb distinction and on the mechanisms that might underlie the emergence of this bias. The final question was whether or not the clarity of the onset of a word influences its segmentation. To address this question, infants' ability to segment verbs was evaluated in two conditions: for verbs starting with a consonant and for verbs starting with a vowel. The hypothesis tested was that the latter ones would be more difficult to segment given stronger phenomena of coarticulation (i.e., the fact that the actual realization of a phoneme depends on the phonemes surrounding it) with their preceding contexts.

The procedure used is the version of the HPP adapted by Jusczyk and Aslin (1995) to explore infants' segmentation of nouns from fluent speech and subsequently used in most of the studies presented in the literature review. The procedure works as follows. Each infant is seated on a caregiver's lap, in the center of a three-sided booth with one light on the center of each of the three panels (see figure 2.1). The light on the center panel is used to center the infant's attention

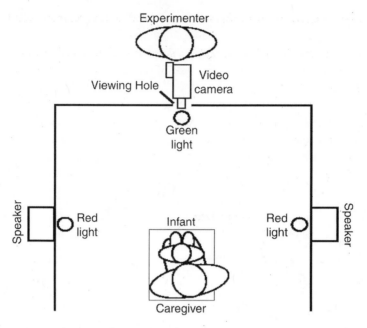

Figure 2.1. Setup for the head-turn preference procedure.

between two consecutive trials. Each trial starts with the flashing of a side light. As soon as the infant orients to the light, a hidden experimenter presses a button and the speech sounds start being presented through the loudspeaker situated behind it. The experimenter keeps the button depressed while the infant is orienting to the light and sound source and releases it when the infant looks away. The sound is presented either until the end of the stimulus or until the infant turns away from the light for more than two seconds. The experimental variable measured in this procedure is the time during which the infant is orienting to the flashing light while a speech stimulus is being played (which corresponds to the total amount of time that the experimenter had the button depressed during a given trial).

The experimental session is organized in two phases. During the familiarization phase, infants are familiarized with two lists of repeated words until 30 seconds of orientation times to each word have accumulated. When this familiarization criterion is reached, the test phase begins, in which infants are presented with four passages. Each passage is made up of six short sentences all containing one occurrence of a target word, appearing in various sentential locations. For each infant, two of the passages correspond to the two words that they heard during familiarization, and two correspond to two other nonfamiliarized or "new" words (which two verbs are used for familiarization is counterbalanced across infants). In this procedure, based on previous studies, infants' recognition in the passages of the words heard in familiarization is indexed by a preference for the passages containing the familiarized words over those containing the "new" words (Kemler Nelson et al., 1995).

Two main experiments were conducted by Nazzi et al. (2005). The first experiment tested infants' segmentation of strong-weak bisyllabic verbs; these words follow the predominant stress pattern of English bisyllabic words in general but the less common pattern for verbs. The words used were two consonant-initial verbs (*ticket, visit*) and two vowel-initial verbs (*orbit, outlaw*). Two of the corresponding passages are as follows:

- The policeman tickets speeding drivers. Meanwhile, the clerk keeps track of how many he tickets. The meter maid tickets people who park illegally. However, diplomats' cars are not ones that she tickets. The new guard tickets trucks blocking the door. A friendly baggage clerk tickets the suitcases.
- The earth orbits the sun once a year. Astronomers know how far Neptune orbits. The comet orbits every 50 years. The scientists don't believe that a quasar orbits. A brand-new satellite orbits around Saturn. A small asteroid orbits the nearest star.

Two groups of infants were tested in the first experiment: 10.5- and 13.5-month-olds. The two age groups exhibited different patterns of orientation times (see figure 2.2). The 10.5-month-olds showed no preference for the passages containing the familiar verbs. In contrast, this preference was present at 13.5 months, suggesting that these older infants could segment the strong-weak verbs from fluent speech. Moreover, there was no effect of onset type at both ages: the younger

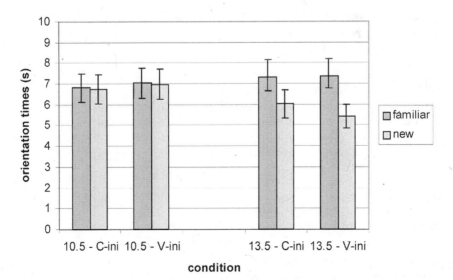

Figure 2.2. Results of the segmentation of strong-weak verbs from fluent speech.

infants failed to segment both the consonant- and the vowel-initial verbs, while the older ones could segment both types of verbs.

The second experiment explored the segmentation of weak-strong bisyllabic verbs. The words used were two consonant-initial verbs (*discount, permit*) and two vowel-initial verbs (*incite, import*). Two of the corresponding passages are as follows:

- The mother often permits her son to help. Her boss permits everyone to take a day off. We know what the red thing permits. In the park, his aunt permits everyone to swing. That's something the teacher never permits. She permits only quiet games.
- The company never imports by airplane. The boss imports the goods across the ocean. Wegman's often imports cheese from France. It's not the same as what your aunt imports. We'll see how much her new thing imports. She imports rice from India.

Three groups of infants were tested in that second experiment: 10.5-, 13.5-, and 16.5-month-olds. The three age groups showed different patterns of orientation times (see figure 2.3). The 10.5-month-olds showed no evidence of segmenting either type of weak-strong words. In contrast, there was evidence that the 16.5-month-olds could segment both types of words. At 13.5 months, the results were intermediate: the consonant-initial verbs were segmented, but there was no indication that the infants were able to segment the vowel-initial verbs.

Several conclusions can be drawn from that first study of the segmentation of verbs. First, it establishes the early segmentation of verbs, which emerges at least

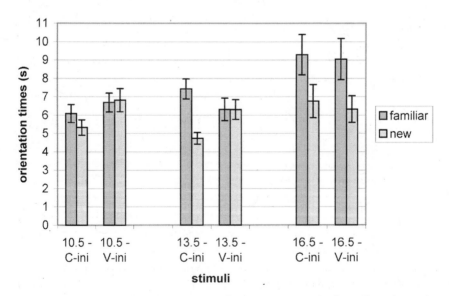

Figure 2.3. Results of the segmentation of weak-strong verbs from fluent speech.

by 13.5 months of age, about when infants start speaking. Note that the study did not investigate the segmentation of monosyllabic verbs, which may be segmented at an earlier age. This first result thus reinforces the finding previously established for nouns that infants may encode sound patterns at the very onset of lexical acquisition by segmenting words from fluent speech.

Second, Nazzi et al.'s (2005) study shows that two factors which have been found to influence noun segmentation also influence verb segmentation: word onset type and stress pattern. Regarding word onset type, evidence was found that for weak-strong verbs (though not for strong-weak verbs), verbs starting with clear onsets (plosive consonants) are segmented earlier than verbs with unclear onsets (vowels). This late segmentation of verbs starting with vowels is consistent with Mattys and Jusczyk's (2001a) findings that infants do not segment monosyllabic nouns such as *ice* before 16 months of age; both studies support that words with vocalic onsets are more difficult to segment.

Regarding stress pattern, the findings for vowel-initial verbs suggest infants' greater difficulty in segmenting weak-strong verbs compared with strong-weak verbs, thus partially replicating the trochaic bias shown for nouns (Jusczyk, Houston, & Newsome, 1999). Importantly, the fact that this strong-weak bias applies to verbs even though the predominant stress pattern of verbs is weak-strong suggests that the acquisition and application of the trochaic bias is not sensitive to differences between lexical classes. Rather, this bias likely extends to items from a range of different lexical categories. Furthermore, note that the two factors of word onset type and stress pattern interacted: although having a vowel onset or iambic stress made an item harder to segment, infants at 13.5 months could deal with these added difficulties unless both types were present.

Nazzi et al.'s (2005) study points to some new factors that may influence segmentation. The first set of factors concern prosody. Nazzi et al. (2005) conducted a comparison between their stimuli and those of Jusczyk, Houston, and Newsome (1999) using the ToBI (Tones and Break Indices) prosodic annotation system (Beckman & Ayers-Elam, 1997; Silverman et al., 1992) and focusing on factors likely to influence segmentation: the presence or absence of prosodic phrases (a sequence of words that cohere by prosodic contour) and pitch accents (i.e., prominence-leading pitch movements) as well as stress pattern realization (Cutler & Darwin, 1981; Ladd, 1996; Pitt & Samuel, 1990; Sorensen et al., 1978; Tyler & Warren, 1987).[3] While these prosodic analyses revealed that not all prosodic cues consistently distinguished the noun and verb stimuli (e.g., realization of stress patterns), two strong prosodic differences were identified. Nouns were more likely than verbs to be clearly followed by a prosodic phrase boundary. In addition, nouns were more likely than verbs to be clearly preceded by a syllable bearing a pitch accent. These two prosodic cues thus provided "more reliable" marking of both edges of the noun stimuli than of the verb stimuli. This finding offers a tentative explanation for the developmental lag observed for the segmentation of verbs from fluent speech, although it remains to be shown whether these differences are reliable cues to nouns and verbs, or whether they are artifactual differences between the noun and verb passages used in these two studies.[4]

The second factor that may also have influenced segmentation is whether or not the infants knew the words preceding the target words. Indeed, the nouns in the noun passages were more often preceded by familiar words than were the verbs in the verb passages, a bias which could also have favored the noun stimuli (Brent & Cartwright, 1996; Rathbun, Bortfeld, Morgan, & Golinkoff, 2002). Note that Rathbun et al. (2002) recently found that infants could detect monosyllabic words (both nouns or verbs) at 6 months, hence earlier than what had been found by Jusczyk and Aslin (1995); this earlier segmentation probably reflects a facilitory effect due to the presence of familiar words such as *Mommy* before the target words.

Summary and Conclusion

In this chapter, we have presented evidence that infants are able to segment words from fluent speech from as early as 7.5 months of age, evidence collected with nouns presented in fluent speech and pseudowords presented in sequences of artificial languages. At an early age, infants demonstrate that sensitivities to linguistic and nonlinguistic details play a role in their ability to recognize words in fluent speech. They are also sensitive to language specific properties of the native language, and this influences their speech segmentation strategies. In particular, English-learning infants seem to use a type of metrical segmentation strategy in which they treat stressed syllables as word onsets.

Following this, we presented evidence showing that in fluent speech there are acoustic and phonological differences between words from various lexical categories. As discussed, the evidence regarding nouns and verbs suggest that the latter might be less salient in the speech stream than the former: shorter durations, lower frequency of appearing in syntactic or prosodic constituent-final positions, and predominant stress pattern being the opposite of that of the majority of English words. These differences raise the question of whether or not the developmental path shown for the segmentation of nouns would extend to verbs.

Accordingly, we presented and discussed the results of the first exploration of infants' segmentation of verbs (Nazzi et al., 2005). Briefly, this study established that verb segmentation emerges early (at the latest by 13.5 months), though later than what had been found for nouns, and extended to verbs evidence regarding the influence on segmentation of two factors already identified by the studies on noun segmentation: word onset type and stress pattern. New factors that might also influence segmentation were also identified: the prosodic factors of pitch accent and phrasal boundary placement, and the familiarity of the items preceding target words.

These new factors could explain the marked developmental lag in verb segmentation observed when comparing the studies by Nazzi et al. (2005) and Jusczyk, Houston, and Newsome (1999). This lag is compatible with the hypothesis that verbs are more difficult to segment than nouns. If this segmentation lag was confirmed in a direct, more controlled comparison of the segmentation of these two lexical categories, then it would raise the question of whether this segmentation lag might contribute to the delayed acquisition of verbs in English. How could one find evidence that this segmentation onset lag could at least partially contribute to the delay that is later observed in the acquisition of verbs in English? One possibility would be to test whether or not the verb segmentation lag would be reduced or reversed in languages in which the noun acquisition bias is not present (e.g., Korean and Japanese). It would also be interesting to determine the time course of the segmentation of other lexical classes, and see if overall a pattern emerges that suggests a link between segmentation onset and lexical acquisition timing.

Acknowledgments The writing of this chapter was supported by a grant from the European Science Foundation EUROCORES program The Origin of Man, Language and Languages to T. N., and a research grant from NIDCD (DC006235) to D. H. We would like to thank everyone at the Infant Language Research Laboratory at Johns Hopkins University for their various contributions to the studies the authors conducted while they were working there, including Eileen Crowley and Natasha Scheitlin for help in recruiting and testing the subjects, all the graduate students and postdoctoral fellows, and last but certainly not least, Peter and Ann Marie Jusczyk. Thanks also to Laura Dilley and Stefanie Shattuck-Hufnagel for their acoustic analyses of the stimuli and to David Horn for helpful comments on previous versions of this chapter.

Notes

1. Alternatively, opposite biases could develop for the two lexical classes, favoring in both cases the segmentation of the words with the predominant stress pattern of their class.

2. Another factor that could influence the longer durations of nouns is the fact that nouns are made up of more phonemes than verbs, even when syllable number is controlled (Kelly, 1996).

3. Duration of the stimuli was not analyzed because differences between the nouns and verbs would have been meaningless given that the nouns and verbs were not phonetically matched.

4. The fact that almost all the words preceding the nouns were monosyllables that could receive a pitch accent, while verbs were preceded by more variable contexts, is compatible with this artifactual possibility.

References

Aslin, R. N. (1993). Segmentation of fluent speech into words: Learning models and the role of maternal input. In B. de Boysson-Bardies et al. (Eds.), *Developmental neurocognition: Speech and face processing in the first year of life* (pp. 305–315). New York: Kluwer Academic.

Au, T. K. F., Dapretto, M., & Song, Y. K. (1994). Input vs. constraints: Early word acquisition in Korean and English. *Journal of Memory and Language, 33*, 567–582.

Beckman, M. E., & Ayers-Elam, G. (1997). Guide to [English] ToBI Labelling, ver. 3. http://ling.ohio-state.edu/Phonetics/E_ToBI/etobi_homepage.html.

Black, M., & Chiat, S. (2003). Noun-verb dissociation: A multi-faceted phenomenon. *Journal of Neurolinguistics, 16*, 231–250.

Bloom, L., Tinker, E., & Margulis, C. (1993). The words children learn. *Cognitive Development, 8*, 431–450.

Brent, M. R., & Cartwright, T. A. (1996). Distributional regularity and phonotactic constraints are useful for segmentation. *Cognition, 61*, 93–125.

Brent, M. R., & Siskind, J. M. (2001). The role of exposure to isolated words in early vocabulary development. *Cognition, 81*, B33–B44.

Bull, D., Eilers, R. E., & Oller, D. K. (1984). Infants' discrimination of intensity variation in multisyllabic stimuli. *Journal of the Acoustical Society of America, 76*, 13–17.

Bull, D., Eilers, R. E., & Oller, D. K. (1985). Infants' discrimination of syllable fundamental frequency in multisyllabic stimuli. *Journal of the Acoustical Society of America, 77*, 289–295.

Cassidy, K. W., & Kelly, M. H. (1991). Phonological information for grammatical category assignments. *Journal of Memory and Language, 30*, 348–369.

Cole, R. A., & Jakimik, J. (1978). Understanding speech: How words are heard. In G. Underwood (Ed.), *Strategies of information processing* (pp. 67–116). New York: Academic Press.

Cole, R. A., & Jakimik, J. (1980). How are syllables used to recognize words? *Journal of the Acoustical Society of America, 67*, 965–970.

Cutler, A. (1990). Exploiting prosodic probabilities in speech segmentation. In T. M. A. Gerry (Ed.), *Cognitive models of speech processing: Psycholinguistic and computational perspectives. ACL-MIT Press series in natural language processing* (pp. 105–121). Cambridge, MA: MIT Press.

Cutler, A., & Carter, D. M. (1987). The predominance of strong initial syllables in the English vocabulary. *Computer Speech and Language, 2*, 133–142.

Cutler, A., & Darwin, C. J. (1981). Phoneme-monitoring reaction time and preceding prosody: Effects of stop closure duration and of fundamental frequency. *Perception and Psychophysics, 29*, 217–224.

Dahan, D., & Brent, M. R. (1999). On the discovery of novel wordlike units from utterances: An artificial-language study with implications for native-language acquisition. *Journal of Experimental Psychology: General, 128*(2), 165–185.

Dehaene-Lambertz, G., & Houston, D. (1998). Faster orientation latencies toward native language in two-month-old infants. *Language and Speech, 41*, 21–43.

Dromi, E. (1987). *Early lexical development.* Cambridge: Cambridge University Press.

Echols, C. H., Crowhurst, M. J., & Childers, J. B. (1997). The perception of rhythmic units in speech by infants and adults. *Journal of Memory and Language, 36*, 202–225.

Eilers, R. E., Bull, D., Oller, D. K., & Lewis, D. C. (1984). The discrimination of vowel duration by infants. *Journal of the Acoustical Society of America, 75*, 1213–1218.

Friederici, A. D., & Wessels, J. M. I. (1993). Phonotactic knowledge and its use in infant speech perception. *Perception and Psychophysics, 54,* 287–295.

Gentner, D. (1983). Why nouns are learned before verbs: Linguistic relativity vs. natural partitioning. In S. A. Kuczaj (Ed.), *Language development: Language, culture, and cognition* (pp. 301–325). Hillsdale, NJ: Erlbaum.

Goldin-Meadow, S., Seligman, M., & Gelman, R. (1976). Language in the two-year-old. *Cognition, 4,* 189–202.

Golinkoff, R. M., Jacquet, R. C., Hirsh-Pasek, K., & Nandakumar, R. (1996). Lexical principles may underlie the learning of verbs. *Child Development, 67,* 3101–3119.

Goodsitt, J. V., Morgan, J. L., & Kuhl, P. (1993). Perceptual strategies in prelingual speech segmentation. *Journal of Child Language, 20,* 229–252.

Gopnik, A., & Choi, S. (1995). Names, relational words, and cognitive development in English and Korean speakers: Nouns are not always learned before verbs. In M. Tomasello & W. E. Merriman (Eds.), *Beyond names for things* (pp. 63–80). Hillsdale, NJ: Erlbaum.

Gout, A. (2001). *Etapes précoces de l'acquisition du lexique.* Unpublished dissertation, École des Hautes Études en Sciences Sociales, Paris, France.

Hauser, M. D., Newport, E. L., & Aslin, R. N. (2001). Segmentation of the speech stream in a non-human primate: Statistical learning in cotton-top tamarins. *Cognition, 78,* B53–B64.

Höhle, B., & Weissenborn, J. (2003). German-learning infants' ability to detect unstressed closed-class elements in continuous speech. *Developmental Science, 6*(2), 122–127.

Houston, D. M. (1999). *The role of talker variability in infant word representations.* Unpublished doctoral dissertation, Johns Hopkins University.

Houston, D. M. (2005). Speech perception in infants. In D. B. Pisoni & R. E. Remez (Eds.), *Handbook of speech perception* (pp. 417–448). Oxford: Blackwell.

Houston, D. M., & Jusczyk, P. W. (2000). The role talker-specific information in word segmentation by infants. *Journal of Experimental Psychology: Human Perception and Performance, 26*(5), 1570–1582.

Houston, D. M., & Jusczyk, P. W. (2003). Infants' long-term memory for the sound patterns of words and voices. *Journal of Experimental Psychology: Human Perception and Performance, 29*(6), 1143–1154.

Houston, D. M., Jusczyk, P. W., Kuijpers, C., Coolen, R., & Cutler, A. (2000). Cross-language word segmentation by 9-month-olds. *Psychonomic Bulletin and Review, 7,* 504–509.

Houston, D. M., Santelmann, L. M., & Jusczyk, P. W. (2004). English-learning infants' segmentation of trisyllabic words from fluent speech. *Language and Cognitive Processes, 19,* 97–136.

Jusczyk, P. W. (1997). *The discovery of spoken language.* Cambridge, MA: MIT Press.

Jusczyk, P. W., & Aslin, R. N. (1995). Infants' detection of the sound patterns of words in fluent speech. *Cognitive Psychology, 29*(1), 1–23.

Jusczyk, P. W., Cutler, A., & Redanz, N. (1993). Preference for the predominant stress patterns of English words. *Child Development, 64,* 675–687.

Jusczyk, P. W., Friederici, A. D., Wessels, J., Svenkerud, V. Y., & Jusczyk, A. M. (1993). Infants' sensitivity to the sound patterns of native language words. *Journal of Memory and Language, 32,* 402–420.

Jusczyk, P. W., & Hohne, E. A. (1997). Infants' memory for spoken words. *Science, 277,* 1984–1986.

Jusczyk, P. W., Hohne, E. A., & Bauman, A. (1999). Infants' sensitivity to allophonic cues for word segmentation. *Perception & Psychophysics, 62,* 1465–1476.

Jusczyk, P. W., Houston, D. M., & Newsome, M. (1999). The beginning of word segmentation in English-learning infants. *Cognitive Psychology, 39*, 159–207.

Jusczyk, P. W., Luce, P. A., & Charles-Luce, J. (1994). Infants' sensitivity to phonotactic patterns in the native language. *Journal of Memory and Language, 33*, 630–645.

Karzon, R. G., & Nicholas, J. G. (1989). Syllabic pitch perception in 2- to 3-month-old infants. *Perception and Psychophysics, 45*, 10–14.

Kelly, M. H. (1992). Using sound to solve syntactic problems: The role of phonology in grammatical category assignment. *Psychological Review, 99*, 349–364.

Kelly, M. H. (1996). The role of phonology in grammatical category assignments. In J. L. Morgan & K. Demuth (Eds.), *Signal to syntax.* Hillsdale, NJ: Lawrence Erlbaum.

Kelly, M. H., & Bock, J. K. (1988). Stress in time. *Journal of Experimental Psychology: Human Perception and Performance, 14*, 389–403.

Kemler Nelson, D. G., Jusczyk, P. W., Mandel, D. R., Myers, J., Turk, A., & Gerken, L. A. (1995). The Headturn Preference Procedure for testing auditory perception. *Infant Behavior and Development, 18*, 111–116.

Klatt, D. H. (1979). Speech perception: A model of acoustic-phonetic analysis and lexical access. *Journal of Phonetics, 7*, 279–312.

Klatt, D. H. (1989). Review of selected models of speech perception. In W. Marslen-Wilson (Ed.), *Lexical representation and process* (pp. 169–226). Cambridge, MA: MIT Press.

Ladd, D. R. (1996). *Intonational phonology.* Cambridge: Cambridge University Press.

Mattys, S., & Jusczyk, P. W. (2001a). Do infants segment words or recurring contiguous patterns? *Journal of Experimental Psychology: Human Perception and Performance, 27*, 644–655.

Mattys, S., & Jusczyk, P. W. (2001b). Phonotactic cues for segmentation of fluent speech by infants. *Cognition, 78*, 91–121.

Mattys, S., Jusczyk, P. W., Luce, P. A., & Morgan, J. L. (1999). Phonotactic and prosodic effects on word segmentation in infants. *Cognitive Psychology, 38*, 465–494.

Mehler, J., Jusczyk, P., Lambertz, G., Halsted, N., Bertoncini, J., & Amiel-Tison, C. (1988). A precursor of language acquisition in young infants. *Cognition, 29*, 143–178.

Morgan, J. L., Shi, R., & Allopenna, P. (1996). Perceptual bases of rudimentary grammatical categories: Toward a broader conceptualization of bootstrapping. In J. L. Morgan & K. Demuth (Eds.), *Signal to syntax* (pp. 263–283). Hillsdale, NJ: Lawrence Erlbaum.

Nazzi, T. (2002). *The emergence of verb segmentation in infancy.* Paper presented at the 13th biennal meeting of the International Society for Infant Studies, Toronto, Canada, April 18–21.

Nazzi, T., Bertoncini, J., & Mehler, J. (1998). Language discrimination by newborns: Towards an understanding of the role of rhythm. *Journal of Experimental Psychology: Human Perception and Performance, 24*, 756–766.

Nazzi, T., Dilley, L. C., Jusczyk, A. M., Shattuck-Hunagel, S., & Jusczyk, P. W. (2005). English-learning infants' segmentation of verbs from fluent speech. *Language and Cognitive Processes, 19*, 97–136.

Nazzi, T., Floccia, C., & Bertoncini, J. (1998). Discrimination of pitch contours by neonates. *Infant Behavior and Development, 21*, 779–784.

Nazzi, T., Iakimova, G., Bertoncini, J., Frédonie, S., & Alcantara, C. (in press). Early segmentation of fluent speech by infants acquiring French: Emerging evidence for cross-linguistic differences. *Journal of Memory and Language.*

Perruchet, P., & Peereman, R. (2004). The exploitation of distributional information in syllable processing. *Journal of Neurolinguistics, 17*, 97–119.

Perruchet, P., & Vinter, A. (1998). PARSER: A model for word segmentation. *Journal of Memory and Language, 39*, 246–263.

Pitt, M. A., & Samuel, A. G. (1990). The use of rhythm in attending to speech. *Journal of Experimental Psychology: Human Perception and Performance, 16*, 564–573.

Polka, L., & Sundara, M. (2003). Word segmentation in monolingual and bilingual infant learners of English and French. In M. J. Sole, D. Recasens, & J. Romero (Eds.), *Proceedings of the 15th International Congress of Phonetic Sciences*, 1021–1024.

Rathbun, K., Bortfeld, H., Morgan, J., & Golinkoff, R. (2002). What's in a name: Using highly familiar items to aid segmentation. Paper presented at the 27th annual Boston University Conference on Language Development, Boston, November 1–3.

Saffran, J. R., Aslin, R. N., & Newport, E. L. (1996). Statistical learning by 8-month-old infants. *Science, 274*, 1926–1928.

Saffran, J. R., Johnson, E. K., Aslin, R. N., & Newport, E. L. (1999). Statistical learning of tone sequences by human infants and adults. *Cognition, 70*, 27–52.

Shi, R., Werker, J. F., & Morgan, J. L. (1999). Newborn infants' sensitivity to perceptual cues to lexical and grammatical words. *Cognition, 72*, B11–21.

Silverman, K., Beckman, M., Pitrelli, J., Ostendorf, M., Wightman, C., Price, P., et al. (1992). ToBI: A standard for labeling English prosody. In J. J. Ohala, T. M. Nearey, B. L. Derwing, M. M. Hodge, & G. E. Wiebe (Eds.), *ICSLP 92 Proceedings: 1992 International Conference on Spoken Language Processing, Volume 2* (pp. 867–870). Department of Linguistics, University of Alberta.

Sorensen, J. M., Cooper, W. E., & Paccia, J. M. (1978). Speech timing of grammatical categories. *Cognition, 6*, 135–153.

Tincoff, R., & Jusczyk, P. W. (1996, July). *Are word-final sounds perceptually salient for infants?* Paper presented at the Fifth Conference on Laboratory Phonology, Evanston, IL.

Tyler, L. K., & Warren, P. (1987). Local and global structure in spoken language comprehension. *Journal of Memory and Language, 26*, 638–657.

van de Weijer, J. (1998). *Language input for word discovery.* Unpublished doctoral dissertation, University of Nijmegen (MPI Series in Psycholinguistics, 9).

Werker, J. F., & Tees, R. C. (1984). Cross-language speech perception: Evidence for perceptual reorganization during the first year of life. *Infant Behavior and Development, 7*, 49–63.

3 Discovering Verbs Through Multiple-Cue Integration

Morten H. Christiansen and Padraic Monaghan

Introduction

Before children can ride a bicycle or tie their shoes, they have learned a great deal about how words are combined to form complex sentences. This achievement is especially impressive because children acquire most of this syntactic knowledge with little or no direct instruction. Nevertheless, mastering natural language syntax may be among the most difficult learning tasks that children face. In adulthood, syntactic knowledge can be characterized by constraints governing the relationship between grammatical categories of words (such as noun and verb) in a sentence. However, acquiring this knowledge presents the child with a chicken-and-egg problem: the syntactic constraints presuppose the existence of grammatical categories because syntactic knowledge is generally couched in terms of categories of words and not in terms of individual words. On the other hand, grammatical categories have little value in and by themselves; rather, they are only useful insofar as they support syntactic constraints. A similar "bootstrapping" problem faces a student learning an academic subject such as physics: understanding momentum or force presupposes some understanding of the physical laws in which they figure, yet these laws presuppose the very concepts they interrelate. But the bootstrapping problem solved by young children seems vastly more challenging, both because the constraints governing natural language are so intricate and because young children do not have the intellectual capacity or explicit instruction available to the academic student. So how does the child solve the bootstrapping problem in language acquisition? In this chapter, we pursue a possible solution in the form of multiple-cue integration.

By 1 year, infants will have learned a great deal about the sound structure of their native language (for reviews, see Jusczyk, 1997, 1999; Kuhl, 1999; Pallier, Christophe, & Mehler, 1997; Werker & Tees, 1999). Thus, when they face the problem of bootstrapping syntax at the beginning of their second year, they are already well acquainted with the phonological and prosodic regularities of their native language. The multiple-cue integration hypothesis suggests that this perceptual attunement provides an essential scaffolding for later learning by biasing children toward aspects of the input that are particularly informative for acquiring syntactic information (e.g., Christiansen & Dale, 2001; Gleitman & Wanner, 1982; and contributions in Morgan & Demuth, 1996; Weissenborn & Höhle, 2001). Specifically, the integration of multiple probabilistic cues derived from the co-occurrence of words (distributional), their sound properties (phonological), and their intonational (prosodic) as well as situational (semantic) context by perceptually attuned general-purpose learning mechanisms may hold the key to how children solve the bootstrapping problem. In this way, multiple cues can provide reliable evidence about linguistic structure that is unavailable from any single source of information.

A further initial strategy that a child may bring to bear on the problem of bootstrapping syntax is to focus on the discovery of nouns and verbs, perhaps the most salient groups of content words in that they refer to objects and actions in the environment. Even in this much reduced version, children's learning task remains formidable given that they are still in the process of making sense of the nonlinguistic world as well. And it is in this context that verbs may be particularly difficult to pin down. Minimally, early verb learning requires that children master three different complex learning tasks. First, children need to be able to segment fluent speech to locate possible verb forms using distributional, acoustic, and other types of language-internal cues (see the other chapters in part I). Second, they must be able to find the appropriate parts of actions to be named among unfolding event sequences involving many types of language-external cues (see chapters in part II). Finally, they have to learn to integrate language-internal and language-external cues in the service of acquiring the form and meaning of verbs (and other words; see chapters in part III).

In this chapter, we discuss how children may accomplish the difficult task of verb learning, focusing on the integration of multiple language-internal cues to verb forms. We first review previous work on multiple-cue integration. We then report results from novel analyses of corpora of English child-directed speech, pointing to different roles for distributional and phonological cues in the learning of nouns and verbs. Finally, we relate the differential roles of cues to differences in semantic support for nouns and verbs in language-external information, and discuss possible implications of our results for the understanding of word learning more generally.

Multiple-Cue Integration in Language Acquisition

There are three sources of information that children could potentially bring to bear on solving the bootstrapping problem: innate knowledge in the form of linguistic universals; language-external information concerning observed semantic relationships between language and the world; and language-internal information, such as aspects of phonological, prosodic, and distributional patterns that indicate the relation of various parts of language to each other.

Although some kind of innate knowledge may play a role in language acquisition, it cannot solve the bootstrapping problem. Even with built-in abstract knowledge about grammatical categories and syntactic rules (e.g., Pinker, 1984), the bootstrapping problem remains formidable: Innate knowledge can only help address the bootstrapping problem by building in universal aspects of language, and relationships between words and grammatical categories clearly differ between languages (e.g., the sound /su/ is a noun in French, *sou*, but a verb in English, *sue*). Crucially, children still have to map the right sound strings onto the right grammatical categories while determining the specific syntactic relations between these categories in their native language. Moreover, there now exists strong experimental evidence that children do not initially use abstract linguistic categories but instead employ novel words as concrete items, thereby challenging the usefulness of hypothesized innate grammatical categories (Tomasello, 2000). Thus, independently of whether or not innate linguistic knowledge is hypothesized to play an important role in language acquisition, it seems clear that other sources of information nevertheless are necessary to solve the bootstrapping problem.

Language-external information is likely to contribute substantially to language acquisition. Correlations between environmental observations relating prior semantic categories (e.g., objects and actions) and grammatical categories (e.g., nouns and verbs) may furnish a "semantic bootstrapping" solution (Pinker, 1984). However, given that children acquire linguistic distinctions with no semantic basis (e.g., gender in French; Karmiloff-Smith, 1979), semantics cannot be the only source of information involved in solving the bootstrapping problem. Another extralinguistic factor is cultural learning, whereby children may imitate the pairing of linguistic forms and their conventional communicative functions (Tomasello, Kruger, & Ratner, 1993). For example, by observing the idiom "John spilled the beans" used in the appropriate context, the child by reproducing it can discover that it means that John has revealed some sort of secret and not that he is a messy eater. However, to break down the linguistic forms into relevant units, it appears that cultural learning must be coupled with language-internal learning.

Though not the only source of information involved in language acquisition, we suggest that language-internal information is fundamental to bootstrapping the child into syntax. However, although language-internal input appears to be rich in potential cues to linguistic structure, there is an important caveat: the individual cues are only partially reliable, and none considered alone provides an infallible bootstrap into language. Thus, a learner could use the tendency for English nouns to be longer than verbs to determine that *elephant* is a noun, but the same strategy would fail for *investigate*. Likewise, although speakers tend to pause at linguistically meaningful places in a sentence (e.g., following a phrase or a clause), pauses also occur elsewhere. And although it is a good distributional bet that a determiner (e.g., *the*) will be followed by a noun, there are other possibilities (e.g., adjectives, such as *big*). To acquire language successfully, it seems that the child needs to integrate a great diversity of multiple probabilistic cues to language structure in an effective way. Fortunately, as we shall see next, there is a growing bulk of evidence showing that multiple probabilistic cues are available in language-internal input, that children are sensitive to them, and that they facilitate learning through multiple-cue integration.

Bootstrapping Through Multiple Language-Internal Cues

We distinguish between three types of language-internal cues: phonological, prosodic, and distributional cues. Phonological information—including stress, vowel quality, and duration—may help distinguish grammatical function words (e.g., determiners, prepositions, and conjunctions) from content words (nouns, verbs, adjectives, and adverbs) in English (e.g., Cutler, 1993; Gleitman & Wanner, 1982; Monaghan, Chater, & Christiansen, 2005; Morgan, Shi, & Allopenna, 1996; Shi, Morgan, & Allopenna, 1998). Phonological information may also help distinguish between nouns and verbs (Monaghan et al., 2005). For example, adults are sensitive to the fact that English disyllabic nouns tend to receive initial-syllable (trochaic) stress whereas disyllabic verbs tend to receive final-syllable (iambic) stress (Kelly, 1988). Moreover, acoustic analyses have shown that even noun-verb ambiguous disyllabic words that change grammatical category but not stress placement can be differentiated by syllable duration and amplitude cue differences (Sereno & Jongman, 1995). Experiments indicate that children as young as 3 years old are sensitive to this stress cue, even though few multisyllabic verbs occur in child-directed speech (Cassidy & Kelly, 1991, 2001). Other potential noun-verb cues in English include differences in word duration, consonant voicing, and vowel types—many of these cues may also be relevant cross-linguistically (see Kelly, 1992, for a review).

Prosodic information provides cues for word and phrasal/clausal segmentation and may help uncover syntactic structure (e.g., Gerken, Jusczyk, & Mandel, 1994; Gleitman & Wanner, 1982; Kemler Nelson, Hirsh-Pasek, Jusczyk, & Wright Cassidy, 1989; Morgan, 1996). Acoustic analyses suggest that differences in pause length, vowel duration, and pitch indicate phrase boundaries in both English and Japanese child-directed speech (Fisher & Tokura, 1996). Infants seem highly sensitive to such language-specific prosodic patterns (Gerken et al., 1994; Kemler-Nelson et al., 1989; for reviews, see Gerken, 1996; Jusczyk & Kemler-Nelson, 1996; Morgan, 1996)—a sensitivity that may start in utero (Mehler et al., 1988). Prosodic information also improves sentence comprehension in 2-year-olds (Shady & Gerken, 1999). Results from artificial language learning experiments with adults show that prosodic marking of syntactic phrase boundaries facilitates learning (Morgan, Meier, & Newport, 1987; Valian & Levitt, 1996). Evidence from event-related brainwave potentials in adults showing that prosodic information has an immediate effect on syntactic processing (Steinhauer, Alter, & Friederici, 1999) further underscores the importance of this cue. Unfortunately, prosody is also partly affected by a number of nonsyntactic factors such as breathing patterns, resulting in an imperfect mapping between prosody and syntax (Fernald & McRoberts, 1996). Nonetheless, infants' sensitivity to prosody provides a rich potential source of syntactic information (Fisher & Tokura, 1996; Gerken 1996; Morgan, 1996).

Information about the distribution of linguistic fragments at or below the word level may also provide cues to grammatical category. Morphological patterns across words may be informative—for example, English words that are observed to have both -ed and -s endings are likely to be verbs (Maratsos & Chalkley, 1980). Artificial language learning results show that adults are better at learning grammatical categories cued by word internal patterns (Brooks, Braine, Catalano, & Brody, 1993; Frigo & McDonald, 1998). Corpus analyses have demonstrated that distributional patterns of word co-occurrence also give useful cross-linguistic cues to grammatical categories in child-directed speech (e.g., Mintz, 2003; Monaghan et al., 2005; Redington, Chater, & Finch, 1998; Redington et al., 1995). Given that function words primarily occur at phrase boundaries (e.g., initially in English and French, finally in Japanese) they may reveal syntactic structure. This is confirmed by corpus analyses (Mintz, Newport, & Bever, 2002) and results from artificial language learning (Green, 1979; Morgan et al., 1987; Valian & Coulson, 1988). Finally, artificial language learning experiments indicate that duplication of morphological patterns across phrase-related items (e.g., Spanish: Los Estados Unidos) facilitates learning (Meier & Bower, 1986; Morgan et al., 1987).

Phonological information may help distinguish between function and content words and between nouns and verbs. Prosodic information provides cues for word and phrasal or clausal segmentation and may help uncover syntactic structure. Distributional information affords cues for labeling and segmentation and perhaps evidence towards syntactic relations. None of these cues in isolation suffice to solve the bootstrapping problem; rather, they must be integrated to overcome the limited reliability of individual cues. Recent connectionist simulations have demonstrated that efficient and robust learning mechanisms exist for multiple-cue integration (Christiansen & Dale, 2001; Reali, Christiansen, & Monaghan, 2003). Despite previous theoretical reservations about the value of multiple-cue integration (Fernald & McRoberts, 1996), analyses of network performance revealed that learning under multiple cues results in faster, better, and more uniform learning. Moreover, the networks were able to distinguish between relevant cues and distracting cues, and performance did not differ from networks that received only reliable cues. The efficacy of multiple-cue integration has also been confirmed in artificial language learning experiments (Billman, 1989; Brooks et al., 1993; McDonald & Plauche, 1995; Morgan et al., 1987).

After one year of exposure to spoken language, children's perceptual attunement is likely to allow them to utilize language-internal probabilistic cues (for reviews, see Jusczyk, 1997, 1999; Kuhl, 1999; Pallier et al., 1997; Werker & Tees, 1999). For example, infants appear sensitive to the acoustic differences between function and content words (Shi, Werker, & Morgan, 1999) and the relationship between function words and prosody in speech (Shafer, Shucard, Shucard, & Gerken, 1998). Young infants can detect differences in syllable number among isolated words (Bijeljac, Bertoncini, & Mehler, 1993)—a possible cue to noun-verb differences. Moreover, infants are accomplished distributional learners (e.g., Gómez & Gerken, 1999; Saffran, Aslin, & Newport, 1996; see Gómez & Gerken, 2000; Saffran, 2003, for reviews), and importantly, they are capable of multiple-cue integration (Mattys, Jusczyk, Luce, & Morgan, 1999; Morgan & Saffran, 1995). When solving the bootstrapping problem, children are also likely to benefit from specific properties of child-directed speech, such as the predominance of short sentences (Newport, Gleitman, & Gleitman, 1977) and exaggerated prosody (Kuhl et al., 1997).

This review has indicated that a range of language-internal cues are available for language acquisition, that these cues affect learning and processing, and that mechanisms exist for multiple-cue integration. Next we present two sets of corpus analysis experiments showing that language-internal cues appear to take on different roles in the context of learning about nouns and verbs in English. Specifically, we have found that phonological cues may be particularly important for learning verbs, whereas distributional information may be more useful for learning about nouns.

Experiment 1: The Importance of Phonological Cues for Verb Learning

In a previous study (Monaghan et al., 2005), we quantified the potential usefulness of phonological and distributional cues for distinguishing between nouns and verbs through a series of corpus analyses of a large corpus of child-directed speech. The method we used to assess this usefulness was discriminant analysis, which attempts to use the cues to carve up a set of words into distinct categories. The extent to which this can be done effectively, matching the actual syntactic categories, can then be assessed. Figure 3.1 is a schematic diagram of the method of distinguishing nouns and verbs, which are represented as dots in a space determined by the set of cues. In essence, discriminant analysis provides a hyperplane through the word space, depicted by the gray-shaded surface, based on the cues that most accurately reflect the actual category distinction. In the figure, the discriminant analysis classifies nouns and verbs effectively, with most nouns occurring above the hyperplane and most verbs positioned below the plane. Our preferred method is to use a "leave-one-out cross-validation" method, which is

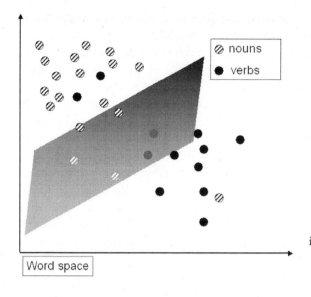

Figure 3.1. Schematic illustration of discriminant analysis of nouns and verbs.

a conservative measure of classification accuracy and works by assessing the accuracy of the classification of words that are not used in positioning the hyperplane. This means that the hyperplane is constructed on the basis of the information on all words except one, and then the classification of the omitted word is assessed. This is then repeated for each word, and the overall classification accuracy can then be determined. The results of the analyses of phonological and distributional cues showed that the use of several cues provides not only more accurate classification than single cues, but better generalization to novel situations. We also found that frequency interacted with the two cues: Distributional cues were more useful for high-frequency words, whereas phonological cues were more reliable for low-frequency words. The integration of phonological and distributional cues resulted in 66.7% correct noun-verb classification. These results indicated the general usefulness of multiple-cue integration in learning syntactic categories. In Experiment 1, we extend this work to determine whether phonological and distributional cues may be differentially useful for learning nouns and verbs. In this study, we generated phonological and distributional cues for the 1,000 most frequent words in child-directed speech and assessed the extent to which these different cue types distinguished each syntactic category from all others.

Method

Corpus Preparation

In order to effectively model the language environment of the child, we used a corpus of child-directed speech. We concatenated all the child-directed speech from the English CHILDES database (MacWhinney, 2000). This amounted to 5,436,855 words. All pauses and turn-taking were marked as utterance boundaries, resulting in approximately 1.4 million utterances. For each word, we derived its phonological form from the CELEX database (Baayen, Pipenbrock, & Gulikers, 1995). Orthographic forms with alternative pronunciations were assigned the most frequent pronunciation from CELEX. Many words in English are syntactically ambiguous: *chair* and *table* have usage as both nouns and verbs, though in most cases there is a clear most frequent usage (*chair* and *table* are usually nouns). CELEX records the frequency of usage of words as different syntactic categories, and so we used this information to label each word with its most frequent usage. The syntactic categories distinguished in CELEX were nouns, adjectives, numerals, verbs, articles, pronouns, adverbs, prepositions, conjunctions, interjections, and contractions (such as *should've, can't*). We counted the number of occurrences of each word in the child-directed speech corpus and selected the 1,000 most frequent words from the CHILDES database and hand-coded those words that did not appear in the CELEX database (mainly comprising proper nouns, interjections, and alternative spellings, such as *mama, mamma*).

Phonological Information

We coded each word for 16 phonological cues that have been posited as useful in distinguishing different syntactic categories in English (Campbell & Besner, 1981; Cutler, 1993; Cutler & Carter, 1987; Gleitman & Wanner, 1982; Kelly, 1992; Kelly & Bock, 1988; Marchand, 1969; Morgan et al., 1996; Shi et al., 1996; Sereno & Jongman, 1990). These cues operate either at the word level, the syllable level, or the phoneme level. Word-level cues concern the properties of the word taken as a whole; syllable-level cues assess the distribution of consonants and phonemes in the syllable; and phoneme-level cues assess the properties of particular phonemes within the word. Table 3.1 summarizes the cues we used in the analyses; for more details of the precise encoding of the cues, see Monaghan et al. (2005).

Distributional Information

The child-directed speech corpus provided the contexts within which each word occurred in one or more utterances, and our distributional cues were designed to exploit this information. We examined the local context of each word from CHILDES in order to gain a reflection of the value of distributional information for categorizing each word. As our measure of distributional information we selected a set of high-frequency words and determined the number of times each word occurred immediately succeeding each of these high-frequency words. The rationale for this was that high-frequency words can be used to promote the categorization of lower-frequency words that follow them. Valian and Coulson (1988) constructed an artificial language in which low-frequency nonsense words

Table 3.1 Phonological cues used in the discriminant analyses of syntactic category

Phonological Cue	Examples		
	monkey	*stretched*	*that*
Word level			
Length in phonemes	5	6	3
Length in syllables	2	1	1
Presence of stress	1	1	0
Syllable position of stress	1	1	0
Syllable level			
Number of consonants in word onset	1	3	1
Proportion of phonemes that are consonants	0.6	0.83	0.67
Proportion of syllables containing reduced vowel	0	0	1
Reduced 1st vowel	0	0	1
-ed inflection	0	1	0
Phoneme level			
Proportion of consonants that are coronal	0	1	1
Initial /ʌ/	0	0	1
Final voicing	0	2	2
Proportion of consonants that are nasals	0.67	0	0
Position of stressed vowel (1: front, 3: back)	3	1	2*
Position of vowels (1: front, 3: back)	2	1	1
Height of vowels (0: high, 3: low)	1.25	2	2.5

*Words with no stress were assigned the median position.

followed only one of two high-frequency nonsense words. Participants were able to learn to group together the lower-frequency words that followed each of the high-frequency words. We selected the 20 most frequent words from the CHILDES database and counted the times that these context words preceded the target word. We then calculated the signed log-likelihood test score for each context–target word pairing (Dunning, 1993; Monaghan et al., 2005). This score reflects the extent to which the target word co-occurs more or less than by chance with the context word in the corpus. High positive values indicate there is a greater than chance co-occurrence between the words, whereas large negative values reflect that the co-occurrence occurs less than by chance. Values close to zero indicate that co-occurrence occurs at chance level. Each of the 1,000 words we examined, therefore, had log-likelihood test scores for the 20 most frequent context words.

Analysis

The potential value of cues for distinguishing the syntactic categories of words was assessed using leave-one-out cross-validation discriminant analysis. For each syntactic category, we labeled words as either belonging to that category or belonging to another category. We used stepwise discriminant analysis which meant that cues were only entered into the analysis if they contributed significantly to making the distinction between words in the category in question and all other words. We performed discriminant analyses employing either the phonological or the distributional cues. In order to compare classification performance for the different syntactic categories, successful classification was weighted by the size of the category—so accuracy greater than 50% reflected better-than-chance performance.

Results and Discussion

Table 3.2 indicates the correct classification of words for each category distinction in the discriminant analyses, employing either phonological or distributional cues. It was not the case that any type of cue resulted in perfect classifications of any syntactic category, though classification was better than chance level of 50% for all analyses. The results supported the prediction that using phonological cues alone resulted in better classification of verbs than of nouns. The results also supported the claim that using distributional cues alone would provide better classification of nouns. Also of note in the results are the particular usefulness of phonological cues for classifying function words—pronouns, prepositions, conjunctions, and interjections all had more than 80% correct classifications with these cues, whereas distributional cues were poor for these word categories.

In order to determine in more detail the role of phonological and distributional cues for distinguishing nouns and verbs, we examined which words were correctly classified by both the phonological and distributional analysis and

Table 3.2 Discriminant analysis classification results using phonological cues and distributional cues for distinguishing each category from all other words

Category	Phonological Classification	Distributional Classification
Noun	61.8	64.3
Adjective	54.8	59.7
Numeral	55.7	62.3
Verb	66.4	62.3
Article	46.9	49.9
Pronoun	83.6	62.9
Adverb	68.1	52.4
Preposition	85.3	62.3
Conjunction	85.6	53.2
Interjection	86.7	57.2
Contraction	63.7	56.4

explored which words were correctly classified using phonological cues only but which were incorrectly classified using distributional cues, and vice versa, the case where distributional cues produced a correct classification but phonological cues resulted in incorrect classification. Finally, we also encoded those words that were classified incorrectly by both analyses. There were two possibilities for the resulting classifications. It may be that the same words are correctly classified by analyses based on both cue types, or it may be that there is complementarity in the classifications: Those words incorrectly classified by, say, the phonological cues, may be correctly classified by the distributional cues. Table 3.3 presents the results, showing the number of words on which the classifications agreed and disagreed. Hierarchical log-linear analysis can then be used to assess whether there are main effects and interactions between the classifications based on the different cue types and the noun-verb category. Table 3.4 shows the results of the one-, two-, and three-way log-linear analyses on the table shown in table 3.3. The one-way analyses refer to main effects in the table, the two-way analyses refer to interactions between two of the factors, and the three-way analysis tests whether there is a three-way interaction in the table.

The one-way effect of noun-verb category can be explained by there being more nouns than verbs. The one-way effects of phonological cues and distributional cues reflected the fact that each classification assigned words to the correct category significantly more than by chance. The two-way effects of noun-verb by phonological cues and noun-verb by distributional cues indicate that the classifications were more successful overall for nouns than for verbs. The two-way effect of distributional cues by phonological cues was due to phonological cues being more

Table 3.3 Correct and incorrect classifications of nouns from other words and verbs from other words in the phonological and distributional discriminant analyses

Nouns	Distributional Classification		
Phonological Classification	Correct	Incorrect	Total
Correct	405	182	592
Incorrect	222	177	399
Total	627	359	986
Verbs	Distributional Classification		
Phonological Classification	Correct	Incorrect	Total
Correct	406	155	561
Incorrect	44	381	425
Total	450	536	986

Table 3.4 Results of hierarchical loglinear analysis

Generating Class	Likelihood Ratio χ^2	df
One-way		6
Noun/verb	489.730	
Phon	530.069	
Dist	551.201	
Two-way		5
Noun/verb × Phon	489.482	
Noun/verb × Dist	529.820	
Phon × Dist	468.349	
Three-way		4
Noun/verb × Phon × Dist	468.101	

"Phon" refers to the classification resulting from the phonological cues, and "Dist" refers to the distributional cue classification. For all likelihood ratio χ^2, $p < .001$.

effective in classifying words than the distributional cues. However, interpretation of these lower-level interactions must be moderated by the three-way interaction.

The three-way interaction suggests that the combination of phonological and distributional information operates differently for nouns and for verbs. The principal differences in the classifications in table 3.3 are the words that the phonological information classifies wrongly. For nouns, the distributional information operates to classify over 50% of these correctly, whereas for verbs, only 44 of 425 incorrect classifications are remedied by the distributional information. Whereas noun classification is benefited by both phonological and distributional information, the addition of distributional information for the verb classifications does not greatly improve classification based on the phonological information alone.

The results of assessing the effects of phonological and distributional information for discriminating words of each syntactic category fit our initial hypothesis well. Phonological information appears to be particularly useful for determining the verb category, but less useful for noun classifications, once distributional information has been taken into account. As an aside, the high accuracy of phonological cues for function words, shown in table 3.2, appears to indicate that phonological information is particularly useful and rich in all cases where distributional information is less accurate as a basis for classification.

Experiment 2: Distributional Cues Work Better for Nouns

The results of Experiment 1 could potentially depend on using a particular type of distributional information. In our Experiment 2, we therefore sought to determine whether other approaches to distributional information may be more useful for distinguishing nouns and verbs as syntactic categories. We considered two forms of distributional information—one in which the information is only about the preceding word (Monaghan & Christiansen, 2004), and one, developed by Mintz (2003), which considers jointly the preceding and succeeding word. We predict that enriched distributional information will benefit classification of both nouns and verbs, but in both cases, classification of nouns will exceed that of verbs.

Mintz (2003) developed an intriguing approach to test the potential assistance that distributional information may provide in classifying words from different syntactic categories. He proposed that a frame formed by linking the preceding and succeeding word would predict with a high degree of accuracy the syntactic category of the intervening word. Put another way, given a particular pairing of preceding (A) and succeeding (B) words, all words (x) that occur within that pair (as AxB) will be of the same syntactic category. To test this prediction, Mintz selected the 45 most frequent A_B pairs of words from subsets of the CHILDES database. He then clustered together all words that occurred inside the A_B frame (i.e., x in the AxB frame). The resulting clusters tended to be of the same syntactic category with very high accuracy (see also chapter 1, this volume). Experiment 2 replicates and extends this study to investigate differentials in classification of nouns and verbs.

Method

Corpus Preparation

We replicated Mintz's (2003) analysis on one of the corpora that he employed: speech spoken to a child aged between 0 and 2 years, 6 months (anne01a-anne23b; Theakston, Lieven, Pine, & Rowland, 2001). We replaced all pauses and turn-taking with utterance boundaries, resulting in 93,269 words distributed over 30,365 utterances. As with the analysis of the large corpus in Experiment 1, syntactic category was taken from CELEX, and all words that were not in CELEX were hand coded. We used a slightly different set of syntactic categories to Experiment 1, to make our results more comparable to the categories used by Mintz: hence we distinguished words into the categories of noun, adjective, numeral, verb, article, pronoun, adverb, conjunction, preposition, interjection, *wh*-word (e.g., *what, where*), and proper noun. Contractions were classified according to the syntactic category of their first element, so *you're* was classified as pronoun, *could've* was classified as verb, and *what's* as *wh*-word.

Analysis

We then selected the 45 most frequent A_B frames from the Theakston et al. (2001) corpus and clustered together all words that intervened in each frame. For example, for the frame *a* _____ *on* the following words occurred and were subsequently clustered together: *puddle, suck, welly-boot, plaster, stamp, tap, wee, sandcastle, spoon, fish, tunnel, bib, video, wee-wee, blanket, nappy, walk, cow, hat, ride, car*. We assessed accuracy by counting the number of correct pairings of words of the same syntactic category (hits) in each cluster, and dividing this by the number of pairings of all words within each cluster (hits + false alarms). In the above example for the *a* _____ *on* frame, accuracy was 100% for this cluster. We assessed completeness by dividing the number of hits by the number of pairings of words of the same syntactic category that occurred in all clusterings (hits + misses). For the *a* _____ *on* frame, any nouns that occurred in any other cluster were counted as misses and reduced completeness. We also measured overall coverage by assessing how many words of each category were classified by the analysis.

In a similar way, we measured the extent to which information only about the preceding word predicted the syntactic category of the following word (Monaghan & Christiansen, 2004). We took the 45 most frequent $A\_$ frames from the Theakston et al. corpus and clustered together all words that occurred after that word (i.e., as an x in Ax). We assessed accuracy and completeness in the same way as the AxB analysis.

Results and Discussion

In the Theakston et al. (2001) corpus, there were a total of 1,249 different nouns and 655 verbs. For the AxB and Ax analyses, the accuracy and completeness results are shown in table 3.5. For the AxB analysis, a greater proportion of verbs were classified, $\chi^2 = 55.36$, $p < .001$. However, accuracy and completeness were both higher for the noun classifications, $\chi^2 = 5810.51$, and $\chi^2 = 77136.21$, respectively, both $p < .001$. Frames that formed clusters including nouns tended to contain only nouns, whereas the verb clusters tended to contain a greater proportion of words from other categories. To a greater degree, nouns tended to occur in the same clusters, whereas verbs were distributed across more clusters.

The Ax analysis resulted in a high coverage, classifying 97.4% of the nouns and 77.9% of the verbs—nearly six times more nouns and twice as many verbs as the AxB analysis (though with lower degrees of accuracy). Thus, a greater proportion of nouns than verbs were classified in the Ax analysis, and accuracy and completeness were both significantly higher for nouns than verbs, all $\chi^2 > 190$, $p < .001$. The clusters containing nouns contained a mean of 32.7 nouns, whereas those containing verbs contained a mean of 20.5 verbs.

Experiments 1 and 2 together indicate that the three different distributional analyses all point to an advantage for classifying nouns over verbs. The clustering of words in AxB and Ax frames is more coherent and accurate for nouns than verbs, as reflected in the advantages for accuracy and completeness analyses in Experiment 2. Nouns tend to be more frequent than verbs, in that more of the most frequent words in a corpus are nouns, in particular, proper nouns. Such a difference

Table 3.5 Accuracy and completeness of AxB and Ax frames analyses for nouns and verbs

AxB	Nouns	Verbs
Total classified	206	205
Accuracy	78%	69%
Completeness	8%	3%

Ax	Nouns	Verbs
Total classified	1217	510
Accuracy	69%	23%
Completeness	9%	3%

in frequency goes some way to explaining why distributional information may be more useful for nouns than verbs—the more information available about the context of a word, the more beneficial that information is going to be. However, frequency cannot account for differences in accuracy of classification. The distributional cues for nouns also supply more detailed information about usage than those provided for verbs. We next discuss why this points towards the greater reliance upon and benefit of word-internal cues for classifying verbs.

General Discussion

In this chapter, we have argued that language-internal information is crucial for solving the bootstrapping problem facing children in early syntax acquisition. The integration of multiple language-internal cues allows young children to get an initial grasp on lexical categories, providing a probabilistic foundation for subsequent acquisition of the syntactic constraints on their native language. Our two experiments have further illuminated the differential contribution of phonological and distributional information to the learning of nouns and verbs from English child-directed speech. Experiment 1 showed that whereas both types of cues were helpful for the discovery of nouns, phonological cues were less useful once distributional cues had been taken into account. Phonological information, on the other hand, was particularly useful for classifying verbs with distributional information providing little additional benefit to overall classification. Experiment 2 further demonstrated that these results were not due to the specific type of distributional information used in Experiment 1. Using the distributional models of Monaghan and Christiansen (2004) and Mintz (2003), we found that whereas more enriched distributional information benefits the classification of both types of words, nouns benefit considerably more than verbs both in terms of accuracy and completeness of categorization. Taken together, Experiments 1 and 2 provide compelling evidence that phonological and distributional cues take on different, partially complementary roles in facilitating the discovery of nouns and verbs in English, with distributional information being more useful for the classification of nouns and phonological information more useful for the classification of verbs.

Our analyses in Experiment 2 further indicate that distributional information is most supportive when early verb learning is concentrated only on certain contexts initially. This is consistent with Tomasello's (1992, 2000) item-based perspective on early syntactic development, suggesting that early word learning, in particular of verbs, is centered on specific words or phrases rather than lexical categories (e.g., *eat* _____, *draw* _____, etc.). Underscoring their importance for verb learning, phonological cues may play an important role in drawing together the disparate verb fragments that were initially highlighted in an item-based fashion by distributional means. Thus, verbs need phonological cues to draw them together into a coherent lexical category because of the item-based nature of their distributional cues. Nouns, on the other hand, do not need phonological cues for this purpose because each noun tends to occur in many more different distributional contexts.

The importance of phonological cues for learning verbs becomes even more evident when language-external information is taken into account. As pointed out by Childers and Tomasello (chapter 12, this volume), nouns tend to be conceptually easier for children to learn in comparison with verbs. Understanding verbs is complicated by the fact that a particular action sequence can be conceptualized in many different ways, and determining which one is the intended one requires the child to determine what perspective a speaker is imposing on the event—the so-called packaging problem (Gentner & Boroditsky, 2001; Gleitman, 1990; Tomasello, 1992—see also chapter 8, this volume). This means that language-external cues are going to be more helpful for discovering nouns than verbs, placing even more importance on phonology as a cue to verb learning.

Not only may nouns be easier to learn because of the conceptual support of language-external cues, but they may also be easier to segment from the speech stream. The same local distributional cues that we found to be reliable for noun classification in Experiments 1 and 2 are also likely to be useful for segmenting nouns from fluent speech. Because good cues—such as *the*, *a*, and *you*—have very low transitional probabilities after them, the onsets of the nouns that tend to follow them will be easy to detect. In this way, the same distributional properties that make nouns easy to classify will also make them easier to discover in the speech stream: nouns are more predictable because they follow good distributional cues. This would suggest a disadvantage for segmenting verbs in early acquisition, and may thus explain the developmental delay in verb segmentation relative to noun segmentation observed by Nazzi and Houston (chapter 2, this volume).

Although we have uncovered several factors that are likely to make verb learning in English more difficult than the learning of nouns, it may be that it is not verbs per se that are hard to learn, but words that are semantically complex. There is an ongoing debate concerning whether nouns are harder to learn than verbs (see chapters 12, 17, and 18 for discussions). A possible consensus is that it is the concreteness of a word that determines its ease of learning, rather than its lexical category (e.g., chapter 14 this volume). Our approach to multiple-cue integration accommodates this perspective. Concrete words will have more reliable language-external cues than more abstract words, and this will facilitate word learning through multiple-cue integration. Words that have a more reliable set of cues supporting them are going to be easier to learn—no matter whether the cues are language-internal or language-external. However, when it comes to associating actions with words, distributional and semantic cues are generally going to be less useful, leaving phonological cues as the perhaps most important cue for the discovery of verbs through multiple-cue integration.

Acknowledgments This research was supported in part by a Human Frontiers Science Program Grant (RGP0177/2001-B). Thanks to Rick Dale, Thomas Farmer, Stanka Fitneva, Roberta Golinkoff, and Luca Onnis for their comments on an earlier version of this chapter.

References

Baayen, R. H., Pipenbrock, R., & Gulikers, L. (1995). *The CELEX Lexical Database* (CD-ROM). Philadelphia: Linguistic Data Consortium, University of Pennsylvania.

Bijeljac, R., Bertoncini, J., & Mehler, J. (1993). How do 4-day-old infants categorize multisyllabic utterances? *Developmental Psychology, 2*, 711–721.

Billman, D. (1989). Systems of correlations in rule and category learning: Use of structured input in learning syntactic categories. *Language and Cognitive Processes, 4*, 127–155.

Brooks, P. J., Braine, M. D., Catalano, L., & Brody, R. E. (1993). Acquisition of gender-like noun subclasses in an artificial language: The contribution of phonological markers to learning. *Journal of Memory and Language, 32*, 76–95.

Campbell, R., & Besner, D. (1981). This and thap—Constraints on the pronuncia-tion of new written words. *Quarterly Journal of Experimental Psychology, 33*, 375–396.

Cassidy, K. W., & Kelly, M. H. (1991). Phonological information for grammatical category assignments. *Journal of Memory and Language, 30*, 348–369.

Cassidy, K. W., & Kelly, M. H. (2001). Children's use of phonology to infer grammatical class in vocabulary learning. *Psychonomic Bulletin and Review, 8*, 519–523.

Christiansen, M. H., & Dale, R. (2001). Integrating distributional, prosodic and phonological information in a connectionist model of language acquisition. In *Proceedings of the 23rd annual conference of the Cognitive Science Society* (pp. 220–225). Mahwah, NJ: Lawrence Erlbaum.

Cutler, A. (1993). Phonological cues to open- and closed-class words in the processing of spoken sentences. *Journal of Psycholinguistic Research, 22*, 109–131.

Cutler, A., & Carter, D. M. (1987). The predominance of strong initial syllables in the English vocabulary. *Computer Speech and Language, 2*, 133–142.

Dunning, T. (1993). Accurate methods for the statistics of surprise and coincidence. *Computational Linguistics, 19*, 61–74.

Fernald, A., & McRoberts, G. (1996). Prosodic bootstrapping: A critical analysis of the argument and the evidence. In J. L. Morgan & K. Demuth (Eds.), *Signal to syntax: Bootstrapping from speech to grammar in early acquisition* (pp. 365–388). Mahwah, NJ: Lawrence Erlbaum.

Fisher, C., & Tokura, H. (1996). Acoustic cues to grammatical structure in infant-directed speech: Cross-linguistic evidence. *Child Development, 67*, 3192–3218.

Frigo, L., & McDonald, J. L. (1998). Properties of phonological markers that affect the acquisition of gender-like subclasses. *Journal of Memory and Language, 39*, 218–245.

Gentner, D., & Boroditsky, L. (2001). Individuation, relational relativity and early word learning. In M. Bowerman & S. Levinson (Eds.), *Language acquisition and conceptual development* (pp. 215–256). Cambridge: Cambridge University Press.

Gerken, L. A. (1996). Prosody's role in language acquisition and adult parsing. *Journal of Psycholinguistic Research, 25*, 345–356.

Gerken, L. A., Jusczyk, P. W., & Mandel, D. R. (1994). When prosody fails to cue syntactic structure: Nine-month-olds' sensitivity to phonological vs. syntactic phrases. *Cognition, 51*, 237–265.

Gleitman, L. (1990). The structural sources of verb meanings. *Language Acquisition, 1*, 3–55.

Gleitman, L., & Wanner, E. (1982). Language acquisition: The state of the state of the art. In E. Wanner & L. Gleitman (Eds.), *Language acquisition: The state of the art* (pp. 3–48). Cambridge: Cambridge University Press.

Gómez, R. L., & Gerken, L. A. (1999). Artificial grammar learning by 1-year-olds leads to specific and abstract knowledge. *Cognition, 70*, 109–135.

Gómez, R. L., & Gerken, L. A. (2000). Infant artificial language learning and language acquisition. *Trends in Cognitive Sciences, 4*, 178–186.

Green, T. R. G. (1979). The necessity of syntax markers: Two experiments with artificial languages. *Journal of Verbal Learning and Verbal Behavior, 18*, 481–496.

Jusczyk, P. W. (1997). *The discovery of spoken language.* Cambridge, MA: MIT Press.

Jusczyk, P. W. (1999). How infants begin to extract words from speech. *Trends in Cognitive Sciences, 3*, 323–328.

Jusczyk, P. W., & Kemler-Nelson, D. G. (1996). Syntactic units, prosody, and psychological reality during infancy. In J. L. Morgan & K. Demuth (Eds.), *Signal to syntax: Bootstrapping from speech to grammar in early acquisition* (pp. 389–408). Mahwah, NJ: Lawrence Erlbaum.

Karmiloff-Smith, A. (1979). *A functional approach to child language: A study of determiners and reference.* Cambridge: Cambridge University Press.

Kelly, M. H. (1988). Phonological biases in grammatical category shifts. *Journal of Memory and Language, 27*, 343–358.

Kelly, M. H. (1992). Using sound to solve syntactic problems: The role of phonology in grammatical category assignments. *Psychological Review, 99*, 349–364.

Kelly, M. H., & Bock, J. K. (1988). Stress in time. *Journal of Experimental Psychology: Human Perception and Performance, 14*, 389–403.

Kemler Nelson, D. G., Hirsh-Pasek, K., Jusczyk, P. W., & Wright Cassidy, K. (1989). How the prosodic cues in motherese might assist language learning. *Journal of Child Language, 16*, 55–68.

Kuhl, P. K. (1999). Speech, language, and the brain: Innate preparation for learning. In M. D. Hauser & M. Konishi (Eds.), *The design of animal communication* (pp. 419–450). Cambridge, MA: MIT Press.

Kuhl, P. K., Andruski, J. E., Chistovich, I. A., Chistovich, L. A., Kozhevnikova, E. V., Ryskina, V. L., et al. (1997). Cross-language analysis of phonetic units in language addressed to infants. *Science, 277*, 684–686.

MacWhinney, B. (2000). *The CHILDES Project: Tools for analyzing talk* (3rd ed.). Mahwah, NJ: Lawrence Erlbaum.

Maratsos, M., & Chalkley, M. A. (1980). The internal language of children's syntax: The ontogenesis and representation of syntactic categories. In K. Nelson (Ed.), *Children's language* (Vol. 2, pp. 127–214). New York: Gardner Press.

Marchand, H. (1969). *The categories and types of present-day English word-formation* (2nd ed.). Munich: C.H. Beck'sche Verlagsbuchhandlung.

Mattys, S. L., Jusczyk, P. W., Luce, P., & Morgan, J. L. (1999). Phonotactic and prosodic effects on word segmentation in infants. *Cognitive Psychology, 38*, 465–494.

McDonald, J. L., & Plauche, M. (1995). Single and correlated cues in an artificial language learning paradigm. *Language and Speech, 38*, 223–236.

Mehler, J., Jusczyk, P. W., Lambertz, G., Halsted, N., Bertoncini, J., & Amiel-Tison, C. (1988). A precursor of language acquisition in young infants. *Cognition, 29*, 143–178.

Meier, R. P., & Bower, G. H. (1986). Semantic reference and phrasal grouping in the acquisition of a miniature phrase structure language. *Journal of Memory and Language, 25*, 492–505.

Mintz, T. H. (2003). Frequent frames as a cue for grammatical categories in child directed speech. *Cognition, 90*, 91–117.

Mintz, T. H., Newport, E. L., & Bever, T. G. (2002). The distributional structure of grammatical categories in speech to young children. *Cognitive Science, 26*, 393–424.

Monaghan, P., Chater, N., & Christiansen, M. H. (2005). *The differential contribution of phonological and distributional cues in grammatical categorization.* Manuscript submitted for publication.

Monaghan, P., & Christiansen, M. H. (2004). What distributional information is useful and usable for language acquisition? In *Proceedings of the 26th annual conference of the Cognitive Science Society* (pp. 963–968). Mahwah, NJ: Lawrence Erlbaum.

Morgan, J. L. (1996). Prosody and the roots of parsing. *Language and Cognitive Processes, 11*, 69–106.

Morgan, J. L., & Demuth, K. (Eds.). (1996). *Signal to syntax: Bootstrapping from speech to grammar in early acquisition.* Mahwah, NJ: Lawrence Erlbaum.

Morgan, J. L., Meier, R. P., & Newport, E. L. (1987). Structural packaging in the input to language learning: Contributions of prosodic and morphological marking of phrases to the acquisition of language. *Cognitive Psychology, 19*, 498–550.

Morgan, J. L., & Saffran, J. R. (1995). Emerging integration of sequential and suprasegmental information in preverbal speech segmentation. *Child Development, 66*, 911–936.

Morgan, J. L., Shi, R., & Allopenna, P. (1996). Perceptual bases of grammatical categories. In J. L. Morgan & K. Demuth (Eds.), *Signal to syntax: Bootstrapping from speech to grammar in early acquisition* (pp. 263–283). Mahwah, NJ: Lawrence Erlbaum.

Newport, E. L., Gleitman, H., & Gleitman, L. R. (1977). Mother, I'd rather do it myself: Some effects and non-effects of maternal speech style. In C. E. Snow & C. A. Ferguson (Eds.), *Talking to children: Language input and acquisition* (pp. 109–149). Cambridge: Cambridge University Press.

Pallier, C., Christophe, A., & Mehler, J. (1997). Language-specific listening. *Trends in Cognitive Sciences, 1*, 129–132.

Pinker, S. (1984). *Language learnability and language development.* Cambridge, MA: Harvard University Press.

Reali, F., Christiansen, M. H., & Monaghan, P. (2003). Phonological and distributional cues in syntax acquisition: Scaling up the connectionist approach to multiple-cue integration. In *Proceedings of the 25th annual conference of the Cognitive Science Society* (pp. 970–975). Mahwah, NJ: Lawrence Erlbaum.

Redington, M., Chater, N., & Finch, S. (1998). Distributional information: A powerful cue for acquiring syntactic categories. *Cognitive Science, 22,* 425–469.

Redington, M., Chater, N., Huang, C. R., Chang, L. P., Finch, S., & Chen, K. J. (1995). The universality of simple distributional methods: Identifying syntactic categories in Mandarin Chinese. In *Proceedings of the Cognitive Science of Natural Language Processing.* Dublin: Dublin City University.

Saffran, J. R. (2003). Statistical language learning: Mechanisms and constraints. *Current Directions in Psychological Science, 12,* 110–114.

Saffran, J. R., Aslin, R. N., & Newport, E. L. (1996). Statistical learning by 8-month-old infants. *Science, 274,* 1926–1928.

Sereno, J. A., & Jongman, A. (1990). Phonological and form class relations in the lexicon. *Journal of Psycholinguistic Research, 19,* 387–404.

Sereno, J. A., & Jongman, A. (1995). Acoustic correlates of grammatical class. *Language and Speech, 38,* 57–76.

Shady, M., & Gerken, L. A. (1999). Grammatical and caregiver cues in early sentence comprehension. *Journal of Child Language, 26,* 163–175.

Shafer, V. L., Shucard, D. W., Shucard, J. L., & Gerken, L. A. (1998). An electrophysiological study of infants' sensitivity to the sound patterns of English speech. *Journal of Speech, Language, and Hearing Research, 41,* 874–886.

Shi, R., Morgan, J., & Allopenna, P. (1998). Phonological and acoustic bases for earliest grammatical category assignment: A cross-linguistic perspective. *Journal of Child Language, 25,* 169–201.

Shi, R., Werker, J. F., & Morgan, J. L. (1999). Newborn infants' sensitivity to perceptual cues to lexical and grammatical words. *Cognition, 72,* B11–B21.

Steinhauer, K., Alter, K., & Friederici, A. D. (1999). Brain potentials indicate immediate use of prosodic cues in natural speech processing. *Nature Neuroscience, 2,* 191–196.

Theakston, A. L., Lieven, E. V. M., Pine, J. M., & Rowland, C. F. (2001). The role of performance limitations in the acquisition of verb-argument structure: An alternative account. *Journal of Child Language, 28,* 127–152.

Tomasello, M. (1992). *First verbs: A case study of early grammatical development.* New York: Cambridge University Press.

Tomasello, M. (2000). The item-based nature of children's early syntactic development. *Trends in Cognitive Sciences, 4,* 156–163.

Tomasello, M., Kruger, A., & Ratner, H. (1993). Cultural learning. *Behavioral and Brain Sciences, 16,* 495–552.

Valian, V., & Coulson, S. (1988). Anchor points in language learning: The role of marker frequency. *Journal of Memory and Language, 27,* 71–86.

Valian, V., & Levitt, A. (1996). Prosody and adults' learning of syntactic structure. *Journal of Memory and Language, 35,* 497–516.

Weissenborn, J., & Höhle, B. (Eds). (2001). *Approaches to bootstrapping: Phonological, lexical, syntactic and neurophysiological aspects of early language acquisition.* Philadelphia: John Benjamins.

Werker, J. F., & Tees, R. C. (1999). Influences on infant speech processing: Toward a new synthesis. *Annual Review of Psychology, 50,* 509–535.

Part II

Prerequisites to Verb Learning: Finding Actions in Events

4   Actions Organize the Infant's World

Jean M. Mandler

Actions are central in organizing the beginning conceptual system. From birth, motion attracts infants' attention. Part of the reason for this might be because early foveal vision is poor and so not much can be gleaned from viewing static objects. However, even if infants cannot see details, an object's translation across the visual field can be attended. It may also be that a bias to attend to motion is built in. The experienced world consists of events, and organisms must be attuned to objects in motion if they are to survive. Whether the bias is due to the immature visual system or has a deeper basis, infants in the first months of life show more advanced discriminations when observing objects in motion than when viewing static objects (Kellman & Spelke, 1983), and many studies of early cognition implicate the importance of events in structuring the infant's burgeoning conceptual system.

In this chapter, I first discuss how infants begin to interpret events and how they represent different kinds of actions. These interpretations tend to be global in nature, with details only gradually added. Then I consider the implications of this organization of conceptual life for the first stage of language learning. In particular, my goal is to characterize the conceptual system that 1-year-olds have available to learn relational terms that deal with motion along paths through space. One might predict from the importance of actions in infants' understanding of events that motion verbs should occur frequently in early speech. This does happen, but it varies by language. The actions that infants conceptualize do not always show up as verbs. In a prepositional language, such as English, many of the actions along paths in space that infants have categorized in the preverbal period, such as going in, out, on, off, up, and down tend to be expressed in early speech by the prepositions alone (e.g., Bloom, Lightbown, & Hood, 1975; Choi & Bowerman, 1991; Tomasello, 1987). The same ideas are expressed by verbs in other languages, such as Korean, with the result that the prominence of verbs in early speech varies in the two languages. Finally, I summarize recent data showing how a common underlying conception of various containment actions in infancy becomes linguistically expressed in quite different ways in Korean and English. This work leads to the conclusion that the proportion of verbs in early speech may neither accurately reflect the knowledge that infants have of actions nor, as has sometimes been speculated, difficulty in parsing actions into their component parts.

How Actions Structure Early Concepts

In recent years we have learned a good deal about the kinds of concepts formed in the first year of life. Most of this literature has emphasized objects, for example, how and when infants differentiate animate from inanimate objects or differentiate various kinds of artifacts, such as vehicles and furniture (e.g., Carey & Spelke, 1994; Mandler, 2004a). I have argued that the first concepts of objects tend to be rather general or global in nature and in many cases are organized around paths of motion. For example, an early concept of *animal* may consist of little more than that animals are objects that start to move by themselves, move in rhythmic but often unpredictable ways, and interact with other objects both directly and from a distance (Mandler, 1992). Such a global concept does not say what animals look like, but rather how they move.

Now this is interesting—objects are being conceptualized, but the conceptualization has to do with actions rather than the way we usually think of objects, as having a particular shape, color, size, parts, and features. It appears to be actions—kinds of movements between interacting objects—that are crucial in getting concepts about objects off the ground. This means, of course, that actions themselves must be conceptualized. I have hypothesized that the earliest concepts stem from attentive processing, especially the attention that is paid to moving objects. In my theory (Mandler, 2004a), it is attention that enables perceptual meaning analysis to take place—this is the process that creates concepts. (I originally called this process perceptual analysis, but that was sometimes interpreted as being a purely perceptual process, so I changed its designation to include its function, namely, meaning creation). Briefly, the theory is that in addition to the automatic perceptual processes that categorize and schematize objects, infants come equipped with a mechanism that redescribes perceptual information into a simpler form that enables ideas to be brought to mind. Infants do not come with innate ideas but rather with a mechanism that enables them to redescribe perceptual information into the concepts with which we think.

Ordinary perception does not require attention, but when attention is directed at something, perceptual meaning analysis can take place and create a concept. Primitive concepts are typically formed from condensed redescriptions of what happens in the events being observed, for example "object starts itself" or "object goes into another object." To understand this process it is important to see that raw perception is too rich and continuous to be used for conceptual thought.

It must be transformed somehow into a simpler format and, importantly, a format that allows access to consciousness. As adults, we admit this kind of transformation when we say we think in words. But infants also think—they make inferences (Mandler & McDonough, 1996), solve problems (Chen, Sanchez, & Campbell, 1997; Willatts, 1997), and recall the past (Carver & Bauer, 1999; Mandler & McDonough, 1995). They do not have words, so there must be a mechanism that transforms perceptual information in a way that enables the same functions.

I have suggested that a plausible format for the redescriptions that perceptual meaning analysis produces is that of the image-schema (Johnson, 1987; Lakoff, 1987). Image-schemas are analog spatial descriptions, usually dynamic in character, that express primitive or fundamental meanings. These representations underlie both the semantic and syntactic meanings of language (e.g., Fauconnier, 1994; Langacker, 2000; Talmy, 1988). They also provide an excellent description of the basic notions that comprise many of the earliest concepts that infants form. Serendipitously, then, image-schemas structure the concepts with which preverbal infants think and also assist them in understanding the language that expresses these concepts.

Common image-schemas are PATH, CONTAINMENT, UP-DOWN, and LINK. All of them are simplifications of spatial structure given by perception. For example, the image-schema PATH is the simplest representation of any object following any trajectory through space, without regard to the characteristics of the object or the details of the trajectory itself—it is merely something moving through space. A very young infant may not get detailed information about the appearance of an object even when attending to it, but can extract a primitive description of something going from one place to another. Further analysis will highlight different aspects of paths and different kinds of paths, for example, upward or downward paths, and will eventually lead to understanding prepositions such as *up* and *down* and verbs such as *climb* and *fall* (Golinkoff, Hirsh-Pasek, Mervis, Frawley, & Parillo, 1995).

CONTAINMENT is a representation of something in any fully or partially enclosed space, that is, a bounded space with an inside and an outside, without specifying details of the appearance of either the contained or the container. Many kinds of contingencies that infants experience can be represented by LINK, which is a family of image-schemas that express dependencies between events by tying them together (Mandler, 1992). For example, a game of peekaboo or one object chasing another can be understood in terms of linked events or linked paths.

In all these cases, image-schemas summarize spatial relations and movements in space. Note that they are *not* visual images (although they may be used in image construction). They are a bit like topological representations, in that they omit many details that we see and that would appear in an image, such as shape and path direction, leaving behind only an irreducible meaning, such as path itself. It should also be noted that image-schemas are a format for storing accessible meanings and cannot themselves be brought to awareness. For that images or words are needed.

From early on, infants attend to the beginnings and endings of object paths. For example, Leslie's work on causal perception showed that infants as young as 4 months attend to the small spatial differences that obtain in causal and non-causal paths (Leslie, 1982; Leslie & Keeble, 1987). Infants notice whether a moving object stops before touching another object, even if the gap is very small. They also notice whether the second object starts up on its own or begins to move only when the first object actually comes in contact with it. Similarly, they notice whether a hand makes contact with an object when it picks it up or merely comes close by (Leslie, 1984).

Infants also are sensitive to the character of the motion on a path. For example, 3-month-olds differentiate biologically correct from incorrect motion of both people and other animals (Arterberry & Bornstein, 2001; Bertenthal, 1993). This discrimination may originally be a kind of automatic perceptual schematizing, but at some point through attentive processing it forms a conceptual package associated with self-motion. Poulin-Dubois, Lepage, and Ferland (1996) reported that 9-month-olds became distressed when seeing a mechanically moving robot start up on its own, suggesting a violation of expectations about how inanimate objects should move. Spelke, Phillips, and Woodward (1995) found that 7-month-olds looked longer at displays in which an inanimate object started to move without contact from another object than when a person did so. Perhaps especially important, infants are sensitive to linked paths, in which one object interacts contingently with another. As young as two months, infants treat objects that act contingently with them as animate, as shown by smiling at them (Frye, Rawling, Moore, & Myers, 1983; Legerstee, 1992; Watson, 1972).

This attention to path information—how objects move and interact with each other—leads to concepts of *animal* and *inanimate thing*. Animals are objects that start themselves, move on rhythmic but somewhat unpredictable paths, and interact with other objects both directly and from a distance. In contrast, inanimate objects do not start themselves but only move due to another object, and when they do move do so along direct paths, and do not interact with other objects from a distance. These primitive definitions involve what objects do, not what they look like. Image-schemas such as ANIMATE PATH, INANIMATE PATH, SELF-MOTION, CAUSED MOTION, and LINKED PATHS describe these notions (Mandler, 1992).

In addition to using path information to characterize animate and inanimate objects, young infants are also sensitive to the goal-directed nature of paths, leading to a concept of an agent. Woodward (1998) found that 5- and 9-month-old infants' attention was focused on the goal of a reach (that is, what happens at the end of a reaching path). She also found that at least by 9 months, infants differentiate between a person grasping an object and apparently unintentionally dropping a hand onto the object; that is, they distinguish between a goal path and a nonpurposeful path (Woodward, 1999). Of obvious importance for learning verbs, Baldwin, Baird, Saylor, and Clark (2001) showed that 10- to 11-month-olds have learned something about the structure of intentional action. They showed the infants videos of everyday purposeful actions, followed by test videos in which the motion was suspended either in the middle of the actions or at their ends. Infants looked longer at the test videos whose structure was interrupted, suggesting that they had conceived of the actions as having beginnings, middles, and ends.

Between 9 and 12 months of age, interpreting behavior in terms of goals is pervasive and abstract in character. A series of studies by Gergely, Csibra, and their colleagues (Csibra, Gergely, Bíró, Koós, & Brockbank, 1999; Gergely, Nádasdy, Csibra, & Bíró, 1995) used computer displays showing geometrical forms moving and interacting in various ways. The data showed that by the end of the first year, infants infants clearly distinguish goal-directed paths from unmotivated trajectories. The displays consisted solely of moving circles, so there was no figural information at all to indicate an agent following a goal. This means that the infants were interpreting (that is, conceptualizing) goals purely on the basis of interactive motion. Twelve-month-olds also apply these interpretations to people who follow either direct or indirect paths to an object (Sodian, Schoeppner, & Metz, 2004). Johnson and Sockaci (2000) reported that 14-month-olds treated purple blobs as agents if they engaged in goal-directed activity. In similar work, Johnson, Slaughter, and Carey (1998) found that when an amorphous object had a face with eyes or had no face but acted contingently with infants, if it turned toward an object, 12-month-olds would follow its "gaze." These various studies on actions strongly suggest that toward the last part of the first year, infants are conceptualizing actions in terms of what actors are trying to do. Image-schemas of AGENCY and SOURCE-PATH-GOAL describe these notions (Lakoff, 1987; Mandler, 2004a).

The global characterization of objects in terms of how they move affects many aspects of infants' behavior. For example, on object-categorization tasks, 7- to 11-month-old infants respond to little models of birds and airplanes differentially, even though they look much alike, but do not respond to dogs and rabbits differentially, even though they look rather different (Mandler & McDonough, 1993). Birds and airplanes differ in the types of paths they take and the way they interact with other objects (also self-motion, of course, although in this case this variable is not likely to be obvious to infants); dogs and rabbits differ on none of these. Poulin-Dubois and Vyncke (2003), using the inductive generalization task (Mandler & McDonough, 1996), found that 14-month-olds generalized animate actions, such as going up stairs or hopping, from one animal to another, but significantly less often to a vehicle. Similarly, the infants generalized inanimate motions, such as going up a ramp and through the air to land on another ramp, from one vehicle to another but significantly less often to an animal.

Some time during this period, infants begin to associate more specific activities with the conceptual classes they have generated. For example, in our work on inductive generalization (e.g., Mandler & McDonough, 1996; McDonough & Mandler, 1998b), we found that when we modeled putting a dog to bed or giving it a drink, 9- to 14-month-olds would use any other animal to imitate these behaviors, but not a nonanimal. (Poulin-Dubois & Vyncke, 2003, showed that these general-izations extend to people.) Fourteen-month-old infants also typically refused to imitate actions we modeled that were inappropriate to a kind, such as putting a vehicle to bed or giving it a drink. At the same time they were quite happy to generalize domain-general behavior, such as being washed or going into a building, across class boundaries, showing nice sensitivity to the kinds of behaviors that characterize animals and vehicles (Mandler & McDonough, 1998b).

It is in this sense that actions organize infants' concepts. It is what things do that determines how infants conceptualize things: In the first instance, animals start themselves, move in rhythmic fashion, and act interactively with other objects from a distance. Artifacts do not move by themselves and do not interact with other objects from a distance. Then animals become creatures that drink and sleep, and artifacts, such as vehicles, become things that get keyed and give rides. (There may be a few early concepts, such as furniture, that are based on more static spatial information, such as where objects are found; see Mandler, Fivush, & Reznick, 1987. It is possible, however, that even categorizing things as "found in the house" or "found in the kitchen" are based on the activities that take place in those locations. This issue has yet to be explored.)

The point that what things do is the basis for concept formation was made many years ago by Nelson (1973), who found that 15-month-olds first identified balls on the basis of shape but decided if they were really balls on the basis of whether they rolled. This principle has also shown up continuously in McDonough's and my research: Infants use parts such as legs and wings to identify something as a member of a class but interpret classes on the basis of what they do. A nice illustration of the effects of this conceptual bias is illustrated in work of Bahrick, Gogate, and Ruiz (2002), who found that 5.5-month-old infants were more likely to process and remember information about what people around them were doing than what they or the objects they used looked like. In these experiments infants watched videos, all of which showed close-ups of faces doing actions such as brushing teeth or hair. Although infants of this age are capable of encoding many face details, neither the objects being used nor the faces of the actors were encoded as well as the activities themselves.

This emphasis on actions at the expense of noticing object details fits well with our work on generalized imitation with older infants, suggesting that infants require a protracted course of learning object details. We found that when we modeled drinking or sleeping with a model dog for 14-month-olds, they were as likely to choose a cat or a rabbit for their imitations as another dog (Mandler & McDonough, 1998b). They tended to be choosier when we modeled activities with cars, typically choosing another car rather than a motorcycle or an airplane. This finding suggests more detailed knowledge about vehicles than about animals (with which the infants we studied have more contact). Other work indicates that even older children know more about artifacts than about natural kinds (Mandler & McDonough, 1998b, 2000). For example, when we modeled activities such as drinking from a cup, 14-month-olds were as likely to use a frying pan for their imitations as a mug. By 20 months they were usually correct, but when we modeled activities with animals and plants, such as giving a little dog a bone to chew on, even 20-month-olds were as likely to make a bird chew on the bone as another dog. Incidentally, these data, in which the same age infants succeed with artifacts and fail with natural kinds (as well as the refusal to imitate incorrect activities), make clear that children's imitations are not just mimicking whatever the experimenter models or what their parents have shown them about toys. They succeed or fail depending on what they have observed about the objects participating in various activities in the real world.[1] In my culture, they tend to be more advanced in their observations about artifacts in daily use than about animals and plants, and this is reflected in how they act out events with models.

In addition to path descriptions of actions—how they begin and end, the different appearance of biological and mechanical paths, and the links between paths—infants also redescribe other spatial relations that might seem more static in nature, but are actually derived from path notions. For example, Quinn and his colleagues have documented how infants gradually acquire an abstract notion of *above* and *below* during the first year. Three-month-olds who are habituated to a picture of a figure above a line dishabituate when the figure is moved to below the line. But they do not dishabituate if a different figure is used in the test; it takes a few more months before infants succeed at this task (Quinn, Cummins, Kase, Martin, & Weisman, 1996). It appears that, at first, relations like above and below are perceptually tied to the particular objects that instantiate the relation. When new objects come along, the spatial relations must be encoded anew. Thus, *above* and *below* are perceptually given in a display of an object above or below a line, and even 3-month-olds encode the spatial relation. To go beyond this and abstract *aboveness* away from the rest of a perceptual display requires further analysis beyond what the perceptual system provides, suggesting that it is an achievement of the conceptual system (Quinn, Polly, Furer, Dobson, & Narter, 2002). Indeed, this is an excellent example of perceptual meaning analysis at work. Although these data concern the static appearance of figures above and below a line, the origin of these concepts appears to be more dynamic in character, involving analysis of paths that go up or down. *Above* and *below* represent the end points of paths that go up or down. For example, Choi and Bowerman (1991) noted that prepositions such as *up* are used first to comment on or request motion along an upward path and only later are used to describe states. Image-schemas of these notions are directed paths and their end points.

The PATH aspect of other image-schemas, such as CONTAINMENT, that might also at first glance appear to be static, is more obvious in the data base. For example, Baillargeon and her colleagues have studied the development of concepts about containment primarily by means of dynamic displays in which objects go in or out of containers or in front of or behind occluders (e.g., Baillargeon & Wang, 2002). Even concepts of support or its lack seem to be derived from observing the circumstances in which objects remain on a surface or fall off it (Baillargeon, 1994). Similarly, concepts of *tight fit* and *loose fit* can be used to describe static spatial relations, but, as I discuss later in this chapter, have been demonstrated in 9- to 14-month-olds in the context of actions that produce these end results (McDonough, Choi, & Mandler, 2003). A few months later, the identical actions are comprehended via prepositions in English and via verbs in Korean (Choi, McDonough, Bowerman, & Mandler, 1999).

To expand a bit about containment, Baillargeon and her colleagues conducted a number of experiments charting the growth in understanding of containment relations between 2.5 and 12 months of age. As young as 2.5 months, infants understand that if something is to go into a container there must be an opening and that something in a container will move where the container moves. By 5 months, infants discriminate between an object fitting tightly or loosely into a container (Spelke & Hespos, 2002). Not until 6 months, however, do they understand that a wide object will not go into a narrower container (Aguiar & Baillargeon, 1998). By around 7.5 months, they know that a taller object will not disappear completely when it is lowered into a shorter container, although as early as 4 months they are successful when the object is lowered behind a shorter screen instead (Hespos & Baillargeon, 2001). This shows how an initial global notion of containment organizes learning—it does not guide learning about all instances of lowering, only those having to do with containers. Baillargeon and her colleagues suggest that as early as 2.5 months, infants have a concept of containment that is basically a distinction between open and closed. Gradually they add quantitative variables to it, such as the size relationships between a container and the contained. This view fits with the simplest concept of containment being represented by an image-schema containment, consisting of an inside, a boundary, and an outside, but it also suggests that the boundary can either be continuous or broken—that is, open or closed. Again, the dynamic nature of image-schema representation captures the action-oriented aspect of containment—opening and closing, going in and going out.

Given that what things do (in the first instance, how they move) is crucial to infants' conceptualizations of objects and the events they take part in, one might expect that attention and consequent perceptual meaning analysis would produce rapid differentiation of various kinds of actions. Yet the principles that govern differentiating objects seem to apply to differentiating actions as well. Our research has shown that it is a slow process to differentiate dogs conceptually from cats or tables from chairs, even though from 3 months of age infants can tell them apart (Mandler & McDonough, 1998a). We have less information about actions, but it seems likely that a similar process operates, even if it begins earlier and perhaps develops more rapidly. Regular path, irregular path, linked path, going in or going out, separating or coming together—these are all very general notions—and although refinements have been learned in some cases by the time that language begins to be learned, still one might expect many early verbs to be overextended in ways similar to the overextension of nouns.

Although overextension of verbs has not been as frequently examined as noun overextensions, it does occur. Bowerman (1996) found similarities between young children's and adults' descriptions of joining and separating actions within three language communities (English, Dutch, and Korean), but the children made fewer distinctions than did the adults, thus overextending a smaller set of verbs or prepositions. For example, Korean children use the word *ppayta* (unfit) for virtually all actions of separation, even though Korean adults use several other words for different varieties of separation. One of her most vivid examples describes the difficulty young Dutch children have with the word *uit* (out). Adult speakers of both English and Dutch make a distinction between actions of "removal from containment" (*out/uit*) and "removal from surface contact" (*off/af*). English-speaking children master this distinction quite readily, presumably because it is consistently made. However, adult Dutch speakers have one noncanonical usage of *uit*, which is to remove clothing from the body, so one takes a shoe "out of" a foot. Bowerman suggests that for Dutch adults, the clothing use of *uit* seems to be stored as a separate sense. But young Dutch learners apparently try initially to construct a single meaning for *uit* that includes both removal from containment and removal from the body. The only meaning consistent with both uses is *removal* itself. As a result, young Dutch children massively overextend *uit* to all kinds of separation. This means, of course, that they must have a nonlinguistic concept of removal or separation. Joining and separating, seem like ideal candidates for image-schema representation, well worth further study in the preverbal period.

Verbs Versus Prepositions

Even if verbs are overextended, because actions are central to infants' understanding of events, one might expect a good many verbs to be among the earliest acquisitions. Rapid verb learning in the early stages of language acquisition does occur in some languages such as Korean (Choi, 1997), but not in others such as English, where object names predominate in lists of the first words. Even in English, however, many investigators report that nouns make up less than half the total vocabulary of language learners in the second year (Bloom, 2000). Nevertheless, much of the literature on first words has focused on nouns, which have been assumed to be easier for young children to learn than verbs and other relational terms. For example, Gentner (1982) suggested that objects form more coherent perceptual packages than events. However, even when nouns dominate early vocabulary in English in terms of number of different words used, relational terms are expressed just as early—there are merely fewer of them (as, indeed, there are in the language). In a longitudinal sample of the speech of English-speaking children in their second year, Choi and Gopnik (1995) reported many more object names than relational words. However, a canonical set of 11 relational words, including *up, down, in, out, on,* and *off,* was used almost as frequently as the more than 300 object words that were recorded, many of which were used only once.

Such a finding indicates a complicating factor in predictions from preverbal understanding of actions to learning verbs: actions—at least of the general path sort that seem to be what infants understand—can be expressed in different ways. In English, much of this work is carried by prepositions. We go in, go out, go up, go down, go on, go off, not to mention go through, go under, go around, go together, and go away. At the same time, a great many English verbs express manner, rather than path, such as *walk, run, swim, dance*, and so forth. Often these are combined, so we walk up, run down, swim across, dance around, and so on. From the point of view of the young English language learner, the manner verbs are many and varied, but there is a ready substitute—those handy prepositions.

Given the importance of spatial information in ours lives, there are surprisingly few prepositions in English. According to Landau and Jackendoff (1993), there are only 55 transitive spatial propositions and many of them are combinations and minor variations on each other, such as *in* and *inside*, *under* and *underneath*, *atop* and *on top of*, and *betwixt* and *between*. In my estimation, about 20 prepositions appear to cover most of the spatial relations commonly expressed in daily speech. In any case, the 6 mentioned earlier (*in, out, on, off, up*, and *down*) are typically the earliest appearing in young English learners' speech.

So young English learners can avoid having to remember the manner verbs of English they have encountered and make do with *go* plus a preposition. In the one-word stage, even *go* can be scrapped because the prepositions convey the relevant path information. That is, in the earliest stages, a preposition such as *up* or *out* acts as an action word just as does a path verb. A child wanting to be picked up can raise her arms and announce "Up!" to communicate successfully the path she wants to be traversed. Parents obligingly fill in the rest of the proposition "pick me up." Even in the two-word stage it would typically be more useful to use a noun plus a preposition, because *go* is at least to some extent implied by the preposition.

The situation is different for young Korean learners. Their language downplays prepositions and uses verbs of motion to express much of the information conveyed by prepositions in English. So Korean infants do not have a small list of all-purpose prepositions available to express actions. Perforce they must learn different verbs for containment events, support events, ascending events, and so forth. Not surprisingly, then, motion verbs loom larger in the earlier vocabularies of Korean children than they do in the vocabularies of English-speaking children (Choi, 1997). At the same time, however, representations of actions in English occur as early in speech as do representations of objects (Nelson, Hampson, & Shaw, 1993), even though the actions are not necessarily expressed as verbs.

An important question that arises is how a presumably identical or at least highly similar preverbal conceptual base becomes translated into verbs in one language and into prepositions in another. To address this process, I suggest we need to revive the notion of semantic primitives (Bierwisch, 1967; E. Clark, 1973;

H. Clark, 1973) albeit in the more modern form of prelinguistic primitives represented by image-schemas. The idea behind the literature on semantic primitives was that relational terms (whether verbs or prepositions) are made up of underlying universal component meanings. To the extent that children understand these notions, learning language should be simplified. Semantic primitives received something of a bad press in the developmental literature. Various predictions that had been made on its basis did not turn out (e.g., Richards, 1979). In addition, Carey (1982) made the important distinction between a meaning component being definitionally primitive and developmentally primitive, pointing out that these need not be the same. Semantic analyses of the adult lexicon often used sophisticated and theory-laden concepts unlikely to be in the new language learner's repertoire. The young child cannot have the same understanding of *brother* as an adult without knowing something about biological relations nor understand the word *buy* without some appreciation of money. This would make it seem unlikely that language acquisition could depend on the universals uncovered by linguistic analyses of the adult lexicon. So it should be developmental primitives (i.e., prelinguistic primitives) we seek to start the process, rather than semantic ones.

On the basis of cross-cultural analyses of language acquisition, Bowerman (1996) also rejected the notion of semantic primitives, even developmental ones. Bowerman suggested that the language specificity of first words in various languages argues against the hypothesis that children start out by mapping relational words, such as verbs and prepositions, onto prelinguistic concepts. She argued that even if there are prelinguistic primitives, perhaps represented by image-schemas as I have suggested, there would have to be a great many of them to account for all the distinctions that various languages make, so many that they would not be of much help in learning a particular language. But infants need prelinguistic primitives to interpret the world long before they talk—a task at least as important as learning to speak. Even though concepts make language learning possible, infants do not form concepts primarily for that purpose.

This "cognitivist" position (Choi, 1997) has been described as saying that relational language is mapped "directly" onto preverbal concepts without taking into account the particulars of the language being learned. Such a position would imply that all children's initial interpretation of relational words is the same regardless of the language they are learning. This view may have been suggested 25 years ago, but I know of no one who would take such a position today. The field has long recognized that there is a complex interplay between preverbal concepts (many of which are indeed likely to be universal) and the details of the language that is being learned. There is no Esperanto that all children start learning. They can and must make use of the distinctions their language offers. At the same time, learning these distinctions must be mapped onto the concepts children bring with them to the language learning task.

This is the true cognitive position. It means that prelinguistic primitives are required, whether they are learned or innate. However, there need not be a vast number of them, even taking all languages into account. When talking about containment, for example, in many cases more distinctions are made than in English, but typically not a great many more. Even in languages some of whose containment terms specify the shape of the container, such as the Mayan language, Tzeltal, there are a few general static terms and only another 10 distinctions or so that are made in conjunction with directional or insertion verbs (Brown, 1994). To my knowledge, there are no data on acquisitions of these distinctions by young Tzeltal language learners. However, if we look at Korean, which makes a number of similar distinctions, infants learn a few of the distinctions first with the variants following over a period of months to years (Choi, 1997). As mentioned earlier, a similar phenomenon was found in Dutch with the notion of removal (Bowerman, 1996). And in a study that included English, Korean, and Tzotzil children (another Mayan language), Bowerman, de Leon, and Choi (1995) found similar patterns of overextension of expressions of actions by young language learners in all three communities. Two-year-old English learners made three distinctions to express a variety of familiar joining and separating actions (verb + *in*, verb + *on*, and *close*), whereas English-speaking adults used six (adding *button*, *fasten*, and verb + *together*). In Korean, children used 7 different verbs to express the same actions, the adults 13. In Tzotzil children made four distinctions and adults nine.[2] Notice that in each of these languages the absolute number of distinctions being made was small (and the children used roughly half the number of terms used by the adults).

The pattern of acquisition seems to be to at first to make a few distinctions and overextend them. One of the virtues of a mechanism of perceptual meaning analysis is that it allows the acquisition of new distinctions at any time that conceptual analysis of perceptual information is carried out. Adults' use of a consistent distinction within a context that the child already understands should direct the child's attentive analysis, enabling discovery of previously overlooked or unattended particulars that the language is specifying. For example, a Korean child who has learned *kkita* to express her concept of *tight-fitting* may overlook the fact that adults use the term only for three-dimensional objects, not two-dimensional ones, and so she may misapply *kkita* to a flat magnet on a refrigerator door.[3] Presumably the first linguistic distinctions children learn are based on two factors: the preverbal concepts they have at their disposal and, within this constraint, the distinctions the language uses most consistently (see Bowerman et al., 1995, for an example of this in Tzotzil, where systematicity takes precedence over perceptual salience of the particles involved).

What we need, then, is a roster of the prelinguistic primitives that allow children their first bootstrapping into language understanding and examples of how these interact with the particulars of the language the children will learn. We are far from such a roster at the moment, but relevant information is beginning to accumulate. As discussed earlier, we have good evidence for a variety of preverbal path concepts, and more are being investigated all the time. Here I will give an example concerning concepts of containment actions and how they become channeled in different ways by Korean and English. The languages differ not only in the aspects of containment that become lexicalized, but also in whether the ideas are expressed by verbs or prepositions. This kind of study exemplifies how a common preverbal conceptual repertoire becomes translated into different linguistic structures.

A Case Study of Learning Prepositions Versus Verbs: "Going in" in English and Korean

topic #5

As an initial search for universal prelinguistic primitives that encompass various containment distinctions, Laraine McDonough, Soonja Choi, Melissa Bowerman, and I studied Korean-learning and English-learning children's first comprehension of words expressing actions of containment (Choi et al., 1999). The languages differ in their expression of containment in two important respects. First, English uses the preposition *in* in conjunction with a few general verbs, such as *put* and *take*, whereas Korean typically uses a variety of different verbs. Second, Korean typically specifies whether containment is tight fitting or loose fitting. More exactly, Korean uses the verb *kkita* (to fit together tightly) for both tight-fitting containment and tight-fitting support, as in putting a ring on a finger or a finger in a ring, thus cutting across the English usages of *in* and *on*. There is another verb *nehta* that means roughly "to put loosely into (or around)," again cutting across the English prepositions *in* and *on*. In addition, there is a verb *nohta* that means "to put loosely on a surface," a distinction not unlike the prototypical meaning of the English preposition *on*. So the language provides a distinction between things going in or things going on but supersedes this distinction in the case in which the thing going in or on results in a tight fit (as in a cassette tape going into its case or a lid being snapped onto a container).

In our first experiment (Choi et al., 1999) we used a technique based on the preferential-looking paradigm of Golinkoff, Hirsh-Pasek, Cauley, and Gordon (1987) and Naigles (1990). In this paradigm, two videos are shown side by side with a single sound source between them that matches the action portrayed in the videos. This paradigm is based on a technique originally devised by Spelke (1976), who used films such as playing peekaboo or playing a tambourine and a single auditory track that matched one or the other. She found that infants preferred to look at the film that matched the auditory input. In the linguistic version of the paradigm, longer looking at the matching screen than at the nonmatching screen is taken to indicate comprehension of the language used.[4]

We made a series of videos showing four kinds of actions. Two actions are expressed in English as putting an object into a container. We call such scenes either *loose-in*, for example, a hand putting a ring loosely into a basket, or *tight-in*, for example, a hand putting a book into a tight slipcover. Watching these scenes, in

English one can ask, "Where is she putting it in?" In Korean two different verbs are used: *nehta* (as in "Where is she putting it loosely in?") and *kkita* (as in "Where is she fitting it tightly?"). The other two kinds of actions are expressed in English as putting an object on something else. We call these scenes either *loose-on*, for example, a hand placing a book on top of another, or *tight-on*, for example, putting a ring tightly on a pole. In either case, one can say, "Where is she putting it on?" These same events are expressed in Korean by the verb *nohta* (as in "Where is she putting it loosely on?") and *kkita* (as in "Where is she fitting it tightly?").

We studied young language learners from English-speaking and Korean-speaking homes on their understanding of *in* and *kkita*, respectively. We paired different scenes of the four types just described and measured which scenes infants looked at when asked, "Where is she putting it in?" in English, or "Where is she fitting it tightly?" in Korean. The kind of scenes we used and the differences in English and Korean words for them are illustrated in figure 4.1. In each case, a woman's hand was shown demonstrating a relation three times in succession, such as putting three pegs tightly into three holes in a board. We could make a straightforward prediction: When a *tight-in* scene such as this was paired with a *loose-on* scene such as placing a book on top of other books, infants from both language communities should look at the same *tight-in* scene. However, when a *loose-in* scene such as tossing rings into a basket was paired with a *tight-on* scene such as putting rings tightly onto a pole, the English-learning children should look at the containment scene, and the Korean-learning children should look at the "support" scene.

These results were confirmed. Up until 18 months looking times were not reliable, but from then on, English-learning infants looked at the scenes appropriate to *in* and Korean-learning infants looked at scenes appropriate to *kkita*. Hence, from as soon as consistent comprehension was found, infants showed they had learned language-specific meanings. Furthermore, in one language these meanings are expressed by prepositions, and in the other by verbs. (Of course, the English-learning children actually heard verb phrases, such, as *putting in*. Yet production data show that English-speaking children first use the prepositions alone, suggesting that the prepositions are conveying the important meanings; see Choi & Bowerman, 1991.)

The question these results raised was how such language-specific learning is possible. What is the knowledge base like that enables Korean-learning children to pick up verbs like *kkita* and English-learning children to pick up prepositions like *in*? Our next experiments began to answer this question (McDonough, Choi, & Mandler, 2003; see also chapter 7, this volume). We studied groups of 9-, 11-, and 14-month-olds, an age range during which we had found that infants do not yet show comprehension of the terms under study. We made more videos showing actions of putting highly varied objects in loose-in, tight-in, loose-on, and tight-on relations so that we could study familiarization to scenes of one type or the other, followed by a preferential-looking test at another scene of the same relation versus a scene of one of the other relations.

Containment-in
Support-on

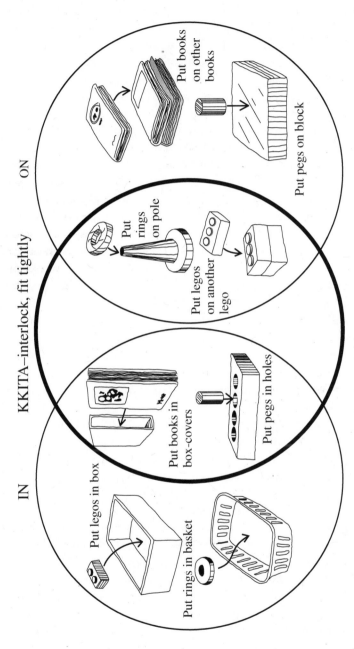

Figure 4.1. Examples of the kinds of containment relations that were studied in Choi et al., 1999, and McDonough et al., 2003. (From "Understanding Spatial Relations: Flexible Infants, Lexical Adults," by L. McDonough, S. Choi, and J. M. Mandler, 2003, *Cognitive Psychology, 46*, 229–259. Reprinted with permission from Elsevier.)

In our first experiment, we studied a contrast of loose-in versus tight-on with babies from an English-speaking community. This contrast conflated containment and support with tightness, but no one had shown familiarization to these abstract conceptualizations in infancy, so we needed to be sure the technique would work. Indeed, more than one colleague was skeptical, and we ourselves were dubious that infants would abstract these notions from the highly varied videos we showed. Happily, the technique did work, and we found that 14-month-olds preferred to look at a novel relation after having been familiarized either with loose-in or tight-on. Eleven-month-olds also preferred the novel relation, but not significantly so. Interestingly, however, the 9-month-olds showed at test a significant preference for the familiar relation, regardless of which one they had been familarized with.

We tested English-speaking adults as well, and they also showed a preference for the novel relation. We also gave the adults an explicit test of understanding the contrast between the two relations. We used an odd-man-out procedure by acting out the events they had seen on the videos. Three of these scenarios were taken from the familiarization videos, and the fourth was the test item of the other relation. Just as with the implicit measure, most of the adults chose the odd-man-out correctly (always justifying their choice by referring to containment or support, not tightness). So we hypothesized that the shift in infancy from a preference for a familiar relation to a preference for a novel relation had to do with whether the younger infants had not yet completely learned this particular contrast. Perhaps 9-month-olds were still exploring these relations or were slower to take them in and so showed a preference for the familiar, whereas, older infants and adults were experienced with them and so preferred novelty. It seemed plausible, but because of the results of the next experiment we believe it was not correct.

In the next experiment, we did the crucial comparison of loose-in with tight-in to see if infants have also abstracted generalized concepts of tight and loose containment from various containment experiences. Spelke and Hespos (2002) showed that 5-month-olds can distinguish the difference between one object fitting tightly in a container and another fitting loosely. But like the Quinn et al. (2002) work referred to earlier, it takes developmental time for infants to move from perception of a spatial relation to a generalization that goes beyond a single instantiation. We familiarized 9-, 11-, and 14-month-olds from both English-speaking and Korean-speaking homes with a series of pairs of either tight-in or loose-in containment relations and then tested to see if they preferred to look at the novel relation. To our surprise, infants throughout this age range from both linguistic communities looked significantly longer at test at the *familiarized* relation, regardless of whether it had been tight-in or loose-in. Clearly they differentiated the two relations, which answered the question we originally asked. But why did they prefer the familiar? Was it because it was a subtle distinction?

Again, we tested adults, this time including Korean speakers, on both the implicit looking measures and the explicit tests described earlier. Now there was a major bifurcation between English and Korean speakers. The English speakers showed no sensitivity to the contrast on either the implicit or explicit test. The Korean speakers, in contrast, showed sensitivity to the contrast on both. The data suggest that years of experience with English damped down the distinction between two kinds of containment, whereas years of experience with Korean maintained the sensitivity. But as for the subtlety issue, even the adult Korean speakers showed the preference for the familiarized relation that we had found for infants from both language groups. It seems hard to maintain that the preference for the familiar was due to the subtle nature of the difference between tight and loose containment, given that all the Korean speakers were sensitive to it. Nevertheless, it is possible that this is the answer. It might just be that containment per se is so much more salient than tightness, that even after years of making the distinction between tight and loose containment, Korean speakers need to confirm the particular relationship being presented, and thus show a preference for the familiar. This is an issue that cries out for research.[5]

Conclusion

I have summarized research that shows the importance of actions in organizing infants' conceptual lives. At first, actions may be conceived of merely as different kinds of motion along paths through space, but over the course of the first year, these conceptions become more detailed. Genuine event conceptions emerge in that certain actions, such as drinking, become linked to particular classes of objects. It may be that actions become differentiated earlier than the objects that participate in these events, but this has not yet been systematically tested. We found that even at 18 months infants often ignored the details of objects in events, such as imitating drinking with a frying pan instead of a cup. What we do not know at this point is whether they would ignore similar differences in actions, such as eating versus drinking. Equally interesting, given that infants do not seem to pay much attention to the details of objects, just when do they learn the shapes that are required to express many containment relations in languages such as Tzeltal? These shape differences (such as bowl-shaped container or taller-than-wide container) typically are so general as not to distinguish, say, a pan from a cup, but they do emphasize the overall shape of objects being manipulated (as is also found in languages such as Chinese that use shape classifiers, such as "flat-thin" or "round-small," to modify nouns). These are all issues in need of research (see Smith, 2003, for work heading in this direction).

Our case study shows that a common set of preverbal conceptualizations of containment actions is mapped equally easily into verbs or prepositions, depending on the language being heard. This result suggests a different slant on some acquisition phenomena. Choi and Gopnik (1995) noted that young Korean speakers show a verb spurt at around 1.5 years, whereas English speakers do not. What if we looked at prepositions instead? To be sure, there could not be a big spurt in preposition types, because, as discussed earlier, they are relatively few, but if one looked at tokens instead, would there be as big a spurt in prepositional use? Of course, as long as one measures percentages of word types a child uses, rather than the frequency of token use, prepositions will always lose, and even adding preposition types to verb types (see Choi, 1997) cannot overcome the problem. Lois Bloom (1973) said that verbs are the heroes of the sentence. As far as early speech is concerned, it might be fair to say that relational terms, whether verbs or prepositions, are the heroes of the sentence. Even the earliest speech describes events and that requires relational words, but these need not be verbs.

I have tried to show in this chapter that by the end of the first year infants have an extensive repertoire of relational concepts that provides enough understanding to learn a host of motion verbs and prepositions. Infants understand that actions are goal directed, have beginnings, middles, and ends, and are often linked to other actions. They conceptualize actions as going into and out of things, behind objects, onto surfaces, up and down, joining and separating, and fitting tightly or loosely. They also conceptualize the difference between causal and noncausal actions and the difference between agents and recipients of action. Furthermore, they have associated specific actions, such as drinking, with animals; others, such as using a key, with vehicles; and still others, such as putting on clothes, with specific body parts. On the other hand, many of the functional aspects of the actions they observe (e.g., cooking, nailing, and keying) almost certainly are still beyond their ken. The causative and instrumental components of verbs may require more analysis than infants have yet brought to bear upon many activities.

I note, however, that the problem of incomplete information is also true for nouns. Nouns are not quite as transparent as they are sometimes made out to be. You can point to a dog, which may help the child learn the word *dog*, but even with objects you cannot point to their meaning—the infant's construal often does not match the adult's. Is this a pan, a cup, or merely something found in the kitchen? Is this a pie, a cake, or merely food? Is this a fox, a dog, or just an animal? In McDonough's and my research on inductive generalization, we found overly broad construals of both natural kinds and artifacts until well into the second year. It is perhaps not surprising, then, that McDonough (2002) found that even 2-year-olds are still uncertain about the extension of many common nouns. In addition to labels, infants need differentiating information, such as particular functions or kinds of behavior. For example, Booth and Waxman (2002) found that 14-month olds who were taught new labels were more likely to categorize novel objects if shown a function for them at the same time.

Although the way that relational concepts are packaged varies more across languages than happens for object concepts, the evidence does not appear strong that verbs and prepositions are intrinsically more difficult for infants to understand. If it turns out that they are, I hypothesize it will not be because they express relations that are more evanescent than objects nor that they require more subtle perceptual parsing. The differences between a dog and a fox seem no less subtle than the differences between stirring and beating a cake mix. As we have seen, infants parse actions into their component parts, and as the work of Bahrick et al. (2002) suggests, it is even possible that young infants learn more details about actions than about objects. A study by Traüble and Pauen (2004) showed that 11-month-olds learning about how novel objects behave were quite sensitive to differences in actions, such as hooking versus inserting, and used this information as a basis for categorizing the objects.

It is true, however, that these are observable spatial functions and many of the functions expressed by verbs do require knowledge of unobservables. Perceptual meaning analysis is directed toward both objects and paths of motion in space, but the purposes of actions—exactly what actors are trying to accomplish (such as cooking things to make them edible)—are not only unobservable but without a considerable store of knowledge may be more difficult for infants to understand than differences in behavior between, say, dogs and cats.

These issues are certainly researchable. We have not yet even explored many characteristics of actions that we know infants can observe and that are available for perceptual meaning analysis. We have good techniques to study prelinguistic primitives and a wealth of analyses of relevant image-schemas available from cognitive linguistics. We are in position to discover the exact mix of preverbal concepts that enable infants to break into the system of verbs and prepositions and the way that these words refine, enhance, or neglect the relational sensitivity that infants bring to the language learning task.

Notes

1. Younger and Johnson (2004) have suggested that because infants do not treat the little models used in the generalized imitation method as symbols that they do not relate the models to the real world. This does not follow. Understanding symbols is a more advanced process than being reminded by a model of something in the world. Furthermore, these authors based their claim on a technique in which, after seeing two videos of real-world scenarios and being presented with a little model of a prop used in one of them, infants were expected to look longer at the "matching" video. It is not clear what psychological principle is being invoked to justify this expectation (see Mandler, 2004b, for discussion).

2. Not all of the individual actions used with the English and Korean samples were tested and a slightly wider range of ages was sampled.

3. Alternatively, of course, she may have not heard the word for "two-dimensional tight-fit" often enough to be able to retrieve it.

4. To be viable, the technique requires roughly equal saliency of the videos. Because we had reason to suspect that infants are more interested in some spatial relations than others, we adopted Naigles's (1990) modification of the design in which, instead of using absolute looking times, we compared children's looking when the target word was present or absent.

5. Casasola and Cohen (2002) showed sensitivity to containment (including both loose and tight fit) in 10-month-olds but did not find a general category of tight-fit (that is, including both tight-in and tight-on). Our paradigms differed somewhat, and we did not test the general category of tight-fit, so again more research is needed.

References

Aguiar, A., & Baillargeon, R. (1998). Eight-and-a-half-month-old infants' reasoning about containment events. *Child Development, 69,* 636–653.

Arterberry, M. E., & Bornstein, M. H. (2001). Three-month-old infants' categorization of animals and vehicles based on static and dynamic attributes. *Journal of Experimental Child Psychology, 80,* 333–346.

Bahrick, L. E., Gogate, L. J., & Ruiz, I. (2002). Attention and memory for faces and actions in infancy: The salience of actions over faces in dynamic events. *Child Development, 73,* 1629–1643.

Baillargeon, R. (1994). How do infants learn about the physical world? *Current Directions in Psychological Science, 3,* 133–140.

Baillargeon, R., & Wang, S. (2002). Event categorization in infancy. *Trends in Cognitive Science, 6,* 85–93.

Baldwin, D. A., Baird, J. A., Saylor, M. M., & Clark, M. A. (2001). Infants parse dynamic action. *Child Development, 72,* 708–717.

Bertenthal, B. (1993). Infants' perception of biomechanical motions: Intrinsic image and knowledge-based constraints. In C. Granrud (Ed.), *Visual perception and cognition in infancy.* Hillsdale, NJ: Erlbaum.

Bierwisch, M. (1967). Some semantic universals of German adjectivals. *Foundations of Language, 3,* 1–36.

Bloom, L. (1973). *One word at a time.* The Hague: Mouton.

Bloom, L. (2000). The intentionality model of word learning: How to learn a word, any word. In R. M. Golinkoff & K. Hirsh-Pasek (Eds.), *Becoming a word learner: A debate on lexical acquisition* (pp. 19–50). New York: Oxford University Press.

Bloom, L., Lightbown, P., & Hood, L. (1975). Structure and variation in child language. *Monographs of the Society for Research in Child Development, 40,* (Serial No. 160).

Booth, A. E., & Waxman, S. (2002). Object names and object functions serves as cues to categories for infants. *Developmental Psychology, 38,* 948–957.

Bowerman, M. (1996). Learning how to structure space for language: A crosslinguistic perspective. In P. Bloom, M. A. Peterson, L. Nadel, & M. F. Garrett (Eds.), *Language and space* (pp. 385–436). Cambridge, MA: MIT Press.

Bowerman, M., de Leon, L., & Choi, S. (1995). Verbs, particles, and spatial semantics: Learning to talk about spatial actions in typologically different languages. In E. V. Clark (Ed.), *Proceedings of the Twenty-Seventh Annual Child Language Research Forum* (pp. 101–110). Stanford, CA: Center for Studies of Language and Information.

Brown, P. (1994). The INS and ONS of Tzeltal locative expressions: The semantics of static descriptions of location. *Linguistics, 32,* 743–790.

Carey, S. (1982). Semantic development: The state of the art. In E. Wanner & L. R. Gleitman (Eds.), *Language acquisition: The state of the art* (pp. 347–389). Cambridge: Cambridge University Press.

Carey, S., & Spelke, E. (1994). Domain-specific knowledge and conceptual change. In L. A. Hirschfeld & S. A. Gelman (Eds.), *Mapping the mind: Domain specificity in cognition and culture* (pp. 169–200). New York: Cambridge University Press.

Carver, L. J., & Bauer, P. J. (1999). When the event is more than the sum of its parts: Nine-month-olds' long-term ordered recall. *Memory, 7*, 147–174.

Casasola, M., & Cohen, L. B. (2002). Infant categorization of containment, support and tight-fit spatial relationships. *Developmental Science, 5*, 247–264.

Chen, Z., Sanchez, R. P., & Campbell, T. (1997). From beyond their grasp: The rudiments of analogical problem solving in 10- and 13-month-olds. *Developmental Psychology, 33*, 790–801.

Choi, S. (1997). Language-specific input and early semantic development: Evidence from children learning Korean. In D. I. Slobin (Ed.), *The crosslinguistic study of language acquisition, Vol. 5: Expanding contexts* (pp. 41–133). Mahwah, NJ: Erlbaum.

Choi, S., & Bowerman, M. (1991). Learning to express motion events in English and Korean: The influence of language-specific lexicalization patterns. *Cognition, 41*, 83–121.

Choi, S., & Gopnik, A. (1995). Early acquisition of verbs in Korean: A cross-linguistic study. *Journal of Child Language, 22*, 497–529.

Choi, S., McDonough, L., Bowerman, M., & Mandler, J. M. (1999). Early sensitivity to language-specific spatial categories in English and Korean. *Cognitive Development, 14*, 241–268.

Clark, E. V. (1973). What's in a word? On the child's acquisition of semantics in his first language. In T. E. Moore (Ed.), *Cognitive development and the acquisition of language* (pp. 65–110). New York: Academic Press.

Clark, H. H. (1973). Space, time, semantics, and the child. In T. E. Moore (Ed.), *Cognitive development and the acquisition of language* (pp. 27–63). New York: Academic Press.

Csibra, G., Gergely, G., Bíró, S., Koós, O., & Brockbank, M. (1999). Goal attribution without agency cues: The perception of "pure reason" in infancy. *Cognition, 72*, 237–267.

Fauconnier, G. (1994). *Mental spaces*. Cambridge, MA: MIT Press.

Frye, D., Rawling, P., Moore, C., & Myers, I. (1983). Object-person discrimination and communication at 3 and 10 months. *Developmental Psychology, 19*, 303–309.

Gentner, D. (1982). Why nouns are learned before verbs: Linguistic relativity versus natural partitioning. In S. Kuczaj (Ed.), *Language development: Vol. 2. Language, thought, and culture* (pp. 301–334). Hillsdale, NJ: Erlbaum.

Gergely, G., Nádasdy, Z., Csibra, G., & Bíró, S. (1995). Taking the intentional stance at 12 months of age. *Cognition, 56*, 165–193.

Golinkoff, R., Hirsh-Pasek, K., Cauley, K., & Gordon, L. (1987). The eyes have it: Lexical and syntactic comprehension in a new paradigm. *Journal of Child Language, 14*, 23–45.

Golinkoff, R. M., Hirsh-Pasek, K., Mervis, C. B., Frawley, W. B., & Parillo, M. (1995). Lexical principles can be extended to the acquisition of verbs. In M. Tomasello & W. E. Merriman (Eds.), *Beyond names for things: Young children's acquisition of verbs* (pp. 185–222). Hillsdale, NJ: Erlbaum.

Hespos, S. J., & Baillargeon, R. (2001). Infants' knowledge about occlusion and containment events: A surprising discrepancy. *Psychological Science, 12*, 141–147.

Johnson, M. (1987). *The body in the mind: The bodily basis of meaning, imagination, and reason*. Chicago: University of Chicago Press.

Johnson, S., Slaughter, V., & Carey, S. (1998). Whose gaze will infants follow? The elicitation of gaze-following in 12-month-olds. *Developmental Science, 1,* 233–238.

Johnson, S. C., & Sockaci, E. (2000, July). *The categorization of agents from actions.* Poster presented at the International Conference on Infant Studies, Brighton, England.

Kellman, P. J., & Spelke, E. S. (1983). Perception of partly occluded objects in infancy. *Cognitive Psychology, 15,* 483–524.

Lakoff, G. (1987). *Women, fire, and dangerous things: What categories reveal about the mind.* Chicago: University of Chicago Press.

Landau, B., & Jackendoff, R. (1993). "What" and "where" in spatial language and spatial cognition. *Behavior and Brain Sciences, 16,* 217–265.

Langacker, R. W. (2000). Why a mind is necessary: Conceptualization, grammar and linguistic semantics. In L. Albertazzi (Ed.), *Meaning and cognition: A multidisciplinary approach* (pp. 25–38). Amsterdam: John Benjamins.

Legerstee, M. (1992). A review of the animate-inanimate distinction in infancy: Implications for models of social and cognitive knowing. *Early Development and Parenting, 1,* 59–67.

Leslie, A. M. (1982). The perception of causality in infants. *Perception, 11,* 173–186.

Leslie, A. M. (1984). Infant perception of a manual pick-up event. *British Journal of Developmental Psychology, 2,* 19–32.

Leslie, A., & Keeble, S. (1987). Do six-month-old infants perceive causality? *Cognition, 25,* 265–288.

Mandler, J. M. (1992). How to build a baby II: Conceptual primitives. *Psychological Review, 99,* 587–604.

Mandler, J. M. (2004a). *The foundations of mind: Origins of conceptual thought.* New York: Oxford University Press.

Mandler, J. M. (2004b). Thought before language. *Trends in Cognitive Science.*

Mandler, J. M., Fivush, R., & Reznick, J. S. (1987). The development of contextual categories. *Cognitive Development, 2,* 339–354.

Mandler, J. M., & McDonough, L. (1993). Concept formation in infancy. *Cognitive Development, 8,* 291–318.

Mandler, J. M., & McDonough, L. (1995). Long-term recall in infancy. *Journal of Experimental Child Psychology, 59,* 457–474.

Mandler, J. M., & McDonough, L. (1996). Drinking and driving don't mix: Inductive generalization in infancy. *Cognition, 59,* 307–335.

Mandler, J. M., & McDonough, L. (1998a). On developing a knowledge base in infancy. *Developmental Psychology, 34,* 1274–1288.

Mandler, J. M., & McDonough, L. (1998b). Studies in inductive inference in infancy. *Cognitive Psychology, 37,* 60–96.

Mandler, J. M., & McDonough, L. (2000). Advancing downward to the basic level. *Journal of Cognition and Development, 1,* 379–404.

McDonough, L. (2002). Basic-level nouns: First learned but misunderstood. *Journal of Child Language, 29,* 357–377.

McDonough, L., Choi, S., & Mandler, J. M. (2003). Understanding spatial relations: Flexible infants, lexical adults. *Cognitive Psychology, 46,* 229–259.

McDonough, L., & Mandler, J. M. (1998). Inductive generalization in 9- and 11-month-olds. *Developmental Science, 1,* 227–232.

Naigles, L. (1990). Children use syntax to learn verb meanings. *Journal of Child Language, 17,* 357–374.

Nelson, K. (1973). Some evidence for the cognitive primacy of categorization and its functional basis. *Merrill-Palmer Quarterly, 19,* 21–39.

Nelson, K., Hampson, J., & Shaw, L. K. (1993). Nouns in early lexicons: Evidence, explanations and implications. *Journal of Child Language, 20,* 61–84.

Poulin-Dubois, D., Lepage, A., & Ferland, D. (1996). Infants' concept of animacy. *Cognitive Development, 11,* 19–36.

Poulin-Dubois, D., & Vyncke, J. (2003). *The cow jumped over the moon: Infants' inductive generalization of motion properties.* Concordia University, Montreal: Unpublished manuscript.

Quinn, P. C., Cummins, M., Kase, J., Martin, E., & Weisman, S. (1996). Development of categorical representations for above and below spatial relations in 3- to 7-month-old infants. *Developmental Psychology, 32,* 942–950.

Quinn, P. C., Polly, J. L., Furer, M. J., Dobson, V., & Narter, D. B. (2002). Young infants' performance in the object-variation version of the above-below categorization task: A result of perceptual distraction or conceptual limitation? *Infancy, 3,* 323–348.

Richards, M. M. (1979). Sorting out what's in a word from what's not: Evaluating Clark's semantic features acquisition theory. *Journal of Experimental Child Psychology, 27,* 1–47.

Smith, L. C. (2003). Learning to recognize objects. *Psychological Science, 14,* 244–250.

Sodian, B., Schoeppner, B., & Metz, U. (2004). Do infants apply the principle of rational action to human agents? *Infant Behavior and Development, 27,* 31–41.

Spelke, E. (1976). Infants' intermodal perception of events. *Cognitive Psychology, 8,* 553–560.

Spelke, E. S., & Hespos, S. J. (2002). Conceptual development in infancy: The case of containment. In N. L. Stein, P. J. Bauer, & M. Rabinowitch (Eds.), *Representation, memory, and development: Essays in honor of Jean Mandler* (pp. 223–246). Hillsdale, NJ: Erlbaum.

Spelke, E. S., Phillips, A., & Woodward, A. L. (1995). Infants' knowledge of object motion and human action. In A. J. Premack, D. Premack, & D. Sperber, (Eds.), *Causal cognition* (pp. 44–77). Oxford: Clarendon Press.

Talmy, L. (1988). Force dynamics in language and cognition. *Cognitive Science, 12,* 49–100.

Tomasello, M. (1987). Learning to use prepositions: A case study. *Journal of Child Language, 14,* 79–98.

Traüble, B., & Pauen, S. (2004, May). *The role of functional knowledge for infant categorization of artifacts.* Paper presented at the International Conference on Infant Studies, Chicago.

Watson, J. (1972). Smiling, cooing, and "the game." *Merrill-Palmer Quarterly, 18,* 323–340.

Willatts, P. (1997). Beyond the "couch potato" infant: How infants use their knowledge to regulate action, solve problems, and achieve goals. In J. G. Bremner, A. Slater, & G. Butterworth (Eds.), *Infant development: Recent advances* (pp. 109–135). Hove, England: Psychology Press.

Woodward, A. L. (1998). Infants selectively encode the goal object of an actor's reach. *Cognition, 69,* 1–34.

Woodward, A. L. (1999). Infants' ability to distinguish between purposeful and non-purposeful behaviors. *Infant Behavior and Development, 22,* 145–160.

Younger, B. A., & Johnson, K. E. (2004). Infants' comprehension of toy replicas as symbols for real objects. *Cognitive Psychology, 42,* 207–242.

5   Conceptual Foundations for Verb Learning: Celebrating the Event

Rachel Pulverman, Kathy Hirsh-Pasek,
Roberta M. Golinkoff, Shannon Pruden,
and Sara J. Salkind

At the critical juncture between words and grammar lie verbs. Verbs appear in children's earliest vocabularies (Choi, 1998; Choi & Bowerman, 1991; Choi & Gopnik, 1995; Fenson, Dale, Reznick, & Bates, 1994; Nelson, 1973; Tardif, 1996). They also serve as the architectural centerpiece of the sentence, specifying argument structure. How young children learn verbs is thus fundamental to our understanding of language acquisition. Most of the research on lexical acquisition has focused on nouns. The tides, however, are turning. Research from the past several years is beginning to illuminate the verb learning process. This chapter focuses on what children know about the conceptual foundations for verb learning.

Though the field is still in its infancy, general (though not unanimous) consensus is emerging: learning verbs is hard. This fact is well documented in the literature and in many of the studies cited in this volume. By way of example, in laboratory tasks, infants appear to fast-map nouns at an earlier age than verbs (Golinkoff, Hirsh-Pasek, Bailey, & Wenger, 1992; Golinkoff, Jacquet, Hirsh-Pasek, & Nandakumar, 1996). Even in languages where verbs occur in the prominent, sentence final position, or in isolation as the result of argument drop, children tend to learn verbs later than nouns (e.g., chapter 17, this volume; Au, Dapretto, & Song, 1994; Bornstein et al., 2004; Caselli, Bates, Casadio, & Fenson, 1995; but see Tardif, 1996). When choosing between a novel object and a novel action, children as old as 5 years have difficulty determining the correct referent for a novel verb in both English and Japanese (Imai, Haryu, & Okada, 2002, 2005; Meyer et al., 2003). Finally, even adults observing interactions between mothers and children on muted videos are less successful at picking out correct referents for verbs than for nouns (Gillette, Gleitman, Gleitman, & Lederer, 1999; Snedeker & Gleitman, 2004).

In light of this mounting evidence, two critical questions arise: First, what makes verb learning so difficult? And second, what does it take to learn a verb? Speculation abounds on the first of these questions. Gentner (1982) offered a menu of differences that might make verb learning harder than noun learning, concluding in 2001 (Gentner & Boroditsky, 2001) that among the key features differentiating the two word classes is the fact that nouns tend to label referents that are more individuated and less relational than the referents labeled by verbs. Snedeker and Gleitman (2004) suggest that the imageability of the referent is also a key distinction, with nouns tending to label referents that are more imageable. Tomasello (1992) contends that verbs are also difficult because they label referents that "unfold in time." Finally, Maguire, Hirsh-Pasek, and Golinkoff (chapter 14, this volume) suggest that there is an amalgamation of features including imageability, concreteness, individuability, and shape that make the referents for nouns more perceptually accessible and hence easier both for conceptual learning and for mapping.

Though we have numerous arguments and counterarguments for why verbs might prove more difficult, we have less data on the second question of what it takes to learn a verb. Do children have the prerequisite knowledge that would enable them to learn verbs as readily as nouns? It is to this question that we now turn.

The Verb Learning Problem

What does it take to learn a verb? Several researchers have identified the theoretical prerequisites for verb learning. Gentner and Boroditsky (2001), for example, write in broad strokes that verb learning requires both the *conceptualization* of actions and events and the *mapping* of words to these events and packages of events. They further argue that the latter might prove more difficult than the former because, across languages, verbs do not package actions and events in the same way. For example, in English one can say, "The man limped down the stairs." In Spanish the sentence would read, "El hombre bajó las escaleras cojeando," and would be translated as, "The man went down/descended the stairs limping." How the man moves, or the *manner* of the action, is embedded within the English verb. In contrast, the manner in Spanish is expressed as a modifier of the verb, with the verb itself indicating only the *path* of the man's motion. Thus, it might take a long time to package the conceptual components for verbs and to map them onto words in a way consistent with the native language. Indeed, Gillette and colleagues (1999) make this point explicitly when they find that conceptually mature adults have difficulty mapping a verb onto an action or relation in their now classic human simulation task.

The question of what it takes to learn a verb was also discussed by Golinkoff and colleagues (2002). They delineated three fundamental tasks required for verb learning to take place: (1) attending to and individuating actions and relations in the environment, (2) forming categories of actions and relations without language, and (3) mapping words to actions (dynamic relations) and action (relational) categories. Though all agree that children must attend to events and dynamic relations to solve the verb learning problem, there has been scant research on infants' knowledge of these conceptual constructs.

Prerequisites for Verb Learning: What We Know

Seeing It All in Motion

One place to begin the investigation is with the infant's attention to motion. Though not all activities, relations, and events include motion (e.g., sleep, explain, outside, between), motion tends to signal the presence of events. Furthermore, there is a rich literature suggesting that infants are very attentive to movement.

By way of example, a number of studies show that infants are better at perceiving objects when they are in motion than when they are statically displayed (Kellman, Spelke, & Short, 1986; Smith, Johnson, & Spelke, 2003; Werker, Cohen, Lloyd, Casasola, & Stager, 1998). In general, infants are more attentive to moving than to stationary objects (Slater, 1989). Further, 9-month-old infants can even form a *representation* of motion to predict the orientation of an object that is rotating *behind* an occluder (Rochat & Hespos, 1996). Attention to movement type (e.g., flexible versus rigid) signals classes of objects that are animate versus inanimate and is critical in determining causality (Cohen & Oakes, 1993; Golinkoff, Harding, Carlson-Luden, & Sexton, 1984; Kotovsky & Baillargeon, 2000; Mandler, 2004; Poulin-Dubois, Lepage, & Ferland, 1996; Rakison, 2003; Wang, Kaufman, & Baillargeon, 2003). Interestingly, while we know a great deal about infants' attention to movement, their understanding of movement has not been studied in its own right. Rather, movement was studied as a tool for discovering infants' understanding of the properties of objects (see Baillargeon, 2004, for a review).

The Great Divide: Using Movement Cues to Parse Events Into Actions

Movement not only offers a perceptual tool for examining objects but also serves as a parsing tool for breaking events into individual actions. Several studies give us insight as to how children might use motion to parse events into segments. Loucks and Baldwin (chapter 9, this volume), for example, present some of the first research in this area. Sharon and Wynn's (1998) studies offer another example. Originally designed to investigate the enumeration of actions, these experiments showed that 6-month-old infants are sensitive to changes in the number of repetitions of an action. Infants in this study could distinguish between two or three repetitions of the same action (jumping) when they occurred in a continuous stream of movement (jumps and falls). It is likely that the infants in this experiment discriminated the sequences based on the number of repetitions of motion segments. Importantly, if infants do have a sense of "number of actions" in a continuous action sequence, they must also have a sense of one action ending and the next beginning. Thus, Sharon and Wynn's experiments provide evidence that infants as young as 6 months can use movement cues to segment events.

Baldwin, Baird, Saylor, and Clark (2001) also present important evidence suggesting that infants as young as 10 months use motion cues to parse sequences of actions. Their study was designed to investigate whether children could home in on an actor's social intent to parse an ongoing stream of action. After familiarizing infants with everyday events (a "cleaning the kitchen" scene), they viewed videos in which pauses were inserted that either interrupted (e.g., *during* the act of hanging up the towel) or allowed completion of (e.g., *after* the towel was hung up) the intended actions. The infants were overwhelmingly more interested in the disrupted actions than the completed ones, suggesting that they were sensitive to the action boundaries within the event. It is possible that this result emerged because children were attending to actor intent. It is equally possible, however, that "perceptual sensitivity to physical and temporal regularities that *coincide with intentions* would enable them to achieve an organized parsing of . . . novel action sequences, even when they do not understand the intentions involved" (Baldwin et al., 2001, p. 715). Thus, the task might be solved through more "impoverished," "bottom-up" parsing strategies that are visual in nature, including movement features such as head turns, gaze direction changes, and changes in body trajectory.

However we interpret this finding, it suggests that infants are sensitive, in some ways, to event structure and that they can parse events from the dynamic flow of action. Taken together, these studies on motion, number, and social intent suggest that infants have the capacity to perceive events and to divide events into individual actions.

Looking Within: Getting a Piece of the Action

The problem of verb learning requires that infants isolate actions and relations from the dynamic stream of events. Learning a relational term like a verb, however, involves more than simply isolating actions. It requires that children are also sensitive to intrinsic (manners) and extrinsic (paths) features of the action. Verbs, for example, tend not to label whole actions. Rather, they label a subset of the many, often simultaneously occurring semantic components of motion events. These components include *motion* (the general fact that motion is taking place), *figure* (the prominent entity in the event), *manner* (the way in which the action or motion is carried out), *path* (the trajectory of the figure with respect to some reference point), *ground* (the reference point for the event's path), and *cause* (the cause of the figure's motion), among others (Talmy, 1985). For example, imagine an event where a man passes through the banner at the end of the New York City

Marathon. The figure is the man, the manner is running, the path is through the banner, the ground is the banner itself, and the cause is the internal motivation for running the race.

Every motion verb conflates a subset of these conceptual components in its meaning such that there is a variety of types of motion verbs. Manner verbs encode motion conflated with manner (e.g., *run, jump, float*). Path verbs encode motion and path (e.g., *enter, circle, descend*). There are also verbs that conflate more than one element along with motion, such as *deplane*, which encodes motion, path, and ground. But no verb encodes everything in a given event. Thus, while all of the elements of motion events may simultaneously meet the eye, only some of them will be relevant to learning any particular verb. As noted earlier, different languages also package event components in different ways (Talmy, 1985). In the majority of languages (e.g., Spanish, Turkish, Greek), path verbs are the most frequent. For example, to express an event in which a woman exited a house as she ran, a native Spanish speaker is most likely to say, "Una mujer *salió* de la casa (corriendo)" (A woman *exited* the house [running]). In many other languages (e.g., English, German, Chinese), manner verbs and cause verbs are most frequent. To express the same event, a native English speaker is most likely to say, "A woman *ran* out of the house." In a small minority of languages (e.g., Atsugewi, a Native American language), verbs most frequently conflate motion and figure. Verbs in these languages often express meanings such as "action/movement of a long, thin object." This variability among verb meanings both within and across different languages requires that the verb learning problem be solved anew for each verb learned, and the most reliable solution varies depending on the language being acquired.

So what in the verb learning process is so difficult for children? To date, the majority of research on verb learning has focused on the mapping problem and on the ways in which older children learn to package conceptual information to master the verb and prepositional system of their native language (e.g., see chapters 4 and 7, this volume). But do children have the conceptual prerequisites needed to build a semantic base for verb learning? Gentner (1982; Gentner & Boroditsky, 2001) hypothesizes that the conceptual prerequisites for the learning of verbs and other relational terms should be largely in place:

> it is important to note that the Natural Partitions hypothesis does not assume that relations themselves are perceived later than objects . . . even those sparse relations that act as predicates over objects are, I suspect, *perceived* quite early. Movement, change, directionality, and so on, seem quite interesting to infants. . . . It is not perceiving relations but packaging and lexicalizing them that is difficult. (Gentner, 1982, p. 326)

Cognitive linguists present a consistent, but largely untested theoretical view. They hold that the types of concepts verbs label, such as path, manner, and cause, may be prelinguistic conceptual primitives from which all other relational terms are constructed (e.g., Mandler, 1991, 2004; Jackendoff, 1983). The challenge for the field is to determine whether these conceptual primitives are indeed in place to support the learning of verbs and relational terms. Research from Choi's laboratory (see chapter 7), from Casasola's laboratory (see chapter 6), and from our laboratories is beginning to address these questions. We are starting to examine whether infants are sensitive to the conceptual primitives that interactively support verb learning. To date, this research is playing out in two main areas: the study of spatial expressions and the study of motion verbs. Spatial expressions, including constructs of containment and support (e.g., *in* and *on*), as well as motion verbs, with components that include constructs like path and manner, offer a perfect looking glass for investigating the conceptual foundations of relational terms. In each case, the construct in question (different types of containment and support, different paths and manners) seems to be perceptually accessible. Further, and importantly, in each case there is considerable cross-linguistic variability. For example, the Korean word *kkita* means "to put tight-fitting," regardless of whether the relation is one of containment (e.g., fitting a peg tightly into a hole) or support (e.g., fitting one Lego block tightly onto another). In English, however, the relevant distinction is between containment (*in*) and support (*on*), regardless of the tightness of fit. With motion verbs, the manner is often expressed in the verb for English speakers (e.g., *run, jump, skid*) while the path is often expressed in the verb for Spanish speakers (e.g., *enter, leave, descend*). Though this research is, quite literally, in its infancy, results are already emerging to suggest that infants are sophisticated observers of actions and relations who attend to conceptual primitives in the ways suggested by both Gentner (1982; Gentner & Boroditsky, 2001) and Mandler (1992, 2004).

Conceptual Primitives for Verb Learning: Spatial Expressions and Motion Verbs

Spatial Expressions

There is a rich literature on spatial expressions (e.g., Bowerman, 1996; Landau, 1996; Landau & Jackendoff, 1993; Meints, Plunkett, Harris, & Dimmock, 2002). Some of the more interesting and now classic findings in this literature came from differences in the way that native Korean and English speakers codified containment and support relations. Choi and colleagues (Choi & Bowerman, 1991; Choi, McDonough, Bowerman, & Mandler, 1999) have found, in both production and comprehension studies, that children categorize spatial relations like containment and support in language-specific ways. In their now classic study, Choi and Bowerman (1991) found that 17- to 20-month-olds' use of spatial words was language-specific. For example, children raised in English-speaking homes used the words *in* and *on* to distinguish between containment events and support events, regardless of fit. Children raised in Korean-speaking homes made a different distinction that cross-cut the English *in* and *on* using the concepts of "tight-fit" or "loose-fit." Choi et al. (1999; see also chapter 7, this volume) found similar results when they looked at the comprehension of language-specific spatial words, like *in* and *on* for English and *kkita* for native Korean. Using a preferential looking paradigm, they found that children as young as 18 months of age comprehend these spatial words and turn their attention towards the events depicting these spatial concepts. Infants raised in English-speaking homes look at an event depicting containment, regardless of tightness of fit, when they hear the word *in*. Children raised in Korean-speaking homes directed their attention towards an event depicting tight fit, regardless of containment or support, when they heard the word *kkita*.

These classic studies raised the question about when the differences that were evident across languages emerge in the course of development. Perhaps the most stunning of the recent demonstrations comes from Hespos and Spelke (2004), who investigated this question with 5-month-old infants. In a habituation task, they presented children with scenes of an object that was fit tightly (or loosely, depending on the condition) in a container. After infants habituated to the event, the experimenters presented either another object that fit tightly or one that fit loosely in the container. The preverbal English-learning infants overwhelmingly demonstrated their ability to distinguish the tight- and loose-fit dimension that is common in containment and support terms used in Korean. In many ways, this experiment is but a replication of one performed by McDonough, Choi, and Mandler (2003) in which 9-month-old infants from both English- and Korean-speaking environments demonstrated that they could discriminate between spatial concepts that are not typically codified in their language.

These empirical demonstrations suggest that, at an early age, infants are predisposed to note the kinds of conceptual divisions within the spatial arena that will be relevant to later language learning. As Mandler (2004) argues, children seem to be able to do perceptual meaning analysis of the sort that will offer a strong foundation for language learning.

Motion Verbs

Motion verbs comprise only a small percentage of the verbs in an adult vocabulary. Yet they offer a promising point of entry for verb research for several reasons. First, motion verbs, like spatial terms, appear relatively early in the corpus of early words (Fenson et al., 1994). Verbs like *fall*, *jump*, and *dance* are among the first set of words to enter the child's budding lexicon. Second, with motion verbs, the referent event is visible to both parent and child. To the extent that words are learned best in periods of joint attention (Adamson, Bakeman, & Deckner, 2005; Carpenter, Nagell, & Tomasello, 1998; Tomasello, 1992), motion verbs thus provide optimal learning opportunities. Third, verbs of motion are generally individuable and imageable, possessing exactly the characteristics that Gentner and Boroditsky (2001) thought would make words more learnable. Fourth, there is some (though limited) knowledge about how events codified in motion verbs are processed (Casasola, Hohenstein, & Naigles, 2003, 2005; Pulverman, Golinkoff, Hirsh-Pasek, & Sootsman-Buresh, 2005; Pulverman, Sootsman, Golinkoff, & Hirsh-Pasek, 2003). Fifth and finally, like the spatial concepts examined above, event components are packaged differently to yield the conceptual bases for verb learning.

Arguably, path is one of the most central concepts for learning relational terms such as verbs because it is the semantic component from which other notions, like animacy and causality, may be derived (Mandler, 2004). By extension, it is equally important to study manner because, in order for a path to be traversed, a manner is required to propel the moving figure. Thus, while the elements of motion to be discussed here are limited, our focus on path and manner will lay a solid foundation for understanding the development of the concepts underlying motion verbs.

In the past few years, we, along with Casasola (chapter 6, this volume; Casasola et al., 2003, 2005), have embarked upon an innovative program of research exploring the cognitive foundations of motion verb learning. Using specially designed stimuli integrated across a variety of studies using multiple experimental paradigms, we have been probing a wide range of subcomponents in the verb learning process and pinpointing infants' strengths and weaknesses with the goal of providing a detailed account of the development of essential pre–verb learning skills. This research has taken place on several fronts. First, we explored infants' attention to motion events with respect to two questions: Do infants notice changes of individual elements of events, and are they able to decompose events into separable elements, such as path and manner? Casasola et al. (2003, 2005) have relevant evidence on event discrimination as well. Second, we investigated the question of event categorization and asked whether infants can form categories of similar paths or manners amidst changes in the perceptual flow. If infants can solve these tasks in nonlinguistic studies, it will further reinforce the view presented above, that infants are perceptually and conceptually prepared to learn verbs.

Attention to Events: Discrimination and Conceptual Decomposition

Path and Manner Research on the parsing of events is rare, so we know relatively little about how infants find individual actions within the flux of dynamic events. Yet there is evidence to suggest that they are competent to detect these actions. Thus, from the standpoint of prerequisites for verb learning, the relevant question becomes one of event decomposition. Can infants attend to aspects of motion or action that will be later codified in relational terms?

Our first pass at this question was with 14- to 17-month-olds in a habituation task (Pulverman, Golinkoff, Hirsh-Pasek, & Sootsman-Buresh, 2005; Pulverman et al., 2003, 2005).[1] Infants viewed silent, computer-animated motion events involving a moving starfish character (the figure) and a stationary ball (the

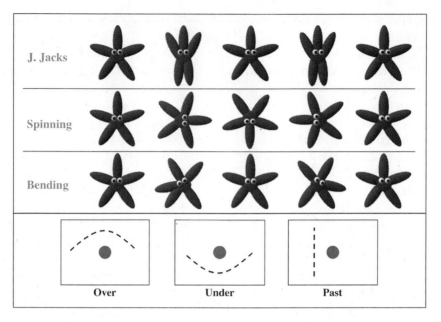

Figure 5.1. Manners and paths used in stimuli. Although illustrated as a series of static postures, the starfish performed the manners as continuous motions.

ground). In the events, the starfish performed an action with both a manner (jumping jacks, spinning, or bending at the "waist") and a path (over the ball, under the ball, or vertically past the ball; see figure 5.1). Once infants became habituated to a single event (e.g., jumping jacks over), they were then tested on four different types of events: (1) a control event identical to the habituation event (e.g., jumping jacks over); (2) an event with the same manner as the habituation event, but a different path (e.g., jumping jacks under); (3) an event with the same path as the habituation event, but a different manner (e.g., spinning over); and (4) an event in which both the manner and path differed from those in all other events (e.g., waist bends past). The results were impressive. Fourteen- to 17-month-old infants had no trouble discriminating between paths or between manners. They readily dishabituated to the path change, the manner change, and the both change events. In short, there was clear evidence that they noticed changes of paths and manners. These initial results motivated several additional studies, all of which affirm the main findings. In our laboratory, Pulverman and Golinkoff (2004) examined attention to path and manner in 7-month-old infants. Using exactly the same habituation task, 7-month-olds successfully dishabituated to changes of manner, changes of path, and changes of both manner and path. This shows that, even before word learning begins, infants notice differences between events that could potentially distinguish between one verb and another. Pulverman and Golinkoff's (2004) study shows that preverbal infants are already equipped with one of the fundamental cognitive tools they will need to learn motion verbs.

A study by Casasola et al. (2003) makes a similar point. In their study, 10-month old children participated in a habituation task in which they viewed videos of more natural action. In the habituation phase, a girl might be seen crawling toward a shrub. In the manner change condition, the girl now walked toward the shrub. In the path change condition, the girl crawled away from the shrub. In the both change condition, the girl walked away from the shrub. Results suggest that 10-month-olds notice both manner and path changes.

Results from all of these studies demonstrate that, even in the first year of life, infants are aware of changes of manner and path. That is, they seem to be sensitive to the conceptual primitives required for later verb learning even in these nonverbal tasks. These studies also raise the question of whether the infants are really responding to path and manner as individual motion components within the event or whether they might be responding to more holistic perceptual changes in events. That is, it is possible that children do not notice a path change per se, but rather that the entire scene has changed. An example might be useful. If path is represented by the color red and manner by the color blue, then we can argue that the children actually note the separable motion components of path and manner, or red and blue. Yet it is possible that they are seeing something analogous to purple and that when we change the path again, for example, to yellow, that the children see green rather than the change from red to yellow. From what we have discussed so far, in the current studies, we cannot distinguish from among these alternatives.

To address this issue in 14- to 17-month-olds, Pulverman and colleagues (Pulverman, Golinkoff, Hirsh-Pasek, & Sootsman-Buresh, 2005; Pulverman et al., 2003) performed a second analysis. They reasoned that, if infants attend to manner and path as particular elements of interest, then all trials in which one of these elements has changed should be treated differently from all trials in which that element remains the same, regardless of whether the other element is the same or different. Furthermore, if manner and path are independent conceptual elements for infants, then reactions to changes of manner and to changes of path should not interact with one another. Thus, to evaluate whether 14- to 17-month-olds treat manner and path as separate elements, an ability we term *conceptual decomposition*, Pulverman et al. analyzed the main effects and interaction of the factors manner and path, each of which had two levels, "same" and "different" (see figure 5.2). The main effects of both manner and path were significant, and no significant interaction between manner and path was found. This pattern of results suggests that, at least for the older children studied on these questions, manner and path may be independent elements within a motion event.

In this nonverbal study, mothers nonetheless filled out the MacArthur Communicative Development Inventory (CDI) Infant Short Form (Fenson et al., 2000) to note the productive and receptive vocabularies of the children, and receptive vocabulary (above or below the expected median for the age range) was

		Manner		
		Same	**Diff.**	
Path	**Same**	Control	Manner Change	**Mean 1**
	Diff.	Path Change	Both Change	**Mean 2**
		Mean 3	**Mean 4**	

Figure 5.2. Calculation of path and manner effects: Path effect = Mean 2 – Mean 1; Manner effect = Mean 4 – Mean 3.

included as a factor in the analysis. Interestingly, a significant interaction was found between the main effect of manner and vocabulary level. The manner effect was greater for the higher vocabulary infants than for their lower vocabulary counterparts. Furthermore, the manner effect was significant only in the higher vocabulary group. There are three possible explanations for these findings, two of which are related to the fact that manner verbs are more frequent than path verbs in English. First, perhaps accumulated knowledge of English verbs teaches infants that manner is important. If this is the case, then the adjustment of attentional biases may possibly be a tool infants use to make further verb learning more efficient. By increasing attention to manner, the likely referents for more verbs should stand out. Second, perhaps some infants happen to pay more attention to manner than others, and learners of English who pay more attention to manner notice the correct referents for more words, promoting higher vocabularies. Third, perhaps an unknown third factor promotes both vocabulary growth and increased attention to manner. Preliminary data from a replication with infants learning Spanish (a language that expresses path more often than manner) supports the second explanation: that attention to manner influences lexical acquisition (Pulverman, Golinkoff, Hirsh-Pasek, & Jackson-Maldonado, 2005; Pulverman, Golinkoff, Hirsh-Pasek, & Sootsman-Buresh, 2005).

The same analysis (omitting the vocabulary factor) performed on the 7-month-olds' data yielded different results. For those young, preverbal infants, a significant interaction of manner and path was found, suggesting that manner and path are not independent elements at 7 months. The results of these two studies show that the ability to treat manner and path as independent elements of motion events develops somewhere between 7 and 17 months of age. Research currently underway on early categorization of motion components allows us to investigate this same question in yet another way, revealing that children might be able to note separable action components by as early as 10 months of age (Pruden, Hirsh-Pasek, Maguire, & Meyer, 2004).

Path and manner offer one example of event discrimination and decomposition that taps into the kinds of perceptual and conceptual constructs that are known to influence later language learning (Langacker, 1987; Mandler, 2004; Talmy, 1985). As a final experiment in this set, however, we wanted to know if infants were also able to detect elements of events that are more subtly codified in the world's languages. Relational terms often mark relative speed (e.g., *The boy ran* versus *The boy sprinted*), though not as frequently as manner or path.[2] Relative speed can be considered a more subtle semantic element in that it is a subcomponent of manner, specifying additional detail about how the action is carried out. Would infants be sensitive to this kind of information in the perceptual stream? An experiment by Salkind (2003; Salkind, Golinkoff, & Brandone, 2005) was designed to find out.

Beyond Path and Manner: Speed Salkind (2003; Salkind et al., 2005) tested 9- to 11-month-old infants' discrimination of repetitive actions performed at different rates. Stimuli were events with a human figure performing complex actions, including both arm and leg movements, such as one might see in an aerobics class. Participants were habituated to an event with one of the actions performed at a particular rate—either 60, 80, 100, or 120 beats per minute. They were then tested on the same action at the same rate and the same action at a new rate, either 20 beats per minute faster or 20 beats per minute slower. Infants looked significantly longer at all of the rate changes, both faster and slower than the original rate, showing that they successfully discriminate rate differences of 20 beats per minute. Salkind's finding that 9- to 11-month-olds can discriminate between the same action performed at different speeds provides evidence that from a very young age, infants are prepared to make at least one of the distinctions that is necessary for learning subtly different manner verbs. Taken together with the studies on path and manner, this result strongly suggests that infants attend to a number of verb-relevant perceptual elements within the motions that they see.

Does Language Itself Influence Attention to Events? The Pulverman, Golinkoff, Hirsh-Pasek, & Sootsman-Buresh (2005) and Pulverman et al. (2003) results suggest that, even in this nonverbal task, language is somehow directly related to children's attention to and conceptual decomposition of motion events. Of course, in a real-world potential verb learning situation, children view motion events accompanied by language. Would the addition of language exert any noticeable change in the way infants approach these tasks? There are two possibilities. On the one hand, research suggests that nouns amplify attention to objects (Baldwin & Markman, 1989) and to categories of objects (Balaban & Waxman, 1997; Waxman, 2003; Waxman & Markow, 1995). Thus, we might expect verbs to amplify attention to motion. On the other hand, the introduction of words might be disruptive to infants' performance because it adds to the processing load of the task. For example, Stager and Werker (1997) found that 14-month-olds could discriminate between two minimal pair syllables (*bih* versus *dih*) when they were presented in the context of a checkerboard that filled a video screen. But when the syllables were presented in the company of objects—as if it were a word learning task—infants could no longer distinguish between the sounds. To investigate the role of language on the processing of motion components, we added language to the Pulverman et al. study.

Pulverman, Brandone, and Salkind (2004) conducted this research with English learning infants between 14 and 17 months of age. The procedure and stimuli are identical to those in Pulverman, Golinkoff, Hirsh-Pasek, & Sootsman-Buresh (2005) and Pulverman et al. (2003), described above, except that language has been added. In the habituation phase, concurrent with the presentation of the motion event, infants hear a novel verb ("He's *jaiming!* Wow! He's *jaiming!* Oh, boy! He's *jaiming!* . . ."). The habituation phase of the experiment thus constituted a potential verb learning situation. Importantly, the test phase of the experiment paralleled the test phase in Pulverman and colleagues' nonlinguistic study. That is, this was *not* a test of verb learning. Instead, the verb was removed from the audio ("Wow! Oh, boy! Wow! . . .") so that the events in the test trials only tap the representation of the event previously formed during the habituation phase. The question is whether the addition of language in the habituation phase of the experiment would influence infants' attention to motion events? The answer is yes. Preliminary results indicate that, in a potential verb learning context, infants learning English notice manner of motion more than they do when watching motion events in silence. Attention to path appears to be unaffected. Furthermore, preliminary results suggest that infants in the potential word learning task look significantly longer at the event with the changed manner than at the event with the changed path, a finding that was not evident in the silent version of the study.

These results suggest, in parallel with Baldwin and Markman (1989), that adding language heightens attention to the visual event. Interestingly, however, language appears to differentially affect infants' responses by increasing attention to only the manner of the event—the most likely referent for novel motion verbs. This finding can be interpreted in a number of ways. First, perhaps this is an instance of "thinking for speaking" (Slobin, 2001), a weak form of linguistic relativity whereby thought *for linguistic purposes* is influenced by one's native language. Under this interpretation, the English-learning infants in this task increased their attention to manner in the potential verb learning situation because manner is the event component most frequently expressed by verbs in English. The second possibility is that increasing attention to manner is a language-general verb learning strategy. Regardless of the language being learned, manner should always be the more likely referent for a novel word. This is because manner concepts are an open set, while path concepts are a closed set. So, even if there are more *tokens* of path terms in a given language, there should nonetheless be more *types* of manner words. A third alternative is more perceptual in nature. If path is considered the more fundamental aspect of these events (Mandler, 2004), perhaps the addition of language serves to bring less potent elements of events, like manner, to the foreground. Extremely preliminary evidence from infants learning Spanish (a language that expresses manner less frequently than path) suggests that infants increase their attention to manner in linguistic contexts regardless of their native language. These data are consistent with both the second (language-general) and third (perceptual) explanations. But regardless of the ultimate reason, Pulverman et al.'s (2004) results are an instance of language heightening attention to the part of events that is most likely to be the referent for a novel verb.

The findings on event discrimination and conceptual decomposition suggest that infants can look within motion events to find the primitives that form the basis for verb learning. Infants notice not only robust (e.g., path and manner) but also more subtle (e.g., speed) perceptual elements that are conflated in the relational terms of languages across the world. Furthermore, the presence of accompanying language in the input seems to promote attention to the elements of events encoded by a greater number of different relational terms. Attention to this information is a key prerequisite for the learning of motion verbs, manner adverbs, and path prepositions. Yet attending to and conceptually decomposing events, while necessary, is not sufficient to prepare infants for the learning of relational terms. To learn action terms, infants must be able to categorize these conceptual building blocks. Research in our laboratories is beginning to address this critical issue as well.

Event Categorization

Verbs and prepositions do not refer to individual events. As Oakes and Rakison (2003, p. 4) have stated, "words refer to *categories* of objects and events" (emphasis added). Just as the noun *chair* refers to dining room chairs, office chairs, and recliners, a motion verb refers to a category of perceptually differing actions. Picture a track star running. Now picture your grandmother running or a cheetah running. These actions look very different, yet they all fall into the category labeled by the English verb *run*. Even when performed by the same person, running can vary dramatically when it occurs on different surfaces, or when performed with different purposes. To complicate matters further, some actions that are perceptually similar fall into different linguistic categories. The action a track star performs when leaping over a hurdle might be considered perceptually similar to the way she runs. How do children ever solve this complicated problem? Why do they call each of these instances, except leaping hurdles, by the same name?

These issues raise a number of ancillary questions. What types of invariants can infants use as a basis for event categories? What kinds of variation can they disregard in their categorization of events? Several studies from our laboratories are among the firsts to address these issues.

Categorizing Human Action

Salkind, Sootsman, Golinkoff, Hirsh-Pasek, and Maguire (2002) were among the first to examine event categorization. They tested 9- to 11-month-old infants' categorization of events based on manner, across a variety of figures. Infants were habituated to one of several complex novel actions, performed by two different female actors in random order. The actions were like those one might see in an aerobics class. Infants were then tested on two novel events: an event with a new actor performing the same aerobic action (in-category event), and an event with the same new actor performing a new aerobic action (out-of-category event). The results suggested that, regardless of the particular combination of actions used in this counterbalanced design, infants could indeed categorize motion events. The children looked significantly longer at the out-of-category test event than at the in-category test event. They also looked longer at the in-category test event than at the last three habituation trials, demonstrating that they discriminated between the new actor and the old actor. Infants formed a category of events based on a common manner *despite* detectable variation in the person performing the action. The ability to find common action across variation in the actor is critical to learning motion verbs. Walking is walking, no matter who is doing it. Salkind et al.'s study shows that, by 9 months of age, infants can categorize events in one of the most fundamental ways necessary for learning manner verbs.

Categorizing Events Based on Path and Manner

Pruden and colleagues extended this research on categorization by investigating whether infants could categorize events based on path across varying manners and based on manner across varying paths (Pruden et al., 2004; Pruden, Pulverman, Hirsh-Pasek, & Golinkoff, 2003). Pruden and colleagues (2004) used English-reared infants between 7 and 15 months of age. The stimuli for these studies were computer-animated motion events involving a starfish and a ball as figure and ground, respectively. Using a superset of the stimuli used by Pulverman and colleagues (Pulverman & Golinkoff, 2004; Pulverman, Golinkoff, Hirsh-Pasek, & Sootsman-Buresh, 2005; Pulverman et al., 2003), six manners (e.g., spinning, jumping jacks, twisting, toe-touching, side bending, and bowing) and six paths (e.g., over, under, around, past, in front of, and behind) were created. In a modified version of the split-screen preferential-looking paradigm (Hirsh-Pasek & Golinkoff, 1996; see figure 5.3), infants viewed events with this animated starfish. Importantly, no linguistic stimuli accompanied these events. Infants were seated on their caregivers' laps in front of a large screen television. Caregivers were asked to close their eyes during the experiment so as not to influence the child's direction of gaze. The amount of time and direction of the child's gaze were recorded.

Infants participated in four phases during the study: (1) the introduction phase, (2) the salience phase, (3) the familiarization phase, and (4) the test phase.

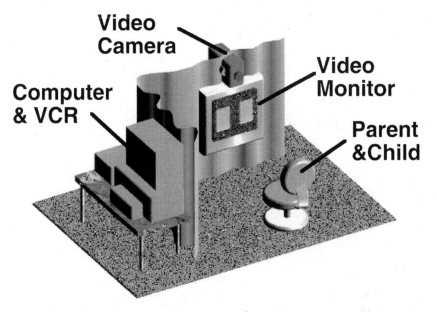

Figure 5.3. The split-screen preferential-looking paradigm.

During the introduction phase, infants were introduced to the animated starfish. During this introduction the starfish moved across the screen from left to right and back while stretching his arms and legs outward.

During the salience phase, infants were simultaneously presented with two event clips side by side. These were the same event clips that would be seen later during the test phase. The purpose of the salience phase was to measure any a priori preference for the event clips to be used in the test phase. The underlying assumption here was that infants would not have an a priori preference for either event clip.

During the familiarization phase, infants were shown four different event clips. Each clip demonstrated the animated star performing both a single manner and a single path. These event clips all demonstrated an exemplar of the category being tested. Finally, during the test phase infants were presented with both an in-category event and an out-of-category event. The purpose of the test phase was to assess whether infants had formed a category.

To test categorization based on path, participants were familiarized with four events on a video screen, one after another, each of which had different manners, but shared a common path (e.g., spinning over followed by twisting over, bending over, and jumping jacks over). They were then tested with two novel events, an in-category event and an out-of-category event, which appeared side by side. The in-category event had a novel manner and the familiar path (e.g., toe-touching over), while the out-of-category event had the same novel manner and a novel path (e.g., toe-touching under). Infants first showed evidence of successful categorization between 10 and 12 months, with these infants looking significantly longer at the in-category event than at the out-of-category event. These findings demonstrate that by 10 to 12 months of age but perhaps not before, infants are able to categorize events based on path, disregarding variations of manner.

To test categorization based on manner, 7- to 15-month-old infants were familiarized with four events with different paths, but the same manner (e.g., spinning over, spinning under, spinning past, and spinning behind). They were then tested on an in-category event with a novel path and the familiar manner (e.g., spinning around), and an out-of-category event with the same novel path and a novel manner (e.g., twisting around). Thirteen- to 15-month-olds looked significantly longer at the out-of-category event than the in-category event, while the younger infants showed no reliable preference. These findings suggest that by 13 to 15 months of age but perhaps not sooner, infants are able to categorize events based on manner, disregarding variations of path.

Pruden et al.'s (2003, 2004) studies show that categorizing events along the lines of an invariant conceptual primitive (like manner or path) does not come "for free." Event categorization skills develop in infancy, with different types of categorization becoming accessible at different points in development. Infants can categorize events based on a common path across varying manners before they can categorize events based on a common manner across varying paths. These findings raise several important points. First, they suggest that infant categorization of actions does not come on line at the same time for each conceptual construct. Some semantic components of events are easier to categorize than others. The second point is that these findings relate to the findings of Pulverman and colleagues (Pulverman, Golinkoff, Hirsh-Pasek, & Sootsman-Buresh, 2005; Pulverman et al., 2003). In order to form categories, infants must be able to isolate the conceptual primitives of path and manner rather than viewing them as interactive wholes. Third, this finding challenges researchers to move beyond a surface view of categorization in which infants are finding merely the invariant feature of the action. Each of these points deserves further elaboration.

The first point, that different categories are formed at different points in development, has been suggested before. Quinn and colleagues (Quinn, Cummins, Kase, Martin, & Weissman, 1996; Quinn, Norris, Pasko, Schmader, & Mash, 1999), for instance, previously showed that the ability to form categories of static spatial relations develops at different times for different spatial relations. For example, infants can form a category of the location "over" before they can form a category of the location "between." Casasola and Cohen (2002) showed that the ability to categorize dynamic events based on their ultimate spatial relations across a variety of figure and ground objects develops on different time scales for different spatial relations. For example, the category "put in" can be formed at an earlier age than the categories "put on" or "put tight-fitting." Finally, in related research, Baillargeon (2004) demonstrates that infants notice different perceptual features within different types of events. Thus, the feature of height is paramount for 4.5-month-olds in an occlusion event but does not surface as a key construct in containment events until children are 7.5 months of age.

The results presented here suggest that path might be more basic than manner for young children. This is consistent with claims forwarded by Mandler (2004) and others who view path as one of the cornerstones for the conceptual development of motion. As Mandler writes, "PATH is the simplest conceptualization of any object following any trajectory through space" (p. 28). It should thus come as little surprise that path seems to be categorized before manner.

The second point is that these data add force to the suggestion that by 10 months of age, children are noting conceptual primitives as separable units rather than as united or interactive perceptual wholes. The infants in Pruden et al.'s (2004) research had to isolate the common element among ever-changing perceptual displays, in this case, path or manner. If the children viewed these dynamic displays as integrative wholes rather than as componential, they could not have solved this task because both test events were novel. Each scene varied by at least one element. Each would thus be viewed as different rather than similar *unless* the child focused on the individual components of the action portrayed (i.e., conceptual decomposition).

Third and finally, Pruden et al.'s (2004) research is but a first step in our understanding of infants' ability to categorize motion events. In these tasks, infants needed only to abstract the invariant perceptual features from the events that they saw. To form the types of event categories that verbs label, children must look beyond these *perceptual* invariants and recognize *conceptual* invariants despite perceptual variation in the event component in question. For example, the manner category "run" applies both to Carl Lewis's running and to Grandma's running, even though these actions perceptually differ. Likewise, the path category "over" applies to both a little over and a lot over, even though the trajectories of the actions are not identical. Can infants form categories of perceptually variable manners and paths? Studies by Salkind and colleagues (Salkind, 2003; Salkind et al., 2002, 2005) begin to shed light on this question.

Categorizing Varying Manners Salkind et al.'s (2002) finding that 9- to 11-month-olds can categorize events based on manner across varying figures (discussed earlier) may have involved categorization of perceptually differing manners. Each particular aerobic action was performed differently by each actor, and these differences were clearly perceptible to adults. However, since it is impossible to determine whether the manner differences were perceptible to infants, we cannot be certain of whether the task included categorization of varying manners. Since detecting the variability of manner introduced by different actors will always be necessarily confounded with discrimination between the actors themselves, we may never be able to determine whether children who cannot yet explicitly answer questions notice such differences of manner in the presence of different actors. But despite the fact that it is unclear whether infants' solution of the Carl Lewis versus Grandma problem is conceptual categorization or merely perceptual, this study shows that they have the ability to overcome the problem.

In another study, Salkind (2003; Salkind et al., 2005) tested infants' categorization of events based on manner across varying rates. Rate is a subcomponent of manner—subtle differences between manner verbs can be based on relative speed (e.g., *run* vs. *sprint*). Thus, this experiment directly addresses the issue of categorization of perceptually varying manners. Stimuli were the same events used in the rate discrimination study described earlier. Each event was comprised of the same female actor performing one of four aerobic actions at either 60, 80, 100, or 120 beats per minute. From the previous discrimination study, we know that infants detect the differences between the rates of these events. Nine- to 11-month-old infants were habituated to three different events in random order, all of which had the same general manner performed at different rates. They were then presented two test events—an in-category event with the same manner at a novel rate and an out-of-category event with a novel manner at the same novel rate. Participants looked significantly longer at the out-of-category event than at the in-category event, showing that, by 9 to 11 months of age, infants are able to categorize manner across varying rates. Since variations in rate or speed are extremely common in the world, this ability constitutes an important foundational skill for learning verbs. Further research is needed to determine the other ways in which infants can categorize perceptually variable manners, and the ways in which they can categorize other perceptually varying semantic components of motion verbs such as path and figure.

In 1982, Gentner hypothesized, "It is not perceiving relations but packaging and lexicalizing them that is difficult." Twenty-two years later, Mandler (2004) added, "our conceptualizing baby is observing what the objects around her are doing in the sense that she is analyzing the paths the objects take" (p. 85). In some ways, the research presented here is a test of the hypotheses that babies are making sense out of the world of events that surrounds them. The field of infant event perception is young, yet data are already beginning to confirm these hypotheses.

Prelinguistic Foundations for Verb Learning

The portrait of infant abilities that is emerging suggests that by the second half of the first year of life, babies begin to parse and categorize events into objects and actions (chapters 4, 6, and 7, this volume; Baldwin et al., 2001; Baillargeon, 2004; Sharon & Wynn, 1998). As babies view the world, they are also capable of looking "within" the individual actions they witness to find components like containment, support, path, and manner that will form the foundations for verb learning. This nascent ability is necessary if we want to explain how children acquire relational terms, but it is not sufficient. To learn these terms, infants must also demonstrate the ability to categorize across instances of path and manner and then to package these primitives in ways used in their native language. Progress on the first of these questions is just beginning, but the evidence suggests that by the second half of the first year, children are beginning to pull invariant features of paths and manners from a changing display. Interestingly, the data also suggest that by 10 months of age, infants see separable components of these actions rather than unanalyzed wholes (e.g., Pruden et al., 2004). The data further suggest that not all action components are created equal. As suggested by Mandler (2004), even for the highly salient features of path and manner, path might prove more accessible than manner and be more basic than manner (Pruden et al.). Finally, language heightens attention to certain features over others, encouraging infants to preferentially notice elements of events encoded by a greater variety of words (Pulverman et al., 2004). This research program is just beginning. There are already, however, several implications of the work. First, this research speaks to questions about event perception in infants. Second, it invites us to reexamine what it is about verbs that makes learning them so difficult relative to learning nouns. Third and finally, this research opens new avenues for further investigation.

The question of what babies have demonstrated in these tasks is of paramount importance. Indeed, the answer to that question is nested in the debates that plague the categorization literature: are these mere perception tests or might they unveil the conceptual primitives that form the foundations for the learning of relational terms (see Rakison & Oakes, 2003, for a review). The research presented in these pages offers no way to disentangle this question. Perhaps in these tasks, children are forming the conceptual foundations that support verb learning. The more parsimonious explanation is that at least they notice the kinds of information in the dynamic display that is embedded in relational terms like motion verbs. Current research in our lab asks whether children would as easily learn dynamic contrasts that are never represented in languages. Salkind (2003; Salkind et al., 2005), for example, is exploring whether infants can categorize events based on rate across varying manners. Languages do not have "rate verbs" with meanings such as "to move at 60 beats per minute." Yet the preliminary results suggest that infants, nonetheless, can form these kinds of categories. "Language-relevant" categories may not be privileged. Young children seem attentive to any number of dynamic perceptual contrasts and language chooses from among these to form the conceptual foundations for relational words. More research is desperately needed to secure this interpretation. Whatever the ultimate explanation, though, there is no doubt that infants have the requisite ability in the first year of life to represent at least some relational concepts.

This raises the second question of why verbs are harder to learn than nouns (though see chapter 18, this volume). The problem might not be in the "world" part of the word-to-world mapping. Children seem to notice and attend to the requisite categories in the environment around them and do so at only slightly older ages than is apparent for object learning. To learn a relational term, however, the child must go beyond just noticing and categorizing a unit like path or manner; she must figure out how to package these components together in ways that are codified in the relational terms of her language. A number of researchers suggest that this is indeed a hurdle for young children (Gentner & Boroditsky, 2001; Imai et al., 2005) and adults (Gillette et al., 1999). The research presented in this chapter suggests even more strongly that the mapping problem might prove the bigger hurdle for young verb learners.

Finally, the research presented here points the way towards new studies that are required if we are to fully understand how children build the conceptual foundations for learning verbs from rather meager perceptual beginnings. Talmy (1985) and Langacker (1987), among others, have identified a host of conceptual primitives that are packaged together to form the verb and prepositional system across languages. One of our goals then is to broaden the scope of the investigation and to do so in a cross-linguistic way. A second avenue of research is to better understand the relationship between the perceptual sensitivities that we have found here and the kind of conceptual categories that form the basis for word learning. Third, it is imperative that we turn attention to the ways in which children map language onto these perceptual and conceptual units. This has been a goal of our research, which is discussed more fully in chapter 14 of this volume.

There is much more to be done in the field, both in terms of the development of infants' event processing abilities and in terms of how infants' understanding of events plays into the learning of relational terms. The investigation of the perceptual and conceptual precursors to language is truly in its infancy. The studies presented here strongly suggest that, in this virgin area of research, infants have competencies heretofore unappreciated and unseen.

Acknowledgments The research reported here and the writing of the chapter were supported by NSF grants #SBR9601306 and SBR9615391 to Hirsh-Pasek and Golinkoff and by NICHD grant #3U10HD25455-0552 to Hirsh-Pasek. We thank our laboratory coordinators, Jennifer Sootsman-Buresh, Dede Addy, Amanda Brandone, Meredith Meyer, Natalie Sheridan, and Meredith Jones whose good work allowed us to concentrate on this project.

Notes

1. In the visual habituation paradigm (Bornstein, 1985), infants are repeatedly presented with the same stimulus or stimuli for as long as they choose to look. When their interest in the stimulus decreases, as determined by a decline in visual fixation time of a predetermined percentage, they are said to be habituated. The habituated infants are then presented with test stimuli that differ from the habituation stimuli in carefully manipulated ways, and with a control stimulus that is equivalent to the event that they saw during habituation. If the differences in the test stimuli are detected, the novelty should attract infants' attention, resulting in longer visual fixation times.

2. Words encoding relative speed must be interpreted with respect to a contextually appropriate norm.

References

Adamson, L., Bakeman, R. D., & Deckner, D. (2005). Infusing symbols into joint engagement: Developmental themes and variations. In L. Namy (Ed.), *Symbol use and symbolic representation: Developmental and comparative perspectives* (pp. 171–195). Mahwah, NJ: Erlbaum.

Au, T. K., Dapretto, M., & Song, Y. (1994). Input vs. constraints: Early word acquisition in Korean and English. *Journal of Memory and Language, 33,* 567–582.

Baillargeon, R. (2004). Infants' reasoning about hidden objects: Evidence for event-general and event-specific expectations. *Developmental Science, 7,* 391–424.

Balaban, M. T., & Waxman, S. R. (1997). Do words facilitate object categorization in 9-month-old infants? *Journal of Experimental Child Psychology, 64,* 3–26.

Baldwin, D. A., Baird, J. A., Saylor, M. M., & Clark, M. A. (2001). Infants parse dynamic action. *Child Development, 72,* 708–717.

Baldwin, D. A., & Markman, E. M. (1989). Establishing word-object relations: A first step. *Child Development, 60,* 381–398.

Bornstein, M. H. (1985). Habituation of attention as a measure of visual information processing in human infants: Summary, systematization, and synthesis. In G. Gottlieb & N. A. Krasnegor (Eds.), *Measurement of audition and vision in the first year of postnatal life: A methodological overview* (pp. 253–299). Stanford, CT: Ablex.

Bornstein, M., Cote, L., Maital, S., Painter, K., Park, S. Y., Pascual, L., et al. (2004). Cross-linguistic analysis of vocabulary in young children: Spanish, Dutch, French, Hebrew, Italian, Korean and American English. *Child Development, 75,* 1115–1140.

Bowerman, M. (1996). Learning how to structure space for language: A crosslinguistic perspective. In P. Bloom, M. A. Peterson, L. Nadel, & M. F. Garrett (Eds.). *Language and space: Language, speech, and communication* (pp. 385–436). Cambridge, MA: MIT Press.

Carpenter, M., Nagell, K., & Tomasello, M. (1998). Social cognition, joint attention, and communicative competence from 9 to 15 months of age. *Monographs of the Society for Research in Child Development, 63*(4, Serial No. 255).

Casasola, M., & Cohen, L. B. (2002). Infant categorization of containment, support and tight-fit spatial relationships. *Developmental Science, 5,* 247–264.

Casasola, M., Hohenstein, J., & Naigles, L. R. (2003, April). Ten-month-old infants' discrimination of manner and path in motion events. In M. Casasola (Chair), *From infancy to adulthood: Exploring the effect of linguistic input on the discrimination of manner and path in motion events.* Symposium conducted at the Society for Research in Child Development Biennial Meeting, Tampa, FL.

Casasola, M., Hohenstein, J. M., & Naigles, L. (2005). Infants' discrimination of manner and path in motion events. Manuscript in preparation.

Caselli, M. C., Bates, E., Casadio, P., & Fenson, J. (1995). A cross-linguistic study of early lexical development. *Cognitive Development, 10,* 159–199.

Choi, S. (1998). Verbs in early lexical and syntactic development in Korean. *Linguistics, 36,* 755–780.

Choi, S., & Bowerman, M. (1991). Learning to express motion events in English and Korean: The influence of language-specific lexicalization patterns. *Cognition, 42,* 83–121.

Choi, S., & Gopnik, A. (1995). Early acquisition of verbs in Korean: A cross-linguistic study. *Journal of Child Language, 22,* 497–529.

Choi, S., McDonough, L., Bowerman, M., & Mandler, J. M. (1999). Early sensitivity to language-specific spatial categories in English and Korean. *Cognitive Development, 14,* 241–268.

Cohen, L. B., & Oakes, L. M. (1993). How infants perceive a simple causal event. *Developmental Psychology, 29,* 421–433.

Fenson, L., Dale, P. S., Reznick, J. S., & Bates, E. (1994). Variability in early communicative development. *Monographs of the Society for Research in Child Development, 59*(5, Serial No. 242).

Fenson, L., Pethick, S., Renda, C., Cox, J. L., Dale, P. S., & Reznick, J. S. (2000) Short form versions of the MacArthur Communicative Development Inventories. *Applied Psycholinguistics, 21,* 95-115.

Gentner, D. (1982). Why nouns are learned before verbs: Linguistic relativity versus natural partitioning. In S. A. Kuczaj, II (Ed.), *Language development: Vol. 2. Language, thought, and culture* (pp. 301–334). Hillsdale, NJ: Lawrence Erlbaum.

Gentner, D., & Boroditsky, L. (2001). Individuation, relativity, and early word learning. In S. C. Levinson (Series Ed.), M. Bowerman & S. C. Levinson (Vol. Eds.), *Language, culture, and cognition: Vol. 3. Language acquisition and conceptual development* (pp. 215–256). New York: Cambridge University Press.

Gillette, J., Gleitman, H., Gleitman, L., & Lederer, A. (1999). Human simulations of vocabulary learning. *Cognition, 73,* 135–176.

Golinkoff, R. M., Chung, H. L., Hirsh-Pasek, K., Liu, J., Bertenthal, B. I., Brand, R., et al. (2002). Young children can extend motion verbs to point-light displays. *Developmental Psychology, 38,* 604–614.

Golinkoff, R. M., Harding, C. G., Carlson-Luden, V., & Sexton, M. E. (1984). The infant's perception of causal events: The distinction between animate and inanimate objects. (Part of above symposium). In L. P. Lipsitt (Ed.), *Advances in infancy research* (Vol. 3, pp. 145–151). Norwood, NJ: Ablex.

Golinkoff, R. M., Hirsh-Pasek, K., Bailey, L., & Wenger, N. (1992). Young children and adults use lexical principles to learn new nouns. *Developmental Psychology, 28,* 99–108.

Golinkoff, R. M., Jacquet, R. C., Hirsh-Pasek, K., & Nandakumar, R. (1996). Lexical principles may underlie the learning of verbs. *Child Development, 67,* 3101–3119.

Hespos, S. J., & Spelke, E. S. (2004). Conceptual precursors to language. *Nature, 430,* 453–456.

Hirsh-Pasek, K., & Golinkoff, R. M. (1996). *The origins of grammar: Evidence from early language comprehension.* Cambridge, MA: MIT Press.

Imai, M., Haryu, E., & Okada, H. (2002). Is verb learning easier than noun learning for Japanese children?: 3-year-old Japanese children's knowledge about object names and action names. *Proceedings of the 26th annual Boston University Conference on Language Development,* 324–335).

Imai, M., Haryu, E., & Okada, H. (2005). Mapping novel nouns and verbs onto dynamic action events: Are verb meanings easier to learn than noun meanings for Japanese children? *Child Development, 76,* 340–355.

Jackendoff, R. (1983). *Semantics and cognition.* Cambridge, MA: MIT Press.

Kellman, P. J., Spelke, E. S., & Short, K. R. (1986). Infant perception of object unity from translatory motion in depth and vertical translation. *Child Development, 57,* 72–86.

Kotovsky, L., & Baillargeon, R. (2000). Reasoning about collisions involving inert objects in 7.5-month-old infants. *Developmental Science, 3,* 344–359.

Landau, B. (1996). Multiple geometric representations of objects in languages and language learners. In P. Bloom, M. A. Peterson, L. Nadel, & M. F. Garrett (Eds.),

Language and space: Language, speech, and communication (pp. 317–363). Cambridge, MA: MIT Press.

Landau, B., & Jackendoff, R. (1993). "What" and "where" in spatial language and spatial cognition. *Behavioral and Brain Sciences, 16,* 217–265.

Langacker, R. W. (1987). Nouns and verbs. *Language, 63,* 53–94.

Mandler, J. M. (1991). Prelinguistic primitives. *Proceedings of the 17th Annual Meeting of the Berkeley Linguistics Society,* 414–425.

Mandler, J. M. (1992). How to build a baby: II. Conceptual primitives. *Psychological Review, 99,* 587–604.

Mandler, J. M. (2004). *The foundations of mind: Origins of conceptual thought.* New York: Oxford University Press.

McDonough, L., Choi, S., & Mandler, J. M. (2003). Understanding spatial relations: Flexible infants, lexical adults. *Cognitive Psychology, 46,* 229–259.

Meints, K., Plunkett, K., Harris, P. L., & Dimmock, D. (2002). What is "on" and "under" for 15-, 18- and 24-month-olds? Typical effects in early comprehension of spatial prepositions. *British Journal of Developmental Psychology, 20,* 113–130.

Meyer, M., Leonard, S., Hirsh-Pasek, K., Imai, M., Haryu, R., Pulverman, R., et al. (2003, November). *Making a convincing argument: A cross-linguistic comparison of noun and verb learning in Japanese and English.* Poster session presented at the 28th Annual Boston University Conference on Language Development, Boston, MA.

Nelson, K. (1973). Structure and strategy in learning to talk. *Monographs of the Society for Research in Child Development, 38*(1–2, Serial No. 149).

Oakes, L. M., & Rakison, D. H. (2003). Issues in the early development of concepts and categories: An introduction. In D. H. Rakison & L. M. Oakes (Eds.), *Early category and concept development: Making sense of the blooming, buzzing confusion* (pp. 3–23). New York: Oxford University Press.

Poulin-Dubois, D., Lepage, A., & Ferland, D. (1996). Infants' concept of animacy. *Cognitive Development, 11,* 19–36.

Pruden, S. M., Hirsh-Pasek, K., Maguire, M. J., & Meyer, M. A. (2004). Foundations of verb learning: Infants categorize path and manner in motion events. *Proceedings of the 28th Annual Boston University Conference on Language Development.*

Pruden, S. M., Pulverman, R., Hirsh-Pasek, K., & Golinkoff, R. M. (2003, April). *Pathways to verb learning: Preverbal infants form action categories.* Poster session presented at the Society for Research in Child Development Biennial Meeting, Tampa, FL.

Pulverman, R., Brandone, A., & Salkind, S. J. (2004, November). *One-year-old English speakers increase their attention to manner of motion in a potential verb learning situation.* Paper presented at the 29th Annual Boston University Conference on Language Development, Boston, MA.

Pulverman, R., & Golinkoff, R. M. (2004). Seven-month-olds' attention to potential verb referents in nonlinguistic events. *Proceedings of the 28th Annual Boston University Conference on Language Development,* 473–480.

Pulverman, R., Golinkoff, R. M., Hirsh-Pasek, K., & Jackson-Maldonado, J. (2005, April). Linguistic relativity in one-year-olds? *English- and Spanish-learning infants' attention to manner and path in silent events.* Poster presented at the Society for Research in Child Development Biennial Meeting, Atlanta, GA.

Pulverman, R., Golinkoff, R. M., Hirsh-Pasek, K., & Sootsman-Buresh, J. L. (2005). *Manners matter: Relating lexical acquisition and event processing.* Manuscript under review.

Pulverman, R., Sootsman, J. L., Golinkoff, R. M., & Hirsh-Pasek, K. (2003). The role of lexical knowledge in nonlinguistic event processing: English-speaking infants' attention to manner and path. *Proceedings of the 27th Annual Boston University Conference on Language Development*, 662–673.

Quinn, P. C., Cummins, M., Kase, J., Martin, E., & Weissman, S. (1996). Development of categorical representations for *above* and *below* spatial relations in 3- to 7-month-old infants. *Developmental Psychology, 32*, 942–950.

Quinn, P. C., Norris, C. M., Pasko, R. N., Schmader, T. M., & Mash, C. (1999). Formation of a categorical representation for the spatial relation *between* by 6- to 7-month-old infants. *Visual Cognition, 6*, 569–585.

Rakison, D. H. (2003). Parts, motion, and the development of the animate-inanimate distinction in infancy. In D. H. Rakison & L. M. Oakes (Eds.), *Early category and concept development: Making sense of the blooming, buzzing confusion* (pp. 159–192). New York: Oxford University Press.

Rakison, D. H., & Oakes, L. M. (Eds.). (2003). *Early category and concept development: Making sense of the blooming, buzzing confusion.* New York: Oxford University Press.

Rochat, P., & Hespos, S. J. (1996). Tracking and anticipation of invisible spatial transformation by 4–8-month-old infants. *Cognitive Development, 11*, 3–17.

Salkind, S. J. (2003, April). *Do you see what I see?* Paper presented at the 4th Annual University of Delaware Linguistics and Cognitive Science Graduate Student Conference, Newark, DE.

Salkind, S. J., Golinkoff, R. M., & Brandone, A. (2005, April). Infants' attention to novel actions in relation to the conflation patterns of motion verbs. In R. M. Golinkoff & K. Hirsh-Pasek (Chairs), *Action packed for language: Prelinguistic foundations for learning relational terms.* Symposium at the Society for Research in Child Development Biennial Meeting, Atlanta, GA.

Salkind, S. J., Sootsman, J. L., Golinkoff, R. M., Hirsh-Pasek, K., & Maguire, M. J. (2002, April). *Lights, camera, action! Infants and toddlers create action categories.* Poster presented at the International Conference on Infant Studies, Toronto, Canada.

Sharon, T., & Wynn, K. (1998). Individuation of actions from continuous motion. *Psychological Science, 9*, 357–362.

Slater, A. (1989). Visual memory and perception in early infancy. In A. Slater & G. Bremner (Eds.), *Infant development* (pp. 43–71). Hillsdale, NJ: Lawrence Erlbaum.

Slobin, D. I. (2001, April). *The child learns to think for speaking: Puzzles of crosslinguistic diversity in form-meaning mappings.* Paper presented at the meeting of the Society for Research in Child Development, Minneapolis, MN.

Smith, W. C., Johnson, S. P., & Spelke, E. S. (2003). Motion and edge sensitivity in perception of object unity. *Cognitive Psychology, 46*, 31–64.

Snedeker, J., & Gleitman, L. R. (2004). Why is it hard to label our concepts? In D. G. Hall & S. R. Waxman (Eds.), *Weaving a lexicon* (p. 293). Cambridge, MA: MIT Press.

Stager, C. L., & Werker, J. F. (1997). Infants listen for more phonetic detail in speech perception than in word-learning tasks. *Nature, 388*, 381–382.

Talmy, L. (1985). Lexicalization patterns: Semantic structure in lexical forms. In T. Shopen (Ed.), *Language typology and the lexicon: Vol. III. Grammatical categories and the lexicon* (pp. 57–149). Cambridge: Cambridge University Press.

Tardif, T. (1996). Nouns are not always learned before verbs: Evidence from Mandarin speakers' early vocabularies. *Developmental Psychology, 32*, 492–504.

Tomasello, M. (1992). *First verbs: A case study of early grammatical development.* New York: Cambridge University Press.

Wang, S., Kaufman, L., & Baillargeon, R. (2003). Should all stationary objects move when hit? Developments in infants' causal and statistical expectations about collision events. *Infant Behavior and Development, 26*, 529–567.

Waxman, S. R. (2003). Links between object categorization and naming: Origins and emergence in human infants. In D. H. Rakison & L. M. Oakes (Eds.) *Early category and concept development: Making sense of the blooming, buzzing confusion* (pp. 213–241). New York: Oxford University Press.

Waxman, S. R., & Markow, D. (1995). Words as invitations to form categories: Evidence from 12- to 13-month-old infants. *Cognitive Development, 29,* 257–302.

Werker, J. F., Cohen, L. B., Lloyd, V. L., Casasola, M., & Stager, C. L. (1998). Acquisition of word-object associations by 14-month-old infants. *Developmental Psychology, 34,* 1289–1309.

6   Precursors to Verb Learning: Infants' Understanding of Motion Events

Marianella Casasola, Jui Bhagwat, and Kim T. Ferguson

By the time they begin acquire language, infants have accumulated a fair amount of knowledge about their world. Perhaps for this reason, researchers who first studied language development believed that children's early words expressed concepts formed independently of language (e.g., Brown, 1973). However, the degree to which infants recruit existing concepts when acquiring language, particularly when it comes to those concepts expressed in verbs and other relational terms, has remained a controversial issue. Whereas some researchers maintain that these concepts are formed independently of language (e.g., Gleitman, 1990; Landau & Jackendoff, 1993; Mandler, 1996), others posit that linguistic input plays an important role in the development of these concepts (e.g., Bowerman & Choi, 2001; Choi, McDonough, Bowerman, & Mandler, 1999; Gentner & Boroditsky, 2001; Gopnik, Choi, & Baumberger, 1996). However, it is possible, as suggested by some researchers, that particular meanings may be formed independently of language while others require linguistic input to develop (Bowerman & Choi, 2001; Carey, 2001). In this chapter, we provide evidence for this last view, demonstrating how particular relational meanings are formed independently of language, whereas others require linguistic input to develop. However, we also add to this view by positing that the contribution of nonlinguistic versus linguistic input in the formation of relational meanings varies not only with the concept in question but also with the developmental point at which the concept begins to develop.

Our goal for this chapter is threefold. We first review the current literature on infants' understanding of motion events, demonstrating that young infants possess a rich understanding of various types of motion events. Findings from our own research show that infants are flexible in the discriminations they make and in the types of categorical representations of motion events that they can form. Second, we show that infants' perceptual and cognitive abilities do not provide them with an understanding of all action events. For particular action events, linguistic input plays an important role in aiding infants' understanding of these events and in organizing these events in a manner required for linguistic expression. As they begin to comprehend relational terms, infants begin to use language to help them acquire a more complete understanding of particular relational meanings. Nonlinguistic processes nonetheless continue to play a central role, but begin to work in conjunction with language in the development of particular relational meanings. Finally, we delineate a developmental progression for infants' understanding of motion events. Specifically, we will demonstrate how developmental changes in infants' ability to form an abstract categorical representation of a dynamic spatial event follows a specific-to-abstract progression, and that language exerts its influence on infants' discrimination and categorization of particular motion events by modulating this progression. Thus, we will demonstrate how the sources of input vary from nonlinguistic input to linguistic input but that the developmental progression remains consistent from the preverbal to the verbal period.

Infants' Nonlinguistic Abilities in Acquiring an Understanding of Motion Events

Young Infants' Discrimination of Motion Events

A large body of research currently exists documenting infants' discrimination and conceptual understanding of motion events. The results of these studies reveal that newborn infants show a preference for moving stimuli over static ones (Slater, 1989) and that they can visually track simple moving stimuli, particularly those with facelike configurations (Morton & Johnson, 1991). Infants use motion to learn about objects. For example, infants depend on movement to develop a concept of animacy (Mandler, 1992; Rakison, 2003; Rakison & Poulin-Dubois, 2001; Spelke, Phillips, & Woodward, 1995), perceive object unity (Johnson & Aslin, 1995; Johnson, Cohen, Marks, & Johnson, 2003; Kellman & Spelke, 1983; Kellman, Spelke, & Short, 1986; Smith, Johnson, & Spelke, 2003), and discriminate between upright and inverted versions of point-light displays of a walking person (Bertenthal, Proffitt, & Cutting, 1984). Motion also seems to be important in the acquisition of object labels. Fourteen-month-old infants map words onto moving but not stationary objects (Werker, Cohen, Lloyd, Casasola, & Stager, 1998). Given the degree to which movement attracts infants' attention (Haith, 1980), it is not surprising that it is so effective in facilitating infants' ability to learn about their environment.

However, most studies that present infants with motion events have focused on infants use of motion to learn about objects. Significantly fewer studies have examined young infants' understanding of motion itself or action events. Gibson, Owsley, and Johnston (1978) found that 5-month-old infants can detect the invariant property of a rigid motion and can differentiate this motion from a novel motion. Bahrick, Gogate, and Ruiz (2002) found that 5-month-old infants discriminate between different repetitive actions performed by an actor (e.g., brushing hair or blowing bubbles). In addition, several studies have documented that infants as young as 6 discriminate between causal versus noncausal launching events (Cohen & Amsel, 1998; Leslie, 1984; Leslie & Keeble, 1987; Oakes, 1994). Studies of infant causal perception have pitted perceptual differences in the launching events against qualitative differences in the causal relation between the objects and have shown that 6-month-old infants respond on the basis of causality rather than the simple perceptual differences among the events.

Discriminating Motion Events Expressed Differently Across Languages

More recently, researchers have begun to investigate infants' discrimination of motion events that differ in how they are described across languages (e.g., Pulverman, Sootsman, Golinkoff, & Hirsh-Pasek, 2002). The research has been inspired, in large part, by the writings of Talmy (1975, 1983, 1985), who described how languages differ in their lexicalization of the components of motion events. Other than the motion itself, Talmy found that the main verb in a given language could also express the figure (the object in motion), the ground (the source, goal, or location of motion), the path (the course followed by the figure), the manner (the way the figure moves), and the cause (whether the motion is agentive or not). For instance, in satellite-framed languages, such as English, one would say, "The girl ran out of the house" where the verb *ran* is an instance of the manner encoded in the verb and the path encoded by a satellite *out*. In contrast, in a verb-framed language, such as Spanish, one would be more likely to say, "La niña entró a la casa corriendo" (The girl entered the house running), where the main verb, *entró*, combines motion with the path of the event, while the manner of the motion is described as a gerund, *corriendo* (Talmy, 1975, 1985; see also Aske, 1989; Berman & Slobin, 1994; Slobin & Hoiting, 1994).

Naigles, Eisenberg, Kako, Highter, and McGraw (1998) found that English and Spanish speakers do differ according to the patterns described by Talmy (1975, 1985). They found that adult English speakers overwhelmingly described a motion event by selecting the manner rather than the path, whereas the Spanish speakers were much more likely to describe the path rather than the manner of motion in the same events. Naigles and Terrazas (1998) found the same to be true with a novel motion event. Although the syntactic frame influenced adult English and Spanish speakers' interpretation of the novel motion verb, speakers of each language were clearly influenced by the predominant semantic pattern of their language when deciding the possible meaning of the novel verb.

Does attention to manner versus path develop from experience with a particular language or does language only direct attention to one component over another? In collaboration with Jill Hohenstein and Letitia Naigles, we explored whether preverbal English-learning infants of 6 and 10 months could discriminate manner and path in a motion event (Casasola, Hohenstein, & Naigles, 2005). Infants viewed manners and paths rated as highly distinct by adult English speakers. Infants were habituated to a single motion event, a video of a girl moving in a particular manner (e.g., skipping) and in a particular path (e.g., toward a bush). Infants then were tested with an event with a familiar manner and familiar path (i.e., the habituation event), an event with a novel manner (e.g., crawling), an event with a novel path (e.g., movement away from the bush), and an event with both a novel manner and a novel path (e.g., the girl crawling away from the bush). Both the 6- and 10-month-old infants easily discriminated the change in manner and the change in path. However, only the 10-month-old infants demonstrated a significant increase in looking time to the novel-manner and novel-path event relative to the events with only a novel manner or only a novel path. This result suggests that, while infants are able to discriminate changes in manner and path by 6 months of age, they do not begin to respond to these elements as distinct components until 10 months of age. The results also indicate that infants do not require experience with English to attend to manner or with Spanish to attend to path but are sensitive to these elements well before they begin to learn words for these events.

Just as the work of Talmy (1983) inspired researchers to begin to explore infants' discrimination of manner and path, Choi and Bowerman's (1991) cross-linguistic study of young Korean- and English-speaking children's descriptions of motion events led researchers to study the spatial concepts available to preverbal infants. Choi and Bowerman found that young Korean- and English-learning toddlers differed in how they organized motion events into semantic spatial categories. Whereas Korean-learning children used the Korean morpheme *kkita* to describe actions resulting in a tight-fitting relation between two objects, such as placing a book in its cover or placing one Lego block on another, English-learning infants described these same dynamic events with the English locative terms *in* and *on*, respectively. This difference is apparent in comprehension as well. Using a preferential-looking paradigm, Choi et al. (1999) found that Korean-learning toddlers comprehended *kkita* as referring to both tight-fit containment and tight-fit support events, whereas English-learning toddlers comprehended *in* as referring to both tight-fit containment and loose-fit containment events. Hence, by their second birthday, English- and Korean-learning toddlers have begun to acquire the semantic spatial categories specific to their language, attending to the spatial distinctions that are linguistically relevant and disregarding those spatial distinctions that are not.

The results reported by Choi and Bowerman (1991) as well as Choi et al. (1999) raise the question of how children acquire the meanings expressed in the English morpheme *in* and the Korean morpheme *kkita*. Do all infants, regardless of linguistic environment, display a sensitivity to the spatial relations of containment and tight fit? There is experimental evidence to suggest that this is the case.

Spelke and Hespos (2002) found that English-learning infants of 5 months discriminate between the action of placing an object in a tight-fit containment relation to a small container and in a loose-fit containment relation to a larger container. Similarly, McDonough, Choi, and Mandler (2003) found that 9-, 11-, and 14-month-old Korean- and English-learning infants could form a spatial category of tight-fit containment events as distinct from a spatial category of loose-fit containment events, demonstrating that, regardless of linguistic background, infants are sensitive to the distinction between tight- and loose-fit containment. Hence, there is converging evidence that preverbal infants can discriminate among a number of spatial distinctions (see also Quinn, 1994; Quinn, Adams, Kennedy, Shettler, & Wasnik, 2003; Quinn, Cummins, Kase, Martin, & Weisman, 1996), including those that are not lexically encoded by their language. Hence, experience with a particular language is not a necessary precursor for infants' ability to discriminate between particular motion events, even when these motion events vary in whether they are lexically encoded.

Forming Spatial Categories Consistent With Semantic Categories

Although infants do not require experience with a particular language to discriminate among particular motion events, a separate question is how infants learn to group spatial events into language-specific semantic spatial categories. When learning to form semantic spatial categories, infants must learn to attend to one type of relation while disregarding other types of relations that may be present. For example, in learning to apply the spatial term *in* to the appropriate array of events, English-learning infants must learn to attend to the containment relation and disregard the distinction between tight-fit containment and loose-fit containment because the English semantic category of *in* includes both types of containment events. The same holds true for infants' acquisition of the semantic category of *on* with tight-fit and loose-fit support. Similarly, infants learning the Korean term *kkita* must attend to the tight-fit distinction and to group tight-fit containment and tight-fit support into a single semantic category. Consequently, infants must not only discriminate a particular spatial relation from another relation, they must also be flexible in how these relations are combined to form either more inclusive or more exclusive spatial categories, depending on the semantic pattern of their language.

To explore infants' ability in grouping the same set of spatial events according to different semantic patterns, English-learning infants of 10 and 18 months were tested on their ability to form a spatial category consistent with the semantic spatial categories of *in*, *on*, or *kkita* (Casasola & Cohen, 2002). During habituation, infants were randomly assigned to view four objects pairs in a containment, support, or tight-fit relation. In the containment and support conditions, infants viewed both tight-fit and loose-fit examples of the relations. Similarly, in the tight-fit condition, infants viewed tight-fit containment and tight-fit support events. Hence, to form each spatial category, infants had to attend to the consistent relation, but disregard the other relations that varied, a task analogous to learning to form the semantic categories of *in, on,* and *kkita.* Following habituation, infants viewed four test trials: an event with familiar objects in a familiar relation, an event with familiar object in a novel relation, an event with novel objects in the familiar relation, and an event with novel objects in a novel relation. The experimental design of the study is presented in table 6.1 with the habituation events described in the top half of the table and the test events in the bottom half of the table.

Both the 10- and the 18-month-old infants habituated to the containment relation demonstrated significantly longer looking times to the novel versus familiar relation, regardless of whether the objects depicting the relation were familiar or novel. This result can be seen in figure 6.1. Because infants' recognition of containment was not tied to familiar objects, they demonstrated that they had formed an abstract categorical representation of containment. In contrast, neither the 10- nor the 18-month-old infants provided evidence of forming a spatial category of support or tight-fit. As is apparent in figures 6.2 and 6.3, 10-month-old infants tended to discriminate between the familiar and novel objects but provided no evidence of discriminating a change in either the support or the tight-fit spatial relation. On the other hand, the 18-month-olds in the support and tight-fit conditions discriminated between the familiar and a novel spatial relation, but only when the objects depicting this relation were familiar (i.e., those seen during habituation). Thus, because infants' recognition of support and tight-fit was dependent

Table 6.1 The experimental design of Casasola and Cohen (2002)

	Condition		
	Containment	Support	Tight-fit
Habituation Event 1:	*Animal in*	*Car on*	**Candle in**
Habituation Event 2:	*Car in*	*Cup on*	**Lego on**
Habituation Event 3:	**Candle in**	*Toy man on*	**Peg in**
Habituation Event 4:	**Peg in**	*Turtle on*	**Toy man on**
Test Event 1: Familiar Objects-Familiar Relation	**Candle in**	Turtle on	Candle in
Test Event 2: Novel Objects-Familiar Relation	Cup in	Peg on	**Turtle on**
Test Event 3: Familiar Objects-Novel Relation	Peg on	Cup in	Peg on
Test Event 4: Novel Objects-Novel Relation	**Turtle on**	Candle in	Cup in

The habituation events are presented in italics in the top portion of the table and the test events are presented in roman type in the bottom half of the table. Events presented in boldface type have a tight-fit relation between the objects.

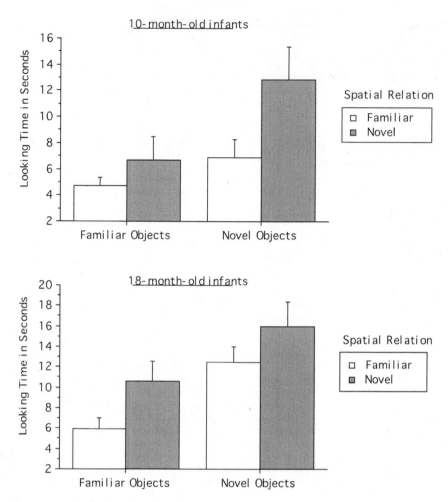

Figure 6.1. The looking times with standard errors of 10- and 18-month-old infants in the containment condition of Casasola and Cohen (2002) to the familiar versus novel spatial relation when the objects were familiar and when they were novel.

on familiar objects, they did not form an abstract categorical representation of these relations.

In sum, these results demonstrate that infants of 10 and 18 months can form an abstract categorical representation of containment, but do not form abstract categorical representations of support or tight-fit (Casasola & Cohen, 2002). The results suggest that preverbal infants are flexible in forming some semantic categories (i.e., containment) but not others (i.e., support or tight-fit). Even 6-month-old infants provided evidence of forming an abstract categorical representation of

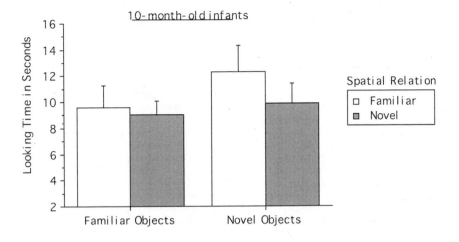

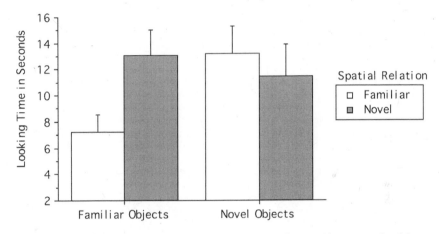

Figure 6.2. The looking times with standard errors of 10- and 18-month-old infants in the support condition of Casasola and Cohen (2002) to the familiar versus novel spatial relation when the objects were familiar and when they were novel.

containment when tested in the same task (Casasola, Cohen, & Chiarello, 2003). However, one concern was that infants relied on simple perceptual cues to discriminate between containment and support events. When habituated to containment events, infants saw the figure (i.e., the object placed in a containment relation) become partially occluded, but the figure never became occluded when placed in a support relation. Hence, infants may have simply responded to perceptual changes in the figure (i.e., becoming occluded during habituation but not during

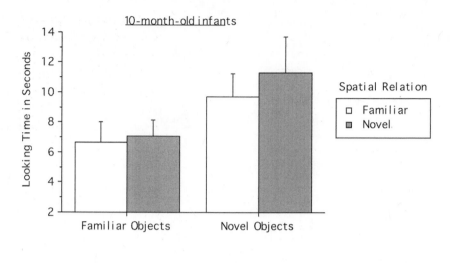

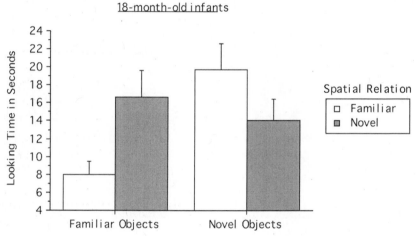

Figure 6.3. The looking times with standard errors of 10- and 18-month-old infants in the tight-fit condition of Casasola and Cohen (2002) to the familiar versus novel spatial relation when the objects were familiar and when they were novel.

the test) rather than to the spatial relation. To rule out this possibility, infants of 6 months were habituated to a single containment event. They then were tested with four test events. The final frame of each test event can be seen in figure 6.4. One test event presented the habituation containment event. A second test event presented a containment event from a higher angle so that the figure was clearly contained but did not become occluded by the container. In a third test event, the figure was placed behind the referent object, so that the figure was as occluded as it had been during habituation but in a novel spatial relation. In a fourth test

Front-angle containment event

High-angle containment event

High-angle behind event

Figure 6.4. One example of the habituation and test events presented to the 6-month-old infants tested in Casasola et al. (2003).

High-angle support event

event, infants viewed the figure placed on the inverted basket so that there was a change in both the occlusion amount of the figure as well as the spatial relation (i.e., support). As can be seen in figure 6.5, the 6-month-olds dishabituated only to the novel relation and not to a change in the occlusion amount of the figure, indicating that infants do not rely on simple perceptual cues to discriminate between

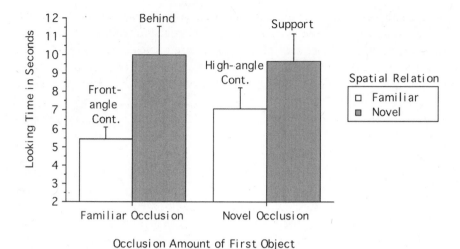

Figure 6.5. The looking times with standard errors of the 6-month-old infants in Casasola et al. (2003) to the familiar versus novel spatial relation when the amount of occlusion was familiar and when it was novel.

containment and support events. Rather, infants can recognize a containment relation across a number of different object pairs and from two different angles.

What Drives Infants' Understanding of Spatial Categorization?

The Role of Perceptual Variability

When the various studies on infants' ability to form an abstract spatial category of containment are viewed together, the results suggest that infants are flexible in how they group containment events into a spatial category. Although infants discriminate between tight-fit containment and loose-fit containment events (McDonough et al., 2003; Spelke & Hespos, 2002), they also are capable of treating these different types of containment relations as equivalent (Casasola & Cohen, 2002; Casasola et al., 2003). Hence, infants form more inclusive or more exclusive categories of containment as a function of the diversity of the exemplars seen during familiarization, analogous to their ability to form more inclusive or exclusive categories of objects (Colombo, McCollam, Coldren, Mitchell, & Rash, 1990). For example, Quinn, Eimas, and Rosenkranz (1993) found that young infants form a category of dogs that excluded cats when the dogs were perceptually similar but not when the dogs were perceptually diverse. Similarly, Oakes, Coppage, and Dingel (1997) demonstrated that infants form more inclusive object categories when the perceptual variability among the exemplars was high, but form more exclusive categories when the perceptual variability among the familiarization exemplars was low. Likewise, if familiarized with only tight-fit containment or only loose-fit containment

(McDonough et al., 2003), infants form an exclusive category of containment, one that discriminates between tight-fit and loose-fit containment. However, if familiarized with both tight-fit and loose-fit containment events (Casasola & Cohen, 2002), infants form a more inclusive category of containment, one that includes both types of containment but excludes other types of spatial relations. The similarity between infants' categorization of objects and their categorization of spatial relations suggests an overlap in the processes underlying infants' categorization across domains.

Does Perceptual Variability Matter in Forming a Spatial Category of Support?

One reason that infants did not form a category of support or tight fit may be because infants in these conditions formed more inclusive categories, one that included the novel relation. For example, infants in the support condition viewed both loose-fit and tight-fit support events during habituation. The tight-fit support events (e.g., a Duplo man placed on a Duplo car) depicted a degree of insertion between the two objects, and infants may have considered the containment event, which has a greater degree of insertion, as corresponding to the support category. If the perceptual variability of the habituation exemplars influences the types of spatial categories that infants form, then infants may form an abstract categorical representation of support if habituated to only loose-fit support events, a support event with no degree of insertion between the objects and one that infants may discriminate as distinct from a containment relation.

To test this possibility, 14-month-old infants were habituated to four loose-fit support events (Casasola, 2005b) using the same design and procedure as Casasola and Cohen (2002). However, infants still did not form an abstract spatial category of support. Similar to the 18-month-olds tested with support by Casasola and Cohen (2002), infants discriminated between the familiar support relation and a novel containment relation only when familiar objects depicting the relations and not novel objects were used. Thus, reducing the perceptual variability of the support relation was not sufficient to facilitate infants' ability to form an abstract categorical representation of support. These results suggest that infants' difficulty with forming an abstract categorical representation of support does not lie with the amount of variability in the habituation events but rather, support appears to be a more difficult spatial category for infants to form than containment. Hence, infants acquire the ability to form particular spatial categories earlier in development than other spatial relations.

The Specific-to-Abstract Progression

How do infants learn to form an abstract categorical representation of a spatial relation? In their research exploring infants' ability to form an abstract categorical representation of above versus below as well as between, Quinn and his colleagues found that 3-month-old infants formed a categorical representation of above versus below only when familiar objects, those seen during familiarization, were used to depict the familiar and novel relations (Quinn, Polly, Furer, Dobson, & Narter, 2002). In contrast, 6-month-old infants formed a categorical representation of these relations when novel objects (i.e., those not seen during familiarization) depicted the familiar and novel relation (Quinn et al., 1996). Similarly, 6-month-old infants depend on familiar objects to discriminate the relation of between from a different relation whereas 9-month-old infants can do so with novel objects (Quinn et al., 2003). Based on these findings, they propose that infants' recognition of a spatial relation proceeds from concrete, with a reliance on familiar objects, to abstract, with infants gaining the ability to recognize a relation independent of familiar objects. Our own results fit with this progression (Casasola & Cohen, 2002). The 18-month-old infants' ability to recognize the support and tight-fit relations were tied to specific objects (i.e., it was concrete), whereas infants' recognition of the containment relation was independent of familiar objects (i.e., it was abstract).

However, the results of Casasola and Cohen (2002) suggested an additional step in the developmental progression. The 10-month-old infants tested on their ability to form a spatial category of support or tight-fit only provided evidence of discriminating between the two test trials with familiar objects and the two test trials with novel objects. These results suggested that infants first acquire the ability to attend to the objects in a dynamic spatial event prior to learning to discriminate the relation. Recent findings provide further evidence for this additional step in the specific-to-abstract progression. Casasola (2005b) randomly assigned 14-month-old infants to view two, four, or six object pairs in a support relation during habituation using the same design and procedure as Casasola and Cohen (2002). The results indicate that the number of object pairs seen during habituation influenced infants' ability to attend to the support relation. Infants who viewed six exemplars during habituation only discriminated the change in objects (see the bottom graph of figure 6.6), the first step in the progression. Infants who viewed four object pairs during habituation only discriminated the spatial relation with familiar but not novel objects, the second step in the progression (see the middle graph of figure 6.6). Finally, infants who viewed two object pairs during habituation discriminated between the familiar and novel relations when the objects were familiar and when they were novel, the last step in the progression (see the top graph of figure 6.6). That is, these infants formed an abstract categorical representation of support, performing at a more developmentally advanced level than the other 14-month-old infants and the 18-month-old infants tested by Casasola and Cohen (2002). Thus, as the number of habituation object pairs decreased, infants advanced further along the specific-to-abstract progression. These results provide further evidence that this progression describes how infants learn to form abstract categorical spatial representation (Casasola, 2005b).

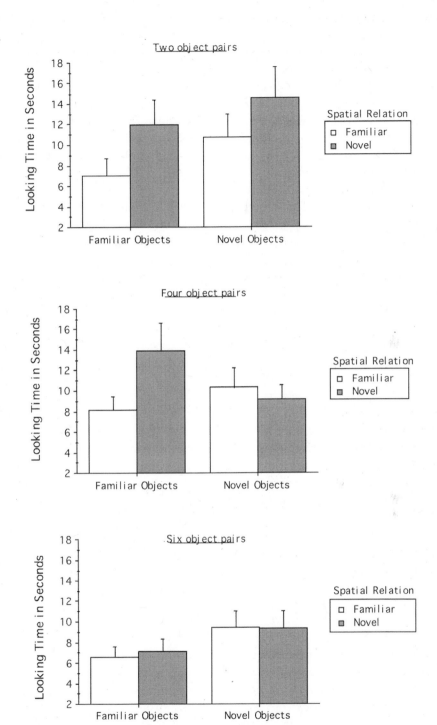

Figure 6.6. The looking times with standard errors of the 14-month-old infants in each condition of Casasola (2005b) to the familiar versus novel spatial relation when the objects were familiar and when they were novel.

Why does the number of object pairs matter for infants learning to form an abstract categorical representation of a spatial relation? The number of object pairs may be important when the relation is not as salient to infants as the objects in the events. Thus, progressively increasing the number of object pairs during habituation, as was the case for infants who were habituated to six object pairs, diverted infants' attention from the support relation to the objects. However, if only two object pairs depicted the support relation, then infants had ample opportunity during habituation to become familiar with the object pairs and then shift their attention to the support relation, providing one explanation for why these infants formed an abstract categorical representation of support. Thus, how salient a spatial event (or any motion event) is relative to the objects is an important factor to consider in how infants learn to discriminate the event as well as form an abstract categorical representation of the event. However, the relative salience of an event versus an object varies across events. There are cases where the motion is more salient than an agent, as was the case in Bahrick et al.'s 2002 study, which found that 5-month-old infants recalled the type of repetitive action in an event, but not the individual person performing the action. There are, however, additional studies that have reported that the type and number of objects presented influence infants' attention to the motion event. For example, Oakes (1994) found that 6-month-old infants could discriminate between causal and noncausal motion events when simple objects, such as circles, were used in the events, but not when more complex objects, such as toy vehicles, were used (Oakes & Cohen, 1990). Ten-month-olds tested in the same study, however, did make this discrimination. Further, Cohen and Oakes (1993) found that 10-month-old infants no longer discriminated between causal and noncausal motion events when multiple object pairs were presented during habituation. Hence, a number of studies converge to demonstrate that the type or number of objects presented during habituation can influence infants' ability to attend to the type of motion event presented. In these cases, it may be because the event is not as salient (or available) to infants as the objects in the events. However, for events that are more salient than the objects, the objects in the events may not be as relevant to how infants learn to discriminate the event.

Developmental Trajectories for Spatial Action Events

The studies reported above demonstrate that infants as young as 6 months can form a category of containment but that infants do not learn to form a category of support until 14 months of age, and even so, only when two objects pairs are presented during habituation (Casasola, 2005b; Casasola et al., 2003). Although 6-month-old infants do not rely on simple perceptual cues to discriminate containment as a distinct relation from support or behind (Casasola et al., 2003), perceptual cues may play an important role in how infants learn to form abstract categorical representations. The perceptual cues associated with containment may be more salient than those associated with support. For example, having one object change in appearance when inserted into the ground object may draw infants' attention to the containment relation, helping them learn about the relation. What is more, containment events appear to be less variable than other relations. Although there are different types of containment events, each is easily defined by encirclement of one object by another. In their work with young children's understanding of verbal instructions with complex spatial relations (e.g., keys in a basket on a coffee table), Plumert and Hawkins (2001) raise this possibility to explain why 3-year-old children describe and find relations that include a containment relation (i.e., *in*) easier than proximity (i.e., *next to*). As young children encounter more difficult spatial tasks, the spatial relation of containment retains its primacy over other spatial relations. Together, the perceptual cues afforded by a containment relation may explain why infants learn to discriminate containment from other types of relations at an earlier point in development.

These possibilities have yet to be tested systematically, leaving open the question of what drives infants to acquire an understanding of particular motion events prior to others. Other researchers similarly have found that young infants demonstrate an understanding of particular types of relations or motion events earlier than others. For example, Quinn found that infants learn to form an abstract categorical representation of above versus below by 6 months but do not form an abstract categorical representation of between until 9 months (Quinn et al., 1996, 2003). Likewise, Hespos and Baillargeon (2001) found that while 3-month-old infants discriminate between physically impossible and impossible occlusion events, they provide no evidence of responding to the same violation in containment events until 7 months of age. Further, Baillargeon and Wang (2002) found that infants attend to particular physical violations in a containment event prior to a covering event. Despite the acquisition of particular concepts prior to others, the manner in which infants acquire the ability to form an abstract categorical representation of a spatial relation nevertheless follows the specific-to-abstract progression.

Are Infants' Nonlinguistic Abilities Enough for Acquiring Relational Meanings?

Taken together, the above findings add to a growing body of knowledge on infants' understanding of motion events. By 6 months, infants can form an abstract categorical representation of containment (Casasola et al., 2003) and above versus below (Quinn et al., 1996) and discriminate changes in manner and path in a motion event (Casasola et al., 2005). By 10 months, infants can form an abstract categorical representation of between (Quinn et al., 2003) and respond to manner and path as organized components of a motion event (Casasola et al., 2005). By 14 months, infants can form an abstract categorical representation of loose-fit support (Casasola, 2005b).

Preverbal infants clearly are acquiring the foundations for the meanings that will be expressed later in verb and other relational terms. However, infants do not acquire all meanings expressed across languages. Infants demonstrate the ability to form a spatial category of loose-fit support when habituated to two objects pairs in this relation (Casasola, 2005b) but do not demonstrate the ability to form a spatial category consistent with the semantic category of *on*, one that includes tight-fit and loose-fit support (Casasola & Cohen, 2002). Likewise, infants do not demonstrate the ability to form a spatial category consistent with the semantic category of *kkita*, one that includes tight-fit containment and tight-fit support. Although infants can discriminate specific instances of the spatial relations from novel relations, they have difficulty forming an abstract categorical representation of these relations. It may be, however, that infants do not learn to do so until motivated by language, a possibility we consider in the next section.

Infants' Understanding of Action Events: Is Language a Bootstrap?

Does Language Aid Infants' Categorization of Dynamic Spatial Events?

Choi and Bowerman (1991) have long argued for the importance of language in the development of young children's spatial concepts. Their study as well as Choi et al.'s (1999) study clearly demonstrate that toddlers are flexible in how they learn to group spatial events into the semantic spatial categories that are specific to their ambient language. Nevertheless, there has not been direct evidence demonstrating a causal link between infants' acquisition of an abstract categorical representation of a spatial relation and experience with specific linguistic input. Results from a study currently underway indicate that 18-month-old infants learning Korean can group tight-fit containment and tight-fit support into a single category, a category that neither 10-month-old infants learning Korean nor 10- or 18-month-old infants learning English can form (Casasola, 2002b). This difference between the younger and the older infants learning Korean as well as between the older infants learning Korean and the infants learning English suggest that it is the older Korean-learning infants' experience with the spatial morpheme *kkita* that aids them in forming a spatial category of tight fit. Of course, nonlinguistic factors, such as cultural differences in Korean and American adults' interaction with their infants, may account for these differences as well. When social and cultural factors are removed, is experience with a particular spatial word sufficient to aid infants in learning to form a spatial category?

Does a Familiar Word Facilitate Infants' Categorization of Support?

Recent work by Loewenstein and Gentner (2005) demonstrate that preschool children's performance on a spatial mapping task improves significantly when the children are provided with familiar labels, such as *in, on,* and *under*. Inspired by these findings, we explored whether the familiar spatial word *on* would lead 18-month-old infants to form an abstract categorical representation of support. Recall that 18-month-old infants have difficulty forming a spatial category of support when habituated to four object pairs in a support relation and when presented with both tight-fit and loose-fit examples of support (Casasola & Cohen, 2002). Based on Bowerman and Choi's (2001) argument and results reported by Loewenstein and Gentner (2005), we hypothesized that hearing a specific spatial word (e.g., *on*) with each example of the support relation during habituation would lead infants to form an abstract categorical representation of support, recognizing the support relation as familiar when depicted by familiar and novel objects. By 18 months, infants comprehend *on* as referring to support events (Meints, Plunkett, Harris, & Dimmock, 2002). Hence, infants of this age may use their experience with the spatial word *on* to attend to the support relation presented in the categorization task and consequently, form a spatial category of support.

Using the same stimuli and design as Casasola and Cohen (2002), infants were habituated to four objects pairs in a support relation, half tight-fit and half loose-fit (Casasola, 2005a). Infants were randomly assigned to one of four auditory conditions. Infants in the silent condition viewed the habituation and test events in silence, an exact replication of the support condition of Casasola and Cohen (2002). Infants in the familiar word condition heard the spatial word *on* presented with each example of support during habituation, in order to document whether adding a specific and familiar spatial word would facilitate infants' ability to form the spatial category of support. Infants in the general language condition heard phrases that directed their attention to the habituation events, but did not include a spatial word, in order to explore whether a facilitative effect of language was due to the presence of *on* or simply due to the presence of language. Infants in the novel word condition heard the novel word *toke* in order to explore if any spatial word would lead infants to attend to form the spatial category. For infants in each of the three language conditions, infants heard the same general, attention-getting phrases while viewing the same test events used in Casasola and Cohen (2002).

The looking times of infants to the familiar support relation versus a novel containment relation in each condition are presented in figure 6.7. Only infants who heard the familiar spatial word *on* during habituation looked significantly longer at the familiar versus novel relation. Additional analyses revealed that infants did so both when the objects were familiar and when they were novel. Thus, only these infants provided evidence of forming an abstract categorical representation of support. In contrast, infants in the general language and novel word conditions failed to discriminate between the familiar and novel relation, even when the objects were familiar. These infants only discriminated the change in objects. Hence, it is not the case that any type of linguistic input leads infants to form a spatial category. Rather, infants appear to use their previous experience with the meaning of the spatial word *on* to focus their attention on the relevant aspect of a dynamic event and facilitate their ability to form an abstract categorical

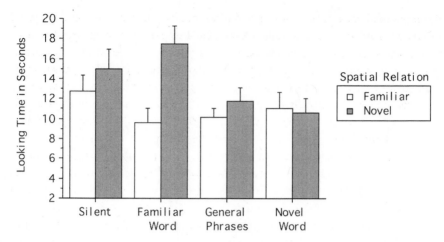

Figure 6.7. The looking times with standard errors of the 18-month-old infants in each condition of Casasola (2005a) to the familiar versus novel spatial relation.

representation of support. These results provide the first experimental evidence for Choi and Bowerman's (1991; Bowerman & Choi, 2001) claims that linguistic input can lead infants to acquire a spatial category that they do not form in the absence of linguistic input. The results also extend the findings reported by Loewenstein and Gentner (2005) by demonstrating that familiar spatial language can aid infants as young as 18 months as well.

Developmental Changes in the Effect of Language on Infants' Spatial Categorization

If infants require experience with spatial language to aid their spatial categorization, then younger infants, who have yet to begin to comprehend spatial locative terms, should demonstrate a very different pattern of response than older infants when provided with linguistic input. We tested infants of 10 months on their ability to form a spatial category of support when hearing the spatial word *on* during habituation, and a second group of 10-month-old infants on their ability to form a spatial category of containment when hearing the spatial word *in* during habituation (Casasola, 2002a). In contrast to the older infants (Casasola, 2005a), the 10-month-old infants did not form a spatial category of support. They also failed to form the spatial category of containment, even though they can form this category when viewing the events in silence (Casasola & Cohen, 2002). Hence, spatial words interfered with 10-month-old infants' ability to attend to the spatial relation. What is more, the infants also did not discriminate between the familiar and novel objects, suggesting that they were overloaded by the addition of the linguistic input.

Infants' difficulty with the task, however, was not due to simply adding linguistic input to the visual events. When general linguistic phrases were added to the habituation and test events in a second study, the 10-month-old infants now discriminated between the familiar and novel objects although they still provided no evidence of attending to the spatial relations. Hence, the general linguistic phrases still yielded a negative impact on infants' performance on the spatial categorization task but less so than when hearing the spatial word. Hence, infants perform most poorly when the spatial word *in* is presented, failing to respond to any changes. Adding linguistic input, and particularly a spatial word, creates too difficult a task for infants, seemingly overloading infants so that they no longer make discriminations they can make when viewing the events in silence. When 10-month-old infants were tested on their ability to form a spatial category of containment when presented with a novel spatial word, *toke*, infants again failed to discriminate changes in the spatial relation and objects. Hence, infants do require familiarity with a spatial word to facilitate their ability to form the spatial category.

In these studies, the novel word *toke* was presented in a very general verb frame, "It goes toke," which might have caused confusion as to the possible referent for the novel word. Although this same general verb frame was used to present the spatial word *on*, 18-month-old infants are familiar with the spatial word and could use their familiarity with the spatial term to direct their attention to the spatial relation. We tested 18-month-old infants on their ability to form a spatial category of support after hearing the novel spatial word *toke* during habituation (Casasola, 2002c), but this time in a verb frame that specified location (i.e., "She puts it toke"). The 18-month-old infants did form a spatial category of support, suggesting that when combined with a familiar verb frame, a novel spatial word can aid 18-month-old infants in forming an abstract categorical representation of support. Not surprisingly, 10-month-old infants do not benefit from hearing the novel spatial word *toke* presented in the verb frame "She puts it toke." Hence, infants must possess a certain degree of linguistic knowledge, either with respect to the specific spatial word presented or the verb frames that specify location (i.e., "She puts it X"), for a specific spatial word to aid their ability to form an abstract categorical representation. This knowledge appears to develop between 10 months and 18 months of age.

Revisiting the Specific-to-Abstract Progression

How does language influence infants' ability to form an abstract categorical representation of a spatial relation? The linguistic input appeared to modulate where infants fell in the specific-to-abstract progression. When the 18-month-old infants viewed support events in silence, they were at the second stage of the progression, discriminating between the familiar and novel relation when the objects were familiar but failing to do so when novel objects were presented (Casasola & Cohen, 2002). However, adding the familiar spatial word *on* to each example of support during habituation aided 18-month-old infants in progressing to the last step of the progression, discriminating between the familiar and novel relation both when the objects were familiar and when they were novel. Similarly, presenting a novel spatial word in the verb frame "She puts it toke" also led infants to form an abstract categorical representation of support. However, adding general linguistic input or a novel spatial word in a general verb frame resulted in 18-month-old infants falling to an earlier step in the progression, failing to respond to the relation between familiar objects but discriminating between the familiar and novel objects. Hence, the nature of linguistic input mattered in whether infants behaved in a more developmentally sophisticated manner or fell back to an earlier point in the progression and behaved similar to younger infants.

Language appears to be interacting with nonlinguistic processes in aiding infants to acquire spatial categories that they do not form without the aid of language. The results of these studies, of course, generate questions: Does language aid infants in forming a spatial category that they would never otherwise form? Or does language simply aid infants in forming a spatial category they would form eventually? This is a difficult question to answer, and the response may differ across the particular event in question. In the case of support, language may be aiding infants to form a spatial category that they would eventually form, even without linguistic input. Fourteen-month-old infants do form a spatial category of support if habituated to only two examples of support and when presented with only loose-fit support (Casasola, 2005b). Whether infants would ever learn to group tight-fit support into the same spatial category as loose-fit support without the aid of linguistic input is uncertain.

Language may play a pivotal role in teaching infants to treat as equivalent those dynamic events that they view as very distinct. Although 18-month-old English-learning infants do not form a spatial category of tight-fit (Casasola & Cohen, 2002), Casasola, Wilbourn, and Yang (in press) were able to teach English-learning toddlers of 21 months to form this spatial category. Toddlers were taught a novel word for four actions that resulted in a tight-fit relation, half tight-fit containment and half tight-fit support. Following exposure to the novel word, toddlers mapped the novel word onto a familiar tight-fit event as well as novel tight-fit support and novel tight-fit containment events. Hence, providing toddlers with a novel spatial word for both tight-fit containment and tight-fit support events taught them to group these events into a single semantic category. These results provide experimental evidence that a novel spatial word motivates toddlers to attend to a spatial relation that they normally disregard in their descriptions of spatial events and to organize a novel semantic category on the basis of this relation. Thus, spatial words themselves can direct attention to a spatial relation and instruct infants and toddlers to treat different types of spatial events as equivalent.

Linking Labels for Actions to Nonlinguistic Concepts: Precursors to Comprehension

One final issue we consider is how infants may begin to link their preverbal understanding of motion events to linguistic labels for these events. Although cross-linguistic variability in the encoding of relational meanings may require infants to reorganize their existing concepts, it may also be the case infants can link a novel word with a specific instance of an action event. One step in word learning involves infants' ability to form links between specific linguistic input and specific events in their environments. There has been much research demonstrating that this ability is in place in infant as young as 13 months with object labels (Woodward, Markman, & Fitzsimmons, 1994). For example, Werker et al. (1998) demonstrated that infants form associations between a word and an object using only the co-occurrence between the two. They used a modified habituation paradigm to ensure that infants could use only the co-occurrence between a word and the object with which it was paired to form the associations when given only a few minutes of exposure (see also Schafer & Plunkett, 1998). Although forming word-object associations is not equivalent to comprehending a word as a label for an object, infants' ability to form an association between a word and an object demonstrates that infants possess one of the necessary precursors for beginning to comprehend language: the ability to link a label with its referent rapidly and with minimal experience. The issue of whether infants can do the same with labels for action events has remained relatively unexplored.

Forming Word-Action Associations

Can 14-month-old infants also learn to associate a novel word to an action event? By 14 months, infants can discriminate between the causal actions of pushing and pulling (Casasola & Cohen, 2000), raising the question of whether infants of this age can associate linguistic labels with these action events. Infants were habituated to a pushing event presented simultaneously with a novel label and to a pulling event presented simultaneously with a second novel label. Infants then viewed two test trials: a same trial (showing a familiar word-action pairing) and a switch trial (showing a novel word-action pairing), as well as a posttest trial to test for fatigue. Infants provided no evidence of discriminating between the same and switch test trials (see figure 6.8, top graph), indicating that they did not form an association between novel word and an action event. When tested in the same task, however, 18-month-old infants did discriminate the same trial from the switch trial (see figure 6.8, bottom graph), indicating that infants learn to form word-action associations with only a few minutes exposure between 14 and 18 months.

Forming Word-Spatial Relation Associations

The 14-month-old infants' difficulty with forming the word-action associations suggests that these associations are more difficult to form than are word-object associations (Casasola & Cohen, 2000). However, infants' difficulty with the task may result because the ability to discriminate between pushing and pulling actions develops between 10 and 14 months of age (Cohen, Bradley, & Casasola, 1995). When

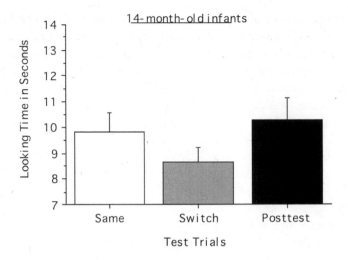

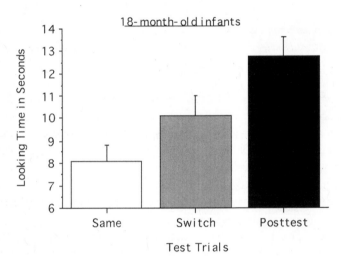

Figure 6.8. The looking times with standard errors of 14-month-old and 18-month-old infants in Casasola and Cohen (2000) to the same, switch, and posttest test trials.

language is added to the task, infants may have difficulty attending to both the linguistic labels and the causal actions (Casasola & Cohen, 2000). However, infants may demonstrate the ability to map a novel word onto an action event if the action event is one that they have learned to discriminate at an earlier point in development. By 6 months of age, infants discriminate between the actions of placing one object in a referent object versus on the referent object (Casasola et al., 2003). Given that this discrimination is acquired earlier than the ability to discriminate between pushing and pulling, can 14-month-old infants learn to associate a novel word with a dynamic containment or support event (Casasola & Wilbourn, 2004)? Infants were tested in the same modified habituation paradigm used by Werker et al. (1998) and Casasola and Cohen (2000). Infants were habituated to a dynamic containment event paired with one novel word and a dynamic support event paired with a second novel word, using Big Bird and a box (see figure 6.9). To ensure that infants would interpret the novel word as referring to the spatial relation presented, each novel word was presented in a sentence (e.g., "Look! She's putting Big Bird *teek* the box. *Teek!*"). The events were presented from both a front and a high angle so that infants could not use perceptual changes in Big Bird's appearance as possible referents for the novel words.

Front-angle containment event

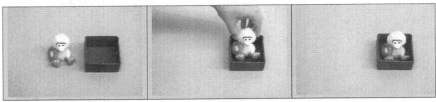

High-angle containment event

Front-angle support event

High-angle support event

Figure 6.9. The front-angle and high-angle containment and support events presented to 14-month-old infants in Casasola and Wilbourn (2004).

Following habituation, infants viewed a same test trial, which maintained the habituation word-relation pairing, and a test trial that presented a switch in the word-relation pairing. Infants looked significantly longer at the switch than at the same test trial, indicating that they had formed an association between the novel word and the relation with which it had been paired during habituation (see figure 6.10). There was no effect of test angle (front or high), indicating that infants were not simply mapping the novel words onto Big Bird or the box, since when there was no change in Big Bird's appearance in the high angle event, but they still looked significantly longer at the switch trial. Thus, 14-month-old infants demonstrated that they were sensitive to the co-occurrence of novel words and spatial relations. They were able to form word-relation associations in the few minutes of exposure to each pairing during habituation, quickly and without interaction with an experimenter, using only the co-occurrence between word and relation as well as the information provided in the linguistic input.

Taken together, both the findings reported by Casasola and Cohen (2000) and Casasola and Wilbourn (2004) show that infants have the cognitive abilities in place to begin to comprehend linguistic labels for particular motion events. Although these studies were not designed to test word learning, they do provide evidence that infants' general cognitive abilities provide them with a sensitivity to note the co-occurrence of a novel word and a particular action event and to link these elements together, even when the amount of experience is limited to only a few minutes. The results also reveal developmental changes in the types of action events to which infants can learn to associate a linguistic label. For infants of 14 months, associating novel words with an action event was easier to do with containment and support events (Casasola & Wilbourn, 2004) than with pushing and pulling events (Casasola & Cohen, 2000), which is not surprising given that in-

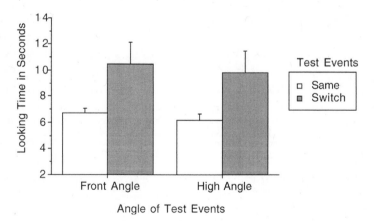

Figure 6.10. The looking times with standard errors to the same versus switch test trials of 14-month-old infants tested with the front-angle versus high-angle events in Casasola and Wilbourn (2004).

fants learn to discriminate between containment and support at 6 months but do not learn to discriminate between pushing and pulling until 14 months (Casasola et al., 2003; Cohen et al., 1995). Also, *in* and *on* are among the earliest spatial words acquired by young children (Clark, 1973). By 15 months, infants comprehend *on* as referring to support events (Meints et al., 2002). Thus, the difference in infants' performance on the task above may reflect differences in learning to comprehend labels for different types of action events.

The results reported also raise an interesting possibility for how infants may learn to form language-specific semantic categories so readily and why they are able to do so from the earliest stages of learning to comprehend particular spatial morphemes (Choi et al., 1999). By 14 months, infants are highly sensitive to the co-occurrence of a particular word and a particular spatial event. In addition to using this sensitivity to form word-relation associations quickly, infants may also use this sensitivity to note which type of relation is always present when a par-ticular spatial term is provided. Although Choi and Bowerman (1991) have offered this process as an explanation for the acquisition of language-specific semantic spatial categories (see also Bowerman, 1989, 1996; Bowerman & Choi, 2001; Choi et al., 1999), the results reported by Casasola and Wilbourn (2004) provide evidence that this argument may be feasible and that by 14 months of age, infants have in place many of the nonlinguistic abilities to begin to acquire relational language.

Conclusion

Both infants' nonlinguistic perceptual and cognitive abilities as well as their understanding of language contribute to the acquisition of the meanings expressed in verbs and other relational terms. For some relational meanings, infants' nonlinguistic abilities are sufficient for acquiring that meaning, as was demonstrated in the case of containment as well as manner and path. For other meanings, such as support and tight fit, infants' nonlinguistic abilities play an important role in the acquisition of these meanings, but alone may not be sufficient. Rather, infants' understanding of language contributes to the development of these relational meanings. More specifically, their comprehension of a specific word and their familiarity with linguistic structures become sources of input for acquiring a partic-ular concept.

The results of various studies also demonstrated how the specific-to-abstract progression exemplifies how infants learn to form an abstract categorical representation of a spatial relation, regardless of whether infants use only their nonlinguistic abilities or whether they use linguistic input to help form a spatial category. To date, we have only tested this progression with respect to infants' categorization of spatial relations. Future investigations will explore if the progression fits with infants' understanding of other types of motion events, such as manner and path in motion events and causal versus noncausal launching events. Because infants' ability to respond to motion events changes across contexts, focusing on the processes that guide their understanding of these events may prove to be the most fruitful in speculating how infants recruit their understanding of motion events in learning relational language. In this manner, we can begin to understand more clearly the relation between thought and language during the first years of development.

Acknowledgments Preparation of this chapter and much of the research reported in it were supported by a Hatch grant from the College of Human Ecology at Cornell University and Grant HD43941-01 from the National Institute of Child Health and Human Development to the first author. We thank Makeba Parramore Wilbourn and Cara H. Cashon for helpful comments on earlier versions of the manuscript.

References

Aske, J. (1989). Path predicates in English and Spanish: A closer look. *Proceedings of the Berkeley Linguistics Society, 15*, 1–14.

Bahrick, L. E., Gogate, L. J., & Ruiz, I. (2002). Attention and memory for faces and actions in infancy: The salience of actions over faces in dynamic events. *Child Development, 73*, 1629–1643.

Baillargeon, R., & Wang, S. (2002). Event categorization in infancy. *Trends in Cognitive Sciences, 6*, 85–93.

Berman, R. A., & Slobin, D. I. (1994). *Relating events in narrative: A crosslinguistic developmental study*. Hillsdale, NJ: Lawrence Erlbaum.

Bertenthal, B. I., Proffitt, D. R., & Cutting, J. E. (1984). Infant sensitivity to figural coherence in biomechanical motions. *Journal of Experimental Child Psychology, 37*, 213–230.

Bowerman, M. (1989). Learning a semantic system: What role do cognitive predispositions play? In M. L. Rice & R. L. Schiefelbusch (Eds.), *The teachability of language* (pp. 133–169). Baltimore, MD: Paul H. Brookes.

Bowerman, M. (1996). Learning how to structure space for language: A cross-linguistic perspective. In P. Bloom, M. A. Peterson, L. Nadel, & M. F. Garrett (Eds.), *Language and space* (pp. 385–436). Cambridge, MA: MIT Press.

Bowerman, M., & Choi, S. (2001). Shaping meanings for language: Universal and language specific in the acquisition of spatial semantic categories. In M. Bowerman & S. C. Levinson (Eds.), *Language acquisition and conceptual development* (pp. 475–511). Cambridge: Cambridge University Press.

Brown, R. (1973). *A first language: The early stages*. Cambridge, MA: Harvard University Press.

Carey, S. (2001). Whorf versus continuity theorists: Bring data to bear on the debate. In M. Bowerman & S. C. Levinson (Eds.), *Language acquisition and conceptual development* (pp. 185–214). Cambridge: Cambridge University Press.

Casasola, M. (2002a, April). *Developmental changes in the effect of linguistic input on infant spatial categorization*. Poster presented at the International Conference on Infant Studies, Toronto.

Casasola, M. (2002b). Exploring the relationship between language-specific semantic spatial categories and infants' nonlinguistic spatial categories. In E. Clark (Ed.), *Proceedings of the thirty-first Stanford Child Language Research Forum* (pp. 1–10). CSLI Publications: http://cslipublications.stanford.edu/CLRF/2002/CLRF-2002-title.html.

Casasola, M. (2002c, July). *Language-specific semantic spatial categories and infants' spatial categories.* Paper presented at the International Congress on Language Development, Madison, WI.

Casasola, M. (2005a). Can language do the driving? The effect of linguistic input on infants' categorization of support spatial relations. *Developmental Psychology, 41,* 183–192.

Casasola, M. (2005b). When less is more: How infants learn to form an abstract categorical representation of support. *Child Development, 76,* 279–290. Manuscript submitted for publication.

Casasola, M., & Cohen, L. B. (2000). Infants' association of linguistic labels with causal actions. *Developmental Psychology, 36,* 155–168.

Casasola, M., & Cohen, L. B. (2002). Infant categorization of containment, support and tight-fit spatial relationships. *Developmental Science, 5,* 247–264.

Casasola, M., Cohen, L. B., & Chiarello, E. (2003). Six-month-old infants' categorization of containment spatial relations. *Child Development, 74,* 679–693.

Casasola, M., Hohenstein, J. M., & Naigles, L. (2005). *Infants' discrimination of manner and path in motion events.* Manuscript in preparation.

Casasola, M., & Wilbourn, M. P. (2004). Fourteen-month-old infants form novel word-spatial relation associations. *Infancy, 6,* 385–396.

Casasola, M., Wilbourn, M. P., & Yang, S. (in press). Can English-learning toddlers acquire and generalize a novel spatial word? *First Language.*

Choi, S., & Bowerman, M. (1991). Learning to express motion events in English and Korean: The influence of language-specific lexicalization patterns. *Cognition, 41,* 83–121.

Choi, S., McDonough, L., Bowerman, M., & Mandler, J. M. (1999). Early sensitivity to language-specific spatial categories in English and Korean. *Cognitive Development, 14,* 241–268.

Clark, E. V. (1973). Nonlinguistic strategies and the acquisition of word meanings. *Cognition, 2,* 161–182.

Cohen, L. B., & Amsel, G. A. (1998). Precursors to infants' perception of the causality of a simple event. *Infant Behavior and Development, 21,* 713–732.

Cohen, L. B., Bradley, K. L., & Casasola, M. (1995, May). *Infants' ability to discriminate between pushing and pulling.* Poster presented at the biennial meeting of the Society for Research in Child Development, Indianapolis, IN.

Cohen, L. B., & Oakes, L. M. (1993). How infants perceive a simple causal event. *Developmental Psychology, 29,* 421–433.

Colombo, J., McCollam, K., Coldren, J. T., Mitchell, D. W., & Rash, S. J. (1990). Form categorization in 10-month-old infants. *Journal of Experimental Child Psychology, 49,* 173–188.

Gentner, D., & Boroditsky, L. (2001). Individuation, relativity, and early word learning. In M. Bowerman & S. Levinson (Eds.), *Language acquisition and conceptual development* (pp. 215–256). Cambridge: Cambridge University Press.

Gibson, E., Owsley, C. J., & Johnston, J. (1978). Perception of invariants by five-month-old infants: Differentiation of two types of motion. *Developmental Psychology, 14,* 407–415.

Gleitman, L. (1990). The structural sources of verb meanings. *Language Acquisition: Journal of Developmental Linguistics, 1,* 3–55.

Gopnik, A., Choi, S., & Baumberger, T. (1996). Cross-linguistic differences in early semantic and cognitive development. *Cognitive Development, 11*,197–227.

Haith, M. M. (1980). *Rules that babies look by: The organization of newborn visual activity*. Hillsdale, NJ: Lawrence Erlbaum.

Hespos, S. J., & Baillargeon, R. (2001). Infants' knowledge about occlusion and containment events: A surprising discrepancy. *Psychological Science, 121*, 141–147.

Johnson, J., & Aslin, R. (1995). Perception of object unity in 2-month-old infants. *Developmental Psychology, 31*, 739–745.

Johnson, S., Cohen, L. B., Marks, K., & Johnson, K. (2003). Young infants' perception of object unity in rotation displays. *Infancy, 4*, 285–295.

Kellman, P., & Spelke, E. (1983). Perception of partly occluded objects in infancy. *Cognitive Psychology, 15*, 483–524.

Kellman, P., Spelke, E., & Short, K. (1986). Infant perception of object unity from translatory motion in depth and vertical translation. *Child Development, 57*, 72–86.

Landau, B., & Jackendoff, R. (1993). "What" and "where" in spatial language and spatial cognition. *Behavioral and Brain Sciences, 16*, 217–265.

Leslie, A. M. (1984). Spatiotemporal contiguity and the perception of causality in infants. *Perception, 13*, 287–305.

Leslie, A. M., & Keeble, S. (1987). Do six-month-old infants perceive causality? *Cognition, 25*, 265–288.

Loewenstein, J., & Gentner, D. (2005). Relational language and the development of relational mapping. *Cognitive Psychology, 50*, 315–353.

Mandler, J. M. (1992). How to build a baby: II. Conceptual primitives. *Psychological Review, 99*, 587–604.

Mandler, J. M. (1996). Preverbal representation and language. In P. Bloom, M. A. Peterson, L. Nadel, & M. F. Garrett (Eds.), *Language and space* (pp. 365–384). Cambridge, MA: MIT Press.

McDonough, L., Choi, S., & Mandler, J. (2003). Understanding spatial relations: Flexible infants, lexical adults. *Cognitive Psychology, 46*, 229–259.

Meints, K., Plunkett, K., Harris, P. L., & Dimmock, D. (2002). What is "on" and "under" for 15-, 18- and 24-month-olds? Typicality effects in early comprehension of spatial prepositions. *British Journal of Developmental Psychology, 20*, 113–130.

Morton, J., & Johnson, M. (1991). The perception of facial structure in infancy. In G. R. Lockhead & J. R. Pomerantz (Eds.), *The perception of structure: Essays in honor of Wendell R. Garner* (pp. 317–325). Washington, DC: American Psychological Association.

Naigles, L., Eisenberg, A. R., Kako, E. T., Highter, M., & McGraw, N. (1998). Speaking of motion: Verb use in English and Spanish. *Language and Cognitive Processes, 13*, 521–549.

Naigles, L. R., & Terrazas, P. (1998). Motion-verb generalizations in English and Spanish: Influence of language and syntax. *Psychological Science, 9*, 363–369.

Oakes, L. M. (1994). The development of infants' use of continuity cues in their perception of causality. *Developmental Psychology, 30*, 748–756.

Oakes, L. M., & Cohen, L. B. (1990). Infant perception of a causal event. *Cognitive Development, 5*, 193–207.

Oakes, L. M., Coppage, D. J., & Dingel, A. (1997). By land or by sea: The role of perceptual similarity in infants' categorization of animals. *Developmental Psychology, 33*, 396–407.

Plumert, J. M., & Hawkins, A. M. (2001). Biases in young children's communication about spatial relations: Containment versus proximity. *Child Development, 7*, 22–36.

Pulverman, R., Sootsman, J. L., Golinkoff, R. M., & Hirsh-Pasek, K. (2002). Infants' nonlinguistic processing of motion events: One year old English speakers are interested in manner and path. In E. Clark (Ed.), *Proceedings of the thirty-first Stanford Child Language Research Forum* (pp. 11–20). CSLI Publications: http://cslipublications.stanford.edu/CLRF/2002/CLRF-2002-title.html.

Quinn, P. C. (1994). The categorization of above and below spatial relations by young infants. *Child Development, 65*, 58–69.

Quinn, P. C., Adams, A., Kennedy, E., Shettler, L., & Wasnik, A. (2003). Development of an abstract category representation for the spatial relation between in 6- to 10-month-old infants. *Developmental Psychology, 39*, 151–163.

Quinn, P. C., Cummins, M., Kase, J., Martin, E., & Weisman, S. (1996). Development of categorical representations for Above and Below spatial relations in 3- to 7-month-old infants. *Developmental Psychology, 32*, 942–950.

Quinn, P. C., Eimas, P. D., & Rosenkrantz, S. L. (1993). Evidence for representations of perceptually similar natural categories by 3-month-old and 4-month-old infants. *Perception, 22*, 463–475.

Quinn, P. C., Polly, J. L., Furer, M. J., Dobson, V., & Narter, D. B. (2002). Young infants' performance in the object-variation version of the above-below categorization task: A result of perceptual distraction or conceptual limitation? *Infancy, 3*, 323–348.

Rakison, D. H. (2003). Parts, motion, and the development of the animate-inanimate distinction in infancy. In D. H. Rakison & L. M. Oakes (Eds.), *Early category and concept development: Making sense of the blooming, buzzing confusion* (pp. 159–192). London: Oxford University Press.

Rakison, D. H., & Poulin-Dubois, D. (2001). Developmental origin of the animate-inanimate distinction. *Psychological Bulletin, 12*, 209–228.

Schafer, G., & Plunkett, K. (1998). Rapid word learning by fifteen-month-olds under tightly controlled conditions. *Child Development, 69*, 309–320.

Slater, A. (1989). Visual memory and perception in early infancy. In A. Slater & G. Bremner (Eds.), *Infant development* (pp. 43–71). Hillsdale, NJ: Lawrence Erlbaum.

Slobin, D. I., & Hoiting, N. (1994). Reference to movement in spoken and signed languages: Typological considerations. *Proceedings of the Berkeley Linguistics Society, 20*, 487–505.

Smith, W. C., Johnson, S. P., & Spelke, E. (2003). Motion and edge sensitivity in perception of object unity. *Cognitive Psychology, 46*, 31–64.

Spelke, E. (1998). Nativism, empiricism, and the origins of knowledge. *Infant Behavior and Development, 21*, 181–200.

Spelke, E. S., Phillips, A., & Woodward, A. L. (1995). Infants' knowledge of object motion and human action. In D. Sperber, D. Premack, et al. (Eds.), *Causal cognition: A multidisciplinary debate*. Symposia of the Fyssen Foundation. New York: Clarendon Press/Oxford University Press.

Talmy, L. (1975). Semantics and syntax of motion. In J. Kimball (Ed.), *Syntax and semantics* (pp. 181–238). New York: Academic Press.

Talmy, L. (1983). How language structures space. In H. L. Pick & L. P. Acredolo (Eds.), *Spatial orientation: Theory, research and practice* (pp. 225–282). New York: Plenum Press.

Talmy, L. (1985). Lexicalization patterns: Semantic structure in lexical forms. In T. Shopen (Ed.), *Language, typology, and syntactic description: Vol. 3. Grammatical categories and the lexicon*. New York: Cambridge University Press.

Werker, J. F., Cohen, L. B., Lloyd, V. L., Casasola, M., & Stager, C. L. (1998). Acquisition of word-object associations by 14-month-old infants. *Developmental Psychology, 34,* 1289–1309.

Woodward, A. L., Markman, E. M., & Fitzsimmons, C. M. (1994). Rapid word learning in 13- and 18-month-olds. *Developmental Psychology, 30,* 553–566.

7   Preverbal Spatial Cognition and Language-Specific Input: Categories of Containment and Support

Soonja Choi

Space offers an important domain of research in which one can study the relation between language and cognition. Virtually from the beginning of life, children explore space and by the time they are a year old—when they begin to talk—they have learned a great deal about spatial relations and spatial actions (Gibson & Spelke, 1983; Piaget & Inhelder, 1967). Within a few months of birth, infants start building up sophisticated knowledge about what to expect in various types of spatial actions such as support and containment (putting things *on* a surface and putting things *in* a container. For example, from 3 months of age, infants explore how objects are supported on surfaces and start distinguishing between situations in which an object will be supported or will fall (Needham & Baillargeon, 1993), and by 7 months of age they can calculate how much contact is needed for an object to be adequately supported by another (Baillargeon & Hanko-Summers, 1990). Infants also build up their knowledge about what to expect in a containment relation: They learn that containers with bottoms can contain things but those without bottoms cannot, that objects in a container will move with the container, and that for an object to be contained it needs to be smaller than the opening of the container (Aguiar & Baillargeon, 1998; Baillargeon, 1995). These findings amply demonstrate that infants have processed a lot of information about spatial actions well before they start producing words.

This early (presumably universal) development of spatial cognition is quite intriguing to linguists and particularly to developmental psycholinguists. This is because languages in fact differ extensively in the way they encode spatial information. First, different languages use different grammatical means to express the spatial relation resulting from a *dynamic* action (e.g., putting x *in* y). In languages like English, the information is typically encoded by prepositions and particles (i.e., closed class words) ("put a book *in* a bag"), while in other languages like Korean, it

191

is typically encoded by verbs (i.e., open class words) ("chayk-ul kabang-ey *nehta*," book-Object bag-Location *put-in*) (Choi & Bowerman, 1991). The two word classes (closed versus open class) typically differ in the level of specificity (Bybee, 1985; Slobin, 2001) they convey. Words in the closed class tend to be more general and grammaticized than words in the open class.

Second, languages differ greatly in the way they semantically categorize spatial relations. Let's take the containment and support relations that infants explore from early on. Although these two relations seem distinct in a straightforward way, it is only so from the perspective of an English speaker (or someone who speaks a similar language in terms of the semantic structure). Recent cross-linguistic studies have shown languages differ in the way they group and partition the containment and support relations (Bowerman, 1996a, 1996b; Bowerman & Choi, 2001; Bowerman & Pederson, 1992; Brown, 1992; Levinson, Meier, & The Language and Cognitive Group, 2003). Bowerman's (1996b) cross-linguistic comparisons with three examples are illuminating. The three examples involve notions of contact, support, and containment: (a) cup on a table, (b) handle on a cupboard door, and (c) apple in a bowl, as shown in figure 7.1. In many languages, relationships involving support by a horizontal surface are treated similarly to relationships involving support by a vertical surface. In English, for example, both (a) and (b) are routinely called *on* and together are different from (c), which is called *in*. But although this strategy seems quite reasonable, not all languages follow it. In Finnish, for example, situations like (b) are grouped linguistically with those like (c) (both are encoded with the inessive case ending *-ssa*, usually translated as "in"), and for (a) a different case ending (the adessive, *-lla*, usually translated as "on") is needed. Bowerman (1996b) suggests that in this system, attachment to an external surface such as (b) can be seen as similar to prototypical containment and different from horizontal support, based on the feature of "intimacy" or "incorporation." In still a third pattern, in Dutch, all three situations are treated as distinct, so different morphemes are assigned to them. Thus, (b) is considered to be similar neither to (a) (*op* in Dutch) nor (c) (*in* in Dutch), as it is characterized with a third spatial morpheme *aan*, that

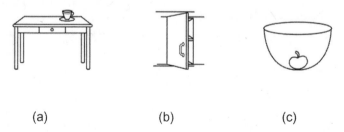

(a)   (b)   (c)

Figure 7.1. Instances of (a) support, (b) attachment, and (c) containment. (From "Learning How to Structure Space for Language: A Crosslinguistic Perspective," by M. Bowerman, 1996, in P. Bloom, M. Peterson, L. Nadel, and M. Garrett (Eds.), *Language and Space* (pp. 385–486). Cambridge, MA: MIT Press.)

is somewhat specialized to relations of hanging and other projecting attachment. And in a fourth pattern, displayed by Spanish, it is quite unnecessary to differentiate among (a), (b), and (c). A single prepositions *en* can be applied to all of them. These cross-linguistic differences suggest that what we have previously considered as universal categories or concepts of containment and support are quite language-specific.

The early development of spatial cognition during the preverbal period on the one hand and the significant cross-linguistic diversity in spatial expressions on the other raise a number of questions about the relationship between cognition and language in the domain of space: (1) What kinds of spatial categories are formed during the preverbal period, and to what extent do the preverbal spatial categories prepare the child for learning the language-specific semantic categories? (2) When do children acquire the language-specific semantic categories? (3) Does linguistic input influence children's spatial cognition, and if so, when does it begin? Different theories would predict different answers to these questions. A modular approach, which argues for independence between the linguistic and cognitive structures (e.g., Jackendoff, 1983; Li & Gleitman, 2002), would hold that conceptual categories are universal and foundational to linguistic structures but that language-specific semantics does not affect children's conceptual structure of space. In sharp contrast, a strong Whorfian hypothesis (Levinson, Kita, Haun, & Rasch, 2002; Pederson et al., 1998; Whorf, 1956) would hold that the language-specific semantic categorization would influence nonlinguistic cognition as children become fluent speakers of their language. Between these two extremes there is a "thinking for speaking" hypothesis (Slobin, 1996), which argues that cognition is influenced by language when it is mediated by linguistic thinking.

For the past several years, my colleagues and I have conducted a series of cross-linguistic studies addressing the above questions and examining the competing theories in a systematic way. Our studies focused on children learning two languages, English and Korean, which differ significantly and interestingly in their spatial semantic systems (see the next section). In these studies, we specifically examined when and how children learning English or Korean develop notions of containment and support relations and acquire the language-specific meanings. Before I report on our findings, however, it is necessary to describe the spatial semantic categories in English and Korean in some detail.

Spatial Semantic Categories in English and Korean

English and Korean classify spatial actions involving containment and support quite differently. The spatial terms *put in* and *put on* in English and *kkita* in Korean are cases in point. The semantic categories referred to by these terms involve at least four distinct features that are packaged differently in the two languages: loose containment, tight containment, loose support, and tight support.

In English, spatial particles *(put) in* or *(put) on* basically distinguish between two relations: containment or support (see figure 7.2). The spatial word *in* is used when the figure (the moving object) ends up contained in or encircled by the ground (the reference object). Note that *put in* is used regardless of whether the containment is tight (e.g., "putting a book tightly into a box-shaped cover") or loose (e.g., "putting a toy in a basket"). The semantic category of *in* in English contrasts with that of *on*. The spatial word *(put) on* is used when the figure ends up being supported or attached by the ground or when it covers or encircles the ground. And again, the meaning of *on* is irrelevant to whether the relation is tight or loose, for example, "putting a Lego piece on another" (tight support) and "putting a block on the surface" (loose support).

The same semantic space is partitioned differently in Korean. In particular, *kkita*, an early-learned verb, picks out a category to do with bringing three-dimensional objects with complementary shapes into an interlocking, tight-fitting relationship. (*Kkita* is a spatial verb. In Korean, information about motion and path is systematically encoded by a set of spatial verbs, whereas in English it is encoded by motion verbs plus path particles, e.g., "put in"; Choi & Bowerman, 1991; Talmy, 1985.) The *kkita* category crosscuts the categories of *put in* and *put on* and extends to some situations that are considered neither "putting in" nor "putting on." This everyday verb

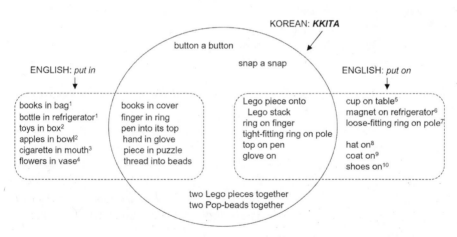

Figure 7.2. Spatial categorization in *in/on* in English and *kkita* in Korean. In Korean, the non-*kkita* events are expressed with different verbs. The gloss here is only approximate: [1]*nehta*, "put *x* loosely in a container"; [2]*tamta*, "put small objects in downward motion in a container that one can carry"; [3]*mwalta*, "hold *x* partially in mouth between teeth"; [4]*kkocta*, "put an elongated object partially into a container or ground"; [5]*nohta*, "put *x* loosely on surface"; [6]*pwuthita*, "attach a flat surface of an object on another"; [7]*nehta*, "put *x* loosely in a container" or *kelta*, "hook *x* on *y*"; [8]*ssuta*, "put *x* to cover head"; [9]*ipta*, "put clothing to cover body"; [10]*sinta*, "put *x* on feet."

has no English counterpart.[1] The crosscutting of the domain of *put in* by *kkita* means that what English treats as a unified category of containment events is, for speakers of Korean, subdivided: "tight-fitting" containment events like putting a book into an exactly matching box cover, described with *kkita*, are treated as a different class of actions from "loose-fitting" containment events like putting an a Lego piece into a box, described with *nehta*. The category of *nehta* encompasses not only loose containment events but also loose encirclement events, for example, putting a loose ring on a pole. Just as Korean breaks down the category of English *put in*, it also subdivides the domain of *put on*. Here, the partitioning is more extensive: attaching a figure to the exterior surface of a ground object with a complementary three-dimensional shape (e.g., putting a top on a pen or a Lego block on a stack of Legos) falls into the "tight fit" category of *kkita*, while juxtaposing objects with flat surfaces (e.g., putting a magnet on a refrigerator) is *pwuchita*; depositing a figure on a roughly horizontal surface (e.g., putting a cup on a table) is *nohta*; and putting a clothing item on the head is *ssuta* (distinguished from putting clothing on the trunk, *ipta*, and on the feet, *sinta*).

In summary, *put in* in English requires the figure to end up in an interior space or volume of the ground, but is indifferent to whether the fit between figure and ground is tight or loose. *Kkita*, in contrast, cares centrally about the fit between a figure or a ground with complementary shapes but is indifferent to whether this fit is obtained by insertion, covering, surface attachment, or encirclement.

Early Acquisition of Spatial Words and Possible Preverbal Structures for Spatial Categorization

When do young children learning English and Korean acquire language-specific spatial semantics of their language? The *when* question is important: If children learning different languages start out with a period of shared meanings for spatial terms (regardless of the language-specific meanings) and only gradually home in on language-specific meanings, it would suggest that a universal conceptual core initially guides semantic learning. But if children acquire language-specific meanings from, let's say, the single word period, it would suggest that early semantic categories are influenced by the linguistic input and that there is an interaction between language and spatial cognition from very early on.

Using a preferential looking method, we examined when children begin to acquire the language-specific meanings of *in* and *kkita* by English-learning (E) and Korean-learning (K) children respectively. As reported in chapter 4, the results showed that E and K children are sensitive to language-specific meanings from as early as 18 months of age. Such an early acquisition of language-specific semantics lead to several points: First, children pay close attention to linguistic input from very early on as their semantic categories are guided by the ambient language from virtually the comprehension period of language development. Second, considering the extensive cross-linguistic differences in spatial classification and given the recent findings that preverbal infants develop significant understanding about what to expect in everyday spatial situations (e.g., Baillargeon, 2002), one can hypothesize that infants also develop a certain level of spatial classification system that is flexible enough to learn the specific system of the target language. But what is the precise nature of preverbal spatial cognition that allows such rapid learning of language-specific semantics? And does language-specific input influence nonlinguistic spatial categorization from early on?

In studying the cognitive preparedness in preverbal infants for learning the language-specific spatial classifications, at least two working hypotheses can be made.

1. Preverbal infants may be nonlinguistically sensitive to a large number of spatial distinctions—larger than needed to learn the target language—at a fairly abstract level, for example, tight versus loose containment, partial versus complete containment, tight versus loose support, attachment versus encirclement, vertical versus horizontal support. These distinctions would not necessarily in themselves define semantic categories associated with spatial morphemes in any particular language, but they would be the foundational building blocks with which children could *construct* such categories by combining them into appropriate configurations through observation of language-specific input. This hypothesis would be in line with the 'semantic primitives for space' approach proposed by Landau and Jackendoff (1993) (see chapter 4).

2. Infants initially do not make well-defined categorization for spatial relations. One version of this possibility is that preverbal infants process instances of spatial configurations at a more individual level: Their knowledge of spatial relations is related to specific context or object. For example, putting a cup on the table, putting a Lego piece onto another, or putting a cap on a bottle is all initially processed as separate relations in the infant's mind because these actions occur in different contexts and involve different types of spatial configuration (e.g., attachment, covering, surface support). Under this hypothesis, linguistic input would play a role in guiding infants to group the actions at a more general level. That is, language would help children notice commonalities across seemingly disparate relations and form spatial categories accordingly (Bowerman & Choi, 2003; Gentner, 2003). More specifically, when Korean children hear caregivers say *kkita* for putting one Lego piece onto another, for putting a cap on a bottle, and for putting a book into its fitted box cover, they come to understand tight fit as the common feature and form the semantic category of *kkita* accordingly (Bowerman & Choi, 2001, 2003).

Notice that both hypotheses require the child to be sensitive to language-specific input to arrive at appropriate semantic categories of the target language. The two hypotheses differ, however, in that in hypothesis 1 linguistic input simply plays a triggering role, whereas in hypothesis 2 linguistic input shapes children's semantic categories. The two hypotheses are of course not necessarily mutually exclusive, in that at a given time, infants may be at different levels of generalization for different types of relation (e.g., containment vs. support; see Casasola & Cohen, 2002). With my colleagues, I explored these hypotheses by testing infants' ability to distinguish between two types of containment and between two types of support based on the tight-fit feature. Thus, four subtypes—let us call them features for convenience—were formed for testing: loose containment, tight containment, loose support, and tight support. These four features are combined in different ways in the two languages (see figure 7.2). In our experimental design, we systematically contrasted these features in such a way that a given contrast is semantically made in one language but not the other.

Preverbal Cognition for Containment and Support, and the Influence of Language

Using a modified version of the preferential looking paradigm employed in our prior research (Choi, McDonough, Bowerman, & Mandler, 1999), we tested the kinds of nonlinguistic distinctions that preverbal children can make. The design consisted of a familiarization period followed by a test period. During the familiarization period, infants were familiarized with one type of spatial relation with six distinct scenes. Figure 7.3 shows the six familiarization scenes for the tight-in relation. The six scenes were presented in three pairs such that on any given trial, two scenes appeared side by side simultaneously, one on each screen. After showing the three pairs (trials 1–3), we showed the same three pairs again in the same order (trials 4–6), but this time with the sides reversed. These familiarization trials were immediately followed by two successive test trials. Each test trial consisted of novel instances of two relations: the same relation with which the child had been familiarized and a novel relation (e.g., one tight-in scene and one loose-in scene). Each trial was 8 seconds long with 2 second intervals between trials.

All relations (in both familiarization and test trials) were presented within dynamic action frames (e.g., putting X tightly in Y). We used a wide variety of objects that were not only perceptually dissimilar (in size, shape, color, or texture) but also drawn from different object classes. All relations were filmed in dynamic actions performed by a person. (To minimize distraction, the person's face was not shown.) In each scene, the person demonstrated the same action three times (e.g., putting three keys tightly into three keyholes one by one).

If participants react systematically to the relational similarities across dynamic events involving widely varying objects, we would expect that their gaze would be systematically drawn to one type of relation: either the familiar or the novel relation (see Hunter, Ames, & Koopman, 1983; McDonough, Choi, & Mandler, 2003; Thelen & Schoner, 2002, for discussion).

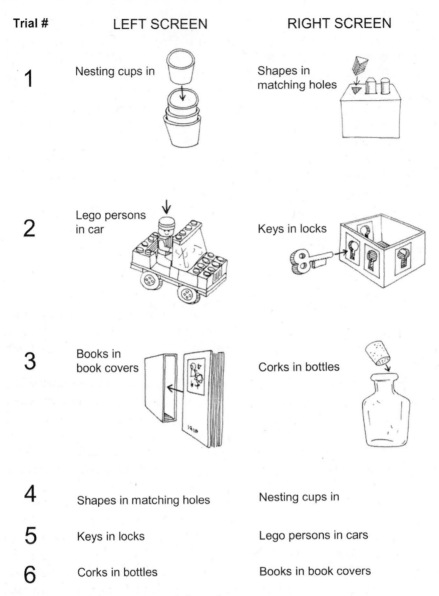

Figure 7.3. Familiarization stimuli for tight-in.

Containment Category: Categories of Loose and Tight Containment

We began our investigation with the category of containment. The question here was whether preverbal infants can categorize two types of containment, loose-fit versus tight-fit containment, as distinct categories. We tested 9-, 11-, and 14-month-olds in

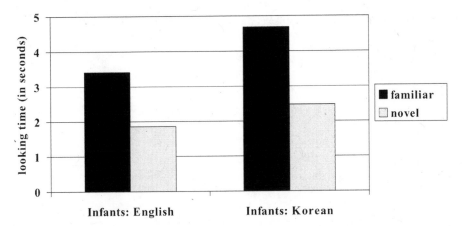

Figure 7.4. Tight-in versus loose-in relations in data from preverbal infants (9-, 11-, and 14-month-olds) raised in English-speaking and Korean-speaking homes.

E and K environments. Half the participants were familiarized with the tight-in and half with the loose-in relation. During the test trials, the two pairs of test scenes juxtaposing the tight-in and loose-in relation were identical in both familiarization conditions.

Results showed the same pattern for all three ages for both languages: Infants in both E and K environments made a distinction between the tight-in and loose-in relations. They looked significantly longer at the familiar relation than at the novel relation during the test trials. That is, those infants familiarized in tight-in looked longer at the tight-in relation during the test trials, and those familiarized in loose-in looked longer at the loose-in relation (see figure 7.4). These data suggest that during the preverbal period, infants can subcategorize the containment relation based on the degree of fit. Furthermore, this ability seems to be nonlinguistically motivated as infants in both E and K environments make the distinction (i.e., preverbal infants in E environments made the distinction although the language does not distinguish them in a systematic way). The finding thus supports our first hypothesis that preverbal infants can make a large number of distinctions that can be packaged differently to learn the language-specific semantics (see chapter 4 for further discussion of this result). But do infants of the same ages also subcategorize the support category on the basis of the tight-fit feature (i.e., loose-on vs. tight-on)?

Support Category: Categories of Loose and Tight Support

In our study on the category of support, our definition of *support* included all the relations that would be called *put on* in English (since we are comparing English and Korean). Such category consists of support by a flat surface (putting a toy on the table), attachment (putting a Lego piece on another Lego), covering (putting a bottle cap on a bottle), and encirclement (putting a ring on a pole). We examined whether infants could subcategorize this support relation on the basis of difference in the tight-fit feature. As in the study for the containment relation, infants (9-, 11-, and 14-month-olds) were familiarized with one type of support relation: either the tight-on relation (e.g., putting Legos on other Legos) or the loose-on relation (e.g., putting toy cups on toy table). See table 7.1 for the full list of familiarization scenes for each relation. During the test trials, both groups were shown two test pairs, each pair consisting of one loose-on relation and one tight-on relation with novel objects, as shown in figure 7.5.

The results were surprising, as they were different from the pattern we saw for the containment category. First, comparisons of the three age groups show that 9-month-olds were different from 11- and 14 month-olds in their preferential looking behavior. Nine-month-olds of both E and K groups did not distinguish between loose-on and tight-on. During the test trials, these infants in both familiarization conditions (loose-on and tight-on familiarization conditions) looked at the two types of relation about the same amount of time (figure 7.6). (E infants looked a little longer at the loose-on relation but the difference was not significant.)

Second, at 11 and 14 months of age, overall, the analysis showed an interaction between scene (familiar vs. novel relation) and familiarization condition. That is, depending on the familiarization condition the children were in, the children

Table 7.1 The familiarization trials showing loose-on and tight-on

Loose-ON familiarization scenes

1. Putting colored blocks of different shapes on top of cylindrical colored posts.
2. Putting small stuffed frogs on colored-paper.
3. Putting Lego people on miniature staircase.
4. Putting plastic shapes on colored foam blocks.
5. Putting toy teacups on toy table.
6. Putting wooden cylinder shape blocks on flat wooden surface

Tight-ON familiarization scenes

1. Putting plastic toy rings tightly on cone-shaped poles.
2. Putting Lego pieces tightly on Lego blocks.
3. Attaching Popbeads on Popbeads.
4. Putting (marker) pentops on (marker) pens.
5. Putting hollow cylinder shape plastic blocks tightly on the matching cylinder shape blocks.
6. Putting matching plastic covers tightly on baby bottles.

All actions were performed three times in succession with three objects of the same type (but typically in different colors and shapes).

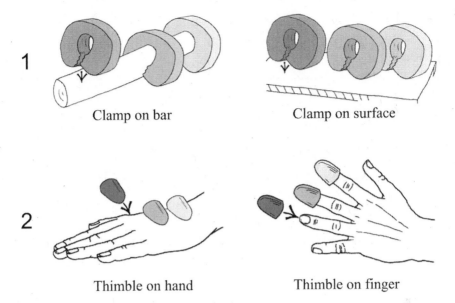

Figure 7.5. Test pairs: tight-on versus loose-on.

differed in whether they preferred the familiar or the novel relation. When each familiarization condition was analyzed separately, it was revealed that the children preferred the tight-on scenes in both familiarization conditions. (For children familiarized with loose-on, tight-on would be the novel relation, and for children familiarized with tight-on, tight-on would be the familiar relation.) More importantly, however, there was a significant cross-linguistic difference in the preference to the tight-on scenes: as can be seen in figure 7.6, the K children preferred the tight-on scenes (to the loose-on scenes) significantly more than the E children did. In fact, tests comparing the difference scores (looking time to tight-on minus looking time to loose-on) show that whereas E children did not differ in their looking preference to tight-on versus loose-on relation, K children looked significantly longer to the tight-on relation than to the loose-on relation. This suggests that K children have a significantly higher interest (or sensitivity) to the tight-on relation than E children do.

Although these results do not show that Korean children categorically distinguish between the loose-on and tight-on relations, they do show that tight-on is a salient relation for 11- and 14-month-old Korean children.[2] (One might argue that the tight-on test scenes were inherently more interesting than the loose-on test scenes for these children, but given that E infants did not show such preference, this interpretation is not likely. The objects in the test trials, i.e., sponge door clamps and thimbles, are fairly novel objects to infants in both cultures.) Why are K children particularly interested in tight-fit support? It is suggested here that

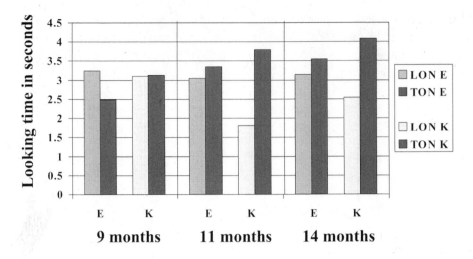

Figure 7.6. Tight-on versus loose-on relations in data from preverbal infants (9-, 11-, and 14-month-olds) raised in English-speaking and Korean-speaking homes.

such interest is linguistically motivated. That is, this cross-linguistic difference for the support category can be explained by the differential linguistic input that the two groups receive: In English the two relations are not distinguished as both are expressed by a single spatial particle *on*, whereas in Korean they are semantically distinguished by two verbs, *kkita* for the tight-fit relation and *nohta* for the loose-support relation.

The data on containment and support, taken together, suggest interesting discrepancies between containment and support relations. For the containment relation, 9-, 11-, and 14-month-old infants distinguish two categories based on the tight-fit feature (i.e., tight-in vs. loose-in). However, use of this feature as a basis for categorization is not generalized to the support relation. For the support relation, 9-month-old infants do not distinguish between tight-on and loose-on. This nondistinction essentially continues through 11- and 14-month-old infants in E environments. In the case of 11- and 14-month-old infants in K environments, however, the infants show heightened sensitivity to the tight-on relation.

These data suggest that the structure of preverbal classification for space is not uniform for all types of spatial relation at a given developmental period. Casasola and Cohen (2002) have reported a developmental difference between the containment and support relations. They found that whereas 18-month-olds could form an abstract category of containment (responding consistently to both familiar and objects being put in a container), they could not form a category at the same abstract level for the support relation. (Eighteen-month-olds could distinguish the support relation from another relation only when familiar objects were involved.) Casasola and Cohen conclude that infants can categorize containment prior to support relationship. Why such difference between the containment and support categories? More specifically for our purpose: Why can't infants subcategorize the support relation on the basis of the tight-fit feature when they can do so for the containment relation? One possible answer may go as follows: Instances of the containment relation are homogeneous (namely, putting X into a ground object with concavity) and thus may readily be grouped into a coherent category without much aid from language, and within this coherent category infants can further subcategorize the relation based on the tight-fit feature. In contrast, instances of the support relation may be viewed as quite diverse in terms of the way support is configured between the figure and the ground object. For example, in the case of "putting a ring on a pole," the relationship of the figure (ring) to the ground (pole) is encirclement, and for "putting a Lego piece on another" it is attachment, and for "putting a bottle cap on bottle" it is covering. In an infant's mind, each of these configurations may be processed as distinct and object specific and may be more salient than the tight-fit feature (see Bowerman & Choi, 2003; Gentner, 2003) as outlined in hypothesis 2 above. Such processing may lead to nondistinction of the two test scenes I presented (i.e., they are equally different from the scenes participants were familiarized with).

Of course, it is also possible that 9-month-old infants treat all types of support relations as similar and thus have formed a single category of support. Such processing would also lead to nondistinction of loose-on and tight-on. However, considering the recent findings of event-specificity in infant cognition and Casasola and Cohen's (2002) findings (as well as cross-linguistic differences on support categories; see below), it is less likely to be the case. Nevertheless, this possibility needs to be tested against hypothesis 2. My lab has begun to do so.

In our studies, the developmental patterns of the containment and support categories also differed in terms of their relations to language. For the containment relation, 9-, 11-, and 14-month-olds showed the same categorization pattern cross-linguistically. But for the support relation, 11- and 14-month-olds in the E environments were different from those in the K environments. In particular, K infants showed a significant preference toward the tight-fit support relation, whereas E infants did not. These language-specific patterns are in the direction of the semantic system of the corresponding adult language, suggesting that language-specific input is guiding infant's spatial categorization regarding the support relation. More concretely, assuming that infants analyze diverse types of support configuration as distinct (as discussed above), K infants are getting special help from the language-specific input (i.e., hearing *kkita* across a variety of situations) to see tight fit as a common feature across various instances of support. It is remarkable that this process begins from 11 months of age.

The differential treatment by preverbal infants for the containment and support categories is in line with some recent findings in infant cognition studies as well as cross-linguistic studies of spatial semantics in adult languages. In infant cognition, there is converging evidence that infants learn about each event category separately. In particular, Baillargeon and her colleagues (Baillargeon, 2002; Hespos & Baillargeon, 2001) have shown that infants' rules about physical events are initially narrow in scope: Infants do not generalize rules or variables acquired about one type of event category (e.g., occlusion) to another (e.g., containment). For example, at 4.5 months, infants understand that a tall object is still visible when it is put behind a short occluder, but they think that a tall object would be completely hidden (i.e., not visible) even when it is put in a short container. So their reasoning about height in an occlusion event is not generalized to a container event. Baillargeon (2002) summarizes, "infants view events involving occluders, containers, and covers as belonging to separate categories, and do not generalize information acquired about one category to the others" (p. 61).

The discrepancy between containment and support is also in line with a recent study conducted by Levinson and his colleagues (Levinson et al., 2003). Levinson et al. conducted a cross-linguistic study of spatial semantic categories using 9 languages of different language families. In this study, the researchers showed some 70 pictures of objects in various spatial relationships and configurations (e.g., apple in bowl, nail in wood, coat on hook, stamp on envelope, cap on bottle) and asked speakers to describe them in their language. On these elicitation data, Levinson et al. conducted a multidimensional cluster analysis to examine which spatial relations are treated semantically similar or different across languages. (Pictures that are ascribed to the same word would be considered similar.) Overall, they found significant differences across the languages, thus seriously challenging stronger versions of the universal conceptual categories hypothesis. Within such cross-linguistic diversity, however, the data showed a converging pattern that is intriguing to the present issue: while the various containment relations are considered similar across most of the languages, various types of support relations form distinct clusters. For example, the relations of on top of, on, over, attachment, and covering are categorized distinctly in different languages. Even what we call good *on* relations in English form distinct clusters in a cross-linguistic comparison: Languages may treat "book on shelf," "tablecloth on table," "tree on mountain," and "man on the roof" as distinct from "cup on table," "cat on mat," or "pen on desk" on the basis of variables such as humanness, type of ground object, and amount of ground covered. Such cross-linguistic diversity for the support relation suggests that there are many different ways to conceptualize or classify various types of support, and language is one of the guiding principles for learners to select a particular way of categorizing them.

Conclusion

In this chapter, I have examined how preverbal infants may be ready to acquire the language-specific semantics on the containment and support relations. Results of our studies suggest that infants analyze the containment and support relations in different ways. Whereas infants categorically distinguished the containment relation on the basis of the tight-fit feature, they did not do so for the support relation. I offered one explanation: the two relations differ in the degree of homogeneity of the spatial configuration, and perhaps that is why subdivision of the relation by tight-fit feature is easier for the containment relation than for the support relation. Our studies also suggest that language plays a differential role for the two types of relation: Whereas no language effects were found for the containment relation, significant language differences were shown for the support category (for 11- and 14-month-olds). This suggests that language interacts with early spatial cognition in specific ways for different types of spatial category.

Our findings, taken together, show that the relation between language and cognition is a complex one from an early stage in child development. We have just begun to explore this complex relationship. Indeed, many questions follow from our findings. For example, what is the precise nature of the way infants analyze various types of the support relation (and other spatial relations)? Does the interaction between language and cognition change over time as children master the language? For example, is the distinction between tight-in and loose-in categories maintained in English-learning children at later stages even though their language does not distinguish them in a systematic way? (See Choi, in press, for some interesting results.) Both developmental psychologists' work on children's cognition and linguists' work on universal and language-specific properties of spatial language will be needed to understand the relation between language and cognition.

Acknowledgments This research was supported by National Science Foundation (BCS-0091493) and National Institute of Health (1R03HD43831-01). I would like to thank Laura Greenig for coordinating every aspect of the study and Emily Wilson and Beth Gravis for their diligent work in recruitment, data collection, and analysis. My deep thanks also go to all the children (and the parents) who participated in the study. In addition, I would like to thank the directors of Chungmaeul, Krada, and Samsung child care centers (in Seoul, Korea) as well as the on-site assistants, Suran Park and Wounwoo Lee. Their help was essential in collecting the Korean data.

Notes

1. English has words such as *tight* and *fit* to refer to tight fit. However, these words are not systematically used to refer to a tight-fit relation as a result of a dynamic action, and their meanings are different from *kkita* in Korean. *Kkita* typically has to do with objects having complementary shapes that interlock tightly in a three-dimensional way. Thus, *kkita* cannot be used in expressions such as "this bed *fits* my size" or "these shoes *fit* loosely."

2. Our preliminary analysis of data from older children suggests that at 24 months, K children (but not E children) can categorically distinguish between loose-on and tight-on.

References

Aguiar, A., & Baillargeon, R. (1998). Eight-and-a-half-month-old infants' reasoning about containment events. *Child Development, 16*(3), 636–653.

Baillargeon, R. (1995). A model of physical reasoning in infancy. *Advances in Infancy Research, 9*, 305–371.

Baillargeon, R. (2002). The acquisition of physical knowledge in infancy: A summary in eight lessons. In U. Goswami (Ed.), *Handbook of childhood cognitive development* (pp. 47–83). Oxford: Blackwell.

Baillargeon, R., & Hanko-Summers, S. (1990). Is the top object adequately supported by the bottom object? Young infants' understanding of support relations. *Cognitive Development, 5*, 29–53.

Bowerman, M. (1996a). Learning how to structure space for language: A crosslinguistic perspective. In P. Bloom, M. Peterson, L. Nadel, & M. Garrett (Eds.), *Language and space* (pp. 385–486). Cambridge, MA: MIT Press.

Bowerman, M. (1996b). The origins of children's spatial semantic categories: Cognitive versus linguistic determinants. In J. J. Gumperz & S. C. Levinson (Eds.), *Rethinking linguistic relativity* (pp. 145–176). Cambridge: Cambridge University Press.

Bowerman, M., & Choi, S. (2001). Shaping meanings for languages: Universal and language specific in the acquisition of spatial semantic categories. In M. Bowerman & S. C. Levinson (Eds.), *Language acquisition and conceptual development* (pp. 475–511). Cambridge: Cambridge University Press.

Bowerman, M., & Choi, S. (2003). Space under construction: Language-specific spatial categorization in first language acquisition. In D. Gentner & S. Goldin-Meadow (Eds.), *Language in mind: Advances in the study of language and cognition* (pp. 387–428). Cambridge: MIT Press.

Bowerman, M., & Pederson, E. (1992). *Cross-linguistic perspectives on topological spatial relationships.* Paper presented at the annual meeting of the American Anthropological Association, San Francisco, December.

Brown, P. (1994). The INs and ONs of Tzeltal locative expressions: The semantics of static descriptions of location. *Linguistics, 32*, 743–790.

Bybee, J. (1985). *Morphology: A study of the relation between meaning and form.* Amsterdam: John Benjamins.

Casasola, M., & Cohen, L. (2002). Infant categorization of containment, support and tight-fit spatial relationships. *Developmental Science, 5*, 247–264.

Choi, S. (in press). Influence of language-specific input on spatial cognition: Categories of containment. *First Language.*

Choi, S., & Bowerman, M. (1991). Learning to express motion events in English and Korean: The influence of language-specific lexicalization patterns. *Cognition, 41*, 83–121.

Choi, S., McDonough, L., Bowerman, M., & Mandler, J. (1999). Early sensitivity to language-specific spatial categories in English and Korean. *Cognitive Development, 14*, 241–268.

Gentner, D. (2003). Why we are so smart? In D. Gentner & S. Goldin-Meadow (Eds.), *Language in mind: Advances in the study of language and cognition* (pp. 387–428). Cambridge: MIT Press.

Gibson, E. J., & Spelke, E. S. (1983). The development of perception. In J. H. Flavell & E. M. Markman (Eds.), *Handbook of child psychology: Vol. 3. Cognitive development* (4th ed., pp. 1–76). New York: Wiley.

Hespos, S., & Baillargeon, R. (2001). Infants' knowledge about occlusion and containment events: A surprising discrepancy. *Psychological Science, 12*(2), 141–147.

Hunter, M. A., Ames, E. W., & Koopman, R. (1983). Effects of stimulus complexity and familiarization time on infant preferences for novel and familiar stimuli. *Developmental Psychology, 19,* 338–353.

Jackendoff, R. (1983). *Semantics and cognition.* Cambridge, MA: MIT Press.

Landau, B., & Jackendoff, R. (1993). "What" and "where" in spatial language and spatial cognition. *Behavioral and Brain Sciences, 16,* 217–238.

Levinson, S. C., Kita, S., Haun, D., & Rasch, B. (2002). Returning the tables: Language affects spatial reasoning. *Cognition, 84,* 155–188.

Levinson, S. C., Meier, S., & The Language and Cognitive Group (2003). "Natural concepts" in the spatial topological domain—adpositional meaning in crosslinguistic perspective: An exercise in semantic typology. *Language, 79,* 485–516.

Li, P., & Gleitman, L. (2002). Turning the tables: Language and spatial reasoning. *Cognition, 83,* 265–294.

McDonough, L., Choi, S., & Mandler, J. (2003). Understanding spatial relations: Flexible infants, lexical adults. *Cognitive Psychology, 46,* 229–259.

Needham, A., & Baillargeon, R. (1993). Intuitions about support in 4.5-month-old infants. *Cognition, 47,* 121–148.

Pederson, E., Danziger, E., Levinson, S., Kita, S., Senft, G., & Wilkins, D. (1998). Semantic typology and spatial conceptualization. *Language, 74,* 557–589.

Piaget, J., & Inhelder, B. (1967). *The child's conception of space.* New York: W. W. Norton.

Slobin, D. I. (1996). From "thought and language" to "thinking for speaking." In J. J. Gumperz & S. C. Levinson (Eds.), *Rethinking linguistic relativity* (pp. 70–96). Cambridge: Cambridge University Press.

Slobin, D. I. (2001). Form-function relations: How do children find out what they are? In M. Bowerman & S. C. Levinson (Eds.), *Language acquisition and conceptual development* (pp. 406–449). Cambridge: Cambridge University Press.

Talmy, L. (1985). Lexicalization patterns: Semantic structure in lexical forms. In T. Shopen (Ed.), *Language typology and syntactic description: Vol. III. Grammatical categories and the lexicon* (pp. 57–149). Cambridge: Cambridge University Press.

Thelen, E., & Schoner, G. (2002). *A dynamic field model of infant habituation.* Poster presented at the International Congress of Infant Studies, Toronto, Canada.

Whorf, B. L. (1956). *Language, thought, and reality: Selected writings of Benjamin Lee Whorf.* Ed. J. B. Carroll. Cambridge, MA: MIT Press.

8 The Roots of Verbs in Prelinguistic Action Knowledge

Jennifer Sootsman Buresh, Amanda Woodward, and Camille W. Brune

In this chapter, we consider infants' prelinguistic action knowledge and how this knowledge might be recruited for verb learning. There are at least two ways in which action knowledge could contribute to verb learning. First, understanding the actions of others is critical for discerning their communicative intentions, and thus provides a foundation for all aspects of language learning not just verb learning (see Tomasello, 1999). Second, infants' action knowledge must provide some of the initial elements of meaning that come to be conveyed in verbs. We focus on the second of these issues, since it is unique to verb learning.

Verbs describe events and relations. As many researchers have noted (e.g., Gentner & Boroditsky, 2001; Gleitman, 1990), the same event can be conceptualized in a multitude of ways. A given action, for example, could be described in terms of the observed physical motion through space, or in terms of a more abstract analysis of the causal or intentional structure of the event (see Edwards & Goodwin, 1986; Huttenlocher, Smiley, & Charney, 1983; Tomasello, 1992). At each level of description, more than one analysis is generally possible. To illustrate, imagine a child running toward and entering a school. At the level of motions, we could choose verbs to focus on the manner of motion or the path the child has taken, for example:

She ran into in the school.
She entered the school in a rush.

And other descriptions are possible from several vantage points:

She hurried to school.
She tried to get in before the bell rang.

Adults' verbs convey these different conceptualizations. Children's first verbs may or may not express these same meanings. Which kinds of meanings appear in the verbs of young learners is, in part, a product of how they conceptualize actions and events.

In early investigations of lexical development, a driving concern was the extent to which infants' first words were grounded in well-organized concepts. This concern was considered in some detail in the case of words than name objects. Some suggested that infants' first object terms did not reflect adult-like conceptual structure, but instead were associated with disorganized clumps of experience or complexive groupings (e.g., Vygotsky, 1962). To illustrate, *cookie* might initially extend to cookies, cookie jars, and kitchens, with more mature word meanings dependent on the putatively late acquisition of the object concept. These proposals were called into question and ultimately ruled out by two lines of evidence. First, investigations of prelinguistic cognition revealed that the conceptual substrate this aspect of the lexicon, namely well-formed object representations, is in place some months before the first words appear (Baillargeon, 1993; Spelke, Breinlinger, Macomber, & Jacobson, 1992). Second, careful observational and experimental work revealed that even 1-year-olds produce and understand words as referring to object categories rather than to undifferentiated clumps of sensory data (Balaban & Waxman, 1997; Huttenlocher & Smiley, 1987; Waxman & Booth, 2003; Waxman & Markow, 1998).

In considering the parallel question of early verb meanings, we first review recent evidence concerning infants' event representations and then the extent to which these aspects of conceptual structure appear in infants' words. We focus on a particular class of events, those involving actions of other people, because verbs describing them are prevalent in children's vocabularies and because recent research has shed light on infants' prelinguistic action representations.

Infants' Action Analysis

Verbs convey varied meanings, but many, especially those used by young children, concern concrete, observable events—in particular, the actions of people. There is rich action information in the infants' milieu. Indeed, infants develop immersed in the actions of social partners. How do infants represent these actions? One possibility is that infants are limited to representing actions as physical motions. Alternatively, infants may, at least in some cases, represent the underlying intentional relations implied by these actions. At the heart of adult action analysis is the understanding that certain actions center on the relation between an agent and the object at which his or her actions are directed (Barresi & Moore, 1996). Many verbs encode these relations. To illustrate, imagine a woman turning to look at and grasp a cup on the table. To adult observers, the relation between the woman and the cup organizes the event. It is in terms of this relation that we would most readily describe it ("She saw the cup," or "She grasped the cup," or "She found the cup," etc.). We can notice other aspects of the event, for example, the path taken by her arms, the exact motion of her head and body as she turns. We have verbs that describe these patterns of motion, but these aspects of the action seem less central than the agent-object relation.

A number of recent studies have investigated whether and under what conditions infants represent actions in terms of intentional relations. As an example, in one study from our laboratory, we asked whether infants represent a common, concrete action—grasping, as centering on the relation between the agent and the object of her action. We used the habituation-dishabituation technique to investigate infants' representations of events like the cup example described earlier. An experimenter, seated between and behind two objects (a bear and a ball) turned to look at and grasp one of the objects (see figure 1 in Woodward, 2003). Infants viewed the same reaching event repeatedly until their attention to it declined. Then we reversed the positions of the two objects and showed infants test events that either varied the agent-object relation or varied the surface properties of the experimenter's motions while preserving the agent-object relation. That is, on new-object trials, the experimenter turned to the same side as during habituation, this time looking at and grasping a different toy. On new-side test trials, she turned to a different side than during habituation, this time grasping the same toy as during habituation. If infants represented the original event in terms of the agent-object relation, we predicted longer looking on new-object trials, which disrupted this relation, than on new-side trials, which preserved it. This is what we found. We tested 7- and 9-month-old infants, and each group responded by looking longer on new-object than new-side trials.

Despite the fact that the woman's motions were different on new-side trials, infants did not seem to find these changes as salient as a change in the agent-object relation. In fact, although both groups showed reliable recovery from habituation on new-object trials, neither group recovered on new-side trials. Adults would be likely to extend the same verbal description to the habituation and new-side events ("She grasped the bear" in each case) but a different description to the new-object event ("She grasped the ball"). Infants represent these events in similar terms. Findings like these have been obtained for a variety of intentional, object-directed actions in infants ranging in age from 3 to 13 months (see Guajardo & Woodward, 2004; Jovanovic et al., 2003; Kiraly, Jovanovic, Prinz, Aschersleben, & Gergely, 2003; Sommerville & Woodward, 2005; Sommerville, Woodward, & Needham, 2005; Sootsman, Morgante, Wilson Brune, & Woodward, 2003; Woodward, 1998, 1999, 2003, 2005; Woodward & Guajardo, 2002; Woodward & Sommerville, 2000).

The example we outlined earlier concerning the woman and the cup involves several kinds of connections simultaneously. The woman attended to the cup, directing her eyes to it, and shifting her body with respect to it, and she also acted on it concretely by grasping it. The latter action, grasping, appears early in infants' action knowledge. By 5 to 6 months, infants represent grasping events as object-directed, even when they are only able to see the grasping hand (Jovanovic et al.,

2003; Woodward, 1998, 1999). This response seems to be driven by knowledge about meaningful human actions. Infants do not interpret as object-directed matched events in which inanimate objects move toward and touch or grasp other objects (Jovanovic et al., 2003; Woodward, 1998), or purposeless or ambiguous human motions (Sommerville & Woodward, 2005; Woodward, 1999; Woodward & Sommerville, 2000; see also Guajardo & Woodward, 2004). Importantly, the inanimate and ambiguous actions exerted the same kinds of influence on infants' overt attention as did purposeful human actions. To illustrate, in one study (Woodward, 1999), infants in one condition saw an experimenter grasp a toy, and infants in another condition saw the experimenter drop her hand onto the toy, palm up, in an apparently purposeless manner. The events in the two conditions were very similar in terms of the experimenter's range of motion and the degree of contact between her hand and the toy. Moreover, the two events directed infants' attention to the object to the same extent. Nevertheless, infants responded to the two events differently: they treated the grasp, but not the back-of-hand event, as object-directed. Thus, infants' responses seem not to be driven by low-level factors, such as the way the actor's hand moved or the way the events entrained their attention.

Attentional Relations

Concrete actions like grasping create observable evidence concerning their object-directedness. These actions make things move. Acts of attention, for example gazing or pointing, do not exert these same kinds of impact on the world. For this reason, attentional relations seem (to developmental psychologists as well as non-scientists) to be more uniquely psychological. When and how do infants come to understand the invisible connection between a person and the object of his or her attention? Researchers have commonly used infants' tendency to orient in responses to an adult's gaze shift as evidence of understanding the act of looking (e.g., Scaife & Bruner, 1975). However, orienting responses could be driven by factors other than an understanding of the "looking" relation (see Corkum & Moore, 1995; Woodward, 2003).

To get clearer evidence on this issue, we adapted our visual habituation technique to ask this question (Woodward, 2003). Infants viewed events like the ones in figure 8.1, except that the woman only looked at the toy; she did not grasp it. Following habituation to one looking event, the positions of the toys were reversed and infants viewed two kinds of test trials: On new-object trials the woman turned to the same side as during habituation, this time looking at a new toy. On new-side trials, she turned to the other side to look at the same toys as during habituation. If infants represent the invisible link between looker and object, we predict longer looking on new-object trials than new-side trials. We tested 7-, 9-, and 12-month-old infants, and infants at each age robustly followed the woman's gaze shifts—they spent much more time looking at the object at which she gazed than at the other object. However, this orienting response did not guarantee that infants recovered the looking relation. Only 12-month-olds looked longer on new-object trials than new-side trials. Seven- and 9-month-olds did not even recover attention during test trials. It was as if they identified the objects as being the same (The woman, the bear, and the ball again. How boring!), without considering the relations between them. A similar study, which included pointing as well as looking, yielded nearly identical findings (Woodward & Guajardo, 2002). Infants followed the experimenter's gaze and point robustly, but only the oldest infants tested, 12-month-olds, responded to the object-directed structure of the pointing action.

These findings fit well with long-standing observations that infants become more organized in their triadic interaction patterns at around this age (Carpenter, Nagell, & Tomasello, 1998) and therefore indicate that this change in social responsiveness is accompanied by a change in social cognition. Moreover, other findings shed further light on infants' understanding of attention. Phillips, Wellman, and Spelke (2002) found that 12-month-old infants understand the regular relations between looking and acting, namely that people tend to look at the objects they are about to act on (see also Sodian & Thoermer, 2004). Brooks and Melzoff (2002) report that at around this same age, infants begin to distinguish between obstructed and unobstructed gaze in social partners, suggesting that they know something about the conditions under which people can see things. Moreover, by shortly after their first birthdays, infants employ their newly minted understanding of attention to inform their interpretation of both emotional expressions (Moses, Baldwin, Rosicky, & Tidball, 2001) and language (Woodward, 2003).

Flexible Action Interpretation

The findings summarized so far indicate that infants are not limited to representing actions in terms of their surface structure but instead have begun to understand the relational structure of action. Infants do not seem to begin with the general expectation that all human motions will be object directed. Instead, they seem to discover the relational nature of particular actions, beginning with familiar actions, such as grasping and gazing. These particular actions are so ubiquitous that they have become, for adults, metaphors for more abstract intentional relations (e.g., "The prize was just beyond my grasp" or "I see what you mean"). However, adults are not limited to understanding certain canonical actions as relational. Instead, we can interpret the same scene through different lenses, focusing on the overt motion or the underlying relations, considering descriptions at different levels of analysis, or from different perspectives.

Recent findings show that by the end of the first year of life, infants engage in flexible action analysis in some situations. For one, they can interpret the same motion as being goal-directed or not based on the physical context in which it occurs or based on the other behaviors of the agent. Illustrating the first of these, Gergely, Csibra, and their colleagues (Csibra, Gergely, Biro, Koos, & Brockbank 1999; Gergely & Csibra, 2003; Gergely, Nasady, Csibra, & Biro, 1995) have found that 12-month-old (and sometimes 9-month-old) infants interpret the same motion, a circuitous motion ending in contact with a goal object, as being goal-directed in some contexts (when the motion circumvents a barrier) but not in others (when no barrier is present) (see also Phillips & Wellman, in press; Sodian, Schoeppner, & Metz, 2004). Illustrating the second, Behne, Carpenter, Call, and Tomasello (2005) have found that infants as young as 9 months of age differentiated between two very similar motions, one carried out in a purposeful manner and the other marked as "accidental" with facial and vocal expressions. When an adult purposefully refused to hand infants a toy, they became frustrated. When the adult "accidentally" failed to hand them the toy, they were less frustrated.

Moreover, infants can represent the complementary roles of two entities in the same event. In one study, Golinkoff (1975) habituated infants to standard plausible events (e.g., a man pushed a woman or a man pushed a table). Fourteen- and 18-month-old infants watched anomalous test events (e.g., table pushed the man) longer than the plausible test events (e.g., woman pushed the man), suggesting that they differentiated the agent and recipient roles (see also Golinkoff & Kerr, 1978). Recent evidence shows sensitivity to different roles during the first year of life. Schoeppner, Sodian, and Pauen (2004) showed 10-month-old infants give-and-take sequences involving two puppets. Infants were habituated to a sequence in which one puppet was always the giver and the other was always the taker. Then, in the test, these roles were reversed on some trials, whereas on other trials the direction motion of the puppets was reversed but their roles stayed the same. Ten- and 12-month-old infants looked reliably longer on role change trials than motion change trials, but only if the exchange was apparently purposeful. Thus, infants seemed to represent the giver and taker roles embedded in the event, suggesting that they have access to the representations needed to eventually acquire verbs like *give* and *take*, which adopt different perspectives on the same event.

Actions at Varying Levels of Analysis

Actions can be described not only at a local level ("She grasped the pen") but also in terms of the overarching plans that drive them ("She wrote a letter"). Mature observers perceive actions in terms of what Zacks and Tverksy (2001) termed *partnomomic hierarchies*, in which subgoals are understood as parts of more abstract plans. Infants begin to represent actions in this way by the end of the first year of life—they attend not only to the local relations between actions and objects, but also to relations between actions and ultimate outcomes (Sommerville & Woodward, 2005; Woodward & Sommerville, 2000). To illustrate, in one study (Sommerville & Woodward, 2005), 12-month-old infants saw an adult reach toward and grasp a cloth that supported a toy and then pull the cloth toward her in order to grasp the toy. The question of interest was whether infants interpreted the adult's grasp of the cloth as directed at the cloth itself (the proximal goal) or instead at the toy (the ultimate goal). To address this question, infants viewed habituation events featuring two different-colored cloths, each supporting a different toy. During habituation trials, an adult pulled one of the cloths in order to obtain the toy. After habituation, the location of the toys was reversed, and infants saw the adult act toward either a new toy (new toy event) or a new cloth (new cloth event). Twelve-month-old infants looked longer at the new toy than new cloth events, indicating sensitivity to the goal of the sequence. This effect depended on the existence of a causal relation between pulling the cloth and obtaining the toy. When we altered the events by taking the toy off the cloth, 12-month-olds did not interpret the actor's grasp of the cloth as directed at the toy.

We also found a developmental change in infants' interpretation of these sequences. Ten-month-old infants, as a group, did not recover the overarching goal of this sequence. However, at this age, infants' goal sensitivity was related to their own ability to implement goal-directed strategies in a similar action task: Infants who produced a high frequency of apparently goal-directed strategies in the action task represented the toy as the actor's goal, whereas those that produced few goal-directed strategies apparently misrepresented the goal of the cloth-pulling sequence as the cloth itself. Thus, under more supportive conditions, perhaps given a simpler relation between the two actions, even 10-month-olds might have recovered the overarching goal.

Conclusions From the Research

The findings of the last several years yield strong evidence that infants have begun to analyze the relational structure of human actions during the first year of life. These findings are consistent with those of studies of nonsocial event analysis. Infants represent causal roles in launching sequences (Leslie & Keeble, 1987), causal chains (Cohen, Rundell, Spellman, & Cashon, 1999), and other physical relations that are encoded by verbs in some languages (Casasola & Cohen, 2002; Choi, McDonough, Bowerman, & Mandler, 1999). We focus on actions because they are pervasive in infants' experience and in their early talk. But we note that they are but one aspect of the infants' emerging ability to represent the relational structure of events.

Taken together, these findings indicate that by the end of the first year of life, infants have the conceptual material relevant for a range of verb meanings, including not only verbs that encode the observable trajectories of moving objects (e.g., *fall*) but also verbs that encode the outcomes of causal sequences (e.g., *open*), intentional actions (e.g., *get*), transactions (e.g., *give*), and psychological states (e.g., *see*). Moreover, there is evidence that in some circumstances infants can interpret an event through more than one lens, considering it for example, as goal-directed or not based on the context, in terms of the complementary roles of two inter-active agents, or in terms of proximal versus ultimate goals. Given that the con-ceptual material exists, when do infants begin to put it into words? We next turn to the question of whether these kinds of meanings are, in fact, expressed in chil-dren's earliest verbs or event words.

The First Action Words

Which aspects of events are first expressed in children's language? Given that re-searchers have been investigating early word learning for more than a century, one might think this question is easily answered. It is not. There is debate about which word forms should be considered relevant to the question. A strict definition would include only words that are members of the syntactic category verb. How-ever, we could also include a variety of words from other grammatical categories that children use to convey information about actions and events. In fact, many of the first words that English-speaking children produce relate to events such as the appearance of a person (e.g., *hi*) or function as a request for an action (e.g., *up*), but they are not verbs. This issue also arises when considering development across languages. Different languages can use different word classes to refer to the same event (see, e.g., Choi & Bowerman, 1991), a fact that complicates cross-linguistic comparisons. Across studies, researchers have adopted different focal sets—driven very often by somewhat different questions. We seek to address two issues: (1) which aspects of action do children first describe? and (2) how does action knowledge contribute to their learning of verbs in particular? Given this dual focus, we consider evidence about verbs as well as other classes of words that children use to describe actions. Beyond deciding which words to consider, it is also necessary to determine what children mean when they use them. This issue is not unique to the study of verb acquisition. The indeterminacy problem describes the infinite number of potential meanings that could be associated with any word. How are researchers to know which of these meanings the child means to convey?

In confronting these problems, researchers have adopted three general meth-ods for investigating the meanings children glean from and convey with verbs and other action terms: analyses of spontaneous speech, laboratory measures of verb comprehension, and laboratory procedures in which novel verbs are trained. We next review the evidence from each of these approaches with a focus on the earli-est event terms and verbs.

Event Words in Natural Discourse

Researchers have long noted that action words appear very early, among the first 50 words in English-speaking children (Benedict, 1979; Bloom, Tinker, & Mar-gulis, 1993; Gopnik & Meltzoff, 1997; Nelson, 1973; Tomasello, 1992). Benedict

(1979) found that 19% and Nelson (1973) found that 13% of the first words seemed to be about actions. Moreover, several of these words could be interpreted as comments on goals (*uh-oh*), perception (*all-gone, look, see*), and other aspects of agents' relations to each other and the world (e.g., *give, bye-bye*). Indeed, Gopnik and Meltzoff (1984) found that infants began to use words such as *uh-oh* and *did it* during periods in which they were honing their problem-solving abilities. This suggests that these terms express newfound insight into the purposes behind babies' own actions.

However, it is often difficult to tell whether these early words name actions or simply accompany them. Many of children's early event words seem to function as performatives, that is, as part of the action rather than the name for it. Children's understanding of these words is idiosyncratic and context specific. For example, Tomasello (1992) reported that in his diary study of his daughter Travis's action words, including verbs, there were several months in which terms were limited to particular performative contexts. At 17 months, Travis used the word *play-play* in the context of banging the piano keys and the word *phone* in response to hearing the telephone ring. Careful cross-context analyses revealed Travis also produced verbs that seemed to name actions. As reviewed next, this finding is consistent with others. By the second half of the second year, many children produce names for actions.

When children produce verbs (or other terms that seem to refer to actions), do they at first name only the physical properties of actions, or can they also name the logical and intentional relations that structure action? In a foundational paper, Huttenlocher, Smiley, and Charney (1983) framed this question and collected initial evidence to address it. Their goal was to use verb production and comprehension as evidence about young children's conceptual representations of actions. They reasoned that if children are able to represent actions not only in terms of physical motions but also in terms of underlying relations and goals, then this should be evident in their use and understanding of verbs that encode these different aspects of action. Given this focus, Huttenlocher and colleagues were particularly interested in verbs such as *dance, run,* and *wiggle,* which name observable patterns of motion, and verbs such as *bring, find,* and *give,* which rely on an understanding of the relational structure of an event and, perhaps, on the agent's goals in acting.

The 22- to 30-month-old children they tested produced and comprehended both kinds of verbs, thus providing initial evidence that they have access to both kinds of action analysis in at least some cases. However, it turned out that these two kinds of verbs were not equally distributed across the child's own actions and those of others. Children produced both kinds of verbs when talking about their own actions (though they used intentional action verbs more often), and they were able to comprehend both kinds of verbs, as evidenced by their ability to respond to commands such as "sit down" and "get X" (see also Goldin-Meadow, Seligman, & Gelman, 1976). In the case of the observed actions of other people, in contrast, children much more readily identified movement verbs than intentional action verbs. Huttenlocher and colleagues suggested that this difference was due to the fact that children only know their own intentional states, not those of others, and that very young children are therefore limited to representing others' actions in terms of movement.

There are two ways in which this conclusion might be true. Children might not know that others have intentions at all. This framing is at odds with the findings, summarized earlier, that infants analyze others' actions not only as physical movements but also, in some cases, as intentional actions. Alternatively, children might understand that others have intentions but be less able to infer a person's particular intention based on observational evidence, particularly for complex events. Determining which particular intention a person has in mind can be a difficult enterprise even for adults. One's own goals may be more salient, or more directly knowable in some cases.

Furthermore, later diary studies (Edwards & Goodwin, 1986; Tomasello, 1992) call the strong form of the conclusion into question because they report that 16- to 18-month-olds sometimes use action words for others' as well as their own actions. For example, Tomasello (1992) reports that at around 16 months of age, Travis used verbs to talk about the movements of other people (e.g., *crying*, *fall-down*) and to request and comment on both her own and others' relational actions (e.g., *move* [*an object*], *get-it*) (see also Edwards & Goodwin, 1986).

Intentional action verbs such as *give* or *find* are about relations. In order to extend them appropriately, children must at least encode the relevant relations (e.g., the relations between giver, object, and recipient). For adults, these actions are also bound up with our understanding of others' psychological states (intentions, perceptions, etc.). It is difficult to know whether babies also represent these aspects of events such as giving or finding. However, more explicit evidence for babies' understanding psychological relations comes from their use of psychological verbs, such as *want* and *see*. We turn next to these verbs.

Many studies have investigated children's use of verbs that, in adult usage, directly encode the psychological nature of intentional relations. In these analyses, a central focus has been the attempt to determine whether children mean to convey information about a psychological relation, or instead use the term as part of an idiomatic expression ("You know what?" versus "I didn't know my shoes were in the basement"). Verbs like *gonna*, *try*, and *mean to* seem express children's intentions from relatively early on. Between 24 and 30 months of age, multiple studies report production of *gonna* (Bartsch & Wellman, 1995; Dunn, 1999; Dunn, Bretherton, & Munn, 1987; Dunn, Brown, & Beardsall, 1991; Fenson et al., 1994). Using the context surrounding children's speech, Bartsch and Wellman (1995) found that 2-year-olds said *gonna* to express goal-directed actions in the immediate future. Six of the 10 children in the sample used these terms first to refer to only their own actions. For three of the children, mental verbs for their own actions and those of others emerged during the same observation. Only one child described others' actions before describing his own actions.

Children also express their intentions using desire terms such as *want* and *need*. For example, Travis, at 23 months of age, replaced her use of *have* and *hold* with *want* (to obtain an object; Tomasello, 1992). By 28 months, nearly all of the children in Bretherton and Beeghly's (1982) sample produced it; of these children, 77% used *want* to talk about themselves and other people. When Bartsch and Wellman (1995) analyzed the context surrounding children's early mental verbs, they found that *want* comprised 97% of 21- to 24-month-olds' desire terms. In their analysis, children's use of *want* was not limited to making requests. Children also used *want* in reference to forming goal-directed action plans, wanting to misbehave, and wanting to act like another person. As Bartsch and Wellman (1995) noted, children's desire terms are intimately linked to actions, "From its earliest appearance, talk about desires seems to rationalize, to explain, and at time to argue for certain actions by appeal to the actors wants" (p. 116).

In addition to goals, children use verbs to comment on perceptual experience by their second birthdays if not before. By 28 months, Bretherton and Beeghly (1982) found that *see* was used by 97% of their sample of 30 children, *look* by 90%, and *watch* by 80%. In all cases, over half of the children used these words to refer to themselves as well as to refer to other people. Children used these words to talk about their own behavior (e.g., "I don't want to see it"), or to request action from another person (e.g., "Don't watch me"). Travis used *look* and *see* at 19 months of age to make a request and to direct another's attention (Tomasello, 1992). By 23 months she used *see* to refer to herself as perceiving something, rather than as a request to direct attention or to comment on what she was doing. This fits with Gopnik and Meltzoff's (1997) review of the CHILDES database, which found that children first produced *see* between 18 and 30 months of age to replace the word *gone* when making a request for something that was no longer in view. Shortly after this, *see* was extended to include situations describing others' ability to see.

Experimental Studies

Naturalistic observations, though rich and ecologically informative, provide a limited window through which to view children's verb knowledge. Children's utterances are driven by pragmatic forces that may lead them to produce some verbs only in limited contexts, for example, to announce their own intentions (Edwards & Goodwin, 1986). As Goldfield (2000) has suggested, the pragmatics of American children's interactions with their mothers often involve requests for noun production (e.g., "What's this called?") and few requests for verb production (e.g., "What's it doing?"). Rather than elicit verb production, parents are more likely to elicit action production (e.g., "What can you make it do?"). Naturalistic evidence concerning children's comprehension may be similarly constrained.

Parents report that their infants understand event words in everyday speech (Fenson et al., 1994). Evidence from parental reports suggests that 50% of

8-month-old infants understand words that are embedded in games and routines (e.g., *peek-a-boo*) and 50% of 12-month-olds understand words associated with actions (e.g., *eat, drink*). These reports are difficult to evaluate because, concerns about parents as informants aside, infants may understand these terms as parts of actions rather than names for actions.

To circumvent these problems, researchers developed more controlled paradigms. In one of the first of these, Goldin-Meadow et al. (1976) assessed 14- to 27-month-old babies' comprehension and production of familiar nouns and verbs in the course of a structured test session in their homes. To distinguish familiar routines from true verb comprehension, they asked babies to produce familiar actions with unusual objects, for example, "Eat the bear." All babies responded correctly at least some of the time, and babies 22 months of age and older responded correctly most of the time. Their items included both verbs that name motions (e.g., *jump* and *run*) and verbs that name relations (e.g., *pick up* and *open*). Babies were less able to produce familiar verbs when asked, "What am I doing?" although some were able to respond some of the time (4 to 16 times out of 30 opportunities).

Goldin-Meadow and colleagues' findings were among the first to show that young 2-year-olds comprehend familiar verbs, even in somewhat unusual contexts (e.g., eating the bear). Forbes and Poulin-Dubois (1997) tested the extent to which 20- and 26-month-olds could extend familiar verbs in comprehension. Using a visual preference paradigm, they showed babies films of a person kicking an object and of a person picking up an object, associating each with the familiar labels *kick* and *pick up*. Then they tested babies' comprehension using films that varied the agent, the manner of the action, or the outcome of the action. For example, in the manner change event, the agent picked up the object with her foot, and in the outcome change she grasped the object with her hand, but then put it down rather than picking it up. Twenty-six-month-olds responded correctly when either the agent or manner changed. That is, they seemed to be able to recognize picking up even when a new person did it or when it was done with the foot. However, they did not respond systematically when the outcome changed. These findings suggest that babies regarded the particular patterns of motion less central to the meaning than the outcome.

An alternative vantage point is to teach babies new verbs in the laboratory. This method, developed by Golinkoff, Hirsh-Pasek, Cauley, and Gordon (1987), asks how babies can learn and extend new verbs and what meanings they attach to them. These studies involve a training session whereby the babies associate a verb label for a novel action. In the subsequent testing session, two actions that differ in one key element appear side by side and the child is asked to look at the named action. This manipulation enables the researcher to ask which elements the child attended to and used to define the novel verb. Researchers have used this method to ask whether babies would more readily attach a novel name to motion patterns versus causative actions in an event.

In one of the first uses of this logic, Naigles (1990) found that 25-month-old children could interpret a novel verb as the name for either a pattern of motion or a causal relation. Children watched films of characters engaging these two kinds of action simultaneously while they heard a novel verb either in a transitive sentence (e.g., "The duck is glorping the bunny") or an intransitive sentence (e.g., "The duck and the bunny are glorping"). Children responded appropriately in both cases, looking at the appropriate video that matched the syntax of the accompanying audio track. These data show not only that 25-month-old children can use syntax to determine the meaning of a novel verb but also that they are flexible in their representation of the event in that they are able to interpret it as a distinctive pattern of motion or as a causative relation. Children could endorse either meaning (see also Fisher, 2002; Naigles, 1996).

The results from these syntactic bootstrapping studies suggest that children can flexibly learn verbs that refer either to patterns of motion through space or to intentional relations. In a more explicit manipulation of the intentional structure of the event, Poulin-Dubois and Forbes (2002) tested whether 21- and 27-month-olds could use an agent's behavioral cues to intentions to learn a novel verb. Children viewed videotapes of paired actions that differed in the extent to which the actor conveyed a goal (e.g., *knocking over* [the actor watches his arm move an object on purpose] versus *toppling* [the actor looks away when his arm accidentally moves an object]). Children in the older group used these intentional behaviors to discriminate the actions where the agent's intention differed and consequently were able to learn distinct verbs for the actions. This suggests that by 27 months of age, children interpret events in terms of intentional structure indicated by overt behavioral cues, and use this information to learn new verbs.

Mind the Gap

Throughout this chapter, we have considered the issue of the level at which children represent actions and level at which they name actions. Recent findings from our laboratory and others indicate that infants understand several kinds of intentional relations by the end of the first year. Interestingly, when children begin to use verbs, they name these intentional relations as readily as patterns of motion. There does not seem to be a period during which infants only talk about observable motions. From the start, they also talk about their own (and perhaps others') intentional relations. However, most of the evidence for production and comprehension of these verbs (like others) comes from studies of 2-year-olds, with robust patterns evident around the second birthday but not earlier. The evidence suggests a notable gap between the beginnings of organized thinking about actions and the emergence of words to describe these actions. In the final section of this chapter, we will consider two possible explanations for this gap.

Tracking Actions Versus Extracting Exemplars

In observing an action, one could consider it as an example of a kind of action (e.g., an instance of seeing). Alternatively, one could consider this action within the ongoing stream of action to make inferences about the agents' likely next actions and responses. Adults can freely adopt either stance and may well do both simultaneously. In fact, in mature reasoning, these two stances inform one another. By attending to a person's prior actions, we can identify exemplars of more abstract actions (e.g., buying, hiding), and this categorization in turn aids online action interpretation.

Here we raise the possibility that infants' initial interpretations of actions may be focused on extracting the meanings of event sequences and making sense of an individual's behavior over time rather than on extracting exemplars of particular kinds of actions. Because the latter is required for verb learning, we speculate that infants may not readily pull out the kinds of units that verbs name. Acquiring a label for an action requires pulling out the exemplar. An accurate representation of a verb, for example, *see*, *want*, or *get*, requires an understanding of the event devoid of the context, that is, without reference to the individual person performing the action and without reference to the specific goal object, or the actions which precede and follow it. Conversely, understanding action in context is at the heart of understanding others' behavior ("She saw it, wanted it, and then got it"). The individual who performs the action, the goal object of the action, and the other actions performed by the agent are critical to making sense of the behaviors of social partners.

The habituation studies we reviewed earlier could be accounted for by infants' adopting either stance. For example, consider the studies in which infants see a person grasp one of two objects. Infants may view each habituation trial as an instance of grasping the ball. Thus, they encode the grasping relation as well as the particular object to which it is directed. Then, in the test, infants may respond to the relative novelty of an action exemplar directed at a new object rather than the old object. Alternatively, infants might seek to link the individual habituation trials together as parts of an extended event in order to predict the agent's next actions. ("She still wants that ball. She's going to want the ball this time too.") In this case, longer looking on new goal trials could indicate a violation of expectation ("Oh, now she wants the bear").

A recent series of studies from our laboratory indicates that by 9 months of age, infants seem to treat the habituation events as part of an ongoing stream of the agent's behavior rather than as isolated exemplars (Sootsman & Woodward, 2004). We used a modified version of the paradigm originally designed to assess infants' understanding of goal-directed actions. Infants in one group saw the typical event from our laboratory. In the habituation event, a person grasped one of two objects on a stage, then in the test the locations of the objects were switched and infants looked longer at the new-goal event than the new-side event. Infants in a second group saw the modified condition. They saw one actor perform the habituation event and a different actor perform the test event. Our reasoning was that if infants do not consider the identity of the agent to be an important part of the event, the results of this condition should be identical to those in the original single-actor condition. If however, infants do know that the identity of the agent is an important part of the event and the behavior of one actor does not necessarily relate to the behavior of a second actor, then the results of this condition should differ. The second response pattern is what we found. Infants did not respond systematically in the test trials, indicating that by 9 months of age, infants' interpretation of an event is tied to the individual who performs it. This is noteworthy because it suggests that infants view the event not just as a series of action exemplars devoid of context (e.g., picking up 1, picking up 2, etc.), but instead view actions as connected to the agent (i.e., *she* is picking up the ball, and now *she* is picking up the ball again). Thus, in the context of this experiment, 9- and 13-month-olds tended to view actions as part of an ongoing behavioral stream and not necessarily as distinct exemplars. To the extent that many real-world interactions require babies to follow the actions of particular social partners, this may make action exemplars difficult to extract.

However, these findings do not mean that there are no conditions under which infants would isolate action exemplars. In the real world, infants see multiple agents acting, and perhaps comparison across agents provides a basis for extracting action categories. We did not test whether infants noted that both agents were grasping rather than hitting or poking. Further research is needed to investigate this issue.

Determining Which Relation Is Being Named

Prelinguistic action knowledge sets the conditions for learning words because it enables the child to represent the relational structure of events. However, as we reviewed earlier, infants can represent a given action from more than one vantage point, for example, considering an action as "grasping the lid," or as part of "opening the box." In fact, understanding events at multiple levels can nominate several possible word meanings, making the task of interpreting what a novel verb means more complex. Interpreting a verb requires that the learner determine which of many possible perspectives the speaker means to take on the event in question (Gentner & Boroditsky, 2001; Gleitman, 1990; Tomasello, 1992). Infants may know that seeing, grasping, and getting, are occurring, but still be uncertain which of these is being named. Furthermore, research described earlier (Naigles, 1990; Fisher, 2002) suggests that children are flexible their interpretations of events—they are able to learn verbs referring to either distinctive patterns of motion or causative relations. Thus, in this case conceptual structure may provide such a rich an array of possible meanings that constraints on learning are necessary to achieve robust verb learning.

One critical source of constraint for verb learning is argument structure. Many researchers (Gleitman, 1990; Gentner & Boroditsky, 2001; Fisher, 2002; Naigles, 1990, 1996) have proposed that the use of syntactic frames is key to learning new verbs. These frames seem to provide information about the packaging of linguistic units required for the establishment of connections between linguistic and conceptual units. As described earlier, by 28 months, children can use different sentence frames to narrow down the possibilities for what a new verb means (Naigles, 1996). We presume that syntax is one of several sources of information on which children can draw (see Hollich et al., 2000; Woodward & Markman, 1998). Its particular importance for verb learning may explain, in part, why the first verbs emerge when they do (Gleitman, 1990).

Conclusion

We began with the question of whether infants possess well-organized action representations that could be recruited for verb learning. Recent findings indicate that they do. Before their first birthdays, infants understand human actions not only as physical motions through space but also as embodying intentional relations of several kinds and at several levels of analysis. Moreover, the evidence from studies of verb acquisition indicates that these representations are expressed in children's earliest verbs. However, by our estimate, perhaps as much as a year elapses between the emergence of well-organized action representations and the first strong evidence for verbs that express them. This gap, we think, points out the fact that having an organized idea does not automatically provide a word meaning. Determining how concepts are expressed in language requires pulling out taxonomic exemplars from the ongoing stream of experience and then determining which of the many possible exemplars are being named. Each of these may present a special challenge in the case of verbs. Infants may focus their action analysis not on extracting exemplars, but instead on predicting what happens next. These processes are not independent. Deciding that this event is an instance of *opening* or *wanting*, for example, requires analyzing the ongoing stream of action. Moreover, having extracted an exemplar, young children face the well-established problem of determining which construal is relevant for the meaning of a verb. In a given scene, grasping, opening, and wanting may all be occurring simultaneously, and learners need more evidence to determine which of these is being named.

Acknowledgments The second author received support from a James McKeen Cattell sabbatical fellowship while preparing this chapter. The research reported was supported by an NIH grant (HD35707-01).

References

Baillargeon, R. (1993). The object concept revisited: New directions in the investigation of infants' physical knowledge. In C. E. Granrud (Ed.), *Visual perception and* cognition in infancy: Carnegie Mellon symposia on cognition (pp. 265–316). Hillsdale, NJ: Erlbaum.

Balaban, M. T., & Waxman, S. R. (1997). Do words facilitate object categorization in 9-month-old infants? Journal of Experimental Child Psychology, 64(1), 3–26.

Barresi, J., & Moore, C. (1996). Intentional relations and social understanding. Behavioral and Brain Sciences, 19, 107–154.

Bartsch, K., & Wellman, H. M. (1995). Children talk about the mind. London: Oxford University Press.

Behne, T., Carpenter, M., Call, J., & Tomasello, M. (2005). Unwilling versus unable? Infants' understanding of intentional action. Developmental Psychology, 41(2), 328–337.

Benedict, H. (1979). Early lexical development: Comprehension and production. Journal of Child Language, 6(2), 183–200.

Bloom, L., Tinker, E., & Margulis, C. (1993). The words children learn: Evidence against a noun bias in early vocabularies. Cognitive Development, 8, 431–450.

Bretherton, I., & Beeghly, M. (1982). Talking about internal states: The acquisition of an explicit theory of mind. Developmental Psychology, 18(6), 906–921.

Brooks, R., & Meltzoff, A. N. (2002). The importance of eyes: How infants interpret adult looking behavior. Developmental Psychology, 38(6), 958–966.

Carpenter, M., Nagell, K., & Tomasello, M. (1998). Social cognition, joint attention, and communicative competence from 9 to 15 months of age. Monographs of the Society for Research in Child Development, 63(4).

Casasola, M., & Cohen, L. (2002). Infant categorization of containment, support and tight-fit spatial relationships. Developmental Science, 5(2), 247–264.

Choi, S., & Bowerman, M. (1991). Learning to express motion events in English and Korean: The influence of language-specific lexicalization patterns. Cognition, 41(1–3), 83–121.

Choi, S., McDonough, L., Bowerman, M., & Mandler, J. M. (1999). Early sensitivity to language-specific spatial categories in English and Korean. Cognitive Development, 14(2), 241–268.

Cohen, L. B, Rundell, L. J., Spellman, B. A., & Cashon, C. H. (1999). Infants' perception of causal chains. Psychological Science, 10(5), 412–418.

Corkum, V., & Moore, C. (1995). Development of joint visual attention in infants. In C. Moore & P. J. Dunham (Eds.), Joint attention: Its origins and role in development (pp. 61–83). Hillsdale, NJ: Erlbaum.

Csibra, G., Gergely, G., Biro, S., Koos, O., & Brockbank, M. (1999). Goal attribution without agency cues: The perception of "pure reason" in infancy. Cognition, 72, 237–267.

Dunn, J. (1999). Making sense of the social world: Mindreading, emotion, and relationships. In P. D. Zelazo and J. W. Astington (Eds), Developing theories of intention: Social understanding and self-control (pp. 229–242). Mahwah, NJ: Erlbaum.

Dunn, J., Bretherton, I., & Munn, P. (1987) Conversations about feeling states between mothers and their young children. Developmental Psychology, 23(1), 132–139.

Dunn, J., Brown, J., & Beardsall, L. (1991). Family talk about feeling states and children's later understanding of others' emotions. Developmental Psychology, 27(3), 448–455.

Edwards, D., & Goodwin, R. (1986). Action words and pragmatic functions. In S. Kuczaj & M. Barrett (Eds.), The development of word meaning (pp. 257–273). New York: Springer-Verlag.

Fenson, L., Dale, P. S., Reznick, J. S., Bates, E., Thal, D. J., & Pethick, S. J. (1994). Variability in early communicative development. Monographs of the Society for Research in Child Development, 59(5).

Fisher, C. (2002). Structural limits on verb mapping: The role of abstract structure in 2.5-year-olds' interpretations of novel verbs. *Developmental Science, 5*(1), 55–64.

Forbes, J. N., & Poulin-Dubois, D. (1997). Representational change in young children's understanding of familiar verb meaning. *Journal of Child Language, 24*(2), 389–406.

Gentner, D., & Boroditsky, L. (2001). Individualism, relativity and early word learning. In M. Bowerman & S. C. Levinson (Eds.), *Language acquisition and conceptual development* (pp. 215–256). Cambridge: Cambridge University Press.

Gergely, G., & Csibra, G. (2003). Teleological reasoning in infancy: The naive theory of rational action. *Trends in Cognitive Sciences, 7,* 287–292.

Gergely, G., Nasady, Z., Csibra, G., & Biro, S. (1995). Taking the intentional stance at 12 months of age. *Cognition, 56,* 165–193.

Gleitman, L. (1990). The structural sources of verb meanings. *Language Acquisition: A Journal of Developmental Linguistics, 1*(1), 3–55.

Goldfield, B. A. (2000). Nouns before verbs in comprehension vs. production: The view from pragmatics. *Journal of Child Language, 27*(3), 501–520.

Goldin-Meadow, S., Seligman, M. E., & Gelman, R. (1976). Language in the two-year-old. *Cognition, 4*(2), 189–202.

Golinkoff, R. M. (1975). Semantic development in infants: The concepts of agent and recipient. *Merrill-Palmer Quarterly, 21*(3), 181–193.

Golinkoff, R. M., Hirsh-Pasek, K., Cauley, K. M., & Gordon, L. (1987). The eyes have it: Lexical and syntactic comprehension in a new paradigm. *Journal of Child Language, 14*(1), 23–45.

Golinkoff, R. M., & Kerr, J. L. (1978). Infants' perception of semantically defined action role changes in filmed events. *Merrill-Palmer Quarterly, 24*(1), 53–61.

Gopnik, A., & Meltzoff, A. N. (1984). Semantic and cognitive development in 15- to 21-month-old children. *Journal of Child Language, 11*(3), 495–513.

Gopnik, A., & Meltzoff, A. N. (1997). *Words, thoughts, and theories.* Cambridge, MA: MIT Press.

Guajardo, J. J., & Woodward, A. L. (2004). Is agency skin-deep? Infants use surface features to interpret goal-directed action. *Infancy, 6,* 361–384.

Hollich, G. J., Hirsh-Pasek, K., Golinkoff, R. M., Brand, R. J., Brown, E., Chung, H., et al. (2000). Breaking the language barrier: An emergentist coalition model for the origins of word learning. *Monographs of the Society for Research in Child Development, 65*(3).

Huttenlocher, J., & Smiley, P. (1987). Early word meanings: The case of object names. *Cognitive Psychology, 19*(1), 63–89.

Huttenlocher, J., Smiley, P., & Charney, R. (1983). Emergence of action categories in the child: Evidence from verb meanings. *Psychological Review, 90*(1), 72–93.

Jovanovic, B., Kiraly, I., Elsner, B., Gergely, G., Prinz, W., & Aschersleben, G. (2003). *The role of effects for infants' perception of action goals.* Unpublished manuscript.

Kiraly, I., Jovanovic, B., Prinz, W., Aschersleben, G., & Gergely, G. (2003). The early origins of goal attribution in infancy. *Consciousness and Cognition 12,* 752–769.

Leslie, A. M., & Keeble, S. (1987). Do six-month-old infants perceive causality? *Cognition, 25*(3), 265–288.

Moses, L., Baldwin, D. A., Rosicky, J. G., & Tidball, G. (2001). Evidence for referential understanding in the emotions domain at 12 and 18 months. *Child Development, 72,* 718–735.

Naigles, L. (1990). Children use syntax to learn verb meanings. *Journal of Child Language, 17*(2), 357–374.

Naigles, L. (1996). The use of multiple frames in verb learning via syntactic bootstrapping. *Cognition, 58*(2), 221–251.

Nelson, K. (1973). Structure and strategy in learning to talk. *Monographs of the Society for Research in Child Development, 38*(1–2).

Phillips, A. T., & Wellman, H. M. (in press). Infants' understanding of object-directed action. *Cognition.*

Phillips, A. T., Wellman, H. M., & Spelke, E. S. (2002). Infants' ability to connect gaze and emotional expression to intentional action. *Cognition, 85,* 53–78.

Poulin-Dubois, D., & Forbes, J. N. (2002). Toddlers' attention to intentions-in-action in learning novel action words. *Developmental Psychology, 38*(1), 104–114.

Scaife, M., & Bruner, J. S. (1975). The capacity for joint visual attention in the infant. *Nature, 253,* 265–266.

Schoeppner, B., Sodian, B., & Pauen, S. (2004). *Encoding action roles in meaningful social interaction in the first year of life.* Unpublished manuscript.

Sodian, B., Schoepner, B., & Metz, U. (2004). Do infants apply the principle of rational action to human agents? *Infant Behavior and Development, 27,* 31–41.

Sodian, B., & Thoermer, C. (2004). Infants' understanding of looking, pointing and reaching as cues to goal-directed action. *Journal of Cognition and Development, 53,* 289–316.

Sommerville, J. A., & Woodward, A. L. (2005). Pulling out the intentional structure of action: The relation between action processing and action production in infancy. *Cognition, 95*(1), 1–30.

Sommerville, J. A., Woodward, A. L., & Needham, A. (2005). Action experience alters 3-month-old infants' perception of others' actions. *Cognition, 96*(1), B1–B11.

Sootsman, J., Morgante, J., Wilson Brune, C., & Woodward, A. L. (2003). *Eyes on the prize: Twelve-month-old infants track the goals of individual agents.* Poster session presented at the meeting of the Cognitive Development Society, Salt Lake City, UT.

Sootsman, J., & Woodward, A. L. (2004). *Nine-month-old infants connect action goals to individual agents.* Poster session presented at the International Conference on Infant Studies, Chicago, IL.

Spelke, E. S., Breinlinger, K., Macomber, J., & Jacobson, K. (1992). Origins of knowledge. *Psychological Review, 99*(4), 605–632.

Tomasello, M. (1992). *First verbs: A case study of early grammatical development.* New York: Cambridge University Press.

Tomasello, M. (1999). *The cultural origins of human cognition.* Cambridge, MA: Harvard University Press.

Vygotsky, L. S. (1962). *Thought and language.* Cambridge, MA: MIT Press.

Waxman, S. R., & Booth, A. (2003). The origins and evolution of links between word learning and conceptual organization: New evidence from 11-month-olds. *Developmental Science, 6*(2), 128–135.

Waxman, S. R., & Markow, D. B. (1998). Object properties and object kind: Twenty-one-month-old infants' extension of novel adjectives. *Child Development, 69*(5), 1313–1329.

Woodward, A. L. (1998). Infants selectively encode the goal object of an actor's reach. *Cognition, 69,* 1–34.

Woodward, A. L. (1999). Infants' ability to distinguish between purposeful and non-purposeful behaviors. *Infant Behavior and Development, 22,* 145–160.

Woodward, A. L. (2003). Infants' developing understanding of the link between looker and object. *Developmental Science, 6,* 297–311.

Woodward, A. L. (2005). The infant origins of intentional understanding. In R. V. Kail (Ed.), *Advances in child development and behavior, Vol. 33* (pp. 229–262). Oxford: Elsevier.

Woodward, A. L., & Guajardo, J. J. (2002). Infants' understanding of the point gesture as an object-directed action. *Cognitive Development, 17,* 1061–1084.

Woodward, A. L., & Markman, E. M. (1998). Early word learning. In W. Damon, D. Kuhn, & R. Siegler (Eds.), *Handbook of child psychology: Vol. 2. Cognition, perception and language* (pp. 371–420). New York: John Wiley and Sons.

Woodward, A. L., & Sommerville, J. A. (2000). Twelve-month-old infants interpret action in context. *Psychological Science, 11,* 73–76.

Zacks, J. M., & Tversky, B. (2001). Event structure in perception and conception. *Psychological Bulletin, 127,* 3–21.

9   When Is a Grasp a Grasp? Characterizing Some Basic Components of Human Action Processing

Jeffery T. Loucks and Dare Baldwin

Countless times each day, we draw inferences about what others are doing and why they are doing it. Such inferences about others' goals and intentions tend to come easily; in fact, it is relatively rare that we are even conscious of mental effort being expended for this purpose. The ease with which we discern goals and intentions seems to belie the actual complexity of the processing involved, however. As people pursue their intentions, the evanescent motions they exhibit tend to be rapid and largely continuous and to involve contact of differing kinds with a diverse set of objects. Our ability to readily make sense of the complex motion array hints at the operation of a powerful cognitive system. Yet surprisingly little is known about the nature of this cognitive system for discerning intentions or the path by which this system is acquired. In this chapter, we examine mechanisms that may assist us, and human infants as well, in identifying actions within the dynamic flow of everyday behavior. We put forward some new ideas about mechanisms for two fundamental aspects of action processing: segmentation of actions within the flow of motion, and action identification. Our overarching goal is to engender new ideas and new avenues of investigation in the study of human action processing.

A basic assumption underlying our approach to explaining skill at identifying actions is that such identification likely arises from the joint operation of multiple mechanisms. For example, one very basic step toward action recognition is to identify individual actions as units or segments within the complex behavior stream. Only observers who are able to pick out relevant units—actions—within the continuously flowing motion stream can begin considering relations—commonalities, differences, causal links, and the like—to other action units. In this sense, skill at identifying and hence categorizing actions relies centrally on skill at segmenting dynamic action. As a first step toward accounting for action recognition, we will turn to what is currently known about the prerequisite skill of action segmentation.

Segmenting the Continuous Motion Flow

Cognitive psychologists and psychophysicists have long been aware of the challenge observers—whether adults or young children—face in extracting relevant segments from complex, dynamic stimuli such as the object world (e.g., segmenting the world into distinct objects; e.g., E. J. Gibson, 1969; J. J. Gibson, 1979; Kellman & Spelke, 1983) and human speech (e.g., segmenting the complex auditory stream into clauses, words, syllables, etc.; Fodor & Bever, 1965; Gleitman & Wanner, 1982; Jusczyk, 1997). Surprisingly, however, the comparable challenge observers face in segmenting human action generally went uninvestigated as a cognitive-perceptual process until quite recently. Social psychologists (e.g., Asch, 1952; Heider, 1958; Newtson, 1973) seem to have been the first to recognize fundamental questions about action segmentation and, in seminal work on this topic, Newtson and his colleagues developed a "breakpoint detection" technique that provided a window on some basic action segmentation phenomena. They documented that observers show high levels of agreement about where meaningful junctures occur in continuous, everyday intentional action, and their research suggests that "breakpoints"—segment boundaries—seem to have a special status in cognitive processing. For example, adults more readily detect frame deletions when these occur at segment boundaries than when they occur internally within segments, and still pictures sampled from boundary portions of the motion stream are more easily interpreted than still pictures sampled from segment-internal portions of behavior (Newtson & Enquist, 1976).

More recently, Zacks and his colleagues (e.g., Zacks & Tversky, 2001; Zacks, Tversky, & Iyer, 2001) have shown that adults who are requested to do so readily segment continuous, everyday action on several levels organized into a partonomic hierarchy (e.g., kitchen cleanup involves larger segments such as loading a dishwasher, with smaller segments nested within, such as grasping the dishwasher door, opening the dishwasher door). They have also identified neurological sites—MT complex and FEF—that seem to be heavily involved in this segmentation process (Zacks et al., 2001).

Our research team has documented that adults' tendency to segment dynamic intentional action is spontaneous; adults engage in segmentation without any direction to do so, and the segmentation they carry out has implications for both their recall and their online processing of such action. For example, we found that adults are better at recalling the locations of tones within a sequence of intentional action when those tones coincided with segment boundaries (points at which intentions are completed) than when those tones occurred midsegment (prior to segment boundaries) (Baird, Baldwin, & Malle, 1999). This recall advantage for boundary tones over midsegment tones emerged both at what we call the *task level* of segmentation (e.g., involving segments such as "wash a dish" and "hang a towel" that subsume a variety of smaller-scale acts) and at what we call the *small-action level* of segmentation (e.g., involving small-scale acts such as "grasp a towel" and "place a towel"). In another study, adults were asked to detect brief flickers (created by changing the color of one frame in a 30 frame-per-second digitized video). As it turned out, they were faster to detect flickers that happened to coincide with segment boundaries than flickers that occurred segment-internally (Baldwin, Pederson, Craven, Andersson, & Bjork, 2005). The latter finding is especially striking because it reveals adults' tendency to segment dynamic action even when this is in no way necessary for the task at hand (i.e., flicker detection).

Infants Segment Dynamic Human Action

Basic skill at action segmentation apparently arises early in life. Several studies have now documented that infants as young as 10–11 months are sensitive to segment boundaries in complex, continuous action. The original study on this topic (Baldwin, Baird, Saylor, & Clark, 2001) utilized a technique that Hirsh-Pasek and colleagues (e.g., Hirsh-Pasek et al., 1987) developed to examine the analogous question about infants' sensitivity to linguistic segments. In the Baldwin et al. study, infants watched as a woman carried out a series of intentional acts in continuously flowing motion: She turned away from a dish rack on noticing a towel on the floor, moved to grasp the towel, walked across the kitchen, and proceeded to hang the towel on a towel rack. The video looped repeatedly, enabling infants to watch this scenario as long as they were willing. This familiarization phase gave infants ample opportunity to process and potentially segment the dynamic motion into individual actions (e.g., grasp towel, place towel). Then infants viewed two test videos in alternating sequence. One—the completing test video—displayed the same scenario except that a 1.5-second still-frame pause was inserted just at the boundary between one segment (i.e., grasp towel) and the next (i.e., place towel). The other—the interrupting test video—differed in just one respect from the completing test video: the 1.5-second still-frame pause occurred segment-internal rather than at the boundary between segments (for half of infants the pause in the interrupting video occurred prior to the segment boundary, and for the other half it occurred after the segment boundary). To illustrate, infants viewing one of the interrupting test videos would see the woman extend an arm in a reach toward the towel. This would be interrupted by a pause, and then action would resume and flow continuously to the end of the scenario. If able to segment the continuously flowing motion depicted in the familiarization video, infants should find the completing test videos rather dull, because the pause only served to accentuate a boundary they themselves already noted. In contrast, the interrupting test video should violate the segmental structure they themselves had extracted from the video during familiarization, and for this reason should strike them as interesting and noteworthy. Thus we predicted that infants would look longer at the interrupting test videos than at the completing test videos. This prediction was borne out. Moreover, a subsequent control study helped to confirm that infants' interest in the interrupting test video did not arise simply due to that video being inherently more salient to them. That is, an independent group of infants viewed the test videos without any prior familiarization. If the interrupting test video elicited longer looking in the first study simply as a result of salience (rather than as a result of the segmentation infants performed during the familiarization phase), then infants should look longer at it even without prior familiarization. But they did not. Instead, infants showed a nonsignificant tendency to prefer to look at the completing test video. Together, these first two studies provided initial evidence that infants only 10–11 months of age are sensitive to the segmental structure of at least some simple everyday intentional actions.

Another recent study (Saylor, Baldwin, Baird, & LaBounty, 2005) confronted infants with a somewhat more challenging segmentation task: infants of 9–11 months watched two displays of dynamic live action simultaneously while listening to centrally presented pure tones that coincided with the segment boundaries of just one of the action scenarios. For instance, in one action scenario a woman sponged off and then organized items on a small bookshelf, while in the other scenario—displayed simultaneously—a woman stocked a miniature chest of drawers with small items. For a given infant, tones matched the completion points for the chest-of-drawers action scenario (e.g., tones occurred just as the woman completed pulling a drawer open, grasping an item, placing an item in a drawer, and the like). For a different infant, tones coincided with completion points for the bookshelf action scenario. We found that infants showed a greater-than-chance proportion of looking at the action for which tones coincided with segment boundaries. As well, we measured infants' looking at the two simultaneous action displays in a silent baseline phase before tones were played. We found that infants' proportion of looking at the matching actions increased relative to their proportion looking at the very same actions during the silent baseline period, thus dispelling the possibility that matching actions engendered more looking simply because infants found them to be inherently more salient. Finally, analyses confirmed that infants' sensitivity to boundary-tone correspondence was as strong upon early viewing of the action scenarios as it was later, when they had viewed the action scenarios several times over. Infants' success in this segmentation task is striking for several reasons. To note correspondence between tones and segment boundaries, infants needed to segment two simultaneous dynamic action scenarios, both of which were relatively novel and involved a variety of novel objects. Moreover, infants showed that they were performing segmentation "online"; they noted tone-boundary correspondences without needing extensive familiarization to the relatively novel action scenarios. All in all, findings from the studies we have conducted thus far point to infants' possessing skills enabling them to readily segment complex, continuous human intentional action.

Sharon and Wynn (e.g., Sharon, 2000; Sharon & Wynn, 1998; Wynn, 1995, 1996) have also documented early action segmentation in infancy; interestingly, however, infants have also failed at segmenting some of the action stimuli Sharon and Wynn have presented to them. The primary focus of their ground-breaking research was to investigate whether infants individuate and enumerate actions, as Wynn and colleagues had previously shown infants capable of doing with respect to objects (e.g., Wynn, 1995). Skill at individuation and enumeration implies that segmentation has occurred; hence positive evidence for individuation or enumeration in these studies also demonstrates segmentation. In some of their studies on this topic, infants watched a puppet engaging in two different kinds of actions: repeated jumping followed by a pause, and then head wagging. Perhaps not surprisingly, given that pauses demarcated action boundaries, infants watching such pause-punctuated motion streams reliably segmented these stimuli (as implied by their success at individuation and enumeration). In a more challenging task presented to infants in some other studies, the puppet's motion was continuous: head wagging moved directly into jumping, for example. With the continuous stimuli, infants typically failed to individuate or enumerate (but see Wynn, 1996, for one exception to this). The precise reason for the failure is not clear. Infants faced with the continuous motion displays may have been unable to detect segment boundaries, and their inability to segment the motion stream undercut individuation and enumeration. If this is correct, the Sharon and Wynn data appear, on the face of it, to fail to replicate infants' success at segmentation of continuous intentional action that we observed in the studies reported earlier. Sharon and Wynn suggested that infants may require considerable experience viewing a particular action scenario to locate segment boundaries within the motion stream if that action scenario lacks pauses at segment boundaries. However, the pattern of findings across all available studies militates against their suggestion. Recall that in our studies (reported earlier), infants readily segmented continuous motion displays, even in the absence of repeated viewing (e.g., Saylor et al., 2005). On the face of it, the whole pattern of findings seems especially puzzling given that Sharon and Wynn presented drastically simplified stimuli (stripped-down cartoons displaying just a simple puppet engaging in two highly distinct repetitive actions) relative to what we showed infants (complex, unrepetitive, live human action, or videos of live action, in complex, everyday settings). If anything, one would have thought infants would have succeeded at segmenting the Sharon and Wynn stimuli rather than our stimuli. One possible explanation is that the very simplicity of the Sharon and Wynn stimuli in fact rendered the segmentation task intractable for infants. This is what would occur if the simplified, stripped-down puppet action failed to capture structural aspects of everyday, human intentional action that infants are sensitive to and can capitalize on for detecting segment boundaries. In other words, the very simplicity of the Sharon and Wynn displays may have rendered them degraded with respect to clues infants ordinarily rely on for segmentation. Our current research investigates the possibility that infants' and adults' skill at action segmentation indeed relies on sensitivity to structure inherent in the flow of behavior.

Structure Detection Facilitates Segmentation

The hypothesis guiding some of our current work is that infants (as well as adults) segment everyday intentional action, at least in part, based on sensitivity to structural properties of the motion stream. Our ideas here share much in common with those of Martin and Tversky (2003), who, like us, propose that viewers capitalize on correlated top-down and bottom-up sources of information (knowledge of what motion patterns arise from specific kinds of intentions on the one hand, and predictable physical characteristics within the motion stream on the other) to segment dynamic human action. Little is known as yet about the details of either of these sources of information for segmentation. A specific goal we are currently pursuing is to gain information about structure-detection skills that may be brought to bear in bottom-up processing. At this phase, we are examining two specific kinds of structure that might play a role in segmentation, though likely there are other sources of structure that we have not yet identified. The kind of intentional action we have considered so far is everyday object-directed intentional action: action that is directed toward achieving goals that involve concrete, and typically inanimate, objects. These are actions like loading luggage onto a cart, polishing a car, wallpapering a living room, or assembling a chest of drawers. Object-directed intentions of these kinds give rise to complex sequences of motion with many subparts (e.g., loading luggage requires numerous instances of grasping, lifting, placing, pushing, adjusting, pulling, and the like). One kind of structure that seems to be exhibited as people carry out such object-directed intentions we will call *structural gestalts*. As people take action to carry out their object-directed intentions, certain physical and temporal properties predictably coalesce within the motion stream; this is true looking across object-directed intentions of many diverse kinds enacted in many different contexts. To illustrate, body parts undergo motion in a predictable sequence and along a characteristic time course as the object of a goal is sighted (e.g., head turn, foveation), approached (body motion and raising of arms in the direction of the foveated object), and contacted (e.g., hands grasp object and manipulation begins). The time course of this sequence gives the concatenation of elements a ballistic quality, with characteristic acceleration and deceleration parameters. What we suggest is that this ballistically enacted gestalt of motion elements tends to coincide with what people (and infants) judge to be a segment within the motion stream.

To test this idea, we adopted a well-documented technique—the point-light format—that pares motion displays down such that purely structural information is presented. Lights are attached to the actor's joints (ankles, knees, wrists, elbows, shoulders, and head) and the action is filmed in the dark. The resulting video displays structural properties of the actor's motions, but the surrounding context in which action takes place and the objects acted upon is utterly absent. In question is whether infants and adults can identify segments within the motion stream when structural information alone is available. If they are sensitive to the kinds of segment-correlated structural gestalts described above, segmentation in the point-light format should be possible. A series of studies that we recently carried out clarify that it is indeed possible, for both adults (Guha, Baldwin, & Craven, 2005) and infants (Baldwin, Neuhaus, Saylor, & Sobel, 2005). Our methodological approach to investigating this question was to use the same paradigms (described earlier) with which we had previously examined adults' and infants' segmentation of everyday intentional action, with the only change being point-light presentation of the motion stream rather than full-light (i.e., normal) presentation. In the case of infants, for example: after being familiarized with a continuous stream of point-light intentional action (e.g., action is filmed with bands of light over the joints as an actor notices a towel on the floor, moves to grasp the towel, and moves across the kitchen to place the towel on the towel rack), 10- to 11-month-old infants displayed longer looking at a test video in which a still-frame pause interrupted an action segment (e.g., the pause occurred in the midst of the motion to grasp or in the midst of the motion to place the towel on the towel rack) than at an otherwise identical test video in which a still-frame pause coincided with the boundary between two segments (e.g., the pause occurred as the grasp of the towel was completed and the motion to place the towel was about to be initiated). A control study revealed that a different group of infants had no starting preference for the interrupting test video over the completing test video (in the absence of prior familiarization), indicating that infants' longer looking at the interrupting test video than the completing test video indeed arose as a result of their spontaneous processing of the point-light video during familiarization. Our findings in the point-light research provide the first evidence to date that adults and infants capitalize on structural information in the motion stream—what one might call bottom-up information—to extract action segments within the flow of behavior.

One implication of our point-light findings is that intentional action is a structurally rich stimulus, and even infants make good use of this structure for segmentation purpose. Interestingly, however, the point-light findings also suggest that structural gestalts inherent in dynamic intentional action are concentrated at a particular level of segmentation—what we have called the small-action level. With adults, we probed segmentation ability for the point-light intentional action at both the task level (involving segments such as "wash dish," "hang towel," "ice cream returned to freezer") and the small-action level (involving subsegments within tasks, such as "grasp towel," "hang towel," "grasp freezer handle," "open freezer door," "place ice cream in freezer," etc.). If you recall, in the full-light context, adults displayed highly reliable segmentation of the continuously flowing motion stream at both the task and small-action levels. We predicted, however, that in the point-light format, adults would display sensitivity to segments only at the small-action level.

This is the level at which structural gestalts most reliably coincide with action segments. At the task level, a segment such as "hang towel" typically groups together a series of small actions, thus involving changes in trajectory, tempo of motion, and the like. Hence task-level units tend not to correspond to single structural gestalts. Small actions, in contrast, tend to correspond to single structural gestalts, and in this sense seem to be highly available structural units within the motion stream. The structural richness inherent in the small-action level of analysis within intentional action makes this a strong candidate for a basic or primary level of segmentation, perhaps akin to the level of the syllable in language (e.g., Bertoncini & Mehler, 1981; Bijeljac-Babic, Bertoncini, & Mehler, 1993; Jusczyk & Derrah, 1987). We might then expect that infants would begin segmenting dynamic human action at the small-action level. As yet, infants' ability to segment intentional action has only been probed at the small-action level; while these findings are certainly consistent with the prediction, clearly our speculation about a basic or primary level of segmentation has not yet been properly put to the test.

Casting certainty aside for a moment, assume that the small-action level is indeed infants' point of entry as they embark on segmentation of dynamic everyday action. How then might infants move from initial sensitivity to these "syllables" within human action to detecting higher-level segments (tasks), comprised of combinations of these small-action units? Sensitivity to statistical regularities in the co-occurrence rates of distinct small-action units should be very helpful in this regard. In undertaking object-directed goal-driven tasks, specific small actions tend to co-occur because each is central to achieving the overarching task-related goal, and in many cases causal principles dictate specific ordering of individual small actions to achieve those higher-level goals. The fact that small actions contributing to task-related goals tend to co-occur means that small actions falling within a task-level segment will have relatively high transitional probabilities, whereas small actions that are part of different task-level segments will tend to have relatively low transitional probabilities. Thus low transitional probabilities serve as a clue to segment boundaries at the task level. To make this concrete, imagine an infant watching a parent moving about the kitchen in the early evening. Some motions are readily segmented via structural gestalts, such as "grasp carrot," "grasp knife," "cut carrot," "place knife," "grasp fridge handle," "open fridge door," and "grasp butter," giving rise to the perception of a string of small actions underway. How does the infant come to appreciate that this motion flow can be analyzed in terms of higher-level tasks such as "chop food" and "get ingredients"? Repeated viewing of such action scenarios would provide infants with information about transitional probabilities, with "grasp knife" and "cut carrot" displaying relatively high transitional probability, as would "grasp fridge handle" and "open fridge door," whereas "place knife" and "grasp fridge handle" would likely display relatively low transitional probability. Infants who are sensitive to these transitional probabilities as a source of information for segmentation would take the low-probability transition as a clue to a segment boundary, helping them to establish "grasp carrot/grasp

knife/cut carrot/place knife" and "grasp fridge handle/open fridge door/grasp butter" as distinct, higher task-level segments.

Infants' language input displays statistical regularities (e.g., Hayes & Clark,
1970) comparable to those we are suggesting may be inherent in human action
(no formal analysis of such statistics within human action has ever been undertaken,
so as yet this is simply a hypothesis). There is now considerable evidence that infants as well as adults spontaneously track such statistical regularities within the
auditory stream and use them as a source of information for segmentation (e.g.,
Aslin, Saffran, & Newport, 1999; Saffran, Aslin, & Newport, 1996). Recently we
began investigating whether adults and infants utilize similar statistical-tracking
skills for detecting segments in novel intentional-action sequences (Andersson,
Baldwin, & Saffran, 2005; Baldwin, Andersson, & Saffran, 2005). Our first study
with adults was modeled directly on the statistical-learning paradigm pioneered
by Saffran et al. (1996). We constructed an "exposure corpus" that included repeated presentation of 12 small actions, each of which involved a simple intentional act involving a bottle and in some cases another object such as a glass or
sponge. The small actions were each sensible, coherent intentional acts in their
own right which, when combined, yielded novel, nonce sequences of intentional
action. This is a direct analog to the Saffran et al. technique of combining phon-
tactically sensible syllables, such as /bi/, /da/, /ku/, /go/, /la/, and /bu/ into novel,
nonce linguistic sequences. Examples of the small actions we used were "stack
bottle on sponge," "poke finger in bottle," "drink from bottle," "peer into bottle,"
"inspect bottom of bottle," and "pour from bottle into hand." The 12 actions were
carried out such that the actor's body position for each of the small actions began
and ended in the same position. This made it possible to combine any small action
with any other small action, so we could randomly select 4 sets of 3 small actions
from the inventory of 12 small actions. The 3 small actions within a set (e.g.,
stack/poke/drink) then always co-occurred in a preset order throughout the exposure corpus (thus transitional probabilities from one small action to the next
within a set, or task, were always 1.0). The four sets (tasks) were then randomly
intermixed, with the constraint that each was seen equally often (in all, 28 times)
over the course of the continuously flowing 20-minute exposure corpus. This
meant that transitional probabilities between small actions in the same task were
high (i.e., 1.0), whereas transitional probabilities for small actions in different
tasks were low (on average 0.30 across the exposure corpus).

In our first study, adult participants were asked to watch the full 20-minute
exposure corpus and told they would be tested on their memory for the sequence of actions at the end. After viewing the exposure corpus, we then tested
their ability to recognize tasks (combinations of three small actions with high
transitional probabilities in the exposure corpus; e.g., stack/poke/drink) as having
been seen before, relative to two kinds of foils, nontasks (three small actions that
they had encountered in the exposure corpus, but never in that combination; e.g.,
inspect/poke/wipe) or part tasks (three small actions that spanned a segment

boundary across tasks in the exposure corpus; e.g., drink/peer/inspect). Figure 9.1 displays still frames depicting the 12 small actions appearing in the exposure corpus. In the test phase, adults watched 16 pairs of video clips, with each pair including one task and either a nontask or a part task (in counterbalanced order across participants), and were asked to indicate which of the two clips in a pair they recalled having seen in their previous experience. Adults readily recognized the tasks as having occurred in their previous viewing; they selected the tasks at rates significantly higher than would be predicted by chance relative to both the nontasks (tasks recognized 82% of the time) and part tasks (tasks recognized 76% of the time). These findings make clear that adults can readily track statistical regularities to guide higher, task-level segmentation of a continuous sequence of novel intentional action.

In research that is underway, we are currently investigating whether infants, like adults, can exploit statistical regularities within a continuous stream of intentional action to extract task-level segments. Infants view the same exposure corpus just described during a familiarization phase and then during a test phase alternately view video clips depicting tasks versus nontasks or tasks versus part tasks. If infants indeed are capable of employing statistical regularities to detect task-level segments within the continuously flowing novel sequence of small actions, then they should become increasingly habituated to the statistically defined segments within the exposure corpus over the course of the familiarization phase. During the test phase, then, they may look longer at the relatively novel nontask and part-task video clips relative to the task video clips, to which their prior exposure would have habituated them. If infants display this pattern, it will be the first evidence to date that captures infants' discovery of segments within novel intentional action. Such findings would also suggest that developments in action processing trade on recruitment of learning mechanisms, such as statistical learning, that are broadly available to facilitate learning across multiple domains.

Segmentation Summary

We now know a little about how adults and infants achieve organized processing of the dynamic motion flow they witness when watching others carry out object-oriented intentions in the world. The continuous motion flow is segmented, with segments at higher levels hierarchically subsuming lower-level segments. The motion flow exhibits considerable structure, and this structure seems to be readily exploited to assist in detecting segments. Structural gestalts seem especially helpful for aiding detection of small-action segments, whereas higher, task-level segments can be identified via sensitivity to statistical structure. We have gained some initial direct evidence for all of these processes in adults and for some of them in infants as young as 10–11 months. However, all of this research is very new, and questions about segmentation of dynamic human action abound. We hope that others will join us in expanding on a promising beginning.

Drink

Poke

Stack

Rattle

Touch

Blow

Peek

Scrub

Inspect

Clink

Pour

Insert

Figure 9.1. Still images of twelve small actions utilized in the exposure corpus.

239

Categorization and Identification

Each and every instance of motion in the world is a unique event (barring video replay, that is, which we will disregard given that access to such replay remains a rare occurrence relative to the volume of action witnessed by most of us each day). Even when one attempts a high-fidelity repetition of a particular act, some parameters of motion through space and time will invariably differ, however minutely. It is fairly obvious, then, that identifying everyday human acts demands operating with categories of action that group motion patterns sharing relevant commonalities in the face of varying degrees of surface variability. We have a sense of grasping actions being "of a kind," for example, despite a diversity of hands and arms, graspable objects, and rates and trajectories of motion being involved across different instances of grasping. Surprisingly, little is yet known about the perceptual and cognitive operations involved in basic action categorization and identification of this kind. Some recent seminal work on this issue provides some intriguing new ideas about human action categorization in both adults and human infants (Finkbeiner, Nicol, Greth, & Nakamura, 2002; Gennari, Sloman, Malt, & Fitch, 2002; Kuhlmeier, Wynn, & Bloom, 2003; Papafragou, Massey, & Gleitman, 2002; Rakison & Poulin-Dubois, 2002). However, little if any of this work focuses on processing of everyday human action or categorizing action in the absence of linguistic cues to processing. Among the things we do not know about categorization of everyday human action is what sources of information people extract from the motion stream to assist in categorizing and identifying actions. In developing ideas about this, we looked to another domain of research that has focused intensively on this very issue—the domain of face processing.

Sources of Information for Identifying Faces

Like action, identifying people's faces is a complex task that we nevertheless accomplish with relative ease a multitude of times each day. We readily identify the faces of family, friends, mere acquaintances, media personalities, and even a variety of imaginary characters (e.g., Mickey Mouse), despite (a) a considerable degree of homogeneity across faces and (b) the fact that faces are viewed from many different perspectives, under different lighting conditions, and in the midst of varying facial expressions. Given this complexity, one of the many questions to ask about such skill is what information in the face we rely on as key to categorizing and identifying an individual's face. Research on face processing suggests there are at least two sources of information people extract from the face which aid in categorization and identification.

In a classic study, Yin (1969) noted that face processing is disrupted when faces are presented upside-down. This so-called face inversion effect manifests itself in a number of ways. Many studies have documented that inversion disrupts recognition and discrimination of faces (Collishaw & Hole, 2002; Diamond & Carey, 1986; Farah, Tanaka, & Drain, 1995; Freire, Lee, & Symons, 2000; Kemp, McManus, & Pigott, 1990; Knight & Johnston, 1997; Lander, Christie, & Bruce, 1999; Leder & Bruce, 2000; Valentine, 1988) and also makes distortion in the face less perceptible (Bartlett & Searcy, 1993; Thompson, 1980). In particular, a weight of research has indicated that inverting the face specifically disrupts the processing of configural information. Thus two separate mechanisms have been postulated to be involved in processing faces: a mechanism sensitive to featural information and a mechanism sensitive to configural information. Featural information has been conceptualized as those parts of the face that are highly defined, local elements such as the eyes, nose, and mouth. Configural information has been conceptualized as more global, spatial-relational properties of the face, such as the distance between the eyes, nose, and mouth.

The distinction between featural and configural information in faces has intuitive appeal: Areas of the face such as the eyes, nose, and mouth are some of the most salient aspects of the face, and information about those parts of the face seems to be crucial in deciding whether a particular stimulus is even a face to begin with. Configural information is not primary in the same way that featural information is, as it depends on having already registered featural information, yet it could certainly be utilized to identify faces when similarity among features is high (e.g., close relatives). Despite the intuitive appeal of the feature/configuration distinction, determining precisely how to define features and configurations has proven to be elusive. A feature can always be redescribed in terms of configural information; likewise, configural information can be redescribed as features. For example, the mouth can be described in terms of its relational properties (e.g., the size of the upper lip in relation to the lower lip). Similarly, the space between the nose and mouth could be thought of as a feature, and in fact is described as such in the field of medicine (i.e., the philtrum). The distinction between features and configurations is not readily defined, probably in part because the distinction seems to be a matter of degree along a continuum rather than an absolute dichotomy. Nevertheless, the uptake of these sources of information may be accomplished by separable processing mechanisms, and it may well be that the perceptual and cognitive system is capable of altering its processing of information from featural to configural, or vice versa, depending on the functional demands of the processing context.

A variety of forms of evidence have been put forward to bolster the claim that featural and configural sources of information are separable in processing. One form of evidence is behavioral, as described earlier: configural information seems to be especially vulnerable to disruption by inversion. The first direct evidence of this effect—that inversion specifically disrupts the processing of configural information—was provided by Freire and colleagues (2000). Since this study served as the basis for the methodology we have developed to study the analogous issue regarding categorization and identification of human action, we shall describe it here in some detail.

Freire et al. (2000) had participants judge whether simultaneously presented photographs of faces were the same or different. These faces differed in terms of featural information or in terms of configural information. Both types of changes were created by digitally manipulating one original black-and-white photograph of a face. A set of feature-change photographs was created by removing the original eyes, nose, and mouth and replacing them with the eyes, nose, and mouth from photographs of other individuals. Another set of configural change photographs was created that retained the original features, but moved them apart varying distances. The first experiment assessed participants' accuracy for detecting featural changes in the upright and inverted formats, while a second study assessed accuracy for detecting configural changes in the two orientations. As the researchers predicted, accuracy did not differ significantly in the two orientations for detecting featural changes, but was significantly lower for detecting configural changes presented in the inverted format as compared to the upright format.

Other behavioral evidence indicates that a different manipulation—low-pass filtering of the face—disrupts the processing of featural information but leaves the processing of configural information intact (Costen, Parker, & Craw, 1996). This finding, coupled with the evidence just described that inversion specifically disrupts configural processing, points strongly toward two independent mechanisms for processing featural versus configural information in faces. Finally, a complementary form of evidence from studies using fMRI and PET scans indicates that the processing of features versus configurations is manifested in distinct neural substrates, although the specific area associated with processing of features is currently under debate (Rossion et al., 2000). The two postulated systems are proposed to both be active when faces are processed in their upright orientation. When processing inverted faces, however, the standard configural template people are accustomed to viewing (eyes above nose, nose above mouth, etc.) is no longer available. Since this template cannot be accessed, the processing of relational information is thought to be disrupted.

Sources of Information for Categorizing and Identifying Actions

Processing of human action has some basic commonalities with face processing: rapid, online processing of visual spatial information is key for categorization and identification to take place; both are highly dynamic stimuli (although only the rare face-processing study has taken this latter characteristic into account (e.g., Thornton, 1998; Thornton & Kourtzi, 2002); and both action and faces are relied upon heavily to assist in inferring others' goals and intentions. For this reason, we wondered whether phenomena analogous to those in face processing, such as the featural/configural distinction, might be observable in action processing. Moreover, many who have investigated face processing have suggested that the dual-source phenomenon is not unique to face processing. We wondered, then, whether a feature/configuration distinction might be made in the action domain, and if so, whether processing of these two kinds of information might be separable, as they seem to be in face processing.

The information exhibited to observers of human action seems to be inherently and even ubiquitously relational in nature. As motion is carried out, body parts move in relation to objects and other body parts over space and time. One might thus assume that all information in the motion stream is configural. Nevertheless, it is worth considering the possibility that people process some portions of the motion stream arising from human action as features. Our idea here is that certain local regions within the motion stream may be highly relevant for action categorization and identification and become elevated in processing to the status of features, at least in some everyday processing contexts, such as making sense of action in terms of intentions and goals. Processing portions of any stimulus with an emphasis on those elements that are the most central to the task—highly relevant, local features—would certainly increase processing efficiency, and this is of course a key issue for processing a complex, dynamic, and evanescent stimulus like human action.

These ideas have an echo in face processing. Features of the face, such as eyes, nose, and mouth, are functionally highly relevant regions. They are the portions of the face that we look to for information on a person's emotional state and for information about a person's speech (which are both central to inferring others' goals and intentions). Moreover, features are likely to be especially relevant for differentiating faces from one another, as the set of faces with highly similar features but distinct configurations (close relatives) seems almost certain to be smaller than the set of faces with highly similar configurations but distinct features (most people other than close relatives).

If we then think of features of human action as highly relevant, local information within the motion stream, useful to categorizing and indentifying actions, what, in a concrete sense, would be an example of such a feature? As a first attempt to grapple with this question, we looked to the action segmentation data that we and others had collected as a source of inspiration. In particular, we considered conceptualizing action features as local detail that is used to categorize and identify the smallest segments of action that people ordinarily pick out in online action processing. To illustrate, then, for an action like taking a drink, the smallest segments that adults typically remark on would be grasping the cup, lifting the cup to the lips, drinking, and setting the cup back onto the table. Identifying motion as an instance of grasping seems to trade heavily on observing a particular type of hand position (local detail) relative to a graspable solid object.

The next step was to characterize configural information in the action context. In the face processing literature, configural information is conceptualized as global, relational information that exists only with respect to features. With this in mind, we initially characterized configural information in action as the spatial and temporal parameters governing the enactment of action features. Such information is more global than the featural information described just above, in that spatial and temporal parameters (e.g., the rate and path with which action is undertaken) often influence the enactment of several features within the motion stream. To return to the example of taking a drink, configural characteristics would be information about what path the arm took through space toward the cup (trajectory) or how fast the cup was approached by the hand (timing).

A First Study

Employing Freire and colleagues' (2000) face inversion methodology, we undertook to assess people's sensitivity to configural and featural changes in the action stream in upright and inverted conditions. The logic of our experimental design was twofold. First, if people extract and make use of both featural and configural sources of information in dynamic human action, they should demonstrate sensitivity to both kinds of changes in the motion stream and should be able to detect them. Second, if these two types of information are at all distinct in action, then inversion might disrupt the detection of configural changes while having detectably less effect on the processing of featural changes. Much like the face, we hypothesized that inversion would disrupt the standard body template that people are accustomed to processing (e.g., head above shoulders, arms above waist, legs below waist, etc.). Without such a body template, configural information—which is global in nature—should be much more difficult to process. Inversion should not have this effect on featural information, as we conceived of features of action as local elements that are strongly encoded and should be recognizable in either orientation.

Although no study had yet probed for such an inversion effect for human action processing, there was reason to regard it as a plausible possibility. Some recent evidence indicates that people's configural processing of human bodies is disrupted with inversion (Reed, Stone, Bozova, & Tanaka, 2003). As well, Shipley (2003) documented that recognition of action in videos of biological motion is also disrupted with inversion.

We started by filming eight standard action videos. The actions depicted in these videos were quite simple and all involved object-oriented intentional actions. A full list of actions and their respective changes can be found in table 9.1. With the standard actions in mind, we then filmed videos that differed from the standard videos in just one respect: either featural or configural information (but not both). Configural-change videos depicted changes in the trajectory or timing of the action, without changing any action features. For example, if the standard video depicted an act of writing (i.e., grasping a pencil and scribbling with it), the configural-change video depicted the same action scenario except for an alteration

Table 9.1 Information about the eight video sets of Study I

Object	Standard Video	Configural Change	Feature Change
bag	orient towards bag and unzip bag	orient head in opposite direction to bag	wipe off bag at zipper area
textbook	open up textbook to a page	open textbook quickly	flip textbook over
cup	grasp top of cup and drink from cup	grasp bottom of cup	sniff contents of cup
book	grasp book and place on book pile	place book down quickly on pile	drop book on book pile
shoulder	brush off shoulder	brush off shoulder in opposite direction	scratch shoulder
grater	grasp, lift and move grater across surface	grasp grater in a robotic fashion	slide grater across surface
pencil	grasp pencil and scribble on sheet of paper	arcing path of motion to reach pencil	erase sheet of paper
knife	chop potatoes on cutting board with knife	increase height and speed of chop	brush potatoes aside with knife

in the path the arm took through space to reach the pencil. Featural-change videos depicted changes in the elements of the action without changing the spatial or temporal contours of the action. For example, the featural-change video for the writing action described above depicted the actor grabbing the pencil but erasing with it rather than writing with it. In this feature-change video, the path to grasp the pencil and the timing properties of the motion stream were the same as those depicted in the standard video.

It is worth noting at this phase that it is of course impossible to alter featural elements of an action scenario while leaving configural elements (trajectory and timing) entirely unaffected. Any change to local detail (e.g., depicting erasing rather than writing) will inevitably alter trajectory and timing information to some small degree. This is of course also true of the face: changing the local features of a face (e.g., substituting one person's eyes for another's) will inevitably also give rise to at least a small degree of change in the configural properties of the face. Thus the distinction between the feature and configural changes in our videos was a matter of degree, rather than an absolute difference, as was also the case in the face research. In any case, however, care was taken to ensure that configural changes altered configural information to a significantly greater degree than featural information, and featural changes altered features while minimizing the degree of configural change in the videos.

Forty adult participants watched pairs of videos (presented serially) and were asked to decide whether the two videos in the pair were the same or different videos. Both feature-change videos and configural-change videos were paired with their respective standard videos to make different pairs, and the configural-change, feature-change, and standard videos were paired with themselves to make an equal number of same pairs. Half of the video pairs they saw were upright and half were inverted. We were concerned about the possibility of carryover effects if participants saw the same video both upright and inverted; hence we opted to restrict participants to seeing a given video in just one format or the other. Our prediction was that the inverted format would diminish accuracy in identifying the videos for configural changes but not for featural changes.

Our findings confirmed the prediction: Configural changes were significantly more difficult to detect in the inverted than in the upright format. Interestingly, the results revealed one departure from findings typically observed in the face-processing literature: Participants in our action-processing research displayed significantly reduced accuracy for feature changes when action was inverted (whereas in the face literature, typically inversion produces no accuracy decrement). Again, however, this inversion-related reduction was significantly smaller for feature changes than the reduction in accuracy that inversion produced for configural changes. It is also worth mentioning there was a significant main effect of the type of change: Featural-change videos were detected with high accuracy upright, whereas configural changes were much harder to detect even when presented upright. Thus, there appears to be selective attention to features when processing everyday action, even in the format in which one is generally accustomed to viewing it. This pattern is frequently reported in the face literature (e.g., Freire et al., 2000; Mondloch, Le Grand, & Maurer, 2002) and is a point we will return to in our discussion. All in all, findings from this study provided the first evidence to date that people extract both featural and configural information from the motion stream in processing everyday, dynamic human action. Strikingly, the inversion manipulation interfered significantly more in people's identification of videos involving configural changes, suggesting that feature and configural information within human action might be processed via distinct mechanisms, as they seem to be when processing faces.

A Second Study

Our initial findings were encouraging, but we began to realize that they were open to interpretations other than the distinction between featural and configural information that we intended to focus on. For one, we realized that the differences we observed in people's success at identifying featural-change versus configural-change videos in the inverted format might be related to how they encoded the videos linguistically rather than to how they directly processed different forms of information in the motion stream. In particular, our featural-change videos had a tendency to be associated with distinct verbs in English relative to the standard videos, while our configural-change videos tended to be associated with the same verbs as their respective standard videos. In the video set described above, for example, people tended to label the action depicted in both the standard and configural-change videos as "writing," whereas the action depicted in the featural-change video they tended to label as "erasing." Initially we were not fazed by this potential linguistic confound, thinking that the fact that feature changes tended to correlate with verb changes was part and parcel of the featural phenomenon. That is, to the extent that features indeed represent highly relevant content within the motion stream, it would not be surprising if our linguistic system captured such differences in the form of distinct verbs. Ultimately, however, we became convinced that it was nevertheless important to control for the possibility that linguistic differences were the sole source of the inversion effect we had obtained, leading us to rework our action stimuli such that featural-change videos were no more likely than configural-change videos to be associated with verb differences relative to the standard videos.

A second alternative—related but nevertheless potentially distinct from the linguistic alternative just described—was that featural-change videos were correlated to a greater degree than configural-change videos with perceived changes in the content of the actor's intention. Perhaps, then, inversion rendered it more difficult for participants to differentiate videos that appeared to depict the same intentional act, rather than directly affecting processing of configural information, per se. Again, our initial reaction on recognizing this intention difference between featural-change and configural-change videos was to regard it as part of the phenomenon under investigation (after all, we were specifically positing that features capture detail that is highly relevant to processing an actor's goals and intentions). However, we came to believe that controlling for this correlate of feature changes would be important to fully substantiating a feature versus configuration distinction. Thus, in our new stimuli featural and configural changes were equated for judgments of change in the actor's intention as well as for verb differences.

In the second study, we also made a concerted attempt to equate our featural-versus configural-change videos with respect to how detectable changes were in the upright format. Recall that in the first study, participants showed higher accuracy for detecting featural changes than configural changes when videos were upright. Inversion served to widen this accuracy difference, in that accuracy in detecting featural changes was less affected than was accuracy in detecting configural changes. However, demonstration of an inversion effect specific to configural changes would be most compelling if the two change types are equated for detection difficulty in the upright format. In order to achieve such detectability scaling of featural and configural changes, the motion properties involved in configural changes were exaggerated relative to the first study, while motion properties involved in featural changes were attenuated.

A subsidiary goal in redesigning our set of videos was to develop stimuli that could serve a dual purpose: (a) to further document a distinction between features

Table 9.2 Information about the eight video sets of Study 2

Object	Standard Video	Configural Change	Feature Change
mug	orient towards mug and move with open palm	do not fully orient head towards mug	move mug with hand clasped around handle
clay	hit clay with side of hand	increase height and speed of hit	hit clay with closed fist
cabinet	close cabinet by pushing with hand	close cabinet with robotic arm motion	close cabinet with one finger flicking
cup	grasp top of cup and move across table	grasp base of cup	grasp top of cup with finger and thumb
book	grasp book and place on book pile	place book down quickly	place book on pile with palm underneath
light	turn on press lamp with fingers	arcing motion to reach and press lamp	turn on lamp with closed fist
grater	push grater across table with hand	push grater more slowly	push grater with two fingers
pencil	grasp pencil and scribble on sheet of paper	scribble in opposite direction on paper	grasp pencil with full hand grip

versus configural information in adults' processing of everyday action with stringent controls introduced and (b) to investigate infants' sensitivity to these as distinct sources of information in dynamic action. The latter goal led us to consider the role of object knowledge in processing the actions depicted in our videos. Some of the actions we had used in the first study did not seem amenable to use with infants, as infants seemed unlikely to possess crucial knowledge of the objects involved. In our new stimulus set we attempted to include only actions that infants seemed likely to be able to readily process.

The complete set of video stimuli for the second study appear in table 9.2. In all other respects, the prediction, design, and procedure were identical to the first study. Strikingly, the findings from this second study were quite different from those of the first. On this occasion, we did not obtain the classic inversion effect in the form it has typically taken in the face-processing literature. That is, inversion elicited reduced accuracy in this second study to a similar degree for featural changes and configural changes (the magnitude of the effect was larger, but not significantly so, for configural changes). Thus, we were not able to provide unequivocal evidence that these are separable sources of information in action processing. Interestingly, despite our attempts to equate detectability of featural and configural changes in the upright format, consistent with the results of the initial study we again observed that our featural changes were significantly easier to detect in the upright condition than were our configural changes. Thus, even after carefully controlling for verb and intention changes and attempting to alter the balance of motion properties to benefit detection of configural changes, featural changes were still selectively attended to when processing dynamic human action. Taken together, both studies provide evidence that featural and configural changes are sources of information people can use to categorize and identify action and that featural information might hold special status in such processing.

Further Substantiating a Feature-Configuration Distinction in Action Processing

The two studies we have reported provided strong initial support for the idea that it is possible to distinguish featural and configural information in human action. We were not, however, able to provide strong evidence that these two sources of information are processed via distinct mechanisms, as had been documented in the face-processing literature. Interestingly, however, recent findings in the face-processing literature parallel those we obtained in our second study regarding action processing (inversion undercuts sensitivity to featural as well as configural changes; Yovel & Kanwisher, 2004), in contrast to what had previously been reported regarding face processing. Even more strikingly, these new face-processing results emerged in the context of research in which the attempt was made to achieve comparable levels of accuracy in detecting featural versus configural changes when faces were upright (just as in our second study we attempted to achieve such equivalent accuracy levels for feature versus configural changes in the upright condition). In both face- and action-processing domains, this pattern of findings is inconsistent with featural and configural properties being processed via distinct mechanisms (a point Yovel & Kanwisher explicitly make as well) but is instead consistent with the idea that features are especially prominent in processing. If features are local detail receiving selective attention in processing, then processing of features should be relatively robust in the face of potential disruption. If configural information, in contrast, is less attended to in processing, it should be relatively fragile in the face of attempts to disrupt it. If this is correct, the featural versus configural distinction should not be characterized with respect to distinct processing mechanisms, but instead is best captured as the difference between processing of key, central aspects of the motion stream (the meat) versus processing of less central, more peripheral aspects (subtleties and nuances).

A consistent finding across our two studies was that feature changes, even those that do not cross verb or intention boundaries, appear to be especially salient in people's processing of dynamic human action. This finding in itself is of great interest, as it demonstrates that not all portions of the motion stream are equal in people's action processing. In the second study we explicitly designed our videos so that featural changes would be of a much smaller magnitude in terms of motion properties than our configural changes. Featural changes tended to manifest across a very small portion of the screen, while configural changes manifested across a broader area. As well, configural changes that altered the temporal structure of the event yielded surface differences in motion velocity which seemed quite striking, whereas featural changes never included temporal changes of any kind. Yet despite what struck us as real differences in magnitude of surface change that favored detection of configural changes, the configural changes were still much harder for participants to detect even when viewing action in the upright format. One goal of future work will be to document the extent of this detectability difference between featural versus configural changes in more objective terms. That is, it will be of interest to learn the degree of objective motion change needed to elicit detection of configural changes relative to that needed to elicit detection of featural changes.

Featural and Configural Information in Categorization and Development

Our findings do provide evidence that features are prominent in people's processing of the motion stream arising from everyday intentional action. Features are local detail—in our videos such local detail often involves specifics of hand motion and positioning—that we suspect observers zero in on because they are highly relevant to determining the content of an actor's goals and intentions and hence offer valuable information for categorizing actions. Configural information, however, also seems to shape observers' inferences about goals and intentions, though it perhaps is not as central in this process as features. Information about the speed or trajectory of action can provide clues about the nature of the objects being acted upon, the emotional state of the actor, or the actor's attitude or beliefs toward the object acted upon. To illustrate, one of the configural changes that we used across both studies was a change of *placing* a book on a pile versus *slamming* it down on the pile. On observing someone produce such a book-slamming action, one might infer that the actor did not care for that particular book, that the actor was for some reason angry, or perhaps even that the actor was squashing a bug that was sitting on the pile of books. As in this example, configural information may either shape one's inferences about the intentional valence of the categorized act of slamming (e.g., complacent versus angry transfer) or on occasion even serve as the basis for altering the action category identified (e.g., bug-squashing rather than book-slamming). In sum, while we suspect that observers selectively attend to featural information in the motion stream to a greater degree than configural information, sensitivity to both sources of information is crucial to a rich analysis of the actor's goals and intentions.

If our analysis is correct, a number of interesting questions arise. A first question of great interest to us is the extent to which sensitivity to featural and configural information might change with development and experience. As we mentioned earlier, it is an open question whether infants are sensitive to both featural and configural sources of information in human action; we are currently undertaking a study to investigate this possibility. If infants are sensitive to featural information, then they should show recovered interest in looking at featural-change videos after having become habituated to our standard videos. Likewise, if infants are sensitive to configural information, they should similarly show looking recovery to configural-change videos after habituation to the standard videos. We may also expect, however, that even young infants do not recover attention to configural changes to the same degree as they do to featural changes, which would be consonant with our findings in adults.

This research will set the stage for investigating how infant sensitivity to featural and configural aspects of the motion stream might be acquired. We suspect that very early in development—the first few months of life—infants are not reliably sensitive to the same set of featural and configural characteristics to which adults exhibit sensitivity. It seems likely that some degree of experience observing a range of actions and a range of causal effects of various actions on various kinds of objects is key to gaining sensitivity to (a) highly relevant local detail to which adults seem to be selectively sensitive and (b) ways in which timing and trajectory information modify processing of such featural elements. For us, a particularly interesting question is the extent to which emerging appreciation of action as goal-directed and intentional is central to a developing sensitivity to featural and configural characteristics of human action. Consider just the featural components of the motion stream: We have suggested that features are especially valuable clues to the basic content of an actor's goals and intentions. Perhaps some dawning understanding of action as goal directed and intentional is necessary for infants to begin to home in on the characteristics of the motion stream that are informative on this point. Alternatively, it seems possible that featural elements come to be attended to selectively by observers of human action simply because statistical processing of the motion stream reveals them to be the most distinctive characteristics within the motion stream or the best predictors of other components of the motion stream. These same questions can be asked regarding developing sensitivity to configural characteristics of the motion stream. A small body of research in the face-processing domain suggests that processing of configural characteristics of the face undergoes gradual, extended development (Brace et al., 2001; Mondloch et al., 2002; though see Cohen & Cashon, 2001, for alternative evidence) and may be developmentally more fragile than processing of features (e.g., configural processing may be subject to critical period effects; Le Grand, Mondloch, Maurer, & Brent, 2003). One possibility is that sensitivity to configural properties of visual stimuli is particularly dependent on the development of expertise in that domain. It will be of great interest to investigate the possibility of similar effects in the domain of action processing.

The ideas we have advanced concerning possible developmental change in processing of dynamic human action clarifies that we suspect that such processing is itself dynamic. This may be as true for adults as it is for infants: that is, the portions of the motion stream that are processed as features versus those processed configurally may be malleable with experience and differ across action contexts. In an experimental setting using novel action, we may be able to manipulate what portions of the motion stream are most relevant for determining the actor's goals and intentions. The processing of these "artificially generated" sources of information may show similar patterns of selective attention to those shown with familiar action.

In our research on featural versus configural information in action to date, we have investigated observers' processing of only one kind of human action: object-oriented intentional action. The featural-configural distinction may or may not be relevant to categorization and identification of other kinds of action, which would include actions such as a variety of forms of dance and distinct kinds of gaits, such as walking, running, hopping, and the like, and may also include actions that simultaneously involve both object-oriented and person-oriented goals, such as social acts of object transfer (e.g., giving and taking). A subsidiary issue here is that identification of the motion stream as an instance of object- or non–object-oriented action may shape how that flow of behavior is processed. That is, depending on what one thinks is going on, one may deem distinctly different local portions of the motion stream to be relevant for processing. It may be possible to design novel action sequences that are ambiguous as to whether they depict object or non–object-oriented action and then observe how processing changes depending on what observers are biased to think they are viewing.

These points in turn clarify that we do not know what information observers utilize to identify action as object oriented. Intuitively one might hazard that object-oriented action is detected when an actor is observed to contact an object. However, the point-light research we described earlier indicates that actually observing an object being contacted is not essential to such identification: Observers are able to infer that a point-light actor is, for example, picking something up off the floor, even though they cannot see either the object (a towel) or the floor, but only the actor's motions across space and time. Our ability to interpret miming is another case in point. Clearly, observers are sensitive to clues within the motion stream itself that point to object-oriented intentions underway. What all this adds up to is that the perceptual and cognitive system for processing human action is obviously exquisitely sophisticated, and achieving a full understanding of this system poses a challenge of great interest for investigators.

Featural/Configural Summary

There appear to be at least two potentially distinct sources of information that people extract from the dynamic motion stream when processing object-oriented intentional action. One source, featural information, is composed of highly relevant, local detail. The other, configural information, is composed of global relations among motion elements. These two sources appear to be differentially attended to: Features appear to play a more prominent role in people's categorization and discrimination of action. Although our research sheds new light on some of the mechanisms that may play a role in action categorization, our current understanding of the processes at work is limited. We hope that others will join forces to pursue investigation of these and related issues.

Recap and Beyond

We began the chapter by stressing the complexity inherent in human action and noting the dearth of information currently available about how we as observers of behavior succeed in interpreting action so readily. Our goal for the chapter was to begin considering how two fundamental tasks—segmentation and categorization or identification—are accomplished as we view others carrying out everyday intentional actions. Regarding segmentation, we find that adults and infants as young as 10–11 months converge on similar segmentation analyses of dynamic human action and engage in such segmentation automatically while processing action online. We also have starting evidence that both adults and infants achieve segmentation, at least in part, via sensitivity to structural patterns inherent in the flow of behavior. We have examined two types of structural information: (a) structural gestalts that coincide with segments across highly diverse action types and action contexts and (b) statistical regularities concerning predictable co-occurrences across specific motion elements. Adults' and infants' processing of point-light versions of everyday intentional action displays clear-cut sensitivity to structural gestalts informative for segmentation, and statistical learning paradigms display solid skills in adults for detecting segments in novel action sequences via tracking of statistical regularities (research testing these issues is currently underway with infants). These findings suggest a new developmental story regarding the acquisition of skills for action processing. Sensitivity to structure inherent in intentional action appears to enable infants to detect relevant segments within continuous, dynamic human action, even when they possess little or no conceptual understanding of what an actor is doing or why the actor is doing this. Armed with the appropriate segments, infants can begin noticing commonalities and differences across segments they extract over time; in effect, they can begin categorizing actions. To fully understand these developmental processes, however, we will first need to gather considerably more information about categorization mechanisms in human action processing, and how they change with development.

For starters, we need to know something about the kind of information observers capitalize on in the stimulus—the motion stream—for purposes of categorization. Face-processing researchers have led the way in meeting this challenge head-on with regard to faces; evidence suggests there are at least two potentially distinct sources of information involved in recognizing and discriminating faces. We utilized their techniques in order to probe this issue with respect to human action. In this beginning research we focused on everyday object-oriented intentional actions like grasping, lifting, and placing. Our findings suggest there are at least two sources of information in action that adults recruited to recognize and discriminate such actions: (a) featural information regarding local detail about small-action segments and (b) configural information regarding global relations among motion elements. These findings provide new information about what properties within the motion stream people take advantage of when identifying and discriminating basic intentional actions and raise a number of interesting questions for future research. For example, examining the neurophysiological underpinnings of such phenomena will clarify whether processing of features and configurations in action and in faces rely on a common neural substrate. In addition, there are important developmental questions to investigate: to what extent do infants capitalize on the same sources of information adults utilize for processing dynamic human action, and how might their use of these sources change with development?

Segmentation and Categorization Online

Human action is a disappearing stimulus; to make sense of it, online processing is essential. However, online processing of such a complex stimulus probably can only be achieved by a massively parallel cognitive system. With respect to segmentation, for instance, we have reason to believe that multiple sources of information—such as structural gestalts, statistical regularities, and knowledge-based ("top-down") expectations—inform observers' identification of action segments within the motion stream. It seems quite likely that the action segmentation we carry out in everyday life relies on parallel engagement of all these sources of information. With respect to categorization, we have reason to believe that adults key on both featural and configural information in the motion flow to identify and discriminate between actions. Almost certainly, both are utilized in parallel in everyday action processing for identification and discrimination purposes. It seems fairly obvious that all of these subprocesses—for both categorization and segmentation—are carried out in parallel as action is observed (and likely a range of other essential processing tasks, such as integration and intentional inference). Presumably, categorization and segmentation not only are executed simultaneously but often mutually influence or even facilitate one another. For example, a structural gestalt occurring in action can give rise to the extraction of a segment, which then demands identification as a member of a category of actions. To illustrate, imagine an actor reaching toward an array of bottles and pausing indecisively before selecting one. The first part of this motion stream emerges as a structural gestalt by itself given the pause and the shift in trajectory as a bottle selection is made. Extracting it as a segment pulls for identification of the class of actions it belongs to; in this case, probably we would call the segment a "reach," which is distinct from the "grasp" segment that follows. Given that reaching and grasping are frequently executed as part of one fluid motion trajectory, one wonders how we might have come to distinguish these as distinct action categories. Perhaps the origin of this "reach/grasp" distinction lies in such instances of hesitation-driven action disfluency. All in all, processing dynamic human action demands uptake of multiple sources of information at many levels of analysis under serious time pressure, and our success at meeting these demands implies the online engagement of a massively parallel, highly interactive, multicomponent cognitive system.

Segmentation and Categorization: Mutual Catalysts in the Ontogeny of Action Processing

In this chapter, we have already made much of the core role that early skills for structure detection may play in enabling infants to achieve appropriate segmentation of action even when they have little understanding of the actions they are witnessing and hence are not yet identifying those actions as members of action categories. In this sense, skills for detecting structure can enable infants to break into initial appropriate analysis of the motion stream, setting the stage for infants to note commonalities and differences across instances of the structure-based chunks they are extracting from the flow of behavior. In this sense, segmentation seems an obvious prerequisite to categorization. But this doesn't mean that segmentation at all levels is fully fledged before categorization of action comes on line. In fact, at levels of analysis, such as the task level, that are higher than the potentially basic or primary small-action level, the opposite directionality—categorization serving as a prerequisite to segmentation—would seem to be common. Earlier we described a concrete example in which segmentation at the task level might depend on categorization at the small-action level: detecting task segments that group together units like "grasp knife," "grasp carrot," and "cut carrot" into a single, task-level segment such as "chop carrot" seems to require that the lower-level small-action segments be both detected and categorized in order to track statistical regularities across co-occurrences of instances of those categories. That is, one would first need to be able to recognize a given structural gestalt as a member of the "cut" category to be able to track conditional probabilities relative to instances of the "grasp" versus "open" categories. In this way, categorization—what Gentner and colleagues would term "recoding" (Gentner & Medina, 1998)—at the small-action level makes structure detection at that level possible, which in turn promotes segmentation, and ultimately recoding (categorization) at the higher level (see Saffran & Wilson, 2003, for a demonstration of this iterative recoding process at work in infants' tracking of statistical regularities in the language domain). In other words, segmentation and categorization act as mutual catalysts to developmental progress in action processing:

Each exerts pressure on the other until the available structure in the motion stream is fully captured.

Universality Versus Variability in Action Processing

We have presented some evidence that both adults and infants exploit structural gestalts to assist in segmenting human action. However, action seems to be especially rich with these segmentation-relevant structural gestalts at one particular level of segmentation—the level of segments that we as adults might categorize as "grasp," "lift," "poke," and so on. Recall, for example, that in our research described earlier, adults readily segmented point-light intentional action at the level of segments like "grasp" and "lift," but they did not do so for higher-level segments like "wash a dish" or "hang a towel." These higher-level segments are comprised of several lower-level segments and thus involve multiple trajectory changes, rate of action changes, and the like (and for this reason they do not cohere as unified structural gestalts). These findings hint that the level of segmentation at which we apprehend action categories like "grasp" and "lift" is in some fashion perceptually basic or primary. If this is correct then it is a level of segmentation that ought to be readily available to infants, and our findings suggest that it is. This means that we should expect some considerable degree of cross-cultural universality in humans' ability to extract segments that give rise to action categories like "grasp" and "lift." In contrast, we should expect a greater degree of variability in segmentation and categorization at higher levels of action processing. These points give rise to some predictions about possible relations between language and action processing. We might expect relatively little impact of the details of the language system on people's segmentation of the primary or basic level of analysis, whereas language might exert detectable influence in the packaging of action at higher levels. In fact there has been considerable discussion of these issues in the linguistics literature (e.g., Pawley, 1987). One example we might offer here is a comparison of English and Tamil (E. Pederson, personal communication). Imagine a scenario in which an actor enters a kitchen, walks toward a table, grasps a banana from a bowl on the table, and then exits the room. In English, we might describe these motions as "Jeff gets a banana." In Tamil, it is not possible to describe this motion stream in the same kind of global form: The language makes it obligatory to describe the action in terms of lower-level actions. That is, in Tamil, the description would be "Jeff picks up a banana and leaves." What we are suggesting is that the English verb "get" encourages English speakers to analyze action sequences at a level of generality that Tamil speakers may not be inclined to note. The potential for such linguistic relativity effects will be an interesting topic for future investigation now that we possess methodologies suited to probing online action processing (and we are in the midst of some initial work along these lines). These ideas make contact more broadly with Talmy's (1985, 1991) analysis of universality versus cultural variability in how verb systems characterize events, which has been extended in interesting ways by a variety of other researchers (e.g., Zheng & Goldin-Meadow, 2002; Loucks & Pederson, 2005; chapter 5, this volume). These ideas also connect with Gentner and colleagues' (Gentner & Boroditsky, 2001) proposal that the events verbs refer to are "linguistically partitioned," meaning that events in and of themselves are not readily individuated and require a push from language to emerge as coherent and nameable entities. For Gentner and colleagues this stands in stark contrast to the concrete objects usually referred to by nouns; they argue that noun referents are "naturally partitioned" by our perceptual and conceptual systems. Our research suggests one small modification to this proposal: events seem naturally partitionable at one level of analysis, the small-action level at which structural gestalts are available. Linguistic partitioning should primarily influence our packaging of events at levels of analysis both higher and lower than this basic or primary level of small actions.

Conclusion

The study of action processing is in its infancy. There is so much to be done. At the same time, the starting point for investigating action processing is far from a tabula rasa: A rich array of methodological tools developed by ingenious researchers to investigate processing in other domains is available. We have borrowed liberally from two other research traditions—the investigations of language and face processing—to examine basic segmentation and categorization phenomena in action processing. Analogous phenomena seem to be emerging across domains: Detection of structural gestalts and statistical regularities assist in segmentation of the motion stream as in language, and observers utilize local versus global information in different ways for identifying and discriminating actions as they do for faces. This suggests that processing in all of these domains recruits general cognitive mechanisms that are broadly available. At the same time, it may well turn out that there are also unique aspects to action processing that depend on mechanisms unlike those found in any other domain. It will be of great interest to discover ways in which acquisition in other domains, such as verb learning in the language domain, shapes action processing as well as to understand more fully what aspects of action processing must be in place for language learning to be possible. We hope that clarity on all these issues will quickly emerge now that action processing is gaining increasing attention as an important focus of investigation in its own right.

Acknowledgments Preparation of this chapter is based upon work supported by the National Science Foundation under Grant No. BCS-0214484. Our thanks to members of our research group for many helpful and inspirational discussions as well as assistance with data collection: Amanda Altig, Annika Andersson, Stephen

Boyd, Alicia Craven, Girin Guha, Eric Olofson, Meredith Meyer, Karen Myhr, and Emily Neuhaus. As well, our thanks to the adults and infants who so generously participated in the research.

References

Andersson, A., Baldwin, D., & Saffran, J. (2005). *Infants' reliance on statistical regularities in dynamic action as a clue to segmentation*. Unpublished manuscript.

Asch, S. E. (1952). *Social psychology*. Englewood Cliffs, NJ: Prentice Hall.

Aslin, R. N., Saffran, J. R., & Newport, E. L. (1999). Statistical learning in linguistic and nonlinguistic domains. In B. MacWhinney (Ed.), *The emergence of language* (pp. 359–380). Mahwah, NJ: Lawrence Erlbaum.

Baird, J. A., Baldwin, D. A., & Malle, B. F. (1999). *Parsing the behavior stream: Evidence for the psychological primacy of intention boundaries*. Unpublished manuscript, University of Oregon.

Baldwin, D. A., Andersson, A., & Saffran, J. (2005). *Adults segment dynamic human action via statistical regularities*. Unpublished manuscript, University of Oregon.

Baldwin, D. A., Baird, J. A., Saylor, M., & Clark, M. A. (2001). Infants parse dynamic human action. *Child Development, 72*, 708–717.

Baldwin, D., Neuhaus, E., Saylor, M., & Sobel, D. (2005). *Infants find structure in action*. Unpublished manuscript, University of Oregon.

Baldwin, D., Pederson, E., Craven, A., Andersson, A., & Bjork, H. (2005). *Change detection speeds up at intention boundaries*. Unpublished manuscript, University of Oregon.

Bartlett, J. C., & Searcy, J. (1993). Inversion and configuration of faces. *Cognitive Psychology, 25*(3), 281–316.

Bertoncini, J., & Mehler, J. (1981). Syllables as units in infants' speech perception. *Infant Behavior and Development, 4*, 247–260.

Bijeljac-Babic, R. J., Bertoncini, J., & Mehler, J. (1993). How do four-day-old infants categorize multisyllabic utterances? *Developmental Psychology, 29*, 711–721.

Brace, N. A., Hole, G. J., Kemp, R. I., Pike, G. E., Van Duuren, M., & Norgate, L. (2001). Developmental changes in the effect of inversion: Using a picture book to investigate face recognition. *Perception, 30*(1), 85–94.

Cohen, L. B., & Cashon, C. H. (2001). Do 7-month-old infants process independent features or facial configurations? *Infant and Child Development, 10*(1–2), 83–92.

Collishaw, S. M., & Hole, G. J. (2002). Is there a linear or a nonlinear relationship between rotation and configural processing of faces? *Perception, 31*(3), 287–296.

Costen, N. P., Parker, D. M., & Craw, I. (1996). Effects of high-pass and low-pass spatial filtering on face identification. *Perception and Psychophysics, 58*(4), 602–612.

Diamond, R., & Carey, S. (1986). Why faces are and are not special: An effect of expertise. *Journal of Experimental Psychology: General, 115*(2), 107–117.

Farah, M. J., Tanaka, J. W., & Drain, H. M. (1995). What causes the face inversion effect? *Journal of Experimental Psychology: Human Perception and Performance, 21*(3), 628–634.

Finkbeiner, M., Nicol, J., Greth, D., & Nakamura, K. (2002). The role of language in memory for actions. *Journal of Psycholinguistic Research, 31*(5), 447–457.

Fodor, J. A., & Bever, T. G. (1965). The psychological reality of linguistic segments. *Journal of Verbal Learning and Verbal Behavior, 4*, 414–420.

Freire, A., Lee, K., & Symons, L. A. (2000). The face-inversion effect as a deficit in the encoding of configural information: Direct evidence. *Perception, 29*(2), 159–170.

Gennari, S. P., Sloman, S. A., Malt, B. C., & Fitch, W. (2002). Motion events in language and cognition. *Cognition, 83*(1), 49–79.

Gentner, D., & Boroditsky, L. (2001). Individuation, relativity, and early word learning. In M. Bowerman & S. Levinson (Eds.), *Language acquisition and conceptual development* (pp. 215–256). Cambridge: Cambridge University Press.

Gentner, D., & Medina, J. (1998). Similarity and the development of rules. *Cognition, 65,* 263–297.

Gibson, E. J. (1969). *Principles of perceptual learning and development.* New York: Appleton-Century-Crofts.

Gibson, J. J. (1979). *An ecological approach to visual perception.* Boston: Houghton-Mifflin.

Gleitman, L. R., & Wanner, E. (1982). Language acquisition: The state of the state of the art. In E. Wanner & L. R. Gleitman (Eds.), *Language acquisition: The state of the art* (pp. 3–48). Cambridge: Cambridge University Press.

Guha, G., Baldwin, D., & Craven, A. (2005). *Finding structure in action.* Unpublished manuscript, University of Oregon.

Hayes, J. R., & Clark, H. H. (1970). Experiments in the segmentation of an artificial speech analog. In J. R. Hayes (Ed.), *Cognition and the development of language* (pp. 221–234). New York: Wiley.

Heider, F. (1958). *The psychology of interpersonal relations.* New York: Wiley.

Hirsh-Pasek, K., Kemler Nelson, D. G., Jusczyk, P. W., Wright Cassidy, K., Druss, B., & Kennedy, L. (1987). Clauses are perceptual units for young infants. *Cognition, 26,* 269–286.

Jusczyk, P. W. (1997). *The discovery of spoken language.* Cambridge, MA: MIT Press.

Jusczyk, P. W., & Derrah, C. (1987). Representation of speech sounds by young infants. *Developmental Psychology, 23,* 648–654.

Kellman, P. J., & Spelke, E. S. (1983). Perception of partly occluded objects in infancy. *Cognitive Psychology, 15,* 483–524.

Kemp, R., McManus, C., & Pigott, T. (1990). Sensitivity to the displacement of facial features in negative and inverted images. *Perception, 19*(4), 531–543.

Knight, B., & Johnston, A. (1997). The role of movement in face recognition. *Visual Cognition, 4*(3), 265–273.

Kuhlmeier, V., Wynn, K., & Bloom, P. (2003). Attribution of dispositional states by 12-month-olds. *Psychological Science, 14*(5), 402–408.

Lander, K., Christie, F., & Bruce, V. (1999). The role of movement in the recognition of famous faces. *Memory and Cognition, 27*(6), 974–985.

Leder, H., & Bruce, V. (2000). When inverted faces are recognized: The role of configural information in face recognition. *Quarterly Journal of Experimental Psychology A, 2,* 513–536.

Le Grand, R., Mondloch, C. J., Maurer, D., & Brent, H. P. (2003). Expert face processing requires visual input to the right hemisphere during infancy. *Nature Neuroscience, 6*(10), 1108–1112.

Loucks, J., & Pederson, E. (2005). *Language and thought in English and Spanish speaker's categorization of motion events.* Unpublished manuscript, University of Oregon.

Martin, B., & Tversky, B. (2003). *Segmenting ambiguous events.* Unpublished manuscript.

Mondloch, C. J., Le Grand, R., & Maurer, D. (2002). Configural face processing develops more slowly than featural face processing. *Perception, 31*(5), 553–566.

Newtson, D. (1973). Attribution and the unit of perception of ongoing behavior. *Journal of Personality and Social Psychology, 28,* 28–38.

Newtson, D., & Enquist, G. (1976). The perceptual organization of ongoing behavior. *Journal of Experimental Social Psychology, 12,* 436–450.

Papafragou, A., Massey, C., & Gleitman, L. (2002). Shake, rattle, 'n' roll: The representation of motion in language and cognition. *Cognition, 84*(2), 189–219.

Pawley, A. (1987). Encoding events in Kalam and English: Different logics for reporting experience. In R. S. Tomlin (Ed.), *Coherence and grounding in discourse* (pp. 329–360). Amsterdam: J. Benjamins.

Rakison, D. H., & Poulin-Dubois, D. (2002). You go this way and I'll go that way: Developmental changes in infants' detection of correlations among static and dynamic features in motion events. *Child Development, 73*(3), 682–699.

Reed, C. L., Stone, V. E., Bozova, S., & Tanaka, J. (2003). The body-inversion effect. *Psychological Science, 14*(4), 302–308.

Rossion, B., Dricot, L., Devolder, A., Bodart, J.-M., Crommelinck, M., de Gelder, B., et al. (2000). Hemispheric asymmetries for whole-based and part-based face processing in the human fusiform gyrus. *Journal of Cognitive Neuroscience, 12*(5), 793–802.

Saffran, J. R., Aslin, R. N., & Newport, E. L. (1996). Statistical learning by 8-month-old infants. *Science, 274,* 1926–1928.

Saffran, J., & Wilson, D. P. (2003). From syllables to syntax: Multilevel statistical learning by 12-month-old infants. *Infancy, 4*(2), 273–284.

Saylor, M. M., Baldwin, D., Baird, J. A., & LaBounty, J. (2005). *Infants' online segmentation of dynamic human action.* Manuscript in preparation.

Sharon, T. L. (2000). Parsing motion for meaning: Infants' individuation of actions from continuous motion. *Dissertation Abstracts International, Section B: The Sciences and Engineering, 60*(9-B), 4934.

Sharon, T. L., & Wynn, K. (1998). Individuation of actions from continuous motion. *Psychological Science, 9*(5), 357–362.

Shipley, T. (2003). The effect of object and event orientation on perception of biological motion. *Psychological Science, 14*(4), 377–380.

Talmy, L. (1985). Lexicalization patterns: Semantic structure in lexical forms. In T. Shopen (Ed.), *Grammatical categories and the lexicon: Language typology and syntactic description, vol. 3* (pp. 57–149). New York: Cambridge University Press.

Talmy, L. (1991). Path to realization: A typology of event conflation. *Proceedings of the seventeenth annual meeting of the Berkeley Linguistics Society* (pp. 480–519). Berkeley, CA: Berkeley Linguistics Society.

Thompson, P. (1980). Margaret Thatcher: A new illusion. *Perception, 9*(4), 483–484.

Thornton, I. M. (1998). The perception of dynamic human faces. *Dissertation Abstracts International, Section B: The Sciences and Engineering, 58*(12-B), 6837.

Thornton, I. M., & Kourtzi, Z. (2002). A matching advantage for dynamic human faces. *Perception, 31*(1), 113–132.

Valentine, T. (1988). Upside-down faces: A review of the effect of inversion upon face recognition. *British Journal of Psychology, 79*(4), 471–491.

Wynn, K. (1995). Infants possess a system of numerical knowledge. *Current Directions in Psychological Science, 4,* 172–177.

Wynn, K. (1996). Infants' individuation and enumeration of actions. *Psychological Science, 7,* 164–169.

Yin, R. K. (1969). Looking at upside-down faces. *Journal of Experimental Psychology, 81*(1), 141–145.

Yovel, G., & Kanwisher, N. (2004). Face perception: Domain specific, not process specific. *Neuron, 44,* 889–898.

Zacks, J. M., Braver, T. S., Sheridan, M. A., Donaldson, D. I., Snyder, A. Z., Ollinger, J. M., et al.(2001). Human brain activity time-locked to perceptual event boundaries. *Nature Neuroscience, 4,* 651–655.

Zacks, J., & Tversky, B. (2001). Event structure in perception and cognition. *Psychological Bulletin, 127,* 321.

Zacks, J., Tversky, B., & Iyer, G. (2001). Perceiving, remembering, and communicating structure in events. *Journal of Experimental Psychology: General, 130,* 2958.

Zheng, M., & Goldin-Meadow, S. (2002). Thought before language: How deaf and hearing children express motion events across cultures. *Cognition, 85,* 145–175.

10 Word, Intention, and Action: A Two-Tiered Model of Action Word Learning

Diane Poulin-Dubois and James N. Forbes

One aspect of young children's word learning is deciding which sound segment to pair with which concept. The regular occurrence of a word with extralinguistic cues helps children learn many words, including concrete nouns. But in the case of other lexical categories, such as verbs, the word-to-world association is more opaque. For instance, noun meanings express concepts, whereas verb meanings express relations among concepts. Novel nouns are frequently produced in ostensive contexts ("This is a dog"), while novel verbs are frequently produced in nonostensive contexts ("The dog barks too often"). In addition to correct word-to-referent mapping, successful word learning requires that children make inferences regarding word extension. A word-to-object mapping has to become a word-to-category mapping. Among researchers in language acquisition, there is consensus that infants are initially equipped with a set of cognitive and social abilities at the start of their word learning careers. The nature of these abilities and how they become gradually recruited at different stages of word learning are now relatively well understood for noun learning (Bloom, 2000; Hollich, Hirsh-Pasek, & Golinkoff, 2000; Woodward, 2000). In this chapter, we show that many of the same abilities are used to acquire novel action words. We first briefly review research on noun-verb asymmetry in young children's early vocabularies and the implications for verb learning. We next review what is currently known about infants' knowledge about the motion properties of objects, as well as their understanding of human actions. We then present a set of experiments from our laboratories that support the hypothesis that toward the end of the second year, there is a shift in the way children learn the meaning of novel action words and generalize these labels to new instances. This shift appears to be grounded in the ability to take into account behavioral cues (e.g., gaze, gesture) that reflect the intentional structure of the action. We also show that toddlers can generalize action words across a relatively broad range of events, although the similarity in appearance of the initial action and the new action becomes more peripheral as children become more experienced word learners.

The early vocabulary of young word learners has often been characterized as biased toward nouns because nouns form the majority of children's early receptive and productive vocabulary, and nouns are acquired earlier than other verb classes (Bates et al., 1994; Bloom, 1998; Fenson et al., 1994; Goldfield, 1993; Goldin-Meadow, Seligman, & Gelman, 1976; Nelson, 1973). This "noun bias" has been reported in a wide range of languages other than English, including French (Poulin-Dubois, Graham, & Sippola, 1995), Italian (Caselli et al., 1995), Spanish (Jackson-Maldonado, Thal, Marchman, Bates, & Gutierrez-Clellen, 1993) and Hebrew (Dromi, 1987). The main theoretical argument for the early dominance of nouns emphasizes conceptual factors, positing that it is easier to acquire labels for objects than labels for verbs because nouns refer to perceptually distinct and coherent units that are stable and consistent across time and context (Gentner, 1982). In contrast, the task involved in learning a label for an action is a cognitively more complex one, as the child needs to abstract the constant elements across a variety of contexts labeled by the verb, and understand the particular relationship between subject and object (Gentner, 1981; Macnamara, 1972). In a recent paper, Gentner and Boroditsky (2001) have developed and expanded upon Gentner's original position by proposing the "Division of Dominance" hypothesis, which posits that words vary along a continuum of cognitive versus linguistic dominance. On the cognitive end of the continuum lie words that refer to perceptually "individuated" items (i.e., concrete nouns). Words that cannot "exist independently" of language are at the linguistic end of the continuum (i.e., determiners and conjunctions). Verbs lie somewhere in the middle of this continuum, as languages vary in the way they choose to lexicalize and package the same event. Consequently, it is argued that verbs are acquired later, and previously learned lexical items, such as nonobject pairs, influence verb learning (Gentner & Boroditsky, 2001).

Is There a Noun-Verb Asymmetry?

Despite the empirical evidence and theoretical support for the noun bias, there is mounting empirical evidence that it might have been overstated. First, it has been pointed out that words for actions or events are also among children's first words, making up to 10% of early vocabularies (Bates et al., 1988; Bloom, 1973; Bloom, Tinker, & Margulis, 1993; Bowerman, 1974; Gopnik & Meltzoff, 1986; Hampson, 1989; Huttenlocher, Smiley, & Charney, 1983; Lieven, Pine, & Barnes, 1992; McCune-Nicolich, 1981; Nelson, 1973; Nelson, Hampson, & Shaw, 1993; Pine,

1992; Tomasello, 1992; Tomasello & Todd, 1983). Thus, although infants might have a strong bias towards interpreting words as object labels, their ability to acquire labels for actions needs to be accounted for.

Second, challenges to the noun bias hypothesis have come from recent cross-linguistic research. It has been argued that the observed noun bias is simply an artifact of the linguistic structure of English and not something universally true (Choi & Gopnik, 1995; Tardif, Gelman, & Xu, 1999). Proponents of this view propose that infants' early lexicon will reflect the linguistic input to which they are exposed, calling attention to the fact that the structural properties of languages differ in their emphasis on nouns. For example, in English, names for objects are most likely to be the loudest element of a sentence and they are often found in sentence final position (Goldfield, 1993; Tardif, Shatz, & Naigles, 1997). These characteristics of English are likely to make nouns the most salient part of the sentence, making it easier for children to attend to them (Slobin, 1973). This is in sharp contrast to S-O-V languages like Korean and Japanese. It should be pointed out that studies on the vocabulary composition of children acquiring Korean (Au, Dapretto, & Song, 1994; Kim, McGregor, & Thompson, 2000) and Mandarin (Gentner, 1982; Tardif et al., 1999) sometimes report a noun bias. Methodological factors might account for this discrepancy: Studies reporting a balanced vocabulary have typically consisted of naturalistic data, whereas studies yielding a noun bias used maternal report data.

Learning Action Versus Object Labels: Experimental Research

A promising approach to assess the relative ease of acquisition of nouns and verbs consists in teaching novel words to children. A handful of lexical training studies have compared the ease of acquisition of nouns and verbs in both infants and preschool age children. Schwartz and Leonard (1984) used an experimental task to teach novel labels for objects and actions to children, ranging in age from 12.5 to 15.5 months, until they were 16 to 18 months. In the "noun" condition, children were presented with an unfamiliar object performing a familiar action, whereas the "verb" condition consisted of a familiar object performing an unfamiliar action. Their results showed that acquiring the novel object was much easier for children. However, children's exposure to the action referents was relatively brief, whereas they were given an extended time to manipulate the objects. Similar studies with older children have also demonstrated a facility in acquiring object labels. For example, children were quicker at producing labels for objects than labels for actions, despite controlling for "number of exposures," "position in a sentence," and "stress and phonology" (Camarata & Leonard, 1986; Camarata & Schwartz, 1985). Similarly, Rice and Woodsmall (1988) demonstrated that it was easier for 3- and 5-year olds to learn object words. Although these studies show certain methodological limitations, they demonstrate that children learning English are consistently better at acquiring labels for objects than labels for actions. Recently, Imai, Haryu, and Okada (2002) used an experimental paradigm to teach preschoolers a label for a novel noun and a novel verb. Children heard a novel label paired with videotapes of an adult acting as an agent and performing an action with an object. The label was embedded with a syntactic frame that made it a noun or a verb. Both 3- and 5-year-olds were able to map the novel noun to the novel object, as they generalized the noun to a new event where the object was present but was used with a different action. However, only 5-year-olds were able to attach the label to the action, and generalize to a new event where the same action was presented with a new object. Indeed, 3-year-olds were much more conservative in their acquisition of verbs, as they could only generalize the label to the verb when the original object-action pairing was maintained and only the agent was different. Although 3-year-olds are demonstrating some rudimentary understanding of verbs, they have not fully grasped the concept, as they appeared to have mapped the verb label on the object and action pairing. Imai et al. (2002) concluded that verb learning is more difficult than noun learning, even for Japanese children who are learning a language that should facilitate verb learning. In an experimental task, Golinkoff, Jacquet, Hirsh-Pasek, and Nandakumar (1996) reported that children were able to generalize nouns at 28 months, whereas they could generalize verbs only at 34 months.

Lexical training studies have also been successfully used to teach infants new words when procedures are used to assess word comprehension. In these tasks, infants are typically trained to associate a label with an object or an event and are then requested to find the referent among a set of exemplars. Recent studies have shown that infants as young as 13 months can be taught new object labels and that by 18 months of age, infants can learn labels for actions in the laboratory (Casasola & Cohen, 2000; Graham & Poulin-Dubois, 1999; Oviatt, 1980, 1982; Schafer & Plunkett, 1998; Werker, Cohen, Lloyd, Casasola, & Stager, 1998; Woodward & Hoyne, 1999; Woodward, Markman, & Fitzsimmons, 1994). Another approach has been to assess infants' interpretation of novel words in an ambiguous context, that is, in contexts in which the word could label an action or an object. In a pioneering study of the object scope principle, Woodward (1993) presented 18- and 24-month-olds with two simultaneous video displays, one showing a static object and the other a substance in motion. When they heard a new label, 18-month-old infants focused on the object rather than the substance in motion, despite a baseline preference for the motion display. Because 24-month-olds did not show this difference, it remains to be determined whether these findings can be confirmed and extended. Furthermore, it is unclear whether infants avoided mapping the label to a substance or to a motion. In a recent direct test of the word-object bias infants were taught a novel label for moving objects with the habituation paradigm and then shown test events in which either the motion or the object are switched in the presence of the original label (Katerelos, Poulin-Dubois, & Oshima-Takane, 2004). Preliminary findings on English- and Japanese-speaking infants suggest that the novel label is preferably mapped to the object when no syntactic cues are available to specify the grammatical form of the label. The methodological challenge of this switch design is to ensure that the two motions and two objects are equally discriminable. In the next section, we review the empirical evidence showing that infants are quite adept at processing dynamic events.

Foundation for Verb Learning: Infants' Knowledge of Object Motion and Human Action

The predominance of nouns in early vocabulary seems to be consistent with research showing precocious detection of object properties and formation of object categories during the first year of life (Mandler, 2000; Spelke, 2000). However, since verbs are also spontaneously produced in the early stages of lexical development and can be taught after a brief exposure, there are most probably cognitive foundations for leaning verbs as well. Since the early verbs or action words denote events, especially actions, infants would need to be adept at processing object motion and human action in order to learn verbs efficiently. First, motion attracts the attention of even very young infants. For example, infants of 2 to 3 months of age prefer to look at moving rather than stationary objects (Kellman & Banks, 1998). Infants as young as 3 months of age can extract motion commonalities when presented with point-light displays of the pendular motion of animals walking in place or the rotary motion of vehicles rolling in place (Arterberry & Bornstein, 2001, 2002). During the first year of life, infants also show sensitivity to a wide range of motion properties, such as trajectory and onset of motion. For instance, infants as young as 3 months discriminate between a point-light display representing a walking motion and an incoherent display (Fox & McDaniel, 1982).

Not only do infants make fine discriminations of motion patterns, but it has been argued that perceptual analysis of object motions provides the foundations for the formation of early object categories (Mandler, 1992; Rakison & Poulin-Dubois, 2001). Studies using tasks such as the object examination or the object manipulation procedure have found that infants as young as 7 months distinguish between global domains such as animal, vehicle, and furniture, even when vastly perceptually dissimilar objects are presented (Mandler & McDonough, 1993, 1998; Oakes, Madole, & Cohen, 1991). According to Mandler (1992), infants can acquire these broad categories by creating abstract representations (image schemas) from the perceptual analysis of the motion of objects. For instance, the category of animals might combine image schemas of self-propelled motion, irregular trajectory, and contingent interaction with other objects. There is some empirical support for this proposal (see Rakison & Poulin-Dubois, 2001, for a review). In a study, infants were shown to be able to associate two different linear trajectories with two different objects by the middle of the second year (Rakison & Poulin-Dubois, 2002). Two recent experiments conducted in the laboratory of one of us (D. P. D.) demonstrate that infants as young as 12 months are adept at generalizing motor activities across a wide range of agents, paving the way for action word extension. Poulin-Dubois and Vyncke (2004) tested 14- and 18-month-olds' ability to associate animals and people with animate motions (e.g., climbing stairs, jumping over a block) and inanimate motions with vehicles (e.g., jumping across a gap, sliding along a U-shaped block). An experimenter modeled each action three times with an appropriate target exemplar, each demonstration accompanied by appropriate vocalizations (e.g., making a dog walk up the stairs while saying, "Tum, tum, tum"). Infants were then given two test exemplars to imitate the action (e.g., a horse and a car). Infants as young as 14 months generalized motion trajectory from one category exemplar to a member of the same object kind. Interestingly, in another experiment infants were also able to generalize the actions modeled with an animal to both a person and another animal, showing a broad concept of agents. Another recent series of experiments using similar stimuli with the infant-controlled habituation paradigm provide converging evidence that conceptual knowledge about the motion of animate and inanimate objects emerge during the second year (Baker, Demke, & Poulin-Dubois, 2004). For example, when habituated to films featuring a dog jumping over a wall, and a car bouncing off the wall, 16- and 20-month-old infants dishabituated to incongruent test events (e.g., a bus jumping over the wall) but not to congruent events (e.g., a cat jumping over the wall). Finally, infants can also generalize activities such drinking, sleeping, and answering the phone across a similar range of agents (Poulin-Dubois, Frenkiel, Johnson, & Nayer, 2004).

In sum, there is much evidence that infants are not only competent in discriminating human actions and object motion but also understand that many different agents are capable of performing the same actions by the beginning of the second year. This makes possible the extension of action verbs to many different agents at a very early stage in early lexical development, analogous to the way nouns are extended to object categories. However, although motion and action processing are the building blocks from which infants can learn the meaning of many concrete action verbs (e.g., *run*, *jump*), other cognitive abilities are needed to establish the reference of others, such as *spill* and *pour*. To learn these verbs, infants must be able to process the psychological aspects of human actions, including the goal-directed aspects of motion. Furthermore, the semantic category of verbs includes references to mental states, mental activities, or attitudes, and so on. In the next section, we review the research on theory of mind in infancy that has documented the understanding of human actions beyond body movements.

Infants' Knowledge of Intentions-in-Actions

Research over the last decade or so has shown that infants develop some implicit form of folk psychology during the first two years of life. They can reason about people's perceptions, desires, and intentions (Flavell, 1999; Meltzoff, Gopnick, & Repacholi, 1999). The concept of intention is used to denote deliberate action as opposed to accidental action as well as to refer to the reason why something is done. Intentions are mental states that integrate the desires and beliefs that provide the reasons for action (Astington, 2001). There is consensus that a full-fledged understanding of intentions as expressions of future goals, or mental states that precede actions, is certainly beyond the grasp of infants insofar as the understanding of intentions in a representational way develops gradually between 3 and 5 years of age (Astington, 2001; Schult, 2002). However, it seems that infants possess a sensitivity to the physical and temporal features of action that correlate with the initiation and completion of intentions (Baird & Baldwin, 2001; Baldwin & Baird, 1999). For example, by 10–11 months, infants detect disruptions to the structure inherent in intentional action, as shown by their reactions when shown video sequences of everyday actions that are interrupted midstream as the actor pursues an intention. Even infants as young as 6 months selectively attend to the features of an event that are relevant to the actor's goal (Woodward, 1998).

In a landmark study on early intention understanding, Meltzoff (1995) showed 18-month-old infants an actor who tried, but failed to complete an action (e.g., an actor was shown attempting to pull apart the ends of an object shaped like a dumbbell) and then gave them the opportunity to manipulate the object. Infants who saw these "failed attempts" were as likely to produce the target action as infants who had seen a demonstration in which the actor achieved his goal. Moreover, infants tended not to produce the unseen, intended action when a mechanical device replaced the human agent. Thus, it appears that 18-month-olds understand that people's actions are driven by underlying goals and intentions and that these mental attributions cannot be extended to inanimate objects. Bellagamba and Tomasello (1999) used the behavioral reenactment technique to examine whether 12- and 18-month-old infants would also make inferences about the intentions underlying another person's unsuccessful attempts to fulfill a goal. They found that only the older infants understood what the actor was attempting to do and thus reproduced behaviour with the same intention.

Another way to explore infants' implicit understanding of intention has been to examine whether infants can discriminate between intentional and accidental actions modeled by an adult and whether they prefer to reproduce the intentional actions. In a recent experiment, an adult modeled actions to infants aged 14 to 18 months (mean age = 16 months) using objects that had two attachments that could be manipulated (e.g., a bird feeder with a movable top and an attached ring that could be pulled) to produce an end result (e.g., inflatable party favor) (Carpenter, Akhtar, & Tomasello, 1998). The demonstrations included both accidental actions (i.e., actor said "Whoops!" while completing the action) and intentional actions (i.e., actor said "There!" while completing the action) that were designed to look as natural as possible. Following the demonstration, infants were given a turn (i.e., "Can you make it work?") and were shown the end result shortly after they reproduced the intentional action. Overall, infants reproduced significantly more intentional than accidental actions and completed the intentional action by itself more often than they produced any other type of response (i.e., both actions or the accidental action only). Moreover, the infants' tendency to reproduce the intentional actions did not increase across trials, ruling out the possibility that they preferentially reproduced this action type simply because they had learned the association between completing the intentional action and viewing the amusing end result. There was no significant relationship between infants' age (which ranged from 14 to 18 months) and their ability to differentiate intentional and accidental actions. Therefore, Carpenter and her colleagues (1998) concluded that infants as young as 14 months of age have some understanding of the intentions of other people. This study was replicated recently with two separate age groups, 14- and 18-month-olds, in order to enhance the possibility of detecting a developmental pattern in the infants' ability to differentiate between accidental and intentional action (Olineck & Poulin-Dubois, 2005). Although infants from both ages imitated more intentional than accidental actions, older children show a better discrimination.

In summary, infants are sensitive to sociopragmatic cues displayed by people when they perform actions such as gestures, gaze, and body posture, by the middle of the second year, if not earlier. This sensitivity appears to be in place around the time that toddlers start to produce concrete action verbs. In the following section, we review lexical training studies from our laboratories that show toddlers can not only learn novel action labels, but also gradually extend these words productively.

Toward a Model of Early Verb Learning

How children determine which aspect of an ongoing event is being referred to, what Tomasello (1995) calls the "packaging problem," remains a central issue for the study of early verb learning. One source of the difficulty naive learners encounter in solving the verb packaging problem is that verbs can be interpreted in terms of numerous semantic elements such as manner of motion (e.g., to walk vs. to run), direction relative to the speaker (e.g., to come vs. to go), the instrument involved (to spoon vs. to pedal), or by the result achieved (e.g., to fill vs. to empty) to list only a few (Gentner, 1982; Talmy, 1985). In addition to learning which aspects of a verb's referent become conflated with verb meaning, children must also interpret actors' behavioral intentions, speakers' semantic intentions, as well as rely on their own semantic and syntactic understanding to overcome the referential obstacles to learning verb meaning (Forbes & Farrar, 1995). Indeed, a growing consensus among researchers in early verb acquisition is that children rely on multiple factors to learn and generalize new verbs. Moreover, these factors are weighted differently as young children's verbal and cognitive abilities develop (Bloom, 2000; Hollich, Hirsh-Pasek, & Golinkoff, 2000). Hollich et al. (2000) argue that young children's word learning proceeds first by their attending to perceptual elements in ongoing events that are conflated with verb meaning and then attending to more social and linguistic cues to word meaning. We review, in some detail, three of our lexical training studies that reveal this shift from young childrens' initial reliance on perceptual information to increasing reliance on more social and linguistic information to learn verbs.

Forbes and Poulin-Dubois (1997) adapted the intermodal preference "looking paradigm" developed by Hirsh-Pasek and Golinkoff (1996) to study developmental differences in young children's representation and generalization of familiar action verbs. The paradigm minimizes task demands for young children and has been useful in determining how very young children's word learning develops from early infancy to after 24 months (Poulin-Dubois, 1995; Reznick, 1990). In our version of the procedure, 24 20-month-olds and 25 26-month-olds were shown videotapes of two adults performing two familiar action verb referents (*kick* and *pick up*) in a series of familiarization, saliency, and test trials. Only children whose parents reported that their children comprehended both target verbs participated. Familiarization trials consisted of presenting a single referent event depicting the familiar verbs. Familiarization trials were introduced as: "Look! She is kicking" (or "picking up"). Referent events were shown one at a time on one of two monitors during familiarization trials. Children were also shown test trials of paired events presented simultaneously on both monitors (viz., kick and pick up). During test trials, the outcome, manner, agent, or instrument differed from the referent events viewed during familiarization trials. For instance, during outcome test trials, *kick* with a different outcome from that shown during familiarization trials and *pick up* with a different outcome from that shown during familiarization trials were shown simultaneously. Control trials were included to verify infants' familiarity with both verbs depicted in the familiarization phase. Test and control trials were introduced as: "Look! Who is kicking? Find kicking." Like previous studies using the preferential looking paradigm, we also included saliency trials which consisted of simultaneously presenting the *kick* and *pick up* referents shown during familiarization trials. During saliency trials, children were not specifically instructed to look at one of the events. Hence, children should have looked equally often (on average) at both referent events, provided neither referent event was intrinsically more salient than the other.

Children's generalization and representation of the action verbs *kick* and *pick up* was inferred from their looking time at the target events during test trials. Children's looking time was not attributable to the saliency of either event. A principle finding was a developmental difference in the younger and older children's ability to locate target actions in which the overall appearance (e.g., manner, agent) differed from the original referent event. Specifically, 26-month-olds generalized both familiar verbs to new referents in which the manner of action or the agent differed from the original referent seen during familiarization trials, whereas 20-month-olds were only able to extend the newly learned word to a new agent. Another principle finding was that children's expressive vocabulary, measured by the MacArthur Communicative Development Inventory: Toddlers (CDI; Fenson et al., 1991), was a better predictor of verb representation and generalization than age. High expressive vocabulary 20-month-olds generalized the familiar verbs to agent changes, whereas low expressive 20-month-olds did not. This finding is especially intriguing since most previous studies of early noun learning using the preferential looking paradigm have failed to find a relationship between looking time at targets and parental report (CDI) of expressive language level (e.g., Hirsh-Pasek & Golinkoff, 1996; Hollich et al., 2000). At first glance, this supports the idea that vocabulary development might be more closely related to children's ability to extend action verbs beyond the original referent action (principle of extendibility), than to children's knowledge that action words label actions (principle of reference) (Golinkoff et al., 1996).

These findings show that young children's representation of familiar action verb meaning changes from 20 to 26 months of age. The convergence of evidence from this and other studies in early verb learning suggests that young children's initial representation of verb meaning is, like the representation of noun meaning, narrowly defined and context specific, which renders them conservative in generalizing verbs (e.g., Forbes & Farrar, 1993; Theakston, Lieven, Pine, & Rowland, 2002; Tomasello, 1992). More specifically, children under 24 months narrowly represent action verb meaning in terms of event appearance, in the same way that young children generalize nouns to perceptually similar objects. By 26 months, children's representation of verb meaning includes proportionally more "essential" elements of semantic meaning (e.g., Behrend, 1990; Forbes & Farrar, 1993, 1995), actors' behavioral intentions (e.g., Baldwin & Baird, 1999; Gergely, Nadasdy, Csibra, & Biro, 1995; Poulin-Dubois & Forbes, 2002), speaker's semantic intentions (e.g., Forbes, Ashley, & Martin, 2003), as well as syntactic form and function relationships (e.g., Naigles & Terrazas, 1998; Slobin, 2001).

Poulin-Dubois and Forbes (2002) looked specifically at young children's ability to infer behavioral cues marking actors' intended actions (e.g., eye gaze, hand gestures) to learn, then generalize novel action verbs. Using a version of the visual preference paradigm, we taught 28 21- and 34 27-month-old children six pairs of novel action verbs. Two of the verb pairs looked very similar in appearance, but differed in terms of the actors' behavioral intentions (e.g., *topple* and *knock over*). One of the verb pairs referred to events that completely differed in appearance as well as in terms of the actors' behavioral intentions (e.g., *insert* and *align*). Familiarization trials were used to introduce six novel action verbs using the verbal prompt: "Watch! She is going to (target verb). She is (target verb). Can you say (target verb)?" Familiarization actions were shown one at a time during the familiarization phase. Test trials consisted of presenting one pair of actions simultaneously on side-by-side monitors (e.g., *align* and *insert*) with the verbal prompt: "Look! Where is (target verb)? Find (target verb)." On test-match trials, children were shown the standard actions seen during familiarization trials. On test-extend trials, children were shown novel examples of the standard actions. Saliency trials were identical to test trials except that children were not specifically instructed to find the referent of a target verb: "Wow! Look at the pictures. See the pictures?" Motivation trials consisted of hand puppets dancing to the beat of accompanying children's songs. Children viewed a total of 35 trials: 12 familiarization, 6 test-match, 6 test-extend, 6 saliency, and 5 interest, all of which lasted 8 seconds.

The primary dependent measure was children's looking time at the target actions, which was converted to a percentage and compared to chance (50%). Twenty-one- and 27-month-olds looked significantly longer than chance at the target actions for *align* and *insert* (different appearance and different actors' intentions) on test-match trials. So even the youngest children could learn at least one of the novel verb pairs. In contrast, only 27-month-olds looked significantly longer than chance at the target actions for *view* and *stack* and *topple* and *knock over* (similar appearance, but different actors' intentions) on test-match trials. Furthermore, as shown in table 10.1, only 27-month-olds looked significantly longer than chance at the target actions for *align*, *insert*, *topple*, and *knock over* on test-extend trials. These results were not due to the saliency of individual actions because looking time at paired actions on saliency trials did not differ from chance.

These findings show that by 27 months, children perceive subtle behavioral cues, such as eye gaze and hand gestures, and interpret these cues as relevant to novel action verb meaning. Of course, these findings afford both a rich and a lean interpretation. A lean interpretation would be that the older children were merely more adept than the younger children at interpreting behaviors such as bringing one's hands to the mouth or eyes, as useful in distinguishing referents labeled by different verbs. A rich interpretation would be that by 27 months, children regularly interpret actors' behavioral intentions as "intentions-in-action" or part of their representation of verb meaning. This latter interpretation is supported by 27-month-olds' ability to extend two of the verb pairs, differing in

Table 10.1 Mean percentage of looking times at target event by test conditions and verb pairs

	21 Months		27 Months	
Verb Pairs	Match	Extend	Match	Extend
Different appearance/different intention				
Align	57.32*	50.95	57.90*	58.98*
Insert	57.97*	55.64	59.83*	56.51*
Same appearance/different intention				
Topple	47.64	52.16	59.79**	56.84*
Knock-over	51.75	45.42	62.66**	56.32*
View	55.08	55.97	56.65*	50.16
Stack	50.86	47.80	57.13*	53.01

actors' behavioral intentions, to previously unseen referents of the just-learned verbs. The rich interpretation is further supported by what is currently known about the development of action analysis and intentional understanding in children from 12 to 36 months of age (Baldwin, Baird, Saylor, & Clark, 2001; Bloom, 2000; Carpenter et al., 1998; Olineck & Poulin-Dubois, 2005). Regardless of the richness of the interpretation, this study shows that children confer a special status to behavioral cues about a person's mental state in acquiring the meaning of action words.

Finally, Forbes et al. (2003) used a participatory lexical training task to further study when actors' behavioral intentions are processed by young children as "intention-in-the-mind," and included in their semantic representation of verb meaning. Using a participatory, live-action verb learning task more closely approximates how young children actually learn words by participating in ongoing events. The ecologically valid design complements and extends the more artificial preferential looking paradigm in determining how and when young children infer actors' and speakers semantic intentions.

Forbes et al. (2003, Experiment 1) taught 16 21-month-olds and 16 27-month-olds the same six novel verbs in one of two conditions: explicit or no explicit speakers' semantic intentions. In the explicit condition, children were told what each verb specifically referred to and were explicitly informed when the novel verb was performed. In the no explicit intentions condition, children were engaged in off-task talk but heard the novel verb form spoken exactly as in the explicit intentions condition, except that the verb did not immediately precede or follow the actions. The six novel action verbs corresponded to three different categories of paired events: (1) different appearance, different agents' behavioral intention; (2) different appearance, same agents' behavioral intention; and (3) same appearance, different agents' behavioral intentions. Because the paired events systematically differed in terms of event appearance and agents' behavioral intentions, the design allows a more precise determination of whether and when young children's action word learning is based on the overall appearance of ongoing events, or on their interpretation of the agent's semantic intentions. The explicit, no explicit intentions manipulation shows whether young children's action verb learning occurs most readily novel verb meaning is communicated explicitly or nonexplicitly.

Each child was seen three times for approximately 30 minutes on each occasion. During each training session, one experimenter modeled a verb pair (in one of six orders) one at a time (six times each). Children's comprehension and production of the verbs was assessed at the end of each session in the order that the verbs were modeled. To test children's comprehension, the experimenter placed both of the action props used during the training session to model the verbs in front of the child and asked: "Can you (target verb)? Show me how you (target verb)." To elicit children's production of the modeled verbs, the experimenter placed both of the action props in front of the child, demonstrated one of the actions, and asked: "What am I doing? Can you say what I'm doing?" Because the elicited production testing procedure involves demonstrating the target verb, children's comprehension was always tested first.

The dependent measure of interest was the mean proportion of times children comprehended and produced (combined) each of the target verbs. The data revealed systematic differences in 21- and 27-month-olds' ability to learn novel action verbs referring to events that systematically differed in terms of appearance and actors' intentions (figure 10.1). The youngest children learned verbs proportionately most often referring to paired events that looked different and in which the actor intended something different. They learned verbs proportionately least often for paired events that looked similar but in which the actors' behavioral intentions differed. In contrast, 27-month-olds learned verbs proportionately most often referring to paired events that differed in terms of the actors' semantic intentions and least often for paired events in which the actors' intensions were identical. Overall, children learned the novel verbs proportionately most often in the explicit semantic intentions condition. However, protocol (explicit versus no explicit intentions) did not differentially affect 21- or 27-month-olds' verb learning on any of the verbs.

In Experiment 2 (Forbes et al., 2003), 16 22- and 16 28-month-olds were taught a different sample of six novel action verbs using the same design and procedures as in Experiment 1. But in Experiment 2, children's verb generalizations rather than their verb learning were measured. During structured testing, children's generalizations of the verbs modeled during the training sessions were assessed by their comprehension and production of the just-learned verbs to

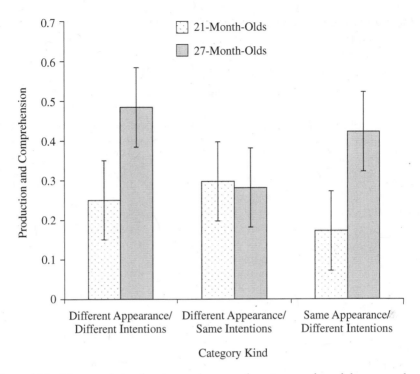

Figure 10.1. Mean verb production and comprehension combined, by age and category kind.

generalization events. The generalization events were similar to those children experienced during the training sessions except that different props were used. For example, four different-colored wrapped bean bags were placed into boxes of the same color to demonstrate the referrent event for the novel verb *match* during the training session. During the verb generalization test session, four different-colored wooden dowels and colored plastic pots were offered as props for children to generalize the verb *match*. Of particular interest was whether children generalized newly learned novel action verbs based on their understanding of the verb's intended meaning or based on their perception of the event to which the verbs referred.

As in Experiment 1, children again systematically differed in their ability to generalize novel action verbs. Surprisingly, 22-month-olds produced and comprehended the paired verbs referring to the different appearance/same agent's behavioral intentions events reliably more often than 28-month-olds. In previous lexical training studies of which we are aware, 22-month-old children typically do not extend just-learned verbs to different referent events. Nor have 22-month-old children outperformed children older by 6 months in any of the lexical training studies of which we are aware. Perhaps lexical training studies relying exclusively on nonparticipatory lexical training tasks, such as the preferential looking paradigm, underestimate children's lexical abilities as well as their representation of word meaning. The other principal findings were that compared to 22-month-olds, 28-month-olds extended proportionately more action verbs to: (1) generalization events differing in appearance and agents' behavioral intentions, as well as (2) generalization events similar in appearance but different in terms of agents' behavioral intentions (see figure 10.2). And as in Experiment 1, children again learned one of the six verbs proportionately most often in the explicit condition. So making the speaker's semantic intentions explicit can facilitate children's ability to learn and extend novel verbs. But children learned and extended ten of the

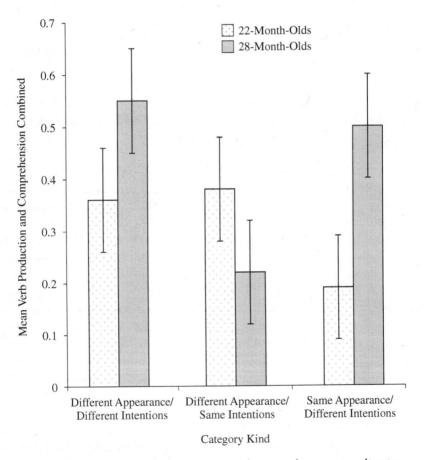

Figure 10.2. Mean verb production and comprehension during generalization trials combined, by age and category kind.

twelve verbs across two studies equally well regardless of whether the speaker's intentions were explicitly stated or implied from the speaker's behavior (see also Tomasello & Barton, 1994).

It would appear that between 21 and 28 months of age, children's verb learning strategy transitions from a reliance on the overall appearance of verb referent events to a reliance on behavioral and linguistic cues about others' semantic intentions. Certainly by 28 months, children regularly encode others' behavioral and verbal semantic intentions as an integral part of their understanding of novel action verb meaning. These conclusions accord with Golinkoff, Hirsh-Pasek, Mervis, and Frawley's (1995) claim that young children's verb learning proceeds first by their attending to event components that are lexicalized in their respective languages, then increasingly attend to social and syntactic cues to verb meaning.

Discussion

Across most languages around the world, children appear to be biased to learn nouns earlier and more rapidly than verbs. This seems counterintuitive given that languages vary in the extent to which they are noun-friendly. According to a recent proposal, word learning falls along a continuum of dominance, anchored at each end by cognitive and linguistic factors, on which verbs fall somewhere in the middle (Gentner & Boroditsky, 2001). In this chapter, we have argued that young children possess advanced skills for processing object motion and human actions, which represent the cognitive foundations for the acquisition of many verbs. For example, by the end of the first year of life, infants can discriminate between different types of motion and have also started to associate different motion types (e.g., linear vs. nonlinear trajectory) with a broad range of category exemplars (Rakison & Poulin-Dubois, 2001). Children also make rapid strides in human action understanding during that same developmental period, particularly in the detection of intentional actions. Consequently, we have argued that children should easily learn verbs that are more cognitively transparent than those which are more "opaque." Indeed, children younger than 24 months learn and extend verbs referring to events differing in appearance more readily than verbs differing in actors' behavioral intentions (Forbes et al., 2003). Moreover, learning the verb *to think* requires a different conceptual representation than learning the verb *to run*. Mental verbs like *to think* refer to mental states, for which referential criteria must be deduced, whereas the meaning of motion verbs like *to run* refer to directly perceptible actions.

Other theorists argue that early word learning is more accurately depicted as a process of children learning the rules of word use rather than agreement of referential intent (e.g., Montgomery, 1997, 2002; Wittgenstein, 1958). Montgomery, for example, argues that young children are not developing mental representations of words referring to objects, events, or internal mental states early on. Rather, they are learning to mimic word use in context (see also Tomasello's, 1992, verb island hypothesis). Later on, children gradually develop the symbolic understanding of word reference as well as the mental representation of word meaning. Moreover, children's mental representations of word meaning differ from those of adults, and change as they experience multiple examples of referents for a specific word (Forbes & Farrar, 1995). Nonetheless, our own experimental research, as well as that of others, shows that toddlers readily learn and extend labels for motion verbs (e.g., *kick*) by the time they are about 18–21 months of age. Our research also shows that learning and extending motion verbs requires infants to process cues about the agent's intentions (e.g., eye gaze, gestures) shortly thereafter.

In accord with the emergentist coalition model (ECM) explanation of young children's language acquisition, we believe that children's word learning is enabled by a conceptual toolbox composing multiple representation abilities for interpreting social, perceptual, and linguistic cues provided by the speaker and the context (Hirsh-Pasek, Golinkoff, & Hollich, 2000). According to the emergentist coalition model, although a wide range of cues are available from the start of word learning, not all cues are utilized by children in the early stages of word learning. What changes with development is the relative weighting of these cues. For example, although 12-month-old infants can notice social eye gaze, they do not use this cue in learning a new noun until later and instead rely on the perceptual salience of the objects to help them learn a new word (Hollich et al., 2000). Our data show that a similar developmental progression is also observed with respect to verb learning, with the perceptual salience of events guiding how the reference of a new action word is established early on. Moreover, a given cue might be used in some contexts later than in others, such as when 21-month-old children use eye gaze from the speaker to map a new word to a referent but cannot use eye gaze from the actor in an event to determine the meaning of a novel action word (Poulin-Dubois & Forbes, 2002).

Findings from our studies reported in this chapter support the idea that word learning develops in several stages, akin to the two-tier developmental lexical principles model proposed by Golinkoff, Mervis, and Hirsh-Pasek (1994). More specifically, it is interesting to note that in Experiment 1 (Forbes & Poulin-Dubois, 1997), 21-month-old children with a limited vocabulary seemed to follow the principle of extendibility to generalize new action words, guiding themselves on the perceptual similarity between the original action and the test actions. Within the same age group, children with a larger vocabulary were able to use the principle of categorical scope, that is, they extended words on the basis of some nonobvious commonalities rather than on perceptual similarity in the same way that children have been shown to generalize nouns to a taxonomic category. At 26 months of age, all children seem to have had enough word-learning experience (median vocabulary over 400 words) to use the categorical scope principle in a flexible way. This is an important finding because no link has been found so far between vocabulary size and performance on the training or testing trials of word learning studies which considered forced choices between the target object and a distracter object (Hollich et al., 2000). The present findings indicate that the categorical scope principle might be better linked to vocabulary development than the reference principle.

The experimental studies we have reviewed only examined some of the cues that children might use in mapping and generalizing a novel word. For example, we modified specific aspects of events and examined how infants represented, learned, and generalized the new words. In our intermodal visual preference paradigm studies, we removed from the auditory prompt all the linguistic cues that signal a verb; nor were any attentional cues provided by the speakers since disembodied voices labeled the events. In the real world and in our studies using a participatory lexical training task, speakers provide sociopragmatic cues (e.g., eye gaze, pointing) when they produce new labels for actions and the input contains syntactic cues. For example, Tomasello and Akhtar (1995) demonstrated that 27-month-old children are able to use adults' pragmatic cues to determine whether the label refers to an object or an action. In the study, children heard an adult pronounce a novel word when presented with a novel object performing a novel action. Pragmatic cues in the situation (novelty to the conversation, or adult gaze) guided the children in attaching the label to the appropriate referent. It remains to be determined what exact role, if any, social cues from the speaker might play in verb learning. Information about precisely which component of the event is being labeled would unlikely be provided by the speaker's eye gaze for action verbs, the way a speaker's gaze can indicate which object is the focus of attention. It is certainly of no use for learning many types of verbs, such as mental state verbs.

Finally, Forbes and Farrar (1995) showed that the context (repeated exposure to the same referent event vs. repeated exposure to different versions of a referent event) in which novel verbs are learned greatly affect young children's initial assumptions about verb meaning. Thus, children's verb learning and extensions are not wholly explicable in terms of children's perceptual, conceptual, linguistic, and social-cognitive skills. The ECM needs to be extended to account for how the context (viz., initial exposure to similar or different examples of events to which verbs refer) of verb learning, as well as other cues that might overlap with those used in noun learning, affect children's verb representation, learning, and extensions.

Acknowledgments Portions of the research were supported by an NIH grant (1R15HD042472-01) awarded to James Forbes and by a grant from the Natural

Sciences and Engineering Research Council of Canada (#2003-03) to Diane Poulin-Dubois.

References

Arterberry, M. E., & Bornstein, M. H. (2001). Three-month-old infants' categorization of animals and vehicles based on static and dynamic attributes. *Journal of Experimental Child Psychology, 80,* 333–346.

Arterberry, M. E., & Bornstein, M. H. (2002). Infant perceptual and conceptual categorization: The roles of static and dynamic stimulus attributes. *Cognition, 86,* 1–24.

Astington, J. W. (2001). The paradox of intention: Assessing children's metarepresentational understanding. In B. F. Malle, L. J. Moses, & D. A. Baldwin (Eds.), *Intentions and intentionality: Foundations of social cognition* (pp. 85–103). Cambridge, MA: MIT Press.

Au, T. K. F., Dapretto, M., & Song, Y. K. (1994). Input vs. constraints: Early word acquisition in Korean and English. *Journal of Memory and Language, 33,* 567–582.

Baird, J. A., & Baldwin, D. A. (2001). Making sense of human behavior: Acrion parsing and intentional inference. In B. F. Malle & L. J. Moses (Eds.), *Intentions and intentionality: Foundations of social cognition* (pp. 85–103). Cambridge, MA: MIT Press.

Baker, R. K., Demke, T. L., & Poulin-Dubois, D. (2004). *Infants' knowledge of the motion trajectories of animals and vehicles.* Manuscript submitted for publication.

Baldwin, D. A., & Baird, J. A. (1999). Action analysis: A gateway to intentional inference. In P. Rochat (Ed.), *Early social cognition: Understanding others in the first months of life* (pp. 215–240). Mahwah, NJ: Erlbaum.

Baldwin, D. A., Baird, J. A., Saylor, M. M., & Clark, M. A. (2001). Infants parse dynamic action. *Child Development, 72,* 708–717.

Bates, E., Bretherton, I., Snyder, L., Beeghly, M., Shore, C., McNew, S., et al. (1988). *From first words to grammar: Individual differences and dissociable mechanisms.* New York: Cambridge University Press.

Bates, E., Marchman, V. A., Thal, D., Fenson, L., Dale, P., & Reznick, S. (1994). Developmental and stylistic variation in the composition of early vocabulary. *Journal of Child Language, 21,* 85–123.

Behrend, D. A. (1990). The development of verb concepts: Children's use of verbs to label familiar and novel events. *Child Development, 61,* 681–696.

Bellagamba, F., & Tomasello, M. (1999). Re-enacting intended acts: Comparing 12- and 18- month-olds. *Infant Behavior and Development, 22,* 277–282.

Bloom, K. (1973). *The setting event as a determinant of infant learning.* Chapel Hill: University of North Carolina Press.

Bloom, L., Tinker, E., & Margulis, C. (1993). The words children learn: Evidence against a noun bias in children's vocabularies. *Cognitive Development, 8,* 431–450.

Bloom, P. (1998). Theories of artifact categorization. *Cognition, 66,* 87–93.

Bloom, P. (2000). *How children learn the meanings of words.* Cambridge, MA: MIT Press.

Bowerman, M. F. (1974). Discussion summary: Development of concepts underlying language. In R. L. Schiefelbusch & L. L. Lloyd (Eds.), *Language perspectives: Acquisition, retardation, and intervention* (pp. 191–209.) Baltimore: University Park Press.

Camarata, S., & Leonard, L. B. (1986). Young children pronounce object words more accurately than action words. *Journal of Child Language, 13,* 51–65.

Camarata, S. M., & Schwartz, R. G. (1985). Production of object words and action words: Evidence for a relationship between phonology and semantics. *Journal of Speech and Hearing Research, 28*, 323–330.

Carpenter, M., Akhtar, N., & Tomasello, M. (1998). Fourteen- through eighteen-month-old infants differentially imitate intentional and accidental actions. *Infant Behavior and Development, 21*, 315–330.

Casasola, M., & Cohen, L. B. (2000). Infants' association of linguistic labels with causal actions. *Developmental Psychology, 36*, 155–168.

Caselli, M. C., Bates, E., Casadio, P., Fenson, J., Fenson, L., & Sanderl, L. (1995). A cross-linguistic study of early lexical development. *Cognitive Development, 10*, 159–199.

Choi, S., & Gopnik, A. (1995). Early acquisition of verbs in Korean: A cross-linguistic study. *Journal of Child Language, 22*, 497–529.

Dromi, E. (1987). *Early lexical development*. New York: Cambridge University Press.

Fenson, L., Dale, P. S., Reznick, J. S., Bates, E., Thal, D., & Pethick, S. (1994). Variability in early communicative development. *Monographs of the Society for Research in Child Development, 59* (Serial No. 242).

Fenson, L., Dale, P. S., Reznick, J. S., Thal, D., Bates, E., Hartung, J. P., et al. (1991). *The MacArthur communicative development inventories: User's guide and technical manual*. San Diego, CA: Singular Press.

Flavell, J. H. (1999). Cognitive development: Children's knowledge about the mind. *Annual Review of Psychology, 50*, 21–45.

Forbes, J. N., Ashley, T., & Martin, A. (2003). *Interpreting others' intentions facilitates toddlers' verb learning*. Paper presented at the meeting of the American Psychological Association, Atlanta, GA.

Forbes, J. N., & Farrar, M. J. (1993). Children's initial assumptions about the meaning of novel motion verbs: Biased and conservative? *Cognitive Development, 8*, 273–290.

Forbes, J. N., & Farrar, M. J. (1995). Learning to represent word meaning: What initial training events reveal about children's developing action verb concepts. *Cognitive Development, 10*, 1–20.

Forbes, J. N., & Poulin-Dubois, D. (1997). Representational change in young children's understanding of familiar verb meaning. *Journal of Child Language, 24*, 389–406.

Fox, R., & McDaniel, C. (1982). The perception of biological motion by infants. *Science, 218*, 486–487.

Gentner, D. (1981). Some interesting differences between verbs and nouns. *Cognition and Brain Theory, 4*, 161–178.

Gentner, D. (1982). Why nouns are learned before verbs: Linguistic relativity versus natural partitioning. In S. Kuczaj (Ed.), *Language development: Language, cognition and culture* (pp. 301–334). Hillsdale, NJ: Erlbaum.

Gentner, D., & Boroditsky, L. (2001). Individuation, relativity and early word learning. In M. Bowerman & S. C. Levinson (Eds.), *Language acquisition and conceptual development* (pp. 215–256). Cambridge: Cambridge University Press.

Gergely, G., Nadasdy, A., Csibra, G., & Biro, S. (1995). Taking the intentional stance at 12 months of age. *Cognition, 56*, 165–193.

Goldfield, B. A. (1993). Noun bias in maternal speech to one-year-olds. *Journal of Child Language, 20*, 85–99.

Goldin-Meadow, S., Seligman, M., & Gelman, R. (1976). Language in the two-year-old. *Cognition, 4*, 189–202.

Golinkoff, R. M., Hirsh-Pasek, K., Mervis, C. B., & Frawley, W. B. (1995). Lexical principles can be extended to the acquisition of verbs. In W. E. Merriman & M. Tomasello

(Eds.), *Beyond names for things: Young children's acquisition of verbs* (pp. 185–222). Hillsdale, NJ: Erlbaum.

Golinkoff, R. M., Jacquet, R. C., Hirsh-Pasek, K., & Nandakumar, R. (1996). Lexical principles may underlie the learning of verbs. *Child Development, 67,* 3101–3119.

Golinkoff, R. M., Mervis, C. B., & Hirsh-Pasek, K. (1994). Early object labels: The case for a developmental lexical principles framework. *Journal of Child Language, 21,* 125–155.

Gopnik, A., & Meltzoff, A. N. (1986). Relations between semantic and cognitive development in the one-word stage: The specificity hypothesis. *Child Development, 57,* 1040–1053.

Graham, S. A., & Poulin-Dubois, D. (1999). Infants' reliance on shape to generalize novel labels to animate and inanimate objects. *Journal of Child Language, 26,* 295–320.

Hampson, P. J. (1989). Aspects of attention and cognitive science. *Irish Journal of Psychology, 10,* 261–275.

Hirsh-Pasek, K., & Golinkoff, R. M. (1996). *The origins of grammar: Evidence from early language comprehension.* Cambridge, MA: MIT Press.

Hirsh-Pasek, K., Golinkoff, R. M., & Hollich, G. (2000). An emergentist coalition model for word learning: Mapping words to objects is a product of the interaction of multiple cues. In R. M. Golinkoff, K. Hirsh-Pasek, L. Bloom, L. Smith, A. Woodward, N. Akhtar, et al. (Eds.), *Becoming a word learner: A debate on lexical acquisition* (pp. 136–164). New York: Oxford University Press.

Hollich, G., Hirsh-Pasek, K., & Golinkoff, R. M. (2000). Breaking the language barrier: An emergentist coalition model for the origins of word learning. *Monographs of the Society for Research in Child Development, 65* (3, Serial No. 262).

Huttenlocher, J., Smiley, P., & Charney, R. (1983). Emergence of action categories in the child: Evidence from verb meanings. *Psychological Review, 90,* 72–93.

Imai, M., Haryu, E., & Okada, H. (2002). Is verb learning easier than noun learning for Japanese children? 3-year-old Japanese children's knowledge about object names and action names. *Boston University Child Language 26th Proceedings, 1,* 324–335.

Jackson-Maldonado, D., Thal, D., Marchman, V., Bates, E., & Gutierrez-Clellen, V. (1993). Early lexical development: In Spanish-speaking infants and toddlers. *Journal of Child Language, 20,* 523–549.

Katerelos, M., Poulin-Dubois, D., & Oshima-Takane, Y. (2004). Is the noun bias universal? A cross-linguistic study of word learning. Manuscript in preparation.

Kellman, P. J., & Banks, M. S. (1998). Infant visual perception. In W. Damon (Series Ed.) & D. Kuhn & R. S. Siegler (Vol. Eds.), *Handbook of child psychology: Vol. 2. Cognition, perception, and language* (5th ed., pp. 103–146). New York: Wiley.

Kim, M., McGregor, K. K., & Thompson, C. K. (2000). Early lexical development in English- and Korean-speaking children: Language-general and language-specific patterns. *Journal of Child Language, 27,* 225–254.

Lieven, E. V., Pine, J. M., & Barnes, H. D. (1992). Individual differences in early vocabulary development: Redefining the referential-expressive distinction. *Journal of Child Language, 19,* 287–310.

Macnamara, J. (1972). Cognitive basis of language learning in infants. *Psychological Review, 79,* 1–13.

Mandler, J. M. (1992). How to build a baby: II. Conceptual primitives. *Psychological Review, 99,* 587–604.

Mandler, J. M. (2000). Perceptual and conceptual processes in infancy. *Journal of Cognition and Development, 1,* 3–36.

Mandler, J. M., & McDonough, L. (1993). Concept formation in infancy. *Cognitive Development, 8,* 291–318.

Mandler, J. M., & McDonough, L. (1998). On developing a knowledge base in infancy. *Developmental Psychology, 34,* 1274–1288.

McCune-Nicolich, L. (1981). Toward symbolic functioning: Structure of early pretend games and potential parallels with language. *Child Development, 52,* 785–797.

Meltzoff, A. N. (1995). Understanding the intentions of others: Re-enactment of intended acts by 18-month-old children. *Developmental Psychology, 31,* 838–850.

Meltzoff, A. N., Gopnik, A., & Repacholi, B. M. (1999). Toddlers' understanding of intentions, desires, and emotions: Explorations of the dark ages. In P. D. Zelazo, J. W. Astington, & D. R. Olson (Eds.), *Developing theories of intention* (pp. 17–41). Mahwah, NJ: Erlbaum.

Montgomery, D. E. (1997). Wittgenstein's private language argument and children's understanding of the mind. *Developmental Review, 17,* 291–320.

Montgomery, D. E. (2002). Mental verbs and semantic development. *Journal of Cognition and Development, 3,* 357–384.

Naigles, L. R., & Terrazas, P. (1998). Motion-verb generalizations in English and Spanish: Influences of language and syntax. *Psychological Science, 9,* 363–369.

Nelson, K. (1973). Structure and strategy in learning to talk. *Monographs of the Society for Research in Child Development, 38* (Serial No. 149).

Nelson, K., Hampson, J., & Shaw, L. K. (1993). Nouns in early lexicons: Evidence, explanations, and implications. *Journal of Child Language, 20,* 61–84.

Oakes, L. M., Madole, K. L., & Cohen, L. B. (1991). Infant habituation and categorization of real objects. *Cognitive Development, 6,* 377–392.

Olineck, K. M., & Poulin-Dubois, D. (2004). Infants' ability to distinguish between intentional and accidental actions and its relation to internal state language. *Infancy, 8,* 91–100.

Oviatt, S. L. (1980). The emerging ability to comprehend language: An experimental approach. *Child Development, 51,* 97–106.

Oviatt, S. L. (1982). Inferring what words mean: Early development in infants' comprehension of common object names. *Child Development, 53,* 274–277.

Pine, J. M. (1992). How referential are "referential" children? Relationships between maternal-report and observational measures of vocabulary composition and usage. *Journal of Child Language, 19,* 75–86.

Poulin-Dubois, D. (1995). Object parts and the acquisition of the meaning of names. In K. E. Nelson & Z. Réger (Eds.), *Children's language* (Vol. 8, pp. 125–143). Hillsdale, NJ: Erlbaum.

Poulin-Dubois, D., & Forbes, J. N. (2002). Toddlers' attention to intentions-in-action in learning novel action words. *Developmental Psychology, 38,* 104–114.

Poulin-Dubois, D., Frenkiel, S., Johnson, S., & Nayer, S. (2005). *Infants' inductive generalization of motion and mental properties to animals and people.* Manuscript submitted for publication.

Poulin-Dubois, D., Graham, S. A., & Sippola, L. (1995). Parental labelling, categorization, and early lexical development. *Journal of Child Language, 22,* 325–343.

Poulin-Dubois, D., & Vyncke, J. (2004). *The cow jumped over the moon: Infants' inductive generalization of motion properties.* Unpublished manuscript, Concordia University, Montreal, Quebec, Canada.

Rakison, D. H., & Poulin-Dubois, D. (2001). Developmental origin of the animate-inanimate distinction. *Psychological Bulletin, 127,* 209–228.

Rakison, D. H., & Poulin-Dubois, D. (2002). You go this way and I'll go that way: Developmental changes in infants' detection of correlations among static and dynamic features in motion events. *Child Development, 73,* 682–699.

Reznick, J. S. (1990). Visual preference as a test of infant word comprehension. *Applied Psycholinguistics, 11*, 145–166.

Rice, M. L., & Woodsmall, L. (1988). Lessons from television: Children's word learning when viewing. *Child Development, 59*, 420–429.

Schafer, G., & Plunkett, K. (1998). Rapid word learning by fifteen-month-olds under tightly controlled conditions. *Child Development, 69*, 309–320.

Schult, C. A. (2002). Children's understanding of the distinction between intentions and desires. *Child Development, 73*, 1727–1747.

Schwartz, R. G., & Leonard, L. B. (1984). Words, objects and actions in early lexical acquisition. *Journal of Speech and Hearing Research, 27*, 119–127.

Slobin, D. I. (1973). Cognitive prerequisites for the development of grammar. In C. Ferguson & D. I. Slobin (Eds.), *Studies of child language development* (pp. 173–208). New York: Holt, Rinehart, and Winston.

Slobin, D. I. (2001). Form-function relations: How do children find out what they are? In M. Bowerman & S. C. Levinson (Eds.), *Language acquisition and conceptual development* (pp. 406–449). New York: Cambridge University Press.

Spelke, E. S. (2000). Core knowledge. *American Psychology, 55*, 1233–1243.

Talmy, L. (1985). Lexicalization patterns: Semantic structure in lexical forms. In T. Shopen (Ed.), *Language typology and syntactic description* (Vol. 3, pp. 57–149). Cambridge: Cambridge University Press.

Tardif, T., Gelman, S. A., & Xu, F. (1999). Putting the "noun-bias" in context: A comparison of English and Mandarin. *Child Development, 70*, 620–635.

Tardif, T., Shatz, M., & Naigles, L. (1997). Caregiver speech and children's use of nouns versus verbs: A comparison of English, Italian, and Mandarin. *Journal of Child Language, 24*, 535–565.

Theakston, A. L., Lieven, E., Pine, J. M., & Rowland, C. F. (1992). Going, going, gone: The acquisition of the verb "go." *Journal of Child Language, 29*, 273–290.

Tomasello, M. (1992). *First verbs*. Cambridge: Cambridge University Press.

Tomasello, M. (1995). Pragmatic contexts for early verb learning. In M. Tomasello & W. E. Merriman (Eds.), *Beyond names for things: Young children's acquisition of verbs* (pp. 115–146). Hillsdale, NJ: Erlbaum.

Tomasello, M., & Akhtar, N. (1995). Two-year-olds use pragmatic cues to differentiate reference to objects and actions. *Cognitive Development, 10*, 201–224.

Tomasello, M., & Barton, M. (1994). Learning words in non-ostensive context. *Developmental Psychology, 30*, 639–650.

Tomasello, M., & Todd, J. (1983). Joint attention and lexical acquisition style. *First Language, 4*, 197–211.

Werker, J. F., Cohen, L. B., Lloyd, V. L., Casasola, M., & Stager, C. L. (1998). Acquisition of word-object associations by 14-month-old infants. *Developmental Psychology, 34*, 1289–1309.

Wittgenstein, L. (1958). *Philosophical investigations* (G. E. M. Anscombe, Trans.). New York: Macmillan.

Woodward, A. L. (1993). The effect of labeling on children's attention to objects. In E. V. Clark (Ed.), *Proceedings of the 24th Annual Child Language Research Forum* (pp. 35–47). Stanford, CA: Center for Study of Language and Information.

Woodward, A. L. (1998). Infants selectively encode the goal object of an actor's reach. *Cognition, 69*, 1–34.

Woodward, A. L. (2000). Constraining the problem space in early word learning. In R. M. Golinkoff, K. Hirsh-Pasek, L. Bloom, L. Smith, A. Woodward, N. Akhtar, et al. (Eds.), *Becoming a word learner: A debate on lexical acquisition* (pp. 81–114). New York: Oxford University Press.

Woodward, A. L., & Hoyne, K. L. (1999). Infants' learning about words and sounds in relation to objects. *Child Development, 70,* 65–72.

Woodward, A. L., Markman, E. M., & Fitzsimmons, C. M. (1994). Rapid word learning in 13- and 18-month-olds. *Developmental Psychology, 30,* 553–566.

11   Verbs, Actions, and Intentions

Douglas A. Behrend and Jason Scofield

Verbs are action words.

The preceding simple definition of verbs has more or less guided the study of children's learning of verbs and their meanings across the first several years of life (e.g. Tomasello & Merriman, 1995). However, this simple definition is also clearly oversimplified—verbs do more than just denote action. Verbs not only denote actions, but also denote the results of those actions, paths of actions, states such as sleep and possession, and many other aspects of the world. Verbs and their argument structures also express grammatically the relations between the multiple elements that play distinct roles in a sentence and in the world.

However, it is not only that verbs can denote many things other than actions and are the key predicates in sentence structure that leads to dissatisfaction with this simple definition. Actions themselves are not simple to conceptualize. In fact, over the past decade a great deal of attention has been paid to children's understanding and appreciation of the mental states that underlie human actions, most notably intentions (see Malle, Moses, & Baldwin, 2001; Zelazo, Astington, & Olson, 1999). Though it should be obvious that verbs can be used to denote not only human actions but the actions of other organisms and inanimate objects as well (e.g. "The plane flew over Missouri"), the relationship between intentions, actions, and the learning of verbs for human actions is a poorly understood and underexplored area of research. In this chapter, we investigate the interrelatedness of human actions, the intentions that guide those actions, and the language used to label and describe those actions. We describe several studies from our program of research, which has for the last several years attempted to empirically document the ways in which intentions, actions, and verbs are related in young children's growing understanding of the physical, mental, and linguistic world around them. Finally, we conclude by suggesting a model in which developmental achievements in both language development and in early theory of mind—as documented by children's growing sophistication in their understanding of the intentional basis of human behavior—mutually and reciprocally influence each other in nontrivial manners. It is also important at this point to state what this chapter is not about, which is the issue of whether young children's word learning, in general, is predicated on an understanding of the referential intentions of others in their environments (e.g., L. Bloom & Tinker, 2001; P. Bloom, 2000; Tomasello, 1999). Though we do, by necessity, discuss this issue, it is not the focus of this chapter.

Verbs

The past 15 years have seen a rapid increase in interest in the acquisition of verbs and their underlying concepts. Perhaps due to the warning of George Miller, whom Medin and Smith (1984) quoted as stating that researchers interested in concept formation appeared to believe that "concept is spelled N,O,U,N" (p. 132), developmental and cognitive scientists alike turned their attention to verbs and their underlying concepts and representations. Much of this first wave of work was dedicated to fundamental issues in the acquisition of verbs and was detailed extensively in the first volume in the developmental literature dedicated exclusively to the topic of verbs (Tomasello & Merriman, 1995).

One of the fundamental issues addressed by this literature was that of comparing verb acquisition to noun acquisition. A number of studies of children's early vocabulary consistently showed that nouns were more common in early lexicons than verbs, often by a wide margin (e.g., Benedict, 1979; Gentner, 1982). Though individual and cross-linguistic differences in the noun advantage existed, the evidence was compelling enough for Gentner (1982) to posit her natural partitioning account of this advantage. Gentner argued, in essence, that verbs are tougher nuts to crack than nouns in large part due to the relational nature of verb concepts and, therefore, they are acquired more slowly and enter the child's lexicon later than nouns. An ensuing line of research was dedicated to testing the generalizability of the noun advantage and the natural partitioning explanation of why verbs are so difficult to learn. Much of this research involved cross-linguistic studies of children's early lexical development, with a focus on languages in which verbs appear in more salient (e.g., sentence-final) positions in natural language than in English and other primarily western languages that had been studied. A number of these studies (e.g., Choi & Gopnik, 1995; Tardif, 1996; Tardif, Gelman, & Xu, 1999) showed that the noun advantage was substantially smaller or nonexistent in children learning the languages in question, such as Korean and Mandarin, and the authors of these studies argued that any noun advantage in early lexical development was probably due to language-specific factors. However, reviews of this literature have come to the conclusion that even with these cross-linguistic studies included, there is strong evidence to support the position that

verbs are observed less frequently in early lexicons across languages and methodologies (Bornstein & Cote, 2004; Gentner & Boroditsky, 2001). Certainly the characteristics of local languages can influence the degree of the noun bias in children's
vocabulary but it seems clear that, ceteris paribus, children find verbs more difficult to learn than nouns.

A second fundamental issue addressed by this first wave of research on verb
meanings was distinctions between different types of verbs, their underlying concepts, and the types of events that these verbs denoted. Common distinctions made
along these lines were between action (or manner) verbs and result (or end-state)
verbs, between manner and path verbs, and between causative and noncausative
verbs. Early work in this area seemed to show a number of distinct patterns in children's acquisition of these different classes of verbs. For example, Huttenlocher,
Smiley, and Charney (1983) showed that very young children's earliest verbs
tended to be verbs for simple intransitive actions such as *run* and other simple action predicates including verb particles such as *up*. When change-of-state verbs first
appeared in children's lexicons, children used these verbs to describe their own actions rather than the actions of others. Huttenlocher et al. argued that this pattern
was due to the fact that young children had access to their own goals and intentions but not to those of other actors in the environment. This argument is not only
relevant to the focus of this chapter but prescient in terms of how it anticipated
the interest in young children's understanding of intentions that followed.

Additional research on early verb learning demonstrated specific biases in
children's learning of novel verbs. Studies by Behrend (1990), Forbes and Farrar
(1993), and Forbes and Poulin-Dubois (1997) showed that children between 2
and 5 years of age have a bias to interpret a novel verb used to label a novel event
with both a clear manner of action and clear result as referring to the result or end
state of the event. This bias also appeared to get stronger as children got older.
Children rarely assumed that a novel verb referred to an instrumental component
of the novel action, and Forbes and Farrar described children's mapping of novel
verbs as "biased and conservative."

Once these relatively consistent biases were established, additional studies
addressed the issue of how stable these biases were and what information in the
word learning environment could influence these biases. Crucial among these
studies were inquiries into syntactic bootstrapping of verb meanings (Gleitman,
1990). Seminal studies by Naigles (1990, 1996) elegantly demonstrated that children could use the syntactic context in which a novel verb was presented to distinguish between causative and noncausative verb meanings. In addition, Behrend,
Harris, and Cartwright (1995) demonstrated that children learning English ad-
justed their learning biases as a function of how the verb was inflected during
training. Specifically, preschoolers were more likely to make action verb interpretations of novel verbs presented with a progressive *-ing* ending than when
presented with the past *-ed* ending. A third set of studies demonstrated that children's verb learning biases could be changed with experience. That is, children's
result verb bias could be overridden if, during training, children saw events with

three different results labeled with a novel verb (e.g., Behrend, 1995; Childers & Tomasello, 2002). Finally, it was shown that word-learning principles similar to those used in noun learning could be applied to verb learning as well (e.g., Golinkoff, Jacquet, & Hirsh-Pasek, 1996).

Thus, the initial wave of interest in and studies on children's verb learning demonstrated that children find verbs more difficult to learn than nouns and that their interpretation of novel verbs used to label human actions are biased, conservative, and susceptible to being overridden by information from the environment. Finally, this research showed that children are able to use multiple sources of information from the linguistic and learning contexts in order to shape the biases they demonstrate when entering into a novel word-learning situation.

Actions

Of course, the statement that verbs are action words raises not only the question of how verbs are learned but also important questions as to how best to define human actions and how children process and understand human action. Though this is not the place to get into a detailed account regarding the nature of human action, it is clear that the issues of the nature of action and children's verb learning are intimately related. It has been argued that the canonical actions are those in which an agent performs an action that produces some effect on the world (e.g., Slobin, 1981). Note that these actions can be described as causative or transitive actions, and, as such, are inherently more complex than simple intransitive actions such as running.

There are several dimensions along which events and the actions that comprise them differ that are relevant to the current discussion. A first dimension involves the number and types of roles that are involved in an action. In the canonical events described by Slobin (1981), there are typically two distinct roles: the actor or agent who performs the action and the patient or subject of that action. Early work in this area by Golinkoff and Kerr (1978) showed that very young children direct a disproportionate amount of their attention to events toward the agent or actor in the event. In addition, Forbes and Poulin-Dubois (1997) showed that toddlers differ in their willingness to extend a verb to an exemplar in which the agent of an action changed. One-year-olds with smaller expressive vocabularies were less likely to extend newly learned novel verbs to exemplars of actions in which the agent differed than 1-year-olds with larger vocabularies or 2-year-olds. This is an intriguing finding, as verbs are usually not restricted to applying to the actions of some agents but not others with the exception of restrictions between major ontological categories (e.g., animate versus inanimate).

Actions also have distinct temporal characteristics. Some have occurred in the past, some are presently occurring, and some have yet to occur. This temporal characteristic is that which is expressed by tense in natural languages. In addition, actions also have distinct temporal contours. Some actions have been completed while some are ongoing; some occur in a smooth, continuous fashion while others occur repetitively or iteratively. These temporal characteristics of events are those characteristics that are expressed in most natural languages by aspect. Though tense and aspect are nearly hopelessly confounded in English, other languages make much clearer distinctions between when an event occurs in time in relation to the utterance (tense) and that action's temporal contour (aspect). Interestingly, the distinction between continuous and completed events in aspect often initially gets conflated with the action verb/result verb distinction in children's early use of verb inflections (Bloom, Lifter, & Hafitz, 1980; Bronckart & Sinclair, 1973). That is, children often use the progressive -*ing* inflection with manner of action verbs and the past -*ed* with result verbs in a way that suggests that they are marking this aspect of verb semantics rather than the temporal profile of the events (see also Behrend et al., 1995; Tomasello, 1992).

Intentions

A final aspect of human actions that is central to this chapter is the fact that most human actions stem from some sort of a prior mental plan or intention. Though the issue of intentions, per se, has been infrequently raised in the verb acquisition literature, the development of the understanding of intentions and intentionality in young children has been a recent and major focus in the literature on early cognitive development, theory of mind, and social cognition. Indeed, there is a vast philosophical literature and debate on the precise nature of intentions and intentionality (see Brentano, 1874/1973; and more recently Dennett, 1987; Searle, 1983), but for our purposes an intention refers to a mental state or plan that precedes the conduct of an action. An intention to perform an action does not always guarantee that the intended action is performed for several reasons. For example an actor may fail in an attempt to produce an intended action or may simply never get the opportunity to perform an intended action, and so on. It also not necessarily true that all actions performed fulfill some specific underlying intention as in the case of accidents—a child who spills a cup of milk typically (though not always!) does not intend to spill it.

Though this preceding discussion makes it clear that there is not a simple isomorphic relationship between intentions and actions, the understanding that most human action is preceded or accompanied by an intentional state is a cornerstone of the young child's developing theory of mind and, more generally, social cognitive capabilities (e.g., Malle et al., 2001). In Dennett's (1987) terms, when we interpret our own and others' actions in terms of the mental states that underlie those actions, we are taking the intentional stance toward those actions. That is, rather than simply relying on physical or other nonmentalistic explanations of others' behaviors, humans appear to be the only species (with chimpanzees the possible exception; see Povinelli, 2001) that regularly attribute behavioral causes to internal, mental states. Thus, a hallmark of the human cognitive apparatus appears to be the ability to go beyond the information given in the behavioral stream and make inferences about the underlying mental causes of the actions that make up the stream.

Indeed, recent research on infants and young children's understanding of intentions has focused on the origins and development of these types of inferential abilities. Research using habituation and preferential looking paradigms with infants has shown that children as young as 6 months of age distinguish between animate and inanimate objects as well as the behaviors that actors will direct towards these different classes of objects (Legerstee, 2001; Legerstee, Barna, & Di-Adamo 2000). Similarly, research by Woodward and her colleagues has demonstrated that infants appreciate that action is goal directed (e.g., Woodward, 1998, 1999; Woodward & Somerville, 2000). For example, Woodward (1998) found that 9-month-olds and, to a lesser extent, 5-month-olds encoded the goal of an actor's reach. That is, after these infants were habituated to a display in which they saw an arm reaching to one of two toys in a display, the infants dishabituated more strongly to a display in which the reach was directed to a different toy in the same location than to the same toy in a new location. Thus, even though the former scene was more perceptually similar to the training events than the latter scene, infants found the reach to the new object to be more different from the habituation events. Woodward inferred that this pattern of responses would only be demonstrated by infants who had inferred that the goal of the actor's reach was to obtain a particular toy and not simply to touch a particular location in the display.

Studies with slightly older infants have expanded upon the notion that infants have a nascent understanding of the intentional nature of human action. In a classic series of studies, Gergely, Nadasdy, Csibra, and Biro (1995) exposed children to an animate-like stimulus that traveled around an obstacle and then touched another similar stimulus. After being habituated to this scene, 12-month-old infants then saw the same scene without the obstacle present. In one version of this scene, the stimulus followed the same path as it did during the habituation events. In the other version, the stimulus took a direct, straight-line path to its goal. Gergely et al. found that children dishabituated more strongly to the scene in which the stimulus took its original path even though this path was identical to the path on which the children had been dishabituated. Gergely et al. concluded that 12-month-olds adopted the intentional stance and interpreted the stimulus's action in terms of an underlying intention to reach a particular goal (see also Csibra, Gergely, & Biro, 1999).

Meltzoff (1995) extended the exploration of children's understanding of intentions to 18-month-olds. Rather than using habituation procedures, Meltzoff pioneered the behavioral reenactment paradigm. In this paradigm, an experimenter models an action for a child, and then the child is given the opportunity to reenact the action with the same materials. Rather than modeling completed actions, however, Meltzoff modeled what appeared to be unsuccessful attempts at a completed action. For example, in one event the experimenter took a strand of beads and dropped the beads on a table next to a cup. When given the opportunity to reenact this behavior, most children did not simply imitate the exact action that had been modeled; rather, children were more likely to produce the presumed intended action (i.e., dropping the beads in the cup) than to precisely imitate the modeled action. A variety of control conditions and a second experiment using a mechanical (i.e., nonintentional) model allowed Meltzoff to conclude that the children's behavior was a consequence of their assuming that the experimenter intended to perform a specific action (e.g., put beads in the cup) and that imitative behavior in this age group is driven by inferences about another's intentions and not simply by a behavioral matching or mimicry process.

This paradigm has been used successfully by a number of other scholars. Some studies have demonstrated that autistic children, who typically do very poorly on tasks dealing with others' mental states (i.e., theory of mind), perform similarly to typically developing children on this task (Carpenter, Pennington, & Rogers, 2001). In addition, Huang, Heyes, and Charman (2002) used this paradigm and argued that at least some of children's tendency to produce the intended action might be a function of the affordances of the objects used as stimuli (see also Charman & Huang, 2002). In any case, the behavioral reenactment paradigm and other procedures in which children's understanding of intentions are inferred through young children's actions on objects (e.g., Carpenter, Call, & Tomasello, 2002) have enabled researchers to study the development of children's intentional understanding in age groups for whom habituation or preferential looking paradigms are not appropriate.

In our own research, we have used variants of these paradigms in order to understand the relations and interactions between children's growing understanding of others' intentions and the language used to express such intentions. We are by no means the first to note and investigate the relations between these two crucial domains in early development. First, producing language is an intentional action that requires plans for both the motor activities involved in speech as well as the content of the speech itself. Second, the act of labeling an object in the world for a listener may be motivated by referential intentions (e.g., Bruner, 1999). That is, a speaker may have some mental plan from which the act of providing a label for a novel or familiar object follows. Moreover, it has been argued recently that the word learner in this scenario must be aware of and comprehend such referential intentions to be able to benefit from such an ostensive provision of a label for an object (e.g., L. Bloom & Tinker, 2001; P. Bloom, 2000, 2002; Tomasello, 1999, 2001). Without such awareness of others' communicative intentions, the process of language development—and word learning in particular—becomes a much more difficult chore. Given the research documenting infants' and toddlers' propensity to interpret others' behavior in terms of their underlying intentions, it certainly does not appear to be a major leap to assume that children understand linguistic acts in terms of their underlying communicative intentions, referential or otherwise.

Rather than focusing on whether children's understanding of others' intentions (referential or otherwise) aid in the process of language acquisition (which it almost certainly does at some level), we have been interested recently in a much more specific question that has been asked very infrequently in the literature: Can the language used by a speaker in the course of producing an action provide a cue to the young child about the intentions of an actor? Specifically, we have asked whether the use of a novel verb uttered by a speaker to label an action can influence children's interpretations of that novel verb (Behrend & Wittek, 2003, 2004), especially when those actions are the sorts of failed attempts often demonstrated in behavioral reenactment paradigms.

To our knowledge, only Tomasello and Barton (1994) have addressed this question, though in a somewhat different manner than our approach. In that research, 2-year-olds were presented with an actor performing a sequence of two actions with a set of common toys. The actor used a novel verb (e.g., "I'm going to *gorp* it") prior to the onset of the action sequence, and then in the course of the two actions said "Oops!" when performing one of those actions. Children were then given the opportunity to play with the toys and to "*gorp*." Children were less likely to produce the action accompanied by "oops" even when that action was performed first (and, therefore, the action most likely being labeled by the verb that preceded the action sequence). In the terms of the current research, children used the experimenter's utterance of "oops" as a cue to the experimenter's intentions, specifically that she did not mean to perform the action that was followed by "oops."

Our Research Program

We and our colleagues have addressed these issues in a series of studies in our labs. In the first study, Angelika Wittek and I used a modified version of the behavioral reenactment paradigm with a large cross-linguistic sample (Behrend & Wittek, 2003, 2004). In this initial study, we simply added the presentation of a novel verb during the demonstration of novel actions in order to see whether the act of the experimenter labeling her action with a novel verb would alter children's reenactments of demonstrations of failed attempts. Specifically, we predicted that when a failed attempt was labeled with a novel verb that children would be more likely to reproduce the failed attempt than when the action was not accompanied by the novel verb. We reasoned that when an actor takes the time to label her action with a novel verb, then that label would provide a cue that the actor's behavior was *intended*, that is, that she really meant to drop the beads *beside* the cup. We tested both German- and English-speaking children between 18 and 30 months of age in this initial study.

This study was followed up by a series of studies (Childers & Behrend, 2003) in which the use of a novel verb to label a failed attempt was directly compared to other types of utterances that accompany actions that can provide cues to an actor's intentions (e.g., "uh-oh" or "oops"). Finally, we will discuss some ongoing research in our lab which turns around the question of the relationship between language and intentions by asking whether having knowledge of an actor's intentions before an action is performed helps young children to learn a novel verb used to label that action.

We (Behrend & Wittek, 2004) first addressed the question of the role played by novel verbs in children's interpretation of other's intentions by making several relatively simple modifications to Meltzoff's (1995) behavioral reenactment paradigm. First, we used Carpenter et al.'s (2001) modification, in which children were given a 20 second manipulation period with the stimuli prior to the demonstration of an action. If during that manipulation period, the child spontaneously performed the target action (e.g., dropping the beads in a cup), then the experimenter demonstrated an alternate target action (or failed attempt) during the demonstration phase of the experiment (e.g., circling the beads around the cup). This was done to control for potential actions suggested by the affordances of the objects (see Huang et al., 2001). Second, half of the actions demonstrated were accompanied by neutral language uttered by the experimenter (e.g., "Watch") and half were accompanied by a novel verb used by the experimenter to label the action (e.g., "Watch me. I'm meeking."). Finally, we used a within-subjects design in which all participants saw four actions, two accompanied by neutral language and two accompanied by novel verbs.

Do Novel Verbs Provide Cues to an Actor's Intentions?

Our participants were 143 children, with an approximately equal number of children in 18-month, 24-month, and 30-month age groups. Half of the children were native American-English speakers (tested in the United States) and half of the children were native German speakers (tested in Germany).

We created four stimulus sets that were modeled after those used by Meltzoff (1995) and Carpenter et al. (2001). Each set included materials that were easily manipulated by children as young as 18 months of age. The order of presentation of the stimulus sets was randomized across participants. With two of the stimulus sets, the experimenter modeled the actual target action for that stimulus set; that is, she put the beads in the cup or pulled the barbell apart. These two events were known as the target trials. For the other two stimulus sets, the experimenter modeled a failed attempt of the target action, that is, she dropped the beads next to the cup or had her hand slip off one end of the barbell while trying to pull it apart. These two events were known as the intention trials. Though it may be somewhat confusing to label these trials with the term intention, we did so in order to be consistent with previous work. The experimenter labeled her action in one of target trials and one of the intention trials with a different novel verb (i.e., "Watch me *meek*" or "Watch me *tam*") and used neutral language including no verb (e.g., "Watch me") during the other target trial and intention trial. Thus, each child was exposed to one instance of each of four trial types: target-verb (TV), target–no verb (TNV), intention-verb (IV) and intention–no verb (INV). Following the demonstration of each action, the experimenter gave the stimuli to the child and said, "Now it's your turn" in the no-verb trials or "Now it's your turn to X" in the verb trials, where X stands for the novel verb. Of course, the German children received all linguistic input in German (for additional details on the procedure, see Behrend & Wittek, 2004).

Thus, in this experiment, the TV and TNV trials were essentially control trials, while the IV and INV trials were the experimental trials. In particular, we were interested in any differences in the children's production of the target action and the failed attempt between the IV and INV trials. If it is the case that young children used the act of the experimenter labeling her action with a novel verb as a cue that the actor intended to perform that action, then we expected that children will be more likely to produce that failed attempt on the IV trials than on the INV trials or be less likely to produce the target action in the IV trials than on the INV trials. We expected this result because we reasoned that the act of labeling an unfamiliar action with a novel verb would make the child more likely to believe that the performed action was, in fact, the intended action.

As our data were categorical in nature, all primary analyses were conducted using logistic regression. Contrary to our hypothesis, children were not significantly more likely to produce the failed attempt on the IV trials (28%) than on the INV trials (21%), though the effect was in the right direction. However, two results suggested that the presence of the novel verb did have an effect on children's interpretations of the intentions of the experimenter. First, when broken down by age group, the 30-month-olds were more likely than either of the younger two age groups to produce the failed attempt. Second, when we looked at the rates of production of the target action (i.e., putting the beads in the cup), significantly fewer children produced the target action on the IV trials (29%) than on the INV trials (50%). We believe this result suggests that although the presence of a novel verb did not significantly increase the rates at which children produced the failed attempt, it was a potent enough cue to the actor's intentions to draw the children away from the presumed intention of the experimenter. Thus, children were less likely to perform the target action and more likely to perform some other action including, at least for the 30-month-olds in our sample, the failed attempt at a target action. To our knowledge, this finding is the first to demonstrate that the simple act of labeling one's actions with a novel verb can influence children's inferences about an actor's intentions. Not only does this finding demonstrate that children can use language as a cue to an actor's intentions, but the fact that these verbs had never been heard before by the children suggests that there may be more important relations between verb learning and intentional understanding.

*Do Novel Verbs Provide Different Cues Than Other Types
of Language?*

Given this initial finding that labeling an action with a novel verb can influence children's inferences about an actor's intentions, a relatively simple follow-up question presented itself. Perhaps the influence of the verb was not due specifically to the verb used by the experimenter to label her action but was due more generally to the fact that language—any language—accompanied the action. In order to test for this possibility, Jane Childers and I (Childers & Behrend, 2003) have conducted a series of studies in which we compared the effects of a novel verb's presence during the demonstration of a novel action with the effects of a linguistic cue such as "oops." Whereas the novel verb, in our view, is a cue that the actor intended to perform the action that was performed, a linguistic cue such as "oops" is a cue that the actor did not intend to perform that specific action. If the influence of language is a general influence, then there should be no difference between a verb condition and an "oops" condition. If, however, the effect of the verb is more specific, then there should be differential patterns of responding to events accompanied by these linguistic forms.

In Experiment 1, we presented 30 2.5-year-old children with a series of four events demonstrated by the experimenter. Each event had both accidental and intentional components. For example in one event a small toy was suspended in a basked hanging from the center of a tripod. When the experimenter retrieved the toy with her hand (intention) she knocked down the tripod (accident). Each such event was demonstrated three times to each child. Depending on the condition to which the child was assigned the experimenter accompanied the action with different language. In the verb condition, the experimenter said, "I'm going to gorp. I'm gorping! Did you see me gorp?" In the oops condition, the experimenter said, "Oops! Uh-oh. Oh dear." In the control condition, the experimenter said, "Watch. Look. Did you see?" Children were then given the stimuli and allowed to play with them for 30 seconds. Children's responses were coded as producing the intentional action, the accidental action, both actions, or other actions.

The results of this first study were disappointing in that there was no difference between the three experimental conditions. Contrary to our hypothesis, children apparently were not using the language that accompanied the action to help them determine which component of the action to imitate. In fact, children were equally likely to produce the intentional and accidental components of the events across all three conditions. However, there was a strong effect for response type. Across all conditions, children were significantly more likely to produce the intended action than the accidental action, even though both actions had been demonstrated during the training phase. In retrospect this result may not have been so surprising. Given prior findings that children will produce an intended action even when that action has not been directly demonstrated (e.g., Behrend & Wittek, 2004; Meltzoff, 1995), it makes sense that children would prefer to produce an intended action when that intention is demonstrated for them and that a linguistic manipulation may not be strong enough to sway children away from this strong intentional bias.

Thus, in a second study, we presented 36 2-year-olds with two simpler events in which just the accidental result was demonstrated. This procedure was thus more similar to that used in the standard behavioral reenactment procedure. One event involved a ramp and a toy truck. All children saw the experimenter place the toy truck at the edge of the ramp and let it go. However, instead of rolling down the ramp, the truck was placed so it fell off the top edge of the ramp onto the table. The second event used an inverted plastic bowl with a slot cut into it. The experimenter took a wooden disk, placed it just above the slot (into which the disk could fit), and released it. Instead of falling in the slot, however, the disk slid down the side of the bowl and came to rest on a tray beneath the bowl. Again each child was assigned either to a verb condition, an oops condition, or a control condition.

Once again in this study, the results did not support the hypothesis, though they were in the expected direction. In this study, children frequently produced the intended action at rates similar to those found using the behavioral reenact-ment paradigm. However, there was again no overall difference in the number of intended actions produced across the three conditions. Though the oops condi-tion, as expected, appeared to enhance this bias to produce the intended action, this condition differed only marginally from the other two conditions combined.

Given these two failed attempts to find the expected effect, we considered another possibility. Given children's strong bias to produce the intended action, perhaps the cue of a novel verb used during the course of an action was not a strong enough signal for children to change their intentional inferences. This may have been especially true for the events and objects in Experiment 2 for which there were clear affordances: A truck rolls down a ramp and a disk fits into a slot that is slightly larger than the disk. We reasoned that the power of a verbal cue to intentionality would be stronger in conditions in which there is not a clear affordance of the objects or in conditions in which there are multiple plausible actions or affordances that can be associated with those objects (see Huang et al., 2002). This interpretation makes sense given the findings that other types of social cues, such as facial expressions used during social referenc-ing by infants and toddlers, are most potent in novel, ambiguous situations (see Feinman, 1982, for a review).

We set out to test this possibility in a third study in which we presented 36 2-year-olds with a series of four novel stimulus sets, each of which had multiple possible actions associated with them. For example, one stimulus set included a spatula with a magnetic strip on its underside and a pretend piece of bread with a magnetic strip on the top. Thus, one could pick up the bread with the spatula either by sliding it underneath the bread (affordance) or by touching the two magnets together and then raising the spatula (novel action). The experimenter then demonstrated a failed attempt at the novel action; in this example, pressing the bottom of the spatula to the top of the bread and then lifting the spatula up without the bread. Children were once again assigned to either a verb condition, an oops condition, or a control condition. Children's responses were then coded as being either a direct imitation of the failed attempt, a production of the intended action (lifting the bread with the magnets), or a production of the afforded action (scooping up the bread with the spatula).

The results of this study were clear and compelling. Not only did children produce many fewer of the afforded actions but there was a significant difference between the verb condition and the oops and control conditions. In the verb condition, children were significantly more likely to reproduce exactly the failed attempt demonstrated by the experimenter and less likely to produce either the intended or afforded action. Though it could be argued that children in this study may not have known about the afforded action because this action was not demonstrated to them, recall that in the basic behavioral reenactment paradigm children are never shown the afforded action and they nonetheless produce it. Indeed, Huang et al. (2002) argue that object affordances are the driving force behind children's responses in the behavioral reenactment paradigm and not children's understanding of the actor's intentions. However, as this last study demonstrated that when a novel verb is used to label an unfamiliar action, this verb can be used as a potent cue to an actor's intention when the action to be performed is ambiguous and not simply afforded by the objects. In other words, though object affordances may play a role in children's responses in these types of paradigms, so do children's inferences about an actor's intentions. Not coincidentally, these conditions (i.e., labeling an unfamiliar action with a set of objects that may have multiple affordances) may be just those conditions that best characterize a child learning a novel action verb through ostension.

Thus, this series of studies replicated, extended, and specified the original results obtained by Behrend and Wittek (2004). First, these studies showed that in conditions in which a clear action is afforded by a set of stimuli, 2-year-old children have a strong tendency to produce the afforded, intended action when a failed attempt is demonstrated. Second, these studies established that different types of language used to accompany an action can lead 2-year-old children to make different inferences about an actor's intentions: Terms such as "oops" can strengthen children's existing tendency to produce the intended action, while a novel verb can weaken it. Third, this strong tendency to produce the intended action can overwhelm the more subtle effect that labeling an action with a novel verb has on children's inferences about another's intentions. Labeling an unfamiliar or unexpected action with a novel verb affects children's intention judgments specifically in those situations in which the intended action is not clearly afforded by the stimuli or situations in which there are multiple plausible actions that can be performed.

But what do these results have to say about verb learning per se? A lot, we think. It should be clear that the situation produced by adding a novel verb to the basic behavioral reenactment paradigm (i.e., labeling an unfamiliar action [prior to the onset of the action] with a set of objects that may have multiple affordances) may be just those conditions that best characterize a child learning a novel action verb through ostension (Tomasello & Kruger, 1992). What our studies make clear is that in addition to considerations about which component of an action a novel verb labels (e.g., Behrend, 1990), the syntactic context in which the verb is used (e.g., Naigles, 1990), and children's basic verb-learning strategies (e.g., Golinkoff et al., 1996), children also use their knowledge of others' intentions and cues to those intentions when making an initial mapping of a novel verb's meaning. In other words, the simple act of labeling an action with a verb may provide multiple, important cues to the verb learner. We pursue this issue even further by asking in the next study whether having a priori knowledge of an actor's intentions can further aid the child who is learning a novel verb.

Does Knowing About Intentions Help Children Learn Novel Verbs?

To this point, our research has been focused on whether language—in the form of a novel verb used to label an action as well as more explicit cues such as "oops"— can inform the young child about an actor's intentions. Certainly it must be the case that children frequently encounter unfamiliar actions in the ongoing behavior stream. For example, while watching a parent work in the kitchen, a child might observe the parent *open* the refrigerator, *wash* the dishes, *grill* the chicken, and so on (cf. Baldwin, Baird, & Saylor, 2001). If the parent chooses to label any of those actions during such a sequence, the act of labeling can not only highlight the specific segment of the behavior stream but can also inform the child that the mother intended to do just what she is doing.

However, given our findings that suggest that a novel verb's impact is greatest in this area when an action is unfamiliar or ambiguous, an obvious additional question can be posed by simply turning the verb-intention relationship on its head: Does having prior knowledge of an actor's intentions aid in the child's learning of a new verb to label an action? Stated another way, will a child perform better in a verb learning experiment when conditions are manipulated such that in some conditions children have an expectation that a particular action is forthcoming while in others children have no such expectation or, at least, a diminished one?

There is some reason to believe that having access to another's intentions may indeed aid the child during verb learning. For example, some early verb learning studies by Tomasello (1995; Tomasello & Kruger, 1992) showed that children performed best on word learning tasks when a novel verb was presented before an action was performed as compared to when the verb was presented while the action was being presented or following the action. Though Tomasello and Kruger (1992) interpreted these results as demonstrating that children may learn words better in nonostensive conditions, an equally likely interpretation could be that children performed better because the act of labeling an impending action signaled to the child the actor's intentions.

More recent research that is highly relevant to this issue was reported by Poulin-Dubois and Forbes (2002). The authors showed that 27-month-olds but not 21-month-olds used behavioral cues to an actor's intentions, such as eye-gaze and direction of reach, to distinguish between actions labeled by novel verbs. Following Searle, Poulin-Dubois and Forbes argued that by early in the second year of life, children make use of an actor's intention-in-action during verb learning. It is interesting to note that this finding can be contrasted with the earlier findings by Tomasello and Kruger (1992) who showed that children tended to learn verbs better when an actor's prior intentions were expressed when the actor labeled an impending action with a novel verb. At the very least, children are able to use cues to an actor's intentions while an action is occurring in ways that the earlier research did not consider.

The distinction between prior intentions and intention-in-actions is a useful one and one in which we are very interested. Specifically, we are interested in the role that knowledge of another's prior intentions plays during novel word learning. As mentioned previously, one way to demonstrate one's prior intention is to label an impending action with a novel verb. However, rather than examining the role played by the timing of the utterance of a novel verb in relation to the performance of an action (i.e., before, during, or after the action was performed; Tomasello & Kruger, 1992), we were interested in examining whether a child could distinguish between individuals who reliably achieve their stated intentions and those who do not when the child needs to make a decision about the meaning of a novel verb. In other words, can children use their knowledge of the reliability with which an actor fulfills prior intentions in order to choose that actor's behavior as a model action for a newly learned verb when contrasted with the behavior of another actor who less reliably fulfills her prior intentions?

Interestingly, a very similar question has been asked recently, but not with regard to verb learning. Koenig, Clement, and Harris (2004) studied whether 3- and 4-year-olds could use an individual's prior "testimony" in order to learn a novel word. Children were exposed to two models, one who correctly labeled a familiar object, and one who incorrectly labeled that object. Subsequently the models used the same novel word to label different objects, and the children were asked to choose which object was the referent of the novel word. In this experiment, children were more likely to choose the label that had been used by the model with a history of prior accurate testimony with regard to her labeling of familiar objects (see also Koenig & Echols, 2003).

Koenig et al. (2004) frame their results in terms of children's ability to rely on testimony given by knowledgeable or trustworthy speakers in order to learn novel words. However, when the words being learned are verbs, it is not simply the trustworthiness of the speaker that must be taken into account, especially when the actor is labeling their own impending action. In the case in which a speaker says, "I am going to X" prior to performing an action, the speaker is not providing testimony inasmuch as she is expressing a prior intention to perform a specific action. Thus, it becomes an interesting question to ask whether young children will use the reliability of another's statement of their intentions when labeling actions in order to learn a novel verb for a new action.

We are currently addressing this question in our laboratory, using a procedure similar to that used by Koenig et al. (2004). Twenty-five 3- and 4-year-old children were shown a videotape of two female adults. During the training phase, each adult in turn said, "Watch me, I'm going to roll the ball," and then performed an action. However, one of the adults rolled the ball, and the other adult bounced the ball. This demonstration was repeated in reverse order with the same individuals performing the same actions. Thus, one adult was established as a "good intender" and the other as a "bad intender."

During the test phase, children were then shown a series of four test trials depicting the same two adults using a novel verb to label novel actions performed with simple objects. For example, in one test trial one of the adults said, "Watch me, I'm going to *meek* the pompom," and proceeded to flick the pompom over her shoulder. The other adult also said, "Watch me, I'm going to *meek* the pompom," and twirled the pompom above the table. After these two demonstrations, the experimenter (not one of the two models) produced the pompom and said, "Okay, now it's your turn to *meek* the pompom." Children's responses were coded as producing one of the two demonstrated actions or as producing an action that had not been demonstrated.

The results of this first study were intriguing and similar to those reported by Koenig et al. (2004). Children showed a greater tendency to produce the action that was performed by the good intender than to produce the action performed by the bad intender, though this was only the case when responses other than the two performed actions were excluded from the analysis. In addition, there was a marginally significant trend for this effect to be stronger in the younger children than in the older children in our sample. These preliminary results suggest to us that children might need additional cues or reminders about which actor was the "good intender" during the test trials. We have modified the procedure and expect that with these additional reminders, all children will show the predicted effect and that we will see fewer irrelevant responses in our sample. Still, we believe that this initial study demonstrates that if a child knows that an actor reliably fulfills their stated intentions, they can then use this information to learn a novel verb for a novel action.

Putting It All Together

The research summarized in this chapter represents our initial efforts to explore the relations between developments in children's understanding of verbs, the words most frequently used to label human actions, and their growing under-standing of intentions, one of the crucial mental states that underlie these actions. Not surprisingly, there appear to be important relations between these two very important aspects of early cognitive and language development. There are three basic findings from these studies that we wish to emphasize. First, children be-tween 18 and 30 months of age change their patterns of responding in a behav-ioral reenactment paradigm when a modeled "failed attempt" is accompanied by a novel verb. Specifically, these children are less likely to produce the successful tar-get action in this condition compared to when the same action is not accompanied by a novel verb. Second, the influence of labeling an action with a novel verb on children's intentional inferences is greatest when an action is not directly afforded by the stimuli or when there are multiple plausible actions to perform. Given children's strong bias to produce a presumed intended action, this finding suggests that children will use language as a cue to an actor's intention when it is unclear just what that intention is. Third, we have preliminary evidence that suggests that knowing the reliability with which an actor fulfills a stated prior intention may aid the child when learning a novel verb used to label a novel action.

These findings, taken together with prior research on children's understanding of intentions and intentional action, suggest that there are important, reciprocal relations between the young child's growing understanding of intentions and the development of the verb lexicon. We speculate here on what those relations might look like and suggest further avenues of research.

First, it seems apparent that infants and young toddlers have substantial com-petencies in their understanding of the intentional basis of human action prior to the time when children start adding verbs to their lexicon (Carpenter, Akhtar, & Tomasello, 1998; Gergely et al., 1995; Woodward, 1998). In addition, infants are also able to parse the ongoing stream of behavior into action segments that corre-spond with the initiation and completion of intentional behaviors (Baldwin & Baird, 2001; Baldwin et al., 2001). Baldwin and her colleagues argue that these low-level action parsing abilities are a key to the infant's abilities to make infer-ences about the underlying intentions of human action. We would add that the abilities to parse the behavior stream and to make intentional inferences late in the first year and early in the second year of life are prerequisites for the child to begin mapping novel verbs onto the actions they observe in their world. It remains intriguing that despite these apparently precocious abilities, the verb lexicon does not begin to grow rapidly until substantially later in the first or second year of life. Thus, while these abilities can be seen as necessary for verb learning, they may not be wholly sufficient, and children may use other general or specific word-learning strategies to aid them during early verb learning (e.g., Golinkoff et al., 1996; Hol-lich, Hirsh-Pasek, & Golinkoff, 2000).

Once the verb lexicon begins to develop in earnest during the third year of life, we believe that children then begin to use their understanding of verbs and their meanings as tools in their own right to help them make more sophisticated sense out of the behavioral stream. Specifically, our finding that children can use information about the reliability of an actor's stated intentions to help them learn a novel verb suggests that by three years of age children can not only use language as a cue to an actor's intentions but they also can use their understanding of others' intentions as a cue to the meaning of a novel verb. Thus, we see a recursive relation between these two domains of early competencies: Children can bootstrap their way into the verb lexicon as a result of their early understanding of language and intentions, and then they can use their growing competencies with verbs to help them further refine their understanding of actors' intentions.

In fact, we believe that this mutually enhancing relationship between intentional understanding and language development have important implications for the development of other cognitive abilities during early childhood, especially those that have to do with the child's understanding of mental states other than intentions. If the child can come to the understanding that not all intentions are realized in behavior, that not all behaviors are the consequences of a specific intention (i.e., failed attempts, accidents, and mistakes), and that how one labels such actions may vary along these lines (e.g., *pour* vs. *spill*), then children may be compelled to look toward other mental states in order to determine why an agent performed a specific action. Indeed, the child's mastery of the understanding of mental states such as knowledge, belief, and desire make major advances during the preschool years (e.g., Perner, 1991; Wellman, 1992), and these advances may depend to some degree on the child's prior understanding of intentional action and the language used to express such actions. Of course, we are not the first to argue that language and theory of mind developments are related in nontrivial ways (see the chapters in Astington & Baird, 2005). However, we believe that our research program is documenting a specific path through which children may achieve a more mature understanding of the relations between the actions that make up the behavior stream and the mental states of the agents who perform these behaviors (see also Olineck & Poulin-Dubois, 2004).

Conclusion

Verbs are action words. But because they are action words, they are also by necessity words that are intimately related to mental states such as intentions that underlie human actions. Though there are other linguistic forms and structures that can be used to express mental states (e.g., modals), the simple act of labeling one's action with a novel verb appears to influence the child's interpretations of that action. We liken this effect to the effect that a novel noun can have when a speaker labels an unfamiliar object. Just as providing a label for an unfamiliar object highlights object-relevant properties such as shape (e.g., Landau, Smith, & Jones, 1988) and category membership (e.g., Waxman & Markow, 1995), providing a label for an unfamiliar action highlights action-relevant properties such as manner of action, the result of the action, and, as we have shown here, the intention that underlies that action. Our plans are to continue to investigate these crucial relations between verb learning and intentional understanding, and to focus more specifically on the mechanisms through which developments in these two domains influence one another.

References

Astington, J. W., & Baird, J. A. (Eds.). (2005). *Why language matters for theory of mind.* Oxford: Oxford University Press.

Baldwin, D. A., & Baird, J. A. (2001). Discerning intentions in dynamic action. *Trends in Cognitive Science, 5,* 171–178.

Baldwin, D. A., Baird, J. A., & Saylor, M. M. (2001). Infants parse dynamic action. *Child Development, 72,* 708–717.

Behrend, D. A. (1990). The development of verb concepts: Children's use of verbs to label familiar and novel events. *Child Development, 61,* 681–696.

Behrend, D. A. (1995). Processes involved in the initial mapping of verb meanings. In M. Tomasello & W. Merriman (Eds.), *Beyond names for things: Young children's acquisition of verbs* (pp. 251–273). Hillsdale, NJ: Erlbaum.

Behrend, D. A., Harris, L. L., & Cartwright, K. B. (1995). Morphological cues to verb meaning: Verb inflections and the initial mapping of verb meanings. *Journal of Child Language, 22,* 89–106.

Behrend, D. A., & Wittek, A. (2003). *Toddlers use verbs as cues to an actor's intentions.* Paper presented at the meetings of the Society for Research in Child Development, Tampa, FL.

Behrend, D. A., & Wittek, A. (2004). *Toddlers use verbs as cues to an actor's intentions.* Unpublished manuscript.

Benedict, H. (1979). Early lexical development: Comprehension and production. *Journal of Child Language, 6,* 183–200.

Bloom, L., Lifter, K., & Hafitz, J. (1980). Semantics of verbs and the development of verb inflection in child language. *Language, 56,* 386–412.

Bloom, L., & Tinker, E. (2001). The intentionality model and language acquisition: Engagement, effort, and the essential tension in development. *Monographs of the Society for Research in Child Development, 66.*

Bloom, P. (2000). *How children learn the meanings of words.* Cambridge, MA: MIT Press.

Bloom, P. (2002). Mindreading, communication and the learning of names for things. *Mind and Language, 17,* 37–54.

Bornstein, M. H., & Cote, L. (2004). *Cross-linguistic analysis of vocabulary in toddlers: Spanish, Dutch, French, Hebrew, Italian, Korean, and English.* Poster presented at the International Conference on Infant Studies, Chicago, IL.

Brentano, F. (1973). *Psychology from an empirical standpoint.* New York: Humanities Press. (Original work published 1874)

Bronckart, J. P., & Sinclair, H. (1973). Time, tense and aspect. *Cognition, 2,* 107–130.

Bruner, J. (1999). The intentionality of referring. In P. D. Zelazo & J. W. Astington (Eds.), *Developing theories of intention: Social understanding and self-control* (pp. 329–340). Mahwah, NJ: Lawrence Erlbaum.

Carpenter, M., Akhtar, N., & Tomasello, M. (1998). Fourteen- through 18-month-old infants differentially imitate intentional and accidental actions. *Infant Behavior and Development, 21*, 315–330.

Carpenter, M., Call, J., & Tomasello, M. (2002). Understanding "prior intentions" enables two-year-olds to imitatively learn a complex task. *Child Development, 73*, 1431–1441.

Carpenter, M., Pennington, B. F., & Rogers, S. J. (2001). Understanding of others' intentions in children with autism. *Journal of Autism and Developmental Disorders, 31*, 589–599.

Charman, T., & Huang, C. (2002). Delineating the role of stimulus enhancement and emulation learning in the behavioural re-enactment paradigm. *Developmental Science, 5*, 25–27.

Childers, J. B., & Behrend, D. A. (2003). *Children expect novel verbs to refer to intentional actions.* Poster presented at the American Psychological Society conference, Atlanta, GA.

Childers, J. B., & Tomasello, M. (2002). Two-year-olds learn novel nouns, verbs, and conventional actions from massed or distributed exposures. *Developmental Psychology, 38*, 967–978.

Choi, S., & Gopnik, A. (1995). Early acquisition of verbs in Korean: A cross-linguistic study. *Journal of Child Language, 22*, 497–529.

Csibra, G., Gergely, G., & Biro, S. (1999). Goal attribution without agency cues: The perception of "pure reason" in infancy. *Cognition, 72*, 237–267.

Dennett, D. C. (1987). *The intentional stance.* Cambridge, MA: MIT Press.

Feinman, S. (1982). Social referencing in infancy. *Merrill-Palmer Quarterly, 28*, 445–470.

Forbes, J. N., & Farrar, M. J. (1993). Children's initial assumptions about the meaning of novel motion verbs: Biased and conservative? *Cognitive Development, 8*, 273–290.

Forbes, J. N., & Poulin-Dubois, D. (1997). Representational change in young children's understanding of familiar verb meaning. *Journal of Child Language, 24*, 389–406.

Gentner, D. (1982). Why nouns are learned before verbs: Linguistic relativity versus natural partitioning. In S. A. Kuczaj (Ed.), *Language development: Vol. 2. Language, thought and culture* (pp. 301–334). Hillsdale, NJ: Lawrence Erlbaum.

Gentner, D., & Boroditsky, L. (2001). Individuation, relativity and early word learning. In M. Bowerman & S. Levinson (Eds.), *Language acquisition and conceptual development* (pp. 215–256). Cambridge: Cambridge University Press.

Gergely, G., Nadasdy, Z., Csibra, G., & Biro, S. (1995). Taking the intentional stance at 12 months of age. *Cognition, 56*, 165–193.

Gleitman, L. (1990). The structural sources of verb meanings. *Language Acquisition: A Journal of Developmental Linguistics, 1*, 3–55.

Golinkoff, R. M., Jacquet, R. C., & Hirsh-Pasek, K. (1996). Lexical principles may underlie the learning of verbs. *Child Development, 67*, 3101–3119.

Golinkoff, R. M., & Kerr, J. L. (1978). Infants' perception of semantically defined action role changes in filmed events. *Merrill-Palmer Quarterly, 24*, 53–61.

Hollich, G. J., Hirsh-Pasek, K., & Golinkoff, R. M. (2000). Breaking the language barrier: An emergentist coalition model for the origins of word learning. *Monographs of the Society for Research in Cognitive Development, 65*.

Huang, C., Heyes, C., & Charman, T. (2002). Infants' behavioral reenactment of "failed attempts": Exploring the roles of emulation learning, stimulus enhancement, and understanding of intentions. *Developmental Psychology, 38*, 840–855.

Huttenlocher, J., Smiley, P., & Charney, R. (1983). Emergence of action categories in the child: Evidence from verb meanings. *Psychological Review, 90,* 72–93.

Koenig, M. A., Clement, F., & Harris, P. L. (2004). Trust in testimony: Children's use of true and false statements. *Psychological Science, 15,* 694–698.

Koenig, M. A., & Echols, C. H. (2003). Infants' understanding of false labeling events: The referential roles of words and the speakers who use them. *Cognition, 87,* 179–208.

Landau, B., Smith, L. B., & Jones, S. S. (1988). The importance of shape in early lexical learning. *Cognitive Development, 3,* 299–321.

Legerstee, M. (2001). Six-month-old infants rely on explanatory inference when relating communication to people and manipulatory actions to inanimate objects: Reply to Gergely (2001). *Developmental Psychology, 37,* 583–586.

Legerstee, M., Barna, J., & DiAdamo, C. (2000). Precursors to the development of intention at 6 months: Understanding people and their actions. *Developmental Psychology, 36,* 627–634.

Malle, B. F., Moses, L. J., & Baldwin, D. A. (Eds.). (2001). *Intentions and intentionality: Foundations of social cognition.* Cambridge, MA: MIT Press.

Medin, D. E., & Smith, E. E. (1984). Concepts and concept formation. *Annual Review of Psychology, 38,* 113–138.

Meltzoff, A. N. (1995). Understanding the intentions of others: Re-enactment of intended acts by 18-month-old children. *Developmental Psychology, 31,* 838–850.

Naigles, L. R. (1990). Children use syntax to learn verb meanings. *Journal of Child Language, 17,* 357–374.

Naigles, L. R. (1996). The use of multiple frames in verb learning via syntactic bootstrapping. *Cognition, 58,* 221–251.

Olineck, K., & Poulin-Dubois, D. (2004). *Developmental change in infants' understanding of intentional and accidental actions.* Poster presented at the International Conference on Infant Studies, Chicago, IL.

Perner, J. (1991). *Understanding the representational mind.* Cambridge, MA: MIT Press.

Poulin-Dubois, D., & Forbes, J. N. (2002). Toddlers' attention to intentions-in-action in learning novel action words. *Developmental Psychology, 38,* 104–114.

Povinelli, D. J. (2001). On the possibilities of detecting intentions prior to understanding them. In B. F. Malle, L. J. Moses, & D. A. Baldwin (Eds.), *Intentions and intentionality: Foundations of social cognition* (pp. 225–248). Cambridge, MA: MIT Press.

Searle, J. R. (1983). *Intentionality: An essay in the philosophy of mind.* New York: Cambridge University Press.

Slobin, D. I. (1981). The origin of grammatical encoding of events. In W. Deutsch (Ed.), *The child's construction of language* (pp. 185–199). London: Academic Press.

Tardif, T. (1996). Nouns are not always learned before verbs: Evidence from Mandarin speakers' early vocabularies. *Developmental Psychology, 32,* 492–504.

Tardif, T., Gelman, S. A., & Xu, F. (1999). Putting the "noun bias" in context: A comparison of English and Mandarin. *Child Development, 70,* 620–635.

Tomasello, M. (1992). *First verbs: A case study of early grammatical develoment.* Cambridge: Cambridge University Press.

Tomasello, M. (1995). Pragmatic contexts for early verb learning. In M. Tomasello & W. E. Merriman (Eds.), *Beyond names for things: Young children's acquisition of verbs* (pp. 115–146). Hillsdale, NJ: Lawrence Erlbaum.

Tomasello, M. (1999). Having intentions, understanding intentions, and understanding communicative intentions. In P. D. Zelazo & J. W. Astington (Eds.), *Developing theories of intention: Social understanding and self-control* (pp. 63–75). Mahwah, NJ: Lawrence Erlbaum.

Tomasello, M. (2001). Perceiving intentions and learning words in the second year of life. In M. Tomasello & E. Bates (Eds.), *Language development: The essential readings* (pp. 111–128). Malden, MA: Blackwell.

Tomasello, M., & Barton, M. E. (1994). Learning words in nonostensive contexts. *Developmental Psychology, 30,* 639–650.

Tomasello, M., & Kruger, A. (1992). Joint attention on actions: Acquiring verbs in ostensive and nonostensive contexts. *Journal of Child Language, 19,* 311–333.

Tomasello, M., & Merriman, W. E. (1995). *Beyond names for things: Children's acquisition of verbs.* Hillsdale, NJ: Lawrence Erlbaum.

Waxman, S. R., & Markow, D. B. (1995). Words as invitations to form categories: Evidence from 12- to 13-month-old infants. *Cognitive Psychology, 29,* 257–302.

Wellman, H. M. (1992). *The child's theory of mind.* Cambridge, MA: MIT Press.

Woodward, A. L. (1998). Infants selectively encode the goal object of an actor's reach. *Cognition, 69,* 1–34.

Woodward, A. L. (1999). Infants' ability to distinguish between purposeful and nonpurposeful behaviors behaviors. *Infant Behavior and Development, 22,* 145–160.

Woodward, A. L., & Sommerville, J. A. (2000). Twelve-month-old infants interpret action in context. *Psychological Science, 11,* 73–77.

Zelazo, P. D., Astington, J. W., & Olson, D. R. (Eds.). (1999). *Developing theories of intention: Social understanding and self-control.* Mahwah, NJ: Lawrence Erlbaum.

Part III

When Action Meets Word: Children Learn Their First Verbs

12 Are Nouns Easier to Learn Than Verbs? Three Experimental Studies

Jane B. Childers and Michael Tomasello

A current controversy in the study of word learning is whether it is conceptually easier to learn nouns as compared to verbs early in development. Using data available at the time, Gentner (1982) showed that across several languages, children's early productive vocabularies appear to be dominated by nouns. From this evidence, she argued that it may be easier for infants to acquire nouns because the referents of nouns are more easily "packaged" than are the referents for verbs. That is, in a simplified view of word learning, the child must attend to appropriate perceptual elements, package them together, and connect them in some way to a spoken word. Perceptual elements that are often referred to by nouns (e.g., concrete objects), tend to be highly cohesive (doggie "parts" are always seen when a dog is present, for example), are viewed across language and culture in the same way (i.e., as objects), and are referred to using the same word type (i.e., nouns). In contrast, the perceptual elements that are connected to individual verbs are not as cohesive because elements of meaning are likely to be distributed across time and space, they are not conceptualized in the same way across languages and cultures (i.e., languages vary in the way verbs refer to different aspects of events), and they may not be universally lexicalized as verbs (e.g., the verb category itself varies across languages).

More recently, Gentner and Boroditsky (2001) have expanded on these ideas by reiterating that they are not proposing that "nouns are easy." They are proposing that, if children are able to conceive of a referent in itself, outside of or before language, it should be easier for the infant to then learn how to refer to that referent using language than it will be to both package the world and learn a new word at the same time. Some nouns, particularly names for concrete objects, are likely to be "preindividuated," or likely to have become concepts or categories, before the word for those concepts is learned. If they are preindividuated and if that coherency in the referent does help word learning, then early vocabularies should have just those types of words. Note that this view is not a "noun first" view; it predicts that any word type that refers to concepts that an infant can easily conceptualize, individuate, or parse will appear earlier in development. Tomasello (2003) added further that some kinds of joint attentional frames and linguistic utterances make the referents of some words particularly transparent for young children, and many of these have to do with the manipulation, exchange, and labeling of objects—the fact that objects are to some degree preindividuated conceptually is an important part of this process.

In recent investigations of Gentner's proposals, researchers have examined children's productive vocabularies across languages. This body of research suggests that, in general, the early productive vocabularies of children learning English, Italian, or Spanish favor nouns (Au, Dapretto, & Song, 1994; Jackson-Maldonado, Thal, Marchman, Bates, & Gutierrez-Clellen, 1993; Tardif, Gelman, & Xu, 1999; Tardif, Shatz, & Naigles, 1997), while children acquiring Mandarin (Tardif et al., 1997, 1999) and perhaps Korean (Gopnik & Choi, 1995; but see also Au et al., 1994; Kim, McGregor, & Thompson, 2000) do not, possibly because nouns are not favored in the input in these languages. A methodological problem inherent in this type of study is that because children use each of their verbs more frequently than they use each of their nouns, spontaneous speech samples tend to underestimate children's noun vocabularies because, relative to individual verbs, the probability that a child will use any particular noun in one hour of sampling is not very high. This has led some researchers to prefer the use of a vocabulary checklist to estimate noun and verb comprehension and production (Caselli, Casadio, & Bates, 1999). For this reason, Tardif et al. (1999) measured Mandarin-speaking children's vocabularies in two ways (spontaneous sample and vocabulary checklist), and the verb advantage mostly disappeared in the results from the vocabulary checklist.

A difficulty in evaluating these differing sets of results is that nouns and verbs appear with different frequencies, in different types of sentences, and in different contexts in these languages. In fact, there are almost no experimental studies that have investigated whether, if the frequency of nouns and verbs is experimentally controlled, children either produce or comprehend nouns more quickly or more frequently than they do verbs. Of the three relevant experimental studies that have been conducted, only one provides evidence to suggest that nouns are easier to learn. Schwartz and Leonard (1984) found that toddlers who were taught 16 new nouns and verbs were able to learn more nouns than verbs and required between 20 and 40 exposures to learn the words they eventually produced. However, the children in their study were learning 16 words at a time with 64 objects and actions presented and named in each session. In two other studies, no differences were found. Tomasello and Akhtar (1995) found that 2-year-olds could learn both novel nouns and verbs with enough exposures, but there was no direct comparison of how many or what kinds of exposures are needed in the two cases. Oviatt (1980) found no indications of noun-verb differences in the comprehension of 1-year-olds. In sum, additional systematic experimental tests of the relative ease of acquisition of nouns and verbs are needed.

In this chapter, we describe three experiments that address the noun-verb question in different ways. In the first experiment, we asked how many times (and on how many days) does a 2-year-old need to hear a word to be able to learn it, and does this differ for nouns and verbs? To address these two basic questions (which, surprisingly, have not yet been addressed fully experimentally), we taught children novel nouns and verbs, varying the number of models and the spacing of the models across days. We then tested children's comprehension and production of these words at various intervals. In addition, we followed the same procedures in teaching children nonverbal novel actions to see whether the same learning principles apply in a nonverbal task.

Thus, the study is one of only a handful studies that address a basic question in word learning—how many exposures are needed and on what schedule? In addition, it addresses an important controversy in the area, whether noun learning is privileged in language development or is not. Moreover, the inclusion of an unnamed new action provides an important comparison point not available in other studies. In the presentation of nouns and verbs in any study (typically seen across different studies and not in the same study), it is common for novel objects in a noun learning study (or condition) to be shown as static objects, while in verb studies (conditions), objects are shown in dynamic events. That means that children learning verbs must attend to moving dynamic events and learn new words at the same time (as they do in everyday life). The no-word new event condition in our study allows us to examine children's ability to remember dynamic events that are tied to new objects and to separate this event ability from their ability to learn a word to refer to new events (verb condition).

However, as is common in noun studies and verb studies, a limitation of this first experiment is that the sentences used to present the nouns and verbs may have favored nouns. Specifically, children in the noun condition heard, for example, "Look at this! This is a wuggy. See? It's a wuggy." while children in the verb condition heard, "Look at this! It's dacking. See? It dacks." Although these sentence structures are similar to each other, the noun phrasing is likely more common in naturalistic settings than is the verb sentence type because verbs often are embedded in sentences that are longer than these. (Again, note that this decision is common across noun and verb studies. Noun studies often use simple frames like the frames in the noun condition here, while verb studies typically use more complex frames—making the comparison of noun and verb learning across studies more difficult.) Thus, in a second study, we taught children four nouns and four verbs over two days, embedding the words in longer sentences (e.g., "The blick's spraying it" or "The dog's blicking it"). Embedding nouns in sentences like these is fairly rare in the noun learning literature, while the presentation of novel verbs in these types of frames is fairly common. This second study thus investigates whether, when nouns and verbs are presented in comparable sentence contexts, controlling the number of exposures, and presenting a dynamic event in both the noun and verb conditions, nouns are easier to learn than are verbs.

A further question concerns whether studies that compare nouns to verbs would produce different results if different types of verbs or different types of action referents were presented. If children find it easier to learn transitive than intransitive verbs, for example, then studies that compare nouns with verbs should be viewed with these considerations in mind. In Study 3, we compare children's ability to learn intransitive and transitive verbs and their ability to understand verbs for self-action as opposed to other action, to determine whether some of these verb and referent types are learned more quickly than are others. We then use these results to discuss whether the findings in the first two studies presented here are influenced by the types of verbs we chose.

Previous Studies of Noun and Verb Learning

Basic research in the area of children's word learning has revealed some general patterns of word learning. For example, research using a parental vocabulary checklist (the MacArthur-Bates Communicative Development Inventory [CDI]; Fenson et al., 1994) has shown that English-speaking 1-year-olds learn about one word a day, and two-year-olds learn about two words a day. In addition, children typically comprehend a word before they produce it (e.g., Benedict, 1979; Fenson et al., 1994; Goldin-Meadow, Seligman, & Gelman, 1976).

However, there is also evidence that some aspects of word learning differ depending on the type of word being learned. For nouns, young children can comprehend (or "fast map") a new noun after only a few exposures (Carey & Bartlett, 1978; Markson & Bloom, 1997; Woodward, Markman, & Fitzsimmons, 1994). Children may have constraints or predispositions that help them connect nouns to objects (e.g., Golinkoff, Mervis, & Hirsh-Pasek, 1994; Markman, 1990); children appear to attend to shape when extending new nouns (e.g., Jones, Landau, & Smith, 1992); and children learning nouns may assume the speaker is referring to a category of objects (e.g., Waxman & Booth, 2000; Waxman & Markow, 1995).

Less is known about the general character of verb learning, perhaps because fewer studies have investigated the acquisition of verbs (e.g., Tomasello & Merriman, 1995). However, a prevailing view of early verb learning is that, compared to nouns, verbs appear to be relatively difficult to acquire. Although verbs (or action words) appear in children's earliest productive vocabularies, these vocabularies often contain many more nouns than verbs (Au et al., 1994; Caselli et al., 1999; Gentner, 1982; Jackson-Maldonado et al., 1993; Tardif et al., 1997, 1999). It is unclear whether children have constraints or biases that guide early verb learning (though they may), and children may or may not fast map verbs as they do nouns (see e.g., Golinkoff, Jacquet, Hirsh-Pasek, & Nandakumar, 1996; Merriman, Marazita, & Jarvis, 1995, for evidence that they do). They appear to benefit from hearing verbs in an impending context (directly before they themselves perform an action) as opposed to during or following the action (Tomasello, 1995; Tomasello & Kruger, 1992). Several studies of verb learning using naturalistic observation and in the laboratory suggest that children are highly conservative in their use of new verbs, tending to use verbs only in the syntactic contexts in which a verb has been heard (Olguin & Tomasello, 1993; Tomasello, 1992) and resisting the extension of new verbs to some new events (Behrend, 1990; Forbes & Farrar, 1993, 1995). Some have tried to extend word learning principles to both nouns and verbs (e.g., Golinkoff et al., 1994; Golinkoff, Hirsh-Pasek, & Mervis, 1995); however, more evidence supporting this type of approach is needed. What seems more likely is that the processes that underlie noun and verb learning differ.

The comparison of nouns to verbs is largely a comparison across different studies, some investigating noun learning and some investigating verb learning. As a consequence, the methods used to teach a noun or verb vary across the studies being compared. We were interested in presenting 2.5-year-old children with new nouns or new verbs in a similar experimental context to examine whether differences in their ability to comprehend or produce the new words could be revealed. In Study 1, we also decided to include a nonverbal (action) condition because recent studies suggest that noun learning either is similar to learning a nonverbal fact (Childers & Tomasello, 2003; Markson, 1999; Markson & Bloom, 1997) or it is not (Waxman & Booth, 2000). This nonverbal action condition is important because it can help to reveal whether children are having difficulty remembering new actions associated with objects or whether the problem lies in learning words that refer to new actions. Three previous studies have included nouns and verbs in a single study (Oviatt, 1980; Schwartz & Leonard, 1984; Tomasello & Akhtar, 1995), and only one of these studies (Schwartz & Leonard, 1984) demonstrates a difference in learning nouns and verbs (favoring nouns). In addition, one noun learning study shows that children can produce a new noun after approximately 6–8 sessions regardless of whether they are exposed to that noun once or twice per session (Schwartz & Terrell, 1983). This finding suggests that the distributed practice effect found across skills and across species (see Dempster, 1996; Underwood, 1961, for reviews) could also apply to children's word learning.

Given the need for studies that examine both noun and verb learning in a single study and the need for systemic investigations of how the number and timing of exposures influences word learning, we designed a study to address the following basic questions: How often does a child need to hear a word to be able to learn it? Is this different for different types of words? And once a word is comprehended or produced, how long will a child remember it?

Study 1: 2-year-old Children Learn Nouns, Verbs, and Nonverbal Actions

We taught three different groups of 2.5-year-old children nouns, verbs, or non-verbal actions over one month (Childers & Tomasello, 2002). Each child in each of the three groups ($n = 12$ per group) was shown six sets of objects, one set for each of six timing of exposures conditions. Each set of objects contained three familiar (warm-up) objects and three novel objects. One novel object in a set was randomly selected as the target object before the study began and the other two served as distracters (see figure 12.1). For the noun group, six nouns (*blick, gep, snarf, wuggy, danu, gazzer*) were randomly assigned to the target objects. The verb group used the same target and distracter objects in the same sets as the noun group. We designed six generic actions that could be performed with any of the novel objects and assigned a novel verb and action randomly to the target before the study began. The six verbs and actions were *keef* (experimenter balances object on two fingers, then flicks it to make the object wobble), *gorp* (experimenter puts object on her knee and lets go so it rolls down her leg), *pud* (experimenter throws the object on the floor, making it bounce) *meek* (experimenter starts the object spinning and the object spins), *dack* (experimenter flicks the object on its end and makes it tumble), and *tam* (experimenter starts the object twirling on its end). In the nonverbal action group, six generic actions were created that could be performed with any of the novel objects. (These actions included the experimenter's actions more than the actions designed for the verbs, which were about the actions of the object.) The six nonverbal actions were experimenter puts object on her head, experimenter catches object in the air, experimenter puts object on floor and spins it around, experimenter puts object on her elbow and moves it up and down, experimenter balances object on the back of her hand, and experimenter rolls object on her knee. The novel words, actions, and target objects were assigned to the sets before the study began and were the same across subjects.

During the study, each object set was randomly assigned to a timing of exposures condition in a counterbalanced manner across children. Two sets were presented on a massed schedule (all exposures on one day) and four were presented in varying distributed schedules. The two grouped schedules were Massed 4 (four exposures on one day) or Massed 8 (eight on one day). Two schedules distributed exposures over 4 days (Daily 4: one per day for 4 consecutive days; Widely Spaced 4: one per day with each exposure day separated by 3 days). Two schedules were designed as a compromise between massed and distributed schedules (Clumped 4: 2 on one day, 3 intervening days, 2 on the second day; and Clumped 8: 2 on one day, 4 on one day, and 2 on one day with 3 days between each exposure day). Two different ordering schedules were created, and half of the children in each word group received each order. Children generally were not exposed to more than two new words in one day.

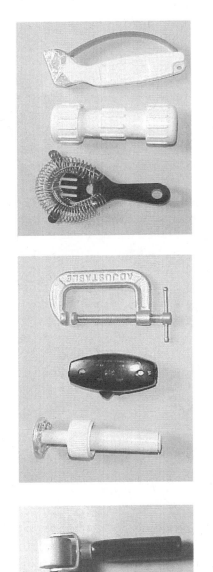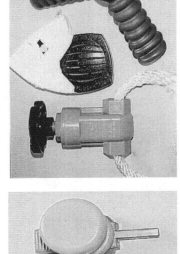

Figure 12.1. Materials for Study 1. The target object is shown as the left object in each set.

In addition to these variations in the timing of exposures, children were tested in both comprehension and production at three intervals: immediately following the learning phase, 24 hours later, and 1 week later.

In the *familiarization phase*, the experimenter produced a plastic bag full of the familiar and novel objects in a set. The experimenter drew out the three familiar objects in a random order and then the three novel ones. She showed each child each object, said something about it (different for different objects and word conditions), gave it to the child to play with, and then asked the child to put it in a bucket. When a nontarget object was introduced, the experimenter showed interest in it and commented by saying things like, "Look at this! It's really neat. See? What color is it? Can you put it in the bucket?" When the target object was shown, the experimenter produced a novel word in the sentence types appropriate to the child's word condition. In the noun condition, the experimenter labeled it with one or more pairs of sentences (depending on the timing conditions): for example, "Look at this! This is a wuggy. See? It's a wuggy. Can you put it in the bucket?" In the verb condition, the three familiar objects were presented with a simple action and familiar verb (e.g., "Look at this. It swims/it rolls/I'm biting it."). For the three novel objects, a novel action was shown as the experimenter picked up the target object while saying, "Look at this! It's dacking. See? It dacks. Can you put it in the bucket?" (The experimenter showed interest in the other two novel objects.) Children in the nonverbal action condition experienced almost the same procedure but instead of a novel verb, the experimenter said, "Look at this! Look what we can do with this. See? Look what we can do with it. Can you put it in the bucket?"

In the *test phase*, children were asked to produce the novel word and then to comprehend the word using a forced choice task. In the noun group, the experimenter started by asking the child to name the three familiar objects (in random order). Then she asked for names of the three novel objects (in random order), saying, "Look at this! What is this called? Can you tell me? What is it?" In the comprehension task, the experimenter showed the child the set of familiar objects and asked the child to point to one of the objects. The experimenter then showed the child the set of novel objects (arrayed randomly) and asked her to choose the target by saying, "Show me the wuggy. Which one's the wuggy? Can you put it in the bucket?"

A similar procedure was followed for the verb group. In the production task, the experimenter asked the child to show her the action (familiar before novel) and to tell her what the action was called ("Look at this! What does it do? What does this do? What is it doing?"). Thus, children were asked to both enact the action and say the verb, and these responses were analyzed separately. In the comprehension task, the experimenter showed the child the three novel objects (arrayed randomly) and asked, "Show me the one that dacks. Which one was dacking? Can you put it in the bucket?" This type of comprehension task was designed for consistency across word conditions. If children remembered the target object but not the associated action, this task would overestimate their knowledge of the verb and action.

In the nonverbal action condition, the experimenter held up each object (familiar before novel) and asked the child to show her the action ("Look at this. What do we do with this? What does this do?"). In the comprehension task, the experimenter enacted the action using her hand (e.g., patting her head) and asked the child to choose the target object (from the novel objects, arrayed randomly), saying, "Show me the one that goes like this. Show me the one that goes like this. Can you put it in the bucket?" As in the verb condition, this comprehension task may reveal more about whether children remembered the target object than whether they remembered the nonverbal action.

Although it was possible that children's responses would vary across the three retention intervals, we found no differences. If children could comprehend or produce a word immediately, they also remembered the word one day and one week later. This finding is consistent with the findings of Markson and Bloom (1997), Carey and Bartlett (1978), and others. However, in our study the spacing condition was a within-subjects variable so that after the immediate test, children were getting "reminders" at each testing session because the word or action was performed by the experimenter in the comprehension test. We also found no differences between the three word groups in children's comprehension abilities. Children were very good at recalling target objects across conditions, supporting the well-known advantage for comprehension over production (e.g., Fenson et al., 1994; Goldin-Meadow et al., 1976; see figure 12.2).

Differences between the word groups and the timing of the exposure conditions were found in children's productions. Nonverbal actions were the easiest to produce; children produced significantly more nonverbal actions than nouns in three timing conditions and more actions than verbs in five conditions. Thus, in general, children found it easier to demonstrate the action an adult had performed with an object than to verbally produce the word they had used for that object (noun) or the word for that associated action (verb).

Children produced almost twice as many nouns as verbs overall (see figure 12.3). We also coded whether children could demonstrate the correct action on the target object in the verb condition, and they could. Both this measure and the nonverbal action results show that children could remember novel actions associated with specific target objects but had difficulty verbally producing the verb itself.

The variations in the timing of exposures affected the two types of words more than it affected the nonverbal actions. Specifically, the two massed conditions (Massed 4, Massed 8) were inferior to the distributed condition (Daily 4) for both nouns and verbs. Also, for both nouns and verbs there was at least one condition with four distributed exposures that was statistically higher than another condition with eight massed exposures.

The current findings provide some experimental support for the idea that nouns are easier to learn than verbs (Gentner, 1982; Gentner & Boroditsky, 2001),

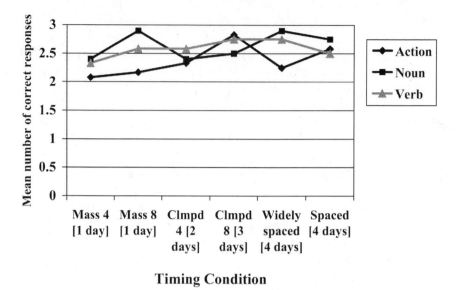

Timing Condition

Figure 12.2. Mean number of correct target choices in comprehension (out of three) as a function of Item Learned and Timing of Exposures in Study 1.

at least for English-speaking children. However, the way we taught and tested our nouns and verbs should be carefully considered. In our study, children in the noun group were asked to map a new word onto a new object (as is common in noun learning). Children in the verb group had to map a new word onto an action that was related to a specific object. Although this allowed us to be able to teach and test the verbs in a way that was similar to the nouns, in everyday contexts, verbs are mostly used for a range of objects. Thus, we could have increased the difficulty in the verb condition by our insistence that they attach the verb to a single object. On the other hand, children in the nonverbal action condition seemed to readily attach new actions to specific objects.

More important perhaps, our verb comprehension task may have favored nouns because the dependent measure was children's choice of the target object that was associated with the new action. In our production test, we asked children in the verb condition to produce both the action and the verb label. Thus, children in this condition were asked to make two responses (reproduce the action and say the verb), while children in the noun condition only needed to make one response (say the noun). On the other hand, testing verb production in this way allowed us to demonstrate that what children in the verb condition were having difficulty accomplishing was not mapping actions to specific objects (they were able to reproduce the action) but learning verbs to refer to these actions—which is the task faced in everyday verb learning situations. A third limitation of this first experiment is that the sentences in which the words were embedded are probably more com-

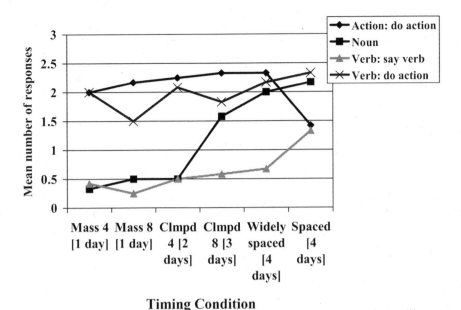

Figure 12.3. Mean number of times word produced (out of 3) as a function of Item Learned and Timing of Exposures in Study 1.

mon for nouns than verbs because verbs often are embedded in longer sentences. In a second study, we taught children nouns and verbs embedded in longer sentences.

Two other difficult decisions were (1) whether to teach the verb in a transitive or intransitive sentence frame ("The ball is meeking" vs. "I'm meeking the ball") and (2) whether to use the verb to describe the child's action or that of an object (or other person). There is some indirect evidence that children learn some kinds of verbs better when they are used for their own actions (e.g., Huttenlocher, Smiley, & Charney, 1983; Roberts, 1983). We explored the consequences of our verb decisions in our third study.

Study 2: Nouns and Verbs Embedded in Sentences

In our second study, we taught 18 2-year-old children (mean age = 2 years, 2 months; range = 2 years, 0 months–2 years, 3 months) and 18 2.5-year-old children (mean age = 2 years, 8 months; range = 2 years, 4 months–2 years, 11 months) four nouns and four verbs over two days. Twelve girls and 23 boys participated. In this study, children, regardless of whether they were learning nouns or verbs, saw novel objects undergoing simple novel actions and always heard the target word embedded in a longer sentence (i.e., words were not in simple labeling phrases or sentence-final). To our knowledge, no other study has directly compared noun and verb learning showing the same objects in the same events and using these types of sentences.

On the first of two days, the experimental session began with the presentation of four familiar objects undergoing actions. The experimenter removed each object from an opaque bag and demonstrated an action for approximately 30 seconds (e.g., pulled an apple in a toy wagon; hit a firetruck with her hand). The experimenter then showed the child the first novel object undergoing an action that was accompanied by a noun or a verb. During this presentation, the child heard four pairs of the novel word. Words were presented one at a time and were demonstrated with a familiar puppet (e.g., a dog). For example, for the first word, the experimenter showed a puppet using a novel object to blow on a carpenter's level (see table 12.1 for a complete list of stimuli). Children hearing nouns first heard, "Look. The blick's spraying it," while children hearing verbs first heard, "Look. The dog's blicking it." The order of the words was set up such that two nouns were always presented one after the other, and two verbs were presented one after the other. Whether the nouns were shown first or the verbs were shown first was counterbalanced across children.

Immediately following the presentation of each new word, children were asked to produce the word. In the noun sets, children heard, "Look at this. What's this? What's this called? Can you tell me? What is it?" In the verb sets children heard, "Look at this. What does this do? What's it doing? Can you tell me? What's it doing?" After the production task for the first word, children were taught a second word and given a second production test for that new word. At the end of the pair of words, both noun or both verb, children were given a comprehension test. In the comprehension test, two familiar object sets (from the four that were introduced before the novel words were presented) were placed randomly with the two novel sets just presented. The experimenter first asked the child to point to one of the familiar objects, and then asked the child to point to each of the novel targets in a random order (e.g., nouns: "Where's the _____? Can you give me the _____? Where is it? Can you point to it?"; verbs: "Where's the one that was _____ing? Which one _____s? Can you point to it?"). Once the child had made a choice of an object set, that set was replaced in the array and available on subsequent test questions. Thus, on every comprehension question, children were able to choose from four object sets, two familiar and two associated with the new words. Children were never choosing between an object set used for a noun and one used for a verb. They were hearing nouns (or verbs) for all four object sets (two familiar and two novel) and then were demonstrating whether they had successfully associated a particular noun (or verb) with a particular set or had not.

The procedure of introducing the new words, eliciting production of each word, and then asking the child to point to the object sets that were associated with each new word was repeated for the next two words with the only difference being two different familiar objects (from the four that had been seen) were used in the second set of comprehension questions. The experimenter returned on a

Table 12.1 Materials for Study 2

"Animate" puppets (agents):
> a dog, a frog, a sheep, a bird

Familiar objects and familiar actions:

Day 1
> grab car off dartboard
> pull apple in wagon
> hit firetruck with hand
> pour strawberry from cup

Day 2
> throw chair in box
> carry cake in basket
> eat pizza slice
> shake rattle

Novel objects and novel actions:

Day 1
> use orange blower to blow on a carpenter's level
> use a rake to rake a brillo pad
> use a paint scraper to flip a coffee-filter-clamp over
> bounce a party horn up and down on a leash

Day 2
> use a magnet on a stick to pick up a paint scraper
> put twisted straw in funnel and turn straw around
> mix drain plug in a hand mixer
> use a roller to roll the top of a black box with a button

Novel nouns and verbs:

blick, blicking	gep, gepping
gazzer, gazzing	wug, wugging
pud, puding	modi, modeing
keef, keefing	snarf, snarfing

second day and repeated the entire process with four new familiar object sets, two new object sets associated with new nouns and two associated with new verbs.

Because the comprehension and production tasks involved different types of test trials with different probabilities for responses, we analyzed each task separately. For the comprehension task, a repeated measures ANOVA was computed with Word (noun, verb) as a within-subjects factor and Age (younger, older) as a between-subjects factor; the dependent variable was the number of correct choices at test. The analysis revealed a main effect of Word, $F(1, 34) = 4.64$,

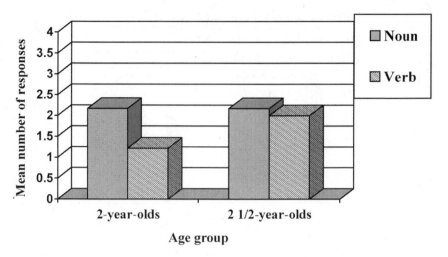

Figure 12.4. Comprehension data from Study 2.

$p < .05$, no main effect of Age, and no interaction. Overall, children comprehended more nouns than verbs (see figure 12.4).

In addition to comparing noun and verb responses to each other, a separate question is whether responses differed from chance. Following each comprehension test question, children were given four object sets from which to choose. Thus, if children were choosing randomly, they should make the correct choice 25% of the time, or on one of the four comprehension trials. One sample t tests with Bonferroni corrections ($p < .025$) were used to compare children's comprehension means to chance. In the younger age, children's responses to the noun comprehension questions (mean = 2.17, $SD = 1.04$) exceeded chance, $t(17) = 4.75$, $p < .001$; children's responses to the verb comprehension questions did not (mean = 1.22, $SD = .94$). In the older age, children's responses to the noun comprehension questions (mean = 2.17, $SD = 1.29$) and verb comprehension questions (mean = 2.00, $SD = 1.37$) exceeded chance, $t(17) = 3.82$, $p < .01$, and $t(17) = 3.09$, $p < .01$ respectively.

To examine children's responses in the production task, a repeated measures ANOVA was computed with Word (noun, verb) as a within subjects factor and Age (younger, older) as a between subjects factor; the dependent variable was the number of correct productions at test. This analysis revealed a trend towards significance for Age group, $F(1, 34) = 4.02$, $p < .06$. Children in the older age produced, on average, approximately one new word (either noun or verb), while children in the younger age did not (see table 12.2).

In Study 1, 2.5-year-old children did not differ in their ability to comprehend new nouns and new verbs. While children in Study 2 across age comprehended more nouns than verbs, the results from the one sample t tests suggest that the

Table 12.2 Results of Study 2 production

	Word Type	
	Noun	Verb
Child Age		
Younger	.44 (.70)	.28 (.57)
Older	.94 (1.09)	.94 (1.25)

Table 12.2 shows the mean number of productions (s.d.) of the four novel nouns and four novel verbs.

advantage for nouns was most evident in the responses produced by the younger 2-year-old children. A difference in the findings of the two studies was that in Study 1, older 2-year-olds produced more nouns than verbs while in Study 2, noun and verb production did not differ. This difference may have emerged because the noun sentence frames in Study 1 were simpler than the verb sentence frames in Study 1 and the noun and verb sentence frames in Study 2. Thus, children's ability to produce new nouns in Study 1 may have benefited from the simple frames in which nouns were heard. A strength of Study 2 is that the presentation of the objects in motion and the use of the same types of sentences for embedding the new words make the noun and verb conditions much more comparable in Study 2 than they were in Study 1. Overall, Study 2 suggests that when these conditions are comparable, evidence for a "noun advantage" is most clearly present in the responses of younger 2-year-olds and not older ones.

A lingering question from both studies is whether the type of verb being learned matters. Is it more difficult for children to learn some types of verbs (e.g., intransitives, verbs for other people's actions) as compared to other types (e.g., transitives, verbs for their own actions)? If there is a difference in children's ability to learn some verbs as compared to others, a noun advantage may be revealed more strongly in some cases (e.g., names for concrete objects vs. words for intransitive or other agent actions) than in others. The final study simply examines whether some verbs are easier for a 2-year-old child to learn.

Study 3: Are Some Types of Verbs Easier to Learn Than Others?

A tricky issue for verb researchers is deciding the type of verb to include in a study. If studying nouns, it is common to include nouns that can be thought of as at the basic level (e.g., Rosch & Mervis, 1975). However, there is no clear "basic level" for verbs, and findings from individual studies may vary for the simple reason that they focus on different types of verbs. For example, in Huttenlocher et al. (1983), "movement" verbs (e.g., *kick, jump, wave*) were contrasted with "multientity change verbs" (e.g., *clean, put down, give*). Forbes and Farrar (1993) focused on a group of novel motion verbs in which "a subject or object (was changed) or being caused to change position or location" (p. 276). Behrend (1990) focused on action verbs (e.g., *pound*) which focus on "the physical movement of an agent without . . . the result of that movement" (p. 682) as opposed to result verbs (e.g., *break*) that refer only to the result and not the way that result was produced. The results from Studies 1 and 2 could be limited by the types of verbs we chose to contrast with nouns in the studies. Study 3 examines two potential influences: whether children are learning transitive or intransitive verbs, and whether children themselves are the agent or not when they are exposed to the new verb. If these two factors emerge importantly in Study 3, then the results from Studies 1 and 2 should be considered with these verb choices in mind.

One reason to believe that children would learn transitive verbs more easily than intransitives would be that transitives conform to a "prototypical" event type in which an agent acts directly on a patient (Slobin, 1985). However, studies of everyday speech in naturalistic contexts do not show a clear advantage for either verb type (e.g., Tomasello, 1992). Our study tests whether an advantage for transitives holds if children are given equivalent experiences with transitive and intransitive verbs (see Naigles, 1990; Hirsh-Pasek & Golinkoff, 1996, for preferential-looking studies of attention to transitive and intransitive sentence frames).

A second question is whether children are better at learning verbs that refer to their own actions (e.g., Huttenlocher et al., 1983). If children are better at learning verbs for their own actions and were presented with verbs for the experimenter's actions or the action of an object in Studies 1 and 2, then those studies may underestimate verb learning. For example, in Huttenlocher et al. (1983, Study 2), 90% of children's (age 24–26 months) utterances with verbs were produced when they were involved in an action in some way. In these utterances, children were either describing their own actions, describing the action of the toys involved, or making a request for action from another person. Huttenlocher et al. concluded that children were mostly using verbs for self-action. However, Edwards and Goodwin (1986) have noted that children in Huttenlocher et al.'s study produced verbs in response to observed action (*come, go,* and *do*) but these uses were discounted. In Huttenlocher et al., Study 3, infants (starting at 1 year) were asked to follow an instruction or point to one of two films and could follow an instruction directed to them before they could point to the correct depiction of a verb in a film. Huttenlocher et al. viewed these results as supportive of a "self-action first" account, but the results could also simply stem from the greater likelihood that children would get practice following commands as opposed to pointing to screens in everyday life. Edwards and Goodwin (1986) found that self and other action emerged differently for different verbs. For example, *pull* and *stuck* were used only for self-action while *shut* and *open* were often used for self-action but also used for other action. They argued that patterns of verb usage for self-action and other action resulted from particular communicative needs. A third study (Roberts, 1983) examined young 2-year-olds' ability to enact an action using their own body in response to sentences (with familiar verbs) that referred to the child as an agent or referred to another person as the agent. Roberts found that young 2-year-old children performed best in this task if they were the agent. A limitation of this study is that the dependent variable, latency to move, was somewhat difficult to measure.

There are only a small number of studies examining self and other action. These studies focus on familiar verbs and do not conclusively show an earlier ability to comprehend or produce new verbs that refer to self as opposed to other action. Much of the data supporting a self-first view is spontaneous production data that could be influenced by the child's desire to talk about particular events, not his or her ability to conceive of or learn words for specific (other agent) events. We introduced novel verbs and controlled the exposure to new verbs for the self or other to ensure the child heard an equal number of exposures to both. We also implemented the same testing procedure to test comprehension and production of verbs with self as agent and other agents. In sum, this study could be important for researchers considering the self-other distinction; however, it is important for understanding Studies 1 and 2 because it could reveal an important situational factor that could have had a major influence in those studies.

In this third study, we taught 24 2-year-old children (mean age = 2 years, 1.5 months; range: 1 year, 10 months–2 years, 4 months) four nouns and four verbs over two days. We varied both the agent who performed the action (child, puppet) and the type of verb presented (transitive, intransitive) in a within-subjects design. That is, each child heard one new verb of each type: a child-transitive verb, a child-intransitive verb, an other-agent transitive verb, and an other-agent intransitive verb, with two verbs presented on each of two days.

Each of the four novel target events could be enacted by the experimenter as either a transitive or intransitive action. For example, in one event, the experimenter squeezed a nasal aspirator into the air (intransitive) or used the aspirator to spray air onto a small table (transitive). In the other three target events, the experimenter moved the top of a soda can crusher back and forth (intransitive) or used the top of the crusher to squeeze a Nerf ball (transitive), used a pasta fork to perform a raking action (intransitive) or used the fork to rake confetti (transitive), and bounced the end of a child safety leash (intransitive) or bounced a banana up and down with the leash (transitive). In addition to these target actions, we designed eight distracter events that corresponded to familiar verbs (*turn*, *pull*, *brush*, *pick up*, *close*, *mix*, *hit*, and *get*).

On the first day, the experimenter introduced one target event and two distracters in a random order. She began by enacting the events one at a time while either producing neutral positive comments for the distracter actions or producing the appropriate verb for the target action. Each verb was produced three times for a single event (impending, ongoing, and completed) before a different event was introduced. In the distracter events the child heard three sentences with similar impending, ongoing and completed action contexts that contained general verbs. In the new verb events, the child heard novel verbs in the three sentence contexts.

If the verb was assigned to the self-agent condition, the experimenter first enacted the event ("Let's play a game. Look what I can do. Now it's your turn.") and then asked the child to enact the event. During the child's enactments, the experimenter produced the new verb (e.g., "You're going to meek it. Wow, can you play the game? You're meeking it. Look. You meeked it."). (If the verb was an intransitive, the same sentence frames were produced without the final pronoun, e.g., "You're meeking.") During the two distracter events, the same procedure was followed; however, the experimenter did not produce the new verb (e.g., "Look at this. Look what this can do. Now it's your turn. You're going to play. You're doing great. Wow. You got a turn.").

In the other-agent condition, the experimenter asked the child to choose a puppet to enact the event. The experimenter then enacted the event with the puppet ("Let's play a game. Look what he can do. Now it's your turn.") and gave the child a turn to enact the event. The experimenter then enacted the event three more times while producing the new verb if appropriate (e.g., "Now it's Big Bird's turn again. He's going to pilk. He's pilking. Look. He pilked."). In the distracter games, the same procedure was followed but no new verb was presented.

Whether children heard self-agent or other-agent sentences, after each event had been shown and the appropriate sentences had been produced three times, the next game in a set was introduced. This process was repeated until the child had played each game in a set three times and heard each verb a total of nine times.

At this point, the experimenter presented the child with a production test (always first) and a comprehension test. In the production test, the experimenter demonstrated each of the three games in the set in a random order and asked the child to produce the verbs. In the child-agent question, the experimenter asked the child to enact the event and then say the verb (e.g., "Now let's play this game. It's your turn. Can you do it? What are you doing?"). In the other-agent question, the experimenter asked the child to choose a puppet first and then asked the question (e.g., "Now watch. It's the [puppet's] turn. Watch what he's doing. What is he doing?").

Following the production questions, the experimenter asked the child two sets of comprehension questions. In the child-agent comprehension question, the experimenter asked the child to choose the correct event from the three presented (one heard with a novel verb and two heard with distracter phrases) and enact the event (e.g., "Now [child's name]. You're going to meek it. You're meeking it. Show me [child's name's] meeking it."). In the other agent comprehension question, the experimenter asked the child to first choose a puppet and then enact the event (e.g., "Now the [puppet]. He's going to pilk. He's pilking. Show me he is pilking."). Both the production questions and the comprehension questions presented in the test phase (child-agent or other-agent first) were presented in a random order.

Given the difference between comprehension and production task demands, the data from each of these was analyzed separately. We first examined children's comprehension of the new verbs using a 2 (Verb: transitive, intransitive) by 2 (Agent Training: other, self) by 2 (Question at Test: other, self) repeated measures ANOVA; the dependent measure was the mean number of events enacted correctly at test. The analysis revealed a trend for Question, $F(1, 23) = 4.02$, $p < .06$, and a significant Agent by Question interaction, $F(1, 23) = 5.24$, $p < .05$. A post-hoc test with Bonferroni corrections revealed that when children initially heard a new verb that referred to their own actions, they were better at responding to questions that referred to their own actions than questions that referred to another agent's actions, $t(23) = 2.51$, $p = .02$ (see table 12.3). This was not true of the verbs in which children saw a puppet agent (i.e., in this case, they were able to respond to either question type). A similar analysis of the production data revealed a significant main effect of Question, $F(1, 23) = 6.27$, $p < .05$. In the production test, children were more likely to produce a new verb when they were asked a question with a puppet as the agent.

We found no effect or interaction of verb type suggesting that transitive verbs did not differ from intransitive verbs in this task (which was similar to the tasks used in Studies 1 and 2). In addition, there was no main effect of agent during training suggesting that, overall, children did not learn these actions better when the verbs were produced when the child was the agent as opposed to when the experimenter was the agent. In the comprehension task, children showed more flexibility if they were not the agent when they learned the new verb. In production, children were more likely to produce the verb (in response to the test question) if the experimenter was the agent, perhaps because they could focus on their productions.

Could these results simply stem from the methodological decision to use a puppet as an agent for the other-agent condition? Note that this choice does not

Table 12.3 Results of Study 3

	Question Type	
Task Agent	Child	Other
Comprehension Child	1.2 (.78)	.7 (.81)
Other	1.0 (.75)	1.1 (.61)
Production Child	.7 (.87)	1.0 (.81)
Other	.8 (.72)	1.0 (.83)

Table 12.3 shows the mean number of trials (s.d.) children comprehended or produced the novel verb out of two ($N = 24$).

directly bear on the important findings Study 3 provides for Studies 1 and 2. The tasks are similar during the learning and test phase in all 3 studies, and Study 3 shows that the use of puppets during the learning phase or test phase does not greatly influence results given these tasks. In addition, the use of puppets does not bear directly on the transitive/intransitive results. The use of a puppet as other agent only has bearing on the ability of the results in Study 3 to address the self-other agent distinction more generally. On the one hand, this use allowed us to present the verbs in a similar way and test for comprehension and production using the same methodology. On the other hand, the child in the comprehension task was always the actual agent because he or she needed to serve as agent in some way to complete the enactments (i.e., in the other-agent comprehension enactment, the child demonstrated using a puppet: "Show me he is pilking.").

Previous research has suggested that children learn new verbs that refer to their own actions before verbs that refer to other agent's actions (e.g., Huttenlocher et al., 1983). However, previous studies have focused on familiar verbs and may have been influenced by many factors including the number of exposures children had with particular agents and these verbs. Children may often hear verbs that refer to their own actions, but our study shows that if they are exposed equally to other agents, they are just as able to learn verbs to refer to these agents' actions—at least from 26 months of age. Importantly, given the similarity in children's responses to transitive and intransitive verbs as well, it is less likely that the findings in Studies 1 and 2 are a product of the particular types of verbs presented, and more likely that the same results also would be found in studies including other verb types.

General Discussion

Our first two studies are two of only a handful of studies (Oviatt, 1980; Schwartz & Leonard, 1984) that have directly compared noun and verb learning in the same study systematically controlling the number of exposures in the laboratory. The results from both Studies 1 and 2 suggest that, all things being equal, 2-year-olds show a more robust ability to learn new nouns as compared to verbs. Thus, we have presented two studies with converging results that support the same conclusion. Moreover, Study 2 is the first study to equate noun and verb conditions in terms of task (children see dynamic events in both conditions) and sentence type (new words are embedded in longer sentences in both conditions), and thus it provides the strongest evidence to date suggesting that nouns are easier to learn than are verbs.

In Study 1, 2.5-year-olds were able to comprehend nouns and verbs across a variety of timing conditions. These children could produce both new nouns and new verbs in what could be thought of as the ideal learning condition—distributed exposures to the new word over about a week. However, they also were able to produce new nouns in less ideal conditions—including a condition in which exposures to the new word are separated by days—but had trouble producing new verbs in these less ideal conditions. This tendency to be less vulnerable to various factors, but only in noun learning, was mirrored in the comprehension findings in Study 2. In Study 2, at 2 years, children had difficulty comprehending new verbs in less ideal learning contexts while showing an ability to comprehend new nouns in these contexts. Taken together, these results show a developmental progression in children's ability to learn new words, as well as providing additional evidence concerning the specific conditions in which nouns are advantaged. That is, younger 2-year-olds may comprehend nouns with fewer exposures as compared to verbs, which may help them to then learn to produce these nouns by 2.5 years with fewer exposures, or greater delays between exposures, as well.

There are differences in noun/verb productions across languages. Experimental studies that control the number and timing of exposures to nouns and verbs in the laboratory, and that include other languages are needed. Children learning English, Italian, and Spanish appear to especially favor nouns (object words) as opposed to other word types in their early vocabularies (Au, Dapretto, & Song, 1994; Gentner, 1982; Jackson-Maldonado et al., 1993; Tardif et al., 1997, 1999) while children acquiring Mandarin Chinese (Tardif, 1996; Tardif et al., 1997, 1999) and perhaps Korean (Gopnik & Choi, 1995; see also Au et al., 1994; Kim et al., 2000) are not as heavily "noun biased."

These differences across languages could be due to differences in linguistic factors between languages, including differences in the morphological complexity of nouns and verbs, as well as cultural factors, including the frequency with which caregivers appear to label objects or talk about actions. For example, in Mandarin, verbs are marked for aspect but not person or number, and the marking for aspect is found in a separate morpheme that does not change the stem (Tardif et al., 1997). Thus, the verb morphology system in Mandarin may be highly transparent (Slobin, 1973) to the child, which may promote verb learning in Mandarin. In addition, Mandarin- and perhaps Korean-speaking parents do not appear to spend as much time focusing on object labels as do English-speaking parents (Gopnik & Choi, 1995; Tardif et al., 1997, 1999). English-speaking parents appear to spend a fair amount of time labeling objects and reading picture books, both of which could promote noun learning (Fernald & Morikawa, 1993; Goldfield, 1993). However, if frequency was the only factor facilitating noun learning, in our study in which frequency was held constant, children should have learned both nouns and verbs, and they did not. Of course our English-speaking children may have been especially practiced in the learning of new nouns as compared to verbs and so studies of this type including children learning other languages are needed.

In addition to linguistic factors (e.g., morphological complexity) and cultural factors (e.g., frequency), there remains a cognitive explanation for the dominance of nouns in early vocabularies. Gentner's (1982) proposal and more recent expansion (Gentner & Boroditsky, 2001) suggests that words for concrete objects should emerge earlier in development because the objects themselves are highly coherent and can be preindividuated and the words that refer to these objects primarily function to denote specific entities by themselves. In contrast, events are conceptualized in different ways across languages, and verbs and other relational terms depend on other words in sentences (e.g., arguments) for meaning. We provide some evidence of the difference between understanding an action and learning a verb in the nonverbal action condition in Study 1. In that study, children were able to demonstrate both new nonverbal actions and new actions that had been accompanied by verbs but had difficulty verbally producing a new verb. Therefore, connecting new verbs to new actions appeared to be more of a problem than was understanding (or packaging) the new actions themselves. Of course it is possible that attending to a new action is so cognitively demanding that children have trouble also attending to the new verb, and this difficulty would fit with Gentner's (1982; Gentner & Boroditsky, 2001) hypotheses. However, our studies demonstrate that the difference between noun and verb learning not only is a difference in understanding objects and events in and of themselves but lies in children's ability to connect new words to these events.

Studies of children's spontaneous speech and parental reports of early vocabularies are important. However, a new focus of word learning researchers could be to begin to investigate more carefully in the laboratory the specific conditions under which children are able to learn nouns or verbs. By gathering more experimental evidence demonstrating when and how children learn nouns compared to verbs, we can then draw inferences about the cognitive difficulties children may face. We have shown that if one wanted a 2- or 2.5-year-old English-hearing child to learn a new noun, it could be presented on a single day (eight exposures) for comprehension or on at least 3 days (that do not have to be consecutive) for production. To teach a child a new verb, a 2.5-year-old need only have the chance to be exposed to that verb on a single day (eight exposures) to begin to comprehend that verb (and this is not enough for a 2-year-old), but needs to hear that verb repeated on consecutive days for about a week to be able to reliably produce that verb. These facts of language learning support a view in which noun learning is more robust and less vulnerable to variations in presentations than is verb learning, perhaps because objects are conceptually "easier" to package.

Acknowledgments Funding for this research was provided in part by a grant from the National Institutes of Health (1R15HD044447-01) to the first author and a second grant from the National Institutes of Health (HD 35854-01) to the second author. We would like to thank Patty Chen, Anna Ciao, Elaine Heard, Jennifer Roscetti, Amanda Snook, and Ignae Thomas for their assistance in data collection and coding. We are also grateful to the parents and children who participated in the studies and the teachers and directors at Alamo Heights Presbyterian Day School, First Presbyterian Church Children's Center, Laurel Heights United Methodist Children's Center, and the University Presbyterian Church Children's Center.

References

Au, T. K., Dapretto, M., & Song, Y. (1994). Input vs. constraints: Early word acquisition in Korean and English. *Journal of Child Language, 33,* 567–582.

Behrend, D. (1990). The development of verb concepts: Children's use of verbs to label familiar and novel events. *Child Development, 61,* 681–696.

Benedict, H. (1979). Early lexical development: Comprehension and production. *Journal of Child Language, 6,* 183–200.

Carey, S., & Bartlett, E. (1978). Acquiring a single new word. *Papers and Reports on Child Language Development, 15,* 17–29.

Caselli, M. C., Casadio, P., & Bates, E. (1999). A comparison of the transition from first words to grammar in English and Italian. *Journal of Child Language, 26,* 69-111.

Childers, J. B., & Tomasello, M. (2002). Two-year-olds learn novel nouns, verbs, and conventional actions from massed or spaced exposures. *Developmental Psychology, 38,* 967–978.

Childers, J. B., & Tomasello, M. (2003). Children extend both words and non-verbal actions to novel exemplars. *Developmental Science, 6,* 185–190.

Dempster, F. (1996). Distributing and managing the conditions of encoding and practice. In E. Bjork & R. Bjork (Eds.), *Handbook of perception and cognition* (2nd ed., pp. 317–344). New York: Academic Press.

Edwards, D., & Goodwin, R. (1986). Action words and pragmatic function in early language. In S. A. Kuczaj & M. D. Barrett (Eds.), *The development of word meaning: Progress in cognitive development research* (pp. 257–273). New York: Springer-Verlag.

Fenson, L., Dale, P., Reznick, J. S., Bates, E., Thal, D., & Pethick, S. J. (1994). Variability in early communicative development. *Monographs of the Society for Research in Child Development, 59,* v–173.

Fernald, A., & Morikawa, H. (1993). Common themes and cultural variations in Japanese and American mothers' speech to infants. *Child Development, 64,* 637–56.

Forbes, J. N., & Farrar, M. J. (1993). Children's initial assumptions about the meaning of novel motion verbs: Biased and conservative? *Cognitive Development, 8,* 273–290.

Forbes, J. N., & Farrar, M. J. (1995). Learning to represent word meaning: What initial training events reveal about children's developing action concepts. *Cognitive Development, 10,* 1–20.

Gentner, D. (1982). Why nouns are learned before verbs: Linguistic relativity versus natural partitioning. In S. A. Kuczaj, II (Ed.), *Language development: Vol. 2. Language, thought and culture* (pp. 301–344). Hillsdale, NJ: Erlbaum.

Gentner, D., & Boroditsky, L. (2001). Individuation, relativity, and early word learning. In M. Bowerman & S. C. Levinson (Eds.), *Language acquisition and conceptual development* (pp. 215–256). Cambridge: Cambridge University Press.

Goldfield, B. A. (1993). Noun bias in maternal speech to one-year-olds. *Journal of Child Language, 20,* 85–99.

Goldin-Meadow, S., Seligman, M., & Gelman, R. (1976). Language in the two-year-old. *Cognition, 4,* 189–202.

Golinkoff, R. M., Hirsh-Pasek, K., & Mervis, C. B. (1995). Lexical principles can be extended to the acquisition of verbs. In M. Tomasello & W. E. Merriman (Eds.), *Beyond names for things: Young children's acquisition of verbs* (pp. 185–221). Hillsdale, NJ: Erlbaum.

Golinkoff, R. M., Jacquet, R. C., Hirsh-Pasek, K., & Nandakumar, R. (1996). Lexical principles may underlie the learning of verbs. *Child Development, 67,* 3101–3119.

Golinkoff, R. M., Mervis, C. B., & Hirsh-Pasek, K. (1994). Early object labels: The case for a developmental lexical principles framework. *Journal of Child Language, 21,* 125–155.

Gopnik, A., & Choi, S. (1995). Names, relational words, and cognitive development in English and Korean speakers: Nouns are not always learned before verbs. In M. Tomasello & W. E. Merriman (Eds.), *Beyond names for things: Young children's acquisition of verbs* (pp. 63–80). Hillsdale, NJ: Erlbaum.

Hirsh-Pasek, K., & Golinkoff, R. M. (1996). *The origins of grammar: Evidence from early language comprehension.* Cambridge, MA: MIT Press.

Huttenlocher, J., Smiley, P., & Charney, R. (1983). Emergence of action categories in the child: Evidence from verb meanings. *Psychological Review, 90,* 72–93.

Jackson-Maldonado, D., Thal, D., Marchman, V., Bates, E., & Gutierrez-Clellen, V. (1993). Early lexical development in Spanish-speaking infants and toddlers. *Journal of Child Language, 20,* 523–549.

Jones, S., Landau, B., & Smith, L. B. (1992). Syntactic context and the shape bias in children's and adults' lexical learning. *Journal of Memory and Language, 31,* 807–825.

Kim, M., McGregor, K. K., & Thompson, C. K. (2000). Early lexical development in English- and Korean-speaking children: Language-general and language-specific patterns. *Journal of Child Language, 27,* 225–254.

Markman, E. M. (1990). Constraints children place on word mearnings. *Cognitive Science, 14,* 57–77.

Markson, L. (1999). *Mechanisms of word learning in children.* Unpublished doctoral dissertation, University of Arizona.

Markson, L., & Bloom, P. (1997). Evidence against a dedicated system for word learning in children. *Nature, 385,* 813–815.

Merriman, W. E., Marazita, J., & Jarvis, L. (1995). Children's disposition to map new words onto new referents. In M. Tomasello & W. E. Merriman (Eds.), *Beyond names for things: Young children's acquisition of verbs* (pp. 147–183). Hillsdale, NJ: Lawrence Erlbaum.

Naigles, L. G. (1990). Children use syntax to learn verb meanings. *Journal of Child Language, 17,* 357–374.

Olguin, R., & Tomasello, M. (1993). Twenty-five-month-old children do not have a grammatical category of verb. *Cognitive Development, 8,* 245–272.

Oviatt, S. (1980). The emerging ability to comprehend language. *Child Development, 51,* 97–106.

Roberts, K. (1983). Comprehension and production of word order in Stage 1. *Child Development, 54,* 443–449.

Rosch, E., & Mervis, C. B. (1975). Family resemblances: Studies in the internal structure of categories. *Cognitive Psychology, 7,* 573–605.

Schwartz, R. G., & Leonard, L. B. (1984). Words, objects, and actions in early lexical acquisition. *Journal of Speech and Hearing Research, 27,* 119–127.

Schwartz, R., & Terrell, B. (1983). The role of input frequency in lexical acquisition. *Journal of Child Language, 10,* 57–66.

Slobin, D. I. (1973). Cognitive prerequisites for the development of grammar. In C. A. Ferguson & D. I. Slobin (Eds.), *Studies of child language development* (pp. 175–208). New York: Springer.

Slobin, D. I. (1985). Crosslinguistic evidence for the language-making capacity. In D. I. Slobin (Ed.), *The crosslinguistic study of language acquisition: Vol. 2. Theoretical issues* (pp. 1157–1249). Hillsdale, NJ: Lawrence Erlbaum.

Tardif, T. (1996). Nouns are not always learned before verbs: Evidence from Mandarin speakers' early vocabularies. *Developmental Psychology, 32,* 492–504.

Tardif, T., Gelman, S. A., & Xu, F. (1999). Putting the noun bias in context: A comparison of English and Mandarin. *Child Development, 70,* 620–635.

Tardif, T., Shatz, M., & Naigles, L. (1997). Caregiver speech and children's use of nouns versus verbs: A comparison of English, Italian and Mandarin. *Journal of Child Language, 24,* 535–65.

Tomasello, M. (1992). *First verbs: A case study of early grammatical development.* New York: Cambridge University Press.

Tomasello, M. (1995). Pragmatic contexts for early verb learning. In M. Tomasello & W. E. Merriman (Eds.), *Beyond names for things: Young children's acquisition of verbs* (pp. 115–146). Hillsdale, NJ: Erlbaum.

Tomasello, M. (2003). *Constructing a language.* Cambridge, MA: Harvard University Press.

Tomasello, M., & Akhtar, N. (1995). Two-year-olds use pragmatic cues to differentiate reference to objects and actions. *Cognitive Development, 10,* 201–224.

Tomasello, M., & Kruger, A. (1992). Joint attention on actions: Acquiring verbs in ostensive and non-ostensive contexts. *Journal of Child Language, 19,* 311–333.

Tomasello, M., & Merriman, W. E. (1995). *Beyond names for things: Young children's acquisition of verbs.* Hillsdale, NJ: Erlbaum.

Underwood, B. (1961). Ten years of massed practice on distributed practice. *Psychological Review, 68,* 229–247.

Waxman, S. R., & Booth, A. (2000). Principles that are invoked in the acquisition of words, but not facts. *Cognition, 77,* B33–B43.

Waxman, S. R., & Markow, D. B. (1995). Words as invitations to form categories: Evidence from 12- to 13-month-old infants. *Cognitive Psychology, 29,* 257–302.

Woodward, A., Markman, E., & Fitzsimmons, C. (1994). Rapid word learning in 13- and 18-month-olds. *Developmental Psychology, 30,* 533–566.

13   Verbs at the Very Beginning: Parallels Between Comprehension and Input

Letitia R. Naigles and Erika Hoff

In the process of acquiring the verbs of their language, young children must go beyond the information given. That is, they must become able to extend the verbs they hear to new settings and new uses. For example, the child who hears his mother tell him not to run must come to know that *run* refers to both his own slow, effortful running and the swifter motion of the older child on the block. Similarly, the child must realize that *eating* refers both to what he does to Cheerios and what the sea lion at the zoo does to fish. With respect to uses, the child must come to know that different agents can run and eat, and that eating can to be done to different things. In this chapter, we address two questions concerning this ability to extend verb meanings past their attested instances. First, when in the course of verb learning do verb meanings become extendable? We present new data concerning 1-year-olds' ability (as well as the lack thereof) to extend familiar verbs to new instances. Second, given that limits to extendability are observable early in verb acquisition (see also Bloom, 2000; Dromi, 1987; Golinkoff, Mervis, & Hirsh-Pasek, 1995; Mervis, Golinkoff, & Hirsh-Pasek, 1991), we look for causes of these limits in children's input. We present new data on the nature of children's verb input which suggests that children's early conservatism may indeed have its roots in how verbs are used by adults, but these roots are neither direct nor transparent. Last, we present these data on children's early verb comprehension and experience as an exploration which probes the limits of current methodology to answer these questions.

The Nature of Children's Verb Meanings During Their Second Year of Life

Evidence From Production

The first thing to note about 1-year-olds' verbs is their existence. That is, even if nouns are the largest category of lexical items from the onset of word learning, there are always at least some verbs present in children's speech as well (Bloom, Tinker, & Margulis, 1993). In fact, diaries have revealed quite extensive verb use—both in terms of types and tokens—before children's second birthdays, on the order of 100+ verb types produced (Braunwald, 1995; Clark, 1996; Tomasello, 1992). What does this early verb use imply about early verb knowledge?

Most descriptions of 1-year-olds' verb use are lists of verbs that children have produced, either spontaneously (Benedict, 1979; Clark, 1996; Marchman & Bates, 1994; Tomasello & Kruger, 1992) or elicited (Goldin-Meadow, Seligman, & Gelman, 1976). While such lists indicate the range of actions and relations that children can talk about, they do not provide information about children's specific, and possibly idiosyncratic, meanings when they produce verbs. In contrast, Huttenlocher, Smiley, and Charney (1983), Braunwald (1995), and Smiley and Huttenlocher (1995) have reported more detailed analyses of children's early verb meanings, all of which suggest that at least some early verb meanings are context-restricted rather than adult-like. In particular, Huttenlocher, Smiley, and Charney (1983) analyzed the spontaneous speech of eight children whose mean length of utterance (MLU) ranged from 1.4 to 1.8 and found that 90% of their verb-containing utterances were produced when the child, as opposed to a parent or other animate agent, was participating in the action. Thus, they concluded that children's first verb meanings refer specifically to self-involved action and do not include actions produced by others. Subsequently, Smiley and Huttenlocher (1995) gathered monthly 5-hour samples of spontaneous speech from 1-year-olds over the 6-month period from 13 to 19 months and analyzed the children's uses of four verbs (in addition to other relational terms), *open, ride, sit,* and *rock.* All of these verbs appeared to be used more commonly with self-initiated than other-initiated action, corroborating the early Huttenlocher, Smiley, and Charney finding of restricted usage; however, Smiley and Huttenlocher also reported that both *rock* and *ride* were used in reference to the movements of both objects and people, suggesting some extendability. For example, *ride* was used to describe both the movement of objects and the movement of people on objects. Unfortunately, Smiley and Huttenlocher did not distinguish between children's initial versus later uses of the verbs within the 6-month period, so it is not clear when such extendability to different agents occurred. Finally, Braunwald (1995) kept diaries of the verb use of her two daughters J and L. While most of their early verbs appeared to be used in conventional ways, one of L's first verbs, *cry,* was used quite idiosyncratically (e.g., "hi cry," "lola [pacifier] cry," pp. 93–94).

opposite of generalization?

In sum, all three studies report instances of context-restricted verb use by 1-year-olds. The most common type of underextension seems to involve a restriction of the agent or experiencer of the action; that is, verbs are initially applied preferentially to self-involved action. It is also important to point out, though, that context-restricted verb use is by no means total, even by 1-year-olds. Each study reports some verbs that are extended to multiple actors.

Evidence From Comprehension

Many researchers who studied children's early verb productions also tested verb comprehension in the same children. These tests typically revealed that the children understood more verbs than they were currently producing (Benedict, 1979; Goldfield, 2000; Goldin-Meadow et al., 1976; Smith & Sachs, 1990). However, these tests are not very informative concerning our question of the extendability of 1-year-olds' verbs, because the comprehension task usually involved asking the children themselves to enact the verbs with familiar props (e.g., "Eat the cookie"). Successful performance on such a task does not reveal whether the children can extend *eating* or *pushing* to agents other than themselves, or to patients not previously encountered, or to manners of eating or pushing heretofore unobserved.

More recently, researchers have used the intermodal preferential looking paradigm (IPL) to assess children's comprehension of verbs used in novel contexts. The IPL enables the presentation of two dynamic video events that are paired with a single verb; the child need only select (via longer looking or pointing) the matching over the nonmatching event to demonstrate verb understanding. All tests of English verb comprehension using IPL to date have assessed, implicitly or explicitly, whether children can extend verbs to new actors (agents, experiencers) and new settings because all of the events have presented actors different from the child participants themselves and settings different from the child participants' experiences. No studies have yet tested—at least explicitly—when children can extend verbs to novel patients or themes.

Huttenlocher, Smiley, and Charney (1983) launched the literature on comprehension of familiar verbs in novel contexts. In their first study, 10 verb pairs were presented, either both movement verbs (e.g., *jump, blow*) or both change verbs (e.g., *bring, put down*). Children saw each pair up to four times and were tested on the same verb each time (e.g., "One is *jump* and one is *blow*. Which one is *blow*? Point."). Only those children who responded correctly all four times received credit for comprehension. The results indicated that movement verbs were successfully understood earlier than change verbs. Huttenlocher et al. did not distinguish the performance of the youngest children (under 30 months of age) from the older children (up to 42 months of age), but even those children with generally poor comprehension performed better with the movement verbs. In general, then, children as young as 22 months of age (the youngest age tested) were able to distinguish some movement verbs performed by unfamiliar actors. In their second

high freq
?

study, children were tested every 1 to 2 months during their second year on com-prehension of seven verbs, *wave, sit, run, kick, jump, put down,* and *get.* The action foils for each verb were not reported; the focus of the study concerned whether the children performed correctly first in the IPL test (with novel actors), or first in an act-out test (with the children themselves as actors). Huttenlocher et al. found that the children demonstrated successful comprehension earlier with the act-out task than with the IPL task, and they concluded that children's earliest verb mean-ings refer primarily to their own actions and are only later extended to the actions of others.

Three subsequent studies have corroborated Huttenlocher, Smiley, and Char-ney's findings, that one-year-olds can distinguish some English verbs. Golinkoff, Hirsh-Pasek, Cauley, and Gordon (1987) tested familiar verb comprehension in 16-month-olds using IPL; they (and all subsequent studies using this method) measured the duration of children's visual fixations rather than their points at the matching screen. Six pairs of actions were presented and six verbs were tested; the test audio was similar in form to that of Huttenlocher, Smiley, and Charney (1983). Golinkoff et al. (1987) reported significant longer looking to the matching screen for only three verbs, *wave, eat,* and *bounce* (but not *turn, drink,* and *clap*). Naigles (1997) tested 17.5-month-olds' comprehension of three pairs of motion verbs (*crawl* paired with *walk, run* paired with *roll,* and *slide* paired with *jump*). Each action in a pair was presented in the same context (e.g., rolling vs. running down the same hill, sliding vs. jumping into the same pool). The test audios were potentially more difficult, though, as these simply asked "Where is running?" dur-ing the test trials without labeling both actions first. Naigles reported significantly longer looking to the matching screen by these 17-month-olds for only one verb, *roll* (27-month-olds successfully comprehended all six verbs).

Forbes and Poulin-Dubois (1997) investigated whether 20-month-olds could extend a familiar verb when aspects of its action had changed. They presented two verb-action pairs for familiarization and then tested whether the children could match the verbs (*kick, pick up*) when the actions had new agents, new manners, or new outcomes. The children were able to distinguish the verbs even when the ac-tions were carried out by new agents, but were unsuccessful with new manners and new outcomes (26-month-olds were also successful with new manners). More recent findings suggest that this ability to extend to new agents is still fragile, though: When trained with novel verbs, 19- to 21-month-olds were unsuccessful at extending these to new actors (Maguire et al., 2002; Poulin-Dubois & Forbes, 2002).

These assessments of 1-year-olds' verb meanings converge on two conclu-sions: (1) early verb meanings are extended, but (2) there are limits on extendabil-ity. That is, each study demonstrated some verb comprehension (on average, one to three verbs), which implicates extendability because certainly the agents and possibly the patients and manners of the actions were different from the chil-dren's previous experience with those verbs. Conversely, though, each study also demonstrated a lack of comprehension with the majority of the verbs tested, thereby implicating a lack of extendability because the children were unable to match common verbs with these new instances of their referent actions. Huttenlocher, Smiley, and Charney (1983) and Forbes and Poulin-Dubois (1997) directly manipulated the actors of each verb; their findings suggest that the primary difficulty lies in extending a verb's actions to new actors. Golinkoff et al. (1987) and Naigles (1997) presented actions that may have differed from the children's previous experience on a number of dimensions. Children's failure to demonstrate comprehension in these studies suggests also that several aspects of the action may be underextended in the verb.

Further complicating the picture of early verb knowledge, comparison of findings across studies also reveals some curious within-verb differences. Verbs that appeared to be easy to comprehend in one study seemed difficult in another. Only Huttenlocher, Smiley, and Charney (1983) tested a large enough set of verbs such that cross-study comparisons of specific verbs could be made; therefore, their verb list with the proportion of children who were correct on each verb (table 3, p. 81) will be the standard against which the findings of the other studies are compared. Differences between studies in ease of acquisition emerge in all three cross-study comparisons. First, Forbes and Poulin-Dubois (1997) reported reliable comprehension of both *kick* and *pick up* with their toddlers, whereas Huttenlocher et al. reported that *kick* was comprehended much better than *pick up*. Second, Golinkoff et al. (1987) found reliable comprehension with *wave*, *bounce*, and *eat*, but not *turn*, whereas Huttenlocher et al. grouped the former two verbs as consistently easier than the latter two. Third, Huttenlocher et al. found that *run*, *walk*, and *jump* were among their easiest verbs, whereas Naigles (1997) did not find reliable comprehension for any of the three. Certainly, the actual stimuli varied across each of these studies; however, each set of researchers also made concerted efforts to ensure that their stimuli were representative of the usual meaning of each verb. One question, then, concerns whether this inconsistency across studies is a mere methodological glitch or is symptomatic of a deeper difficulty in the study of early verb acquisition.

Overall, the research on children's early verb use—including studies of both production and comprehension—supports the claim for some limits on the extendability of children's early verbs. Clearly, children are not able to use or understand their verbs with a wide range of actors, patients, or manners. Given that these limitations exist, the next question we address concerns their causes.

Causes of Under-Extended Verb Meanings

Three causes of limited extendability have been proposed: the absence of a principle of extendability that applies to the class of verbs (Golinkoff, Hirsh-Pasek, Mervis, Frawley, & Parillo, 1995; Mervis et al., 1991), restricted input with the verbs children know (Huttenlocher, Smiley, & Charney, 1983; Smiley & Hutten-locher, 1995), and restricted conceptual underpinnings of verb meanings (Huttenlocher et al., 1983). Mervis et al. (1991) included a principle of extendability in their first tier of word learning principles; the absence of this principle in very young word learners was posited to explain why such children underextended their very first words (e.g., Harris, Barrett, Jones, & Brooks, 1988). Because toddlers begin to extend their *nouns* to new instances before they do so with *verbs* (e.g., Golinkoff et al., 1987; Fernald, Pinto, Swingley, Weinberg, & McRoberts, 1998), Golinkoff et al. (1995) postulated that the principle of extendability needed to be "reacquired" for verbs. The argument was that the relevant extendable meaning components for verbs (e.g., manner and outcome of action, actor, theme) were different from those for nouns (e.g., shape, size, and color of object). Yet because all studies to date of 1-year-olds' verb comprehension have yielded evidence of some extendability, it is not clear that a principle is lacking. What needs to be explained is not the complete absence of extendability, but instead its limited or restricted application.

In one attempt to explain early limitations on verb extendability, children's verb input has been compared with their noun input (recall that verb extendability typically emerges later in development than noun extendability). In all of these comparisons, verbs appear to be presented in less straightforward fashions than nouns. For example, Tomasello and Kruger (1992) analyzed maternal talk during dyadic toy play and found that whereas mothers commonly presented nouns while actually pointing to their referents, they frequently presented verbs just before the actions were performed. Similarly, Clark and Wong (2002) performed a detailed analysis of six corpora from the CHILDES database (MacWhinney, 2000), focusing on parents' explicit offers of new or unfamiliar words (e.g., "That's a jaguar" or "What is she doing?"). Fully 84% of all such explicit offers referred to nouns and only 5% referred to verbs, suggesting that verbs are offered to children in much less direct ways. Finally, Tardif, Gelman, and Xu (1999) compared the number of verbs and nouns produced when mothers were reading books and engaged in toy play with mechanical toys, blocks, stuffed animals, and vehicles. Tardif et al. found that mothers produced the most nouns when engaged in book reading, and they produced significantly more verbs than nouns when engaged in play with mechanical toys. In sum, when compared with noun input, verb input seems less clear (verbs do not coincide temporally with their referent actions) and explicit (verbs are rarely introduced directly), as well as more contextually variable (verbs are more likely to be used when playing with specific types of toys). The different training experiences may contribute to children's reluctance to extend verbs to new instances when they are already extending nouns (see also Goldfield, 2000; Sandofer, Smith, & Luo, 2000).

Input differences that might account for limitations on extendability have also been observed *within* the domain of verbs. For example, verbs differ in the frequency with which they are produced by caregivers and children appear to be sensitive to such frequency differences. Naigles and Hoff-Ginsberg (1998) found that verbs that were used more frequently by mothers when children were just beginning multiword speech were the same words that the children produced more frequently 10 weeks later (see also Choi & Gopnick, 1995). Of course, frequency of use by children does not directly implicate the ability to extend verbs, as early frequent uses could simply be repetitions of the same form-meaning relation. However, Naigles and Hoff-Ginsberg also investigated an aspect of children's verb use that was closely related to extendability; namely, the use of verbs in different sentence frames (so-called syntactic diversity). Verbs that are more syntactically diverse are more likely to be used in reference to different aspects of actions; for example, utterances including *eat* in different frames, such as "Doggie eats hamburger," "Doggie eats noisily," and "Doggie ate it up," extend *eat* with a different theme, manner, and outcome, respectively. Naigles and Hoff-Ginsberg (1998) found that maternal input influenced children's extendability qua syntactic diversity, in that verbs which were used more frequently and with greater syntactic diversity by mothers were more likely to be used in more syntactically diverse utterances by their children 10 weeks later.

Naigles and Hoff-Ginsberg's (1998) findings suggest that children are paying attention to verb frequency and syntactic diversity in their input and that these properties of input assist children in extending their verbs to new instances. However, Huttenlocher and her colleagues (Huttenlocher, Smiley, & Charney, 1983; Smiley & Huttenlocher, 1995) have observed some limitations to the role of input frequency in accounting for children's verb extendability. Recall that Huttenlocher et al. found, in both production and comprehension, that children seem to use their verbs preferentially to refer to their own actions rather than others' actions. At first blush, this preference could be attributed to the children's input: In their analyses of child-directed speech, Huttenlocher, Smiley, and Charney (see also Huttenlocher, Smiley, & Ratner, 1983) reported that parents of 24-month-olds used verbs more frequently to refer to the child's action than another's action. However, two aspects of this input did not match the children's output. First, the ratio of verbs describing child-initiated to other-initiated action was 2:1 in the input but 9:1 in the children's productions. Huttenlocher et al. argued that if children were just following their input, this child-action bias should not be so pronounced (but see Singleton & Newport, 2004, for evidence in the grammatical domain of children's output demonstrating more pronounced regularization than their input). Second, in the input, this child-action bias was greater for movement verbs than for change verbs; however, in their output children referred to themselves more when using change verbs than when using movement verbs. These inconsistencies between maternal input and child output led Huttenlocher and her colleagues to propose that children's early verb meanings preferentially refer to their own actions because of their conceptual limitations. That is, they first represent action concepts—and so verb meanings—in terms of themselves and only later become able to extend those concepts and verb meanings to the actions of others.

Two primary causes, then, can be implicated in children's initial limitations on verb extendability: One is the child's own conceptual limits, perhaps an initial inability to see similarities between her own and others' actions. The second is the children's input, perhaps being less informative in the relevant ways for verbs than for nouns. Notice, though, that the first cause was proposed just because of the perceived failure of the second: Huttenlocher, Smiley, and Ratner's (1983) analyses showed that children's input did not match their own verb uses. Yet it is possible that this failure was viewed too broadly. For example, Huttenlocher et al.'s input data concerned subclasses of verbs, not individual verbs, so it is not clear whether the mismatch between input and child verb use existed for the same verbs. Moreover, it is not clear from Huttenlocher et al.'s analyses how input frequency and the child-action bias interacted; for example, verbs more frequent in the input might elicit considerable child verb use irrespective of their adherence to a child-action bias. Thus, questions remain concerning the extent to which children's verb use is a function of their input.

Summary and Prospectus

Converging evidence has indicated that children's early verb meanings are extendable but only to a limited extent. That is, in comprehension paradigms where extendability is assessed directly, the majority of verbs tested are not well understood by 1-year-olds. Furthermore, the exact verbs that are well understood at this age varies considerably from study to study. Converging evidence from studies of children's input indicates that the speech they hear may be at least partly responsible for this limited extendability, as verbs are presented overall less clearly than nouns, and some verbs are presented in more diverse ways than others. However, the link between children's input and their restricted verb meanings is not yet straightforward and direct. In particular, no studies have yet investigated whether the exact verbs that are used in restricted or unclear ways by adults are the same ones that are extended less by children. Here we present two research efforts aimed at elucidating (a) the nature of the verb input 1-year-old children receive and (b) the extendability of many of those same verbs in 1-year-olds' lexicons.

Study 1: The Frequency of Early-Acquired Verbs in Child-Directed Speech

The initial goal of Study 1 was to document the use in child-directed speech of the same verbs whose comprehension would be tested in Study 3—albeit in other children. In our first effort to do this we armed ourselves with a varied collection of toys and visited four mothers with 14-month-old children. We gave some thought to the particular toys we brought, seeking to provide occasions for the use of the verbs whose frequency we sought to document (e.g., mechanical toys to elicit more verbs overall, a ball for the verb *roll*, etc.). The only structure we provided was to ask the mothers to play with the toys with their children, and we asked to observe a mealtime. It was immediately clear that this first effort was failing to provide us with a representative sample of the "child input" we sought to describe. Verbs that we know appear early in children's vocabularies (such as *kiss*) did not appear at all in our samples (we were not there for family members' departures or for bedtimes). Also, we heard *roll* from one mother who liked rolling a ball with her child and we heard no examples of *roll* from a mother who chose not to play with the ball at all.

At this point, we had discovered what remains the central finding of these input studies—that the frequency with which (at least some) verbs are used is highly dependent on the situation. We remained interested, however, in documenting frequency and other parameters of verb use in input of early acquired verbs in order to provide companion data for the study of early verb comprehension. Thus, we found four new mothers with young children, we eliminated some verbs, such as *kiss*, from our target list, and we moved to a more controlled procedure. We describe that study and its findings below.

Method

The participants were four English-speaking monolingual caregivers with children between the ages of 13 and 15 months. Caregiver-child interaction was videotaped for a total of 140 minutes for each dyad over two days, yielding a combined speech sample over 9 hours in duration and including nearly 2,000 utterances. On each day of observation, the procedure for collecting speech samples was to provide the caregiver with seven different toys, one at a time to ensure that each toy was played with. The toys were a ball, a device for blowing bubbles, a pretend lawn mower that produced bubbles as it was pushed, plastic play food, and jack-in-the-box, a pop-up toy, and a child's tape recorder with a tape of songs. There were 17 targeted verbs: *blow, bounce, clap, drink, eat, jump, listen, look, push, roll, sing, sit, talk, throw, turn, walk,* and *wave.* From the videotape records, each caregiver utterance that contained a token of any of the target verbs was transcribed, and the toy being played with was noted.

Results

For these analyses, only the frequency of occurrence of each verb was calculated. Other aspects of input, though important (e.g., syntactic diversity), can only be assessed if the verbs occur at all, and the purpose of this study was to ascertain how frequently, and across what diversity of contexts, each verb occurred. The frequency of each verb in the entire speech sample, combined across mothers and toys, is presented in figure 13.1. The same frequency data presented by toy context are presented in figure 13.2 for those verbs with nonzero frequencies.

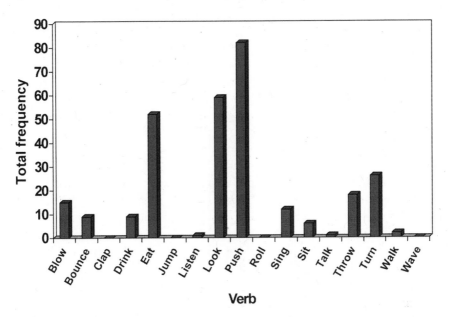

Figure 13.1. Total frequency of 17 early-acquired verbs in a 2,000-utterance corpus of speech addressed to 14-month-olds.

These data make two points about the nature of verb use in child-directed speech, which are cautions to those who would study the input young verb learners receive. The first point, made by the data presented in figure 13.1, is that even 9 hours of adult–child interaction is insufficient to produce a representative sample of usage for many verbs—verbs that we know must appear in input because children use them early in development. The frequencies of *clap, jump, roll,* and *wave* were zero, and fully half of our list of early-acquired verbs had frequencies in 9 hours of input that were lower than 10, suggesting that even for verbs that appear in a speech sample of this size, frequency estimates may be unreliable.

The second point, made by the data presented in figure 13.2, is that the frequency of many verbs is highly dependent on the context in which mother and child are interacting. The verb *drink* was used only in play with toy food; *sing* and *talk* were used only with the toy tape recorder; *throw* was used only with the ball. In fact, a total of 6 of the 13 attested verbs were restricted to use in one context. Other verbs, such as *eat, push,* and *turn,* were well distributed across at least three toy contexts. But it was also the case that diversity across contexts was not a guarantee of high usage: *walk* and *sit* appeared in multiple contexts but at low frequencies. Finally, the standout verb was *look,* which was both high in frequency in several contexts and appeared with at least some frequency in most contexts.

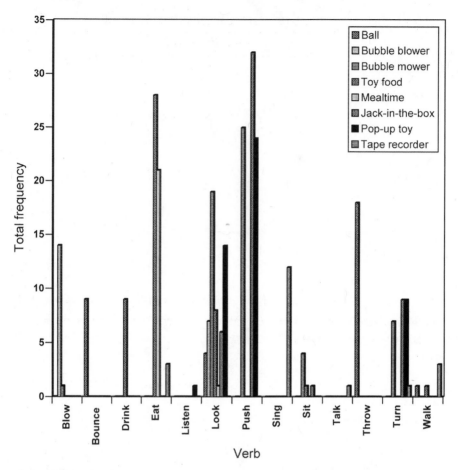

Figure 13.2. Total frequency of 17 early-acquired verbs by contexts of use.

Discussion

In sum, this exploratory study revealed that even very common verbs seem to be difficult to sample in child-directed speech, that the frequency of many verbs appeared to depend heavily on the particular toy being played with, and also that for a few verbs, frequency was both high and consistent across contexts. This latter finding seemed reminiscent of a distinction made by Rice and Bode (1993; see also Clark, 1993, 1996; Goldberg, 1999; Snedeker & Gleitman, 2004), between high-frequency verbs with general all-purpose meanings (so-called GAP verbs) and lower frequency verbs that might have more specialized meanings. Study 2, then, asked whether GAP and non-GAP verbs appeared differently in spontaneous speech, using a larger sample of mothers and more verbs. We also sought to

Table 13.1 GAP and non-GAP verbs

GAP Verbs	Non-GAP Verbs	
Come	Drop	Listen
Do	Fall	Move
Go	Give	Open
Get	Work	Pull
Look	Know	Push
Make	Jump	See
Need	Lay	Sit
Put	Lie	Take
Want	Like	Think
	Run	Wave

document the use of both motion verbs and those describing internal states. Finally, we also broadened the contexts investigated: in addition to mealtime and toy play, we assessed maternal verb use when dressing the child and when reading to him or her. Our question was, did frequency of verb use also differ across these broader contexts, and were different classes of verbs differentially affected by context?

Study 2: The Effect of Context of the Frequency of Verbs in Child-Directed Speech

Method

Transcripts of mother-child interaction that were collected as part of a larger study provided the database. The sample included 63 mothers and their 2-year-old children, who were videotaped in four different settings: mealtime, dressing, book reading, and toy play, for an average total of approximately 57 minutes of interaction and an average of 949 child-directed utterances ($M = 238$ per setting) for each dyad. Thirty verbs were identified as early-acquired verbs on the basis of previous research (Naigles & Hoff-Ginsberg, 1998). Nine of these were on Rice and Bode's (1993) list of GAP verbs and 19 were not. The GAP and non-GAP verbs are listed in table 13.1. The verbs were also categorized as describing motion or internal state (see table 13.2). Transcripts of the interactions were searched, using SALT (Miller & Chapman, 1985), for instances of those verbs.

Results

On average, the GAP verbs were more frequent than the non-GAP words. When all 30 verbs were ranked from highest to lowest frequency, the GAP verbs had a

Table 13.2 Motion and internal state verbs

Motion		Internal State
Come	Push	Think
Go	Put	Know
Lay	Pull	Need
Move	Lie	See
Sit	Run	Want
Open	Give	Look
Take	Drop	Like
Fall	Jump	Listen

mean rank of 8.4 and the non-GAP verbs had a mean rank of 19.1. Moreover, as Naigles and Hoff-Ginsberg (1995) previously reported with this dataset, the internal state verbs were more frequent (mean rank = 10) than the motion verbs (mean rank = 13.1). The rates of maternal use by setting for GAP and non-GAP verbs are presented in figure 13.3, and for internal and motion verbs in figure 13.4.

Visual inspection of figures 13.3 and 13.4 suggests that frequency of occurrence varies by setting. One-way repeated measures ANOVAs revealed significant effects of setting for each class of verbs (GAP, non-GAP, motion, and internal state; Fs [3, 165] range from 20.34 to 40.83, all $ps < .001$). The biggest effect of setting comes from the book-reading context: All four categories of verbs were most frequent during book reading, and 20 of the 30 individual verbs followed this pattern. Moreover, both GAP and internal state verbs were especially frequent

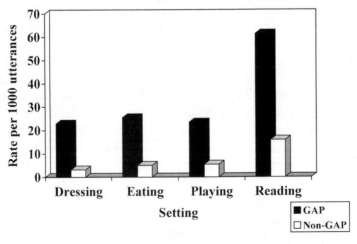

Figure 13.3. Frequency of occurrence of GAP and non-GAP verbs in a 63-mother corpus by setting.

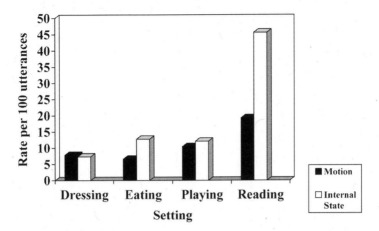

Figure 13.4. Frequency of occurrence of motion and internal state verbs by setting.

in this context, manifesting their greatest differential with non-GAP and motion verbs, respectively.

These analyses of setting by verb class mask, however, differences in the effects of setting on individual verbs. We operationally defined a setting effect for an individual verb as occurring when the frequency of occurrence of that verb in one setting was more than twice the frequency of occurrence of that verb in at least one other setting. Using this definition, as mentioned earlier, book reading yielded setting effects for 20 of the 30 verbs; that is, book reading yielded the highest frequency of occurrence of that verb, and its frequency was more than twice that of at least one other setting. Of the other verbs, two had their highest frequency of occurrence in the dressing setting (*need, pull*), three in the eating setting (*drop, sit, want*), and four in the playing setting (*jump, listen, move, work*). We also investigated whether setting effects occurred when the book reading setting was omitted; that is, whether a given verb in one of the dressing, eating, or playing settings occurred more than twice as frequently as in one of the other two settings. Such setting effects were observed for many of the verbs, as shown in table 13.3.

Two findings of Study 2 are of particular interest. First, all three settings yielded some high-frequency effects (playing yielded high frequencies of occurrence for eight verbs, dressing for six verbs and eating for four verbs) and some low-frequency effects (dressing yielded low frequencies of occurrence for nine verbs, eating for eight verbs, and playing for seven verbs). Thus, it is not the case that some settings are better, overall, for sampling verb use. Instead, some settings facilitate use of some verbs and not others. Second, 11 of the 16 non-GAP verbs (69%), but only five of the nine GAP verbs (55%) displayed these idiosyncratic patterns. Thus, it appears that non-GAP verbs are more subject to setting

Table 13.3 Setting effects with book reading omitted

Verb	Frequent Setting	Infrequent Setting
Fall	eating, playing	dressing
Get	dressing	playing
Go	playing	dressing, eating
Lay	dressing	eating, playing
Lie	dressing	eating, playing
Like	playing	dressing
Look	playing	dressing, eating
Make	playing	dressing
Pull	dressing	eating, playing
Push	playing	eating, dressing
Put	dressing, playing	eating
Run	eating	dressing, playing
See	playing	dressing
Take	eating	playing
Think	eating	dressing
Wave	dressing	eating, playing

effects than GAP verbs; as predicted, these latter verbs are represented more equally across settings. This difference was much smaller in the motion-internal state comparison, where 56% of the former verbs and 50% of the latter verbs displayed such setting effects.

Discussion

Study 2 corroborated the findings of Study 1: The frequencies with which verbs are used varied highly by context, whether context is defined narrowly as the presence of a given object (e.g., a ball vs. toy food) or broadly as involving book reading versus mealtime. Book reading elicited the most verbs at the highest frequencies (as well as the most speech overall), but verb use across the other three settings was quite idiosyncratic. Interestingly, non-GAP verbs as a class displayed setting effects the most; apparently, verbs more specific or specialized in meaning are also more specialized in the contexts in which they appear.

What might these setting effects lead us to predict about early verb acquisition or comprehension? First, verbs that appear in more settings in child-directed speech might be acquired earlier (although as Study 1 showed, more contexts does not necessarily equal higher frequency). Second, though, is the possibility that what these setting effects reveal is that obtaining a representative sample of children's input from which one might derive predictions regarding verb acquisition is a perilous enterprise. Thus, in an exploratory rather than hypothesis-testing mode, we turn to the study of early verb comprehension.

Study 3: English Verb Comprehension

Method

Participants

Twenty-four children were included in the final sample. They ranged in age from 17 to 20 months, with a mean age of 18.97 months ($SD = 0.97$). Approximately equal numbers of boys and girls were included. Six additional children were tested but excluded due to the following: parent interference during viewing (three children), looking to one side during the test trials more than 80% of the time (one child), and multilingual status (two children). At the time of participation, the children's production vocabulary was assessed via a checklist their mothers filled out (Rescorla, Hadicke-Wiley, & Escarce, 1991); overall, the children produced an average of 98.96 words ($SD = 73.71$), of which an average of 9.58 ($SD = 10.75$) were verbs. The participants' mean age and vocabulary size by audio condition is listed in table 13.4. All of the children were being raised in English-speaking homes; nearly all were of European heritage. Participants were recruited through files of newspaper birth announcements and contacted by telephone.

Apparatus

The children watched videos on side-by-side monitors while sitting on their parents' laps. A centering light illuminated when both screens were blank, and a video recorder between the monitors filmed the children's faces. The videos were presented on two synchronized VCRs. Parents, who wore visors to shield their eyes, were explicitly instructed not to engage the children while watching the videos, not to point to the videos, and not to produce the verbs. Children whose parents did any of these things were excluded.

Stimuli and Design

The six test verb pairs were chosen with two main purposes in mind. First, given the variability in verb comprehension noted in the introduction to this chapter, we

Table 13.4 Participant information, Study 3

Audio Condition	Age	Mean Overall Vocabulary	Mean Verb Vocabulary
A	19.82 (0.46)	134.55 (74.03)	15.00 (11.62)
B	18.25 (0.62)	68.85 (60.86)	5.0 (7.69)

preferred to assess verbs whose comprehension had already been attested in at least one previous study. Therefore, we chose *eat, wave, jump, roll, throw, blow*, and *open* as some of our test verbs (e.g., Benedict, 1979; Goldin-Meadow et al., 1975; Golinkoff et al., 1987; Huttenlocher, Smiley, & Charney, 1983; Naigles, 1997). Our selection of verbs was limited by the fact that each needed to be easily depicted on video; this ruled out such early verbs as *come, go*, and *get*. Second, we also wanted our test-foil pairs to differ minimally rather than maximally in their actions, so that successful comprehension could be attributed to a verb meaning that was specified in detail rather than general. For example, (unlike) Golinkoff et al. (1987), we chose verb pairs that could involve the same patient (e.g., the same ball used for *roll* and *throw*). And unlike Huttenlocher et al. (1983), we chose verb pairs whose action involved the same body part (e.g., *wave* paired with *clap* rather than *kick*). Thus, *eat* was paired with *kiss* as both involved the actor's mouth, *jump* was paired with *sit* as both involved vertical motion, *roll* was paired with *throw* as both involved the actor's hands (and horizontal motion), *blow* was paired with *cry* as both involved the actor's face, and *open* was paired with *close* as both involved the actor's hands (and the same object).

Twelve 6-second actions were filmed using an adult female actor. The actions are described in table 13.5; note that each action of a pair was performed with the same prop, if props were included, and that both actions in a pair were performed according to the same timing. The test audios are also presented in table 13.5; note that the direct object, when produced, was always "it."

The action clips were then arranged according to the layout shown in table 13.6. Each trial lasted 6 seconds; the intertrial interval (when both screens were blank) was 3 seconds long. The audio for each trial was first produced during these 3 seconds and then repeated when the trial appeared. During the first two trials, each action was presented singly paired with a neutral audio ("Look what she's doing!"). During the third trial, the actions were presented simultaneously, paired again with a neutral audio; this served as the control trial for stimulus salience. The fourth trial presented the test audio ("Look, she's eating/kissing it") paired with the two simultaneously presented actions. This layout was presented a total of six times such that each child was tested on six of the twelve verbs. The

Table 13.5 Verb/action pairs

Verb/action pair	Audio (B/A)
Eat/Kiss a carrot	She's eating it/kissing it!
Jump/Sit on a chair	She's jumping/sitting!
Close/Open a small cooler	She's closing it/opening it!
Blow/Cry into a tissue	She's blowing/crying!
Throw/Roll a ball	She's throwing it/rolling it!
Clap/Wave	She's clapping/waving!

Table 13.6 Layout of videos

Trial #	Video 1	Audio	Video 2
1	Girl eats carrot	"What's she doing?"	Blank
2	Blank	"What's she doing now?"	Girl kisses carrot
3	Girl eats carrot	"She's on both screens!"	Girl kisses carrot
4	Girl eats carrot	"Look, she's eating it!"	Girl kisses carrot

side of the matching screen was counterbalanced across participants in each audio condition, as well as within participants so that the match occurred equally on the left and right sides. Eleven of the children (6 girls and 5 boys) heard the A audio whereas 13 of the children (7 girls and 6 boys) heard the B audio. Both audios were spoken by the same adult female voice, using child-directed intonation.

Procedure and Coding

Children spent a few minutes in the laboratory playroom getting used to their surroundings, then accompanied their parent into the IPL room. The child sat on his or her parent's lap facing the two monitors. The experimenter left the room during the session.

The children were videotaped while watching the videos; their eye movements were coded from the tapes in real time by an observer who could not hear the stimulus audio and so could not know which side was the matching video (see Naigles, 1996, 1998; Naigles & Gelman, 1995; Naigles & Kako, 1993, for similar coding procedures). The children's direction and duration of looking was coded for each action pair during the salience (trial 3 in table 13.6) and test trials, measured in hundredths of a second. Trials in which the child did not look at the center light for a minimum of 0.3 seconds, and in which the child had not looked at either screen (once the events appeared) for a minimum of 0.3 seconds, were excluded. A total of 7.6% of the trials were unusable; these empty cells were filled with the group mean for that verb. Each child was coded at least twice; if the coders did not agree on visual fixation for the test trials for each of the six pairs (within approximately 0.5 seconds), a third (and sometimes fourth and fifth) coder viewed the video until two coders were found to be in agreement. An average of 3.96 coders was necessary to achieve agreement on each participant (range = 2–5). The chronologically earlier of these two coders-in-agreement was selected as the one whose coding was included in the analysis. Reliability was assessed as in Naigles (1998); reliability was high, with an average r^2 of 0.98. The dependent measure was proportion of looking time to the matching screen during each test trial as compared with the proportion of looking time to the matching screen during the corresponding salience trial.

Results

Our major question concerned whether the children understood the verbs; that is, whether they looked longer to the matching screen during the test trials when the verbs were presented. Figure 13.5 displays the findings for both groups of children across verbs. Averaged across verbs, the children who heard the A audio looked longer at the matching screen during the test trials than during the salience trials; however, the children who heard the B audio showed no difference between trials. A four-way ANOVA with two between-subjects variables (Audio condition [2] and Gender [2]) and two within-subjects variables (Verb [6] and Trial [2]) was performed. A main effect of Trial was obtained ($F[1, 20] = 7.58$, $p = .012$, $MSE = 0.0562$), as well as a significant interaction of Audio condition and Trial ($F[1, 20] = 4.98$, $p = .035$). Planned comparisons with each audio condition separately confirmed that the children in the A condition looked at the matching screen significantly more during the test trials than during the salience trials; all 11 of these children manifested this shift. No significant effect was found for the children in the B condition; only 8 of the 13 children preferred the matching screen more during the test trials than during the salience trials.

No significant main effects or interactions were found with the Verb variable, which suggests that neither the A nor the B verbs differed among themselves in comprehensibility. However, we were interested in whether the children in the A condition preferred the matching screen for all six verbs, and whether the children in the B condition preferred the matching screen for any of their six verbs. Therefore, 12 paired one-way *t* tests were conducted, comparing children's looking times during the salience and test trial for each verb. The results revealed that the

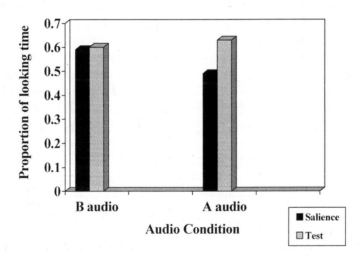

Figure 13.5. Percentage of looking time to the salience and test trials by audio condition.

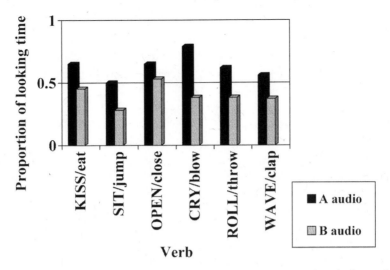

Figure 13.6. Percentage of looking time to the A actions (capitalized) for each action pair.

children significantly preferred the matching screen for *kiss, sit, cry,* and *wave* (*t*s [10] = 1.90 to 2.43, *p*s = .042 to .017), all of which appeared in the A condition. None of the other verbs' salience-test comparisons reached significance.

It is also of interest to know whether the children's looking preferences during the test trials varied by audio condition, for each verb. Thus, a second analysis compared the children's looking times during the test trial only, as the percent of looking to the action labeled by the A audio. For example, the looking time of the 11 children who heard "kiss" to the video of "kissing the carrot" (i.e., the match) were compared with the looking times of the 13 children who heard "eat" to the same video (i.e., the nonmatch). Did the audio make a difference? The results are shown in figure 13.6; verb comprehension could be inferred if the percent of looking time is greater for the A audio than for the B audio. Six two-sample one-way *t* tests (one for each verb pair) were performed, and five of the six—all but the *open/close* comparison—reached significance (*t*s [22] = 1.83 to 3.7, *p*s = .04 to .0006).

Why did the children who heard the A audio perform so much better than those who heard the B audio? Although this was not part of the design, the children in the A condition were both older by about a month, and had larger vocabularies, than the children in the B condition. Both of these differences were statistically significant (Age: *t*[22] = 6.93, *p* < .01; Vocabulary: *t*[22] = 2.38, *p* < .05). Scrutiny of the data also revealed that the girls in the A condition had particularly high vocabularies (*M* = 189.17, *SD* = 37.94) compared with the boys in that condition (*M* = 69.0, *SD* = 45.35), the girls in the B condition (*M* = 67.86,

$SD = 70.91$) and the boys in the B condition ($M = 70.00$, $SD = 53.40$). We thus were curious as to whether age or vocabulary size was the better predictor of looking time to the matching screen. All pairwise zero-order correlations among age, total vocabulary, verb vocabulary, percent looking time to the matching screen during the test trial only, and percent shift toward the matching screen from the control to test trials were calculated. Age and total vocabulary, total vocabulary and verb vocabulary, and the two IPL measures all yielded significant correlations ($rs = .447, .94$, and $.744$, respectively, all $ps < .05$). Finally two AN-COVAs were performed, one with age as the covariate and one with vocabulary as the covariate. When the variance due to age or vocabulary was removed, there was no difference between the A and B conditions. Thus, two conclusions are possible: either good verb comprehension is only the province of older and more verbal 1-year-olds, or the verbs presented to the B group just happened to be more difficult.

Discussion

These findings demonstrate several things about 1-year-olds' verb comprehension. First, children at this age do understand some familiar verbs in novel contexts, with new actors and/or props. That is, even though our *kissing* action involved an unknown actor and a very novel patient (i.e., the carrot), the action itself was clearly distinctive enough—and had been extended enough in the children's lexicons—that they could identify it reliably. Clearly, then, at least some verb meanings have become decontextualized by the time children are 18–19 months of age. As such, these findings corroborate and extend those of previous researchers: Like Forbes and Poulin-Dubois (1997), Golinkoff et al. (1987), and Huttenlocher, Smiley, and Charney (1983), we found that children under 22 months of age could understand familiar verbs when extended to a new actor. We believe that our findings are even more robust than these earlier ones, because some of our child participants demonstrated comprehension of five of the six verbs they heard (the highest percentage of any previous study). Moreover, our method was more challenging because the verbs were not labeled until the test trials whereas both Golinkoff et al. and Huttenlocher et al. primed the children during the familiarization trials by saying "one is X-ing and one is Y-ing." Our test-foil pairs were also only minimally different, such that the ability to distinguish sitting from jumping or waving from clapping involved fairly precise representation of the relevant action (i.e., not just vertical motion in relation to a chair or horizontal motion with the hands). So far, then, our findings are in accord with those gathered previously: One-year-old children can extend their verb meanings to quite novel situations.

   In line with the questions we raised in the introduction to this chapter, we performed two further comparative analyses with our data: First, we investigated whether our specific verb findings matched those found previously. That is, are the verbs found to be well-understood in Study 3 also well understood in other studies? Second, we investigated whether our specific verb findings from Study 3 matched the patterns of use in input found in Studies 1 and 2. That is, are those verbs that were used in more diverse or frequent contexts by adults the same verbs that were well-understood by our 1-year-old child participants?

With regard to the first question, it appears once again that the verbs that our child participants comprehended were not the ones that other researchers have found to be easily understood by toddlers. In particular, in table 13.7 we present our calculations of performance from our Study 3 and five other studies. Three of these were comprehension studies in which the child participants acted out the actions using themselves as the actors and one was Huttenlocher, Smiley, and Charney (1983; the other IPL studies did not include enough of the target verbs to enable a comparison). The fifth column of data is drawn from the listed norms of production of these verbs at 18 months, based on the MCDI checklist (Dale & Fenson, 1996). Each column presents the percent of children demonstrating knowledge of some subset of the 12 test verbs. Two things are immediately observable: First, the comprehension studies vary dramatically in actual rate of performance, even though the children are all in the same age range: Goldin-Meadow et al. (1976) and Huttenlocher et al. (1983) found that most of their children perform well with both the understood (U) and not understood (N) verbs, whereas Goldfield found that most of her children perform poorly with both types of verbs. Second, only three of the five studies yield the same pattern of results as our Study 3, that children perform better with the U verbs than with the N verbs. Two conclusions are thus possible: either that tests of verb comprehension in toddlers have not yet reached a standard of validity and reliability, as replication across studies seems very low, or that patterns of specific verb comprehension in toddlers are extremely idiosyncratic. Perhaps, again unlike with nouns, there is no "stock" set of content-rich verbs that young children learn. The variations in input observed in Studies 1 and 2 would certainly be consistent with the latter conclusion.

With regard to the second question, though, there does not appear to be a direct correspondence between the verbs that were used in multiple contexts in Studies 1 and 2 and the verbs that were comprehended best in Study 3. In particular, if one were to rank the seven relevant verbs in Study 1 on the basis of their frequency and diversity across contexts, *eat, throw*, and *blow* would surely rank higher than *clap, jump, roll*, and *sit* (see figures 13.1 and 13.2). These verbs might be expected to be better understood, yet Study 3 found significant comprehension for none of the highly-ranked verbs. Instead, two of the verbs that were hardly used at all, in Study 1, were among those well understood in Study 3. The results of Study 2 are even more challenging to cast in a form that is comparable with those of Study 3. The two types of verbs that were used preferentially by mothers in the high-frequency book-reading context, and which appeared at high rates across contexts, were just those that are most difficult to test using IPL (i.e., GAP

Table 13.7 Comparison of Study 3 with other published studies

	Study 3	CDI-18 mo.	Benedict	G-M et al.	Goldfield	H et al.
				Percentage of Children Demonstrating Knowledge of These Verbs		
Method	C: IPL	P: checklist	C: act out	C: act out	C: act out	C: points
Mean Age or Age Range	17–20 months	18 months	9–17 months	14–26 months	20 months	22–40 months
Verbs comprehended[a]	78 (5)	22.53 (3)	50 (2)	75 (3)	5 (3)	84 (1)
Verbs not comprehended[b]	55 (7)	17.33 (7)	21 (6)	94.4 (6)	11.4 (4)	75.6 (5)

CDI = Child Development Inventory, Dale & Fenson (1996).

Benedict = Benedict (1979).

G-M et al. = Goldin-Meadow et al. (1976).

Goldfield = Goldfield (2000).

H et al. = Huttenlocher et al. (1983).

C = comprehension study; P = production study.

[a] = kiss, sit, cry, wave, roll.

[b] = eat, jump, open, close, blow, clap, throw.

Numbers in parentheses indicate the number of verbs included in each calculation.

verbs and internal state verbs). Thus, we have not (yet) found support for input as a causal factor in the extendability of children's first verbs.

General Discussion: Lessons Learned

The motive behind these studies of early verb input and verb comprehension was to study the development of the verb lexicon from its beginnings. We believed, and still believe, that the central questions of when and in what ways children go beyond the information they are given with respect to verb acquisition would be answered if we could document the nature of the information given in the input and the extendability of children's first verbs. What our studies have demonstrated is that the devil may be in the implementation of this research plan.

Documenting the nature of children's input requires either recording every-thing children hear or obtaining a representative sample. Although there is a sub-stantial literature that has documented the nature of children's input on the basis of speech samples, it has done so in terms of average properties of child-directed speech across caregivers (e.g., Naigles & Hoff-Ginsberg, 1995), or it has described individual caregivers in terms of average properties of speech across utterances (e.g., MLU) and the rate of high-frequency events (e.g., directives; Hoff-Ginsberg, 1991). Even in these cases, there are documented effects of context, which means that children's language experience is both a function of how their caregivers use language and the settings in which they spend their time (Hoff-Ginsberg, 1991). These difficulties notwithstanding, it is possible to get sufficiently accurate data on children's verb input to account for some properties of children's early verb use (Naigles & Hoff-Ginsberg, 1998). What the present findings suggest, though, is that this requires a great deal of data and works better for some verbs than for others. In particular, Study 1 revealed that, even with nine hours of maternal talk and the presence of toys designed to invoke our target actions, many verbs de-scribing those actions were produced rarely or not at all. Study 2 highlighted the fact that, even within a relatively large sample of caregivers (i.e., 63 mothers), many of our target verbs occurred in only one or two of our four contexts. Thus, drawing conclusions about the extent to which input influences early verb mean-ings (beyond the fact that, of course, it must) is perilous with current methods of input sampling. Child verb use not directly reflected in the input sampled could be attributed to conceptual issues, but could also be a function of the input not sampled.

The problems involved in measuring extendability at the very beginning of verb acquisition are equally challenging. The basic issue is that different kinds of extendability are all interconnected. The decision to depict an extended meaning of a given verb comes with numerous interdependent choices; we describe three of these here. First, assessments of agent extendability with conventional (i.e., not nonsense) verbs will inevitably assess manner extendability as well, because new agents are likely to perforsm an action differently from the way the child performs it. However, the degree of difference across agents may vary depending on the specific action and so verb. For example, an adult's eating or running is probably very different from a child's, but an adult's waving may not be so different. Second, assessments of patient extendability are also likely to assess manner extendability, as actions can be carried out differently with different patients; again, though, the degree of difference across patients may vary across verbs. For example, eating a carrot looks different from eating a lollipop or a bowl of cereal; in contrast, throwing a ball may not look so different from throwing a stick. Third, in the IPL format, assessments of lexical comprehension—and so extendability—are based on comparison with a foil. Thus, assessments of verb extendability could vary as a function of the similarity between the target and foil. In Study 3, we selected our foils to be similar to the targets on many dimensions (e.g., the body part used to perform the action, whether the direction of motion was vertical or horizontal). We might have obtained "better" comprehension of the B verbs if the foils had been different on some of these dimensions; for example, if the foil for *eat* had been brushing hair or shaking the head, or if the foil for *opening the box* had been kicking or throwing the box.

In sum, the absence of significant findings of verb comprehension—and so extendability—could still be attributed, as Huttenlocher, Smiley, and Charney (1983) originally claimed, to the child's restricted meaning for that verb. The child may not recognize the action when it is instantiated by another individual. However, our data raise the possibility of two other factors operating. First, perhaps the child's meaning for that verb has been extended to other agents and other patients, but the actor in the video performed the action with a prop such that the action looks very different from what is represented in the child's lexicon. Second, perhaps the child has not learned that verb yet because its relevant actions have not appeared with the verb with sufficient frequencies and/or contexts in the child's experience.

In study after study, the findings are that 1-year-old children do know some verbs; moreover, the meanings for these verbs have been extended beyond the child's own experiences. However, establishing *which* verbs they know, let alone *how well* they know them, has proven to be the challenge. Perhaps a more appropriate conclusion to draw is that one-year-olds' verb knowledge is individually idiosyncratic; that is, there may be no general set of verbs that all one-year-olds can be confidently predicted to know. This was highlighted in the introduction to this chapter, when we contrasted the specific verb findings of Golinkoff et al. (1987), Huttenlocher, Smiley, and Charney (1983), and Naigles (1997), and in the discussion of Study 3, when we investigated whether the verbs known vs. unknown in our study patterned similarly in five other studies. Preliminary data from Linda Smith's lab (personal communication, December 2003) corroborates this individuality. Smith has found that the set of verbs that 1-year-olds produce overlap little; that is, each child uses his or her own idiosyncratic set. Part of the challenge in establishing children's verb vocabularies surely comes from difficulties, such as those described above, involved in verb assessment, but we also believe that the idiosyncratic nature of the verbs children know can be traced to the idiosyncratic nature, especially the enormous context-specificity, of the ways adults use verbs when talking to children.

Thus, we end this chapter with a suggestion for an alternative route for further studies of children's first verbs. Rather than examine verb knowledge cross-sectionally and at a single point in time, we believe that what is needed are intensive studies of individual children, who are studied longitudinally from their first use of their first verb. Moreover, because the topic of interest concerns the child's ability to extend verbs to new agents, patients, and variants of actions, and because children's uses are likely to be as context-specific as their caregivers', it becomes of crucial importance to directly record every usage rather than assume that a sample of speech every month will include the relevant data. What we are recommending is a return to the diary method, which has already been used to great effect for studies of children's first words (e.g., Dromi, 1987) and first nouns (e.g., Harris et al., 1988), but which has never been used to study the very first instances of children's very first verbs. Tomasello's (1992) case study of his daughter is the only study that comes close; however, its data are limited to the child's first verb combinations; her single-word uses with her verbs, and the meanings of these uses, were not reported. We have begun such an intensive diary study of children's first verbs (e.g., Naigles, Vear, & Hoff, 2002; Vear, Naigles, Hoff, & Ramos, 2001), with the intent of shedding further light on when and how children's verb meanings are learned.

References

Benedict, H. (1979). Early lexical development: Comprehension and production. *Journal of Child Language, 6*, 183–200.

Bloom, L., Tinker, E., & Margulis, C. (1993). The words children learn: Evidence against a noun bias in early vocabularies. *Cognitive Development, 8*, 431–450.

Bloom, P. (2000). *How children learn the meanings of words.* Cambridge, MA: MIT Press.

Braunwald, S. (1995). Differences in the acquisition of early verbs: Evidence from diary data from sisters. In M. Tomasello & W. Merriman (Eds.), *Beyond names for things: The acquisition of verbs* (pp. 81–114). Hillsdale, NJ: Erlbaum.

Choi, S., & Gopnick, A. (1995). Early acquisition of verbs in Korean: A cross-linguistic study. *Journal of Child Language, 22*, 497–530.

Clark, E. (1993). *The lexicon in acquisition.* Cambridge: Cambridge University Press.

Clark, E. (1996). Early verbs, event types, and inflections. In C. Johnson & J. Gilbert (Eds.), *Children's language* (Vol. 9, pp. 61–73). Mahwah, NJ: Erlbaum.

Clark, E., & Wong, X. (2002). Pragmatic directions about language use: Offers of words and relations. *Language in Society, 31*, 181–212.

Dale, P., & Fenson, L. (1996). Lexical development norms for young children. *Behavior Research Methods, Instruction, and Computers, 28*, 125–127.

Dromi, E. (1987). *Early lexical development*. Cambridge: Cambridge University Press.

Fernald, A., Pinto, J., Swingley, D., Weinberg, A., & McRoberts, G. (1998). Rapid gains in speed of verbal processing by infants in the 2nd year. *Psychological Science, 9*, 72–75.

Forbes, J., & Poulin-Dubois, D. (1997). Representational change in young children's understanding of familiar verb meaning. *Journal of Child Language, 24*, 389–406.

Goldberg, A. (1999). The emergence of the semantics of argument structure constructions. In B. MacWhinney (Ed.), *The emergence of language* (pp. 197–211). Mahwah, NJ: Erlbaum.

Goldfield, B. (2000). Nouns before verbs in comprehension versus production: The view from pragmatics. *Journal of Child Language, 27*, 501–520.

Goldin-Meadow, S., Seligman, M., & Gelman, R. (1976). Language in the two-year-old. *Cognition, 5*, 189–202.

Golinkoff, R., Hirsh-Pasek, K., Cauley, K., & Gordon, L. (1987). The eyes have it: Lexical and syntactic comprehension in a new paradigm. *Journal of Child Language, 14*, 23–45.

Golinkoff, R., Hirsh-Pasek, K., Mervis, C., Frawley, W., & Parillo, M. (1995). Lexical principles can be extended to the acquisition of verbs. In M. Tomasello & W. Merriman (Eds.), *Beyond names for things: Young children's acquisition of verbs* (pp. 185–221). Hillsdale, NJ: Erlbaum.

Harris, M., Barrett, M., Jones, D., & Brooks, S. (1988). Linguistic input and early word meaning. *Journal of Child Language, 15*, 77–94.

Hoff-Ginsberg, E. (1991). Mother-child conversation in different social classes and communicative settings. *Child Development 62*, 782–796.

Huttenlocher, J., Smiley, P., & Charney, R. (1983). The emergence of action categories in the child: Evidence from verb meaning. *Psychological Review, 90*, 72–93.

Huttenlocher, J., Smiley, P., & Ratner, N. (1983). What do word meanings reveal about conceptual development? In T. Seiler & W. Wannenmacher (Eds.), *Concept development and the development of word meanings* (pp. 211–233). Berlin: Springer-Verlag.

MacWhinney, B. (2000). *The CHILDES project: Tools for analyzing talk* (3rd ed.). Mahwah, NJ: Lawrence Erlbaum.

Maguire, M., Hennon, E., Hirsh-Pasek, K., Golinkoff, R., Slutzky, C., & Sootsman, C. (2002). Mapping words to actions and events: How do 18-month-olds learn a verb? In B. Skarabela et al. (Eds.), *BUCLD 26 Proceedings* (pp. 371–382). Somerville, MA: Cascadilla Press.

Marchman, V., & Bates, E. (1994). Continuity in lexical and morphological development: A test of the critical mass hypothesis. *Journal of Child Language, 21*, 339–366.

Mervis, C., Golinkoff, R., & Hirsh-Pasek, K. (1994). Early object labels: The case for a developmental lexical principles approach. *Journal of Child Language, 21*, 125–156.

Miller, J. F., & Chapman, R. S. (1985). *SALT: Systematic Analysis of Language Transcripts*. Madison: University of Wisconsin Language Analysis Laboratory.

Naigles, L. (1996). The use of multiple frames in verb learning via syntactic bootstrapping. *Cognition, 58* 221–251.

Naigles, L. (1997). Are English-speaking one-year-olds verb learners, too? In E. Clark (Ed.), *Proceedings of the 28th annual Child Language Research Forum* (pp. 199–212). Stanford: CSLI.

Naigles, L. (1998). Developmental changes in the use of structure in verb learning. In C. Rovee-Collier, L. Lipsitt, & H. Haynes (Eds.), *Advances in infancy research* (Vol.12, pp. 298–318). London: Ablex.

Naigles, L., & Gelman, S. A. (1995). Overextensions in production and comprehension, revisited: A study of *dog, cat,* and *cow. Journal of Child Language, 22,* 19–46.

Naigles, L., & Hoff-Ginsberg, E. (1995). Input to verb learning: Evidence for the plausibility of syntactic bootstrapping. *Developmental Psychology, 31,* 827–837.

Naigles, L., & Hoff-Ginsberg, E. (1998). Why are some verbs learned before other verbs? Effects of input frequency and structure on children's early verb use. *Journal of Child Language, 25,* 95–120.

Naigles, L., & Kako, E. (1993). First contact: Biases in verb learning with and without syntactic information. *Child Development, 64,* 1665–1687.

Naigles, L., Vear, D., & Hoff, E. (2002). *Syntactic flexibility is revealed in children's first verb uses: Evidence from a cross-sectional diary study.* Paper presented at the International Conference on Infancy Studies, Toronto, April.

Poulin-Dubois, P., & Forbes, J. (2002). Toddlers' attention to intentions-in-action in learning novel action words. *Developmental Psychology, 38,* 104–114.

Rescorla, L., Hadicke-Wiley, M., & Escarce, E. (1993). Epidemiological investigation of expressive language delay at age two. *First Language, 13,* 5–22.

Rice, M. L., & Bode, J. V. (1993). GAPS in the verb lexicons of children with specific language impairment. *First Language, 13,* 113–131.

Sandofer, C., Smith, L., & Luo, J. (2000). Counting nouns and verbs in the input: Differential frequency, different kinds of learning? *Journal of Child Language 27,* 561–586.

Singleton, J., & Newport, E. (2004). When learners surpass their models: The acquisition of ASL from inconsistent input. *Cognitive Psychology, 49,* 370–407.

Smiley, P., & Huttenlocher, J. (1995). Conceptual development and the child's early words for events, objects, and persons. In M. Tomasello & W. Merriman (Eds.), *Beyond names for things: The acquisition of verbs* (pp. 21–62). Hillsdale, NJ: Erlbaum.

Smith, C., & Sachs, J. (1990). Cognition and the verb lexicon in early lexical development. *Applied Psycholiguistics 11,* 409–424.

Snedeker, J., & Gleitman, L. (2004). Why it is hard to label our concepts. In Hall & Waxman (Eds.), *Weaving a lexicon* (pp. 257–294). Cambridge, MA: MIT Press.

Tardif, T., Gelman, S., & Xu, F. (1999). Putting the "noun bias" in context: A comparison of English and Mandarin. *Child Development, 70,* 620–635.

Tomasello, M. (1992). *First verbs: A case study of early grammatical development.* Cambridge: Cambridge University Press.

Tomasello, M., & Kruger, A. (1992). Joint attention on actions: Acquiring verbs in ostensive and non-ostensive contexts. *Journal of Child Language, 19,* 311–333.

Vear, D., Naigles, L., Hoff, E., & Ramos, E. (2001). *An investigation of the syntactic flexibility within young children's early verb development: Evidence from a cross-sectional diary study.* Paper presented at the Early Lexicon Acquisition Conference, Lyon, France, December.

14   A Unified Theory of Word Learning: Putting Verb Acquisition in Context

Mandy J. Maguire, Kathy Hirsh-Pasek, and Roberta Michnick Golinkoff

The last decade has witnessed unparalleled research on the study of early verb learning. Rather than projecting a coherent story of how children learn their first verbs, however, the literature seems to offer a set of somewhat disjointed facts. For example, most concur that nouns are generally learned before verbs (Gentner, 1982). Words like *shoe* and *car* appear in children's lexicons before words like *run* and *drive*. Most, but not all, also find this pattern to be universal (Bornstein et al., 2004). On the other hand, research demonstrates that some verbs appear in children's earliest vocabularies and that this verb preference is especially pronounced in languages like Chinese (Tardif, Gelman, & Xu, 1999) and Tzeltzal (Brown, 2001). Finally, we not only find that some verbs arrive very early, but also that some nouns like *passenger* (Hall & Waxman, 1993; Keil & Batterman, 1984) defy the universal trend by arriving relatively late in development. As yet no theory has been able to explain all of these findings in a unified, coherent way. This is the goal of this chapter.

Here we build on suggestions by Gentner and Boroditsky (2001) and Gleitman and her colleagues (e.g., Gleitman & Gleitman, 1992; Snedeker & Gleitman, 2004; Gleitman, Cassidy, Nappa, Papafragou, & Trueswell, 2005) to suggest that the contrasting findings emerging in the verb learning literature may not be about nouns and verbs, but about word learning in general. We argue for a comprehensive approach to word learning that accounts for why some words are learned before others, regardless of form class. Words that label more perceptually accessible concepts might be learned early while those that label abstract or relational concepts require additional support from social and linguistic sources and are thus learned late. We further propose that this pattern will hold not only for words *across* syntactic classes like nouns and verbs, but also for words *within* syntactic classes (see chapter 18, this volume; Snedeker & Gleitman, 2004). In this chapter, we expand our broad-based developmental theory of word learning (the emergentist coalition model [ECM]; Hollich et al., 2000) to illuminate how children acquire language with a specific focus on verb acquisition. In so doing, we demonstrate how the theory of word learning originally developed for the understanding of noun learning can encompass the study of verbs. We also explain a persistent paradox in verb learning—why some verbs appear early even though the class of verbs is generally hard to master.

This chapter is divided into three parts. First, we review the traditional account of verb learning highlighting why verbs in general are so difficult to learn. Second, we present the tenets of the ECM, how the ECM accounts for noun learning, and how it can be extended to verbs. Here we introduce a continuum that spans all word classes to explain why some nouns and verbs are learned early while others are learned late. Finally, we conclude that our framework for verb learning offers a coherent view of the current literature and an explanation for what we have dubbed the *verb learning paradox*: why in general verbs are harder than nouns, and why some verbs nonetheless appear early in children's vocabularies.

The Traditional Account: Verbs Are Hard

In 1982, Gentner wrote a classic article articulating the many reasons why verbs might be harder to learn than nouns. Her work spurred a flurry of activity that spanned 25 years of prolific research from languages that covered the globe (Behrend, 1995; Brown, 2001; Choi & Bowerman, 1991; Choi & Gopnik, 1995; Fisher, 2002; Forbes & Farrar, 1993; Gallivan, 1988; Gleitman & Gillette, 1995; Golinkoff et al., 2002; Golinkoff, Hirsh-Pasek, Mervis, Frawley, & Parillo, 1995; Hirsh-Pasek, Naigles, Golinkoff, Gleitman, & Gleitman, 1988; Imai & Haryu, 2001; Imai & Gentner, 1997; Naigles, 1990, 1996; Poulin-Dubois & Forbes, 2002; Sandhofer, Smith, & Luo, 2000; Slobin, 2001; Smiley & Huttenlocher, 1995; Snedeker & Gleitman, 2004; Tardif, 1996; Tardif et al., 1999; Tomasello & Merriman, 1995). Though there is still some debate (chapter 18, this volume), most conclude that verbs are universally harder to learn than nouns (see Bornstein et al., 2004). Accumulating research also echoes suggestions made by both Gentner and Boroditsky (2001) and Snedeker and Gleitman (2004; Gleitman et al., 2005) that the problem in verb learning might be more about mapping a specific verb onto an action or event than about learning the underlying relational concepts that the verb or relational term encodes.

The Mapping Dilemma

Picture a child running to a sliding board, climbing the ladder, sliding down, and skipping around the slide to mount the ladder again. When compared to the paltry number of nouns that describe this scene (e.g., *boy, ladder, sliding board, ground*, etc.), the choice of verbs is abundant. This example defines the difficulties inherent in verb learning relative to noun learning. If the scene were accompanied by a novel verb, say, *blicking*, children would have many different possibilities for what that novel verb might mean, from playing to running to smiling. That is, children would face the "packaging problem" (Gentner, 1982; Tomasello, 1995) and relatedly what Gleitman and Gleitman (1992) discuss as a kind of "perspective problem" (Gleitman, 1990) in discerning the meaning of *blicking*. The packaging problem refers to the fact that many elements of meaning can be encoded in a single verb. Gentner (1982) writes,

> A language has more degrees of freedom in lexicalizing relations between coherent objects than in lexicalizing the objects themselves. Thus, for verbs and other relational terms, children must discover how their language combines and lexicalizes the elements of the perceptual field. . . . verb meanings are learned as part of a system of semantic distinctions. (pp. 324–325)

The perspective problem, in contrast, addresses which aspect of a scene the speaker highlights based on the verb used. For example, "The dog fled from the cat" offers one perspective while "The cat chased the dog" offers another perspective on the exact same scene. The perspective problem captures the fact that observation of a scene is insufficient to "nail" the meaning of a verb; additional linguistic information is needed to capture the speaker's view on an event.

The packaging and perspective problems are two among many factors that make verbs harder to learn than nouns (Gentner, 1982; Golinkoff, Jacquet, Hirsh-Pasek, & Nandakumar, 1996). Importantly, they are also problems that relate to how children map words onto concepts rather than problems central to the conceptual foundation for relational terms. That is, accumulating evidence from both adults and children suggest that the verbs might be harder to learn than nouns because it is more difficult to figure out the mapping between word and world when relational terms are involved. Research during the past 10 years provides ample evidence of mapping difficulty.

Even Adults Have Trouble Mapping Verbs

Perhaps the strongest data on the difficulty of mapping verbs comes from studies by Gleitman and her colleagues (Gillette, Gleitman, Gleitman, & Lederer, 1999; Snedeker & Gleitman, 2004). In their human simulation studies, adults viewed a series of silent video clips of a mother and child playing. A beep or nonsense word occurred coincident with either the missing noun or verb. The participants' job was simply to guess what word the speaker might have used in place of the beep. The findings were dramatic. Adults, who presumably had no conceptual difficulties with the objects and events represented on the tapes, correctly guessed the missing nouns in 45% of the cases. In stark contrast, the proportion of correct guesses for verbs was a paltry 15%. In fact, if only responses for mental verbs were considered, the proportion of correct verb guesses dropped to zero. Mapping from action or mental state to word is considerably more challenging than mapping from object to word.

Children Also Struggle With Mapping Verbs

Research in our lab with young children also offers a dramatic example of the mapping problem. Following our work with noun acquisition, we assumed that once children formed a category of actions they would easily attach a label to this category and extend that label to similar exemplars.

A series of tasks began to examine this untested assumption. We started with actions that seemed to be relatively straight forward, intransitive whole body actions (see also chapter 11, this volume). In a nonlinguistic habituation study, Salkind, Sootsman, Golinkoff, Hirsh-Pasek, and Maguire (2002) introduced a set of novel aerobic actions, each consisting of a person doing an action that involved movement of both the arms and legs. For example, one action was a modified jumping jack, in which the legs kicked out as in jumping jacks, but the arms reached up in alternation. Salkind et al. (2002) habituated toddlers 9 to 11 months of age to video clips of two different females performing the same novel jumping jack action. When attention dropped below a criterion, children saw three clips, order counterbalanced across subjects: (1) a control clip of the jumping jack action from habituation, (2) a novel actor performing the familiar jumping jack action, and (3) the same novel actor performing a novel action (knee lifts with arms punching forward).

If babies recognized the action, they should be bored with the control clip. If they noted that a new agent was present, they should watch the novel actor/old action significantly more than the control event. And if they could distinguish between the new action and the old action, then they should watch novel actor/novel action event longest of all. The findings indicated that half of the children in the sample with the largest comprehension vocabularies on the MacArthur (mean = 23) could form a category of action despite a change in the actor. This finding was replicated in a fully counterbalanced design with three different full-body actions. Thus, in a nonlinguistic task, toddlers with more language skill than their peers distinguish between novel actions—above and beyond changes in the actor—by as early as 10 months of age (see figure 14.1).

Mapping Labels to Action Categories

The natural next step was to ask whether children could map a verb to the action category they had formed. Here we used the intermodal preferential looking paradigm (Golinkoff, Hirsh-Pasek, Cauley, & Gordon, 1987; Hirsh-Pasek & Golinkoff, 1996), with looking time as the dependent variable. Based on the ease with which

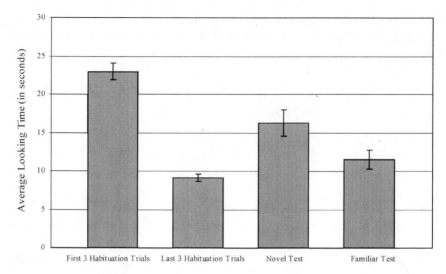

Figure 14.1. Results of Salkind et al. (2002). Mean visual fixation time to the last three habituation trials, novel agent/familiar action test trial, and novel agent/ novel action test trial by high vocabulary 10-month-olds.

children discriminated and categorized the actions in Salkind et al. (2002) and our success with prior comprehension studies (e.g., Hirsh-Pasek & Golinkoff, 1996), we started with 18-month-olds. After all, in Hollich et al. (2000), 12-month-olds were learning novel object labels with only a few exposures and in Pruden, Hirsh-Pasek, Golinkoff, and Hennon (in press), babies at 10 months of age were able to learn a novel object label! Surely by 18 months of age, children should be able to learn a novel verb.

Children sat on a parent's lap watching a large screen television. During the training portion of each study, they saw one of the target actions (e.g., modified jumping jacks) as they heard sentences describing the event ("Hey, she's blicking!"). We created two conditions in which children were trained on two novel action names. The children in Condition 1 saw only one actor performing the target action multiple times. The children in Condition 2 saw four actors, each performing the target action. Prior research suggested that children are conservative in their verb extensions (Forbes & Farrar, 1993). Thus, it might make it easier to extend the new verb to a new agent if they saw multiple actors carrying out the same novel actions. During test trials, children saw a completely new actor performing the target action on one side of the screen and a different novel actor performing a new intransitive action on the other side of the screen.

To our surprise, children at all ages tested (18, 24, and 30 months) uniformly failed to map the word onto the correct action. They watched the old and new actions to the same degree at test. Given the ease with which children formed nonlinguistic categories of these actions by 10 months of age, we wondered why mapping a verb to these same categories was so difficult nearly 2 years later.

More Verb Learning Failures

Though English-speaking children have an early noun bias, many claim that children speaking other languages have a verb bias (Choi, 2000; Choi & Bowerman, 1991; Choi & Gopnik, 1995; Sandhofer et al., 2000; Tardif, 1996; Tardif et al., 1999; Tardif, Shatz, & Naigles, 1997; yet see Kim, McGregor, & Thompson, 2000, for conflicting results). Perhaps the difficulty children have in learning verbs is not about the mapping of words to relations, but rather a problem specific with word mapping in English. Our recent research in English and Japanese, however, suggests that the mapping problem exists across languages.

In our cross-linguistic experiment, English-speaking (Meyer et al., 2003) and Japanese-speaking (Imai, Haryu, & Okada, 2003, in press; chapter 17, this volume) 3- and 5-year-olds participated in a preferential pointing task. Participants saw a person doing an unfamiliar action with an unfamiliar object. Children were exposed to one of three between-subject conditions. In the first, noun condition, they were asked to "Look at the blick," drawing for a noun interpretation. In the bare-frame verb condition, children heard a novel verb in a bare syntactic frame while watching the scene ("Look, blicking! Watch blicking!"). In the "rich-syntax verb" condition, children were given additional syntactic information ("Look, she's blicking it!").

During test trials, children simultaneously saw the old object engaged in a new action in one scene, and the old action being performed with a new object in the other scene (see figure 14.2). At test, children again heard the noun ("Where's the blick?"), bare verb ("Where's blicking?"), or rich syntax audio ("Where's she blicking it?").

In both languages, 3- and 5-year-olds had no difficulty mapping the noun to the object in the noun condition. Further, in both languages, 3-year-olds were unable to map the verb to the action in either language, performing at chance levels. This finding challenges the assumption that all words are initially interpreted as nouns or objects by young children (see also Echols & Marti, 2004; Kersten & Smith, 2002; chapter 19, this volume). It also clearly demonstrates that children can map words to objects before they do so for actions. Most important, it demonstrates the difficulty even 3-year-olds have mapping a verb to an action, regardless of native language. The proposed differences emerged only in the pattern of result for the 5-year-olds.

At age 5, Japanese children correctly mapped the verb to the novel action in both verb conditions. Five-year-old English-speaking children, however, still had trouble mapping the verb to the novel action in the bare-frame verb condition. They could not solve the mapping problem unless they were given rich syntax in

	TRAINING
	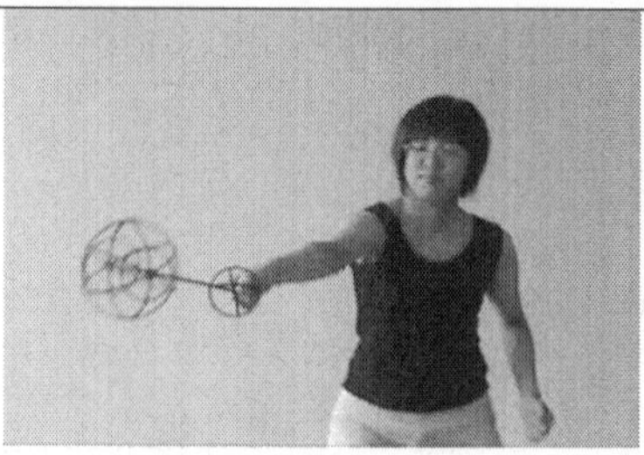
Noun	"Look, at the blick!"
Bare-frame	"Look, blicking!"
Rich-syntax	"Look, she's blicking it!"
	TEST
	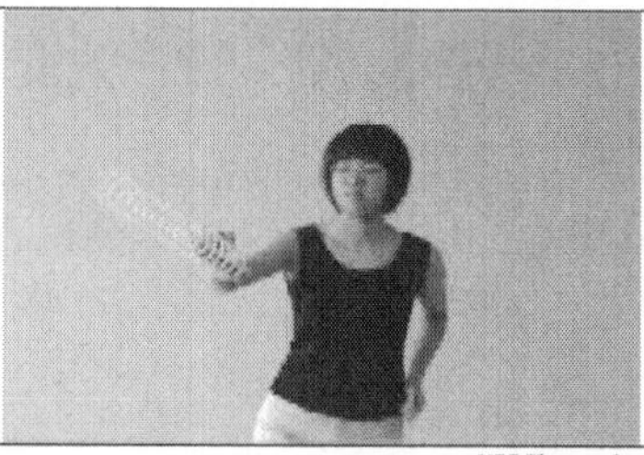 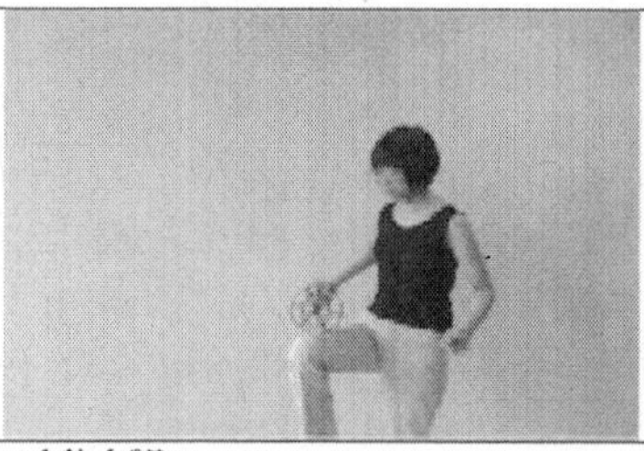
Noun	"Where's the blick?"
Bare-frame	"Where's blicking?"
Rich-syntax	"Where's she blicking it?"

Figure 14.2. Stimuli from Meyer et al. (2003) comparing noun and verb learning based on syntactic cues available.

the form of a full sentence ("She's blicking it") during training. In this condition, children seemed to infer that the pronoun *it* appearing after the verb blocked the noun interpretation for the word.

The differences between the two language groups can be explained in terms of grammatical differences between English and Japanese. While it is rare for transitive verbs to appear in bare frames in English, it is acceptable and common in Japanese because it licenses argument dropping. As a result, the bare frame was unnatural for transitive verbs in English, making mapping more difficult for English-speaking children.

What is most striking about these studies is the late age at which children in both language groups map a word to an action. It is not until 5 years of age that any consistency is seen in verb mapping (see chapter 17, this volume). This finding has recently been replicated in Chinese (Haryu et al., in press). Mapping from word to world is difficult in lab-based studies regardless of the language being learned.

Additional Studies Attest to the Difficulty of Verb Learning

The studies noted above make clear that children's struggles with the packaging problem are not based solely on conceptual problems in forming categories of actions, nor on general problems with mapping (they readily mapped nouns to objects). The problems children encounter appear to be in mapping words to actions. Several other studies converge on the same interpretation. Childers and Tomasello (2002; chapter 12, this volume) tested where the breakdown occurred in verb learning. They attempted to teach 2-year-olds new nouns and verbs in either massed or distributed learning paradigms with responses in either comprehension or production. Findings revealed that children could learn an action associated with a particular object, but nonetheless demonstrated difficulty learning a word for that action. These findings suggest that children are not having a conceptual problem, but something about mapping that retards verb acquisition. Verbs were considerably more difficult to master (especially to produce) than either nouns or action-object pairings without language.

In sum, regardless of age, conceptual abilities, experience, or the specific language to be learned, mapping verb labels is hard even when the underlying non-linguistic category is formed easily. It is no wonder that the literature has been shaped by a noun versus verb debate in which nouns are deemed easy to learn while verbs are thought of as difficult. The goal of the study of language development, however, is not to find separate theories of word learning for different word classes, but rather to find one unified theory to explain all word learning.

Toward a Broad-Based Developmental Theory of Word Learning

The Emergentist Coalition Model

The ECM (Hollich et al., 2000; see also chapter 10, this volume) holds the promise of creating a unified theory of word learning. Developed to explain the course of early word learning and the developmental transformations it undergoes, the ECM states that children have access to a number of different inputs (perceptual, linguistic, and social) for uncovering the referent of a new word. The model answered the call made by many who investigate word learning in terms of a complex, multifactor, interactive theory (e.g., Baldwin & Tomasello, 1998; Bloom, 1993; Nelson, 1996; Woodward & Markman, 1998). As Hollich et al. (2000) wrote, .

> A hybrid view of word learning, this theory characterizes lexical acquisition as the emergent product of multiple factors, including cognitive constraints, social-pragmatic factors, and global attentional mechanisms. The model makes three assumptions: (a) that children cull from multiple inputs available for word learning at any given time, (b) that these inputs

are differentially weighted over development, and (c) that children develop emergent principles of word learning, which guide subsequent word acquisition. (p. v)

Although this theory was developed for noun learning, the ECM's position is that the acquisition of all lexical items is driven first by children's reliance on perceptual information and later through attention to social and linguistic information. Evidence from a number of sources suggests not only that young children place more weight in perceptual information for mapping words to concepts (chapter 11, this volume; Forbes & Farrar, 1993; Smiley & Huttenlocher, 1995), but that in mapping words, they move to a reliance on more social and linguistic information through development (Fisher, 2002; Fisher, Hall, Rakowitz, & Gleitman, 1994; Hirsh-Pasek & Golinkoff, 1996; Hirsh-Pasek et al., 1988; Hollich et al., 2000; Naigles, 1996). Importantly, children are sensitive to both linguistic and social information in the input from a very early age (Hollich et al., 2000). Yet, early in word learning, around 10 months of age (Hirsh-Pasek, Kochanoff, Newcombe, & de Villiers, 2005), they put initial stock in perceptual cues that guide word-to-world mapping. Thus, the word *cup* will be easier to learn in the presence of a cup than will a more perceptually abstract noun *patriot*. Indeed, Bird, Franklin, and Howard (2001), Gillette et al. (1999), and our own work (Lannon et al., 2005) show that words appearing in the earliest vocabularies are the most perceptually accessible across both verbs and nouns and are those that more readily generate mental images.

At this early stage, children also approach word learning from their own point of view rather than from the speaker's point of view. For example, in the presence of an interesting and a boring object, the youngest child of 12 months is likely to assume that the word "goes with" the more interesting object, even if the adult is naming the more boring object and nonverbally indicating it through the social cue of eye gaze. The 19-month-olds followed a speaker's eye gaze to learn a novel name for a boring object. They used subtle social cues to decipher word meaning (Hollich et al., 2000; chapter 15, this volume).

Linguistic cues to word learning become prominent at about the same age. For example, 24-month-olds can use grammatical cues such as the frame in which a verb appears to discern the meaning of a novel verb (Fisher, 1996; Hirsh-Pasek & Golinkoff, 1996; Naigles, 1990, 1996). Echols (1988) also found that children could direct their attention to an object when asked to look at *the blick*, and to an action when *blicking* was requested.

According to the ECM theory, the words children initially learn will be perceptually tied and contextually bound. This will be the case irrespective of syntactic word class. Word learning, however, requires that children learn words in circumstances in which perceptual cues are not available. Words like *idea* and *think* have weak perceptual links. They are also weak in the imagery they generate. Thus, to learn any word—noun or verb—children must coordinate perceptual, social, and linguistic inputs to uncover more precise word meanings. The ECM is blind to word class. It operates as a general framework for explaining vocabulary acquisition across word classes. Thus, children's earliest words might be organized and learned, not by linguistic word classes, but on the basis of other overlapping features. It is important to note that we are not making the claim that linguistic form class does not exist for the young child. Indeed, to use and interpret words correctly in sentences, children must be aware of the linguistic role that words play in sentences. For the development of early vocabulary, however, we are suggesting that linguistic form class, per se, is not what drives the word learning system. An alternative emerging from neuropsychology and developmental cognitive psychology is presented in figure 14.3.

Rethinking the Noun-Verb Dichotomy

Borrowing from literature suggesting that all concepts encoded by words fall along a single continuum of abstractness, we will introduce the SICI continuum (see figure 14.4). Described in greater detail below, SICI is an acronym for shape, individuation, concreteness, and imageability. Following work by Golinkoff et al. (1995), Bird, Howard, and Franklin (2000b, 2003), Black and Chiat (2003), Gentner and Boroditsky (2001), and Gillette et al. (1999), we next describe how together the SICI continuum and the ECM explain not only noun learning but also illuminate the verb learning paradox and the developmental path children follow as they learn verbs. Consistent with Gillette et al. (1999) and Gentner and Boroditsky (2001), children can map words onto verbs if the actions they denote are relatively concrete. Mastery of verb mapping, like noun mapping, requires the use of

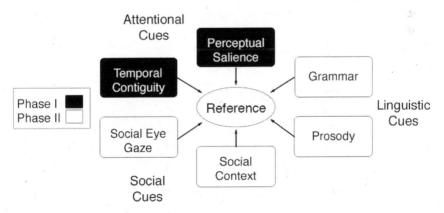

Figure 14.3. The weighting of the cues that contribute to word learning over developmental time in the emergentist coalition model. (From "Breaking the Language Barrier: An Emergentist Coalition Model for the Origins of Word Learning," by G. J. Hollich et al., 2000, *Monographs of the Society for Research in Child Development*, 65[3]. Reprinted with permission.)

grammatical and social inputs that lessen the ambiguity of the verb referent. Here we explore what it means to be relatively concrete for both nouns and verbs.

The SICI Continuum

In reaction to the field's initial focus on noun acquisition, many researchers branched out and focused on the acquisition of other syntactical classes such as adjectives (Waxman & Klibanoff, 2000), verbs (Fisher, 2002; Golinkoff et al., 1995; Huttenlocher, Smiley, & Charney, 1983; Maguire et al., 2002; Merriman, Evey-Burkey, Marazita, & Jarvis, 1996; Naigles & Hoff-Ginsberg, 1995, 1998; Tomasello, 1995), and pronouns (Campbell, Brooks, & Tomasello, 2000). As a result, much of our current understanding of language acquisition is compartmentalized and is primarily based on syntactic class. For many this seemed to be a natural partition, resulting in a flurry of research that compared the learning of nouns to verbs (see Tomasello & Merriman, 1995, for a review; see also Bornstein et al., 2004). Syntactically, nouns and verbs clearly perform different roles. Additionally, there is evidence showing that nouns and verbs are processed differently. This evidence is clear in language acquisition (Gentner, 1982; Imai et al., 2003; Meyer et al., 2003; Sandhofer et al., 2000; Theakston, Lieven, Pine, & Rowland, 2002) and in adult neurolinguistic research with brain damaged patients (for a review see Gainotti, Silveri, Daniele, & Giustolisi, 1995), using event related potentials (ERPs; Brown, Marsh, & Smith, 1973; Khader, Scherag, Streb, & Rösler, 2003; Molfese, Burger-Judisch, Gill, Golinkoff, & Hirsch-Pasek, 1996), and functional magnetic resonance imaging (fMRI; Cappa & Parani, 2002; Damasio & Tranel, 1993) research.

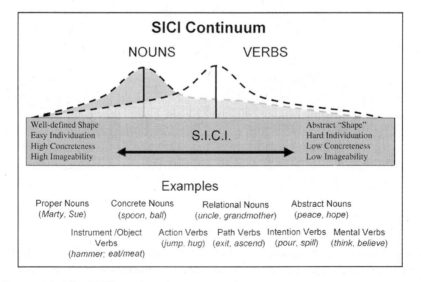

Figure 14.4. The SICI continuum.

On the other hand, more recent research indicates that nouns and verbs might not fall neatly into a dichotomous categorical system from a conceptual point of view. Rather, there might be more of a continuum between the processing of nouns and verbs (Bird, Howard, & Franklin, 2000a, 2003; Black & Chiat, 2003; Gentner & Boroditsky, 2001; Gillette et al., 1999). For example, aphasic dissociations between nouns and verbs are more ambiguous than originally proposed, with subtle abilities and faults between and within syntactical categories (Bird et al., 2000a; Durks & Masterson, 2003). Further, researchers often oversimplify the classifications noun and verb by testing thin categories of objects and actions and making inferences about the general categories of nouns and verbs. Investigators often overlooked the considerable overlap between concepts encoded in the nouns and verbs of a language (consider, for example, "*Eating* is a fun activity" vs. "She is *eating* her lunch"; but see Nelson, 1995).

Many now propose that children's difficulties in learning verbs lie not in the syntactical category of verb per se but in abstracting and mapping complex, relational, semantic information compared to simpler information (Gentner & Boroditsky, 2001; Smiley & Huttenlocher, 1995). Verbs as a class tend to be more conceptually abstract than nouns, and this distinction is even more drastically drawn when we limit the study of noun and verb categories to objects and actions (Snedeker & Gleitman, 2004). Yet, when we consider the range of nouns, from *cup* to *justice*, and verbs, from *running* to *being*, these categories begin to blur. This view suggests that the word learning problem children face is to learn words that fall on a continuum of concepts. The question that arises is how we should characterize this continuum.

As previously noted, SICI is an acronym for the many factors that scale the difficulty of learning a particular word (shape, individuation, concreteness, and imageability). In creating this continuum, we again borrow from Gentner and Boroditsky (2001), Snedeker and Gleitman (2004), research in neurolinguistics (Bird et al., 2000b; Black & Chiat, 2003), and our own work (Golinkoff et al., 1995, 2002). We use SICI instead of relying on any single feature of the continuum for two reasons. First, the literature uses these terms somewhat loosely, and different terms are used across related but different literatures (as in neuroscience). Rather than select any one term to label the continuum, we use an amalgamation. Second, to the extent that these factors play a role in word learning, it is unclear at this time how much weight each one should be given. Thus, because all of these features appear to be important in understanding the continuum of concepts, we take a broad view.

SICI: S Is for Shape

Golinkoff et al. (1995) argued that early in verb learning, and analogous to the shape bias in noun learning (Smith, 2000), young children abstract the "shape" of the main event (as Pinker, 1989, called it) when they observe an action. Indeed,

Golinkoff et al. (1995) predicted that the first kinds of verbs children would learn and extend would be those that lent themselves to the abstraction of an invariant shape (like *dancing*) as opposed to those verbs that described less visible actions (like *thinking*):

> the shape of an event is different from that of objects, for which shape refers to a persistent, palpable object contour. For actions, shape lasts only as long as the event and refers to the overall configuration of the action. To say that the child abstracts the shape of the main event . . . allows the infant to lose the detail of each individual event (i.e., to "bleach" it) and to represent a class of events with a single representation. (p. 198)

Although Golinkoff et al. (1995) did not scale various verbs for the likelihood that they share a common shape (the verb *dancing* would undoubtedly get a higher score than the verb *wishing*, but lower than *walking*, for example), they did bring this notion to ground in two different studies. Golinkoff et al. (1995) asked whether toddlers could fast map and extend new action names as younger toddlers had shown with object names (Golinkoff, Hirsh-Pasek, Bailey, & Wenger, 1992). Thirty-seven-month-olds saw static pictures with various Sesame Street characters performing actions, some familiar and some novel (see figure 14.5). In response to a novel verb, toddlers selected the unknown action demonstrating mutual exclusivity in verb labels. Further, they then extended the new verb to another character whose body showed the same shape, for example, arms and one leg extended for an arabesque. In this experiment stimuli were static, two-dimensional drawings so it was unclear whether children could extend verb labels to ongoing actions. However, the findings showed the importance of body shape in extending a verb label.

In a second article, Golinkoff et al. (2002) presented children (mean age 37 months) with "point light" displays of actions. Point light displays show only dots of light on the major joints (elbow, shoulders, knees, etc.) of a human performing an action in the dark. In this study, children were shown four pairs of eight possible, known actions (kicking, dancing, etc.) in point light displays on a split screen. The scene was accompanied with a verb label corresponding to one of the two actions. For example, children heard "Look at her dancing!" when dancing and kicking were shown. Despite the fact that children only saw lights moving about on a screen, they were able to find the match in the intermodal preferential looking paradigm (Hirsh-Pasek & Golinkoff, 1996) when asked to locate a particular action. These findings suggest that children extend verbs based on an averaged representation of what that action looks like, its "verbal essence" (Golinkoff et al., 2002). "Verbs of motion have . . . *a typical appearance, a physiognomy*" (Marconi, 1997, p. 159, emphasis added).

Since research has established that a major basis of noun extension (although not the only basis—see Kemler Nelson, Russell, Duke, & Jones, 2000; Golinkoff et al., 1995) is shared shape (Smith, 2000), perhaps it is not surprising that when

Figure 14.5. Stimuli from Golinkoff et al. (1996) showing three known actions (eating, sleeping, and reading) and one unknown action ("arabesquing"). Shape cues were potent in determining verb extensions. (From "Lexical Principles May Underlie the Learning of Verbs," by R. M. Golinkoff, R. Jacquet, K. Hirsh-Pasek, and R. Nandakumar, 1996, *Child Development, 67,* 3101–3119. Reprinted with permission.)

possible, children use shape for verb extension. Undoubtedly object shape is more reliable and consistent than the generalized shape of actions that unfold in time. Nonetheless, verbs could be scaled for how much shape consistency they offer (Golinkoff et al., 1995). This argument was originally made within word class, but we propose it extends across them. *Dancing* is also more consistent in shape than the verb *thinking*, but it is also more consistent in shape than the noun *idea*. Thus, there may be substantial overlap across word classes in terms of a shape continuum.

SICI: I Is for Individuation

Other researchers agree that the complexity of the concept a word labels influences word learning. Gentner and Boroditsky (2001) posited a continuum they labeled the Division of Dominance to understand why nouns are acquired before verbs. At the cognitive dominance end of the continuum, items are individuable and available from observation of the world. For example, the referent of a concrete noun like *cup* can be readily observed in the world, as can the referent of any proper name for an individual. Anchoring the linguistic dominance end of the continuum are grammatical elements, such as determiners and conjunctions, which can only be learned through language; there is no individuable element in the world that corresponds to *and*. Gentner and Boroditsky placed verbs and spatial prepositions closer to the linguistic dominance end. Thus, to learn a verb, the child has to know at least some language because "their meanings are linguistically embedded . . . invented or shaped by language to a greater degree than is the case for concrete nouns" (p. 216). Yet Gentner and Boroditsky recognized that not all nouns are at the cognitive end of the dominance continuum. Not all nouns label concrete objects available for inspection in the world. Nouns like *uncle* (meaning male sibling of one of my parents) that specify kinship relations and are defined within a system fall closer to the middle of the continuum.

Gentner and Boroditsky posit that the individuability of a concept determines the ease with which it can be learned. On this theory, in general, verbs lie at the more difficult end of this continuum and are thus harder to learn compared to nouns. Though Gentner and Boroditsky's continuum allows for distinctions within word class, they did not fully explore the possibility of overlap between word categories. Here we argue that this individuation continuum may be extended in this way to help explain all of word learning.

SICI: C Is for Concreteness and I Is for Imageability

The concepts of concreteness and imageability have also be discussed in relation to the noun-verb distinction (Bird et al., 2000a, 2000b; Bird, Franklin, & Howard, 2001; Black & Chiat, 2003; Gillette et al., 1999). In much of the literature on memory and aphasia, the terms *concreteness* and *imageability* are used interchangeably. Here we include both to stay consistent with that work. *Imageability* is defined as the ease with which a word gives rise to a sensory mental image (Paivio, Yuille, & Madigan, 1968). This is distinct from *concreteness* (Paivio et al., 1968), which refers to the ability to see, hear, and touch something. Imageability thus includes, for example, emotion words like *joy* or *hate* that one can imagine but not touch. Imageability ratings generally occur on a 7-point scale from "not imageable at all" (1) to "extremely imageable" (7); (Bird et al., 2001; Gillette et al., 1999). Ratings of imageability would ordinarily, however, be highly correlated with ratings of concreteness (Paivio et al., 1968).

Imageability ratings are more predictive of word acquisition than the grammatical categories of noun and verb. Bird et al. (2001) found that regardless of grammatical category (including verbs and function words), age of acquisition is significantly correlated with imageability. Further, imageability can predict the ease with which one can determine the referent of a novel word in context. In the human simulation study by Gillette et al. (1999), adults' difficulty in identifying absent verb labels compared to noun labels disappeared completely when imageability was controlled:

> it is not a difference between nouns and verbs per se that accounts for the ease with which words are identified. . . . The account is a more mundane and ultimately tautological one, namely that only observables— the most "picturable" or "imaginable" items—can be efficiently acquired by observational operating alone." (p. 153)

Thus, imageability, even for adults, determines the ease with which a novel word is identified, regardless of syntactic class. This further supports the claim of a continuum spanning across word class and allowing for overlap between word classes instead of a dichotomy for understanding noun and verb acquisition.

In sum, words can be thought of as falling on a continuum that characterizes the reliability and consistency of their shape, the ease with which they can be distinguished from other items in the scene (individuability), whether they can be observed in the world at all and are manipulable (concreteness), and how readily they yield a mental image for adults (imageability). Importantly, while nouns differ in their position on this continuum, so do verbs. In fact, nouns and verbs can even overlap in where they fall.

If we couple SICI with a general word learning theory, in this case the ECM, we might gain some purchase on the way the earliest words are learned. Children's earliest words will likely be at the more concrete, shape-based end of this continuum across word classes. Thus, a noun like *cup* will be learned prior to *uncle* and the verb *kiss* will be learned before *think*.

How the ECM, in Combination With the SICI Continuum, Helps Us Understand Verb Learning

Verbs in general lie on the more abstract end of the SICI continuum. As a result, mapping is more ambiguous and requires children to utilize multiple cues to narrow down candidate meaning.

A major tenet of the ECM is that children begin by relying on perceptual information and shift their attention to social and linguistic information in learning words. A large body of research supports this claim with respect to noun learning (see Hollich et al., 2000, for a review). Here we expand this argument by showing similar support within the class of verbs and across word classes. Support for this argument is in three parts. First, we suggest that children's early vocabularies reveal that words are learned through a perceptual bias. Second, we review evidence for the increased use of social cues as children master verb acquisition. Third, we review empirical support for the children's increased use of linguistic cues in uncovering verb meaning. In the end, we argue that given the SICI continuum as a conceptual base, the ECM can explain both word mapping for nouns and verbs.

Initial Perceptual Bias in Verb Concepts

Many of the verbs that appear early in children's vocabularies follow the characteristics of words on the concrete end of the SICI continuum. Throughout the literature, the argument for a perceptually biased, concrete word learner is made in a number of ways. One argument is that children's early verbs are more likely to be available to perception (such as *eat* or *run*) as opposed to later verbs that cannot be as readily observed (such as *think, wish,* or *dream*) (chapter 4, this volume; Smiley & Huttenlocher, 1995; Snedeker & Gleitman, 2004). A second version of this argument is that children's early verbs are more likely to be used in specific contexts and linked to routines as opposed to used more broadly in a wider range of contexts (see chapters 13 and 18, this volume). A third version of the perceptually biased verb learner is that children's early verbs are more likely to require fewer inferences about the speaker's intentions and goals than later verbs (e.g., *pour* versus *spill*) (chapters 10 and 11, this volume; Behrend, 1995; Smiley & Huttenlocher, 1995). A last version of this argument is that children's early verbs are more likely to be used in limited, nonmetaphorical extensions as opposed to broader extensions (Behrend, 1995; Forbes & Farrar, 1993). The evidence that children's initial verb meanings are quite perceptually based, as the ECM would predict, is extensive for each of these overlapping arguments.

Further research with both nouns and verbs suggests that children's early word meanings are relatively concrete compare to those of adults (Gentner, 2003). For example, children use abstract relational terms, like *uncle*, without any apparent understanding of the kinship system implied. Instead, they interpret such complex relational nouns as more concrete, perceptually based concepts, for example, an uncle is a nice man with a pipe (Keil & Batterman, 1984). This conforms to predictions of the ECM and suggests that children interpret more complex, relational nouns as falling at the more concrete end of the SICI continuum than they really do. Children map *uncle* not as an abstract kin relationship (i.e., a parent's brother), but as a perceptually salient feature, for example, "the man who looks like my dad and plays football with me" (see also Hall & Waxman, 1993).

Evidence in verb learning also shows that the verb meanings children encode are more concrete than adults' meanings (Forbes & Farrar, 1993; Maguire et al., 2002; Smiley & Huttenlocher, 1995). For example, Gallivan (1988) interviewed children (ages 3 to 5 years) and adults about the meaning of 10 verbs common in early vocabularies. While children gave definitions concerning perceptual similarities between exemplars (agent, object, and instrument), adults gave more conceptual responses, such as the intentions of the agents and descriptions of the scene. These findings support the theory that younger children use perceptual information as a basis for their understanding of verbs, while adults use more informative aspects such as intentions of the actor.

Forbes and Farrar (1993) taught 3-year-olds, 7-year-olds, and adults novel verbs for novel actions and asked them to judge whether the verb applied to new situations. There was a developmental progression in which adults were more liberal in their extensions than 7-year-olds, and 7-year-olds were more liberal than the very conservative 3-year-olds. For 3-year-olds there could be very few perceptual changes, for example in the result or the instrument, for the novel verb to be extended to a new exemplar. Thus, the conceptualization of the novel verb was much more concrete on the SICI continuum for 3-year-olds than 7-year-olds or adults, who could abstract the meaning from the perceptual scene.

Additionally, Theakston et al. (2002) showed that even for apparently simple verbs like *go*, children between the ages of 2 and 3 years do not have a single, unified concept of *go* despite its frequent use. Instead, at younger ages there were very specific situations for each grammatical instantiation of the word *go*. Thus, while children appeared to use a verb competently, they really used it with many different, unrelated meanings.

How do children move beyond their perceptual biases? According to the ECM, they become increasingly able to mine the social and linguistic cues afforded to them as they learn concepts further along the SICI continuum.

Use of Social Cues

Two forms of intentional understanding are vital to learning novel verbs: (1) inferring the speaker's attentional focus and communicative intent (Baldwin, 1995; Tomasello, Strosberg, & Akhtar, 1996) and (2) inferring the intent of the actor (chapter 10, this volume; Poulin-Dubois & Forbes, 2002; Smiley & Huttenlocher, 1995).

Akhtar and Tomasello (1996) showed that children infer the intent of a speaker to name a novel action when they learn a label for an action that they never saw performed! Here the experimenter told the child that she would *meek* Big Bird. Then after searching, the experimenter informed the child that she could not find Big Bird. The target action was then performed with other objects, but never labeled. As a test, a novel object appeared and the children were asked to *meek* Cookie Monster. These children were still able to produce the action with the novel object at the same rate as children who heard the label as the action was performed. Thus, children used the intent of the speaker to interpret the meaning of the novel verb.

Children not only need to be able to follow the intent of the speaker with respect to which aspect of an event is receiving a label, but to understand the intent of the actor in order to learn the names of similar actions. Poulin-Dubois and Forbes (2002) found that 27-month-olds but not 21-month-olds could use social cues when distinguishing between novel actions that looked quite similar except for barely detectable social information. Specifically, 27-month-olds attended to the subtle cue of eye gaze when determining whether a verb meant something like *topple* or *knock over* when viewing the same action. At this young age, children understand that actions can look similar but have distinct labels because of the intentions of the actor.

Another example of children's ability to utilize subtle social cues comes from the work of Imai, Haryu, Okada, Lianjing, and Shigematsu (chapter 17, this volume) with Chinese-speaking children. When they discovered that even children as old as 5 years could not map a novel verb to a novel action, they reasoned that it might have something to do with the social cues available in the scene. Prior to hearing an unseen speaker offer a label for a novel action performed on a novel object, the actor held up the object that was to be used for a few seconds. Imai et al. reasoned that the extra seconds during which the object was held up may have suggested that the new word was a noun. When the extra seconds of object holding was removed, many more children now attached the new word to the new action.

Children's exquisite sensitivity to social cues when the speaker and the actor were the same also surfaced in a study by Behrend and Wittek (2003; chapter 11, this volume). An actor performed a novel intended action (putting a string of beads into a cup) or a novel unintended action (dropping the string of beads next to the cup) either accompanied by a novel verb label or without a verb. Behrend and Wittek hypothesized that if the unintended action was given a label, children would believe the action was intentional. Results, though not as strong as predicted, did show that 30-month-olds were more likely than younger children to reproduce the unintentional looking action (dropping beads next to the cup) if it was labeled during training. Thus, children take the presence of a verb as a sign that a novel action is being named. On the other hand, the weakness of this effect is also informative for it shows the overwhelming influence of intentionality on children's understanding of human actions. Children ordinarily avoid labeling a seemingly unintended action (see also Childers & Behrend, 2003).

To fully master verb learning requires a strong understanding of both actor and speaker intent. Many potential referents for verbs exist simultaneously. Being able to interpret speaker and actor intent is essential to arriving at the correct verb meanings.

Use of Linguistic Cues

Syntactic frames serve to constrain the possible interpretations of a novel verb, because frames have semantic implications for the verbs that appear in them (Fisher, 2002; Fisher et al., 1994; Gleitman & Gillette, 1995; Naigles, 1990, 1996). For example, a child may hear "bring" while holding a doll and could assume the word means *bring, carry,* or *walk*. But if the child hears "Are you bringing me the doll?" the use of two objects in the frame verb-noun phrase-noun phrase suggests that *bring* is a verb of transfer, eliminating *hold, carry,* and *walk* (Naigles, 1996).

Research using the intermodal preferential looking paradigm found that by 2 to 2.5 years of age children are sensitive to the implications different verb frames have for meaning (Hirsh-Pasek & Golinkoff, 1996; Hirsh-Pasek et al., 1988; Naigles, 1996; see also chapter 15, this volume). For example, children who heard a verb in a transitive sentence frame such as "Oh, see Big Bird glorping Cookie Monster" watched a causal event in which Big Bird made Cookie Monster do something more than they watched a noncausal event in which Big Bird and Cookie Monster performed a novel action together. The opposite result occurred when children heard an intransitive sentence such as, "Oh, see Big Bird is glorping with Cookie Monster!" Hearing this sentence, children watched the noncausal event more than the causal event (Hirsh-Pasek, Golinkoff, & Naigles, 1996). This finding indicates that by around 2 years children understand that cause is encoded in a transitive sentence frame. Other empirical support for the role that linguistic information plays in cueing verb meaning comes from work by Fisher (2002; Fisher et al., 1994; chapter 15, this volume) and Naigles (1990, 1996; Naigles & Kako, 1993; chapter 13, this volume). These findings indicate, as predicted by the ECM, that by around the second year, toddlers are beginning to use grammatical cues in their language to narrow the possible referents of a novel verb.

Children can also use information in the syntactical frame to decipher which aspect of an event a verb labels. Maguire (2004) tested toddlers' ability to use prepositions to interpret a novel verb label. Twenty-five- and 31-month-olds saw video clips of an animated character ("Starry") performing one manner across four different paths in relation to a stable ball. Starry could spin over the ball, spin under the ball, spin past the ball, and spin in front of the ball. The scenes were labeled in one of two ways: either with the correct preposition ("Look, Starry's blicking over the ball. Now he's blicking under the ball"), or without a preposition ("Look, Starry's blicking"). During the test trials, toddlers were shown a novel manner across one of the familiar paths (e.g., bending over the ball) or the familiar manner across a new path (e.g., spinning behind the ball) and were asked to "Look at Starry blicking." Only in the condition where children were offered additional linguistic information in the prepositional phrase, did they successfully extend a novel verb to the manner of the action.

Thus, as children develop they become better able to use all of the resources available (perceptual, social and linguistic) to them in deciphering word meanings. While perceptual cues can help to a large degree with nouns, words that lie on the more abstract end of the SICI continuum are less accessible through perceptual cues alone. These require social and linguistic support to narrow down the candidate meaning for a word. Because verbs generally, though not always, lie on the more abstract end of the continuum, mapping most verbs and some nouns awaits children's ability to coordinate use of the multiple cues at their disposal in the service of word learning. The result is that abstract, relational words are not fully mastered until children can recruit these resources successfully.

A More Coherent and Unified View of Word Learning

We began with a statement of the facts on noun and verb learning that have predominated in our literature. Traditionally, the literature in our field finds that verbs are harder to learn than nouns. Perhaps we can explain the differences in noun and verb learning through appeal to a broad-based theory of word learning (ECM) that is blind to form class. Building on Snedeker and Gleitman (2004) and Gentner and Boroditsky (2001), we suggest that words lie on a continuum from more concrete to more abstract. As we move conceptually towards the more abstract end of the continuum, mapping from word to world becomes too ambiguous to solve without added support from social and linguistic cues. The ECM predicts that children will first map words onto concepts that are more perceptually salient, only later recruiting social and linguistic cues in the service of word learning. This will be true for all words, including nouns, verbs, and even adjectives. This broader view of vocabulary building turns our attention to common mechanisms that might be responsible for learning words providing a more parsimonious story of vocabulary acquisition. Further, the argument for a broader framework for word learning helps us better understand the emerging and often contrasting pattern of findings that have evolved in our literature.

Next we return to the facts about verb learning we pointed out at the start of the paper, facts that seemed unrelated and possibly incoherent. Armed with the ECM, we have a grasp now on what those facts mean and how they fit together.

1. Why are nouns generally learned before verbs? Because on average, nouns, especially object nouns of the sort studied in our literature, fall at the more concrete end of the SICI continuum than do verbs. These more imageable words are learned earlier than less imageable words, regardless of syntactic class (Bird et al., 2001). Preliminary data in our labs (Lannon et al., 2005) suggests that adult ratings of imageability correlate with age of acquisition on standardized material checklists, like the MacArthur Communicative Inventory (Fenson et al., 1994) irrespective of word class in both English and Chinese.

2. Why does this pattern appear to be universal (Bornstein et al., 2004)? Despite the fact that verbs in some languages appear to be favored, research suggests that even in those languages verbs are generally more difficult to learn than nouns. For example, languages like Chinese and Japanese allow the verb to appear in isolation or in potent sentence final position. Nonetheless, research conducted in laboratory settings reveals that children often struggle with learning new verbs even when in situations where they readily learn new nouns (chapter 17, this

volume; Meyer et al., 2003). This is because the packaging and perspective problems are universal to verbs across languages.

3. Why do some verbs appear in children's earliest vocabularies, a finding that is especially pronounced in languages like Chinese (Tardif et al., 1999) and Tzeltzal (Brown, 1998)? We have discussed two reasons why some verbs appear early in children's vocabularies for at least two reasons. First, the verbs that appear in these languages are on the more concrete end of the SICI continuum. Although the average noun is more concrete than the average verb, there is variability around the mean. There is within-class variation on the SICI continuum just as there is between-class variation in where items fall. As Snedeker and Gleitman (2004) have argued, motion verbs will be acquired earlier than mental verbs. Similarly, those verbs that are more perceptually available and contextually bound will be learned before verbs that are not. The specificity of verbs in other languages may explain their early acquisition. For example, in Tzeltzal there are different, context-specific verbs for "eat meat" (*ti'*), "eat soft things" (*lo'*) and "eat crunchy things" (*k'ux*) (Brown, 2001). Each of these verbs is produced by children in the one-word stage. The specificity of their meanings may make them easier to acquire than the more abstract English *eat*. Those verbs found at the concrete end of the SICI continuum are easier to acquire, just as the ECM and SICI would predict. Indeed, Tardif (chapter 18, this volume) suggests that the early verbs learned by Chinese children are more perceptually accessible and context bound, a finding echoed by Naigles and Hoff (chapter 13, this volume).

The second explanation for children's early verbs comes from the apparent contradiction of children using verbs like *think* and *know* that seem to fall at the abstract end of the SICI continuum. Here the research suggests that children might have only partial knowledge of the meanings of these verbs (Gallivan, 1998; Theakston et al., 2002). That is, while children may use these verbs, they probably do not use them in adult-like ways.

Thus, the verbs that enter children's vocabularies early have meanings that are either (1) accessible to a young child through perception and context-specificity, or (2) have meanings that are different than adult meanings by being less abstract than they appear. The predictions of the ECM, combined with the SICI continuum, help explain why verbs appear in early vocabularies even though the class of verbs is learned relatively late.

4. Finally, why are the conceptual meanings of some nouns like passenger or uncle acquired relatively late in development? As with verbs, nouns demonstrate within class variability on the SICI continuum. Indeed, sometimes the noun distribution will overlap with the verb distribution because these nouns are more abstract. Like verbs, these more difficult nouns can enter children's vocabularies early, but when they do, their meanings are not the same as adult meanings. Such is the case with nouns like *passenger* and *island*, which for children are rooted in perceptually based, concrete notions (Hall & Waxman, 1993; Keil & Batterman, 1984). Just as with verbs, learning abstract relational nouns will require the coordination

of social and linguistic information in additional to perceptual cues. In short, a wide-angle lens on word learning helps to explain what appear to be divergent findings in the verb learning literature.

Conclusion

During the past 10 years, the study of word learning has become more inclusive. Instead of focusing solely on ways in which children learn object nouns, we now have data on how children learn verbs, adjectives, and pronouns. It is possible that each word class will require different learning rules. For example, the packaging and perspective problems might be unique to verbs and adjectives. Yet an alternate and perhaps more parsimonious approach to the study of word learning posits that one framework might be able to account for all word learning and that differences in noun and verb learning might be a product of natural variation among the kinds of things that these syntactic form classes tend to label. The ECM offers one such unified account. It is an account that is sensitive to data from linguistics, psychology, and neuropsychology. It also allows us a way to explain seemingly disparate findings in a coherent way.

Acknowledgments The research reported here and the writing of the chapter were supported by NSF grants SBR9601306 and SBR9615391 to both authors and by NICHD grant 3U10HD25455-0552 to Hirsh-Pasek. We thank our laboratory coordinators, Dede Addy, Amanda Brandone, Meredith Meyer, and Meredith Jones, whose good work allowed us to concentrate on this project, and Josh Pasek who helped us streamline the arguments for this chapter.

References

Akhtar, N., & Tomasello, M. (1996). Two-year-olds learn words for absent objects and actions. *British Journal of Developmental Psychology, 14,* 79–93.

Baldwin, D. A. (1995). Understanding the link between joint attention and language. In C. Moore & P. J. Dunham (Eds.), *Joint attention: Its origins and role in development* (pp. 131–158). Hillsdale, NJ: Lawrence Erlbaum.

Baldwin, D. A., & Tomasello, M. (1998). Word learning: A window on early pragmatic understanding. In E. V. Clark (Ed.), *Proceedings of the Stanford Child Language Research Forum* (pp. 3–23). Cambridge: Cambridge University Press.

Behrend, D. A. (1995). Processes involved in the initial mapping of verb meanings. In M. Tomasello & W. E. Merriman (Eds.), *Beyond the names for things: Young children's acquisition of verbs* (pp. 251–275). Hillsdale, NJ: Lawrence Erlbaum.

Behrend, D. A., & Wittek, A. (2003, April). *Toddlers use verbs as cues to an actor's intentions.* Paper presented at the meetings of the Society for Research in Child Development, Tampa, FL.

Bird, H., Franklin, S., & Howard, D. (2001). Age of acquisition and imageability ratings for a large set of words, including verbs and function words. *Behavior Research Methods, Instruments, and Computers, 33*, 73–79.

Bird, H., Howard, D., & Franklin, S. (2000a). Little words—not really: Function and content words in normal and aphasic speech. *Journal of Neurolinguistics, 15*, 209–237.

Bird, H., Howard, D., & Franklin, S. (2000b). Why is a verb like an inanimate object? Grammatical category and semantic category deficits. *Brain and Language, 72*, 246–309.

Bird, H., Howard, D., & Franklin, S. (2003). Verbs and nouns: The importance of being imageable. *Journal of Neurolinguistics, 16*, 113–149.

Black, M., & Chiat, S. (2003). Noun-verb dissociations: A multi-faceted phenomenon. *Journal of Neurolinguistics, 16*, 231–250.

Bloom, L. (1993). *The transition from infancy to language: Acquiring the power of expression*. New York: Cambridge University Press.

Bornstein, M., Cole, L., Maital, S. K., Park, S. Y., Pascual, L., et al. (2004). Cross-linguistic analysis of vocabulary in young children: Spanish, Dutch, French, Hebrew, Italian, Korean and American English. *Child Development, 75*, 1115–1140.

Brown, P. (1998). Children's first verb in Tzeltal: Evidence for an early verb category. *Linguistics, 36*, 713–753.

Brown, P. (2001). Learning to talk about motion UP and DOWN in Tzeltal: Is there a language-specific bias for verb learning? In M. Bowerman & S. C. Levinson (Eds.), *Language acquisition and conceptual development* (pp. 512–543). Cambridge: Cambridge University Press.

Brown, W. S., Marsh, J. T., & Smith, J. C. (1973). Contextual meaning effects on speech evoked potentials. *Behavioral Biology, 9*, 755–761.

Campbell, A. L., Brooks, P., & Tomasello, M. (2000). Factors affective young children's use of pronouns as referring expressions. *Journal of Speech and Hearing Research, 43*, 1337–1349.

Cappa, S., & Perani, D. (2002). The neural correlates of noun and verb processing. *Journal of Neurolinguistics, 16*, 183–189.

Childers, J. B., & Behrend, D. A. (2003). *Children expect novel verbs to refer to intentional actions*. Poster presented at the American Psychological Society Conference, Atlanta, GA.

Childers, J. B., & Tomasello, M. (2002). Two-year-olds learn novel nouns, verbs, and conventional actions from massed or distributed exposures. *Developmental Psychology, 38*, 967–978.

Choi, S. (2000). Caregiver input in English and Korean: The use of nouns and verbs in book-reading and toy-play contexts. *Journal of Child Language, 27*, 69–96.

Choi, S., & Bowerman, M. (1991). Learning to express motion events in English and Korean: The influence of language-specific lexicalization patterns. *Cognition, 41*, 83–121.

Choi, S., & Gopnik, A. (1995). Names, relational words, and cognitive development in English and Korean speakers: Nouns are not always learned before verbs. In M. Tomasello & W. E. Merriman (Eds.), *Beyond the names for things: Young children's acquisition of verbs* (pp. 63–80). Hillsdale, NJ: Lawrence Erlbaum.

Damasio, A. R., & Tranel, D. (1993). Nouns and verbs are retrieved with differently distributed neural systems. *Proceedings of the National Academy of Sciences, USA, 90*(5), 4957–4960.

Durks, J., & Masterson, J. (2003). Editorial. *Journal of Neurolinguistics, 16*, 59–65.

Echols, C. H. (1988, April). *The identification of words and their meanings in the transition into language*. Paper presented at the International Conference on Infant Studies, Atlanta, GA.

Echols, C. H., & Marti, C. N. (2004). The identification of words and their meanings from perceptual biases to language-specific cues. In D. G. Hall & S. R. Waxman (Eds.), *Weaving a lexicon* (pp. 41–78). Cambridge, MA: MIT Press.

Fenson, L., Dale, P. S., Reznick, J. S., Bates, E., Thal, D., & Pethick, S. J. (1994). Variability in early communicative development. *Monographs of the Society for Research in Child Development, 59* (5, Serial No. 242).

Fisher, C. (1996). Structural limits on verb mapping: The role of analogy in children's interpretations of sentences. *Cognitive Psychology, 31*, 41–81.

Fisher, C. (2002). Structural limits on verb mapping: The role of abstract structure in 2.5-year-olds' interpretations of novel verbs. *Developmental Science, 5*, 55–64.

Fisher, C., Hall, D. G., Rakowitz, S., & Gleitman, L. R. (1994). When it is better to receive than to give: Syntactic and conceptual constraints on vocabulary growth. *Lingua, 92*, 333–375.

Forbes, J. N., & Farrar, J. M. (1993). Children's initial assumptions about the meaning of novel motion verbs: Biased and conservative? *Cognitive Development, 8*, 273–290.

Gainotti, G., Silveri, M., Daniele, A., & Giustolisi, L. (1995). Neuroanatomical correlates of category-specific semantic disorders: A critical survey, *Memory, 3*, 247–264.

Gallivan, J. (1988). Motion verb acquisition: Development of definitions. *Perceptual and Motor Skills, 66*, 979–986.

Gentner, D. (1982). Why nouns are learned before verbs: Linguistical relativity versus natural partitioning. In S. A. Kuczaj II (Ed.), *Language development: Vol. 2. Language, thought, and culture* (pp. 301–334). Hillsdale, NJ: Lawrence Erlbaum.

Gentner, D. (2003). Why are we so smart? In D. Gentner & S. Goldin-Meadow (Eds.), *Language in mind: Advances in the study of language and thought* (pp. 195–236). Cambridge, MA: MIT Press.

Gentner, D., & Boroditsky, L. (2001). Individuation, relativity and early word learning. In M. Bowerman & S. C. Levinson (Eds.), *Language, culture, and cognition: Vol. 3. Language acquisition and conceptual development* (pp. 215–256). New York: Cambridge University Press.

Gillette, J., Gleitman, H., Gleitman, L., & Lederer, A. (1999). Human simulations of vocabulary learning. *Cognition, 73*, 135–176.

Gleitman, L. (1990). Structural sources of verb meaning. *Language Acquisition, 1*, 3–55.

Gleitman, L., Cassidy, K., Nappa, R., Papafragou, A., & Trueswell, J. (2005). Hard words. *Language Learning and Development, 1*, 23–64.

Gleitman, L., & Gillette, J. (1995). The role of syntax in verb learning. In P. Fletcher & B. MacWhinney (Eds.), *The handbook of child language* (pp. 413–427). London: Blackwell.

Gleitman, L., & Gleitman, H. (1992). A picture is worth a thousand words: The role of syntax in vocabulary acquisition. *Current Directions in Psychological Science, 3*, 31–35.

Golinkoff, R. M., Chung, H. L., Hirsh-Pasek, K., Liu, J., Bertenthal, B. I., Brand, R., et al. (2002). Point-light displays as a key to early verb learning. *Developmental Psychology, 4*, 604–615.

Golinkoff, R. M., Hirsh-Pasek, K., Bailey, L., & Wenger, N. (1992). Young children and adults use lexical principles to learn new nouns. *Developmental Psychology, 28*, 99–108.

Golinkoff, R. M., Hirsh-Pasek, K., Cauley, K. M., & Gordon, L. (1987). The eyes have it: Lexical and syntactic comprehension in a new paradigm. *Journal of Child Language, 14*, 23–45.

Golinkoff, R. M., Hirsh-Pasek, K., Mervis, C. B., Frawley, W. B., & Parillo, M. (1995). Lexical principles can be extended to the acquisition of verbs. In M. Tomasello & W. E. Merriman (Eds.), *Beyond the name for things: Young children's acquisition of verbs* (pp. 185–222). Hillsdale, NJ: Lawrence Erlbaum.

Golinkoff, R. M., Jacquet, R., Hirsh-Pasek, K., & Nandakumar, R. (1996). Lexical principles may underlie the learning of verbs. *Child Development, 67*, 3101–3119.

Hall, D. G., & Waxman, S. R. (1993). Assumptions about word meaning: Individuation and basic-level kinds. *Child Development, 64*, 1550–1575.

Haryu, E., Imai, M., Okada, H., Li, L., Meyer, M., Hirsh-Pasek, K., et al. (in press). *Noun bias in Chinese children: Novel noun and verb learning in Chinese, Japanese, and English preschoolers.* Proceedings of the Boston Child Language meetings.

Hirsh-Pasek, K., & Golinkoff, R. (1996). The preferential looking paradigm reveals emerging language comprehension. In D. McDaniel, C. McKee, & H. Caims (Eds.), *Advances in infancy research, Vol. 8* (pp. 53–73). Norwood, NJ: Ablex.

Hirsh-Pasek, K., Golinkoff, R. M., & Naigles, L. (1996). *The origins of grammar: Evidence from early language comprehension.* Cambridge, MA: MIT Press.

Hirsh-Pasek, K., Kochanoff, A., Newcombe, N., & de Villiers, J. (2005). Using scientific knowledge to inform preschool assessment: Making the case for "empirical validity." *Social Policy Report, 19*(1), 3–19.

Hirsh-Pasek, K., Naigles, L., Golinkoff, R. M., Gleitman, L. R., & Gleitman, H. (1988, October). *Syntactic bootstrapping: Evidence from comprehension.* Paper presented at the Boston University Conference on Language Development, Boston, MA.

Hollich, G. J., Hirsh-Pasek, K., Golinkoff, R., Brand, R., Brown, E., Chung, H. L., et al. (2000). Breaking the language barrier: An emergentist coalition model for the origins of word learning. *Monographs of the Society for Research in Child Development, 65*(3).

Huttenlocher, J., Smiley, P., & Charney, R. (1983). Emergence of action categories in the child: Evidence from verb meanings. *Psychological Review, 90*, 72–93.

Imai, M., & Gentner, D. (1997). A crosslinguistic study of early word meaning: Universal ontology and linguistic influence. *Cognition, 62*, 169–200.

Imai, M., & Haryu, E. (2001). Learning proper nouns and common nouns without clues from syntax. *Child Development, 72*, 787–802.

Imai, M., Haryu, E., & Okada, H. (2003). Is verb learning easier than noun learning for Japanese children? 3-year-old Japanese children's knowledge about object names and action names. In B. Skarabela, S. Fish, & A. H.-J. Do (Eds.), *Proceedings of the 26th Annual Boston University Conference on Language Development* (pp. 324–335).

Imai, M., Haryu, E., & Okada, H. (in press). Is verb learning easier than noun learning for Japanese children? 3-year-old Japanese children's knowledge about object names and action names. *Proceedings of the 26th Annual Boston University Conference on Language Development.*

Keil, F. C., & Batterman, N. (1984). A characteristic-to-defining shift in the development of word meaning. *Journal of Verbal Learning and Verbal Behavior, 23*, 221–236.

Kemler Nelson, D. G., Russell, R., Duke, N., & Jones, K. (2000). Two-year-olds will name artifacts by their functions. *Child Development, 71*, 1271–1288.

Kersten, A. W., & Smith, L. B. (2002). Attention to novel objects during verb learning. *Child Development, 73*(1), 93–109.

Khader, P., Scherag, A., Streb, J., & Rösler, F. (2003). Differences between noun and verb processing in a minimal phrase context: a semantic priming study using event-related brain potentials. *Cognitive Brain Research, 17*, 293–313.

Kim, M., McGregor, K. K., & Thompson, C. K. (2000). Early lexical development in English- and Korean-speaking children: Language-general and language specific patterns. *Journal of Child Language, 27*, 225–254.

Lannon, B., McDonough, C., Ma, W., Hirsh-Pasek, K., Golinkoff, R. M., & Tardif, T. (2005). *The role of imageability in early word learning: Evidence from English and Chinese*. Manuscript in preparation.

Maguire, M. J. (2004). *Children's use of universal and language-specific cues in verb learning*. Unpublished dissertation, Temple University, Philadelphia, PA.

Maguire, M. J., Hennon, E. A., Hirsh-Pasek, K., Golinkoff, R. M., Slutzky, C. B., & Sootsman, J. (2002). Mapping words to actions and events: How do 18-month-olds learn a verb? In B. Skarabela, S. Fish, & A. H. J. Do (Eds.), *Proceedings of the Boston University Annual Conference on Language Development* (pp. 371–382). Somerville, MA: Cascadilla Press.

Marconi, D. (1997). *Lexical competence*. Cambridge, MA: MIT Press.

Merriman, W. E., Evey-Burkey, J. A., Marazita, J. M., & Jarvis, L. H. (1996). Young two-year-olds' tendency to map novel verbs into word actions. *Journal of Experimental Child Psychology, 63*, 466–498.

Meyer, M., Leonard, S., Hirsh-Pasek, K., Golinkoff, R. M., Imai, M., Haryu, R., et al. (2003). *Making a convincing argument: A cross-linguistic comparison of noun and verb learning in Japanese and English*. Poster presented at the Boston University Conference on Language Development, Boston, MA.

Molfese, D. L., Burger-Judisch, L. M., Gill, L. A., Golinkoff, R. M., & Hirsh-Pasek, K. (1996). Electrophysiological correlates of noun-verb processing in adults. *Brain and Language, 54*, 388–413.

Naigles, L. (1990). Children use syntax to learn verb meanings. *Journal of Child Language, 17*, 357–374.

Naigles, L. (1996). The use of multiple frames in verb learning via syntactic bootstrapping. *Cognition, 58*, 221–251.

Naigles, L. R., & Hoff-Ginsberg, E. (1995). Input to verb learning: Evidence for the plausibility of syntactic bootstrapping. *Developmental Psychology, 31*, 827–837.

Naigles, L. R., & Hoff-Ginsberg, E. (1998). Why are some verbs learned before other verbs? Effects of input frequency and structure on children's early verb use. *Journal of Child Language, 25*, 95–120.

Naigles, L., & Kako, E. (1993). First contact in verb acquisition: Defining a role for syntax. *Child Development, 64*, 1665–1687.

Nelson, K. (1995). The dual category problem in the acquisition of action words. In M. Tomasello & W. Merriman (Eds.), *Beyond names for things: Young children's acquisition of verbs* (pp. 223–250). Hillsdale, NJ: Lawrence Erlbaum.

Nelson, K. (1996). *Language in cognitive development*. New York: Cambridge University Press.

Paivio, A., Yuille, J. C., & Madigan, S. A. (1968). Concreteness, imagery and meaningfulness values for 925 nouns. *Journal of Experimental Psychology, 76*, 1–25.

Pinker, S. (1989). *Learnabilty and cognition: The acquisition of argument structure*. Cambridge, MA: MIT Press.

Poulin-Dubois, D., & Forbes, J. N. (2002). Toddlers' attention to intentions-in-action in learning novel action words. *Developmental Psychology, 38*, 104–114.

Pruden, S., Hirsh-Pasek, K., Golinkoff, R. M., & Hennon, E. (in press). The birth of words: Ten-month-olds learn words through perceptual salience. *Child Development*.

Salkind, S., Sootsman, J., Golinkoff, R. M., Hirsh-Pasek, K., & Maguire, M. J. (2002, April). *Lights, camera, action! Infants and toddlers create action categories.* International Conference on Infant Studies. Toronto, Canada.

Sandhofer, C., Smith, L., & Luo, J. (2000). Counting nouns and verbs in the input: Differential frequencies, different kinds of learning? *Journal of Child Language, 27,* 561–585.

Slobin, D. I. (2001). Form-function relations: How do children find out what they are? In M. Bowerman & S. C. Levinson (Eds.), *Langauge acguisition and conceptual development* (pp. 406–449). Cambridge, MA: Cambridge University Press.

Smiley, P., & Huttenlocher, J. (1995). Conceptual development and the child's early words for events, objects, and persons. In M. Tomasello & W. E. Merriman (Eds.), *Beyond the names for things: Young children's acquisition of verbs* (pp. 21–62). Hillsdale, NJ: Lawrence Erlbaum.

Smith, L. B. (2000). Learning how to learn words: An associative crane. In R. M. Golinkoff, K. Hirsh-Pasek, L. Bloom, A. Woodward, N. Akhtar, M. Tomasello, & G. Hollich (Eds.), *Breaking the word learning barrier: What does it take?* (pp. 51–80). New York: Oxford University Press.

Snedeker, J., & Gleitman, L. (2004). Why is it hard to label our concepts. In G. H. Waxman (Ed.), *Weaving a lexicon* (pp. 257–294). Cambridge, MA: MIT Press.

Tardif, T. (1996). Nouns are not always learned before verbs: Evidence from Mandarin speakers' early vocabularies. *Developmental Psychology, 32,* 492–504.

Tardif, T., Gelman, S. A., & Xu, F. (1999). Putting the "noun bias" in context: A comparison of English and Mandarin. *Child Development, 70,* 620–635.

Tardif, T., Shatz, M., & Naigles, L. (1997). Caregiver speech and children's use of nouns versus verbs: A comparision of English, Italian, and Mandarin. *Journal of Child Language, 24,* 535–565.

Theakston, A. L., Lieven, E. V. M., Pine, J. M., & Rowland, C. F. (2002). Going, going, gone: The acquisition of the verb 'go.' *Journal of Child Language, 29,* 783–811.

Tomasello, M. (1995). Pragmatic contexts for early verb learning. In M. Tomasello & W. E. Merriman (Eds.), *Beyond the names for things: Young children's acquisition of verbs* (pp. 115–146). Hillsdale, NJ: Lawrence Erlbaum.

Tomasello, M., & Merriman, W. E. (Eds.). (1995). *Beyond the names for things: Young children's acquisition of verbs.* Hillsdale, NJ: Lawrence Erlbaum.

Tomasello, M., Strosberg, R., & Akhtar, N. (1996). Eighteen-month-old children learn words in non-ostensive contexts. *Journal of Child Language, 23,* 157–176.

Waxman, S. R., & Klibanoff, R. S. (2000). The role of comparison in the extension of novel adjectives. *Developmental Psychology, 36,* 571–581.

Woodward, A. L., & Markman, E. M. (1998). Early word learning. In D. Kuhn & R. S. Siegler (Eds.), *Handbook of child psychology: Vol. 2. Cognition, perception, and language* (pp. 371–420). New York: John Wiley.

15   Who's the Subject? Sentence Structure and Verb Meaning

Cynthia Fisher and Hyun-joo Song

Even very young children use the syntax of sentences to interpret new words. In many experiments, children between the ages of 2 and 5 assigned different interpretations to made-up verbs, depending on the sentence structure in which the verb was presented (e.g., Fisher, 1996, 2000, 2002; Fisher, Hall, Rakowitz, & Gleitman, 1994; Naigles, 1990, 1996; Naigles & Kako, 1993). Such findings tell us that observed events are not the only influence on verb interpretation even for very young children; sentence structure provides useful cues as well. The proposal that sensitivity to sentence structure guides the acquisition of verb meaning is known as syntactic bootstrapping (Gleitman, 1990; Landau & Gleitman, 1985).

But how could syntactic bootstrapping work? What aspects of sentence structures are informative to young children, and what semantic information is conveyed to young children by the structure of sentences?

The meaning conveyed by a sentence structure must necessarily be very abstract (e.g., Fisher, Gleitman, & Gleitman, 1991; Pinker, 1994). The sentences in (1) are all transitive yet contain verbs differing greatly in their meanings, ranging from action on an object (*kicked*) to perception (*saw*) and abstract causation (*justified, pleased*).

(1) a. Emma kicked John.
   b. Emma saw John.
   c. The conversation justified all their hopes.
   d. John's sincerity pleased Emma.

The diversity of meanings of transitive verbs should be no surprise. Sentence structures vary principally in the number and type (e.g., noun phrases versus sentence complements) of arguments and the positioning or marking of those arguments (e.g., subject versus object). Therefore, by its very nature, sentence structure yields information about aspects of a verb's meaning that affect the number and type of arguments—essentially its semantic structure rather than its semantic content (e.g., Fisher et al., 1991; Grimshaw, 1990).

Elsewhere we have proposed a simple procedure for one form of early syntactic bootstrapping (Fisher, 1996; Fisher et al., 1994; Gillette, Gleitman, Gleitman, & Lederer, 1999), which capitalizes on the relational nature of both sentences and verb meanings (e.g., L. Bloom, 1970; Braine, 1992; Fisher et al., 1991; Gentner, 1982). For example, transitive verbs have two noun phrase arguments and describe semantic two-place predicates—relationships between the referents of those noun phrases. Intransitive verbs have only one noun phrase argument and denote semantic one-place predicates—states, activities, or properties of the single named referent. Once children can identify some nouns, they could assign different meanings to transitive and intransitive verbs by aligning a sentence containing two noun phrases with a conceptual predicate relating the two named entities in the current scene, and a sentence containing one noun phrase with a conceptual predicate centrally involving the single named entity in the current scene.

Consistent with this proposal, a series of experiments has yielded evidence that the number of noun phrases in the sentence is meaningful to young preschoolers. In several studies, 3- and 5-year-olds (Fisher, 1996) and 2.5-year-olds (Fisher, 2002) learned transitive or intransitive made-up verbs used to describe unfamiliar agent-patient events. The identity of the subject and object referents was hidden by using ambiguous pronouns, yielding sentences that differed only in their number of noun phrases (e.g., "She's pilking [her] over there!"). Children were asked to choose the participant in each event whose actions were described by the verb ("Which one pilked [the other one] over there?"). Children more often chose agents as the subjects of transitive than intransitive verbs. A similar sensitivity to argument number has been found in a preferential-looking task with children 21 and 26 months old (Fisher & Snedeker, 2002).

These findings suggest that children might achieve an early separation of the input sentences by transitivity and interpret these sentences in line with their argument number, simply by counting the nouns in each sentence. To the extent that this early separation of transitive from intransitive depends simply on identifying some nouns, it could provide a guide to sentence interpretation and verb learning before the child has learned crucial syntactic features of the native language (e.g., Fisher et al., 1994).

In this chapter, we address a further question: Can sentences tell children more than simply how many and what participants are involved? Once a learner knows enough about the native language to identify one noun phrase in a sentence as its grammatical subject, she might use that information to guide sentence interpretation. This type of knowledge shows its influence quite early in development. For example, English-learning children as young as 16 to 18 months old interpreted word order appropriately in transitive sentences such as "Big Bird is tickling Cookie Monster" (Hirsh-Pasek & Golinkoff, 1996). Very young children pick up on language-specific cues like word order and use them in sentence interpretation.

But can this information be used, in principle and in practice, in interpreting sentences with unknown verbs? To address this question, we need to ask, essentially, what it means to be the subject of a sentence.

The Semantics of Subjects (Versus Nonsubjects)

The subjects of sentences can be of many semantic kinds, as shown by the italicized phrases in (1): transitive subjects include animate agents (1a), experiencers (1b), events (1c), and abstract stimuli (1d), to name just a few. The semantic diversity of subjects might lead us to believe that the transitive subject category has no unified meaning (e.g., Marantz, 1982; Pinker, 1994). In principle, the semantic role played by the subject could be determined entirely by the semantics of individual verbs with no abstract semantic information that spans the set of transitive verbs conveyed by placement in subject position. If so, then no semantic information could be retrieved based on word order or other cues to subject identity until the meaning of the verb is known; the verbs themselves, in this view, would be learned by observation of world events constrained by the set of arguments in the sentence.

On the other hand, despite the manifest variety of subject meanings, the intuition that subjects share some abstract semantic similarity has long held sway in psycholinguistics and linguistic theory. Proposed semantic descriptions of what it means to be the subject fall into two general (and not mutually exclusive) classes: those based on roles in events, and those based on the perspective adopted by the speaker (e.g., Dowty, 1991; Talmy, 1983).

Event-Dependent Roles

The traditional linguistic view of the linking of each verb's arguments with grammatical positions in sentences relies on the notion of thematic roles. Thematic roles represent the abstract similarity among roles in different events, such as the agents and patients of various causal actions (e.g., Jackendoff, 1990). Despite persistent lack of agreement on a common set of roles, thematic roles or something very much like them help to explain striking cross-linguistic similarities in the linking of semantic argument types with grammatical positions (see papers in Wilkins, 1988).

An influential characterization of thematic roles was advanced by Dowty (1991). He proposed a contrast between a prototype concept of agent and patient and a simple subject selection principle: The argument of a transitive verb with more of the semantic entailments of a protoagent is linked to subject position, while the argument with more of the semantic entailments of a protopatient is linked to direct object position. Entailments of protoagency include volitional involvement, sentience, causation, and movement. Protopatient entailments include undergoing a change of state. Dowty's protorole proposal raises the possibility that children might learn new verb meanings "by 'semantic default,' i.e. by taking it for granted that the subject and object arguments have the full complement of possible proto-role entailments appropriate to each of these grammatical relations" (p. 605).

Similar proposals have been advanced in psycholinguistics. Clark and Begun (1971) investigated the semantics of transitive subjects by asking people to rate the semantic naturalness of sentences whose subjects had been replaced by noun phrases taken from a hierarchy ranging from humans (e.g., *Fred*) to abstract mass nouns (e.g., *sincerity*). Noun phrases higher on this hierarchy could nearly always sensibly replace subject nouns lower on the hierarchy, while the reverse arrangement—replacement of higher subject noun phrase types by lower—tended to lead to semantic anomaly. Clark and Begun suggested that the default interpretation of a transitive subject includes the features [+*human*], [+*animate*], and [+*concrete*]. A related conclusion was reached by Osgood and Bock (1977), based on spontaneous picture descriptions: Multiple features of various entities and their roles in a situation determined which would be mentioned as the subject of a sentence; these included agency and concreteness.

In sum, grammatical subjects tend to denote entities of certain types (human, animate, concrete) playing a subset of roles in events (e.g., causation, volitional involvement, motion). These findings are consistent with the longstanding consensus in linguistic theory that roles that are more prominent in a hierarchy of event-dependent thematic roles are linked to subject position (e.g., Fillmore, 1977; Grimshaw, 1990; Jackendoff, 1990).

Perspective-Dependent Views

Other accounts suggest that features of the events denoted by verbs, including categories of participants and the roles they play, do not entirely predict the linking of semantic arguments with grammatical roles. For example, in (2), *give* and *receive* differ, not in the event participants required by the two verbs (both require a giver, a receiver, and an object given), but in which role the verb treats as more prominent and thus which role is assigned to subject position. Such verbs are troublesome for a view that attempts to predict argument linking entirely from characterizations of roles in events. Either the giver or the recipient can be chosen as grammatical subject, depending on whether the speaker intends to talk about giving or getting.

(2) Phil gave a book to Lenny.
    Lenny received a book from Phil.

Cases like *receive* could be viewed as simple exceptions to an otherwise general tendency to link the (more agentlike) *giver* with the subject role. On the other hand, some observers have argued that the fundamental asymmetry between subject and nonsubject positions in sentences signals a focus- or perspective-dependent semantic asymmetry that is independent of event-dependent thematic roles (Gleitman, Gleitman, Miller, & Ostrin, 1996).

For example, Talmy (1983) suggested, based on an analysis of spatial descriptions, that the subject's role could be described as the conceptual figure, whose location or role relative to a reference or ground object is the main issue of the sentence (see also Clark, 1990; Kuno, 1987). Appeals to the prominence or importance of various aspects of an event for the meanings of particular verbs crop up in other analyses: For example, Pinker (1989) described the semantic difference between *give* and *receive*, or *hit* and *be hit by*, in terms of which part of a complex conceptual-semantic representation is construed as the "main event" of the sentence; Dowty (1991) suggests that assignment of theme and goal roles to direct versus indirect object position depends on whether the meaning of the verb is more centrally concerned with the theme's motion or the resulting effect on the goal location (see also Gropen, Pinker, Hollander, & Goldberg, 1991).

This view suggests a subtly different default interpretation of the subject role: the subject of a sentence could be interpreted not as playing a particular event-dependent role but as playing a role construed as more prominent for a particular verb. Both *give* and *receive* entail the same event roles but focus on different aspects of the same events.

The role of speaker perspective in subject choice can be seen in descriptions of spatial arrays: the same array tends to be described as a circle above a square if the speaker's eye is cued to fall first upon the circle, but as a square below a circle if the speaker's eye is cued to fall first upon the square (Forrest, 1996; Osgood & Bock, 1977). Nappa, January, Gleitman, and Trueswell (2004) reported similar findings for descriptions of pictures in which people give and receive, for example. In language production, the choice of subject is influenced by the direction of the speaker's attention.

The Semantic Prominence of Subjects

Notice the similarity of these two views. In both, grammatical subjects are linked to whichever argument is more prominent in a ranking of conceptual-semantic roles. Prominence can be predicted in part based on the participant roles themselves: languages have many verbs for describing the actions of animate causal agents on patients, for example. In addition, however, evidence for the role of speaker or verb perspective in subject choice suggests that the nature of conceptual-semantic representations allows at least some flexibility in which participant role is represented as more prominent. Various event-dependent and perspective-dependent accounts of subject selection differ greatly in their theoretical assumptions but share the fundamental insight that the syntactic prominence of subjects corresponds to an abstract semantic or conceptual prominence.

For our present purposes, if either of these views is correct, then it means something to be the subject of a sentence, after all. Might children make use of this default interpretation of subjects—as the more prominent argument in a conceptual-semantic structure—in their interpretations of sentences? If so, then once children can identify which noun phrase in a sentence is the subject, they will know not only which participants the verb relates but which participant's role should be construed as more prominent.

To address this question, the empirical strategy taken in this chapter is to explore two complementary predictions of the notion that listeners interpret sentence structures as encoding the conceptual-semantic prominence of a verb's arguments. First, many properties of events that make one participant's role more prominent than another should influence the interpretation of sentences that comment on those events. Some participants in events will make better conceptual figures than others (Talmy, 1983) or have more of the mobile, sentient, active, causal, properties that suggest proto-agency (Dowty, 1991; see also Clark & Begun, 1971; Osgood & Bock, 1977). These factors should affect sentence interpretation by influencing what conceptual structures are readily available to be mapped onto a sentence. Second, if the subject-object asymmetry provides a clue about semantic prominence, it should be possible to induce the listener to adopt a particular perspective on an event by specifying a sentence subject. A subject clearly given in a sentence should lead the hearer to select a conceptual-semantic relation in which the subject referent is the most prominent.

Both predictions are confirmed for adult listeners, who assume that the subject referent plays a more prominent role even where the verb specifies an inherently symmetrical relationship between its two arguments (Gleitman et al., 1996). For example, the verbs in (3) and (4) denote symmetrical relations—two objects match each other and two people meet to the same degree. Nevertheless, adults judged the first member of each pair, in which the subject referent was smaller, more mobile, or less famous than the object referent, as more natural than the second (Gleitman et al., 1996). The role of the participant that was seen as more dynamic or potentially changeable made a more plausible sentence subject. Other things being equal, one is more likely to seek a button to match a dress than the reverse, and ordinary citizens are more likely to try to meet movie stars than the reverse. Importantly, however, sentences with a less obvious subject choice (as in 3b or 4b) are interpretable; they simply suggest a less ordinary prominence ordering of the verb's arguments. Sentence (3b), for example, might be appropriate for a fancy jeweled button, a family heirloom.

(3) a. The button matches the dress.
    b. The dress matches the button.
(4) a. My sister met Meryl Streep.
    b. Meryl Streep met my sister.

The experiments reported here began to explore what preschool children think it means to be the subject of a sentence, testing both predictions of the semantic prominence interpretation of the subject role. Experiment 1 used a novel verb learning task to assess children's default interpretations for new transitive verbs. Children interpreted made-up transitive verbs describing displays in which the dynamic properties of two participants varied. If children interpret the subject/object asymmetry as a cue to the relative semantic prominence of the verb's arguments, then properties of event participants that suggest they play dynamic roles in events should make them good conceptual figures, thus plausible subjects of verbs. Experiment 2 pits explicit subject choice in a sentence against a strong bias in sentence interpretation, to test the hypothesis that properties that make an event participant a very plausible subject can be overridden by the mention of a different participant in subject position in a sentence.

In the final section of this chapter, we will relate these findings to recent evidence that even young children treat grammatical subject referents as more prominent entities in their representation of a multisentence story and therefore as more likely antecedents for a pronoun (Song & Fisher, 2005).

Experiment 1

This experiment manipulated two properties of participants in an event—motion and animacy. Many studies have documented an influence of animacy on the production and comprehension of sentences with known verbs by both adults and children. Animate nouns more often appear as sentence subjects than inanimate ones (e.g., Bock, Loebell, & Morey, 1992; Clark & Begun, 1971). A bias toward animate subjects can be seen in children's earliest sentences (e.g., L. Bloom, 1970; Bowerman, 1973; Brown, 1973). Sentences with animate rather than inanimate subjects are rated as more natural by adults (e.g., Clark & Begun, 1971; Corrigan, 1986); similarly, 2-year-olds more readily learned to place a token on the actor in a picture described by a transitive sentence when the subjects of action verbs were animate (Corrigan, 1988; Corrigan & Odya-Weis, 1985). Childers and Tomasello (2001) reported that 2.5-year-olds were better able to learn new transitive verbs when the verb was presented with pronoun arguments that signaled an animacy contrast (e.g., "He's pilking it"). In sum, animates tend to be subjects in production and are easily interpreted as subjects in comprehension.

However, neither for adults nor for young children are all subjects animate (e.g., Bloom, Miller, & Hood, 1975; Pinker, 1984). The preference for animate subjects in production and comprehension depends on the fit of an animate noun with roles that could be assigned by a particular verb. For example, 2-year-olds identified inanimate subjects of stative verbs such as *hide* and *hurt* as easily as animate subjects (Corrigan, 1988; Corrigan & Odya-Weis, 1985). At least in English, animacy effects on sentence interpretation may be due not to a direct link between subjects and animates but to the potential of animate entities to take on more prominent roles in conceptual-semantic structures (Bloom, Miller, & Hood, 1975; Bock et al., 1992).

Similarly, motion itself should make a participant in a situation a likely prominent argument (Gleitman et al., 1996; Talmy, 1983). Animacy and motion can be thought of as components of the kind of active causality that is prototypical agency (e.g., Dowty, 1991; Slobin, 1985). By manipulating animacy and mobility in noncausal events, this experiment explored whether these dynamic properties make event participants good conceptual figures and thus good subjects for novel verbs.

In Experiment 1, children interpreted novel transitive verbs with ambiguous pronoun arguments (e.g., "It's pilking it" or "It pilks it"). Interpretation of the novel verbs was assessed in a forced-choice task: children were asked to choose the participant in each event that was the subject of the novel verb (e.g., "Which one's pilking/pilks the other one?"). This task provided a simple way of determining which participant in each event was considered to be the most likely subject. The use of nonsense verbs and ambiguous pronouns in these sentences gave the children no information about which participant's perspective the new verb promoted. Their only recourse in interpreting these sentences was therefore to fall back on default assumptions about the interpretation of sentences.

The events described by these verbs involved no causal act of one participant on the other but merely the motion or location of one participant relative to another. This feature was important: a simple agent-patient event would invite observers to represent a particular relationship between the two participants even in the absence of a verb description. Thus children might interpret a novel verb as a translation of a familiar verb suggested by the scene (e.g., Pinker, 1994). The motion and location events used in Experiment 1 were designed to suggest no particular relation between the two participants. To evaluate the success of this manipulation, responses in the transitive verb interpretation task were compared to a control condition in which children were simply asked to pick one of the two participants in each event. The novel verb in its ambiguous transitive sentence frame should direct observers to represent a relationship between the two participants and thus to any asymmetry in the roles each could play; this asymmetry should be less evident in the absence of a sentence to interpret.

Method

Participants

The participants were 60 3-year-olds (mean age 3 years, 3 months; range 2 years, 10 months to 4 years, 0 months), 30 boys and 30 girls, all native speakers of English. Participants were recruited through a database compiled from birth announcements in the local newspaper. Twenty children were assigned to each of the three conditions described below (sentence-progressive, sentence-present, and no sentence). An equal number of boys and girls were assigned to each condition, with mean age balanced across groups. Four children did not complete the task and were replaced in the design. A comparison group of 30 adults (22 women and 8 men), also native speakers of English, was included; 10 were assigned to each condition. The adults were undergraduates at the University of Illinois, who received course credit or a small payment for their participation.

Stimuli

Simple location or motion displays involving puppets and toys were videotaped. The displays were of five different types, designed to systematically vary the mobility and animacy of two participants. The item types are defined in table 15.1. Motion displays were those in which one object moved and the other was still. All four possible combinations of animate and inanimate items were included, as shown in the top of table 15.1. The same pattern was established for displays in which one character was animate and the other inanimate; these are shown in the lower part of table 15.1. All combinations of mobile and immobile participants were included, with one exception: there were no events in which both participants moved because of difficulties making these appear noncausal. Given the overlap between the animacy and motion displays so defined, this resulted in 5 different item types; four brief (5–6 seconds in length) events of each type were constructed, for a total of 20 videotaped scenes.

The use of pretend animates allowed animacy and motion to vary separately. While children can of course tell the difference between toy animals and real ones, many studies have found consistent animacy effects on children's language comprehension and production using pseudo-animates (e.g., Bates et al., 1984; Lempert, 1984), and even some objects whose only animate-like properties were pasted-on eyes (Jones, Smith, & Landau, 1991). Nevertheless it must be kept in mind that the motion in these events was real, but the animacy was not.

Table 15.1 Examples of motion and location events, Experiment 1

	Object 1	Object 2	
Motion Displays	Moving	Not Moving	Example Event
Both animate	+animate	+animate	A raccoon walks behind a lion.
Both inanimate	−animate	−animate	A toy car rolls up to a flashlight.
Animate moves	+animate	−animate	A penguin moves past a watering can.
Inanimate moves	−animate	+animate	A fire truck rolls up to a giraffe.
Animacy Displays	Animate	Inanimate	
Both immobile	−moving	−moving	A bear leans against a chair.
Animate moves	+moving	−moving	A penguin moves past a watering can.
Inanimate moves	−moving	+moving	A fire truck rolls up to a giraffe.

missing +moving +moving

The animate creatures were all animals rather than humans, so that the pronoun *it* could be used to refer to both animates and inanimates. Inanimate objects that moved included vehicles and other objects that could roll, and these were always set in motion off screen; half the time they rolled to a natural stop on screen, and half the time they continued out of sight. Inanimate objects that did not move were all static inanimates (e.g., a wrapped present, a plastic watering can). Animate objects that moved were manipulated by a hidden puppeteer. All objects, animate and inanimate, were selected to be familiar to children. Each object appeared in only one event, and the left-right position of the dynamic (animate and/or mobile) object was counterbalanced within event type. Care was taken to match the two objects in each event for size, brightness, and complexity. The events were arranged in a random order with the constraint that no more than two events of the same type appeared in a row. This order and its reverse were each presented to half of the subjects in each condition. An 8.5" by 11" picture of each event was used in the forced-choice task (see below). Pictures were selected to avoid focusing attention on either participant: each object was roughly centered in its half of the picture page, and took up about the same amount of space.

Procedure

All participants were tested individually in a quiet lab room under one of the conditions described below. When parents accompanied their children into the room, they sat behind the children and were asked not to speak during the task.

Sentence Conditions Transitive sentences containing novel verbs were presented to children as descriptions of each event. Twenty nonsense syllables were used as the novel verbs (e.g., *trab, crast, gluff*), randomly assigned to events for each child. Children in the sentence-progressive condition heard the verbs in the progressive aspect (e.g., *trabbing, crasting, gluffing*), and those in the sentence-present condition heard the verbs in the simple present tense (e.g., *trabs, crasts, gluffs*). Only ambiguous pronouns were used (e.g., "It's crasting it" or "It crasts it"). The progressive is frequently used in novel verb learning studies to unambiguously identify a nonsense syllable as a verb (Brown, 1957) but also imposes additional semantic restrictions. Action or process predicates occur in the progressive (e.g., "John is walking") while stative terms cannot (e.g., "Steve is resembling Bill"). Thus the sentence-present condition was included to determine whether any focus on dynamic participants in Experiment 1 was due to the use of the progressive aspect or to a more general preference for dynamic subjects. The *-s* ending is ambiguous between a present-tense verb and plural noun reading of a novel word; however, children should be able to use the sentence frame itself to identify a verb as an argument-taking predicate (Landau & Stecker, 1988; McShane, Whitaker, & Dockrell, 1986). The use of the two sentence conditions also provided an opportunity for a replication of the effect of a transitive sentence within Experiment 1.

The procedure for the two sentence conditions was as follows: An unfamiliar doll was introduced, who sometimes used "funny new words" when telling about what he saw on a TV screen. On each trial, the experimenter first said the new verb in its sentence and encouraged the child to repeat the sentence. The experimenter then played the videotaped scene twice, repeating the sentence just before each showing of the event, and finally revealed the still photograph of the videotaped event, asking "Which one is (verb)-ing the other one?" or "Which one (verb)-s the other one?" This process was repeated for each of the 20 scenes.

No-Sentence Condition The no-sentence condition was included to assess the children's baseline tendency to choose animate or moving objects in these events. The experimenter introduced the unfamiliar doll and told the children that they would see pictures on the TV and their job was to pick pictures for the doll. Each scene was presented twice with no preceding sentence other than an instruction to watch the screen. The experimenter then revealed the still picture and asked the child, "Which one do you want to pick?"

Children in all three conditions usually pointed without hesitation; if the response was unclear, the experimenter prompted the child to point again. The procedure took about ten minutes. Adult subjects were also tested individually; in the adult version of this task the story involving the unfamiliar doll was omitted, but all other instructions were the same.

Results and Discussion

Children's and adults' interpretations of novel transitive verbs were systematically influenced by the animacy and mobility of the objects in each display. Table 15.2a shows the proportion of moving object choices across all four item types (16 events) in which one object moved and the other did not. Table 15.2b shows the proportion of animate choices across the three item types (12 events) with one animate and one inanimate participant. Note again that these sets of events overlap somewhat (see table 15.1); thus tabulations of moving and animate choices are partially intersecting characterizations of the tendency to make dynamic choices. The events in which animacy and motion were in conflict are also reported separately in table 15.2c. The near-chance performance of children and adults in the no-sentence condition suggests that the stimuli and procedure contained no covert hints as to which item in each scene the observer was intended to choose. The ambiguous sentences, however, did provide a hint: both children and adults systematically chose moving or animate participants as the subjects of the novel transitive verbs. The difference between sentence and no sentence conditions emerged in the same way whether the verbs were progressive (*crasting*) or not (*crasts*).

These patterns were tested in separate ANOVAs examining the proportion of moving and animate choices. Analyses by subjects took age group (child vs. adult) and condition (sentence-progressive, sentence-present, and no-sentence) as

Table 15.2 Pointing responses, Experiment 1

a. Mean (SD) proportions of moving choices in motion displays (16 events)

| | Sentence | | | |
Group	Progressive	Present	No Sentence	Mean
3-year-olds	.70 (.16)	.63 (.21)	.48 (.14)	.60 (.19)
Adults	.81 (.17)	.76 (.22)	.62 (.19)	.73 (.21)
Mean	.74 (.17)	.67 (.22)	.52 (.17)	

b. Mean (SD) proportions of animate choices in animacy displays (12 events)

| | Sentence | | | |
Group	Progressive	Present	No Sentence	Mean
3-year-olds	.58 (.15)	.57 (.15)	.44 (.17)	.53 (.17)
Adults	.76 (.14)	.69 (.08)	.52 (.18)	.66 (.17)
Mean	.64 (.16)	.61 (.14)	.46 (.18)	

c. Mean (SD) proportions of moving object choices in conflict displays (4 events)

| | Sentence | | | |
Group	Progressive	Present	No Sentence	Mean
3-year-olds	.65 (.22)	.62 (.24)	.55 (.28)	.61 (.24)
Adults	.58 (.37)	.60 (.32)	.70 (.28)	.62 (.32)
Mean	.62 (.28)	.62 (.26)	.60 (.28)	

between-subjects factors; item analyses examined the same variables as within-items factors.

Presentation condition had a significant effect on choices of moving objects, $F1(2, 84) = 9.51$, $p < .001$; $F2(2, 30) = 17.77$, $p < .001$, and adults chose moving objects significantly more often than children did, $F1(1, 84) = 10.83$, $p < .001$; $F2(1, 15) = 9.85$, $p < .01$; age and condition did not interact, $F1(2, 84) < 1$; $F2(2, 30) < 1)$. The effect of sentence condition remained significant when only the 3-year-olds were tested: Moving choices were reliably more frequent in both sentence-progressive, $t1(38) = 4.70$, $p < .001$; $t2(15) = 4.70$, $p < .001$, and sentence-present conditions, $t1(38) = 2.70$, $p < .01$; $t2(15) = 2.88$, $p < .05$, than in the no-sentence condition.

Similarly, presentation condition had an effect on choices of animate objects, $F1(2, 84) = 12.28$, $p < .001$; $F2(2, 22) = 9.57$, $p < .001$, and adults chose animates more frequently overall than children did, $F1(1, 84) = 14.13$, $p < .001$; $F2(1, 11) = 5.83$, $p < .05$; these two factors again did not interact, $F1(2, 84) < 1$; $F2(2, 22) < 1)$. The tendency to choose animates more often in each of the two sentence conditions than in the no sentence condition remained significant for the 3-year-olds alone in a subjects analysis and was marginally reliable in the items analysis; sentence-progressive: $t1(38) = 2.90$, $p < .01$; $t2(11) = 1.82$, $p = .096$; sentence-present: $t1(38) = 2.58$, $p < .05$; $t2(11) = 1.78$, $p = .103$.

Thus children and adults tended to select moving rather than still objects and animate creatures rather than inanimate things as likely subjects of transitive verbs in both sentence conditions. The age difference, unrelated to the influence of the sentence, appears to reflect a simple tendency for children to be less consistent than adults in this task.

What about the subset of events in which animacy and motion are in conflict? In these cases, an animate creature stood immobile while an inanimate object moved. Choices for these items are shown in table 15.2c. There was no effect of age or condition on the proportion of moving object choices ($F < 1$), and the interaction between the two factors was not significant, $F(2, 84) = 1.24$, $p > .25$. In these conflict events, animacy and motion seem to have been weighted roughly equally.

Children and adults systematically preferred dynamic—moving or animate—participants in events as subject referents in the absence of information from a familiar verb or from the placement of a familiar noun in subject position as to what kind of relation was described by the verb. Children and adults were less likely to choose moving or animate objects when there was no sentence to be interpreted. This suggests that the sentence directed observers' attention to aspects of each video clip that were not obvious without a sentence—a situation involving the two participants in which the dynamic participant's role becomes more prominent. This effect of a novel transitive verb did not depend on the use of the progressive aspect. Given no sentence to interpret, on the other hand, the choice of participants depended not on the prominence of possible roles, but on visual salience in the picture, which was carefully matched for these items.

In their own speech, young children tend to make dynamic entities the subjects of sentences, including animates or pseudo-animates and objects that appear, disappear, and change in the child's environment (e.g., L. Bloom, 1970; Bowerman, 1973; Brown, 1973; Lempert, 1984; Tomasello, 1992). The results of Experiment 1 provide evidence that they do the same when interpreting a novel verb: Not being told which participant was the subject and not knowing the verb, children assumed that the subject of a transitive sentence referred to the participant they saw as the more central player in the event. Animacy and motion should have similar effects on this mapping process. A moving object is clearly playing a dynamic role, and while animacy is not itself a role in a relation, it is a categorization that has consequences for what roles are possible (Bock et al., 1992; Fillmore, 1977).

Experiment 2

Experiment 1 documented biases affecting children's interpretations of novel verbs in transitive sentences. If these biases were the only influence on children's acquisition of verbs, then children might take all verbs to be action words. But nonactional predicates like *want, see, hear, have,* or *get* (in the sense of *receive*) appear among the first verbs used by many children (e.g., Bowerman, 1973, 1990; L. Bloom, 1970; Bloom, Lightbown, & Hood, 1975; Landau & Gleitman, 1985), and children just under 3 years old can learn to produce passives appropriately with unfamiliar verbs (Brooks & Tomasello, 1999). Experiment 2 pits the bias toward dynamic subjects against a verb's attested subject in a sentence, asking children to interpret sentences that make less obvious assignments to the subject role. These sentences violate documented preferences in children's interpretation of events, but should be interpretable if children can use subject selection as a cue to verb meaning even when it violates these preferences.

As mentioned in the introduction to this chapter, even 16- to 18-month-olds know that the subject of *tickle* plays a different role from its object and use that knowledge to interpret sentences (Hirsh-Pasek & Golinkoff, 1996). Bates et al. (1984) have found that 2-year-olds interpreting sentences with familiar verbs can use clear evidence of assignment to subject position (word order in English) to override plausibility, tending to act out sentences like "The rock kicked the dog" in accord with their word order. Knowing what *kick* means, young children adapt the role of the kicker to fit a rock, as adults do in interpreting sentences with odd subject-verb combinations (Gentner & France, 1988).

Previous results also reveal that placement of a familiar noun in subject position influences preschoolers' interpretation of novel verbs. Fisher et al. (1994) showed 3- and 4-year-olds and adults videotaped scenes of familiar actions with two participants. Each scene was described with a nonsense verb presented in one of two different sentence contexts, as shown in (5), or in isolation (e.g., "Pilking!"). Listeners were asked to paraphrase the novel verb. When novel verbs were presented in isolation, children and adults tended to agree that one participant's role in each scene was more prominent than the other's. For example, observers preferred to describe one scene as chasing rather than running away; similar biases were found for other events. Despite such preferences, assignment of one participant to subject position appropriately affected children's interpretations. However, the scenes presented to children by Fisher et al. were designed to be fairly balanced in the salience of the two participants' roles. In the event described in (5), for example, while observers agreed that the chaser's role was more prominent, the fleeing rabbit moved on its own, and was easy to see as also playing a dynamic role.

(5) a. The skunk is pilking the bunny. (*chasing*)
    b. The bunny is pilking the skunk. (*fleeing*)

The goal of Experiment 2 was to determine whether children could take assignment to subject position, without the aid of a familiar verb, as a cue to what relation the verb describes and do so even if the subject choice demands a quite nonobvious view of an event. Experiment 2 combined the pronoun disambiguation task of Experiment 1 with the novel verb paraphrasing method introduced by Fisher et al. (1994) to examine this question. Four- and 5-year-olds watched videotaped events showing a human agent acting on a passive human patient in some novel way. Causal events like these are most likely to be described by transitive verbs with agent subjects (e.g., Braine, Brody, Fisch, Weisberger, & Blum, 1990; Fisher et al., 1994; Naigles & Kako, 1993; Slobin, 1985).

Novel transitive verbs, with either the agent or the patient participant named in subject position, were used to describe these scenes. The children first watched two training examples of each causal event. In these examples, people dressed as animal characters enacted the event, and the sentences assigned one of them to subject position (e.g., "The pig pilks the bunny!" vs. "The bunny pilks the pig!"). At the end of the second training trial, the child was asked "Which one pilked the other one?" to ensure that he or she had attended to the sentence, and accepted its assignment of event participants to argument positions. Following this training procedure for each event, the children watched a third enactment of the event, this time with people in ordinary clothing. The events were described for a third time with a transitive sentence ("She pilks her!"), and the child was asked (a) to point out which one pilks the other one and (b) to paraphrase what the sentence might mean.

Our predictions were as follows. If preschoolers interpret subject choice in a sentence as evidence about the relative semantic prominence of the verb's two arguments, then sentences that place less dynamic participants in subject position should nevertheless be systematically interpretable. This should be true whether the subject participant is the agent of a causal action or not. Simply put, children should interpret each verb as describing an event or relation in which the subject participant is treated as playing the more prominent role. When the subject participant is the agent of the action, this should be easy: the novel verb can be interpreted as literally describing that participant's causal actions. In contrast, when the chosen subject participant is the passive recipient of the videotaped action, children should be guided toward less literal, more abstract interpretations. For instance, children might interpret the verb as referring to the inferred mental states or motives of the participants. If so, then this result could provide a hint as to how children acquire their early abstract verb vocabulary (e.g., *like* and *want*) despite a powerful bias toward dynamic subjects.

Method

Participants

Twenty-four 4- and 5-year-old children (mean age = 4 years, 11 months, range 4 years, 1 month to 5 years, 7 months), 12 girls and 12 boys, participated in this experiment. All of the children were native speakers of English. The participants were assigned to one of two sentence conditions described below (agent subject vs. patient subject) as well as to one of two orders in which stimulus events were presented. An equal number of boys and girls were assigned to each condition/order group.

Stimuli

Experimental Events Four action scenes were videotaped, each approximately 7–10 seconds long. Each scene depicted one person moving another in some novel way. In one event, for example, the agent repeatedly rotated the patient on a tall swivel stool by pulling on a scarf wrapped around the patient's waist. In each case, the patient's role in the event was entirely passive: In the same event, for example, the swivel stool was too tall for the patient's feet to touch the floor, making it clear that she could not cause her own motion. Three enactments of each action were filmed, differing in the identity of the participants. Each action was shown first carried out by people costumed as a monkey and a duck, then by people costumed as a pig and a rabbit, and finally by two women in everyday clothes. The versions with animal actors were training events, and those with people in ordinary clothes were test events.

The left-right positioning of the agent and patient in the training and test events was counterbalanced, and the agent never appeared on the same side in the second training event and the test event for the same action. Each actor appeared in only one test event. The events were shown in two orders, one the reverse of the other.

Familiarization Items The experimental items described above were preceded by four familiarization video clips to ensure that the children identified the costumed animal characters by name. Each scene showed one of the animal pairs (monkey and duck, pig and rabbit) standing side by side waving. Each pair was shown twice with the left-right positions of the pair counterbalanced. These items were presented in an invariant order.

Sentences Each action was described by a nonsense verb in a transitive sentence. In the training sentences, the identity of subject and object in each sentence was made clear by the use of familiar animal names. For children in the agent-subject condition, the agent of the salient causal event was also the subject of the sentence. For children in the patient-subject condition, the passive patient of the depicted causal event was the subject of the sentence. For example, if one group of children heard "The bunny [verb]s the pig," the other group heard "The pig [verb]s the bunny." All test sentences were of the form "She [verb]s the other girl." These test sentences were ambiguous, and identical in the agent-subject and patient-subject conditions. Four nonsense syllables (*gish, pilk, braff, stipe*) were randomly assigned to the four actions, separately for each subject.

vb for X U.

Procedure

Children were tested individually in a quiet room in their preschool or in the laboratory. Handwritten records of the child's responses were kept by the experimenter; verbal responses were checked for accuracy against audiotapes of the sessions. After a few minutes of warm-up interaction with the experimenter, the task was introduced as follows: An unfamiliar doll who sometimes used "words we don't know" was introduced, and the child was asked to help figure out what the doll meant. The task began with the familiarization events in which children identified the animals (e.g., "Which one's the monkey? Point!"). The two training versions of each action were then shown in a standard order—the monkey-duck pair and then the pig-rabbit pair. On each training trial the experimenter said the nonsense verb in its sentence context while playing the associated scene. The linguistic context of each verb included an initial instruction to look at the subject of the sentence before the action began (e.g., "Look at the monkey!" or "Look at the duck!"), followed by the stimulus sentence (e.g., "The monkey [verb]s the duck" or "The duck [verb]s the monkey") uttered while the action was underway. The stimulus sentence was repeated in a second repetition of the training event. At the end of the second training event, the child saw a still frame of the midpoint of the event and was asked to indicate, by pointing on the video screen, which participant's role was described by the novel verb: "Which one [verb]ed the other one? Point!" Since the subject of the sentence had just been named, this served to ensure that the children had noted the argument assignment of the novel verb. At this point the child's choice was corrected if it mismatched the subject choice of the stimulus sentence: The experimenter repeated the original sentence, reminding the child that this was what the doll had said, and pointed to the correct subject.

Each trial ended with the test event for the novel verb item. The experimenter simply said "Now look!" before the action began, and then said the test sentence ("She [verb]s the other girl") during the action. This sequence was repeated, and after the second presentation of the test event, the child saw a still frame of the midpoint of the event and was asked "Which one [verb]ed the other girl? Point!" The child's choice was recorded, with no correction. Since the subject of the sentence for the test event had not been named, children's responses provided a measure of whether they had learned which role in the event was designated subject by the novel verb. Finally, the experimenter asked the child what she or he thought the sentence meant, encouraging guessing if no answer was forthcoming. In pilot testing, children's paraphrases were often ambiguous as to which participant's actions or reactions were described (e.g., "helping her," with no spontaneous pointing to either character). Therefore, unless the child spontaneously pointed, the experimenter always followed up the paraphrase with an immediate probe: "Which one is?" or "Who is?" and asked the child to point. This enabled the experimenter to determine the intended subjects of nearly all paraphrases. The experimenter kept handwritten notes of the child's verbal and pointing responses.

Coding Children's attempts to paraphrase the nonsense verbs were taken from the experimenter's notes, checked for each child against the audiotape of the session. Paraphrases were first sorted into categories based on which participant the paraphrase focused on—the agent or the patient of the action event. Responses in which the causal agent was the grammatical subject were coded as agent-perspective responses, and those in which the patient was the grammatical subject were coded as patient-perspective responses. Most paraphrase subject choices were explicitly marked in the experimenter's notes based on the child's pointing responses when prompted "Who is?" Importantly, paraphrases that take the patient as subject did not describe the causal action itself; the designation "patient" was chosen simply to yield a uniform classification of paraphrases. There were no passive sentences such as "getting pulled [by her]" among the children's responses.

Children often used more than one sentence in their paraphrases, with different subject choices given. Clauses presented as separate sentences or conjoined with *and, then,* or *when* were coded separately, as it was not possible to tell which the child intended as the primary paraphrase. Examples are shown in (6), with separate clauses italicized. Example (6a) has two paraphrases, the first coded patient-perspective and the second coded agent-perspective; (6b) has three paraphrases, the first two agent-perspective and the third patient-perspective. Clauses or verb phrases that were complements of a main verb were not coded as separate paraphrases. Examples are shown in (7): example (7a) was coded as a single agent-perspective paraphrase, and (7b) was coded as a single patient-perspective paraphrase. A few responses mentioned only one participant and were coded as taking that participant's perspective even though the participant was not mentioned in subject position. For example, the response, "There's a bag on her [patient's] back" would be coded as a patient-perspective response.

(6) a. She's [patient] trying to stay there. *And then she [agent] tried to pull.*

   b. She (agent) put her in that wagon that's all. *You push and pull her* and she (patient) sits right there.

   c. Someone's putting a rope around the other girl, *and the other girl sits in a chair.*

(7) a. She [agent] did something that the other girl didn't want her to do.

   b. Means helping; this girl [patient] is helping that girl get across.

The responses were further classified as either a literal or an extended description of the event. These categories were designed to capture semantic differences in the paraphrases beyond choice of focus on the causal event's agent or patient, and to assess directly the possibility that "patient-subject" stimulus sentences would draw

Super Subjective

children's attention away from literal action descriptions of the causal event. Literal descriptions were those that mentioned only actions and objects that were visible in the event: Two examples are shown in (6b): the actions of pushing and pulling and "sitting right there" are clearly visible in the video. All of the other examples shown in (6) and (7), however, include extended elements, not limited to physical or mechanical descriptions of the observed events. These include inferences about events that may have occurred prior to the videotaped event ("putting a rope around" and "putting her in that wagon"), about the motives or covert actions of the participants ("helping," "didn't want her to," "trying to stay there"), or introduce elements not visible in the video. This coding system resulted in four response categories: literal or extended descriptions taking the agent's or the patient's perspective. As the examples in (6) show, these four categories are not mutually exclusive. Children could and did generate more than one kind of response within a single trial and across the four trials.

A few paraphrases fit none of these categories clearly and were classified as other (9, or 9.4% of trials). These included sentences that mentioned neither of the people in the event (e.g., "the wagon goes and goes"), mentioned both in subject position (e.g., "They wanna drag each other"), or in which the subject of the child's paraphrase could not be determined. Sometimes children failed to produce any paraphrase (on 11, or 11.5% of trials).

All of the children's responses were coded by a second rater who was blind to the sentence condition in which each response was produced. The two raters agreed on 94.4% of coding decisions.

Results and Discussion

Children's pointing responses revealed that they learned which participant each verb assigned to subject position and applied this knowledge to a new use of the verb in an ambiguous sentence. They did so even when this assignment was in conflict with a very strong bias to place the visibly more dynamic participant in subject position. As shown in table 15.3, children in the agent-subject condition were much more likely to choose agents as subjects than were children in the patient-subject condition. An ANOVA on the proportion of agent choices with sentence condition (agent-subject vs. patient-subject) as a between-subjects factor, and trial (training vs. test) as a within-subjects factor, revealed an effect of sentence condition, $F(1, 22) = 81.52$, $p < .001$. There was no difference between proportions of agent choices for the training and test trials, $F(1, 22) < 1$, and no interaction between trial and sentence condition, $F(1, 22) = 1.05$. Thus children accepted the subject choice given in the training trials, remembered it, and extended it to a new enactment described by the same verb.

Following their choice in training trials, children were corrected if they had chosen in conflict with the training sentence. Children in the patient-subject condition were corrected 21% of the time (when they chose agents; see table 15.3),

Table 15.3 Mean (SD) proportion agent choices in pointing task, Experiment 2

| Trial Type | Sentence Condition | | Mean |
	Agent-Subject	Patient-Subject	
Training	.94 (.11)	.21 (.33)	.57 (.44)
Test	1.00 (.00)	.17 (.34)	.58 (.49)

and children in the agent-subject condition were corrected 6% of the time (when they did not choose agents). The trend for children in the patient-subject condition to require correction more often than children in the agent-subject condition was not significant, $t(22) = 1.43$, $p = .17$. The direction of this trend, however, is consistent with the strong bias toward dynamic subjects documented in Experiment 1 and reminds us that semantic and conceptual information and syntactic cues should interact in determining what children learn about a new verb.

Crucially, children's paraphrases indicated that they took the subject assignment in the stimulus sentences as information about the meaning of each novel verb. As shown in table 15.4, children produced agent-perspective paraphrases much more frequently than patient-perspective paraphrases; children also produced many more literal than extended paraphrases. However, both of these preferences were sharply reduced in the patient-subject sentence condition.

An ANOVA with sentence condition as a between-subjects factor and with paraphrase perspective (agent or patient) and paraphrase type (literal or extended) as within-subject variables revealed main effects of both response factors: agent perspective paraphrases were more common than patient-perspective paraphrases, $F(1, 22) = 9.11$, $p < .01$, and literal paraphrases were more common than

Table 15.4 Mean (SD) proportion each paraphrase type, Experiment 2

| Paraphrase Type | Sentence Condition | | Mean |
	Agent-Subject	Patient-Subject	
Agent-perspective			
Literal	.75 (.28)	.27 (.36)	.51 (.40)
Extended	.02 (.07)	.21 (.30)	.12 (.23)
Either	.77 (.25)	.46 (.42)	.62 (.38)
Patient-perspective			
Literal	.17 (.22)	.06 (.11)	.12 (.18)
Extended	.02 (.07)	.31 (.34)	.17 (.28)
Either	.19 (.22)	.38 (.38)	.28 (.32)
Other	.08 (.16)	.10 (.17)	.09 (.16)
No response	.08 (.16)	.15 (.34)	.12 (.27)

extended paraphrases, $F(1, 22) = 8.37$, $p < .01$. Both of these response factors interacted with sentence condition. Agent-perspective paraphrases were significantly more common in the agent-subject than in the patient-subject sentence condition, $F(1, 22) = 4.42$, $p < .05$. Literal paraphrases were significantly more common in the agent-subject than in the patient-subject sentence condition, $F(1, 22) = 19.99$, $p < .001$. The two response variables also interacted: agent-perspective paraphrases were much more likely than patient-perspective paraphrases to be literal, $F(1, 22) = 27.82$, $p < .001$. The three-way interaction between paraphrase subject choice, paraphrase type, and sentence condition was not significant, $F(1, 22) = 2.54$, $p = .125$. Finally, there was no main effect of sentence condition ($F < 1$), indicating that the overall proportion of codable responses did not differ across the agent- and patient-subject sentence conditions.

This pattern of results demonstrates the effect of subject choice in a transitive sentence on children's interpretations of a novel verb. Children are biased to assign the agents of causal actions to subject position, both in their own productions and in their interpretations of others' sentences (e.g., Braine et al., 1990; Fisher et al., 1994; Naigles & Kako, 1993). Moreover, in this experiment, subject assignment in a sentence significantly affected what the children learned about a new verb. When a plausible causal agent appeared in subject position, children assumed that the verb gave a fairly literal description of the causal event itself. When the patient of the salient causal act appeared in subject position, children searched for an interpretation that treated that participant's role in the event as prominent. This led many children to consider more abstract inferences about the scene in view, including the characters' histories and motives. Simply by telling children which character was the subject, we told them which one the sentence (and therefore the novel verb) was about.

The 4- and 5-year-olds tested in Experiment 2 must be considered quite advanced verb learners. This age group was selected for this task because we judged they would be better able to paraphrase the sorts of abstract perspectives on our video stimuli required to sensibly interpret the "patient-subject" verbs. However, several considerations lend plausibility to the prediction that younger children routinely assign a similarly abstract semantic prominence to subject referents. First, the results of Experiment 1 tell us that 3-year-olds tested in a simpler task assume that the more prominent, dynamic participant in an event is referred to by the subject of a novel verb. They did so even in events with no causal action; thus at least by 3, children's preference for dynamic subjects is not limited to the agent subjects of prototypical transitive verbs. Second, a previous study showed that 3- and 4-year-olds can use the choice of subject in a transitive sentence to direct their attention toward one of two perspectives on the same event, and thus interpret an unknown verb as describing something akin to chasing or scaring versus something like running away from (Fisher et al., 1994). The present results with older children extend this finding to a case in which the alternative interpretation is much more abstract and thus less likely to have occurred to children independently of the sentence.

General Discussion

Children's interpretations of novel verbs in these experiments were consistent with the hypothesis that they assigned a prominence-based default meaning to the role of subject in transitive sentences. In Experiment 1, 3-year-olds and adults assumed that ambiguously presented transitive verbs described the role of an animate or mobile participant. This was true even in the absence of a morphological cue (the progressive -ing) that the novel verb denoted a continuing process or activity and even though neither participant could easily be construed as a causal agent. The preference for dynamic choices was reduced when listeners were not asked to interpret a sentence, suggesting that the transitive verbs drew listeners' attention to the asymmetry in participants' possible roles.

The tendency of animates and moving objects to make plausible subjects of novel transitive verbs is consistent with findings that children and adults readily interpret noun phrases with dynamic referents as the subjects of familiar verbs (e.g., Bates et al., 1982; Bates, McNew, MacWhinney, Devescovi, & Smith, 1984; Corrigan, 1986, 1988; Corrigan & Odya-Weis, 1985) and that children's earliest relational terms are likely to be those that describe the comings and goings of people and objects (e.g., Bloom, Lightbown, & Hood, 1975; Huttenlocher, Smiley, & Charney, 1983; Lempert, 1984; Tomasello, 1992). Similar biases appear in adults' comprehension and production of sentences and have been interpreted as due to the plausibility of animate or moving objects as the logical subjects of many conceptual predicates (e.g., Bock et al., 1992; Clark & Begun, 1971).

Other things being equal, 3-year-olds, like adults (e.g., Clark & Begun, 1971; Gleitman et al., 1996), consider some participants in scenes more plausible sentence subjects than others. Moving or animate (and thus potentially mobile or changeable) entities make good conceptual figures, thus good sentence subjects.

If unfettered by sentence structure cues, the bias toward dynamic subjects should lead children to systematically misinterpret stative verbs as action verbs. However, the findings of Experiment 2 suggest that children can take subject choice as evidence about the verb's perspective on the scene. In Experiment 2, even quite nonsalient choices of sentence subject in the stimulus sentences influenced interpretations of novel transitive verbs. Four- to 5-year-olds took the subject of a sentence as the more prominent participant in the new verb's semantic structure. Given the nature of the stimulus events, the patient-subject sentence led children toward more abstract interpretations of the verbs. These results provide striking evidence that preschoolers interpret a sentence subject as a semantically prominent argument within the sentence.

Subjects and Discourse Themes

Further evidence for young children's interpretation of the subject role as the more prominent character in a sentence's meaning comes from our own recent studies of children's comprehension of pronouns (Song & Fisher, 2005). Responses both in an elicited imitation task and in a looking-preference comprehension task revealed evidence that 3-year-olds preferred to interpret ambiguous pronouns as referring to the subject (or first-mentioned noun phrase) of the preceding context sentences. These findings suggest that placement in subject position in previously-encountered sentences made one character more prominent or accessible in the child's representation of the situation described by the story.

For example, in looking-preference comprehension experiments, 3-year-olds saw pictures on two video monitors as they listened to short stories like the one shown in (8). The final (test) sentence of the critical stories contained an ambiguous pronoun. The stimulus pictures and sentences were designed so that the test pronouns were ambiguous for several seconds: For example, in the test sequence shown in (8), *kite* is the first word that uniquely establishes the referent of the pronoun subject (because only one pictured character has a kite). In half of the trials, the pronoun turned out to refer to the character invoked as subject in the context sentences (continued-subject trials), while in the other half of the trials, the pronoun referred to the nonsubject character (shifted-subject trials). We measured children's visual fixations to the two pictured characters during the test sentence, to determine whether children recruited discourse context cues in their comprehension of an ambiguous pronoun.

(8) Context: See the turtle and the bunny.
    The turtle takes the bunny to the store.
    Test: What does he have? Look, he has a kite!

In three experiments, children looked longer during the test sequence at the character who had been established as the subject of the context story, and thus were more accurate in continued- than shifted-subject items. For example, in the story shown in (8), children tended to look at the turtle when they heard *he* in the test sentence. Thus children treated as more prominent or important those referents that had been mentioned in grammatical subject position, and were sentence-initial, in the context stories. Note in (8) that this was true even though both characters were mentioned equally often in the context sentences. The more prominent referents made better antecedents for a subsequent pronoun subject.

Ongoing experiments have been designed to tease apart order of mention and grammatical role (Song, 2004). Children participated in the same task, with the exception that in half of the critical trials the two characters appeared in subject and nonsubject position as before (e.g., "The turtle went with the bunny to the store"), while in half both characters jointly served as subject (e.g., "The turtle and the bunny went to the store"). Preliminary findings reveal a preference for the first-mentioned character in later pronoun interpretation following context sentences with a singular subject but not following conjoined-subject context sentences. These findings suggest that sentence-initial position itself was not responsible for the subject continuity preference in our earlier experiments.

Taken together, these findings suggest that children as young as 3 are sensitive to the connection between subjects and discourse topics. Children's comprehension of a sentence is affected not only by their current knowledge of its words and syntactic structure, but also by the prominence of each referent in a representation of the discourse; our findings show that referent prominence is affected by some of the same factors that affect coreference processing in adulthood, including, centrally, assignment to subject position. We have speculated that this connection could arise naturally because of children's default interpretation of the subject of each sentence as its most semantically prominent argument (Song & Fisher, 2005). Upon interpreting each sentence in a story or discourse, children are invited to create a representation of its meaning that takes the grammatical subject referent as the more prominent participant. In a sense, the syntactic asymmetry between subject and nonsubject arguments is one of the cues that determines the listener's attention to various participants' roles in the events under discussion.

Requirements for Syntactic Bootstrapping

Evidence that young children assign a default interpretation to sentence subjects in terms of some sort of semantic prominence further constrains our theories of the relationship between meaning and syntax in acquisition. Here we briefly sketch a theory of verb learning that is consistent with these and other findings.

A Preliminary Division of the Linguistic Data Based on Number of Nouns

Previous findings that children interpret verbs differently given only information about the verbs' number of arguments suggested an initial way in which observable surface properties of sentences could be intrinsically meaningful to young children (Fisher et al., 1994; Fisher, 1996, 2002). Once children can identify some nouns, they could assign different meanings to transitive and intransitive verbs by aligning a sentence containing two referential terms with a conceptual representation relating the two named entities, and a sentence containing one noun phrase with a conceptual representation centrally involving its single referent. Because the number of nouns in the sentence is a probabilistic indicator of the number of arguments of the verb, these preliminary syntactic hints could boost the probability of correct verb interpretations even before the surface markings of subject and object in a particular language are identified (e.g., Fisher et al., 1994).

Why not test ditransitives?

Prominence in Conceptual-Semantic Representations

The experiments presented here began to explore what semantic information sentences might provide once children can identify the subject noun phrase in a sentence, and revealed evidence that children can interpret the subject role in terms of the relative semantic prominence of a verb's arguments. As suggested in earlier work (e.g., Fisher et al., 1994; Gleitman, 1990), the choice of subject, in addition to the set of arguments, can serve as a sort of linguistic zoom lens to direct the listener's attention toward a particular perspective on an event.

How does the choice of subject influence children's interpretation of sentences? How do children figure out that the subject noun phrase—as marked in the child's native language—encodes some sort of semantic prominence? It is clear that a significant amount of learning is involved in this step. Most obviously, different languages use different means to formally identify the subject and object in transitive sentences: English relies heavily on word order but also uses subject-verb agreement; other languages use case markers or agreement markers on the verb to mark grammatical roles, and permit freer word order. In addition, languages differ in the relative importance of various conceptual-semantic dimensions for subject selection (e.g., Aissen, 1999).

Event-Dependent and Perspective-Dependent Roles: Reprise In the introduction to this chapter, we argued that multiple linguistic and psycholinguistic accounts of the linking of semantic and grammatical roles suggest that an abstract asymmetry in semantic prominence maps onto the difference between subjects and objects. These include event-dependent roles such as Dowty's protoagent and protopatient and perspective-dependent roles such as Talmy's figure and ground. Thus far for our purposes we have argued simply that both kinds of asymmetries give rise to a useful default interpretation for subjects in acquisition. On either view, a subset of participant roles should make more plausible subjects than others (as in Experiment 1), and an explicit choice of subject will invite the child to interpret the subject referent as playing a prominent role (as in Experiment 2).

This does not require, however, that we collapse the two kinds of roles into a single general notion of semantic prominence. As we pointed out in the introduction, event- and perspective-dependent roles are orthogonal. Thematic roles such as protoagent and protopatient reflect abstract similarities across different verbs' semantic entailments (e.g., *like* requires a sentient being who experiences a certain emotional state [liking] relative to a particular object), and predict how their arguments will be mapped onto grammatical positions. The perspective difference between subject and nonsubject, in contrast, appears to be somewhat independent of the event-dependent meanings of particular verbs—and unlike the link between subjects and agents, applies to all subjects, not just active transitive subjects. Dowty (1991) suggested that subjects are more "in perspective" because of the typical association between subjects and discourse topics; this is essentially the converse of our argument, summarized above, that subject noun phrases might naturally gain discourse prominence because of the semantic prominence of subjects (Song & Fisher, 2005).

[Margin handwritten note:] Connects previous + current work

Consistent with the logical independence of event roles and perspective on an event, we suspect that multiple independent dimensions of conceptual-semantic prominence determine what aspects of events adult and child observers attend to and which arguments in those relations they prefer as the syntactic subjects of transitive verbs (e.g., Grimshaw, 1990). Aissen (1999) has proposed an optimality theory version of just such a view: Her proposed dimensions of semantic promi- nence include a thematic role scale on which protoagents outrank protopatients, a discourse topicality or accessibility scale, and a person-animacy scale on which first- and second-person arguments (*you* and *me*; local persons in the discourse) outrank third-person arguments (*them*) and animates (especially humans) outrank inanimates. Aissen argues that these prominence scales tend to be aligned har- monically, with structurally prominent sentence positions (subjects » nonsub- jects) expressing arguments that are prominent on relevant conceptual-semantic dimensions.

On this view, multiple semantic prominence scales and a preference for map- ping arguments that are prominent on a conceptual-semantic dimension onto structurally prominent positions in sentences, are part of the built-in capacity for language acquisition. This type of account can easily explain our results: Once children have learned enough about the syntax of the native language to identify the subject of a sentence, they should be able to assign a default interpretation to subjects in terms of multiple dimensions of semantic prominence: They should in- terpret the subject as having as many protoagent properties as possible given the constraints of the situation, as being prominent in the discourse setting, and as be- ing high on a person-animacy scale. Learning a particular language's grammar will include learning how the subject is marked, and determining the relative ranking of the constraints ruling out subjects that are not agents, not topical, or inanimate.

The Meanings Come First Any form of syntactic bootstrapping assumes that appropriately structured conceptual representations are in place before the ac- quisition of a language. For our present purposes, we need to document the language-independent existence of multiple dimensions of conceptual-semantic prominence (e.g., animate vs. inanimate, topic vs. nontopic) that are proposed to map onto the difference between subjects and objects.

Considerable evidence suggests that infants naturally factor their representa- tions of events into conceptual predicates and arguments, and systematically dis- criminate the different roles in events (for reviews, see P. Bloom, 2000; Fisher & Gleitman, 2002). Some of the most striking evidence for this conclusion comes from learners who are isolated from ordinary exposure to a language and therefore have to invent one on their own. Deaf children who are exposed to no sign lan- guage model invent gestural communication systems termed *home sign* (Goldin- Meadow, 2003). The sentences of these invented systems show clear evidence of language-like predicate-argument structure: Signs glossed as verbs occur with pre- dictable sets of nounlike arguments (*eat* has two arguments, *sleep* only one); as in conventional languages, arguments we would gloss as playing the same roles appear in consistent positions across verbs and sentences. Apparently children need not learn from linguistic exposure that there exists a fundamental distinction between arguments and predicates, that eating entails an eater and a thing eaten, or that the agentlike argument of *eat* is importantly similar to the agentlike argument of *give* or *hit*. These findings suggest that abstract categories akin to protoagent and protopatient are likely to be part of the cognitive endowment children bring to the language learning process.

There is also some evidence that agents are treated as prominent participants in events by prelinguistic infants. For example, studies of 10-month-olds' perception of simple collision events revealed that they were more likely to detect a change in the identity of the agent or striking object than of the object that was hit (Cohen & Oakes, 1993). Striking evidence for the attention-grabbing properties of agents or first movers comes from a word-learning study by Grace and Suci (1985): They taught 17.5-month-olds names for puppets in action scenes and found that the infants more readily learned the new words if the referent puppet was the agent of a causal action than when it was the patient. This suggests that the infants gave more of their attention to the agents while watching the scenes; this allocation of attention made it easier to learn a new name for the agent puppet.

Prelinguistic infants develop considerable knowledge about the differences between animate and inanimate motion and causality (see Gelman & Opfer, 2002, for a review). Moreover, infants show a wide variety of perceptual preferences that lead them to pay more attention to animate than inanimate objects. These include a preference for faces (e.g., Johnson & Morton, 1991), for human motion (e.g., Legerstee, Pomerleau, Malcuit, & Feider, 1987), and for human voices (e.g., Glenn, Cunningham, & Joyce, 1981). Children approach language with an unsurprising bias to attend to the actions of humans or other animates.

An interesting hint of the role of animacy in the development of grammar comes from studies of the creation of Nicaraguan Sign Language, a language invented by several generations of deaf children at a school for the deaf in Nicaragua (e.g., Senghas, Coppola, Newport, & Suppalla, 1997). At a particular point in the development of Nicaraguan Sign Language, Senghas et al. found no transitive verbs that permitted animate direct objects. A causal event in which an animate agent acted on an animate patient required two verbs to license the two animate nouns (e.g., *girl push boy fall*). This is not an unusual pattern in the world's languages: Given the strong association of animacy and subjects, it is common for animate direct objects to require special marking (e.g., Comrie, 1981).

Finally, infants develop sensitivity to the direction of others' attention; many have argued that sensitivity to the flow of attention in social interactions, though obviously imperfect in both children and adults, is one of the cognitive foundations of language acquisition (e.g., P. Bloom, 2000; Tomasello, 2000). By the end of the first year of life, infants can share joint attention on an object with a communicative partner and by 16 to 18 months, interpret a communicative partner's eye gaze and gesture as cues to the likely referents of her words (e.g., Baldwin & Moses, 1996). Joint attention affects early language production as well. For example, Skarabella and Allen (2002) found that 2-year-olds learning Inuktitut were more likely to omit from their sentences the objects of joint attention with their listener, suggesting that they were correctly treating them as situationally "given"; children also omitted nouns for entities just mentioned in the conversation. Such evidence suggests the beginnings of a sensitivity to topicality or givenness in interactions with others.

This brief section merely glances at a vast literature on conceptual development in infancy, and its relationship to language development. Given this sketch of relevant findings, however, it seems plausible that dimensions of conceptual-semantic prominence much like those discussed above precede the acquisition of language and are part of the innate endowment that makes lexical and syntactic acquisition possible.

Final Comments: Verb Learning and Syntax Acquisition

We have argued that once children can identify the subject of a multiargument sentence as structurally prominent, they could assign a default interpretation to sentences containing a novel verb by assuming that the subject referent plays a semantically prominent role in the conceptual relation named by the verb. What counts as prominent will be determined by the situation and by the multidimensional attentional and representational biases of human perceivers.

But how do children identify the subject? Many possibilities exist; one that appeals to us relies on multiple, and individually faulty, sources of constraint to determine the hierarchical structure of sentences (see, e.g., Fisher & Gleitman, 2002; Keenan, 1976; Pinker, 1987). For example, children could identify the subject as structurally prominent in a two-argument sentence based on its association with any of several types of conceptual-semantic prominence (proto-agency, animacy, person, topicality). Other cues include the prosodic structure of the sentence (e.g., Fisher & Tokura, 1996; Gerken, Jusczyk, & Mandel, 1994), and the distributional structure of the sequences of linguistic forms themselves.

This multiple-constraints view comports with recent views of the role of distributional learning in syntax acquisition (see Newport, 2000, for review). A general finding in computational linguistics is that relatively simple assumptions and algorithms can go some distance toward sorting words into grammatical categories (e.g., Mintz, 2003; Redington, Chater, & Finch, 1998), and toward uncovering the hierarchical constituent and dependency structure of the clause (e.g., Klein & Manning, 2002), unaided by semantic or phonological cues. The preponderance of recent evidence suggests that in many domains human learners are intricately attuned to the statistics of their experience, and show great facility in detecting and using multiple probabilistic indicators of a common underlying structure in the world (see Kelly & Martin, 1994). A multiple-constraints view of syntax and lexical acquisition builds on the possibility that even partial information in each relevant domain (prosody, distributional cues to grammatical categories and phrase structure, and semantics) can reduce error, and that the shortcomings of each information source can be compensated for by others (e.g., Gillette et al., 1999; Hollich et al., 2000; Seidenberg & MacDonald, 1999).

For example, the alignment of partial sentence representations and conceptual representations sketched in our work (e.g., Fisher et al., 1994) would permit a useful probabilistic distinction between transitive and intransitive verbs, giving the child a significantly better chance of interpreting verbs as their speaker intended. Given that working out links between something like thematic roles and grammatical positions plays a key role in both verb and syntax acquisition (e.g., L. Bloom, 1970; Grimshaw, 1981; Pinker, 1989), it may be crucial that children have early access to an approximate division of the linguistic data into transitive and intransitive: it is transitive subjects, not all subjects, that tend to be agents. A probabilistic division of the linguistic data into one- and two-argument sentences could allow the child to begin with the domains within which semantic-syntactic mappings will be most regular.

We have suggested, following Aissen (1999; see also Manning, 2003), that multiple types of conceptual-semantic prominence may play a role in identifying the subject category of the native language and therefore in interpreting sentences. The supposition of "soft" or probabilistic links between syntax and meaning has advantages for theories of both verb and syntax acquisition. In particular, probabilistic links between form and meaning permit cross-linguistic variation. In English, subjects tend to be agents, to be animate, to be first- or second-person, and to be discourse-old. None of these patterns is categorical in English, but all show up as powerful tendencies. For example, passives, which have patient subjects, are more likely if the resulting sentence's subject is animate (Ferreira, 1994; Lempert, 1984), discourse-old (Weiner & Labov, 1983), or first- or second-person (Manning, 2003). Languages differ in how strongly they restrict various pairings of syntactic and semantic prominence; a model in which a single privileged semantic feature triggers the subject category cannot explain such cross-linguistic variation (e.g. Manning, 2003; Pinker, 1987).

To the extent that sentence structures can be roughly interpreted by alignment with conceptual structures, sentences can begin to influence verb interpretation as soon as children can recognize some nouns, and they become more informative as the child learns to identify the subject of the sentence. The sentence structure provides information about which event participants are relevant and which should be interpreted as playing a more prominent role in the conceptual relation named by the verb. What roles count as prominent among a verb's multiple arguments seems to depend on multiple conceptual-semantic dimensions. Recognition of the multiple conceptual-semantic correlates of subject status may be indispensable to an adequate theory of verb learning and syntax acquisition.

Acknowledgments The research reported in this chapter was supported by NIH grants R55 OD 34715 and R01 HD44458, by the Research Board of the University of Illinois, and a dissertation research grant from the University of Illinois to the second author. We thank Renée Baillargeon, Kay Bock, Susan Garnsey, Lila Gleitman, and Kristine Onishi for many helpful comments, and Jennifer Ferrer, Choonkyong Kim, Lalita Pourchot, and the members of the language acquisition lab for their help in data collection. The parents, staff, and children of the Montessori School of Champaign-Urbana and the University of Illinois Child Development Lab preschool are also particularly thanked for their participation.

References

Aissen, J. (1999). Markedness and subject choice in optimality theory. *Natural Language and Linguistic Theory, 17*, 673–711.

Baldwin, D. A., & Moses, L. J. (1996). The ontogeny of social information gathering. *Child Development, 67*, 1915–1939.

Bates, E., MacWhinney, B., Caselli, C., Devescovi, A., Natale, F., & Venza, V. (1984). A cross-linguistic study of the development of sentence interpretation strategies. *Child Development, 55*, 341–354.

Bates, E., McNew, S., MacWhinney, B., Devescovi, A., & Smith, S. (1982). Functional constraints on sentence processing: A cross-linguistic study. *Cognition, 11*, 245–299.

Bloom, L. (1970). *Language development: Form and function in emerging grammars*. Cambridge, MA: MIT Press.

Bloom, L., Lightbown, P., & Hood, L. (1975). Structure and variation in child language. *Monographs of the Society for Research in Child Development, 40* (serial no. 160).

Bloom, L., Miller, P., & Hood, L. (1975). Variation and reduction as aspects of competence in language development. In A. Pick (Ed.), *Minnesota Symposia on Child Psychology* (Vol. 1, pp. 3–55). Minneapolis: University of Minnesota Press.

Bloom, P. (2000). *How children learn the meanings of words*. Cambridge, MA: MIT Press.

Bock, J. K., Loebell, H., & Morey, R. (1992). From conceptual roles to structural relations: Bridging the syntactic cleft. *Psychological Review, 99*, 150–171.

Bowerman, M. (1973). Structural relations in children's utterances: Syntactic or semantic? In T. E. Moore (Ed.), *Cognitive development and the acquisition of language* (pp. 197–213). New York: Academic Press.

Bowerman, M. (1990). Mapping thematic roles onto syntactic functions: Are children helped by innate linking rules? *Linguistics, 28*, 1253–1289.

Braine, M. D. S. (1992). What sort of innate structure is needed to "bootstrap" into syntax? *Cognition, 45*, 77–100.

Braine, M. D. S., Brody, R. E., Fisch, S. M., Weisberger, M. J., & Blum, M. (1990). Can children use a verb without exposure to its argument structure? *Journal of Child Language, 17*, 313–342.

Brooks, P. J., & Tomasello, M. (1999). Young children learn to produce passives with nonce verbs. *Developmental Psychology, 35,* 29–44.

Brown, R. (1957). Linguistic determinism and the part of speech. *Journal of Abnormal and Social Psychology, 55,* 508–523.

Brown, R. (1973). *A first language.* Cambridge, MA: Harvard University Press.

Childers, J. B., & Tomasello, M. (2001). The role of pronouns in young children's acquisition of the English transitive construction. *Developmental Psychology, 37,* 739–748.

Clark, E. (1990). Speaker perspective in language acquisition. *Linguistics, 28,* 1201–1220.

Clark, H. H., & Begun, J. S. (1971). The semantics of sentence subjects. *Language and Speech, 14,* 34–46.

Cohen, L. B., & Oakes, L. M. (1993). How infants perceive a simple causal event. *Developmental Psychology, 29,* 421–433.

Comrie, B. (1981). *Language universals and linguistic typology.* Chicago: University of Chicago Press.

Corrigan, R. (1986). The internal structure of English transitive sentences. *Memory and Cognition, 14,* 420–431.

Corrigan, R. (1988). Children's identification of actors and patients in prototypical and nonprototypical sentences types. *Cognitive Development, 3,* 285–297.

Corrigan, R., & Odya-Weis, C. (1985). The comprehension of semantic relations by two-year-olds: An exploratory study. *Journal of Child Language, 12,* 47–59.

Dowty, D. (1991). Thematic proto-roles and argument selection. *Language, 67,* 547–619.

Ferreira, F. (1994). Choice of passive voice is affected by verb type and animacy. *Journal of Memory and Language, 33,* 715–736.

Fillmore, C. J. (1977). The case for case reopened. In P. Cole & J. M. Sadock (Eds.), *Syntax and semantics: Vol. 8. Grammatical relations* (pp. 59–81). New York: Academic Press.

Fisher, C. (1996). Structural limits on verb mapping: The role of analogy in children's interpretation of sentences. *Cognitive Psychology, 31,* 41–81.

Fisher, C. (2000). From form to meaning: A role for structural analogy in the acquisition of language. In H. W. Reese (Ed.), *Advances in child development and behavior* (Vol. 27, pp. 1–53). New York: Academic Press.

Fisher, C. (2002). Structural limits on verb mapping: The role of abstract structure in 2.5-year-olds' interpretations of novel verbs. *Developmental Science, 5,* 56–65.

Fisher, C., & Gleitman, L. R. (2002). Language acquisition. In H. F. Pashler (Series Ed.) & C. R. Gallistel (Volume Ed.), *Stevens' handbook of experimental psychology: Vol. 3. Learning and motivation* (pp. 445–496). New York: Wiley.

Fisher, C., Gleitman, H., & Gleitman, L. R. (1991). On the semantic content of subcategorization frames. *Cognitive Psychology, 23,* 331–392.

Fisher, C., Hall, G. D., Rakowitz, S., & Gleitman, L. R. (1994). When it is better to receive than to give: Syntactic and conceptual constraints on vocabulary growth. *Lingua, 92,* 333–375.

Fisher, C., & Snedeker, J. (2002, October). *Counting the nouns: Simple sentence-structure cues guide verb learning in 21-month-olds.* Paper presented at the Boston University Conference on Language Development.

Fisher, C., & Tokura, H. (1996). Acoustic cues to linguistic structure in speech to infants: Cross-linguistic evidence. *Child Development, 67,* 3192–3218.

Forrest, L. B. (1996). Discourse goals and attentional processes in sentence production: The dynamic construal of events. In A. E. Goldberg (Ed.), *Conceptual structure, discourse, and language* (pp. 146–161). Stanford, CA: CSLI.

Gelman, S. A., & Opfer, J. E. (2002). Development of the animate-inanimate distinction. In U. Goswami (Ed.), *Handbook of childhood cognitive development* (pp. 151–166). Malden, MA: Blackwell.

Gentner, D. (1982). Why nouns are learned before verbs: Linguistic relativity versus natural partitioning. In S. A. Kuczaj (Ed.), *Language development: Vol. 2. Language, thought and culture* (pp. 301–334). Hillsdale, NJ: Erlbaum.

Gentner, D., & France, I. M. (1988). The verb mutability effect: Studies of the combinatorial semantics of nouns and verbs. In S. L. Small, G. W. Cotrell, & M. K. Tanenhaus (Eds.), *Lexical ambiguity resolution in the comprehension of human language* (pp. 343–382). Los Altos, CA: Morgan Kaufman.

Gerken, L. A., Jusczyk, P. W., & Mandel, D. R. (1994). When prosody fails to cue syntactic structure: Nine-month-olds' sensitivity to phonological versus syntactic phrases. *Cognition, 51,* 237–265.

Gillette, J., Gleitman, H., Gleitman, L., & Lederer, A. (1999). Human simulations of vocabulary learning. *Cognition, 73,* 135–176.

Gleitman, L. R. (1990). The structural sources of verb meanings. *Language Acquisition, 1,* 3–55.

Gleitman, L. R., Gleitman, H., Miller, C., & Ostrin, R. (1996). Similar, and similar concepts. *Cognition, 58,* 321–376.

Glenn, S. M., Cunningham, C., & Joyce, P. F. (1981). A study of auditory preferences in nonhandicapped infants and infants with Down's syndrome. *Child Development, 52,* 1303–1307.

Goldin-Meadow, S. (2003). *The resilience of language.* New York: Psychology Press.

Grace, J., & Suci, G. J. (1985). Attentional priority of the agent in the acquisition of word reference. *Journal of Child Language, 12,* 1–12.

Grimshaw, J. (1981). Form, function, and the language acquisition device. In C. L. Baker & J. J. McCarthy (Eds.), *The logical problem of language acquisition* (pp. 165–182). Cambridge, MA: MIT Press.

Grimshaw, J. (1990). *Argument structure.* Cambridge, MA: MIT Press.

Gropen, J., Pinker, S., Hollander, M., & Goldberg, R. (1991). Affectedness and direct objects: The role of lexical semantics in the acquisition of verb argument structure. *Cognition, 41,* 153–195.

Hirsh-Pasek, K., & Golinkoff, R. (1996). *The origins of grammar.* Cambridge, MA: MIT Press.

Hollich, G. J., Hirsh-Pasek, K., Golinkoff, R. M., Brand, R. J., Brown, E., Chung, H., et al. (2000). Breaking the language barrier: An emergentist coalition model for the origins of word learning. *Monographs of the Society for Research in Child Development, 65.*

Huttenlocher, J., Smiley, P., & Charney, R. (1983). Emergence of action categories in the child: Evidence from verb meanings. *Psychological Review, 90,* 72–93.

Jackendoff, R. (1990). *Semantic structures.* Cambridge, MA: MIT Press.

Johnson, M. H., & Morton, J. (1991). *Biology and cognitive development: The case of face recognition.* Oxford: Blackwell.

Jones, S. S., Smith, L. B., & Landau, B. (1991). Object properties and knowledge in early lexical learning. *Child Development, 62,* 499–516.

Keenan, E. L. (1976). Toward a universal definition of "subject." In C. N. Li (Ed.), *Subject and topic* (pp. 303–333). New York: Academic Press.

Kelly, M. H., & Martin, S. (1994). Domain-general abilities applied to domain-specific tasks: Sensitivity to probabilities in perception, cognition, and language. *Lingua, 92,* 105–140.

Klein, D., & Manning, C. D. (2002). A generative constituent-context model for improved grammar induction. *Proceedings of the 40th Annual Meeting of the Association for Computational Linguistics,* 128–135.

Kuno, S. (1987). *Functional syntax*. Chicago: University of Chicago Press.

Landau, B., & Gleitman, L. R. (1985). *Language and experience: Evidence from the blind child*. Cambridge, MA: Harvard University Press.

Landau, B., & Stecker, D. (1988). Objects and places: Geometric and syntactic representations in early lexical learning. *Cognitive Development, 5,* 387–312.

Legerstee, M., Pomerleau, A., Malcuit, G., & Feider, H. (1987). The development of infants' responses to people and a doll: Implications for research in communication. *Infant Behavior and Development, 10,* 81–95.

Lempert, H. (1984). Topic as a starting point for syntax. *Monographs of the Society for Research in Child Development, 49.*

Manning, C. D. (2003). Probabilistic syntax. In R. Bod, J. Hay, & S. Jannedy (Eds.), *Probabilistic linguistics* (pp. 289–342). Cambridge, MA: MIT Press.

Marantz, A. (1982). On the acquisition of grammatical relations. *Linguistische Berichte, 80/82,* 32–69.

McShane, J., Whittaker, S., & Dockrell, J. (1986). Verbs and time. In S. Kuczaj & M. Barnett (Eds.), *The development of word meaning: Progress in cognitive developmental research* (pp. 275–302). New York: Springer-Verlag.

Mintz, T. H. (2003). Frequent frames as a cue for grammatical categories in child directed speech. *Cognition, 90,* 91–117.

Naigles, L. (1990). Children use syntax to learn verb meanings. *Journal of Child Language, 17,* 357–374.

Naigles, L. R. (1996). The use of multiple frames in verb learning via syntactic bootstrapping. *Cognition, 58,* 221–251.

Naigles, L., & Kako, E. (1993). First contact in verb acquisition: Defining a role for syntax. *Child Development, 64,* 1665–1687.

Nappa, R., January, D., Gleitman, L. R., & Trueswell, J. (2004, March). *Paying attention to attention: Perceptual priming effects on word order*. Paper presented at the 17th Annual CUNY Sentence Processing Conference.

Newport, E. L. (2000). A nativist's view of learning: How to combine the Gleitmans in a theory of language acquisition. In B. Landau, J. Sabini, J. Jonides, & E. L. Newport (Eds.), *Perception, cognition and language: Essays in honor of Henry and Lila Gleitman* (pp. 105–119). Cambridge, MA: MIT Press.

Osgood, C. E., & Bock, J. K. (1977). Salience and sentencing: Some production principles. In S. Rosenberg (Ed.), *Sentence production: Developments in research and theory* (pp. 89–140). Hillsdale, NJ: Erlbaum.

Pinker, S. (1984). *Language learnability and language development*. Cambridge, MA: Harvard University Press.

Pinker, S. (1987). The bootstrapping problem in language acquisition. In B. MacWhinney (Ed.), *Mechanisms of language acquisition* (pp. 399–441). Hillsdale, NJ: Erlbaum.

Pinker, S. (1989). *Learnability and cognition*. Cambridge, MA: MIT Press.

Pinker, S. (1994). How could a child use verb syntax to learn verb semantics? *Lingua, 92,* 377–410.

Redington, M., Chater, N., & Finch, S. (1998). Distributional information: A powerful cue for acquiring syntactic categories. *Cognitive Science, 22,* 425–469.

Seidenberg, M. S., & MacDonald, M. C. (1999). A probabilistic constraints approach to language acquisition and processing. *Cognitive Science, 23,* 569–588.

Senghas, A., Coppola, M., Newport, E. L., & Supalla, T. (1997). Argument structure in Nicaraguan Sign Language: The emergence of grammatical devices. In E. Hughes, M. Hughes, & A. Greenhill (Ed.), *Proceedings of the Boston University Conference on Language Development* (pp. 550–561). Boston: Cascadilla.

Skarabela, B., & Allen, S. (2002). The role of joint attention in argument realization in child Inuktitut. In B. Skarabela, S. Fish, & A. H. J. Do (Eds.), *BUCLD 26: Proceedings of the 26th annual Boston University Conference on Language Development* (pp. 620–630). Boston: Cascadilla.

Slobin, D. I. (1985). Cross-linguistic evidence for the language-making capacity. In D. I. Slobin (Ed.), *The cross-linguistic study of language acquisition* (Vol. 2, pp. 1157–1249). Hillsdale, NJ: Erlbaum.

Song, H. (2004). *The influence of discourse representation on young children's pronoun interpretation*. Unpublished dissertation, University of Illinois, Champaign, IL.

Song, H., & Fisher, C. (2005). Who's "she"? Discourse structure influences preschoolers' pronoun interpretation. *Journal of Memory and Language, 52*, 29–57.

Talmy, L. (1983). How language structures space. In H. Pick & L. Acredolo (Eds.), *Spatial orientation: Theory, research, and application* (pp. 225–282). New York: Plenum Press.

Tomasello, M. (1992). *First verbs: A case study of early grammatical development*. New York: Cambridge University Press.

Tomasello, M. (2000). *The cultural origins of human cognition*. Cambridge, MA: Harvard University Press.

Weiner, J., & Labov, W. (1983). Constraints on the agentless passive. *Journal of Linguistics, 19*, 29–58.

Wilkins, W. (1988). *Syntax and semantics 21: Thematic relations*. San Diego: Academic Press.

Part IV

How Language Influences Verb Learning: Cross-Linguistic Evidence

16   Verb Learning as a Probe Into Children's Grammars

Jeffrey Lidz

Let us begin this chapter by asking what constitutes an explanation in linguistics and in the field of language development. Since Chomsky's (1957, 1965) seminal work in generative grammar, the research program of linguistic theory has been set toward circumscribing the set of possible human languages. In an idealization of this program, one must first construct a set of phenomenological descriptions of individual languages. This description leads to the construction of individual grammars, viewed as the relevant cognitive state achieved by the speakers of those languages. Next, the comparison of particular grammars leads to the formation of general principles that underlie all of these grammars.[1] That is, we aim to understand the cognitive code that is shared by all humans who have the ability to acquire a language. Thus, the goal of comparative linguistics is not merely to account for the properties of extant languages but to use the existing languages to develop hypotheses about what patterns of properties might occur in other yet to be encountered languages. More generally, the goal of modern linguistics is to identify the range and limits of cross-linguistic variation to understand the cognitive principles that underlie the spectrum of human language.

For the field of language acquisition, the ultimate goal is to explain how language acquisition is possible and how it unfolds over time under varying conditions of exposure. To be sure, given the complexity of the acquisition task, language learners will take advantage of any source of information they can, including at least their core conceptual knowledge (Baillargeon, 1998; Spelke, 2000), their pragmatic and social abilities (Baldwin & Baird, 1999; Bloom, 2000; Carpenter, Nagell, & Tomasello, 1998; Diesendruck & Markson, 2001; Woodward, 1999), their logical competence (Halberda, 2004), and their domain-general statistical learning mechanisms (Gómez, 2002; Gómez & Gerken, 1999; Saffran, Newport, & Aslin, 1996). But just as surely, learners are constrained in how they approach the language learning problem (Crain, 1991; Gelman & Williams, 1998; Markman, 1989; Newport & Aslin, 2000). There are certain hypotheses that learners simply do not consider, either because they are outside of their computational capacity, because the properties consistent with those hypotheses are not apprehended by the relevant perceptual or conceptual systems, or because they lie outside the range of what human languages allow.

Restricting our attention to the last source of constraints, we return to the explanatory goals of linguistics. One of the fundamental hypotheses of generative grammar is that the linguistic constraints that limit the hypotheses that learners consider in acquiring a language are exactly those constraints that limit cross-linguistic variation (Baker, 2001; Chomsky, 1981, 1986; Hornstein & Lightfoot, 1981; Jackendoff, 2001; Pinker, 1989). On this view, then, hypotheses about the cognitive code underlying the limits of linguistic variation are also hypotheses about constraints on language acquisition (Crain & Thornton, 1998; Lidz & Musolino, 2002; Thornton, 1990).

In this chapter, I explore this possibility in the domain of verb learning. I first consider constraints on possible verbs that are deduced from linguistic description and analysis and then examine whether we find their effects in the acquisition of verbs. If it is true that cross-linguistic constraints parallel constraints on acquisition, we should be able to see those constraints in action both at the level of language description and in language development. Indeed, that is precisely what we find, lending support, at least in the domain of verb learning, to the view that research on language acquisition profits and can be guided by research on mature linguistic systems.[2]

The general framework of inquiry simultaneously applies both linguistic and behavioral research methods, with the aim that conclusions derived from one methodology provide testable hypotheses for the other. By integrating linguistic research with research on language acquisition, we can triangulate on the principles and constraints that both guide language acquisition and delineate the boundaries of possible languages.

Methodologically, this chapter takes advantage of children's use of syntax to guide verb learning. Given that children show a sensitivity to syntactic structure in assigning meaning to verbs, we can use this sensitivity to probe their knowledge of the kinds of grammatical constraints on verbs that are active in adult language. If the syntax of a novel verb is important for the identification of that verb's meaning, then to the extent that children can learn a novel verb's meaning, it follows that they have the syntactic knowledge that triggers that acquisition. Given this general perspective, then, we can use verb learning as a probe into children's knowledge of the mapping between syntax and semantics. In cases where we understand the relationship between syntax and verb meaning, children's acquisition of a given verb's meaning can tell us how and whether the relevant piece of syntactic knowledge plays a role in the acquisition process.

The chapter proceeds as follows. In "What Is a Verb Such That We Can Learn It?" I describe the basic grammar of verbs, identifying certain aspects of verb representation that are universal and certain that are more variable. By starting from a detailed understanding of the syntax and semantics of verbs, we can identify clear questions about how verb learning proceeds and about the role of inherent constraints in verb learning. In "Verb Learning and the Syntactic Bootstrapping Hypothesis," I describe some basic findings on verb learning, arguing that these findings enable us to develop tests of those properties of verb meaning identified in the previous section. The conclusion then goes on to describe a set of results that test possible constraints on language learners that are derived from detailed linguistic description. By taking advantage of principles derived from linguistic research, we can begin to identify the correct balance between the learner and the environment in verb learning.

What Is a Verb Such That We Can Learn It?

A crucial aspect of the meanings of verbs is that they represent generalizations over categories of events.[3] Further, a crucial aspect of events is that they have participants. Consequently, a fundamental property of verbs is that they take arguments that realize these participants. That is, a jumping event is not a jumping event unless there is someone who jumps. Concomitantly, the verb *jump* requires the sentence it occurs in to include a phrase making reference to the jumper. Similarly, hitting requires two participants (a hitter and a hittee) and so the verb *hit* requires two syntactic arguments. From the perspective of verb learning, then, the learner must minimally identify the number of participants entailed by the concept denoted by the verb.

Beyond identifying the participants entailed by an event, different kinds of events have different kinds of participants. It follows, then, that different verbs can take arguments of different types. For example, *think* expresses an event in which an individual stands in a relation with a proposition whereas *eat* expresses an event involving two individuals. Accordingly, *think* can take a sentential complement whereas *eat* take a noun phrase complement, since the former expresses a proposition and the latter an individual.

(1) a. Al thinks *that the election was rigged*.
    b. Al ate *a sandwich*.

Two things are important to note here. First, the mapping between syntactic types and semantic types is largely universal, and hence a potential consequence of grammatical architecture. In no language do verbs whose meanings require propositional arguments systematically occur only with noun phrase arguments.[4] Likewise, in no language are individual entities uniformly expressed as clauses. Second, there is not a one-to-one mapping between semantic argument types and syntactic argument types. A verb that expresses a relation between an individual and a proposition can take a noun phrase complement, as long as that noun phrase can be interpreted as referring to a proposition (Grimshaw, 1979):

(2) a. Sally knows *what time it is.*
    b. Sally knows *the time.*

The sentential complement (*what time it is*) and the noun phrase complement (*the time*) both express the same proposition, so the semantic requirements of the verb are met independently of the syntactic type of the argument.

In this regard, however, it is important to note that the syntactic requirements of a verb cannot be reduced to the semantic requirements of the concept denoted by that verb. Compare *know* with *wonder* (Grimshaw, 1979; Pesetsky, 1982):

(3) a. Kim wonders what time it is.
    b. *Kim wonders the time.

Here, the noun phrase (*the time*) is not allowed even though we know independently (from sentences like 2b) that it can express the relevant meaning. Hence, there must be some syntactic requirements associated with verbs that are independent of their meaning. Hence, learning a verb entails identifying this kind of syntactic restriction.

The independence of syntactic and semantic types can also be seen by comparing the verbs *like* and *enjoy* in (4):

(4) a. She liked the concerto.
        She enjoyed the concerto.
    b. She liked hearing the concerto.
        She enjoyed hearing the concerto.
    c. She liked to hear the concerto
        *She enjoyed to hear the concerto.

Although *like* and *enjoy* express essentially the same relation, only the former can occur with an infinitival complement. In sum, some syntactic requirements of a verb are derivable from semantics (that propositional arguments can be realized as sentential complements), but others are not and must therefore be included as information associated with that verb in the lexicon.

We can therefore add to the list of tasks for the verb learner the ability to identify (a) the semantic types of the participants entailed by the verb, (b) the mapping between semantic types and syntactic types, and (c) any idiosyncratic properties of the verb that restrict that mapping (e.g., whatever explains the difference in complementation possibilities found between *know* and *wonder* or between *like* and *enjoy*). Property (a) is a property of the concept denoted by the verb; property (b) is a property of language in general which could be used to help identify property (a); property (c) is a property of particular lexical items, beyond the constraints that are due to grammatical architecture as a whole.

Finally, knowing what the arguments of a verb are and what syntactic categories they are realized in is not sufficient to understanding the verb. A speaker must also know how those arguments are mapped to syntactic positions. That is, why does the noun phrase *Kim* occur as the subject of *know* while the propositional argument occurs as the object? Why is the meaning associated with *know* expressed as in (2) and not as in (5)?

(5) *What time it is knows Kim.

This question is typically referred to as the linking problem (Carter, 1976), and concerns the relationship between the meanings of individual verbs and the positions that their arguments take in the syntactic structure of a sentence. One of the fundamental discoveries of research in linguistics regarding the syntax of verbs is that the linking properties of verbs are not arbitrary (Carter, 1976; Gruber, 1965; Jackendoff, 1972, 1983, 1990). Rather, the syntactic positions of a verb's arguments are largely predictable from the meaning of that verb (Baker, 1988; Grimshaw, 1990; Levin, 1993; Levin & Rappaport, 1986; for experimental evidence, Fisher, Gleitman, & Gleitman, 1991; Kako, 1999). Consequently, verbs that share meaning also share important properties of syntactic distribution. For example, verbs that refer to causative events involving a change of state (e.g., *break, melt, close*) can participate in the "causative-inchoative" alternation, whereas verbs that do not express a change of state (*hit, see, eat*) cannot (Fillmore, 1967; Grimshaw, 1990; Jackendoff, 1990; Levin & Rappaport-Hovav, 1995):

(6) a. Chris broke the vase.
     b. The vase broke.
     c. Chris hit the vase.
     d. *The vase hit.

Similarly, in the domain of locative verbs (i.e., verbs expressing the movement of some object [the figure] to a location [the ground]), verbs that describe the manner of motion (*pour, spill, shake*) require the figure to occur as the direct object, whereas verbs that describe a change of state (*fill, cover, decorate*) require the ground to occur as the direct object (Gropen, Pinker, Hollander, & Goldberg, 1991; Kim, Landau, & Phillips, 1998; Pinker, 1989; Rappaport and Levin, 1988):

(7) a. Edward poured water into the glass.
     b. *Edward poured the glass with water.
     c. *Edward filled water into the glass.
     d. Edward filled the glass with water.

Thus, the language learner must come to know the systematic mapping between verb meaning and syntactic structure. These mapping principles are not part of a given verb's representation, given that they hold for whole subcategories of verbs, but one way to tell whether a verb has been acquired correctly is to determine whether it shows the appropriate mapping to syntax for its category of meaning.

Certain verbs also seem to be more restricted in their distribution than their meaning alone would predict. For example, whereas the verbs *give* and *donate*

express essentially the same relation, only the former occurs in both the prepositional dative and the double object construction:

(8) a. Georgia gave her paintings to the museum.
     b. Georgia gave the museum her paintings.
     c. Georgia donated her paintings to the museum.
     d. *Georgia donated the museum her paintings.

What this tells us is that certain verbs must have additional information as part of
their lexical representation that restricts their distribution. Wherever a verb appears to violate the general linking properties of the language, that verb must be
additionally specified to correctly limit its distribution.

Putting this all together, we can see that the task of the verb learner is to identify from experience a rich concept that entails a set of participants of various
semantic types. In order to do this, the learner must identify the correct mapping
from semantic types to syntactic types and from semantic arguments to syntactic
positions. Simply put, verbs express who did what to whom. Hence, learning a
verb requires the ability to identify the participants of the event it denotes. Thus,
to know what a novel verb refers to, one must be able to identify in the sentence
those phrases that serve as the arguments of the verb and to determine what
semantic type (e.g., object, proposition, property, etc.) those arguments realize.

Importantly, certain aspects of the mapping from form to meaning are cross-
linguistically stable, while others are cross-linguistically variable. From the perspective of verb learning, then, we can take these cross-linguistic properties as
hypotheses regarding constraints on verb learning that may come from within the
learner himself. Those properties that are cross-linguistically stable (e.g., the mapping from propositions to clauses) potentially constrain children's hypotheses
about the verbs they are learning. Whereas those properties that vary either across
or within languages (e.g., whether a verb takes a tensed or infinitival complement)
should not so constrain acquisition.

Before we can examine how constraints on language acquisition derived from
linguistic description operate, we must first discuss the motivations behind the
methodology of using verb learning as a probe for these constraints.

Verb Learning and the Syntactic Bootstrapping Hypothesis

A well-known problem for the acquisition of language generally and of words in
particular is the stimulus-free nature of language use (Chomsky, 1959). Extralinguistic context is not a very good predictor of what someone is going to say. For
example, when looking at a Rembrandt painting, one might say, "Dutch," "It's
crooked," "I prefer abstract expressionism," "Remember our camping trip last sum-
mer?" or just about anything else. Hence, if the language learner is to learn about
what is being said on the basis of what is happening in the world, the lack of reliable

correlations between language and events represents a serious obstacle to the learner. Worse, even when someone is talking about the here and now, the world makes available many different possible descriptions of the visible scene. Consider a scenario in which a boy and his mother are flying a kite. A novel word used in this context might refer to the kite, the string, wind, boredom, excitement, clouds, blue, flying, waiting, saying, hoping, thinking, breathing, and so on. Given the multiplicity of interpretations of any given context, the learner faced with a novel word needs to determine which of the objects, events, and properties made available by perception that word refers to. A theory of word learning must therefore determine a procedure by which alternatives are eliminated. At minimum, such a theory must allow the learner to compare across situations to narrow down the hypotheses. But even allowing for cross-situational comparison, a word-to-world pairing procedure still cannot overcome Quine's (1960) co-occurrence problem: rabbits always occur with rabbit ears, jumping always occurs with legs, giving always occurs with receiving, and sugar always occurs with sweetness.

Recent findings document that this problem is particularly severe for the case of verbs. Verb use even by mothers of very young children lines up very poorly with ongoing events (Lederer, Gleitman, & Gleitman, 1995). And as we have seen, observation makes available many salient verblike descriptions of a single observed event (Gillette, Gleitman, Gleitman, & Lederer, 1999; Gleitman, 1990; Landau & Gleitman, 1985).

As a way to overcome the difficulties of observational learning of verb meaning, the syntactic bootstrapping hypothesis posits that one important source of additional information lies in the systematic relationships between verb meaning and syntactic structure (Fisher, 1994; Fisher, Gleitman, & Gleitman, 1991; Landau & Gleitman, 1985; Snedeker & Gleitman, 2004). Because they can find a reliable mapping between syntax and lexical semantics, children make use of this mapping in learning verb meanings.

The syntactic bootstrapping hypothesis finds support in several results. First, maternal speech in several languages maps a highly overlapping verb meaning set onto the same range of complement structures (Lederer et al., 1995; Lee, Nelson, & Naigles, 2003). Children as young as 16 months old have been shown to be sensitive to properties of heard speech that could render aspects of these linkages useful, for example, the semantic differences between subjects and objects (Hirsh-Pasek, Golinkoff, DeGaspe-Beaubien, Fletcher, & Cauley, 1985). Indeed, there is some evidence that some syntax-semantics correspondences at this level are unlearned. Isolated deaf children project about these same structures for the same predicate meanings in their self-invented gestured languages (Feldman, Goldin-Meadow, & Gleitman, 1978; Goldin-Meadow & Mylander, 1984; Senghas, Coppola, Newport, & Supalla, 1997).

There is also evidence that young children make use of structural evidence in their verb learning. For instance, by about 24 months they will use information from the number of noun phrases in the utterance to choose between situationally plausible interpretations that differ in argument number of a novel verb (Fisher, 1996; Naigles, 1990). Children of this age have also been demonstrated to be sensitive to syntactic cues in learning the specially problematic verbs like *chase/flee*, which differ only by the perspective they take on the events they denote (Fisher, 1994; Fisher, Hall, Rakowitz, & Gleitman, 1994). Finally, in an act-out task in which children were presented with verbs that they already knew in novel syntactic frames, young children systematically altered the meaning of the verb to fit the meaning associated with the syntactic frame (Naigles, Gleitman, & Gleitman, 1993). For example, asked to act out "Noah comes the elephant to the ark," they pick up first Noah, then the elephant, and move them together to the ark. That is, ditransitive *come* must mean something like *bring*. In this sense, young children are *frame compliant,* altering their construal of the verb to fit its new linguistic environment.

All of these findings go to the idea that the learning procedure in some way makes joint use of the structures and situations that co-occur with verbs to converge on their meanings. Neither source of evidence is strong or stable enough by itself, but taken together they significantly narrow the search space.

The fact that children can use syntax as one source of information in learning novel verbs allows us to ask questions not only about how children learn verbs but also about the existence of constraints on verb learning. Here, we can ask whether children are limited in their verb learning by the same kinds of constraints that appear to hold across languages. That is, we can take information about what a possible verb is or about what a possible linking pattern is by looking for cross-linguistically stable generalizations and then ask whether children also exhibit those constraints in their acquisitions. The idea behind this reasoning is that linguistic universals derive from principled constraints on what a possible human language is. Thus, to the extent that these constraints can be found in verb learners, we add to the evidence in support of these constraints as part of the cognitive code underlying language acquisition. Looked at from another angle, cross-linguistically stable generalizations provide us with hypotheses about constraints on verb learners, which can then be tested on children who are in the process of developing a lexicon. In contrast, to the extent that a property of verb meaning or linking can vary cross-linguistically, we expect to find that property to be highly sensitive to aspects of the linguistic environment since it will depend not on principled constraints from the learner, but on the observation of the particular language being learned (i.e., the linguistic input).

Experimental Investigations of Grammatical Constraints

We now turn to three studies that examined these questions. What we will see is (1) that children rely on universal cues to verb meaning even when those cues are less reliable in the input than other cues, (2) that universal restrictions on verb-syntax pairings are obeyed by learners while cross-linguistically variable restrictions are not, and (3) that universal aspects of semantic representation can be found to guide very young verb learners' acquisition of novel verbs.

Constraints on Argument Number

One way that children's use of syntax to learn verb meanings has been documented involves tests of the way that children extend known verbs into syntactic contexts that they have not previously heard them in (Lidz, 1998; Naigles et al., 1993; Naigles, Fowler, & Helm, 1992). In these experiments, 2-, 3-, and 4-year-old children used objects from a Noah's ark playset to act out sentences presented to them by the experimenter. By examining systematicities in their act-out behavior, particularly when the sentence presented is a novel and apparently ungrammatical one, these experiments enable us to examine the role of syntax in guiding children's interpretations.

As noted above, when presented with novel uses of familiar verbs, children's act-outs were frame compliant, relying on information in the syntax to guide their interpretations (Naigles et al., 1993). Thus, for a sentence like "The zebra comes the giraffe to the ark," children acted out a scene in which the zebra brings the giraffe to the ark, showing that the extra argument is interpreted as a causal agent. By the same token, "the giraffe brings to the ark" is acted out with the giraffe coming to the ark, with no causal agent. What these studies show is that children can use syntax to broaden the scope of the events that they think a novel verb refers to. Although *come* expresses only motion toward a location in the adult language, if this verb is presented with an additional syntactic argument, children who have not yet settled on a representation for the verb's meaning will take that additional syntactic argument as evidence that the verb can also express caused motion.

The close connection between transitivity and causation found in these studies represents a particularly interesting case to examine. It is a linguistic universal that causative events are expressed with transitive structures and that noncausative events are expressed in intransitive structures. But is this universal a principled consequence of grammatical architecture or simply the fact that it can be observed in the input? Do children learn about the connection between causativity and transitivity through their experience with the language, or rather do their expectations about this relation color their perception of the linguistic input they are exposed to?

The problem here is that there are two possible explanations for children's behavior in any syntactic bootstrapping experiments. First, children could behave the way they do because they have learned by examining their input that there is a connection between causation and transitivity. Alternatively, children could behave this way because they expect there to be such a connection. Given that causatives are universally expressed as transitives, how can we find out whether children's use of transitivity to infer causation is due to their first having learned

ungrammatical stimulus

that the language is this way or whether they approach the task of verb learning with this principle to guide them?

Lidz, Gleitman, and Gleitman (2003) examined this question by looking at Kannada-learning children's use of syntax to guide verb learning. As noted, all languages show a strong connection between causation and transitivity. However, one thing that varies cross-linguistically in this domain is whether the alternation between causative and noncausative verbs is morphologically marked (see Comrie, 1985; Haspelmath, 1993; among others). For example, in many languages the intransitive variants are basic and an additional causative morpheme is added to indicate causation. In other languages, the transitive variants are basic and an additional anticausative morpheme is added to indicate the lack of causation. In still other languages, both strategies exist for different verbs. Thus, the addition and subtraction of arguments is used universally to mark the alternation whereas the presence of verbal affixes to mark the alternation varies both cross-linguistically and within a language.

We pitted the universal property of argument number against the cross-linguistically variable property of morphology in Kannada, a language with causative morphology, in order to separate out the effect of inherent constraints on the learner from the effect of the language environment. The reason Kannada was the appropriate probe language concerned the abundance of the morphological cue to causativity (see Lidz, 2003, for the details of causation in Kannada). In Kannada, any verb can be made causative through the addition of a causative morpheme. Moreover, whenever this morpheme is present, the causal interpretation is entailed. Finally, in Kannada, as in all languages, many verbs with two arguments (e.g., *see, climb*) are not interpreted causally. Given this pattern of facts, the causative morpheme is a more reliable surface cue for causation than is the number of arguments.

Because the presence of the causative morpheme guarantees a causal interpretation but the presence of two arguments is only probabilistically associated with causal interpretation, this language offers some insight into the source of children's use of argument number to guide their interpretations. If children use the most reliable cues in the input to determine the syntax to semantics mapping, then we would expect children learning Kannada to rely more heavily on the causative morpheme as an expression of causativity than on the number of arguments. On the other hand, if children are guided by expectations about the syntax-semantics mapping that are based on the principles of grammatical architecture that are responsible for grammatical universals, then children should rely more heavily on argument number than causative morphology. In the latter case, children would be expected to ignore the most reliable cue in the input in favor of the less reliable cue determined by inherent grammatical constraints.

In order to test these possibilities, Lidz et al. (2003) used the Noah's ark methodology described briefly above. Children were presented known verbs with either one or two noun phrase arguments and either with or without the causative morpheme. The predictions were as follows. If children approach the language learning problem open-mindedly and look for the most reliable features of the input, then children were expected to honor the morphological cue over the syntactic one. That is, when presented with "the giraffe came-cause" (i.e., with the causative morpheme added to the verb), we would expect them to interpret this causatively and thus act out something in which some other animal made the giraffe come. By the same token, such children were expected to treat "the zebra came the giraffe" (with no causative morphology) as noncausative. On the other hand, if children are predisposed to take the number of arguments as indicative of event structure, then they were expected to ignore the causative morphology and treat "the giraffe came-cause" as no different from "the giraffe came" and to treat "the zebra came the giraffe" as causative.

The data were clear. Very young Kannada-learning children treated argument number as an indication of causativity and failed to treat causative morphology as an indication of causativity, despite the fact that the latter is the more reliable cue. These data are shown in figure 16.1, which represents the proportion of causative act-outs provided by children as a function of argument number and the presence versus absence of causative morphology. In sum, children acted out two noun phrase sentences as causative and one noun phrase sentences as noncausative, independent of the presence or absence of the causative morpheme.

In effect, these children ignored the more reliable morphological cue to verb meaning and instead relied on the syntactic cue (noun phrase number). This result provides evidence for the priority of the principle aligning syntactic phrases with

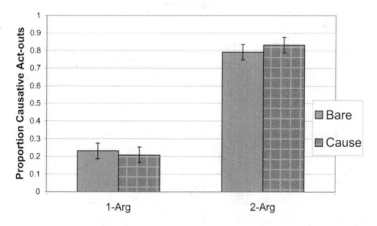

Figure 16.1. Proportion of causative act-outs by 3-year-old learners of Kannada in one-argument versus two-argument contexts with and without causative morphology.

semantic participants and for the unlearned nature of this constraint on verb-syntax linking. The observation that learners discarded the best cue in favor of a weaker one reveals the active role that learners play in acquiring verb meanings. Learners use argument number as a cue to verb meaning not because it is there in the input, but because they expect to find it there.[5] Thus, the connection between causal meaning and transitivity appears to be a guiding constraint on verb learning rather than a learned response to the input.

Constraints on Argument Type

The method of testing children's extensions of known verbs into novel contexts has also been used to investigate children's knowledge of the connection between syntactic and semantic types of arguments and the range of possible verb meanings.

As discussed above, some aspects of the mapping from event participants to syntactic categories are universal, while other aspects are more variable both within and across languages. Thus, a propositional argument can be realized as a tensed clause ("John thinks that Mary will win") or an infinitival clause ("John expects Mary to win") but not as a noun phrase referring to an individual (*"John thinks the winner"). The choice of tensed or untensed clause, however, is subject to lexical variability and must be learned on a verb by verb basis. Similarly, some change-of-state verbs that can occur with one argument ("the vase dropped") can also occur with two ("I dropped the vase"), while others happen not to allow this alternation ("the vase fell" vs. *"I fell the vase"). But verbs in this class never have their arguments realized as sentential complements (*"John falls that it is Bill"; *"John drops Bill to be here").

Given the existence of principled constraints on the syntax-semantics mapping, as well as lexically specific constraints, we can ask whether children are limited in the ways that they are willing to extend known verbs in accordance with these constraints. To do this, Lidz, Gleitman, and Gleitman (2004) compared children's understanding of known verbs in two kinds of ungrammatical syntactic contexts. In the "near" contexts, verbs were presented in environments that are permitted by language in general, but not by English, as in (9). In the "far" contexts, these verbs were presented in contexts that are not permitted by any language, as in (10).

(9) Near extensions. Possible in principle, but not in English.
    a. *The zebra falls the giraffe.
    b. *The zebra thinks the giraffe to go to the ark.
(10) Far extensions. Not possible in any language.
    a. *The zebra falls that the giraffe goes to the ark.
    b. *The zebra thinks the giraffe.

The reasoning behind this manipulation was this: If children are constrained to allow only those mappings that are licensed by the grammatical architecture, then we should expect to find that children distinguish these two types of extensions, showing frame compliant behavior in the near contexts, but not in the far contexts. When presented with a far extension, one that is not consistent with universal constraints on complement types, children should not show frame compliant behavior.

This expectation was met. We found that children relied on the syntactic structure to guide their act-out behavior only when the novel verb-sentence pairing was a possible pairing in principle (but not in practice). Three-year-old children were significantly more likely to act out frame-compliant responses in near contexts than in far contexts. In the cases in which the novel syntactic structure would violate principles mapping syntactic argument type to semantic argument type, children performed non-frame-compliant actions that relied more heavily on what they already knew about the verb. In other words, children accepted extensions of known verbs into new syntactic frames only when the verb-frame pairing was one that might have been possible. Because all of the test items in this study were ungrammatical sentences in the adult language, children had no prior experience with these materials. Yet, they distinguished these materials precisely along the lines that grammatical architecture would predict, accepting only extensions of known verbs into constructions that could be possible for some other related verb (or for a verb with the same meaning in some other language).

This finding suggests that children's knowledge of the syntax-semantics mapping guides their acquisition of novel verbs even when they are at a stage when their lexical representations for certain verbs have not solidified. In other words, some aspects of the syntax to semantics mapping do not have to be learned. Rather they serve as inherent constraints that guide learners' hypotheses regarding verb meanings and that block them from accepting certain verb-frame pairings. At the same time, of course, we see the role that linguistic experience will ultimately play. In exactly the cases that fall within the range of possible mappings between verbs and frames (i.e., the "near" cases), children are flexible and must rely on their experience with particular verbs to properly constrain this flexibility.

Constraints on Verb Meaning

Beyond the role of constraints on the syntax-semantics mapping, we can also ask whether aspects of lexical-semantic representation itself can be examined through experimentation with young verb learners. If cross-linguistic analysis reveals a universal of semantic representation for certain types of events, then we should also be able to find that this representation guides verb learning. To examine this possibility, we return to the acquisition of causatives.

Examination of causative verbs cross-linguistically reveals that their meanings are internally complex. Evidence for this internal complexity comes from several sources. First, in many languages there is a morphological operation that converts intransitive verbs into causative verbs. Thus, alongside a pair like (11) in English, we find a pair like (12) in Kannada.

(11) a. The ice melted.
      b. The sun melted the ice.
(12) a. Barf-u karg-i-tu.
          ice-NOM melt-PST-3SN
          "The ice melted."
      b. Surya barf-annu karag-is-i-tu.
          sun ice-ACC melt-CAUS-PST-3SN
          "The sun melted the ice."

Because the meanings are alike in the two languages, what this suggests is that there is an unpronounced piece of semantic representation in the English causative (11b) that adds causativity to the change of state meaning contributed by the root. Second, certain adverbials can take scope either over or under the causative element, suggesting that it is present in the semantic representation. For example, (13) is ambiguous.

(13) John melted the ice again.

One interpretation of this sentence is that John had some ice, melted it, refroze it, and then remelted it. On this reading, the adverbial includes the causation in its scope. What happens again is John's causing the ice to melt. Another interpretation of the sentence, however, is that while John only melted the ice once, it had already been in a melted state. Here, imagine that there was a block of ice that melted and that Bill froze it. If John then took the ice out of the freezer and applied heat, we could say (13), even though it was the first time John melted the ice. Thus, the adverbial can take scope only over the result subevent of the complex event. For further discussion, see McCawley (1968) and von Stechow (1996).

Bunger and Lidz (2003) asked whether children had access to the internal structure of such events, representing them as having subparts, as in (14), where the first subpart of this structure (X do something) specifies the causing subevent, or the means, and the second subpart (Y become state) specifies the resulting change of state (Dowty, 1979; Hale & Keyser, 1993; Jackendoff, 1990; Levin & Rappaport-Hovav, 1995).

(14) ([X do something] CAUSE [Y become state])

This study took advantage of a prior result on syntactic bootstrapping using the preferential looking paradigm. Studies carried out by Naigles and associates (Naigles, 1990, 1996; Naigles & Kako, 1993) have demonstrated that given a scene depicting two simultaneous events (a causative event and a noncausative continuous event), the structure of the sentence in which a novel verb is presented can influence a child's interpretation of the meaning of that verb. Specifically, children who hear a novel verb in a transitive sentence (X is gorping Y) interpret it as labeling the causative action, whereas those who hear the novel verb in an intransitive sentence (X and Y are gorping) interpret it as labeling the continuous, noncausative, action.

If syntax can guide the difference between and causative and noncausative interpretation and if causative events have internal structure, we reasoned that syntax should also be useful in distinguishing which aspect of a single internally complex event is labeled.

To determine whether children are like adults in representing causative events as having internal structure, we conducted a preferential looking study in which 2-year-old children saw internally complex causative events labeled by a novel verb occurring in distinct syntactic structures. Children were first familiarized to an event of direct causation (e.g., a girl bouncing a ball) described by a novel verb. The syntactic frame in which the novel verb was presented varied across children in four ways: control ("Look at that"), transitive ("The girl is pimming the ball"), unaccusative ("The ball is pimming"), or multiple frame (transitive + unaccusative: "The girl is pimming the ball. Do you see the ball pimming?"). This training phase was followed by a test phase in which children heard the novel verb ("Where's pimming now?") while they saw, on opposite sides of the screen, the separate subevents depicting the means (the girl patting a ball, but no bouncing) and the result (the ball bouncing with the girl standing idly by) of the complex causative presented during training.

Because the unaccusative variant of a causative verb labels the result subevent without making reference to the means, we predicted that subjects in the unaccusative and multiple-frame conditions would be more likely than subjects in the transitive and control conditions to interpret the novel verb as referring to the result subevent. This prediction was borne out, as shown in figure 16.2. At test, subjects in the unaccusative and multiple-frame conditions demonstrated a significant preference for the result subevent. Subjects in the no word and transitive conditions showed no significant preference for either subevent. Thus, when the syntax focused children's attention on the result of a given causative event, they interpreted a novel verb as describing that subevent.

This study provides further evidence, then, that observation of the syntactic behavior of a novel verb provides information about the kind of event that the verb labels. Note that if the syntactic nature of the input did not influence the interpretations that subjects assigned to novel verbs in this study, then we should not have observed this difference in attention at test between the unaccusative and multiple-frame conditions on the one hand and the no-word and transitive conditions on the other. Importantly, cross-linguistic analysis leads us to believe that all causative verbs denote events with internal structure. Consequently, we predicted that children should assign internal structure to the meanings of novel causative verbs. This prediction was borne out. If the subjects in this experiment were not

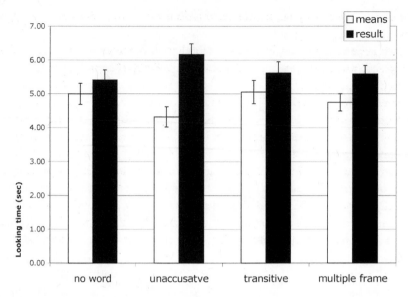

Figure 16.2. Mean visual fixation to means versus result subevent at test, by condition. Difference in attention to the means versus result subevent was significant in the unaccusative and multiple frame conditions.

representing the causative events as having internal structure, the syntax would not have been able to guide them to these different interpretations: that is, if their representations of these causative events did not include a result subpart, then even subjects in the unaccusative and multiple-frame conditions would not have been able to tease that subevent apart from the whole event. Thus, we see that children are constrained to hypothesize meanings for novel verbs in just the ways that those verbs are represented cross-linguistically in adult languages.

Conclusion

In sum, the studies presented here support a general framework of inquiry in which linguistic description and theory-building provide testable hypotheses for constraints on language acquisition. Principles of grammar that are found to be invariant across languages should be evident as constraints on learners. Properties of grammar that vary across languages should not so constrain language learners. In the present case, we have examined the role of syntactic constraints on verb meaning and verb syntax in guiding verb acquisition. In this domain, we find that children are limited in their hypotheses about verb meaning and verb syntax by precisely those constraints that are posited by linguistic description, lending further support to those constraints as principled aspects of the cognitive code underlying human language.

It is important to note, however, that although the work I have described focuses on constraints from the learner, this focus by no means diminishes the contribution of the input and linguistic experience in the development of the syntax and semantics of verb representations. In the cases where there are no inherent constraints guiding acquisition, we expect to see a larger role of the input. Indeed, this role has been documented for the acquisition of argument structure preferences that play a role in parsing (Snedeker & Trueswell, 2004), learning which verbs encode exceptions to general linking principles (Naigles et al., 1992), and identifying the set of syntactic frames that a verb occurs in (Hoff & Naigles, 2002), among various other properties. Thus, the theory of verb-learning that develops is not one that is myopically focused exclusively on constraints from the learner or on the role of the input, but rather on the important interactions between the two.

Notes

1. This is an idealization of the research program because in reality research in all of these areas is conducted simultaneously.

2. Of course the reverse should also be true. Conclusions from language acquisition can and should guide the development of explanatory linguistic theories. See Grodzinsky and Reinhart (1993), Snyder and Stromswold (1997), Thornton and Wexler (1999), and Lidz and Musolino (2004), for some examples in the domain of syntax and semantics.

3. This already represents a simplification, since it is difficult to define the category of verbs semantically. There are many verbs whose meanings are states (John is *sitting* on the floor), relations (John *knows* who stole the bacon), or properties (John *appears* to be late). Worse, there are events that are realized in other syntactic categories (The *earthquake* was frightening; The children are *noisy* today). And the very same concept can sometimes be realized in multiple lexical categories (The results *surprised* me; The results were *surprising* to me; The results were a *surprise* to me). For the present purposes, this simplification is benign, though ultimately a better understanding of grammatical categories needs to be developed. See Baker (2005) and Croft (1991) for discussion.

4. A word of caution is in order here as well. In some languages, embedded clauses are case marked, typically a property of noun phrases. However, it is possible in such languages to distinguish noun phrases that are clausal from those that are not, allowing us to maintain the basic generalization.

5. We should add that Kannada-speaking adults eventually do acquire this special ("language specific") feature of their language; after all, to say that they did not would mean that the Kannada language had changed. So it is reassuring to find, as we did, that Kannada adults—unlike their young offspring—show sensitivity both to argument

number and to the causative morpheme when they participate in the Noah's ark experiment.

References

Baillargeon, R. (1998). Infants' understanding of the physical world. In M. Sabourin & F. Craik (Eds.), *Advances in psychological science: Vol. 2. Biological and cognitive aspects* (pp. 503–529). Hove, England: Psychology Press/Erlbaum.

Baker, M. (1988). *Incorporation*. Chicago: University of Chicago Press.

Baker, M. (2001). *The atoms of language*. New York: Basic Books.

Baker, M. (2005). *Lexical categories*. Cambridge: Cambridge University Press.

Baldwin, D. A., & Baird, J. A. (1999). Action analysis: A gateway to intentional inference. In P. Rochat (Ed.), *Early social cognition: Understanding others in the first months of life* (pp. 215–240). Mahwah, NJ: Lawrence Erlbaum.

Bloom, P. (2000). *How children learn the meanings of words*. Cambridge, MA: MIT Press.

Bunger, A., & Lidz, J. (2004). Syntactic bootstrapping and the internal structure of causative events. In A. Brugos, L. Micciulla, & C. E. Smith (Eds.), *Proceedings of BUCLD* (pp. 74–85). Cambridge, MA: Cascadilla Press.

Carpenter, M., Nagell, K., & Tomasello, M. (1998). Social cognition, joint attention, and communicative competence from 9 to 15 months of age. *Monographs of the Society for Research in Child Development, 255*.

Carter, R. (1976). Some constraints on possible words. *Semantikos, 1*, 27–66.

Chomsky, N. (1957). *Syntactic structures*. The Hague: Mouton.

Chomsky, N. (1959). Review of B.F. Skinner's *Verbal Behavior*. *Language, 35*, 26–58.

Chomsky, N. (1965). *Aspects of the theory of syntax*. Cambridge, MA: MIT Press.

Chomsky, N. (1981). *Lectures on government and binding*. Dordrecht: Foris.

Chomsky, N. (1986). *Knowledge of language: Its structure origin and use*. New York: Praeger.

Comrie, B. (1985). Causative verb formation and other verb-deriving morphology. In T. Shopen (Ed.), *Language typology and syntactic description, III: Grammatical categories and the lexicon* (pp. 309–348). Cambridge: Cambridge University Press.

Crain, S. (1991). Language acquisition in the absence of experience. *Behavioral and Brain Sciences, 14*, 597–612.

Crain, S., & Thornton, R. (1998). *Investigations in universal grammar*. Cambridge, MA: MIT Press.

Croft, W. (1991). *Syntactic categories and grammatical relations*. Chicago: University of Chicago Press.

Diesendruck, G., & Markson, L. (2001). Children's avoidance of lexical overlap: A pragmatic account. *Developmental Psychology, 37*(5), 630–641.

Dowty, D. (1979). *Word meaning and montague grammar*. Dordrecht: Reidel.

Feldman, H., Goldin-Meadow, S., & Gleitman, L. (1978). Beyond Herodotus: The creation of language by isolated deaf children. In J. Locke (Ed.), *Action, gesture and symbol* (pp. 351–414). New York: Academic Press

Fillmore, C. (1967). The grammar of hitting and breaking. In R. Jacobs & P. Rosenbaum (Eds.), *Readings in English transformational grammar* (pp. 120–133). Waltham, MA: Ginn.

Fisher, C. (1994). Structure and meaning in the verb lexicon: Input for a syntax-aided verb learning procedure. *Language and Cognitive Processes, 9*, 473–517.

Fisher, C. (1996). Structural limits on verb mapping: The role of analogy in children's interpretations of sentences. *Cognitive Psychology, 31*(1), 41–81.

Fisher, C., Gleitman, H., & Gleitman, L. (1991). On the semantic content of subcategorization frames. *Cognitive Psychology, 23*, 331–392.

Fisher, C., Hall, G., Rakowitz, S., & Gleitman, L. (1994). When it is better to receive than to give: Structural and cognitive factors in acquiring a first vocabulary. *Lingua, 92*, 333–376.

Gelman, R., & Williams, E. M. (1998). Enabling constraints for cognitive development and learning: A domain-specific epigenetic theory. In D. Kuhn & R. Siegler (Eds.), *Cognition, perception, and language: Vol. 2, Handbook of child psychology* (5th ed., pp. 575–630). New York: John Wiley and Sons.

Gillette, J., Gleitman, L., Gleitman, H., & Lederer, A. (1999). Human simulation of vocabulary learning. *Cognition, 73*(2), 135–176.

Gleitman, L. (1990). Structural sources of verb learning. *Language Acquisition, 1*, 1–63.

Goldin-Meadow, S., & Mylander, C. (1984). Gestural communication in deaf children: The effects and non-effects of parental input on early language development. *Monographs of the Society for Research in Child Development, 49*.

Gómez, R. L. (2002). Variability and detection of invariant structure. *Psychological Science, 13*, 431–436.

Gómez, R. L., & Gerken, L. A. (1999). Artificial grammar learning by one-year-olds leads to specific and abstract knowledge. *Cognition, 70*, 109–135.

Grimshaw, J. (1979). Complement selection and the lexicon. *Linguistic Inquiry, 10*, 279–326.

Grimshaw, J. (1990). *Argument structure.* Cambridge, MA: MIT Press.

Grodzinsky, Y., & Reinhart, T. (1993). The innateness of binding and coreference. *Linguistic Inquiry, 24*, 69–101.

Gropen, J., Pinker, S., Hollander, M., & Goldberg, R. (1991). Syntax and semantics in the acquisition of locative verbs. *Journal of Child Language, 18*, 115–151.

Gruber, J. (1965). *Studies in lexical relations.* PhD dissertation, MIT.

Halberda, J. (2004). *Is this a dax which I see before me? Use of the logical argument disjunctive syllogism supports word learning in children and adults.* Unpublished manuscript.

Hale, K., & Keyser, S. J. (1993). On argument structure and the lexical expression of syntactic relations. In K. Hale & S. J. Keyser (Eds.), *The view from building 20* (pp. 53–110). Cambridge, MA: MIT Press.

Haspelmath, M. (1993). More on the typology of causative inchoative relations. In B. Comrie & M. Polinsky (Eds.), *Causatives and transitivity* (pp. 87–120). Amsterdam: Benjamins.

Hirsh-Pasek, K., Golinkoff, R., DeGaspe-Beaubien, F., Fletcher, A., & Cauley, K. (1985). *In the beginning: One word speakers comprehend word order.* Paper presented at Boston University Conference on Language Development, Boston.

Hoff, E., & Naigles, L. (2002). How children use input to acquire a lexicon. *Child Development, 73*, 418–433.

Hornstein, N., & Lightfoot, D. (1981). *Explanation in linguistics.* London: Longman.

Jackendoff, R. (1972). *Semantic interpretation in generative grammar.* Cambridge, MA: MIT Press.

Jackendoff, R. (1983). *Semantics and cognition.* Cambridge, MA: MIT Press.

Jackendoff, R. (1990). *Semantic structures.* Cambridge, MA: MIT Press.

Jackendoff, R. (2001). *Foundations of language.* Oxford: Oxford University Press.

Kako, E. (1999). *The event semantics of syntactic structure.* PhD dissertation, University of Pennsylvania.

Kim, M., Landau, B., & Phillips, C. (1998). Cross-linguistic differences in children's syntax for locative verbs. In A. Greenhill, H. Littlefield, & C. Tano (Eds.), *Proceedings of BUCLD* (pp. 337–348). Cambridge, MA: Cascadilla Press.

Landau, B., & Gleitman, L. (1985). *Language and experience: Evidence from the blind child*. Cambridge: Harvard University Press.

Lederer, A., Gleitman, L., & Gleitman, H. (1995). Verbs of a feather flock together: Structural properties of maternal speech. In M. Tomasello & E. Merriam (Eds.), *Acquisition of the verb lexicon* (pp. 277–297). New York: Academic Press.

Lee, J., Nelson, J., & Naigles, L. (2003). *Syntactic bootstrapping: A viable strategy for Mandarin verb learners*. Paper presented at BUCLD, Boston.

Levin, B. (1993). *English verb classes and alternations*. Chicago: University of Chicago Press.

Levin, B., & Rappaport, M. (1986). The formation of adjectival passives. *Linguistic Inquiry, 17*, 623–661.

Levin, B., & Rappaport-Hovav, M. (1995). *Unaccusativity*. Cambridge, MA: MIT Press.

Lidz, J. (1998). Constraints on the syntactic bootstrapping procedure for verb learning. In A. Greenhill, M. Hughes, H. Littlefield, & H. Walsh (Eds.), *Proceedings of Boston University Conference on Language Development* (pp. 488–498). Cambridge, MA: Cascadilla.

Lidz, J. (2003). Causation and reflexivity in Kannada. In V. Dayal & A. Mahajan (Eds.), *Clause structure in South Asian languages* (pp. 93–130). Dordrecht: Kluwer.

Lidz, J., Gleitman, H., & Gleitman, L. (2003). Understanding how input matters: Verb-learning and the footprint of universal grammar. *Cognition, 87*, 151–178.

Lidz, J., Gleitman, H., & Gleitman, L. (2004). Kidz in the 'hood: Syntactic bootstrapping and the mental lexicon. In G. Hall & S. Waxman (Eds.), *Weaving a lexicon*. Cambridge, MA: MIT Press.

Lidz, J., & Musolino, J. (2002). Children's command of quantification. *Cognition, 84*, 113–154.

Lidz, J., & Musolino, J. (in press). The quantificational status of indefinites: The view from child language. *Language Acquisition*.

Markman, E. M. (1989). *Categorization and naming in children: Problems of induction*. Cambridge, MA: MIT Press.

McCawley, J. (1968). The role of semantics in grammar. In E. Bach & R. T. Harms (Eds.), *Universals in linguistic theory* (pp. 124–169). New York: Holt, Rinehart and Winston.

Naigles, L. (1990). Children use syntax to learn verb meanings. *Journal of Child Language, 17*, 357–374.

Naigles, L. R. (1996). The use of multiple frames in verb learning via syntactic bootstrapping. *Cognition, 58*, 221–251.

Naigles, L., Fowler, A., & Helm, A. (1992). Developmental changes in the construction of verb meanings. *Cognitive Development, 7*, 403–427.

Naigles, L., Gleitman, H., & Gleitman, L. (1993). Syntactic bootstrapping and verb acquisition. In E. Dromi (Ed.), *Language and cognition: A developmental perspective* (pp. 87–102). Norwood, NJ: Ablex.

Naigles, L., & Kako, E. T. (1993). First contact in verb acquisition: Defining a role for syntax. *Child Development, 64*, 1665–1687.

Newport, E. L., & Aslin, R. N. (2000). Innately constrained learning: Blending old and new approaches to language acquisition. In S. C. Howell, S. A. Fish, & T. Keith-Lucas (Eds.), *Proceedings of the 24th Annual Boston University Conference on Language Development* (pp. 1–21). Somerville, MA: Cascadilla Press.

Pesetsky, D. (1982). *Paths and categories*. PhD dissertation, MIT.

Pinker, S. (1989). *Learnability and cognition*. Cambridge, MA: MIT Press.

Quine, W. V. O. (1960). *Word and object*. Cambridge, MA: MIT Press.

Rappaport, M., & Levin, B. (1988). What to do with theta-roles. In W. Wilkins (Ed.), *Syntax and semantics 21: Thematic relations* (pp. 7–36). New York: Academic Press.

Saffran, J. R., Newport, E. L., & Aslin, R. N. (1996). Word segmentation: The role of distributional cues. *Journal of Memory and Language, 35*, 606–621.

Senghas, A., Coppola, M., Newport, E. L., & Supalla, T. (1997). Argument structure in Nicaraguan Sign Language: The emergence of grammatical devices. In E. Hughes, M. Hughes, & A. Greenhill (Eds.), *Proceedings of the 21st Annual Boston University Conference on Language Development: Vol. 2*. Somerville, MA: Cascadilla Press.

Snedeker, J., & Gleitman, L. (2004). Why it is hard to label our concepts. In G. Hall & S. Waxman (Eds.), *Weaving a lexicon*. Cambridge, MA: MIT Press.

Snedecker, J., & Trueswell, J. (2004). The developing constraints on parsing decisions: The role of lexical-biases and referential scenes in child and adult sentence processing. *Cognitive Psychology, 49*(3), 238–299.

Snyder, W., & Stromswold, K. (1997). The structure and acquisition of English dative constructions. *Linguistic Inquiry, 28*, 281–317.

Spelke, E. S. (2000). Core knowledge. *American Psychologist, 55*(11), 1233–1243.

Thornton, R. (1990). *Adventures in long distance moving: The acquisition of complex wh-questions*. PhD dissertation, University of Connecticut.

Thornton, R., & Wexler, K. (1999). *Principle B, VP-ellipsis and interpretation in child grammar*. Cambridge, MA: MIT Press.

von Stechow, A. (1996). The different readings of *wieder* again: A structural account. *Journal of Semantics, 13*, 87–138.

Woodward, A. L. (1999). Infants' ability to distinguish between purposeful and non-purposeful behaviors. *Infant Behavior and Development, 22*, 145–160.

17 Revisiting the Noun-Verb Debate: A Cross-Linguistic Comparison of Novel Noun and Verb Learning in English-, Japanese-, and Chinese-Speaking Children

Mutsumi Imai, Etsuko Haryu, Hiroyuki Okada,
Li Lianjing, and Jun Shigematsu

To understand the nature of lexical development, it is crucial to investigate how children learn a wide range of word classes, including nouns, verbs, and adjectives, along with closed class words such as prepositions and classifiers. An important question is whether a particular type of concept, over others, universally invites children to name it at early stages of word learning to serve as the entry point into language, that is, whether there is, in Gentner's words, "an initial set of fixed hooks with which children can bootstrap themselves into a position to learn the less transparent aspects of language" (Gentner, 1982, p. 328). A number of researchers have proposed that basic-level object nouns serve such a function and argue that the basic-level object categories reflect the natural clustering of the world and are hence conceptually privileged (e.g., Gentner, 1982; Gentner & Boroditsky, 2001; Rosch, 1978). On the other hand, some researchers disagree with this view, arguing that the relative dominance of a particular type of words in the early lexicon is determined by distributional and structural properties of children's native language, and hence that the class of words that children learn earliest should differ across different languages (e.g., Choi & Gopnik, 1995; Tardif, 1996).

In this chapter we address this issue, reporting results from a series of cross-linguistic studies that examined how English-, Japanese-, and Chinese-speaking children generalize newly learned nouns and verbs. Based on the results, we evaluate the two competing positions in the noun-verb debate. We then explore universal and language-specific factors that affect the ease or difficulty of early noun and verb learning.

Current Debate Concerning the Universal Advantage in Noun Learning

In her natural partition hypothesis, Gentner (Gentner, 1982; Gentner & Boroditsky, 2001) has proposed that nouns will predominate over verbs in children's initial vocabularies because the meanings of concrete nouns are easier for children to discover than those of verbs and other relational terms, because the concepts which nouns typically denote (e.g., balls, cups, dogs) are individuated from the environment in the world and hence are already prepackaged to be named when children start learning language. In contrast, relational concepts, which are typically denoted by verbs, are not as obviously accessible as basic-level object categories, as verbs are cross-linguistically variable in their semantic structure and their meanings cannot be learned independently of the semantic system of the language. Gentner thus predicted that noun learning is universally easier than verb learning, independent of the structural and distributional properties of the language that children are learning.

Some researchers have challenged this view, however, arguing that verbs can be learned faster and easier than nouns if verbs predominate in the input (Choi & Gopnik, 1995; Tardif, 1996). For example, in some languages, including Chinese, Korean, and Japanese, arguments (both subjects and objects) are often dropped from a sentence. As a result, verbs tend to appear more frequently than nouns in the maternal input (e.g., Choi & Gopnik, 1995; Kim, McGregor, & Thompson, 2000; Ogura, 2001; Tardif, 1996). Based on this observation, some researchers predicted that children who are learning these languages should learn verbs earlier, hence more easily, than nouns (e.g., Choi & Gopnik, 1995; Tardif, 1996).

Mixed results have been reported with respect to whether Chinese-, Korean-, or Japanese-speaking children learn verbs earlier than nouns, however. Some studies reported the predominance of verbs in Mandarin-speaking (Tardif, 1996) and Korean-speaking (Choi, 2000) children's early productive vocabularies. However, other studies reported approximately equal proportions of nouns and verbs (Choi & Gopnik, 1995). Yet some other studies reported that the proportion of nouns was higher than verbs in Korean (Au, Dapretto, & Song, 1994; Kim et al., 2000) and in Japanese (Ogura, 2001; Yamashita, 1997) children.

Limitations of Checklist or Production Data as an Index for Relative Noun-Verb Advantage

Why are there such discrepancies in the literature concerning the noun-verb debate? It seems that the discrepancies have in large part arisen from the fact that the studies reviewed above relied on either maternal reports using checklist inventories or production data. While these methodologies no doubt are very useful and provide us with invaluable data for understanding how children build up their vocabulary, there are some limitations inherent in these methodologies when we rely on them as a sole index for relative ease or difficulty of noun and verb learning.

Relative Use of Nouns and Verbs Differ Across Different Contexts

In the studies using either checklist or production data, the relative proportion of nouns and verbs in children's early vocabulary is taken to be an index of the relative ease or difficulty of noun learning and verb learning. However, the relative proportion of nouns and verbs may vary depending on the context in which the production data are collected even within a single language (Choi, 2000; Ogura, 2001; Tardif, Gelman, & Xu, 1999). Thus, samples collected in different contexts may yield different results. Given this, it is difficult to draw a definitive conclusion about whether nouns are learned more easily than verbs (or vice versa) in a particular language based on production data alone.

Using a Word Does Not Guarantee the Full Mastery of the Meaning of the Word

A further limitation in using the proportion of nouns and verbs in children's vocabulary as the index of relative ease of noun versus verb learning is that the fact that a word learner "knows" a word does not necessarily mean that she has acquired the full meaning of the word. In other words, children may use a particular word in a particular situation appropriately, but the total number of situations in which they could use the word appropriately may be much more limited than situations in which the word is used by adults (Bowerman, 1980; Dromi, 1987). For example, a child may use the verb *throw* when she sees someone throwing a ball, but she may not fully understand that when one throws something, one can throw not only balls but any object that can be held with one's hand. She may also not realize that one can throw things in many different ways (e.g., with two hands or one hand, underhand or overhand, etc.), but one cannot throw things using legs (Forbes & Poulin-Dubois, 1997; see also Huttenlocher, Smiley, & Charney, 1983). This problem applies to verbs more severely than nouns because verb meanings are often made up of a combination of abstract semantic features.

Here, we report an interesting anecdote that clearly shows that using a verb in certain context does not mean that the child understand the full, adult-like meaning of it. In Japanese, there are two verbs, *ageru* and *kureru*, corresponding to the English verb *give*. However, the two must be clearly distinguished and cannot be used interchangeably. *Ageru* is used when the giver gives something to someone other than the speaker, while *kureru* is used when the giver gives something to the speaker. Thus, if a mother gives a candy to a child, the child must say, "Okaasan

(Mother) ga (nominal particle) ame (candy) wo (accusative particle) kure-ta (give me-past)," but when the mother gives a candy to the child's sister, the child must say, "Okaasan ga ame wo ageta (give someone other than myself)." Mika, a 4-year-old girl, had been using *ageru* since she was 2.5 years old, and the adults around her had assumed that she knew the meaning of this verb. However, at 42 months old, she said "Ojiichan (grandfather) ga (nominal particle) ame (candy) wo (accusative particle) age-ta (ageru-past, "give to other than self")" when noting that her grandfather gave her a candy, where she should have said "ojiichan ga kureta," because the receiver of the candy was herself, the speaker. Her aunt (the first author) asked her to repeat what she had just said to confirm if it was just a slip of the tongue. She used *ageru* again with confidence. This shows that even though she used *ageru* correctly in many situations, her representation of the meaning was not quite adult-like in the sense that it did not include the crucial semantic component of whether or not the recipient of giving is the speaker. Nonetheless, if her mother had been asked to fill out a vocabulary inventory when Mika was only 2 years old, she would have definitely checked off *ageru*, thinking that Mika had already learned the word.

Our Approach: Learning New Nouns and New Verbs Introduced During a Dynamic Action Event

Given the limitations in using the relative dominance of nouns and verbs in children's earliest vocabulary as the index of the relative ease or difficulty of noun and verb learning in young children, we decided to approach the question by asking how easily (and correctly in the adult sense) children learning different languages extend newly learned nouns and verbs to new instances in experimental settings. A merit of this paradigm is that it allows us to assess the general knowledge children possess about the given word class rather than the knowledge of the meanings of specific words, which must vary across different individuals depending on their specific experiences with the words.

The principles governing the extension of nouns and verbs are very different. An object can appear in many different actions. For example, a ball can be rolled, thrown, kicked, and so on. Thus, when a noun is introduced in a scene in which the referent object is used in a particular action, in extending it, children must know that the noun should be extended on the basis of the sameness of the object per se but not on the basis of the sameness of the action with which the object is used. Likewise, an action can be done with many different objects. For example, we can throw a ball, a Frisbee, a stone, a disk, or almost anything we can lift up with our hands. Thus, in extending a verb that has been mapped onto an action involving an object, the object must be separated from the action and be treated as a variable that can be changed.[1]

In this chapter, we report the results of a cross-linguistic study that investigated how young children learning English, Japanese, or Chinese map novel nouns and verbs onto ongoing action event scenes and how they extend the novel words. Specifically, we asked whether children understand two basic principles for noun extension and verb extension: (a) a noun gets extended on the basis of the sameness of the referred object, and the particular action in which the object is used is not relevant for noun extension; (b) a verb gets extended on the basis of the sameness of the action, and the objects (both the agent and theme object) that appear in a particular action event are variables that can be replaced across different instances of the event referred to by the verb. Before describing the studies, however, we briefly discuss some linguistic properties of the three languages and discuss predicted patterns based on the linguistic comparisons.

Distributional and Structural Properties of English, Japanese, and Mandarin Chinese

Comparing children learning English, Japanese, and Chinese is extremely interesting because the three languages are different from one another along the dimensions that have been assumed to affect the relative ease or difficulty of verb learning by children. Argument dropping is allowed in Japanese and Chinese but not in English. This means that in Japanese and Chinese, when the arguments can be inferred from the context, it is possible that a verb is the only word in the sentence. As a consequence of this linguistic property, children learning Japanese or Chinese tend to hear verbs more frequently than children learning English do. As mentioned earlier, because of this distributional property, some researchers predict that children learning Japanese or Chinese will learn verbs earlier (and hence more easily) than nouns (Choi & Gopnik, 1995; Tardif, 1996). However, at the same time, this property may lead to the opposite prediction. It has been proposed that inferring the meaning of a verb is very difficult even for adults without cues from the argument structure (Gillette, Gleitman, Gleitman, & Lederer, 1999), and that children do utilize the structural cues in inferring verb meanings (e.g., Fisher, 1996). Thus, one could make the prediction that verb learning should be more difficult for children who are learning a language that occasionally allows argument dropping. (In fact, in Japanese, argument dropping occurs more than occasionally—it is usually dropped when the speaker believes that the arguments can be inferred from the context.)

The second dimension is the presence of morphological inflection in verbs. On this dimension, Chinese contrasts not only to English but also to Japanese. While verbs are inflected in both English and Japanese, they are not in Chinese. In other words, nouns and verbs are not morphologically distinguished in Chinese (Erbaugh, 1992). Remember that in Chinese and Japanese, verb arguments are often dropped, and the verb alone can constitute a sentence in the language. In the case of Japanese, even when this occurs, verbs can be identified by inflectional morphology. That is, when a verb is produced without the arguments, as in "Mite (Look), X-teiru (X-ing)," one can tell that the word X is a verb. However, in Chinese, when a word is produced on its own (and this can happen in a conversational discourse), it is difficult to tell whether it is a noun or a verb. In other words, one can identify a novel word as a verb only when it is embedded in an argument structure (see Li, Bates, & MacWhinney, 1993, for a discussion of how Chinese-speaking adults determine grammatical classes of words and their thematic roles in sentence processing). It is of great theoretical interest to see whether the morphological simplicity of Chinese makes verb learning even easier when compared to Japanese (Tardif, 1996).

Given these distributional and structural properties of English, Japanese, and Chinese, comparing children of these three language groups should provide us with invaluable insights onto the question of what linguistic factors might influence early verb learning.

How Japanese-, Chinese-, and English-Speaking Children Map Novel Nouns and Verbs Onto Dynamic Action Events: Cross-Linguistic Comparisons

The Task and Procedure

In this study, 3- and 5-year-old children from three language groups—Japanese, Mandarin Chinese, and English—were tested (Haryu et al., 2005; Imai, Haryu, & Okada, 2005; Meyer et al., 2003). The children were all from monolingual families living in Japan (a suburban Tokyo metropolitan area), China (Beijing), and the United States (Philadelphia), respectively.

Six sets of video action events served as stimulus materials. Each set consisted of a standard event and two test events. In each standard event, a young woman was doing a novel repetitive action with a novel object. The two test events were variants of the standard event. In one, the same person was doing the same action with a different object (action-same-object-change, henceforth AS) from the standard event. In the other, the person was doing a different action with the same object (action-change-object-same, henceforth OS; see figure 17.1 for a sample set; also see table 1 in Imai et al., 2005, for a complete description of the actions and the objects used in the stimuli).

The standard event was presented on a computer monitor for about 30 seconds. While watching the standard event, a child heard either a novel noun or a novel verb, depending on the condition. The child was then shown the two test videos and was asked to which event the target word should be extended.

Conditions and Instructions

Our major interest was to examine whether Japanese-, Chinese-, and English-speaking children understand the basic principles governing noun generalization and verb generalization, so in all three language groups, children learned either six novel nouns or six novel verbs. In addition, we wished to see whether dropping of the verb arguments affects children's performance in learning novel verbs. Thus, in

(a) Standard

(b) Action-Same-Object Difference (AS)   (c) Object-Same-Action-Difference (OS)

Figure 17.1. Sample stimulus set used in the novel noun/verb learning study.

English and Japanese, we presented the verbs in two different forms: one with full arguments (full argument verb condition) and the other with no arguments (bare verb condition). In providing the arguments, in English, the pronoun *she* served as the subject, and *it* as the object of the sentence (e.g., "Look, she is X-ing it"). In Japanese, the word *oneesan* (girl) is used for the subject, and *nanika* (something) was used in referring to the novel object.

As we noted earlier, in Chinese, when both arguments are dropped, one cannot tell whether the word is a verb or a noun. We thus conducted only the noun and the full argument verb conditions. In the noun and the full argument verb conditions, special care was taken so that there was absolutely no ambiguity over whether the target word was a noun or a verb, respectively. In presenting the verb in the full argument verb condition, an aspect marker *zai*, which marks the imperfective aspect and is usually used in expressing an ongoing action, accompanied the verb along with the subject *ayi* (the girl) and the theme object "yi-(one) ge (generic classifier) dongxi (thing)" (i.e., something).[2] The conditions carried out in each language and the corresponding instructions are given in table 17.1.

Predicted Patterns

What patterns are predicted? If children understand that a noun refers to an object and that the particular action in which it is used is irrelevant to the meaning of the noun, we would expect them to select the OS event when asked to extend a novel noun. If they understand that a verb maps to an action, and that the agent and the theme object of the action event are both variables that can be changed across different instances of the event referred by the verb, they would select the AS event in extending a novel verb.

The question of most importance is whether children would perform equally well in learning novel nouns and verbs. If there is any asymmetry between noun learning and verb learning, it is extremely interesting to see whether there are any cross-linguistic differences in the pattern of novel noun and verb learning. If the universal noun advantage view is correct, we may expect that children in all three languages perform better in learning new nouns than new verbs. On the other hand, if the relative ease of noun and verb learning is determined by distributional properties of the input language, we may expect that Japanese- and Chinese-speaking children do better in extending new verbs than English-speaking children. If structural properties of language such as morphological simplicity affect the ease of word learning (Tardif, 1996), we might expect that Chinese children perform even better than Japanese children, as Chinese verbs are morphologically simpler than Japanese verbs.

Children's Performance in Novel Noun Learning

Children in all three languages in both age groups succeeded in the novel noun extension task. They extended a novel noun to the same object/different action event, and there was no cross-linguistic or developmental difference. Thus, 3-year-olds, regardless of the language they are learning, have a clear understanding that nouns refer to objects and that the actions in which the referent object is used are irrelevant to the noun meaning.

Children's Performance in Novel Verb Learning

In contrast to the success in the novel noun learning task, in none of the language groups were 3-year-olds able to successfully extend novel verbs (see table 17.2). It is not until they are 5 years old that children reliably can extend a novel verb to an event involving the same action but a different object. In this sense, the results suggest that learning a new verb is more difficult than learning a new noun. With this overall pattern in mind, however, we should also note that the performance of Japanese-, Chinese-, and English-speaking children was not totally uniform. In fact, we found intriguing cross-linguistic differences in the pattern of novel verb learning. Specifically, the condition in which 5-year-olds successfully extended newly learned verbs varied across the three languages, which in turn suggests that children speaking different languages rely on different cues in learning verbs. Below, we describe how children of the three language groups generalized novel verbs in our task, starting with Japanese children.

Table 17.1 Conditions carried out in the three languages and the corresponding instruction

Language	Condition	Instruction During Verb Presentation	Instruction for Test
English	Noun	"Look! This is an X!"	"Where is the X? Can you point to the X?"
	Bare verb	"Look! X-ing"	"Where is X-ing?"
	Full argument verb	"Look! She is X-ing it"	"Where is she X-ing it?"
Japanese	Noun	"Mite (Look)! X-ga (nominal particle) aru (exist)" (Look! There is (an) X)	"X-ga aru (exist)-no (nominal particle)-wa (topic particle) docchi (which movie)?" (In which (movie) is there (an) X?)
	Bare verb	"Mite (Look)! X-teiru (X-progressive)" (Look, X-ing)	X-teiru-no (genetive particle)-wa (topic particle) docchi (which movie)-wa (topic particle) docchi (which movie)?" (In which (movie) is (she) X-ing?)
	Full argument verb	"Mite (Look)! Oneesan (girl) ga (nominal particle) nanika (something)-wo (accusative particle) X-teiru (X-progressive)" (Look, she is X-ing something)	"Oneesan (girl) ga (nomial particle) nanika (something)-wo (accusative particle) X-progressive no (genetive particle) docchi (which movie)-wa (topic particle) docchi (which movie)?" (In which (movie) is she X-ing something?)
Chinese	Noun	"Ni (you) kan (look)! Nali (there) you (exist) ge (classifier) X" (Look! There is (an) X)	"Na (which) zhang (quantifier) tu (picture) li (within) you (exist) ge (classifier) X?" (In which picture is there (an) X?)

458

Full argument verb zai only	"Ni (you) kan (look)! Ayi (girl) zai (progressive) X yi (one) ge (classifier) dongxi (thing) ne (mode marking particle)" (Look, (a) girl is X-ing something)	"Na (which) zhang (classifier) tu (picture) li (within) ayi (aunt) zai (progressive) X yi-(one) ge (classifier) dongxi (thing)?" (In which picture is she X-ing something?)
Full argument verb 3 sentences with different auxiliaries	"Ni (you) kan (look)! Ayi (girl) zai (progressive) X yi (one) ge (classifier) dongxi (thing) ne (mode marking particle)" (Look, (a) girl is X-ing something)	"Na (which) zhang (classifier) tu (picture) li (within) ayi (aunt) zai (progressive) X yi-(one) ge (classifier) dongxi (thing)?"
	"Ni (you) kan (look)! Ayi (girl) zhengzai (progressive) X yi (one) ge (classifier) dongxi (thing) ne (mode marking particle)" (Look, (a) girl is X-ing something)	"Ayi (aunt) zai (progressive) X yi-(one) ge (classifier) dongxi (thing) de (progressive) tu (picture) shi (is) na (which) yi-(one) ge(classifier)" (In which picture is she X-ing something?)
	"Ni (you) kan (look)! Ayi (girl) yizhizai (progressive) X yi (one) ge (classifier) dongxi (thing) ne (mode marking particle)" (Look, (a) girl is always X-ing something)	

Table 17.2 Proportion of action-same-object-change responses in each of the noun, bare verb, full argument verb conditions in Japanese-, English-, and Chinese-speaking 3- and 5-year-olds

Language	Age	Noun	Bare Verb	Full Argument Verb
Japanese	3-year-olds	0.27[a]	0.64	0.39
	5-year-olds	0.08[a]	0.85[b]	0.69
English	3-year-olds	0.14[a]	0.49	0.42
	5-year-olds	0.09[a]	0.56	0.70[b]
Chinese	3-year-olds	0.15[a]	—	0.06[a]
	5-year-olds	0.06[a]	—	0.24[a]
	6-year-olds	—	—	0.52
	8-year-olds	—	—	0.72[a]

[a]Significantly below chance, $p < 0.05$. The children selected the object-same choice significant above chance. [b]Significantly above chance, $p < 0.05$.

Japanese-Speaking Children

Five-year-olds, but not 3-year-olds, showed understanding of the principle that verbs get extended on the basis of the sameness of actions, and that the objects that appear in a particular action event are variables that can be replaced across different instances. While the 5-year-olds extended a novel verb to the action-same-object-change test at reliably above chance level, the 3-year-olds showed only chance-level performance (Imai et al., 2005). To our surprise, Japanese children performed better when the verb was presented without the arguments than when it was presented with an explicit mention of the arguments (Haryu et al., 2005).

A series of follow-up studies were conducted to specify the nature of the Japanese 3-year-olds' chance level performance in novel verb generalization (Imai et al., 2005, Study 2). Chance-level performance in a forced-choice task must be interpreted with special caution because there are multiple possibilities to account for this phenomenon. One possibility is that some children may have mapped the verb to the object rather than the action ignoring the verb morphology (i.e., -teiru). A second possibility is that they might have thought that a novel verb could refer not only to the action but also to the object used in the action. If the 3-year-olds in this study had indeed made this assumption, they should have found both test events plausible. A third possibility, in contrast to the second, is that 3-year-olds may have thought that the verb referred to the action only with that particular object. In other words, the 3-year-olds were labeling the action-object interaction. If this was the case, they should have found neither test event plausible. Finally, the task may have involved a greater information-processing load than 3-year-olds could handle. To make a choice in this paradigm, children had to mentally process three ongoing action events simultaneously, holding the standard event in their working memory while watching the two test events.

Given that all three stimuli were ongoing video events, this may have overloaded the 3-year-olds' information processing capacity.

To circumvent the processing load problem, we replicated the original study using a yes-no paradigm. That is, instead of selecting one of the two scenes, children saw one test event at a time while watching the standard next to it. Thus, the demand of information processing should have been greatly decreased in this task. To examine the three possibilities introduced above, we included a scene of the object lying still on a table (still object, henceforth SO) in addition to the AS and OS events in the test. If the 3-year-olds thought that the new verb would refer to the object, they would extend the word to the SO scene but not to the action with a different object (AS). If they thought that a novel verb could refer to either an action or an object involved in the action, they should accept all of the test items, including the SO test. On the other hand, if they thought that a novel verb refers to an action with a particular object, they should reject any of the test stimuli as a referent of the verb in this study.

It turned out that the Japanese 3-year-olds clearly rejected the still object, which means that they did not think that a verb could refer to an object. The rate of "yes" responses was not different across the AS test and OS test, both of which fell at the chance level. These results suggest that Japanese 3-year-olds assume that verbs refer to the action-object interaction. In their verb meaning representation, the core meaning (i.e., the action) is not separated from the theme object, and as a result, their generalization of novel verbs is overly conservative: they do not extend a novel verb to the same action if the object involved in the action is replaced with a different object.

Given these results, in another follow-up study we examined whether Japanese 3-year-olds would extend a verb to the same action when the agent was changed but the same object was retained. This question is worth examining, since Maguire et al. (2002) recently reported that the 18-month-olds did not extend the verb to the exact same action done by a new person even after hearing the verb with the identical action acted by four different people. We thus tested whether 3-year-olds would extend a verb to a scene in which a different actor was doing the same action as the original event with the same object, again using the yes-no procedure (Imai et al., 2005, Study 3). In this case, the children had no problem extending the verbs to the same action.

In summary, the pattern of the results from Japanese children suggest that 3-year-olds do tolerate a change in the actor but are unwilling to extend a newly learned verb to a new instance when the theme object is changed. This indicates that they do not fully understand the basic principle for verb extension, that verbs are extended on the basis of the action independent of the object. Five-year-olds did seem to understand this principle well and were able to apply it immediately in a novel verb learning situation. Interestingly, however, they were able to do so when the arguments of the verb were omitted but not when they were explicitly mentioned. (We will discuss the possible reason later in the chapter.)

English-Speaking Children

In spite of the linguistic differences between English and Japanese, English-speaking children's performance in the novel verb extension task was overall very similar to that of Japanese children: 3-year-olds showed chance-level performance, while 5-year-olds were able to extend a novel verb to the AS test (Meyer et al., 2003).

There was one important difference between Japanese-speaking and English-speaking groups, however. Unlike Japanese children, who performed above chance in the bare verb condition but not in the full argument verb condition, English-speaking 5-year-olds were able to extend the verb to the AS test reliably above chance only when the verb arguments were specified ("Look, she is X-ing it"). They selected the AS tests only 55.6% of the time when the verb arguments were omitted. This difference suggests that the structural characteristics of children's native language might influence the structural form in which children expect to hear a verb.

Chinese-Speaking Children and Adults

The results from Chinese-speaking children were utterly surprising. Unlike Japanese- and English-speaking children, both 3- and 5-year-olds selected the OS test at highly above chance level in the full argument verb condition. This means that they mapped the novel verb to the object instead of the action. As shown in table 17.3, the Chinese-speaking 3- and 5-year-olds consistently selected the OS test regardless of whether the word was presented as a noun or a verb.

Given these surprising results from Chinese-speaking children, we tested monolingual Mandarin-speaking adults living in Beijing, China, to see how they performed in the task. The Chinese-speaking adults who were assigned to the verb (with full arguments) condition selected the AS test 100% of the time. These results suggest (1) that it was perfectly clear to Chinese-speaking adults that the target novel word presented in the full argument verb condition was indeed a verb and (2) that there was a large developmental shift from an object-naming bias to an action-naming bias in Chinese speakers.

To identify the age at which this shift takes place, we further tested 6- and 8-year-old Mandarin Chinese–speaking children in the full argument verb condition (see table 17.3). In the full argument verb case, the 6-year-olds selected the AS test at chance (52.2%). At 8 years of age, Chinese-speaking children finally extended a novel verb to the AS test significantly above chance level (72%).

Did Additional Linguistic Cues Help?

Given the surprising results from the Chinese speakers, we conducted a few different versions of the full argument verb condition, trying to find a condition under which Chinese children (at least 5-year-olds) could reliably extend the verb to the action even when the object is changed.

Table 17.3 Proportion of the AS response in Chinese-speaking children in the noun, bare verb, and full argument verb conditions tested with the original stimulus set and the revised stimulus set in which the object-holding segment was removed

Stimuli	Age	Noun	Full Argument Verb 2-syllable word, zai only	Full Argument Verb 1-syllable word, zai only	Full Argument Verb 1-syllable word, 3-sentence frames
Original	3-year-olds	0.15[a]	0.06[a]	0.25[a]	0.34
	5-year-olds	0.06[a]	0.24[a]	0.34	0.39
	6-year-olds	—	0.52	—	—
	8-year-olds	—	0.72[b]	—	—
Object-holding part removed	3-year-olds	0.32[a]	—	—	0.41
	5-year-olds	0.27[a]	—	—	0.88[b]

[a]Significantly below chance, $p < 0.05$. The children selected the object-same choice significant above chance. [b]Significantly above chance, $p < 0.05$.

First, the number of syllables in the word was changed. In the original study, we prepared novel words (both nouns and verbs) with two syllables. This was because two-syllable words were most common for both nouns and verbs. However, verbs referring to simple actions, such as *jump*, *kick*, and *run*, tend to be monosyllabic words. Thus, we constructed monosyllabic nonsense words and replicated the full argument verb condition with them. Although this manipulation lifted the AS response a little, no statistically reliable difference was obtained (table 17.3).

We then provided additional linguistic cues to indicate that the novel word was a verb. In the original instruction in the full argument verb condition, the experimenter said "Ayi (girl) zai (progressive) X (novel word) yi (one) ge (classifier) dongxi (thing) ne (mode marking particle)" (She is X-ing something). In this instruction, the novel word X could be unambiguously identified as a verb by the structure of the sentence, in particular, by the word order and the presence of the aspect marker *zai*. However, *zai* is also used as a verb, meaning roughly "to exist" or "to be present (at a place)." In this case, the word that comes after *zai* is usually a noun. Young children thus could have been confused because of this homonymous use of *zai* and mistakenly assumed that the word was a noun. We thus presented the verb in three different sentences using three different auxiliaries, namely, *zai*, *zhengzai*, and *yizhizai*, all of which mark the progressive aspect, to provide even clearer and stronger clues that the novel word was a verb. However, again, this manipulation did not bring a statistically reliable increase in the Chinese-speaking children's performance.

Chinese-Speaking Children Are Sensitive to Subtle Extralinguistic Cues

So far, the results suggested that Chinese children as old as 5 years of age could not extend newly learned verbs to the same action in the face of a change in the object even when a novel word was presented in such a way as to make it clear that it was a verb. It is possible that the lack of morphological distinction between nouns and verbs makes it difficult for Chinese children to extract the extension principle for verbs, in contrast to the general assumption in the literature that Chinese is a verb-friendly language. At the same time, there must be conditions under which Chinese preschoolers, especially 5-year-olds, can extend to novel verbs to the action in the face of a change in the object. What cue do they need in addition to linguistic cues? We suspected that that the difficulty in identifying a word's grammatical form class solely from structural cues such as morphological marking or word order leads Chinese children to rely heavily on extralinguistic cues.

Upon reflection, in this light, there is one property of our stimuli that may have given Chinese children a subtle cue that the object is the one that should be attended to in the event. We created the standard video clips in such a way that the actor holds the object for a moment (for about half a second) before starting the action. We did so to make sure that children see the object clearly; the details of the object may not be clearly observable when it is in motion. Of course, the novel word was presented after the action started whether it was presented as a noun or a verb. It should be stressed that the object was not unnaturally highlighted in the original stimuli, and it did not affect Japanese- or English-speaking children. However, if Chinese children were very sensitive to extralinguistic, situational cues, this first segment of the video might have lead Chinese children to think that the object was in a way "topicalized."

To test this possibility, we removed the segment of the video clip in which the actor was holding the object. In the new video, thus, the object was already in motion at the very start of the event presentation. We replicated the full argument verb condition with Chinese-speaking 3- and 5-year-olds with this version of the stimuli. We again presented the monosyllabic nonsense words in three sentences with three different aspect marking auxiliaries to highlight that the word was a verb to give the children as much linguistic support as possible.

Consistent with our expectation, this manipulation—removing the half-second segment of the video clip in which the object was held still—indeed brought a drastic change in Chinese-speaking children's performance in the verb learning task and their performance was now equivalent to the level of performance by Japanese- or English-speaking children. The Chinese-speaking 3-year-olds were now at the chance level, just like Japanese- and English-speaking 3-year-olds, and the Chinese-speaking 5-year-olds now selected the AS test above chance level, just like their Japanese- and English-speaking counterparts (see table 17.3). We then conducted the noun condition with Chinese-speaking 3- and 5-year-olds using this revised stimuli to see whether they could still select the OS test and confirmed that they had no problem in doing so. Thus, it was not the case that Chinese-speaking children mapped the novel word simply to the most salient component of the event, whether it was a noun or a verb. They were able to extend a novel verb to the same action only when the action was maximally salient, but even under this condition, they had no problem in mapping a novel noun to the object. Taken together, this shows that Chinese-speaking 5-year-olds can extend novel verbs to the same action with a different object, but they need support from contextual or perceptual cues in order to do so. When contextual cues are in conflict with linguistic cues, it appears that Chinese-speaking preschoolers rely more heavily on extralinguistic cues than linguistic cues, unlike Japanese- or English-speaking children. It may be that the lack of obvious morphological distinction between nouns and verbs leads Chinese-speaking children to be more attentive to extralinguistic cues than Japanese or English-speaking children are.

Implications for Theories of Lexical Development and Verb Learning

In this chapter, we have approached the question of whether learning of nouns (object names) is universally privileged over learning of verbs by asking how well

children from three different language groups—Japanese, Chinese, and English—
learn novel nouns and verbs introduced during ongoing action events. Two findings from the cross-linguistic studies were particularly important for the question:
(1) children in all three language groups succeeded in extending a novel noun to
the same object appearing in a different action at 3 years of age but did not succeed in generalizing a novel verb to the same action involving a different object
until 5 years of age or later; (2) 5-year-olds succeeded in the verb learning task,
but the condition under which they showed the best performance differed across
languages. We now discuss the implications we might draw from our results for
theories of verb learning as well as theories of lexical development in general.

Comparison of Novel Noun Learning and Novel Verb Learning in Experimental Settings

In the studies reported in this chapter, 3-year-olds learning three different languages
could extend a newly introduced noun to the same object used in a different action,
while in no language group could 3-year-olds extend a newly introduced verb to the
same action carried out with a different object. A very similar pattern of results was
reported by Kersten and Smith (2002) with English-speaking children. As reviewed
earlier, in their study, English-speaking 3-year-olds were unwilling to extend a novel
verb to the same motion when the agent object was changed. Yet, parallel to the results from our own studies, the 3-year-olds in their study were willing to apply the
same noun to the same object even though it appeared in a different motion.

Our cross-linguistic novel noun/verb learning study and Kersten and Smith's
(2002) study with English-speaking children both showed that young children
learn novel nouns more easily than novel verbs when the ease or difficulty was
measured by how well and how willingly young children extend newly learned
words to new instances (see also Golinkoff, Jacquet, Hirsh-Pasek, & Nandakumar,
1996). The advantage of novel noun learning over novel verb learning is also observed when we compare the ease with which young children form object-label
associations and action-label associations. Werker, Cohen, Lloyd, Casasola, and
Stager (1998) demonstrated that 14-month-old infants were able to form associations between novel labels and novel objects. Using the same experimental
paradigm as in Werker et al. (1998), Casasola and Cohen (2000) tested whether
14- and 18-month-old infants were able to form associations with novel labels and
novel actions and found that it was not until 18 months that infants could associate a novel action with a novel label.

With slightly older children, Childers and Tomasello (2002) also showed that
children learn the noun-object link easier than the verb-action link. In one condition, they showed 2.5-year-old English-speaking children three different novel objects and taught them their noun labels. In another condition, they showed the
children three novel actions performed with three novel objects and taught them
three novel verbs corresponding to the three actions. In the third condition, they

simply taught three novel actions with three novel objects. The 2-year-olds remembered both objects and actions very well, yet their memory of the object-noun link was twice as good as their memory of the action-verb link.

The contrast between novel noun learning and novel verb learning in young children becomes even more prominent when we compare the conservatism children repeatedly show in extending novel verbs to the liberal, yet principled, fashion in which same-age or even younger children generalize newly learned nouns (e.g., Golinkoff, Hirsh-Pasek, Bailey, & Wenger, 1992; Haryu & Imai, 2002; Imai & Gentner, 1997; Imai, Gentner, & Uchida, 1994; Imai & Haryu, 2001; Landau, Smith, & Jones, 1988; Markman, 1989). In particular, in different studies we have demonstrated that Japanese-speaking 2-year-old children are able to flexibly map a novel noun not only to a basic-level object category but also to a subordinate category, a substance, or to a unique individual, depending on the perceptual or conceptual nature of the named entity and its familiarity. This flexible pattern of noun extension should be noted all the more because ontologically distinct subclasses of nouns—nouns denoting object kinds, nouns denoting substance kinds, and nouns denoting unique individuals—are not grammatically distinguished in Japanese (Haryu & Imai, 2002; Imai & Gentner, 1997; Imai & Haryu, 2001; see also Imai & Haryu, 2004).[3]

In summary, previous research has shown that children map a novel noun to its referent more easily than they map a novel verb to its referent (Cassasola & Cohen, 2000; Childers & Tomasello, 2002; Werker et al., 1998). Furthermore, it appears that young children find it easier to extend novel nouns than to extend novel verbs, as they extend a newly learned noun to instances other than the originally named object in principled ways, while they are reluctant to extend a newly learned verb to other instances with only a change in the object involved in the action (Imai et al., 2005; Kersten & Smith, 2002; Maguire et al., 2002). Thus, the pattern of results from novel noun and verb learning seems to converge on the conclusion that novel noun learning is easier than novel verb learning.

Influence of Language-Specific Properties on Verb Learning

So far, we have argued for the universal advantage of noun learning over verb learning. Furthermore, there was a striking cross-linguistic similarity in the developmental pattern in novel verb learning. The 3-year-olds in any of the three language groups were not successfully able to extend a novel verb to the same action when the patient object was changed, but in all three languages in the optimal condition, 5-year-olds succeeded in extending novel verbs. At the same time, however, the condition in which 5-year-olds succeeded as well as the ease with which children learn novel verbs appears to be different across the three languages.

Following the common assumption in the literature that learning an argument-dropping language gives an advantage to verb learning (Choi & Gopnik, 1995; Tardif, 1996), we had expected that Chinese- and Japanese-speaking children might perform better than English-speaking children in the novel verb learning task. Furthermore, we had suspected that Chinese-speaking children might show even higher performance than Japanese-speaking children because of the morphological simplicity of Chinese verbs (Tardiff, 1996). Contrary to these predictions, Chinese-speaking children did not perform any better than Japanese- or English-speaking children. In fact, in conditions in which the action was not made particularly salient over the object, Chinese-speaking children showed greater difficulty in learning novel verbs than English- or Japanese-speaking children. Chinese-speaking children were extremely sensitive to contextual cues when learning novel verbs for action events, and unless the action was made very salient, Chinese-speaking 5-year-olds were not able to map a novel verb to the action. It should be noted that Chinese-speaking children did not determine the novel word form class solely based on contextual (or perceptual) saliency of the event, as they were able to map novel nouns to the objects under the action-salient situation. Given this, it seems reasonable to conclude that nouns are easier to learn than verbs for Chinese-speaking children, just as for Japanese- or English-speaking children. Furthermore, verb learning may be even more difficult for Chinese-speaking children than Japanese- or English-speaking children in conditions in which children must infer the meaning of a verb under circumstances in which strong contextual cues are not provided.

At present, we can only speculate on the reason Chinese-speaking children were so sensitive to contextual cues, even to the extent that linguistic cues that are apparent to Chinese-speaking adults were bluntly overridden. As discussed earlier, one important linguistic property that sets Chinese against Japanese and English is the lack of morphological distinction between nouns and verbs. Thus, unlike the case with Japanese or English, Chinese speakers cannot determine the grammatical form class of a word by morphological markings. Furthermore, even though word order provides a cue for determining the form class of each word in the sentence, it is only probabilistic: Although the basic word order is SVO, there other word orders: OSV, SOV, and VOS are also found in the spoken language (Li et al., 1993). Thus, to identify the grammatical class of each word in the sentence and assign its thematic roles to it, Chinese speakers have to coordinate semantic, syntactic, semimorphological grammatical cues such as aspect markers, object markers, and passive markers in "a complex system of mutual constraints" (Li et al., 1993, p. 193). This linguistic property may lead Chinese-speaking children to rely more on extralinguistic, contextual cues than on linguistic cues in novel word learning.

It is also noteworthy that the condition in which children performed best in our novel verb extension task was different for English- and Japanese-speaking children. The action events used in our research involve only three elements, an actor, an action, and an object. Thus, even when children heard a verb without the explicit mention of the subject and the object of the sentence, it should have been easy to infer what the dropped arguments would have been. In Japanese, it is natural to drop the arguments when the speaker thinks that the hearer can infer them from the observational or pragmatic cues. From the Japanese point of view, it was obvious that the subject was the actor and the theme object was the novel object, and hence it was more natural that the arguments be dropped in this case. Japanese children in fact could have been distracted by hearing this unnecessary information. In sharp contrast, English-speaking 5-year-olds extended the verb to the AS test only when the verb was accompanied by the pronouns *she* and *it*. It appears that the English-speaking children would not extend a novel verb when the verb was presented in an unusual structural form, even though the arguments of the verb could have been easily inferred from observation of the event.

Taken together, universally shared cognitive factors and language-specific linguistic factors both matter for early word learning, but it appears that the former is more prominent than the latter, given the striking similarity in the developmental pattern in the novel noun/verb learning task across the three languages of very different linguistic properties.

Progressive Development of Verb Meanings

The results of our cross-linguistic novel noun/verb learning study support the view that object naming is advantaged over verb learning, as discussed above. At the same time, it needs to be explained why children as old as 3 years had so much difficulty in our verb extension task even though they comprehend and produce many verbs (e.g., Choi & Bowerman, 1991; Choi & Gopnik, 1995; Golinkoff, Hirsh-Pasek, & Schweisguth, 2001; Tardif, 1996). We have no intension of claiming that children cannot learn verbs until 5 years of age. The point we would like to make instead is that young children's verb meanings develop progressively and that it takes a substantial amount of time before they finally obtain fully adult-like representations of verb meanings. Remember the example of the Japanese verb *ageru* we described earlier. The child started using the verb when she was 26 months old, but at 4-1/2, she still had not acquired the fully adult-like meaning of it.

The pattern of success and failure in young children's verb learning in experimental settings also supports this idea. First, as demonstrated by Casasola and Cohen (2000), children seem to become able to associate a novel causal action to a novel label at around 18 months of age. However, it is highly unlikely that 18-month-olds would be willing to extend a newly learned verb to the same action when one of the two objects (either the agent or the patient) or both objects are changed, given the results by Maguire et al. (2002). As reviewed earlier, these researchers demonstrated that English-speaking 18-month-olds were not willing to extend a newly learned verb to the same intransitive action when the actor was changed from the original scene even after they had been trained on the verb-action association with four different agents. Golinkoff et al. (1996) demonstrated that 3-year-old English-speaking children could extend a novel verb to the same intransitive action by a different actor, but the 3-year-olds in Kersten and Smith's (2002) study failed to do so.[4] In our studies (Haryu et al., 2005; Imai et al., 2005; Meyer et al., 2003), in none of the three languages were 3-year-olds willing to extend a verb to the same action when an object (the agent in their case and the theme object in our case) was changed.

In summary, previous results from novel verb learning studies suggest that children do learn verbs as early as 18 months, but their representation of verb meanings at initial stages is incomplete and fragile. It seems to take some time for children to acquire the full, adult-like meaning for many verbs. It also seems to take quite some time for the basic principle for verb meaning extension—that verbs get extended on the basis of the same action or relation while the objects are variables that can be changed from situation to situation—to become solidified enough to be applicable under very stringent circumstances when external aids such as social and perceptual support are not provided, and a new verb is associated only with a single instance.

Fast-Mapping May Not Be Beneficial for Verb Learning

What does it take for a word learner to infer the meaning of a verb? What do they need to know to extend a verb to other instances correctly? The principle of verb extension we dealt with in this chapter—that verbs get extended to a new situation with a different agent or a different object, as long as the action is the "same"—is a very basic extension principle that holds for almost all verbs, and it is an important first step toward adult-like representation of verb meanings. However, word learners also need to know that different types of verbs employ different criteria for extension. Some verbs should be extended on the basis of sameness of manner, while others should be extended solely on the sameness of results, yet others should be extended on the basis of the sameness of direction or trajectory of motion. Furthermore, here, the notion of "being the same" does not mean "being identical," as, for example, there are many ways of walking, turning, throwing, hopping, climbing, ascending, and so on. Children thus first need to know which semantic aspect (such as manner, path/direction/trajectory, and result) they should attend to in extending the particular verb they are learning, and they then need to extract what constitutes the "sameness" for the given semantic aspect in the verb in question (see Maguire et al., 2002, for a similar point). This process of extracting sameness—or discovering the "invariant component" in other words—and using it as the basis for extension is exactly like analogical mapping based on abstract higher-order relations.

Seen this way, the way children learn nouns and verbs may be very different, and for a good reason. Children as young as 2 years of age are willing to fast-map the meaning of a noun after only observing it to get associated with a single referent (e.g., Golinkoff et al., 1992; Haryu & Imai, 2002; Imai & Gentner, 1997; Imai et al., 1994; Imai & Haryu, 2001; Landau et al., 1988; Markman, 1989). This may be in large part because the structure of the noun lexicon is hierarchical and coherent, and also because the meaning of a noun is largely predictable from the perceptual nature of the named entity due to a high correlation between conceptual and perceptual properties in concrete entities. For example, the (concrete) noun lexicon is divided into two distinct ontological classes, the class of objects and the class of substances, and determination of the class membership of a given entity (i.e., whether this thing is an object or a substance) is largely, if not completely, supported by the entity's perceptual nature, such as its solidity, boundedness, and shape complexity (Imai & Gentner, 1997; Imai & Mazuka, 2003; Smith, Columga, & Yoshida, 2003). Once the named entity's ontological class membership is determined, the extension principles are rather simple (or at least much simpler than those for verbs). When the word is determined to be an object name, it should be extended by shape; when it is determined to be a substance name, it should be extended by material (Soja, Carey, & Spelke, 1991). Given this coherent and cleanly structured noun lexicon, it is relatively easy for children to come up with assumptions about the noun lexicon (e.g., what kinds of nouns are there in the noun lexicon, what kinds of noun correspond to what kind of conceptual classes, how different kinds of nouns are syntactically marked, what perceptual and conceptual factors are most useful in inferring word meanings, etc.), and with these assumptions, it is likely that children can successfully fast-map a new noun to its meaning with only a single instance (Imai & Haryu, 2004).

The verb lexicon is not as cleanly structured as the noun lexicon, and the cross-linguistic variability is much greater than the noun lexicon (Gentner, 1982). Even though there seems to be only a small set of semantic components that are universally lexicalized in motion/action events (e.g., such as figure, ground, manner, and path), the component that is most likely to be packaged into verb meanings varies across different languages (Talmy, 1985). Furthermore, within each language, the lexicalization pattern is only probabilistic. For example, even though English is a manner-dominant language, there are quite a few verbs that lexicalize path of the motion (e.g., *enter, ascend, descend*). Syntactic argument structures provide clues for the inference of verb meanings at a global level (e.g., whether the action involves change of state of the patient object, whether it is spontaneous and self-moved, or whether it only happens by some external force, etc.). However, as there are so many different classes of verbs that take different argument alternation patterns in different semantic domains (Levin, 1993), inferring the specific meaning of a verb from a single instance with one syntactic argument structure would be difficult and could even be harmful (Naigles, 1996).

Seen in this light, the different strategies children take in learning nouns and verbs may be quite reasonable and optimal. In learning nouns, they generate assumptions about noun extension at very early stages of lexical development, and by applying these assumptions, they fast-map a newly encountered noun to its meaning with a single instance. In learning verbs, in contrast, they do not seem to easily generate such assumptions about verb extension. Children extract abstract, widely applicable rules for verb meaning extension quite slowly, only after learning different verbs in an "island-like" fashion for a substantial period of time (cf. Tomasello, 2000). Considering the structure of the verb lexicon, this is probably a more beneficial strategy than fast-mapping.

Concluding Remarks: Interaction Between Universal and Language-Specific Factors in Early Word Learning

One of the important questions in the literature of lexical development is whether a particular word class is easier for children to learn over others, and what factors determine the relative ease or difficulty of word learning. The results from the cross-linguistic novel noun/verb learning study reported in this chapter support the view that noun learning is universally advantaged over verb learning, as children of three very different languages performed better in learning novel nouns than in learning novel verbs. At the same time, the cross-linguistic pattern of novel verb learning points to the influence of linguistic properties on the ease of novel verb learning as well as on cues children utilize in inferring verb meanings. Interestingly, however, it was not the distributional property of nouns vs. verbs, but the structural properties of the language that had a greater influence here. Contrary to the general assumption in the literature (Gentner, 1982; Tardif, 1996), morphological simplicity in the Chinese language may magnify the difficulty children experience in learning a new verb (see Erbaugh, 1983). Note, however, that the lack of the form class information within the subclasses of nouns does not seem to make novel noun learning difficult for Japanese-speaking children (see note 3; see also Imai & Gentner, 1997; Imai & Haryu, 2001, 2004). This suggest that availability of cues from syntax for the inference of word meanings interacts with the nature of the concepts for a given word class.

Early word learning takes place within a dynamic interaction among children's universal cognitive disposition, distributional and structural properties of the language they are learning, and nature of concepts (e.g., the degree of abstractness, complexity of meaning, perceptual accessibility, etc.) denoted by words. In this interaction, the relative dominance among these factors seems to be hierarchically ordered. Based on the pattern of results in the word learning literature, it is probable that conceptual factors take precedence over linguistic factors in the hierarchy. As we reviewed throughout the chapter, it has been repeatedly observed that, across different languages, children learn labels of objects more readily and easily than labels of actions, and that they generalize nouns more willingly than verbs. Linguistic factors, either structural or distributional, do affect word learning but not to the degree that they can override conceptual constraints.[5]

Taken together, what is important for future research is not so much the question of which of the two factors—universal conceptual constraints and language specific properties—is more important, but the question of how the two factors interact with one another.

Acknowledgments This research is supported by the Ministry of Education Grant (# 15300088) and the Keio University Mori Grant to Mutsumi Imai. We thank Kathy Hirsh-Pasek, Roberta Golinkoff, Hua Shu, and Victoria Muehleisen for insightful comments on earlier versions of the chapter.

Notes

1. Of course, verbs put some constraints on the types of arguments they can be used with. A piece of fabric cannot be smashed, so the verb *smash* cannot take *fabric* as an argument. However, within the range of the semantic constraints, different objects can occur as the argument of the verb.

2. However, we did not set up the *"zai* + verb" alone (without the arguments) pattern, since native speakers of Chinese judged this pattern unnatural.

3. For example, when a novel individuated object (either animate or inanimate) was labeled with a novel noun, Japanese-speaking 2-year-old children spontaneously generalized the noun to other objects that were similar to the original in shape (but not in other perceptual dimensions) assuming it to be a basic-level object category name. At the same time, they could relax this default assumption quite readily. When a novel noun was associated with a substance, they generalized it on the basis of material identity, ignoring the sameness in shape (Imai & Gentner, 1997). When a familiar animal was named, they interpreted it to be a proper name of the named animal (Imai & Haryu, 2001). When a named object was inanimate and was a typical member of the familiar category, they mapped the new noun to a category subordinate to a old, familiar one, but when the inanimate object was an atypical member of the familiar category, they mapped the new label to a new basic-level category, restructuring the boundary of the old, familiar category by excluding the named object from it (Haryu & Imai, 2002).

4. This difference in the results could be attributed to the difference in the stimuli. While Golinkoff et al. (1996) used still pictutes, Kersten and Smith (2002) used animated events.

5. Interestingly, an analogous pattern has been witnessed in the learning of object names and substance names. Imai and Gentner (1997; see also Imai & Mazuka, 2003) examined how Japanese- and English-speaking children project word meanings when a novel noun was presented in association with a range of entities with different levels of individuation (i.e., highly individuated complex-shaped objects, simple-shaped solid substances that can be construed either as individuated objects or unindividuated solid substance, and clearly unindividuated substances). Imai and Gentner showed that the ontological distinction between objects and substances is universally available at the beginning stage of word learning, and this conceptual understanding constrains noun learning whether or not this ontological distinction is marked by the grammar of the language children are learning. At the same time, the way in which language divides the individuation continuum affected the pattern of word meaning projection for simple shaped solid substances, whose status of individuation was perceptually ambiguous.

References

Au, T. K.-F., Dapretto, M., & Song, Y. K. (1994). Input vs. constraints: Early word acquisition in Korean and English. *Journal of Memory and Language, 33*, 567–582.

Bowerman, M. (1980). The structure and origin of semantic categories in the language learning child. In M. L. Foster & S. H. Brandes (Eds.), *Symbol as a sense: New approaches to the analysis of meaning* (pp. 277–299). New York: Academic Press.

Casasola, M., & Cohen, L. B. (2000). Infants' association of linguistic labels with causal actions. *Developmental Psychology, 36,* 155–168.

Childers, J., & Tomasello, M. (2002). Two-year-olds learn novel nouns, verbs, and conventional actions from massed or distributed exposures. *Developmental Psychology, 37,* 698–705.

Choi, S. (2000). Caregiver input in English and Korean: Use of nouns and verbs in book-reading and toy-play contexts. *Journal of Child Language, 27,* 69–96.

Choi, S., & Bowerman, M. (1991). Learning to express motion events in English and Korean: The influence of language-specific lexicalization patterns. *Cognition, 42,* 83–121.

Choi, S., & Gopnik, A. (1995). Early acquisition of verbs in Korean: A cross-linguistic study. *Journal of Child Language, 22,* 497–529.

Dromi, E. (1987). *Early lexical development.* Cambridge: Cambridge University Press.

Erbaugh, M. (1983). Acquisition of Mandarin syntax: "Less" grammar isn't easier. *Chinese Language Teatchers Association Journal, 22,* 51–63.

Erbaugh, M. (1992). The acquisition of Mandarin. In D. S. Slobin (Ed.), *The crosslinguistic study of language acquisition, Vol. 3* (pp. 373–456). Hillsdale, NJ: Lawrence Erlbaum.

Fisher, C. (1996). Structural limits on verb meaning: The role of analogy in children's interpretations of sentences. *Cognitive Psychology, 31,* 41–81.

Forbes, J., & Poulin-Dubois, D. (1997). Representational change in young children's understanding of familiar verb meaning. *Journal of Child Language, 24,* 389–406.

Gentner, D. (1982). Why nouns are learned before verbs: Linguistic relativity versus natural partitioning. In S. A. Kuczaj (Ed.), *Language development: Vol. 2. Language, thought, and culture* (pp. 301–334). Hillsdale, NJ: Erlbaum.

Gentner, D., & Boroditsky, L. (2001). Individuation, relativity, and early word learning. In M. Bowerman & S. Levinson (Eds.), *Language acuiqisition and conceptual development* (pp. 257–283). Cambridge: Cambridge University Press.

Gillette, J., Gleitman, H., Gleitman, L., & Lederer, A. (1999). Human simulations of vocabulary learning. *Cognition, 73,* 135–176.

Golinkoff, R., Hirsh-Pasek, K., Bailey, L. M., & Wenger, N. R. (1992). Young children and adults use lexical principles to learn new nouns. *Child Development, 28,* 99–108.

Golinkoff, R., Hirsh-Pasek, K., & Schweisguth, M. (2001). A reappraisal of young children's knowledge of grammatical morphemes. In J. Weissenborn & B. Höhle (Eds.), *Approaches to bootstrapping: Phonological, lexical, syntactic and neurophysiological aspects of early language acquisition* (pp. 167–188). Amsterdam: John Benjamins.

Golinkoff, R., Jacquet, R. C., Hirsh-Pasek, K., & Nandakumar, R. (1996). Lexical principles may underlie the learning of verbs. *Child Development, 67,* 3101–3119.

Haryu, E., & Imai, M. (2002). Reorganizing the lexicon by learning a new word: Japanese children's inference of the meaning of a new word for a familiar artifact. *Child Development, 73,* 1378–1391.

Haryu, E., Imai, M., Okada, H., Li, L., Meyer, M., Hirsh-Pasek, K., & Golinkoff, R. (2005). Noun bias in Chinese children: Novel noun and verb learning in Chinese, Japanese and English preschoolers. In A. Brugos, M. Clark-Cotton, & S. Ha (Eds.), *Proceedings of the 29th Annual Boston University Conference on Language Development* (pp. 272–283). Sommerville, MA: Cascadilla Press.

Huttenlocher, J., Smiley, P., & Charney, R. (1983). Emergence of action categories in the child: Evidence from verb meanings. *Psychological Review, 90,* 72–93.

Imai, M., & Gentner, D. (1997). A crosslinguistic study on constraints on early word meaning: Linguistic influence vs. universal ontology. *Cognition, 62,* 169–200.

Imai, M., Gentner, D., & Uchida, N. (1994). Children's theories of word meanings: The role of shape similarity in early acquisition. *Cognitive Development, 9,* 45–75.

Imai, M., & Haryu, E. (2001). Learning proper nouns and common nouns without clues from syntax. *Child Development, 72,* 787–802.

Imai, M., & Haryu, E. (2004). The nature of word learning biases and their roles for lexical development: From a cross-linguistic perspective. In D. G. Hall & S. R. Waxman (Eds.), *Weaving a lexicon* (pp. 411–444). Cambridge, MA: MIT Press.

Imai, M., Haryu, E., & Okada, H. (2005). Mapping novel nouns and verbs onto dynamic action events: Are verb meanings easier to learn than noun meanings for Japanese children? *Child Development, 76,* 340–355.

Imai, M., & Mazuka, R. (2003). Re-evaluation of linguistic relativity: Language-specific categories and the role of universal ontological knowledge in the construal of individuation. In D. Gentner & S. Goldin-Meadow (Eds.), *Language in mind: Advances in the issues of language and thought* (pp. 430–464). Cambridge, MA: MIT Press.

Kersten, A. W., & Smith, L. (2002). Attention to novel objects during verb learning. *Child Development, 73,* 93–109.

Kim, M., McGregor, K. K., & Thompson, C. K. (2000). Early lexical development in English- and Korean-speaking children: Language-general and language-specific patterns. *Journal of Child Language, 27,* 225–254.

Landau, B., Smith, L. B., & Jones, S. S. (1988). The importance of shape in early lexical learning. *Cognitive Development, 3,* 299–321.

Levin, B. (1993). *English verb classes and alternations.* Chicago: University of Chicago Press.

Li, P., Bates, E., & MacWhinney, B. (1993). Processing a language without inflections: A reaction time study of sentence interpretation in Chinese. *Journal of Memory and Language, 32,* 169–192.

Maguire, M., Hennon, E., Hirsh-Pasek, K., Golinkoff, R., Slutzky, C., & Sootsman, J. (2002). Mapping words to actions and events: How do 18-month-olds learn a verb? In B. Skalabela, S. Fish, & A. Do (Eds.), *Proceedings of the 26th Annual Boston University Conference on Language Development* (pp. 371–382). Sommerville, MA: Cascadilla Press.

Markman, E. M. (1989). *Categorization in children: Problems of induction.* Cambridge, MA: MIT Press.

Meyer, M., Leonard, S., Hirsh-Pasek, K., Imai, M., Haryu, E., Pulverman, R., & Addy, D. (2003, November). *Making a convincing argument: A crosslinguistic comparison of noun and verb learning in Japanese and English.* Paper presented at the 28th Annual Boston Conference on Language Development, Boston University, Boston, MA.

Naigles, L. (1996). The use of multiple frames in verb learning via syntactic bootstrapping. *Cognition, 58,* 221–251.

Ogura, T. (2001). *Meishi yuui, doushi yuui ni oyobosu hahaoya no gengo nyuryoku no kentou.* (Influence of maternal input in the distribution of nouns and verbs in early vocabulary.) Ministery of Education and Science Grant Report. Kobe, Japan: Kobe University.

Rosch, E. (1978). Principles of categorization. In E. Rosch & B. B. Lloyd (Eds.), *Cognition and categorization* (pp. 28–46). Hillsdale, NJ: Erlbaum.

Smith, L., Columga, E., & Yoshida, H.(2003). Making an ontology: Crosslinguistic evidence. In D. H. Rakison & L. M. Oakes (Eds.), *Early category and concept development: Making sense of the blooming, buzzing conflusion* (pp. 275–302). New York: Oxford University Press.

Soja, N., Carey, S., & Spelke, E. (1991). Ontological categories guide young children's inductions of word meaning: Object terms and substance terms. *Cognition, 38,* 179–211.

Talmy, L. (1985). Lexicalization patterns: Semantic structure in lexical forms. In T. Shopen (Ed.), *Language typology and syntactic description* (Vol. 3, pp. 57–149). New York: Cambridge University Press.

Tardif, T. (1996) Nouns are not always learned before verbs: Evidence from Mandarin speakers' early vocabulary. *Developmental Psychology, 32,* 492–504.

Tardif, T., Gelman, S., & Xu, F. (1999). Putting the "noun bias" in context: A comparison of English and Mandarin. *Child Development, 70,* 620–635.

Tomasello, M. (2000). The item based nature of children's early syntactic development. *Trends in Cognitive Sciences, 4,* 156–163.

Werker, J. F., Cohen, L. B., Lloyd, V. L., Casasola, M., & Stager, C. L. (1998). Acquisition of word-object associations by 14-month-old infants. *Developmental Psychology, 34,* 1289–1309.

Yamashita, Y. (1997). The effect of saliency in input on the acquisition of nouns and verbs: Innate constraints or language-specific input? *Naruto Eigo Kyoiku (Naruto College of Education Research Papers), 11.*

18 But Are They Really Verbs? Chinese Words for Action

Twila Tardif

Over the past decade, several studies of Mandarin- and Cantonese-speaking children's early vocabulary development have provided converging evidence for the fact that Chinese-speaking children's vocabularies have a very different proportion of nouns and verbs than comparable samples of English speakers and speakers of most other languages, except perhaps Korean (see Choi, 2000; Choi & Gopnik, 1995; Kim, McGregor, & Thompson, 2000). Moreover, although individual child characteristics, activity context, and measurement instruments all have significant effects on the extent to which a child's vocabulary may appear to contain nouns or verbs, every context and instrument in which Chinese- and English-speaking children's vocabularies has been compared directly has yielded reliable and highly significant differences. English-speaking children's vocabularies, on average, contain a much higher proportion of nouns than verbs as well as a higher proportion of nouns than Chinese-speaking children. In contrast, Chinese-speaking children's vocabularies contain roughly equal numbers of nouns and verbs and a much higher proportion of verbs than English-speaking children (Tardif, 1996; Tardif, Gelman, & Xu, 1999; Tardif, Shatz, & Naigles, 1997). Thus, although I would not argue that Chinese children have a "verb bias," the fact that verbs are learned so early and in such great numbers in Chinese needs to be explained.

The focus of this chapter is on what properties Chinese verbs may have to facilitate the process of verb learning in Chinese, much as properties of nouns may afford the learning of nouns (compare Gentner, 1982; Gentner & Boroditsky, 2001). More generally, I believe that important insights can be obtained from an examination of the nature of Chinese- and English-speaking children's early vocabularies. Certainly nouns have many properties that make them easy to learn, but why are they not learned at the same rates across languages? Moreover, why do Chinese-speaking children learn so many verbs as well as (and often instead of) concrete nouns? As many authors have commented (Gentner, 1982; Gentner & Boroditsky, 2001; Tardif, 1996; Tardif et al., 1997; Tomasello, 2003) Chinese is a "verb-friendly" language. Specifically, several aspects of the input (e.g., frequency and placement of nouns vs. verbs), morphological transparency, and pragmatic emphases on "naming" versus "doing" games may act in tandem with (as in English) or against (as in Mandarin) any cognitive biases that children might bring to the task of word learning and result in varying proportions of nouns and verbs in children's early vocabularies across languages. However, I believe there is an additional factor that has not been emphasized in previous treatments of why English and Chinese might be different.

In Chinese, but not English, verbs are highly specified and there is little resorting to "general purpose" or "light" verbs as there is in English simply because these general-purpose verb terms do not exist. In contrast, Chinese speakers often resort to general-purpose types of nouns (e.g., *che1*, vehicle) even though they have more specific labels which would correspond to the myriad of specific object nouns that young children acquire early in English (e.g., *car, truck, motorcycle, bicycle, bus*). Previous theories on the nature of word learning and particularly those focused on explaining the noun bias have discussed various features of nouns and verbs that may work together with innate perceptual and conceptual constraints to facilitate the learning of nouns and hinder the learning of verbs. However, in this chapter, I would like to suggest that some of these features may not be true across all languages. Specifically, whereas these prior theories have allowed for cross-linguistic differences in specific features such as syntactic markings and inflections, word order, and differences in the extent to which manner and path are lexicalized within the verb itself, I am suggesting that we need to also consider the nature of the words themselves and how they are organized into a coherent noun or verb lexicon in a particular language. In essence, I am responding to a question that Liz Bates posed to me (personal communication, 2002) regarding the following findings in Chinese—"But are they really verbs?" With respect to Liz and to foreshadow my conclusions, they are most certainly verbs in every formal sense of the term. However, I would also argue that they are not the same kinds of verbs (or nouns) that we have in English, and a deeper understanding of cross-linguistic differences in what verbs (and nouns) really are, I feel, may go a long way toward explaining the phenomenon. For urging me to think through this issue, I owe a debt of gratitude to Liz for posing the question in the first place.

Documenting the Phenomenon

Before explaining the phenomenon, however, it is important to clarify the nature of the difference between Mandarin and English with respect to verb (and noun) acquisition. Several previous studies have demonstrated, in separate samples of children and using various methods of counting nouns and verbs, that Mandarin Chinese–speaking children do not have the same predominance of nouns in their early vocabularies as English-speaking children (Tardif, 1996; Tardif et al., 1997, 1999). More recently, this has been found for Cantonese-speaking children in Hong Kong as well (Leung, 2001). However, each of these samples were relatively small and relied primarily on naturalistic speech samples (although Tardif et al., 1999, also administered a pilot version of the MacArthur-Bates Communicative Development Inventory [CDI], a parental-report checklist measure of early vocabulary) with children who were typically beyond the earliest stages of vocabulary acquisition. This has led some authors (e.g., Gentner & Boroditsky, 2001) to conclude that Chinese children probably do show a noun bias in their earliest stages of vocabulary learning but that it was not captured in these studies because they examined toddlers who were beyond the earliest stages of language acquisition. Moreover, other researchers (e.g., Au, Dapretto, & Song, 1994; Caselli et al., 1995; Tomasello, 2003) have suggested that the CDI, because it is based on mothers' knowledge of their children's vocabularies over multiple contexts and situations, would be a more appropriate instrument for examining the actual content of children's vocabularies than spoken language measures, which may overestimate the words that children use more frequently. In other words, naturalistic samples may be biased by counting more word types for those words that appear more frequently as tokens (see Richards, 1987, for an expansion of this argument). Indeed, Mandarin-speaking children and their caregivers produce more verb tokens as well as verb types. However, when the type-token ratios for children's nouns and verbs in the Tardif (1996) Mandarin sample were examined, they did not differ. More importantly, I have also argued (Tardif 1996, 2005) that Mandarin-speaking children have access to more verb types than English-speaking children and that English-speaking children have access to more noun types than Mandarin-speaking children. Nonetheless, without examining comparable samples of English and Mandarin on a measure that is not susceptible to a frequency effect, it is difficult to demonstrate this convincingly.

Thus, the focus in this section will be on preliminary data from three large scale norming studies of the MacArthur-Bates CDI (Fenson et al., 1993)—the original English sample, as well as both the Putonghua (Mandarin) and Cantonese CDI norming samples (Tardif, Fletcher, Liang, & Zhang, 2002).

Each of these three samples includes approximately 1,600 children, with roughly 70 children at each monthly age group from 8 to 30 months, with equal numbers of girls and boys at each age group. In addition, all three samples are relatively well distributed in terms of parents' levels of education and socioeconomic status and are generally representative of urban and suburban populations in each location. Direct comparisons of these samples to examine the overall patterns of word types that appear in children's early vocabularies as well as the nature of the words themselves, will allow us to more clearly understand the nature of the cross-linguistic differences between English and Chinese.

Importantly, we also consider two different dialects of Chinese, Mandarin and Cantonese, which differ in many phonological, lexical, and syntactic properties—so much so that some linguists (e.g., Ramsey, 1987) have suggested that, from a linguistic perspective, they are only dialects inasmuch as French and Italian could be considered dialects of Romance.

As with the naturalistic data reported in earlier studies, even the large-sample CDI results show clear noun-verb differences between children who were learning English versus those learning Mandarin or Cantonese as their first language (Tardif et al., 2002). Importantly, this was true at all levels of vocabulary development. As can be seen from figure 18.1, both Mandarin- and Cantonese-speaking children had fewer nouns and more verbs than English-speaking children at every level of vocabulary development examined by the CDI. In figure 18.2, which examines the ratios of nouns to nouns + verbs in English and Mandarin, it is even more obvious that this was more true for children who had only 1–5 words in their vocabularies than it was for children who had 600 or 700 words. What is particularly striking about these data is that, when side-by-side comparisons are made, verbs appear to develop at roughly the same time (and with similar growth curves) as closed class items in English, whereas they develop early and are more parallel with the growth of nouns in Mandarin and Cantonese. And yet, despite enormous differences in the nature of closed class items across English and Chinese, both the Mandarin and Cantonese samples showed a similar, delayed, development of closed class items as the English-speaking children. Thus, even on the CDI with

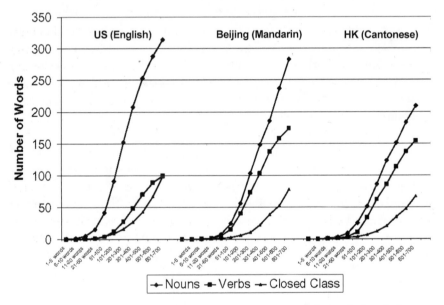

Figure 18.1. Mean number of common nouns, "action words," and closed class items from infant and toddler samples in norming studies of the English ($n = 1652$), Mandarin ($n = 1588$), and Cantonese ($n = 1556$) communicative development inventories, by total vocabulary size.

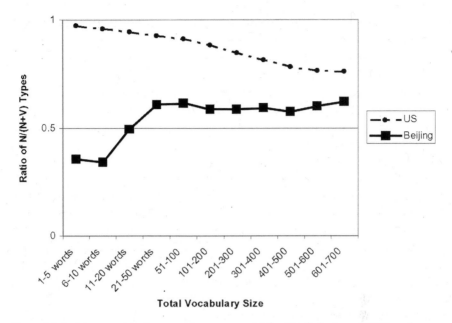

Figure 18.2. Mean ratio of noun / (noun + verb) for English- (*n* = 1517) and Mandarin-speaking (*n* = 1321) children in CDI norming samples, by total vocabulary size.

large samples of children at varying ages and levels of language development, English- and Chinese-speaking children differ with respect to how predominant and easily both nouns and verbs are acquired in each language. Statistically, this translates into a highly significant word type by location interaction, controlling for both age and total vocabulary, $F(2, 5098) = 1689.91$, $p < .0001$, with English-speaking children producing more nouns and fewer verbs than either the Mandarin- or Cantonese-speaking children.

The next question, then, given how reliably this finding has appeared (using naturalistic samples in home environments, controlled contexts of natural speech sampling in the laboratory, and even the CDI), is why Chinese-speaking children have so many verbs in their early vocabularies. Previous studies have focused on the role of input and activity context, as discussed below, but, as mentioned above, I will propose that it is not just input, but that the nature of the categories "verb" and "noun" also differ across languages.

Is It Input?

Several studies point toward the role of input—the speech that children hear directed specifically toward them—both in supporting the noun bias in languages like English and in not supporting the noun bias in languages like Mandarin. In

Tardif et al.'s (1997) study, Mandarin-speaking caregivers produced more verb types and tokens than noun types and tokens, placed verbs at the ends of utterances, and had fewer morphological alterations to verbs than to nouns. In contrast, English- and Italian-speaking caregivers showed more morphological alterations on the verbs, placed nouns at the ends of utterances, showed a much smaller difference between verb and noun tokens than the Mandarin-speaking caregivers, and, most importantly, neither the English-nor the Italian-speaking caregivers produced more verb types than noun types. These input frequency differences were replicated in Tardif et al.'s (1999) study of English- and Mandarin-speaking caregivers in three controlled laboratory contexts (book reading, toy play, mechanical toy play), where again Mandarin-speaking caregivers (and their children) showed a significantly greater token frequency for verbs, but also a significantly greater number of verb types than the English-speaking caregivers.

Similar findings have been reported for Korean (Choi, 2000) and for Tzeltal (Brown, 1998), but it is not clear that the type difference between nouns and verbs or even the contrast with English is true for Japanese (Ogura, Murase, Yamashita, & Mahieu, 1999). If frequency of types as well as tokens is important, it is not surprising that high proportions of verbs are reported for Mandarin-, Korean-, and Tzeltal-speaking toddlers, but not for English-, Italian-, or Japanese-speaking children.

Another way of considering the role of input is to consider not just the words themselves but also the clarity of cues that caregivers provide for children when they are trying to call their attention to a specific noun or verb in ongoing speech. Gleitman and colleagues (Gillette, Gleitman, Gleitman, & Lederer, 1999) addressed this issue by filming a group of English-speaking caregivers interacting with their language-learning toddlers and extracting segments of the videos where the caregivers were emphasizing a particular noun or verb (a target word). These segments were then shown to a group of undergraduate students with the target word removed in order to test how likely the students would be to guess the target word. Their findings, for this native English-speaking sample watching native English-speaking caregivers, were that the students were much more accurate at guessing the nouns than they were at guessing the verbs and that the imageability of the words themselves did not predict the accuracy of their guesses. Gillette et al. (1999) take these findings to suggest that not only are nouns conceptually simpler than verbs but that it is also easier to identify which noun-object mapping is intended than it is to identify which verb-action mapping is intended. I would argue that for English this finding is most certainly true, but that it is unlikely to hold up for Chinese. Indeed, in a study reported by Snedeker, Li, and Yuan (2003), cross-linguistic differences were found in this very same task. Specifically, English-speaking college students were very inaccurate at identifying the translation-equivalents of nouns used by Mandarin-speaking caregivers in the same types of adult-child interactions used in the Gillette et al. study and were in fact more accurate at guessing the translation-equivalents of Mandarin verbs than they were at guessing the English verbs. Second, a group of Mandarin-speaking college students were also more accurate at guessing the Mandarin verbs than the translation-equivalents of English verbs and at guessing the translation-equivalents of English nouns versus the Mandarin nouns. This input language by word type interaction suggests, in fact, that not only does the linguistic input (type and token frequency, placement of words in an utterance) vary across languages, but so does the nonlinguistic input. In addition to the possibility that caregivers in different cultures may engage in different activities with their children (see Fernald & Morikawa, 1993; and discussion of context effects found by Tardif et al., 1999), the nonlinguistic cues offered by native English- and native Mandarin-speaking caregivers also vary to the extent that even when one cannot understand the language being spoken, accuracy in making word-to-world mappings will be in the direction of emphasis for the language being spoken, not in the direction of emphasis for one's native language.

Thus, there are plenty of reasons from the input (linguistic and nonlinguistic) alone for why Mandarin-speaking children might be more readily able to learn verbs than English-speaking children. Nonetheless, I believe a full account of why Mandarin-speaking children learn as many verbs (and as few common nouns) as they do is not complete until we also consider the nature of the verbs themselves.

Are Chinese Verbs Really Verbs?

To answer the question, "But are they really verbs?" one has to consider the question of what makes a verb a verb. For the present purposes, I will focus on two issues: (1) the acquisition and use of syntactic markers that are unique to the category of verbs, and (2) the semantics of these words as words that encode "one or more entities undergoing changes of state" (Tomasello, 1992, p. 6). For the first, I will demonstrate that Mandarin-speaking children demonstrate early acquisition of these markers (i.e., soon after they first begin to combine words) and that they use these markers in conjunction with verbs in everyday speech. For the second, I will examine the most frequent words that appear in children's vocabularies, as measured on the CDI in English and Mandarin, and specifically contrast the most frequent "action words" in each of these languages. For each of these ways of considering the question, my answer is most definitely yes, Chinese verbs are verbs. However, there is a remaining sense in which verbs in Chinese (and Korean and Tzeltal) are quite different from those in English and it is this last sense, I believe, that can help us to understand why Chinese speakers have such an easy time with verbs (and perhaps a harder time acquiring common nouns than expected by current theories which map cognitive predispositions onto form class categories).

Misconception 1: Chinese Does Not Have Form Classes

Several authors (e.g., Kao, 1990) have argued that perhaps verbs in Chinese are not really verbs because Chinese allows for much flexibility in the assignment of words to word classes, and this may in fact account for why there appear to be so many verbs in Chinese children's early vocabularies—because they are not really verbs in the grammatical sense of the term. Although this is an extreme position, many authors (e.g., Bates, Chen, Tzeng, Li, & Opie, 1991; Li, Jin, & Tan, 2004) have taken a milder form of this position. In this view, it is assumed that although class-ambiguous words occur in many languages, including English, the proportion of verbs than can occur freely as nouns or nouns that can appear as verbs with no morphological changes is greater in Chinese than for other languages. Instead, I argue that this is a misconstrual of both English and Chinese for adults (see also Chan & Tai, 1995) and even more so for children's earliest verbs.

In fact, of the 20 most frequent action words (verbs) in the vocabularies of 16-month-olds in the English and Mandarin norming studies for the CDI, a much larger number of the English verbs can be turned into nouns (without changes in morphology or pronunciation) than the Chinese verbs. If we examine the list shown in table 18.1, fully 12 of the English verbs can be used as nouns by placing them in a sentence with a general-purpose verb such as "have/take a [target]" (e.g., have a bite/drink/cry). Others (e.g., *go, tickle*) are more marginal, but likely to be frequently nominalized in adult-to-child speech, whereas only three (*eat, open, see*) of the 20 most common verbs for 16-month-olds are resistant to this type of nominalization. In Mandarin, the comparable transformation would be to add a numeral-classifier compound (e.g., *yi-ge*), with the general classifer *-ge4*. Under this rule (or any other rule that transforms verbs into nouns without changing morphology), only one of the Mandarin verbs (*niao4*, pee) could be transformed into a noun. Six others (*chi1*, eat; *zou3*, walk; *he1*, drink; *kai1*, open; *chuan1*, wear; and *ti1*, kick) frequently appear in verb-object compounds (e.g., *chi1 fan4*), but only two of these compounds (*chi1 fan4, zou3 lu4*) are synonymous with the verb in isolation. Instead, most of these common Mandarin verbs have free substitutions of objects and do not change form class unless they are transformed grammatically in a nominalizing phrase (i.e., verb + *de*, a nominalizing marker). Even this process, which is much like the process of creating a gerund in English, would not occur with great frequency for most of these verbs. Note that even for verbs which are semantically similar across English and Mandarin such as *bao4* (hug), the English verb but not the Mandarin is form-class ambiguous. Thus, for children's earliest verbs, at least, it is simply not the case that Mandarin has more words that can be both nouns and verbs than English (see also Chan & Tai, 1995, for a comparison of denominal verbs in modern adult Mandarin versus English).

Table 18.1 Twenty most frequent action words on CDI for English and Mandarin 16-month-olds

Mandarin Word	Percentage of Children Who Use It	English Equivalent	Nominalized in Mandarin	English Word	Percentage of Children Who Use It	Nominalized English?
Bao4	74.3	Hug/hold	No	*Go*	23.6	Abstract
Da3	60	Hit	No	*Bite*	23.6	Yes
Na2	55.7	Take/bring/grab with ha	No	*Drink* (act)	20.8	Yes
Yao4	48.6	Want/think	No	*Cry*	19.4	Yes
Chi1	45.7	Eat	No	*Eat*	19.4	No
Zou3	40	Walk/leave/go	No	*Kiss*	19.4	Yes
He1	38.6	Drink	No	*Open*	18.1	No
Kai1 (men2)	37.1	Open (a door)	No	*Hug*	18.1	Yes
Niao4	35.7	Pee	Yes	*See*	16.7	No
Bei1	35.7	Carry on back	In fixed term bei1bao1	*Tickle*	15.3	Marginal
Get3	34.3	Give	No	*Stop*	15.3	Yes
Lai2	34.3	Come	No	*Sleep*	15.3	Yes
Chuan1	32.9	Wear (clothes)	No	*Love*	13.9	No
Qin1	32.9	Kiss	No	*Walk*	13.9	Yes
Ti1	32.9	Kick	No	*Touch*	12.5	Yes
Mo1	30	Touch	No	*Dance*	12.5	Yes
Diao4	30	Drop	No	*Read*	12.5	No
Kan4	28.6	Look	No	*Play*	12.5	Limited
Fei1	28.6	Fly	No	*Swing* (act)	12.5	Yes
Kai1 (che)	28.6	Drive (a car)	No	*Watch* (act)	11.1	Yes

Misconception 2: Chinese Children Use Verbs as Bare Forms,
Not Inflected Forms

Another way one might argue that the Chinese verbs reported on the CDI are not really verbs is if children are producing them as bare forms. In this view, although the lexical items may be verbs in the adult lexicon, when children are producing them at the one-word stage, they may simply be producing them as holophrases such as Lois Bloom's (1970) "mommy sock" example in which the words that are uttered may have a whole host of meanings that go beyond the forms themselves. Tomasello (1992) also makes this argument for several of his daughter's early noun forms as well as for children's early words more generally. Although detailed data on how children are actually using words is necessary to fully address this question, the issue of whether Mandarin-speaking children are producing verbs in isolation versus verbs together with appropriate syntactic markings is something that can be addressed both with the CDI data and with the naturalistic data that have already been collected for Mandarin-speaking toddlers.

Despite the fact that Mandarin allows frequent ellipsis of grammatical markers and verbal arguments, prompting some to suggest it presents a worst-case scenario for syntactic bootstrapping, there is quite a large degree of predictability in which verbs receive arguments and which do not, even in adult-to-child speech (Lee, Nelson, & Naigles, 2003). Moreover, although the particular syntactic differences between nouns and verbs are different from English and not as easily identified in inflectional processes such as plurals or tense, the differences between nouns and verbs in Mandarin are both numerous and obvious to the listener, particularly when word order and specific constructions are taken into account. Among other distinguishing features, both Chao (1968) and Li and Thompson (1981) argue that nouns, but not verbs, are modifiable by a preceding numeral-classifier compound (e.g., *yi1-ben3 shu1*; one-CL [classifying marker] book); cannot be modified by monosyllabic adverbs such as negative markers (e.g., **bu4 shu1*; *not book); and can typically be substituted into a possessive phrase such as *wo3-de shu1* (my book). In contrast, verbs, but not nouns, can be preceded by the negative markers *bu4* or *mei2*; may be preceded by *bie2* (don't) and other auxiliaries; may receive aspect marking with the preverbal marker *zai4* or the postverbal markers *zhe*, *le*, or *guo4*; and may be followed by various types of resultative verb constructions indicating the extent or direction of the verb (e.g., *kan4-wan2 le*, read-finish ASP = finished reading).

In our CDI data, Mandarin-speaking children were reported to use syntactic markings on verbs at roughly the same ages and stages of language acquisition as English-speaking children. As shown in figure 18.3, by 24 months of age, over 80% of Mandarin-speaking children in our CDI sample were reported to combine words, and roughly 50% of children produced one or more of the markers used on nouns and verbs. Thus, it is clear that by 24 months of age Mandarin-speaking children are using verb-specific syntax and, in this sense, are producing verbs and

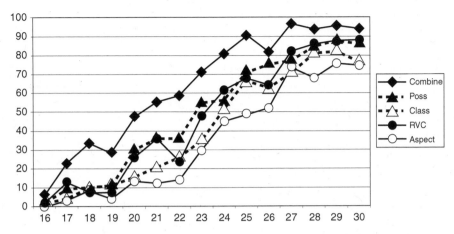

Figure 18.3. Proportion of children reported to "sometimes" or "often" combine words and use syntactic markers for nouns (possessive and classifiers) and verbs (resultative verb complements and perfective aspect marker *le*) from ages 16 to 30 months in Beijing CDI norming study (*n* = 1069).

not just words that happen to be verbs in the adult speech but are not marked as verbs by the child.

Nonetheless, the above data do not examine whether children are making distinctions between nouns and verbs by using these markings uniquely for nouns and verbs or whether they are using them indiscriminately. In order to examine this question, Tardif and Zhang (2003) reported an analysis of the five most frequent action verbs (*na2, zuo4, chi1, da3, zou3;* grab, sit, eat, hit, walk/go) and the five most frequent object nouns (*che1, qiu2, mao1, bi3, deng1;* car/vehicle, ball, cat, pen/writing instrument, light) in every child utterance from the monthly transcripts of the 10 children in the Tardif (1996) corpus. In this analysis, a total of 1,267 sentence frames were examined from the 20- to 26-month-old children. And although the vast majority of words (a higher proportion of nouns than verbs) were produced in isolation, as shown in table 18.2, when children did use syntactic markers there was almost no overlap for the unique noun (numeral + classifier; possessive) and verb (negative; aspect; resultative verb complement) modifiers. The one exception to this was for two uses of the negative marker *mei2* (not [have]) with the noun *che1* (car/vehicle). In fact, although negative markers are not permitted to directly modify nouns, the marker *mei2* (not) often appears as a shortened form of *mei2 you3* (not have) when preceding bare nouns, even in adult speech, and its status as a pure negative marker versus a negative verb form is debatable (Chao, 1968).[1]

Thus, it is clear that Mandarin speakers, and presumably Cantonese speakers as well, use syntactic markings for nouns and verbs from a very early age and that

Table 18.2 Syntactic markings on target words in child Mandarin

Syntactic Marker	Object Nouns	Action Verbs
Bare Form	112 (58.9%)	259 (24%)
Uncodable	41 (21.6%)	52 (4.8%)
(Num) + (CL) + target	28 (14.7%)	0
Pro / NA + de + target	3 (1.6%)	0
Neg + target	2 (1.0%)	139 (12.9%)
Target + aspect	0	36 (3.3%)
Target + RVC	0	5 (0.05%)
Total tokens	190	1077

Note: Num, numeral; CL, classifier; Pro, pronoun; NA, proper name; de, *de*, a possessive marker; Neg, negative; RVC, resultative verb complement.

they use them appropriately such that only noun markings are used with nouns and only verb markings are used with verbs. A remaining issue, however is how flexible they are in using these markings. Do Mandarin- and Cantonese-speaking children use sentence structures and syntactic markings on verbs flexibly with relatively free substitution (as is allowed by the verb properties), as Tomasello (1992, 2000) argues is necessary to demonstrate that they have the syntactic category of "verb," or do they use them in a piecemeal fashion, using some markings with some verbs but not yet with others, at rates mimicking the frequencies heard in the input? For Mandarin, these analyses have yet to be done, but if we were to extrapolate from both English and Tzeltal (Brown, 1998), we might predict that once children acquire a critical mass of verbs in their vocabularies, they do become flexible users of the syntax. The interesting difference is that for Mandarin and Tzeltal, because large numbers of verbs are learned early, one would predict that this critical mass of verbs and, by extension, "verb" as a syntactic category, would be acquired much earlier in the word-learning process than it is for English.

Misconception 3: Chinese Verbs Are Not Really What We Would Call Verbs in English—They Are Simpler Types of Predicates or Possibly Even Nouns

A final way in which Mandarin verbs might not be considered verbs is if their meanings are different from what we mean by a verb in English. To use Tomasello's (1992) definition, in order to be considered a verb, a word must encode something about a change of state rather than be a simple directional (e.g., *up* as it is often used in English child speech) or other placeholder for more complex verbal meanings. To examine this more closely, let us consider the 100 most frequent words acquired by 16-month-old English- and Mandarin-speaking toddlers on the CDI. The number of items that fall into the categories people, common nouns (including animals, body parts, clothing, food and drink, small household objects, toys, vehicles, and outside things and places), adjectives (descriptive words), verbs (action words), games and routines, sound effects, and closed class (quantifiers, pronouns, time words, direction words, and classifiers) from the CDI norming samples in both English and Mandarin are shown in table 18.3. As expected, most of the top 100 words for English-speaking toddlers are common nouns. Two thirds of the most common 100 words, in fact, are nouns, and only three of the top 100 words in English are verbs. In contrast, only one third of the top 100 words in Mandarin are common nouns, and this is paralleled by almost as many verbs. Even when the category of people is considered together with common nouns, just under half of the top 100 Mandarin words for 16-month-olds are nominals, whereas English-speaking 16-month-olds have almost three quarters of their vocabularies filled with nominals. Although some authors (e.g., Gentner & Boroditsky, 2001; Gillette et al., 1999) are satisfied that this demonstrates that Mandarin conforms to the general cognitive predispositions children have toward learning nouns, I believe that stopping at this conclusion prevents us from fully understanding not only how children learn

Table 18.3 One hundred most frequent word types on English and Mandarin CDI for 16-month-olds

Category	English Items	Mandarin Items
Predicate-like		
Action words	3	27
Descriptive words	4	7
Games/routines	11	8
Total	18	42
People	6	17
Common nouns		
Animals	12	8
Body parts	11	1
Clothing	4	3
Food/drink	10	11
Furniture/rooms	3	0
Household items	10	2
Outside things	6	3
Toys	7	3
Vehicles	3	1
Total	66	32
(Common nouns + people)	(72)	(49)
Closed class		
Pronouns	2	0
Quantifiers	1	2
Other		
Sound effects	11	11

verbs in Mandarin but how words are learned by children more generally. Understanding what is really different about Mandarin-speaking children's early lexicons can provide us with clues to understanding the deeper principles underlying the predispositions.

What is most surprising in the Mandarin data is not that children do not acquire as many common nouns as English (although this too is worthy of exploration, as I discuss below), but that they acquire so many verbs. Almost one third (27) of the top 100 words for the Mandarin-speaking 16-month-olds were verbs, whereas English-speaking children had only three. This is a ninefold difference. For common nouns, the difference is only twofold. Although some of the differences might be explained by input alone, I believe that differences in the semantic properties of both nouns and verbs in these two languages may help explain the rest of the anomaly.

However, it is important to clarify that the semantic properties of these categories are not different in the sense that verbs in Chinese are really what are called nouns in English or, to be less extreme, other predicate-like categories. For the case with nouns, it should suffice to examine the most common 20 verbs in 16-month-olds vocabularies, as shown in table 18.1. Clearly, each of these verbs, even in Mandarin, is a word that describes an action or change of state and not an entity. Moreover, even when categories such as descriptive words and games and routines are included in the data, there is still a highly significant difference across languages. Finally, when the actual terms that are described in each of these categories are examined, they are surprisingly similar across languages. For instance, in English, the most common descriptive terms are *hot, all gone, yucky*, and *pretty*, whereas they are *mei2 le!* ("gone"), *da4* ("big"), *tang4* ("hot"), and *chou4* ("stinky") in Mandarin. Thus, it is not the case that the Mandarin verbs are not really verbs in the sense of being what one would count as adjectives or other types of predicates on the English CDI.

So How Are Verbs Different in Chinese?: "Are They Really Verbs?" Revisited

According to Gentner (1982, p. 304), "the Natural Partitions view predicts that terms denoting objects and entities will be acquired first across languages and that these terms will be nominals." This is echoed in her more recent view, whereby the combination of "natural partitions" and "relational relativity" (that "noun meanings are given to us by the world" whereas "verb meanings are more free to vary across languages," Gentner, 1981, p. 169) leads to the proposal that "children learn some object names before relational terms" (Gentner & Boroditsky, 2001, p. 217). In both discussions, there is a "division of dominance" such that cognitive and perceptual categories and experience aid in children's mapping of words to the world for proper names and concrete nouns, whereas linguistic experience is required for the acquisition of closed class items, with kinship terms, verbs, and prepositions lying in between. Although the general claim that children acquire some words by relying on perceptual and conceptual cues, and that others are acquired by relying more heavily on linguistic experience must be true, I suggest that this particular continuum of categories is not equally applicable across languages. In fact, Gentner and Boroditsky (2001) allude to this issue in their discussions of English-speaking children's acquisition of different types of nouns and verbs and of cross-linguistic data pertaining to their hypothesis (particularly with respect to Brown's [1998] work in Tzeltal and de Leon's [2001] findings for Tzotzil). Nonetheless, examining this question more closely with reference to the nature of verb (and noun) semantics in English and Mandarin will be particularly informative as to why Mandarin appears to break the rule.

Several authors (e.g., Clark, 1993; Goldberg, 1999) have made a distinction between "light" and "heavy" verbs and argued that light, or "general-purpose," verbs such as *go*, *do*, and *make* are acquired earliest and used most frequently in children's verb vocabularies. Nonetheless, there may be cross-linguistic differences in this as well (Clark, 2003). In her discussion of why Tzeltal-speaking children appear to acquire so many verbs, Brown (1998) challenged this notion and suggested that, in contrast, Tzeltal-speaking children tend to acquire heavy verbs in their early stages of vocabulary learning. I would argue that Mandarin-speaking children acquire both types of verbs and that they use heavy verbs with much greater frequency than English-speaking children. For instance, in English, *go* and *put* are used more than twice as often as any other verbs when talking about intransitive and transitive motion, respectively (Clark, 2003). In Mandarin, this is not the case— the verbs for *go* (*zou3/qu4*) are among the most common intransitive verbs in Tardif's (1996) corpus, but these two Mandarin verbs are more specific than the English equivalent and not used with much greater frequency than other verbs such as *look* (*kan4*), *come* (*lai2*), *sit* (*zuo4*), *ascend* (*shang4*), or *descend* (*xia4*). For transitive motion verbs, *grab* (*na2*) is the most common, followed by *hit* (*da3*), *eat* (*chi1*), and other verbs, with *put* still appearing frequently but not as frequently as any of these other verbs (Tardif, 2001).

In the English and Mandarin CDI data presented above, both light and heavy verbs appear as common verb types for 16-month-olds. Thus, even for English, heavy verbs—those which provide strong cues to the subject/agent or object/patient of the verb—can be acquired early. Nonetheless, in English, these words are not acquired as early as many common nouns, as evidenced by the relative rankings of these words on the CDI. In English, for instance, the most common object noun is *ball*, ranking number 6, followed by *dog* at rank number 9. The most common action words are *go* (a light verb) and *bite* (a heavy verb), with a tied ranking of 81 and 48 object nouns preceding these two verbs. For Mandarin, the most common object noun is *egg*, ranking number 10, followed by *light* at rank 17. The most common action words are *hug/hold* (a heavy verb, with a human agent holding another human patient in the arms) at rank 5 and *hit* (neither very heavy nor very light, since a human agent using a hand is implied but not required—an instrument could be instead of a bare hand—and any number of potential objects or beings could serve as the patient) at rank 10. Thus, for Mandarin, the action words appear just as early and are just as common as object nouns, whereas object nouns clearly appear earlier and more frequently in English-speaking children's early vocabularies.

Mandarin, like Korean and Tzeltal (Brown, 1998; Choi, 1998; Choi & Bowerman, 1991), encodes much more into the verb than English. Examples of this difference abound, and Choi and Bowerman (1991; Bowerman & Choi, 2001) discuss this for Korean in terms of spatial properties, but I believe the difference is more broad than that. Consider, for example, the verbs *carry* and *push*. In English, *carry* refers to carrying a backpack (on the shoulders or back), carrying a baby, carrying a serving dish, carrying a purse, and a number of different ways of transporting objects with one's body. In Mandarin, distinct verbs are used for different ways in which objects might be carried (i.e., on the back, *bei1*; held in one's arms, *bao4*; flat on two hands, *duan1*; dangling in one hand, *ling2*; etc.). To distinguish among these different forms of carrying, Chinese (both Mandarin and Cantonese) uses distinctly different morphological forms such that there is nothing common or transparent in the morphology of each of these verbs that would allow the child to infer the English term *carry*. Indeed, it would be incorrect and result in a different understanding if one tried to use a single verb to represent these various meanings. In English, even though there are distinct terms for many specific actions—one can press, topple, shove, or squish something—one tends to resort to a general purpose verb, together with a preposition and the relevant object noun when talking about actions (i.e., *push down, push over, push away*, etc.) particularly in face-to-face communications where it is obvious what kind of pushing (or other motion) is involved.

The opposite is true for nouns. Specifically, I would argue that, in Chinese, many nouns, and particularly nouns of everyday use, are light. This became particularly evident when we began the process of translating and piloting the CDI in Mandarin and Cantonese. Although both of these Chinese languages have an indefinitely large number of specific nouns to describe all kinds of household objects, toys, and everyday items that a child might come into contact with, when we put these terms on the instrument, two types of phenomena became glaringly obvious. First, many distinct English nouns had common root terms in Chinese. For example, in English, *rooster* and *hen* are both types of *chickens* and each of these words appear on the CDI, with over 50% of 24-month-olds in the English sample able to say *chicken* and 20% or more able to say *rooster* and *hen* (Dale & Fenson, 1996). In Chinese, all three terms share a common root, *ji1* (*chicken*), and *hen* and *rooster* are productive variations with the prefixes *mother* (*mu3-ji1*) and *male* (*gong1-ji1*). Although it is acceptable to consider these as separate words, the problem comes when additional male-female or adult-juvenile distinctions are made with other animals—the same prefixes are used over and over again. In English, *mare* and *cow* have no obvious morphological relations to *hen*, despite the fact that they are all females. In Chinese, however, the females of all three species would be referred to as *mu3* plus the common term for the species. In other cases, such as for the category vehicles, the English terms are again highly distinctive (e.g., *motorcycle, bicycle, truck, car, taxi, bus, train*, etc.), whereas the Chinese terms could certainly be considered as separate words, but they also share a common root (e.g., *mo2tuo2che1, zi4xing2che1, ka3che1, jiao4che1, chu1zu1che1, gong1gong4qi4che1, huo3che1*, etc.). In both of these cases, when we piloted the CDI with Mandarin-speaking parents, they objected to many of the specific noun terms as either being completely redundant (e.g., in the case of hens, chickens, and roosters) or as too difficult (e.g., in the case of the names of different rooms and several items that were commonly used in Chinese households).

Thus, in Chinese everyday speech, the most frequent nouns are not those that are specific and identify individual objects at the basic level as in English, but in fact are what would seem (to an English speaker) to be more general terms identifying classes of objects. But to a Chinese speaker, these are the basic level terms, much as general-purpose light verbs (e.g., *go, put, carry, push*) are the basic level for describing common actions in English. And, similar to the way that English speakers use more and different types of specific nouns, Chinese uses many more distinct and specific verbs. As a final example of this, consider the responses of an English speaker and a Mandarin speaker when asked how one traveled to work. In Mandarin, one might answer any of the following *qi2/zuo1/kai1 che1 lai2 de* ("rode/sat/drove vehicle come" = came by riding/sitting/driving), where the specific vehicle of transportation is not specified, but how one interacted with the vehicle (riding/sitting in/driving) is. In English, one could easily have omitted the verb and said "by bicycle/bus/car," with the emphasis instead on highly distinct and specific names for different types of vehicles.

In sum, then, English and Chinese appear to resort to general purpose terms for different types of words, and this goes beyond matters of simple preference to the issue of what is acceptable or not in a given language. For instance, it would be considered incorrect and indeed childish to refer to all vehicles (including trains and fire trucks) as cars in English, whereas Chinese speakers can do this by simply using the root term *che1*. Which particular vehicle is meant would be inferred from context or the use of an associated verb (e.g., *ride* vs. *drive*), or, if required, one could use the specific term when there is ambiguity (e.g., *zuo4 huo3che1* vs. *zuo4 gong1gong4qi4che1*, "sat on a train" vs. "sat on a bus"). Similarly, it would be incorrect to refer to all pushing motions as *tui1* ("push open/away") in Chinese, whereas English speakers do this quite naturally. Thus, in addition to having different assumptions about which terms (nouns or verbs) need to be lexicalized in a given situation, English and Chinese also differ in how nouns and verbs are lexicalized, at least insofar as when general purpose versus specific terms must be used. In some ways, this also brings back an issue raised by Snedeker et al. (2003) in the discussion of their cross-linguistic findings. One possible explanation, they felt, for the cross-linguistic differences was that the English-speaking mothers were using basic level terms for the target nouns in English, but different terms were used for Chinese. They suspected that there may have been problems with the stimuli that they chose for the Chinese dyads since the study had first been conducted in English, but I suspect instead that the differences may reflect real and interesting differences in how one refers to objects in each of these languages. Again, there is a corollary with verbs—English has many general purpose verbs and specific ones when specificity is needed, but Chinese has specific verbs for basic actions without an easily available general purpose term to describe them. Thus, whereas English speakers may have used either the general purpose verb or a more specific verb, Chinese speakers would have used only the more specific verb and this (together with more concrete cues to the specific verb) may have accounted for the greater precision with which even English speakers guessed which verbs were meant by the Chinese mothers.

So . . . Are They Really Verbs?

By every formal account, I would argue that the verbs in Mandarin-speaking children's early vocabularies are verbs, at least inasmuch as the verblike words that English-speaking children have trouble acquiring are verbs. Yet, in addition to the multiple ways in which verbs are emphasized in Mandarin adult-to-child speech (see Tardif et al., 1997), the nature of Mandarin verbs also makes its easier to acquire more verbs than children do in English. It is not that English does not have many specific verbs; it does. It is also not the case that Chinese verbs are uniformly more "nouny" in the sense that they are all heavy and encode so much of the ground or of the instrument (Talmy, 1985) into the verb that the nouns are redundant. In fact, many of the most frequent verbs in the Mandarin children's vocabularies are also the most frequent verbs in English, although there are differences as well. The main difference is that, in English, adults (as well as children) tend to use more general purpose verbs to approximate meaning and then use prepositions, nouns, and other parts of speech to more fully specify the meaning. In Mandarin, verbs are used for very specific meanings (without the addition of distinguishing prepositions). In contrast, Mandarin nouns tend to be general, whereas they tend to be highly specific in English. When one counts up the number of distinct types that children have in their vocabularies, then, it is not surprising that children tend to acquire large numbers of the word class that is emphasized (via frequency, utterance position, and specificity of meaning in everyday use) in their language.

The fact that Mandarin-speaking children acquire so many verbs, whether one terms them verbs or something else, is what challenges us to consider what is special about Chinese. I believe it also challenges us to think about whether, ultimately, the distinctions between nouns and verbs are equally relevant across languages. More importantly, understanding the nature of the differences between early verb acquisition in English and Mandarin can also help us to understand better how children come to learn words and, when they do use cognitive biases to help them learn words, what the inherent features of these biases might be, regardless of which form class they might map onto in a particular language. Word learning, by its nature, is multidimensional—children (the learners) come to the task with both inborn and learned predispositions, adults (the models) come to the task with habits of speaking and interacting as well as assumptions about what language is and whether and how to teach their children language, and the words themselves were created through thousands of generations of use to represent categories, events, and all that is speech-worthy in our lives, with rules for combining them that have been codified into a grammar. Quine's (1960) posing of the "gavagai" problem, while interesting, fails to take all of these issues into account—it assumes a naive listener in an unstructured environment learning a word that might be presented in the same way, regardless of the particular speaker or listener and their shared assumptions, or of the immediately preceding context and surrounding environment.

The evidence presented in this chapter speaks clearly to the fact that verbs are privileged in Chinese, in much the way nouns are privileged in English. Regardless of which measures are used, whether one is looking at adult or child speech, or even the contexts in which the speech occurs, Mandarin speakers highlight verbs in their everyday spoken language. Although we may have answered one question—are they really verbs?—a number of even more difficult questions arise once we start to realize that the prevalence of verbs in Chinese may reflect a fundamental difference in how language systems have chosen to represent meaning.

Acknowledgments Thanks to all of the parents and children who participated in these studies, to Tracy Chan, Kawai Leung, Shanping Qiu, and Hongli Zhang, who helped with the data collection and analysis, as well as to my collaborators Paul Fletcher, Susan A. Gelman, Weilan Liang, Virginia Marchman, Letitia Naigles, Marilyn Shatz, Fan Xu, and Zhixiang Zhang, without whom this research would not have been possible. Thanks also to Susan Gelman and Virginia Marchman, who provided insightful comments on an earlier draft of this chapter. The examinations of Beijing and Hong Kong children's vocabularies and grammar were supported by Hong Kong Research Grant's Council Earmarked grants CUHK4031/97H to the author and HKU 7158/99H to Paul Fletcher.

Note

1. Nonetheless, even this marker was used conservatively directly in front of nouns, despite the fact that disappearance or the inability to find objects was a common topic of conversation for these toddlers. Instead, it tended to be used in isolation, or in utterances where the noun was fronted and the negative marker appeared after the noun in a topic-comment type of structure, rather than in the typical pretarget structure observed with verbs.

References

Au, T. K., Dapretto, M., & Song, Y. K. (1994). Input vs. constraints: Early word acquisition in Korean and English. *Journal of Memory and Language, 33,* 567–582.

Bates, E., Chen, S., Tzeng, O., Li, P., & Opie, M. (1991). The noun-verb problem in Chinese aphasia. *Brain and Language, 41,* 203–233.

Bloom, L. (1970). *Language development: Form and function in emerging grammars.* Cambridge, MA: MIT Press.

Bowerman, M., & Choi, S. (2001). Shaping meanings for languages: Universal and language specific in the acquisition of spatial semantic categories. In M. Bowerman & S. C. Levinson (Eds.), *Language acquisition and conceptual development* (pp. 475–511). Cambridge: Cambridge University Press.

Brown, P. (1998). Children's first verbs in Tzeltal: Evidence for an early verb category. *Linguistics, 36*(4), 715–753.

Caselli, M. C., Bates, E., Casadio, P., Fenson, J., Fenson, L., Sanderl, L., et al. (1995). A cross-linguistic study of early lexical development. *Cognitive Development, 10,* 159–200.

Chan, M. K. M., & Tai, J. H.-Y. (1995). From nouns to verbs: Verbalization in Chinese dialects and East Asian languages. In J. Camacho & L. Choueri (Eds.), *Sixth North American Conference on Chinese Linguisitcs. NACCL-6* (pp. 49–74). Los Angeles: University of Southern California Press.

Chao, Y. R. (1968). *A grammar of spoken Chinese.* Berkeley: University of California Press.

Choi, S. (1998). Verbs in early lexical and syntactic development in Korean. *Linguistics, 36,* 755–780.

Choi, S. (2000). Caregiver input in English and Korean: Use of nouns and verbs in book-reading and toy-play contexts. *Journal of Child Language, 27*(1), 69–96.

Choi, S., & Bowerman, M. (1991). Learning to express motion events in English and Korean: The influence of language-specific lexicalization patterns. *Cognition, 41,* 83–121.

Choi, S., & Gopnik, A. (1995). Early acquisition of verbs in Korean: A cross-linguistic study. *Journal of Child Language, 22,* 497–529.

Clark, E. V. (2003). *First language acquisition.* Cambridge: Cambridge University Press.

de Leon, L. (2001). Why Tzotzil (Mayan) children prefer verbs: The role of linguistic and cultural factors over cognitive determinants. In M. Almgren, A. Barreña, M. J. Ezeizabarrena, I. Idiazabal, & B. MacWhinney, et al. (Eds.), *Research on Child Language Acquisition: Proceedings of the 8th Conference of the International Association for the Study of Child Language* (pp. 947–969). Somerville, MA: Cascadilla Press.

Fenson, L., Dale, P., Reznick, J. S., Thal, D., Bates, E., Hartung, J., et al. (1993). *MacArthur Communicative Development Inventories: User's guide and technical manual.* San Diego: Singular.

Fernald, A., & Morikawa, H. (1993). Common themes and cultural variations in Japanese and American mothers' speech to infants. *Child Development, 64*(3), 637–656.

Gentner, D. (1981). Some interesting differences between nouns and verbs. *Cognition and Brain Theory, 4,* 161–178.

Gentner, D. (1982). Why nouns are learned before verbs: Linguistic relativity versus natural partitioning. In S. A. Kuczaj (Ed.), *Language development: Vol. 2. Language, thought, and culture* (pp. 301–334). Hillsdale, NJ: Erlbaum.

Gentner, D., & Boroditsky, L. (2001). Individuation, relativity, and early word learning. In M. Bowerman & S. Levinson (Eds.), *Language acuiqisition and conceptual development* (pp. 257–283). Cambridge: Cambridge University Press.

Gillette, J., Gleitman, H., Gleitman, L., & Lederer, A. (1999). Human simulations of vocabulary learning. *Cognition, 73,* 135–176.

Kao, M. K. (1990). Guanyu hanyu de cilei fenbie (On the differentiation of lexical classes in Chinese). In M. K. Kao (Ed.), *Yuyanxue lunwenji (Linguistic essays of Kao Ming Kai)* (pp. 262–272). Beijing, China: Commercial Press.

Kim, M., McGregor, K. K., & Thompson, C. K. (2000). Early lexical development in English- and Korean-speaking children: Language-general and language-specific patterns. *Journal of Child Language, 27,* 225–254.

Lee, J., Nelson, J., & Naigles, L. R. (2003). *Syntactic bootstrapping: A viable strategy for Mandarin verb learners.* Paper presented at the Boston University Conference on Language Development.

Leung, V. Y. K. (2001). *Cantonese-speaking children's early acquisition of nouns and verbs.* Unpublished manuscript, The University of Hong Kong.

Li, C. N., & Thompson, S. A. (1981). *Mandarin Chinese: A functional reference grammar.* Berkeley: University of California Press.

Li, P., Jin, Z., & Tan, L. H. (2004). Neural representations of nouns and verbs in Chinese: An fMRI study. *Neuroimage, 21,* 1533–1541.

Ogura, T., Murase, T., Yamashita, Y., & Mahieu, A. (July, 1999). *Acquisition of nouns and verbs in Japanese children.* Poster presented at Eighth International Congress for the Study of Child Language, San Sebastian, Spain.

Quine, W. V. (1960). *Word and object: An inquiry into the linguistic mechanisms of object reference.* New York: Wiley.

Ramsey, S. R. (1987). *The languages of China.* Princeton, NJ: Princeton University Press.

Richards, B. (1987). Type/token ratios: What do they really tell us? *Journal of Child Language, 14*(2), 201–209.

Snedeker, J., Li, P., & Yuan, S. (2003). Cross-cultural differences in the input to early word learning. *Proceedings of the Twenty-Fifth Annual Conference of the Cognitive Science Society.* Mahwah, NJ: Lawrence Erlbaum.

Talmy, L. (1985). Lexicalization patterns: Semantic structure in lexical forms. In T. Shopen (Ed.), *Language typology and syntactic description, Vol. 3: Grammatical categories and the lexicon* (pp. 57–149). Cambridge: Cambridge University Press.

Tardif, T. (1996). Nouns are not always learned before verbs: Evidence from Mandarin speakers' early vocabularies. *Developmental Psychology, 32,* 492–504.

Tardif, T. (2001). A context for the noun bias: Comparative studies of English, Italian, and Mandarin. In A. Almgren, A. Barreña, M. J. Ezeizabarrena, I. Idiazabal, & B. MacWhinney (Eds.), *Proceedings of the VIIIth International Association for the Study of Child Language, Volume 2: Syntax, morphology and the lexicon* (pp. 970–980). Medford, MA: Cascadilla Press.

Tardif, T. (2005). The importance of verbs in Chinese. In P. Li (Ed.), *Handbook of East Asian Psycholinguistics Vol. 1: Chinese*. Cambridge: Cambridge University Press.

Tardif, T., Fletcher, P., Liang, W. L., & Zhang, Z. X. (July, 2002). *Nouns and verbs in children's early vocabularies: A cross-linguistic study of the MacArthur Communicative Development Inventory in English, Mandarin, and Cantonese*. Poster presented at joint conference of International Association for the Study of Child Language and Society for Research in Communication Disorders, Madison, WI.

Tardif, T., Gelman, S. A., & Xu, F. (1999). Putting the "noun bias" in context: A comparison of English and Mandarin. *Child Development, 70*, 620–635.

Tardif, T., Shatz, M., & Naigles, L. (1997). Caregiver speech and children's use of nouns versus verbs: A comparison of English, Italian, and Mandarin. *Journal of Child Language, 24*, 535–565.

Tardif, T., & Zhang, H. L. (2003, April). *Early word combinations in Mandarin*. Talk presented at biennial meeting of the Society for Research in Child Development, Tampa, Florida.

Tomasello, M. (1992). *First verbs: A case study of early grammatical development*. New York: Cambridge University Press.

Tomasello, M. (2000). Do young children have adult syntactic competence? *Cognition, 74*, 209–253.

Tomasello, M. (2003). *Constructing a language: A usage-based theory of language acquisition*. Cambridge, MA: Harvard University Press.

? not grammatical objects?

19   Influences of Object Knowledge on the Acquisition of Verbs in English and Japanese

*Alan W. Kersten, Linda B. Smith,
and Hanako Yoshida*

This chapter reviews the evidence for an influence of object knowledge on verb learning. A number of lines of research provide evidence that the meanings of verbs are more general and flexible than are the meanings of nouns. In particular, the same verb can have markedly different meanings in the context of different objects and the different nouns that label them, whereas the meanings of nouns are relatively stable across different contexts. This flexibility in the meanings of verbs may have implications for verb learning. In particular, a child may need to learn about an object and the types of motions it is capable of before being able to understand what a verb may mean in the context of that object. This leads to the prediction that children should learn verbs more readily in the context of familiar objects than in the context of unfamiliar objects. Moreover, children who are presented with a verb in the context of an unfamiliar object may pay as much attention to that object as to its motion, in order to learn about the object and the types of motion it is capable of. Support for both of these predictions comes from recent research by Kersten and Smith (2002), who presented children with novel verbs, each of which was accompanied by both a particular object and a particular motion. Children were found to attend just as strongly to unfamiliar objects as to motions. In contrast, when verbs were presented in the context of familiar objects, children attended more strongly to motions than to those objects, learning more about those motions than they did when those motions were performed by unfamiliar objects. The remainder of the chapter discusses whether object knowledge influences the learning of all verbs, or only certain types of verbs. In particular, attention to object structure during verb learning is compared in children learning English, a language that most frequently employs intrinsic manner of motion verbs, and in children learning Japanese, a language that most frequently employs extrinsic path of motion verbs.

Introduction

Imagine that you are exploring previously uninhabited terrain and you come across a creature unlike any you have ever seen before. It has five legs, two on each side and one attached to the rear, is covered with scales like a fish, and is as large as a cow. Now imagine that as you approach this creature, it detects your presence, jumps into the river next to which it was standing, and propels itself away, using the legs at its sides like oars and its rear leg like a rudder. When later describing this event to your friends, a likely account would be, "I discovered a new creature, which I am calling a pentapod, but when I tried to get a closer look it jumped into the river and swam away."

This scenario demonstrates an important difference between nouns and verbs in the types of meanings that they convey. This creature is unlike any you have seen before, and thus it requires a new noun label, namely *pentapod*. Its mode of locomotion in the water is also unlike any you have seen before, using its legs un- like any other creature you have encountered, and yet it is quite natural to make use of an existing verb, *swim*, to describe this motion.

This scenario is of course quite far-fetched, but this same basic phenomenon has occurred repeatedly throughout the history of language. For example, with the advent of electronic communications in the late twentieth century, a new noun, *e-mail*, was coined. The existing stock of nouns in the English language was appar- ently insufficient to describe this new form of communication, and thus a new noun was added to the language. No doubt quite shortly thereafter, this new noun was used in a sentence, perhaps "I just sent you an e-mail." Although in the past, the verb *send* had been used to describe the physical transmission of an object from one location to another, it was apparently quite natural to extend its use to the transmission of bits through cyberspace. Thus, when presented with a new (virtual) object to be described and a new way of acting upon that object, a new noun was required but an existing verb was sufficient.

Experimental Evidence for Greater Flexibility in Verb Meanings Than in Noun Meanings

The preceding examples suggest that the meanings of basic-level nouns are rela- tively specific and unchanging, and thus when a new object has to be labeled, a new noun is required. In contrast, the meanings of verbs are more general and flexible, and thus when a new action needs to be labeled, the meaning of an old verb can be extended to include this new action. A number of lines of research provide support for this view. First, Gentner (1981) has noted that the average verb has more dictionary senses than does the average noun when the two classes of words are matched in frequency. This finding suggests that when a new action needs to be described, instead of adding a new verb to the language, an existing verb may acquire a new sense to accommodate this new action.

Second, Gentner and France (1988) have demonstrated that adult speakers of a language are much more willing to extend the meaning of a verb than to extend the meaning of a noun in order to allow comprehension of a seemingly anomalous sentence. In particular, they presented participants with sentences in which the noun and the verb were semantically mismatched, such as "The butterfly pondered," and asked them what these sentences meant. Participants were much more likely to alter the verb to be consistent with the noun (e.g., interpreting *pondered* to mean "hovered in one spot for a long time") than they were to alter the noun to be consistent with the verb (e.g., interpreting *butterfly* to mean "a person wearing bright clothes"). This finding suggests that a verb may acquire a new sense simply by being used in combination with a new noun.

Third, Kersten and Earles (2004) used a memory paradigm to demonstrate that the meaning of a verb changes more in the context of different nouns than does the meaning of a noun in the context of different verbs. They presented participants with simple intransitive sentences such as "The ball bounced" and instructed participants to remember either the noun or the verb from each sentence. Participants who were instructed to remember nouns were later tested for recognition memory of each of those nouns (e.g., *ball*), either in the context of the same verb it had accompanied earlier (e.g., *bounced*), or in the context of a different verb (e.g., *rolled*). Similarly, participants who were instructed to remember verbs were later tested for recognition memory of each of those verbs (e.g., *bounced*), either in the context of the same noun that it had accompanied earlier (e.g., *ball*), or in the context of a new noun (e.g., *quarter*). Recognition memory for verbs was found to be strongly dependent upon reinstatement of the same noun that had accompanied a verb earlier. In contrast, reinstatement of a verb had little effect on memory for a noun. This combination of findings suggests that the meanings of nouns are relatively stable across different semantic contexts. The meanings of verbs, on the other hand, are much more variable across semantic contexts. This makes it difficult to recognize that a verb presented in one semantic context had previously been encountered in a different semantic context, because the meanings encoded by the verbs may be quite different on the two occasions.

Implications for Verb Learning

If the meanings of verbs are indeed more general and flexible than are the meanings of nouns, this may have implications for verb learning in children. Research dating back to Posner and Keele (1968; 1970) has revealed that categories involving a great deal of variability take longer to learn than do categories whose exemplars cluster tightly around the prototype. Thus, if verbs indeed involve greater generality (and thus variability) in their meanings than do nouns, one may make the prediction that it should take children longer to learn the meanings of verbs than to learn the meanings of nouns.

This prediction appears to be largely supported, as documented by Gentner (1981, 1982; Gentner & Boroditsky, 2001). There remains a great deal of debate, however, about whether the earlier acquisition of nouns than of verbs is a universal phenomenon, or whether it is dependent upon how nouns and verbs appear in a particular language. For example, some have argued that verbs may be acquired earlier than nouns in languages such as Korean and Mandarin, in which verbs appear more frequently than nouns in parental speech to children, and appear more often in salient sentence positions (Choi & Gopnik, 1995; Gopnik & Choi, 1995; Tardif, 1996). Even in these languages, however, whether there is a verb advantage or a noun advantage in children's early speech depends on the way nouns and verbs are counted. In particular, whereas there is an apparent verb advantage when direct observation is used to assess a child's vocabulary, there is evidence of a noun advantage when a parental checklist method is used (Au, Dapretto, & Song, 1994; Tardif, Gelman, & Xu, 1999). Moreover, in most other languages that have been studied, a clear noun advantage is evident regardless of how nouns and verbs are counted. Thus, the consensus view that emerges from this research is that nouns enjoy an overall advantage over verbs in acquisition but that the size of this advantage is influenced by the way nouns and verbs appear in a particular language.

Evidence from child language acquisition is thus consistent with the view that the greater variability of verb meanings makes them more difficult to acquire than nouns. More specific predictions are possible, however, if one analyzes the sources of variability in verb meanings. In all of the examples presented so far, the extension of an existing verb's meaning to include some new scenario has resulted from the use of that verb in combination with a new object, or else in combination with a new noun used to label an object. The clearest example of this phenomenon comes from the research of Gentner and France (1988) involving semantically mismatched nouns and verbs. In this research, when a verb (e.g., *pondered*) was used in combination with a noun that it had not previously accompanied (e.g., *butterfly*), the verb took on a new meaning (e.g., hovered in place). This finding suggests a mechanism by which verbs may take on new meanings. In particular, when a verb is used in combination with a noun that it had not previously accompanied, the characteristics of the object labeled by the noun may be combined with the general meaning of the verb to produce a new interpretation of that verb. If this process were repeated over and over again in many different speakers, either through independent discovery or social transmission, the result would be the standardization of a new sense of the verb to accommodate that new object.

The results of Gentner (1981) and Kersten and Earles (2004) may represent the end product of this mechanism for extending the meanings of verbs to cover new objects. In particular, when a verb starts to be consistently used in combination with a new object, a new sense for that verb may emerge. In contrast, when a new object needs to be labeled, a new noun may be created rather than adding a new sense to an existing noun. Thus, over time, verbs may accrue new senses at a greater rate than nouns, accounting for Gentner's (1981) finding that the average verb has more senses than the average noun. Furthermore, if the different senses of a verb represent the use of that verb in combination with different objects, then these different senses should be elicited by the use of that verb together with different nouns. Thus, in Kersten and Earles's (2004) study of recognition memory for nouns and verbs, when a verb was presented at encoding in the context of a noun, this may have brought to mind a particular sense of the verb associated with the object labeled by that noun. When that same verb was presented along with a different noun at retrieval, this may have brought to mind a different sense of the verb, making it difficult to remember having seen that verb before.

If the variability in the meanings of verbs stems from the use of verbs in combination with different objects, then further predictions are possible regarding the acquisition of verbs. In particular, in order to understand what a verb means in a given instance, it may be necessary to know something about the object whose actions are being predicated. For example, in order to understand the meaning of the verb *run* in a sentence, it is important to know whether the object doing the running has two legs (as in the case of a human), four legs (as in the case of a horse), or no legs (as in the case of an engine). Thus, one may make the prediction that children should show faster learning of a novel verb when that verb is used to describe the actions of a familiar object than when the verb is used to describe the actions of an unfamiliar object. Second, one may make the prediction that when children are presented with a novel verb in the context of an unfamiliar object, they will attempt to learn about the nature of an object in order to try to understand what a verb may mean in the context of that object.

Naturalistic studies of verb use in children are difficult to evaluate with regard to these predictions, because it is hard to determine whether a verb used by a child was learned in the context of familiar or unfamiliar objects. Two different findings provide suggestive evidence, however, in favor of the prediction that children should show faster learning of verbs in the context of familiar objects. One is the previously described finding that in most languages that have been studied, nouns are learned earlier than verbs (Gentner & Boroditsky, 2001). One possible interpretation of this finding is that children need to learn about nouns and the objects they label before they can learn the meanings of verbs. A second finding comes from Bloom (1981), who observed that verb use is rare in the one-word period, whereas it is much more common when children start putting two words together, with these two-word combinations often comprising a noun and a verb. On the basis of this result, Bloom proposed that children learn verbs in combination with nouns rather than in isolation, suggesting that knowledge of objects is necessary before one can learn how to use verbs in the context of those objects.

Most experimental studies of verb learning also fail to provide evidence regarding these predictions because they exclusively employ the motions of familiar objects as stimuli. There have been several studies that have portrayed the motions of unfamiliar objects, however, and these studies provide support for the prediction that children focus on unfamiliar objects when learning a verb, perhaps in order to learn about the nature of those objects and the types of motions they can take part in. First, in the classic study of Brown (1957), children were presented with cards depicting novel actions involving novel objects and substances. Each card was accompanied by a novel count noun, mass noun, or verb. Children were later presented with three cards, one that matched the original on the action, one that matched the original on the object, and one that matched the original on the substance, and were asked to choose which of these three cards was the best example of the word heard earlier. When children were presented with a novel verb, they were most likely to select the card involving the same action, but 33% of their choices still involved novel objects and substances. This finding could be interpreted to suggest that children who were presented with a novel verb focused not only on the actions being performed, but also on the objects and substances involved in those actions.

The results of Brown (1957) are suggestive at best with regard to the present predictions, however, because no actual motions were presented, thus deviating from the typical verb learning scenario. More recent evidence involving actual motions comes from the research of Behrend (1990) and Forbes and Farrar (1995). Both of these studies involved presenting children with novel verbs accompanied by video clips involving people performing novel actions with novel instruments. Children were later presented with video clips involving changes to one or more attributes of these events and were asked whether each of these video clips still depicted an example of a verb heard earlier. Both studies revealed a tendency for young children to reject an event as being an example of a previously presented verb if the instrument depicted in the event had changed. This again could be taken to suggest that children focused to some extent on the object involved in an action when attempting to learn a verb for that action, perhaps in order to learn about the nature of that object and what could be done with it.

The results of Behrend (1990) and Forbes and Farrar (1995) thus provide evidence that children learning a verb attend to a novel object playing the role of instrument in an event. More recent research by Kersten and Smith (2002) provides evidence that children learning a verb also attend to a novel object playing the role of agent in an event. In this research, 3.5- to 4-year-old children were presented with novel, buglike creatures moving around on a television screen. Each such event was accompanied by a novel verb. Two different verbs were presented, corresponding to two different motions and two different creatures carrying out those motions. In particular, the verb *morping* always accompanied an event involving a creature with a rounded, orange body with red spots on it, moving toward a second creature such that the two ended up in contact with one another (see figure 19.1). In contrast, the verb *spogging* always accompanied an event

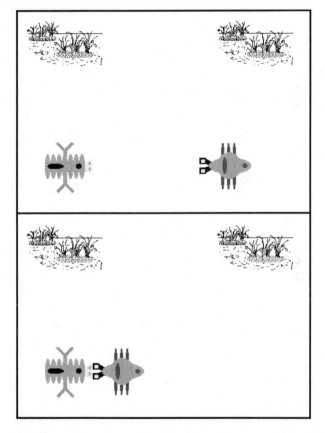

Figure 19.1. Two frames of an example event from Kersten and Smith (2002) Experiment 1. The upper frame depicts the starting positions of the two characters, whereas the lower frame depicts their positions at the end of the event. (From "Attention to Novel Objects During Verb Learning," by A. W. Kersten and L. B. Smith, 2002, *Child Development*, 73, p. 97. Copyright 2002. Adapted with permission.)

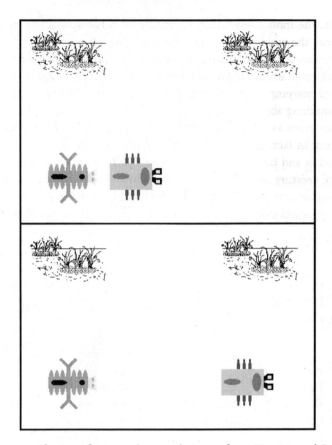

Figure 19.2. Two frames of a second example event from Kersten and Smith (2002) Experiment 1. The upper frame depicts the starting positions of the two characters, whereas the lower frame depicts their positions at the end of the event. (From "Attention to Novel Objects During Verb Learning," by A. W. Kersten and L. B. Smith, 2002, *Child Development*, 73, p. 99. Copyright 2002. Adapted with permission.)

involving a creature with a rectangular, purple body with gray spots on it, moving away from a second creature (see figure 19.2). Thus, children could potentially have mapped a verb onto the motion depicted in an event, the creature carrying out that motion, or both.

The extent to which children attended to these two different types of information was measured by subsequently presenting children with a number of test events and asking children if each of these events was still an example of the verb *morping*. Some events were identical to previous examples of *morping*, some involved the correct motion but the wrong creature (i.e., the creature previously associated with the verb *spogging*), some involved the correct creature but the wrong motion (i.e., the motion previously associated with the verb *spogging*), and some involved both the wrong creature and the wrong motion.

The results of this experiment are depicted in the left column of figure 19.3. Children accepted events involving the correct motion and the correct creature as examples of *morping* a high percentage of the time, indicating that they had learned something about the meaning of this new verb. Children were less likely to accept an event as an example of morping if either the motion or the creature was incorrect. In fact, children were just as likely to reject an event involving the correct motion and the wrong creature as they were to reject an event involving the correct creature and the wrong motion. This suggests that children were attending just as strongly to the object in motion as they were to the motion itself. This result provides evidence in favor of the prediction that children will attend to

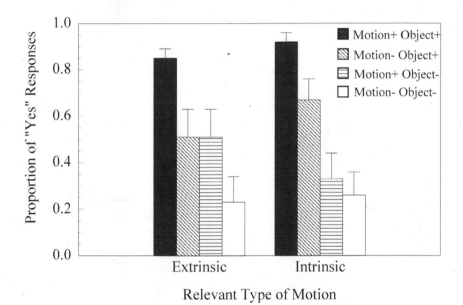

Figure 19.3. Combined results of Kersten and Smith (2002) Experiments 1 and 2. The results of Experiment 1, in which extrinsic motion was relevant, are depicted on the left. The results of Experiment 2, in which intrinsic motion was relevant, are depicted on the right. The *y* axis depicts the proportion of "yes" responses to the question, "Is this one morping?" Motion+ object+ events involved both the correct motion and the correct object. Motion– object+ events involved the correct object performing the wrong motion. Motion+ object– events involved the correct motion performed by the wrong object. Motion– Object– events involved the wrong object performing the wrong motion. (From "Attention to Novel Objects During Verb Learning," by A. W. Kersten and L. B. Smith, 2002, *Child Development, 73,* p. 103. Copyright 2002. Adapted with permission.)

a novel object when learning a verb, perhaps in order to learn about the nature of the object and the types of motion it is capable of.

The study of Kersten and Smith (2002) also provides evidence for the first prediction that children will learn a verb more readily in the context of a familiar object than in the context of a novel object. In particular, Kersten and Smith compared verb learning in the context of unfamiliar objects, namely the buglike creatures described previously, and in the context of familiar objects, namely cars and trucks. In both conditions, a given verb was always accompanied by a particular motion as well as a particular object carrying out that motion. For example, in the familiar objects condition, the verb *morping* always accompanied an event in which a car moved toward a van, such that the two ended up in contact at the end of the event. In contrast, the verb *spogging* always accompanied an event in which a truck moved away from the van. Thus, children could potentially have associated the verb *morping* with a motion, an object (i.e., a car), or both, just as in the unfamiliar objects condition.

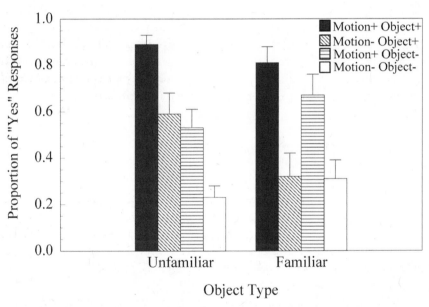

Figure 19.4. Results of Kersten and Smith (2002) Experiment 3. The y axis depicts the proportion of "yes" responses to the question "Is this one morping?" Motion+ object+ events involved both the correct motion and the correct object. Motion– object+ events involved the correct object performing the wrong motion. Motion+ object– events involved the correct motion performed by the wrong object. Motion– object– events involved the wrong object performing the wrong motion. (From "Attention to Novel Objects During Verb Learning," by A. W. Kersten and L. B. Smith, 2002, *Child Development*, 73, p. 105. Copyright 2002. Adapted with permission.)

The results of this experiment are depicted in figure 19.4. As can be seen, children in the familiar objects condition focused much more strongly on motions than on objects. In particular, children in the familiar objects condition were more likely to reject an event involving the correct object (i.e., a car) performing the wrong motion (i.e., moving away), than they were to reject an event involving the correct motion (i.e., moving into contact) performed by the wrong object (i.e., a truck). In contrast, children in the unfamiliar objects condition attended equally to objects and motions, in replication of the experiment described above. Comparing across the two conditions, children in the familiar objects condition were significantly more likely than children in the unfamiliar objects condition to reject an event involving the correct object but the wrong motion as an example of *morping*. If one takes the ability to associate a verb with a motion as one's measure of verb learning, then this result provides evidence in favor of the prediction that children should learn verbs more readily in the context of familiar objects than in the context of unfamiliar objects.

There is thus support for both of the above predictions regarding influences of object knowledge on verb learning. In particular, there is evidence that children learn verbs more readily in the context of familiar objects, perhaps because knowledge of an object and what it is capable of constrains the possible meanings of a verb in the context of that object. Furthermore, there is evidence that children learning verbs in the context of unfamiliar objects attend to those objects as well as the motions they are performing, perhaps because they are attempting to learn about those objects and the types of motions they are capable of.

The Generality of Influences of Object Knowledge on Verb Learning

The research described in the previous section provides evidence for an influence of object knowledge on verb learning. The question remains as to how general such influences are. In particular, does object knowledge influence the learning of all verbs, or is this influence limited to certain classes of verbs, with other classes of verbs being learned relatively independently of object knowledge?

A prediction that different classes of verbs will be differentially influenced by object knowledge comes from the research of Kersten (1998a, 1998b, 2003). Kersten proposed a distinction between two different classes of motion verbs. Extrinsic motion verbs involve the motion of an object with respect to a frame of reference external to that object, such a second object. For example, the verb *collide* describes the motion of one object into contact with a second object. In contrast, intrinsic motion verbs involve the motions of the parts of an object with respect to the object itself. For example, the verb *run* in the context of a human being describes the ways the arms and legs move with respect to the body of the human during locomotion. The terms extrinsic and intrinsic motion are closely related to the linguistic terms path and manner of motion (see e.g., Talmy, 1985), although extrinsic and intrinsic motion are more explicit about the nature of the perceptual information underlying those terms (see Jackendoff, 1987, for a related distinction). Thus, any differences in the processing of extrinsic motion and intrinsic motion verbs are likely to generalize to differences in the processing of path and manner of motion verbs.

Kersten (1998a) proposed that the meanings of intrinsic motion verbs are strongly dependent upon the nature of the object whose motion is being described. For example, the meaning of the verb *run* is very different in the context of the nouns *person, horse*, and *engine*. The reason for this close relationship between objects and intrinsic motions is that intrinsic motions are defined in terms of the relative motions of the parts of an object, and thus intrinsic motions are strongly dependent upon the way the parts of an object are configured. For example, the verb *run* describes pendular motions of the arms and legs with respect to the body when used in conjunction with a human being, but in the context of an object that does not have arms or legs (e.g., an engine), a very different meaning is brought to mind.

Kersten proposed a mechanism to account for this dependence of intrinsic motion verbs on object structure. In particular, he proposed that object categories (as well as the nouns that refer to these categories) include information not only about the static configuration of the parts of an object, but also about the typical ways those parts move in relation to one another. Stated differently, object categories are defined not only in terms of the static shape of an object, but also how the shape of an object changes over time. The role of an intrinsic motion verb, then, may be to select which of the various intrinsic motions associated with an object is relevant in a given instance. In particular, an intrinsic motion verb may carry only a generic meaning when used in isolation, but this generic meaning may be compared to each of the more specific intrinsic motions associated with an object in order to select one of these motions as being relevant. For example, the meaning of the verb *run* may mean little more than "to move rapidly" when used in isolation. When used in combination with the noun *person*, however, a more specific interpretation is selected involving the motions of arms and legs. If this same verb is used in conjunction with the noun *engine*, a very different interpretation is selected, involving the motions of valves and pistons. This mechanism thus accounts for the apparent dependence of intrinsic motion verbs on object structure, because the same verb will select different intrinsic motions when used in conjunction with different nouns.

In contrast to intrinsic motion verbs, Kersten (1998a) proposed that the meanings of extrinsic motion verbs are relatively independent of the nature of the objects carrying out those motions. Because the motion of an object is defined in terms of a frame of reference external to the object, the detailed structure of an object is irrelevant to the meanings of these verbs. For example, when describing the meaning of the verb *collide*, the two objects involved can be conceptualized as points or undifferentiated blobs, with those two points or blobs moving into contact with one another.

Kersten (1998a, 1998b) used a miniature artificial language learning task to provide evidence that intrinsic motion verbs are more dependent than extrinsic motion verbs on the meanings of the nouns that accompany them. Adult participants were presented with a series of animated events, similar to the ones employed by Kersten and Smith (2002). Each such event was accompanied by a sentence involving a novel noun and verb, such as "The zeebee is morping," presented orally through headphones. Each noun was related not only to the static characteristics of one of the bug-like creatures appearing in an event, but also a particular intrinsic motion, namely the way the legs of a bug moved in relation to its body (see figure 19.5), and a particular extrinsic motion, namely the direction the creature moved in relation to a second bug appearing on the screen. Thus, a participant could potentially have associated a noun with an intrinsic motion, an extrinsic motion, or both. Each verb was also related to a particular intrinsic motion and a particular extrinsic motion. Thus, a participant could similarly have associated a verb with an intrinsic motion, an extrinsic motion, or both.

After viewing a number of learning events, participants were tested on their knowledge of relations between nouns and verbs and the two different kinds of motion. Two different kinds of test trials were presented. In one type of trial, participants were tested on their knowledge of motions associated with individual nouns and verbs. In each such trial, participants were presented with two events, one after the other, and were asked to choose which of the two events was the better example of a particular noun or verb. The two events in a trial differed either on intrinsic motion or extrinsic motion. Each trial thus tested for knowledge of the relation between a particular noun or verb and a particular type of motion. For example, if the verb *morping* had always accompanied events in which one creature moved into contact with a second creature, a test of this relation would have involved presenting one event involving a creature moving into contact with a second creature, and a second event involving a creature moving away from a second creature, and asking participants which of these two events was the better example of the verb *morping*.

A second type of test trial involved presenting participants with combinations of nouns and verbs that had never gone together before. The nouns and verbs appearing in these combinations in fact made opposing predictions with regard to intrinsic motion and extrinsic motion. This second task was thus similar to the task of Gentner and France (1988) in which participants were asked to interpret combinations of nouns and verbs that were semantically mismatched. For example, if the noun *zeebee* had always accompanied events in which one creature moved into contact with a second creature, and the verb *spogging* had always accompanied

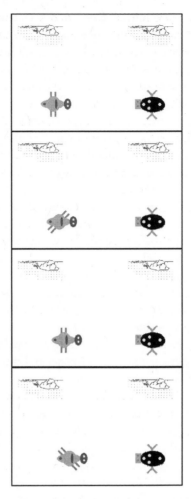

Figure 19.5. Four frames of an example event from Kersten (1998a), providing an example of an intrinsic motion of one of the buglike creatures. In the first frame, the creature starts the event with its legs at its sides. In the second frame, the creature angles its left legs forward and its right legs back as the creature as a whole moves forward. In the third frame, the legs of the creature return to its sides as the creature advances once more. In the fourth frame, the creature angles its right legs forward and its left legs back as the creature advances further. The legs of the creature would then return to its sides, starting the process over again. This sequence would continue until the end of the event, which in this event would occur when the two creatures came into contact with one another. (From "A Division of Labor Between Nouns and Verbs in the Representation of Motion," by A. W. Kersten, 1988, *Journal of Experimental Psychology: General, 127*, 34–54. Published by the American Psychological Association. Adapted with permission.)

events in which one creature moved away from a second creature, participants would now have been presented with the sentence "The zeebee is spogging." Participants were asked to choose which of two events was better described by each such sentence. In half of these trials, the two events in a test trial differed only on extrinsic motion. For example, one event may have involved a creature moving toward a second creature and one event may have involved a creature moving away from a second creature. In other trials, the two events differed only on intrinsic motion. In particular, one event involved a creature that moved its legs in the same way that previous zeebees had done, whereas the other event involved a creature that moved its legs in a manner consistent with previous examples of the verb *spogging*.

A measure of the influence of object knowledge on the interpretation of a motion verb can be derived by comparing participants' performance in these two types of test trials. For example, as a measure of the influence of object knowledge on the interpretation of an extrinsic motion verb, one can compare the likelihood of choosing the extrinsic motion associated with a verb when that verb appears alone, to the likelihood of choosing that same extrinsic motion when the verb appears with a semantically mismatched noun. The prediction from Kersten (1998a) is that nouns should have relatively little influence on the interpretation of extrinsic motion verbs, and thus participants should perform similarly on tests of extrinsic motion, regardless of whether or not a verb appears with a semantically mismatched noun.

One can also derive a measure of the influence of object knowledge on the interpretation of an intrinsic motion verb by comparing performance across these two types of test trials. The prediction from Kersten (1998a) is that nouns should have a much greater influence on tests of intrinsic motion than on tests of extrinsic motion. Thus, participants should be much less likely to choose the intrinsic motion associated with a verb when that verb appears with a semantically mismatched noun, compared to when that verb appears alone.

This analysis was applied to the results of the three experiments conducted by Kersten (1998a, 1998b) in which a direct comparison of intrinsic motion and extrinsic motion was possible. The results of this analysis are depicted in figure 19.6. The y axis in figure 19.6 represents the percentage decrease in verb-consistent responding resulting from the addition of a semantically mismatched noun. As can be seen, the addition of a semantically mismatched noun had relatively little influence on the interpretation of an extrinsic motion verb. In particular, participants chose the extrinsic motion associated with the verb almost as often in the presence of a semantically mismatched noun as they did when the verb appeared alone. In contrast, the addition of a semantically mismatched noun had a much greater influence on the interpretation of an intrinsic motion verb. In particular, participants were much less likely to select the intrinsic motion associated with a verb when that verb was accompanied by a noun associated with a different intrinsic motion.

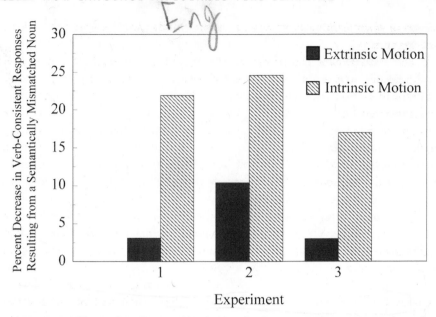

Figure 19.6. Effects of a semantically mismatched noun on the interpretation of extrinsic motion verbs and intrinsic motion verbs in three different experiments: (1) Kersten (1998a) Experiment 2, (2) Kersten (1998a) Experiment 5, and (3) Kersten (1998b) Experiment 1. The y axis represents the decrease in the percentage of choices consistent with the verb resulting from the addition of a semantically mismatched noun. For example, the leftmost bar for each experiment represents the percentage of trials in which participants chose the correct extrinsic motion associated with a verb when that verb was presented in isolation, minus the percentage of trials in which participants chose the extrinsic motion associated with a verb when that verb was presented along with a noun that was associated with a different extrinsic motion. The rightmost bar similarly represents performance on trials testing knowledge of intrinsic motion.

These results are consistent with the idea that the meanings of extrinsic motion verbs are less dependent upon object structure than are the meanings of intrinsic motion verbs. In particular, the meaning of an extrinsic motion verb may remain largely the same regardless of the nature of the objects carrying out that motion. These results may have implications for verb learning. In particular, a child may not need to learn about the nature of an object before learning the meaning of an extrinsic motion verb in the context of that object. Instead, that object may need only to be conceptualized as a point or a blob, allowing children to represent the motions of this point or blob with respect to its surroundings. Thus, one may make the prediction that children will exhibit less attention to object structure when learning an extrinsic motion verb than when learning an intrinsic motion verb.

Some support for this prediction comes from the research of Kersten and Smith (2002), who examined attention to novel objects during both the learning of extrinsic motion verbs and the learning of intrinsic motion verbs. In particular, in Experiment 1 of Kersten and Smith (2002), a particular verb (e.g., *morping*) was always accompanied by a particular object, which always moved on a particular path with respect to a second creature on the television screen (i.e., an extrinsic motion). In contrast, in Experiment 2, a particular verb was always accompanied by a particular object with a particular way of moving its legs (i.e., an intrinsic motion). Comparing across these two experiments, children were more likely to attend to novel objects when learning intrinsic motion verbs than when learning extrinsic motion verbs (see figure 19.3). In particular, children were more likely to reject an event on the basis of a change in object when the relevant type of motion was intrinsic than when the relevant type of motion was extrinsic.

The fact remains, however, that children exhibited significant attention to objects even in the context of an extrinsic motion verb. This finding would appear to be inconsistent with the theory that attention to object structure is not necessary to learn the meaning of an extrinsic motion verb. A possible reconciliation of these results with this theory, however, comes from the fact that all of the children in the research of Kersten and Smith (2002) were native English speakers. As pointed out by a number of researchers (e.g., Gennari, Sloman, Malt, & Fitch, 2001; Naigles & Terrazas, 1998; Slobin, 1996; Talmy, 1975), the most commonly used class of motion verbs in the English language describes the manner of motion of an object (e.g., *run, walk, skip, saunter*). Although the correspondence between manner of motion and intrinsic motion is not perfect, many of these verbs also fall into the category of intrinsic motion verbs. Because the interpretation of an intrinsic motion verb is strongly dependent upon the nature of the object carrying out that motion, children learning English may develop a general tendency to focus on objects in a verb learning context. Children may thus exhibit this tendency not only when they are learning an intrinsic motion verb, but also when they are learning an extrinsic motion verb, as in Experiment 1 of Kersten and Smith (2002).

Some evidence for this conjecture comes from a comparison of the results of Kersten and Smith (2002) on verb learning to the results of a study by Landau and Stecker (1990) examining the learning of novel prepositions. Landau and Stecker presented 3- and 5-year-old children with novel objects in different locations on a box. For some children, this arrangement was accompanied by a novel noun. In particular, children were told "This is a corp." For other children, this arrangement was accompanied by a novel preposition. In particular, children were told "This is acorp my box." Children were then tested on whether they thought these novel terms referred to objects, locations, or both. Children in the noun condition were found to attend exclusively to the object, ignoring the location of that objects. In contrast, children in the preposition condition attended exclusively to location, ignoring the identity of an object. Thus, whereas children in Kersten and Smith's (2002) study of verb learning attended just as strongly to objects as to motions, children in Landau and Stecker's (1990) study of preposition learning ignored objects and attended only to a static relation involving that object.

Although Landau and Stecker (1990) only presented children with static arrangements, their results may still have some bearing on the learning of motion words such as verbs. In particular, some of the first motion terms that English-speaking children learn are prepositions such as *in*, *out*, *up*, and *down* (Bowerman, 1978; Farwell, 1977; Gentner, 1982; Gopnik & Choi, 1995; Greenfield & Smith, 1976; McCune-Nicolich, 1981; Nelson, 1974; Smiley & Huttenlocher, 1995; Tomasello, 1987). As pointed out by Jackendoff (1987) and Talmy (1985), the motions described by such prepositions tend to be extrinsic in nature, describing the path of an object with respect to an external reference point. Thus, whereas verbs in English are learned in the context of intrinsic motion, prepositions may be learned primarily in the context of extrinsic motion. If the interpretation of extrinsic motion is indeed less dependent upon object structure than is the interpretation of intrinsic motion, this may explain the different results of Landau and Stecker (1990) and Kersten and Smith (2002). In particular, children in the study of Kersten and Smith (2002) may have attended to objects during verb learning because of their experience of learning a large number of intrinsic motion verbs, whose meanings are strongly dependent upon object structure. In contrast, children in the study of Landau and Stecker (1990) may not have attended to objects during preposition learning because of their experience of learning prepositions that convey extrinsic motion, whose meanings are less dependent upon object structure.

Attention to Novel Objects During Verb Learning in Japanese

The findings described in the previous section provide some evidence that extrinsic motion is less dependent upon object structure than is intrinsic motion. English-speaking children may thus attend strongly to object structure when learning verbs because of their prior learning of large numbers of intrinsic motion verbs. If this is the case, one may make the prediction that children who speak a language that makes less frequent use of intrinsic motion verbs and more frequent use of extrinsic motion verbs should show reduced attention to object structure during verb learning. One such language is Japanese. According to Slobin (2004), the most commonly used type of motion verb in Japanese describes the path of an object, a clear example of extrinsic motion. Thus, if extrinsic motion is indeed less dependent upon object structure than is intrinsic motion, one may make the prediction that Japanese children should attend less to object structure during verb learning than do English-speaking children.

Kersten, Smith, and Yoshida (2005) tested this prediction by presenting 4- to 5.5-year-old Japanese- and English-speaking children with the stimuli employed by Kersten and Smith (2002). The method for the English-speaking children was identical to that used in Experiment 1 of Kersten and Smith (2002). The method for the Japanese children was the same, except that all of the instructions were presented in Japanese by a native speaker and Japanese-sounding novel words were employed. In particular, English-speaking children heard "This one is morping" when they saw an event in which a creature with a rounded, orange body with red spots on it moved into contact with a second creature, whereas Japanese children heard "Kore wa mobette-iru yo" ("This is mobetting") when they saw this event. In contrast, English-speaking children heard "This one is spogging" when they saw an event in which a creature with a rectangular, purple body with gray spots on it moved away from a second creature, whereas Japanese children heard "Kore wa sokutte-iru yo" ("This is sokutting") when they saw this event. Thus, children could have associated these novel words with a particular creature, a particular motion, or both.

As in the study of Kersten and Smith (2002), children were tested by presenting them with events that were either identical to or somewhat different from the previous examples of a particular verb, and asking them if these were still examples of that verb. Some of these events were identical to previous examples of the verb, some involved the correct motion performed by wrong creature, some involved the correct creature performing the wrong motion, and some involved both an incorrect creature and an incorrect motion. English-speaking children were asked the question "Is this one morping?" along with each such test event, whereas Japanese children were asked "Kore wa mobette-imasuka?" ("Is this mobetting?"). If a prior language learning history involving a preponderance of extrinsic motion verbs indeed causes Japanese children to attend less to object structure during verb learning, then Japanese children would be expected to be less likely than English-speaking children to reject an event as an example of a verb as a result of a change in the creature participating in that event.

The results of this study, however, revealed nearly identical patterns of performance in the two language groups. In particular, both groups were more likely to reject an event as an example of a verb as a result of a change in motion than as a result of a change in the creature carrying out that motion. A change in creature also produced a significant reduction in children's willingness to accept an event as an example of a verb, however. The magnitude of this effect was almost identical in Japanese- and English-speaking children, suggesting that the two groups of children attended similarly to object structure during verb learning.

This result runs counter to the prediction that speakers of a language that makes frequent use of extrinsic motion verbs should exhibit less attention to object structure during verb learning than do speakers of a language that makes more frequent use of intrinsic motion verbs. There are a number of possible explanations for this discrepancy. One explanation is that the proposed distinction between intrinsic and extrinsic motion verbs in their sensitivity to object structure is wrong. Stated in a more positive light, an influence of object knowledge on the interpretation of a verb may be an even more general phenomenon than originally proposed, applying to verbs in general rather than just to specific classes of verbs. Thus, the meanings of extrinsic motion verbs, as well as the meanings of intrinsic motion verbs, may be dependent upon the nature of the object whose motions are being predicated, encouraging children to attend to object structure in order to help them determine what a verb may mean in the context of a particular object.

A second possibility is that the similar pattern of performance in Japanese and English-speaking children derives from the fact that English and Japanese are not entirely different in their verb conflation patterns. In particular, English as well as Japanese employs extrinsic path of motion verbs (e.g., *come, arrive, enter, exit*), although they may not be used as frequently as intrinsic manner of motion verbs (Naigles, Eisenberg, Kako, Highter, & McGraw, 1998). Moreover, Japanese as well as English employs intrinsic manner of motion verbs (Koike, 2003), although they may not be used as frequently as are extrinsic path of motion verbs (Slobin, 2004). The fact that children learning Japanese are sometimes confronted with intrinsic motion verbs, whose meanings are strongly dependent upon object structure, may encourage them to attend to object structure to help them determine the meaning of these verbs. If this happened with sufficient frequency, it could potentially cause Japanese children to develop a general strategy of attending to object structure during verb learning, similar to that seen in English-speaking children.

This idea could explain the apparent discrepancy between the results of Landau and Stecker (1990) on preposition learning in English and the results of Kersten et al. (2005) on verb learning in Japanese. The most likely type of motion to be conveyed by each of these word types is extrinsic motion. Japanese verbs also sometimes convey intrinsic motion, however, and thus Japanese children may learn that attention to object structure is sometimes useful in order to learn the meaning of a verb. In contrast, the use of English prepositions to convey intrinsic motion may be much rarer (Jackendoff, 1987; Talmy, 1975).[1] Thus, English-speaking children may generally be able to learn the meanings of prepositions without reference to the nature of the object whose motion is being described, accounting for Landau and Stecker's finding that English-speaking children ignore object structure when learning prepositions.

If Japanese children's attention to object structure during verb learning indeed results from the existence of intrinsic motion verbs in Japanese, then it remains possible that children who are exposed to a language that does not employ intrinsic motion verbs will not develop a tendency to focus on object structure during verb learning. It is not clear if any such languages exist, however. For example, Romance languages such as Spanish are frequently cited as examples of languages in which the use of extrinsic path of motion verbs is preferred (see e.g.,

Gennari et al., 2001; Slobin, 1996; Talmy, 1985), but intrinsic manner of motion verbs are still preferred in certain contexts even in Spanish (Naigles et al., 1998; Naigles & Terrazas, 1998).

A third possible account of the similar patterns of performance in Japanese and English-speaking children is that attention to object structure during verb learning does not represent a verb learning strategy per se but rather represents a generalization of a tendency acquired in the context of learning nouns. In particular, there is now a substantial body of evidence suggesting that attention to object shape increases over early word learning, as children acquire a large vocabulary of shape-based nouns (e.g., Gershkoff-Stowe & Smith, 2004; Smith, 1999). One possible explanation for children's attention to objects during verb learning is that a tendency to focus on object shape, acquired in the context of noun learning, generalizes to the learning of other types of words such as verbs. If the meanings of intrinsic motion verbs are in fact strongly dependent upon the nature of the object in motion, then this attention to object shape may actually be beneficial to verb learning, especially for children learning languages such as English that frequently employ intrinsic motion verbs. This attention to objects may be less useful when learning verbs in a language such as Japanese that more frequently employs extrinsic motion verbs, but may occur nonetheless as a result of prior noun learning.

This account could explain the verb learning results of Kersten and Smith (2002) and Kersten et al. (2005) by proposing that there exist multiple, competing influences on children's attention in a verb-learning context. In particular, children may learn at a relatively early age to attend to object shape in word-learning context, as a result of learning a large number of nouns that can be readily discriminated on the basis of shape. This attention to shape may not be limited to a noun-learning context, but rather may generalize to the learning of other types of words such as verbs and adjectives (see Smith, Jones, & Landau, 1992, for evidence with regard to adjectives). As children later start to learn large numbers of verbs, they may learn that attention to motion is also useful in the context of verb learning. The performance of children in the studies of Kersten and Smith (2002) and Kersten et al. (2005) may reflect a combination of these two influences. In particular, cues to a word-learning context may elicit attention to object shape, whereas the syntactic and morphological markers of a verb may elicit attention to motion, resulting in attention being directed to both of these types of information.

This account could also explain why Japanese- and English-speaking children perform so similarly in a verb learning task despite the differences in the types of motion encoded by verbs in the two languages. In particular, attention to object structure may reflect one's prior noun learning history, and this noun learning history may be quite similar for speakers of the two languages. Although Japanese and English nouns differ with regard to the count/mass distinction (Imai & Gentner, 1997; Soja, Carey, & Spelke, 1991), animate objects such as the buglike creatures employed in the Kersten et al. (2005) study are treated as count nouns in both languages. Thus, the presence of an animate object may elicit attention to object shape in speakers of both languages, even in a verb learning context.

This account leaves open the possibility that differences in the verb learning performance of Japanese- and English-speaking children may emerge later in development. In particular, young children may exhibit a universal tendency to focus on objects in a word learning context, a tendency that was acquired in the context of learning nouns. As children get older, syntactic cues may become increasingly important in driving attention to different attributes of a stimulus, overwhelming this more general tendency to focus on objects. Thus, differences between Japanese- and English-speaking children may become evident only after this initial tendency to focus on objects is overcome. It would be interesting to test whether adult speakers of English and Japanese differ in any measurable degree in their verb learning performance given the different structure of their languages.

Further research is needed to determine which of these explanations best accounts for the similarity in the performance of Japanese and English-speaking children in a verb learning task. For example, an approach that could be used to test for influences of one's prior noun learning history on subsequent verb learning would involve testing speakers of different languages in a context in which their prior noun learning histories differed. For example, English and Japanese differ in their treatment of simple objects such as bricks, with English treating them as count nouns (i.e., a brick), and Japanese treating them as mass nouns (i.e., a piece of clay). Thus, Japanese-speaking children learn to attend to the substance of such an object in the context of a novel noun, whereas English-speaking children attend to its shape (Imai & Gentner, 1997). If Japanese- and English-speaking children were presented with the motions of such an object along with a novel verb, they could be tested to see to what extent they attended to the shape and substance of the object, as well as its motion. If attention to objects during verb learning reflects one's prior noun learning history, then Japanese- and English-speaking children would also be expected to attend differently to shapes and substances in a verb learning context.

Conclusion

The research reviewed in this chapter provides evidence that children attend not only to motions but also to object structure when learning verbs. This strategy may reflect the nature of verb meanings, which vary considerably in the context of different objects. Thus, children may attempt to learn about an object and the types of motion it is capable of in order to help them figure out what a verb means in the context of that object. Different types of verbs may differ in the extent to which they are dependent upon object structure, however. In particular, intrinsic motion verbs, which describe the relative motions of the parts of an object, may be strongly dependent upon the static configuration of those parts. Extrinsic motion verbs, on the other hand, which describe the motion of an object as a whole with respect to an external reference frame, may not be as dependent on object structure. Instead, one may be able to conceptualize the objects taking part in these motions as points or blobs, without needing to flesh out the detailed structure of these objects.

Evidence for a distinction between intrinsic motion and extrinsic motion verbs in their dependence on object structure is still quite limited. Speakers of English and Japanese, two languages that differ in their use of intrinsic and extrinsic motion verbs, show similar patterns of attention to objects and motions in a verb learning task. This may suggest that attention to object structure is useful not only in the learning of intrinsic motion verbs but also in the learning of extrinsic motion verbs. Alternatively, attention to object structure during verb learning may reflect a generalization of tendencies acquired in a noun learning context. These tendencies may be useful when learning an intrinsic motion verb, encouraging attention to the structure of an object and thus allowing children to constrain the possible meanings of the verb. These tendencies may be less useful when learning extrinsic motion verbs. Further research involving the motions of novel objects is needed in order to better understand the role of object knowledge in the acquisition of verbs.

Acknowledgments This research was supported by NICHD Grant R01MH60200-05. Animated examples of the stimuli used in this research are available at http://www.science.fau.edu/psychology/akersten/home.html.

Note

1. When used as verb particles in combination with particular verbs, prepositions do sometimes convey intrinsic motions. For example, the verb-particle combination *reach out* describes a way of moving the arms in relation to the body, making it an example of intrinsic motion. Such uses may represent metaphorical extensions of the more basic meanings of these prepositions, however, which appear to primarily convey locations and motions with respect to an external reference frame (Lindner, 1982).

References

Au, T. K., Dapretto, M., & Song, Y. K. (1994). Input vs. constraints: Early word acquisition in Korean and English. *Journal of Memory and Language, 33*, 567–582.

Behrend, D. A. (1990). The development of verb concepts: Children's use of verbs to label familiar and novel events. *Child Development, 61*, 681–696.

Bloom, L. (1981). The importance of language for language development: Linguistic determinism in the 1980s. *Annals of the New York Academy of Sciences, 379*, 160–171.

Bowerman, M. (1978). The acquisition of word meanings: An investigation of some current conflicts. In P. J. Johnson-Laird & P. C. Wason (Eds.), *Thinking: Readings in cognitive science* (pp. 239–253). New York: Cambridge University Press.

Brown, R. (1957). Linguistic determinism and the part of speech. *Journal of Abnormal and Social Psychology, 55*, 1–5.

Choi, S., & Gopnik, A. (1995). Early acquisition of verbs in Korean: A cross-linguistic study. *Journal of Child Language, 22*, 497–529.

Farwell, C. B. (1977). The primacy of goal in the child's description of motion and location. *Papers and Reports in Child Language Development, 13*, 126–133.

Forbes, J. N., & Farrar, J. M. (1995). Learning to represent word meaning: What initial training events reveal about children's developing action verb concepts. *Cognitive Development, 10*, 1–20.

Gennari, S. P., Sloman, S. A., Malt, B. C., & Fitch, W. T. (2002). Motion events in language and cognition. *Cognition, 83*, 49–79.

Gentner, D. (1981). Some interesting differences between verbs and nouns. *Cognition and Brain Theory, 4*, 161–178.

Gentner, D. (1982). Why nouns are learned before verbs: Linguistic relativity versus natural partitioning. In S. Kuczaj II (Ed.), *Language development, volume 2: Language, thought, and culture* (pp. 301–334). Hillsdale, NJ: Erlbaum.

Gentner, D., & Boroditsky, L. (2001). Individuation, relativity, and early word learning. In M. Bowerman & S. Levinson (Eds.), *Language acquisition and conceptual development* (pp. 215–256). Cambridge: Cambridge University Press.

Gentner, D., & France, I. M. (1988). The verb mutability effect: Studies of the combinatorial semantics of nouns and verbs. In S. L. Small, G. W. Cottrell, & M. K. Tanenhaus (Eds.), *Lexical ambiguity resolution: Perspectives from psycholinguistics, neuropsychology, and artificial intelligence* (pp. 343–382). San Mateo, CA: Kaufman.

Gershkoff-Stowe, L., & Smith, L. B. (2004). Shape and the first hundred nouns. *Child Development, 75*, 1098–1114.

Gopnik, A., & Choi, S. (1995). Names, relational words, and cognitive development in English and Korean speakers: Nouns are not always learned before verbs. In M. Tomasello & W. E. Merriman (Eds.), *Beyond names for things: Young children's acquisition of verbs* (pp. 63–80). Hillsdale, NJ: Erlbaum.

Greenfield, P. M., & Smith, J. H. (1976). *The structure of communication in early language development.* New York: Academic Press.

Imai, M., & Gentner, D. (1997). A cross-linguistic study of early word meaning: Universal ontology and linguistic influence. *Cognition, 62*, 169–200.

Jackendoff, R. (1987). On beyond zebra: The relation of linguistic and visual information. *Cognition, 26*, 115–122.

Kersten, A. W. (1998a). A division of labor between nouns and verbs in the representation of motion. *Journal of Experimental Psychology: General, 127*, 34–54.

Kersten, A. W. (1998b). An examination of the distinction between nouns and verbs: Associations with two different kinds of motion. *Memory and Cognition, 26*, 1214–1232.

Kersten, A. W. (2003). Verbs and nouns convey different types of motion in event descriptions. *Linguistics, 41*, 917–945.

Kersten, A. W., & Earles, J. L. (2004). Semantic context influences memory for verbs more than memory for nouns. *Memory and Cognition, 32*, 198–211.

Kersten, A. W., & Smith, L. B. (2002). Attention to novel objects during verb learning. *Child Development, 73*, 93–109.

Kersten, A. W., Smith, L. B., & Yoshida, H. (2005). Attention to novel objects during verb learning in Japanese and English-speaking children. Manuscript submitted for publication.

Koike, Y. (2003). The acquisition of Japanese motion verbs: Lexicalization types and the interaction between verbs and particles. *Dissertation Abstracts International Section A: Humanities and Social Sciences, 64*, 880.

Landau, B., & Stecker, D. S. (1990). Objects and places: Geometric and syntactic representations in early lexical learning. *Cognitive Development, 5*, 287–312.

Lindner, S. (1982). What goes up doesn't necessarily come down: The ins and outs of opposites. In K. Tuite, R. Schneider, & R. Chametzky (Eds.), *Papers from the eighteenth regional meeting of the Chicago Linguistic Society* (pp. 305–323). Chicago: University of Chicago.

McCune-Nicolich, L. (1981). The cognitive bases of relational words in the single word period. *Journal of Child Language, 8*, 15–34.

Naigles, L., Eisenberg, A., Kako, E., Highter, M., & McGraw, N. (1998). Speaking of motion: Verb use in English and Spanish. *Language and Cognitive Processes, 13*, 521–549.

Naigles, L. R., & Terrazas, P. (1998). Motion-verb generalizations in English and Spanish: Influences of language and syntax. *Psychological Science, 9*, 363–369.

Nelson, K. (1974). Concept, word, and sentence: Interrelations in acquisition and development. *Psychological Review, 81*, 267–285.

Posner, M. I., & Keele, S. W. (1968). On the genesis of abstract ideas. *Journal of Experimental Psychology, 77*, 353–363.

Posner, M. I., & Keele, S. W. (1970). Retention of abstract ideas. *Journal of Experimental Psychology, 83*, 304–308.

Slobin, D. I. (1996). Two ways to travel: Verbs of motion in English and Spanish. In M. Shibatani & S.A. Thompson (Eds.), *Grammatical constructions: Their form and meaning* (pp. 195–219). Oxford: Clarendon Press.

Slobin, D. I. (2004). The many ways to search for a frog: Linguistic typology and the expression of motion events. In S. Strömqvist & L. Verhoeven (Eds.), *Relating events in narrative: Vol. 2. Typological and contextual perspectives* (pp. 219–257). Mahwah, NJ: Erlbaum.

Smiley, P., & Huttenlocher, J. (1995). Conceptual development and the child's early words for events, objects, and persons. In M. Tomasello & W. E. Merriman (Eds.), *Beyond names for things: Young children's acquisition of verbs*. Hillsdale, NJ: Erlbaum.

Smith, L. B. (1999). Children's noun learning: How general processes make specialized learning mechanisms. In B. MacWhinney (Ed.), *The emergence of language: 28th Carnegie Symposium on Cognition* (pp. 277–304). Mahwah, NJ: Erlbaum.

Smith, L. B., Jones, S. S., & Landau, B. (1992). Count nouns, adjectives, and perceptual properties in children's novel word interpretations. *Developmental Psychology, 28*, 273–286.

Soja, N. N., Carey, S., & Spelke, E. S. (1991). Ontological categories guide young children's inductions of word meaning: Object terms and substance terms. *Cognition, 38*, 179–211.

Talmy, L. (1975). Semantics and syntax of motion. In J. Kimball (Ed.), *Syntax and semantics* (Vol. 4, pp. 181–238). San Mateo, CA: Academic Press.

Talmy, L. (1985). Lexicalization patterns: Semantic structure in lexical forms. In T. Shopen (Ed.), *Language typology and linguistic description: Vol. 3. Grammatical categories and the lexicon* (pp. 57–149). New York: Cambridge University Press.

Tardif, T. (1996). Nouns are not always learned before verbs: Evidence from Mandarin speakers' early vocabularies. *Developmental Psychology, 32,* 492–504.

Tardif, T., Gelman, S., & Xu, F. (1999). Putting the noun bias in context: A comparison of English and Mandarin. *Child Development, 70,* 620–635.

Tomasello, M. (1987). Learning to use prepositions: A case study. *Journal of Child Language, 14,* 79–98.

20 East and West: A Role for Culture in the Acquisition of Nouns and Verbs

Tracy A. Lavin, D. Geoffrey Hall,
and Sandra R. Waxman

How do verb learning and noun learning differ? The consensus in the early word learning literature is that children acquire nouns earlier and more rapidly than verbs (e.g., Bates et al., 1994; Benedict, 1979; Gentner, 1982; Huttenlocher & Smiley, 1987; Macnamara, 1972; Nelson, 1973). This pattern has been widely interpreted as an indication that verb learning relies on a more sophisticated apprehension of the semantic and syntactic structure of language than does noun learning. Two versions of this argument have been put forth: one is based on a syntactic bootstrapping view of verb learning and focuses primarily on the different linguistic requirements of learning nouns and verbs; the second is based on a natural partitions account of the differences between nouns and verbs and addresses the perceptual and conceptual differences in the concepts labeled by nouns and verbs. Both views make similar predictions about the course of early noun and verb learning.

According to the syntactic bootstrapping account (e.g., Gleitman, 1990; Gleitman & Gleitman, 1992; Landau & Gleitman, 1985; Naigles, 1990), the acquisition of verbs is delayed relative to the acquisition of nouns because nouns (particularly those with concrete, imageable referents) can be acquired through direct observation of the real world contexts in which they are heard. This contextual information is available from the beginning of lexical development; however, it does not provide adequate support for verb learning. Acquiring verbs depends not just on direct observations of the world, but also on the linguistic information that is conveyed through the argument structures in which verbs occur. This linguistic information is not available to young children until they have developed some understanding of the relationship between sentence structure and verb meaning in the particular language they are acquiring. By this account, the delay in verb learning is a logical consequence of relying on argument structure to infer the meaning of a novel verb.

The natural partitions and relational relativity hypotheses (Gentner, 1982; Gentner & Boroditsky, 2001) also predict a delay in the onset of verb learning but focus on different issues. At stake here is the observation that there is a real world distinction between the concepts labeled by nouns and those labeled by verbs. Relatively speaking, the referents of nouns come in tidy preindividuated packages that are easy to pick out and serve as good candidates for word learning. The relational concepts labeled by verbs are more nebulous and (even for concrete, observable actions) the mapping between verbs and the particular aspects of the world that they encode is highly variable across languages (e.g., in some languages verbs of motion encode manner of motion while others encode path of motion; Papafragou, Massey, & Gleitman, 2002). By this account, the mapping between nouns and their referents is relatively stable and straightforward and should, therefore, be accessible to the youngest word learners; however, the variable nature of the mapping between verbs and their referents across languages implies that children need to discover the language-specific semantic patterns of verbs in their particular language before they can start acquiring verbs.

On one hand, all is well. Two distinct theories of word learning, addressing the problem from different perspectives, both converge on the same prediction: noun learning should precede verb learning in development. There is good empirical evidence in support of the prediction: children do show the expected noun bias in their early word learning. On the other hand, something is missing. Logically, according to the syntactic bootstrapping story, once learners begin to recover and utilize argument structures to arrive at verb meaning—once the problem has been solved—verb learning should surge ahead. Similarly, according to the natural partitions story, once learners begin to unravel the language-specific semantic patterns of verbs, verb learning should advance dramatically. Yet this does not seem to be the case. Despite the fact that children have at least some of the necessary verb learning structures in place by their second birthday, noun learning seems to outstrip verb learning from the outset of lexical acquisition until the third birthday (Gentner, 1982). For example, Naigles (1990, 1996) has shown that by 2 years of age, toddlers can use syntactic structure to draw suitable inferences about the meaning of a novel verb. Choi, McDonough, Bowerman, and Mandler (1999) have shown that, by 18 months, children have worked out some of the important language-specific semantic patterns associated with relational terms. If children can solve the problems associated with verb learning by the age of two, why then does verb learning lag behind noun learning for at least another full year?

Before addressing this question, let us first consider the current status of the "noun bias" in the study of early word learning. The position that all children learn many nouns and few verbs early in their word learning careers has been the subject of some controversy. A number of researchers have argued that early word learning is not *universally* characterized by an early emphasis on nouns. On the other hand, several researchers have argued that the noun bias is, in fact, a universal feature of early word learning. Choi and Gopnik (1995; Gopnik & Choi, 1995;

Gopnik, Choi, & Baumberger, 1996) have collected data showing that children acquiring Korean as their first language learn nouns and verbs at an equivalent rate. Similarly, Tardif and her colleagues (Tardif, 1996; Tardif, Gelman, & Xu, 1999; Tardif, Shatz, & Naigles, 1997) have shown that children acquiring Mandarin do not show a delay in verb learning relative to noun learning. These findings suggest that children can proceed with efficient verb learning at or around the time that noun learning takes off. However, a number of studies have yielded contradictory findings showing that children acquiring a wide variety of languages, including Dutch, French, Hebrew, Italian, Japanese, Kaluli, Korean, Mandarin, Navajo, Spanish, and Turkish, do show a delay between noun and verb learning that is similar to the pattern seen in English-learning children (Au, Dapretto, & Song, 1994; Bornstein et al., 2004; Fernald & Morikawa, 1993; Gentner, 1982; Gentner & Boroditsky; 2004; Kim, McGregor, & Thompson, 2000).

On the surface, the question of the universality of the noun bias in early word learning appears to be a relatively straightforward empirical one. If it is clear that children acquiring English show a noun bias, it should be equally clear that children acquiring other languages either do or do not show a noun bias, whichever the case may be. However, the introduction of cross-linguistic comparisons into the study of early word learning raises a number of difficult methodological issues. The core issue revolves around the problem of discovering and counting all the words in any child's vocabulary. That is, in order to determine whether a child acquiring a particular language shows a noun bias in her word learning, one must first determine how many nouns and verbs she has in her vocabulary. This already difficult problem is further complicated by the fact that different approaches to measuring early vocabulary have produced different results and by the fact that any cross-linguistic differences may be either exaggerated or obscured through interactions with different methods of assessing vocabularies.

Two general approaches to measuring early vocabularies have been used, and the differences in the results of different studies are likely the result of biases in these approaches. One method involves gathering naturalistic samples of children's productive speech and extrapolating on that basis the relative proportions of nouns and verbs in children's vocabularies. The second method uses maternal reports (e.g., MCDI checklists) to gather information from mothers about their children's vocabularies. Studies that rely on speech samples usually indicate that children acquiring some languages (e.g., Korean or Mandarin) do not show a noun bias in their early word learning, while those relying on maternal reports tend to report a universal noun bias. Why might these measures yield such different outcomes? Both approaches have systematic biases that can distort estimates of the words in children's vocabularies. On the one hand, checklist measures inflate the proportion of nouns in children's vocabularies (Pine, Lieven, & Rowland, 1996): Mothers seem to be more exhaustive in their reports of the nouns their children know than of the verbs. To make matters worse, this exaggeration is particularly pronounced for American mothers compared to Chinese mothers (Tardif et al., 1999). On the other hand, children's speech samples are not unproblematic either, because the type and number of words children produce vary widely as a function of several factors, including the context in which the sample is gathered. Children tend to emphasize nouns during book reading sessions and verbs during play sessions (Tardif et al., 1999). These differences become particularly problematic in the context of cross-linguistic research because the available evidence indicates that American children produce relatively more nouns during book reading and Chinese children produce relatively more verbs during play sessions (Tardif et al., 1999). One solution to these methodological problems is to combine several methods of assessing vocabularies. It is not clear, though, that composite measures would resolve the matter because the systematic biases of each measure seem to play out differently for children acquiring different languages. Thus, there is no guarantee that the various means of counting vocabulary items will balance each other out to provide a cleaner index of word learning.

Despite these concerns, one clear point does emerge from the cross-linguistic research: Regardless of which language is studied and which vocabulary measure is used, verb learning never outstrips noun learning. Although a noun bias may not be a universal feature of word learning, there is no evidence for a verb bias. This state of affairs suggests that the predictions made by the syntactic bootstrapping and natural partitions hypotheses are widely borne out. On the other hand, though the advantage for noun over verb learning is never reversed, it does appear to vary across children who are learning different languages. Because these cross-linguistic differences in the relative rates of noun and verb learning cannot be accounted for by either syntactic bootstrapping or natural partitions, it is important to investigate other factors that may influence the course of noun and verb learning.

One step in this direction, is to avoid entirely the problematic task of counting words in children's vocabularies and to opt instead for a laboratory-based word learning task. This approach would allow us to investigate factors that influence the process of word learning rather than relying on some measure of its outcome. Several factors relevant to the acquisition of nouns and verbs have already been given considerable attention, including features of the language and social/pragmatic cues to word meaning. With respect to languages, typically, the emphasis is on structural features, like word order, morphology, or noun ellipsis, that differ across languages. For example, for children exposed to English, nouns might be more salient or more frequent than verbs in the input; for children exposed to languages like Mandarin or Korean, verbs might be more salient or more frequent than nouns (e.g., Gentner, 1982; Tardif et al., 1997). However, although there is some evidence that the distribution of words in the input influences the pattern of lexical development (e.g., Naigles & Hoff-Ginsberg, 1998), children's vocabularies clearly reflect more than just the frequency and salience of words in the input (Gentner, 1982)—otherwise, children's first words would consist of items like *the* and *you*.

With respect to social and pragmatic factors, there is a growing consensus that lexical development is a multiply determined process (e.g., Hall & Waxman, 2004; Hollich et al., 2000; Woodward & Markman, 1998)—that word learners exploit a variety of sources of information—and, in particular, that social-pragmatic cues can be (one of several) reliable guides to the meaning of novel words (e.g., Clark, 1997; Tomasello, Kruger, & Ratner, 1993). Recent work has focused on children's understanding of intentional cues as guides to meaning (e.g., Baldwin et al., 1996; Poulin-Dubois & Forbes, 2002; Tomasello & Barton, 1994); however, many other aspects of the social contexts in which children acquire novel words can potentially provide reliable information about word meaning. Recent work in cultural psychology suggests that in different cultures, social cues may emphasize different sources of information and, in particular, some cultures may highlight information that supports noun learning and others may highlight information that supports verb learning.

Evidence that different cues to word learning might be more or less salient in different cultures comes from research showing that members of Eastern cultures tend to engage preferentially in a holistic style of reasoning, while members of Western cultures tend to engage in more analytic reasoning. These differences have been demonstrated in a variety of domains (Markus & Kitayama, 1991; Nisbett, Peng, Choi, & Norenzayan, 2001). Two lines of research—one focusing on categorization and the other involving memory and attention—suggest that, as a consequence of their analytic reasoning style, members of Western cultures may be particularly attentive to sources of information that are helpful in acquiring nouns, while members of Eastern cultures, as a consequence of their holistic reasoning style, may be more attentive to verb-relevant sources of information.

In categorization tasks, Easterners have shown a preference for relational categories while Westerners show a preference for taxonomic categories (Ji, Zhang, & Nisbett, 2004). For example, when shown pictures of a monkey, a panda, and a banana and asked to choose two items that form a category, Chinese participants are more likely to choose the monkey and the banana (focusing on the relation "eat") and Americans are more likely to choose the monkey and the panda (forming a taxonomic category like "mammals" or "animals"). In memory tasks, Easterners seem to be attentive to relationships between objects, while Westerners are more attentive to the objects themselves, especially salient focal objects. For example, Masuda and Nisbett (2001) showed Japanese and Americans animated underwater scenes and later asked participants to describe what they had seen. The Japanese made more references than the Americans to relationships between different objects in the scene and between objects and the background. The Americans focused more on describing individual objects.

This difference in focus could be relevant to the acquisition of nouns and verbs. Individual objects and taxonomic categories are usually labeled with nouns while thematic relations are generally captured by verbs. If Westerners are particularly attentive to the kind of information that is most useful in learning nouns and

Easterners are more attentive to information useful for learning verbs and if these cultural differences are in place early enough in development to play a role in the initial stages word learning, then we should expect to find systematic cultural differences in early lexical development. Western children should be more focused on learning nouns and Eastern children should be more focused on learning verbs. As a result, Western children may acquire many more nouns than verbs in the early stages of word learning—not simply because of the learning requirements of nouns and verbs, but because noun-relevant information is more salient in Western cultures. Eastern children may show more of a balance between noun learning and verb learning because their cultural experiences make them more attuned to verb-relevant information, which may reduce the impact of the more stringent requirements imposed on verb learning.

In recent work, we have extended an experimental task developed by Gillette, Gleitman, Gleitman, and Lederer (1999) to explore the role of cultural factors in word learning. The task involves simulating, for adult participants, some of the conditions of early word learning. In particular, participants view spontaneous mother-toddler interactions from which all linguistic information has been deleted—on the assumption that linguistic information is unavailable to very young word learners. The question is, What information can participants recover from the nonlinguistic contextual information? Gillette et al. (1999) hypothesized that when faced with these conditions in typical early word learning scenarios, children can learn nouns but not verbs, for which they need more linguistic information. If this is true, then adults should also be able to learn nouns but not verbs when faced with a simulation of these conditions—according to the logic of the task.

The simulation of early word learning is accomplished by showing adults short videos of mothers interacting with their toddlers. The videos are presented without sound so that participants are provided with rich contextual information but no linguistic information. The videos depict scenarios in which mothers use particular target words, and the participants' task is to determine what those words are. Some of these target words are nouns and the others are verbs. Although identifying an already acquired word for an adult is undeniably different from learning de novo a novel word for a toddler, the task does offer information concerning the differences involved in learning a noun versus a verb for a learner armed only with contextual information as a guide to meaning.

As predicted, Gillette et al. (1999) found that participants were more successful in identifying the target words that were nouns (45% of targets correctly identified) than those that were verbs (15% of targets correctly identified). These results were interpreted as showing that adults in a simulated vocabulary learning task, just like children engaged in real word learning, can successfully identify nouns on the basis on nonlinguistic contextual information but they need more information in order to correctly identify verbs. Under this interpretation, these findings provide support for a syntactic bootstrapping view of verb learning. There is, however, an alternative interpretation: it is also possible that the (Western)

participants in the Gillette et al. (1999) study performed especially well in the identification of target nouns because they were particularly attentive to noun-relevant information. This alternative could not be explored within the Gillette et al. (1999) design because all of the participants were Westerners; however, we have used a modified version of the same design to address just this possibility.

We adapted the simulated vocabulary learning task in two ways to consider the role of cultural factors. First, we included both Eastern and Western participants. If Easterners are more attentive than Westerners to verb-relevant information, then they should show better success with verbs in the simulated vocabulary learning task. Second, we modified the procedure so that we would be able to gain more insight into the question of whether Easterners and Westerners do, in fact, attend to different kinds of information. Unlike Gillette et al. (1999), we did not provide participants with any information concerning the lexical categories of target words. As a result, we expected that participants who were more attentive to noun-relevant information would include relatively more nouns among their responses, and that participants who were more attentive to verb-relevant information would include relatively more verbs.

Except for these two modifications, our simulated vocabulary learning task was very similar to the procedure developed by Gillette and her colleagues (1999). Participants watched video clips of Western, English-speaking mothers interacting with their toddlers. They saw silent video clips of mothers using particular target words while interacting with their toddlers. The participants' task was to guess what those words were. The scenes were drawn from video footage of four mothers interacting with their 18- to 25-month-old toddlers. Each of the mother-toddler pairs was videotaped in their own home while engaging in a naturalistic free play session. Sixteen target words (8 nouns and 8 verbs) were selected from among the most frequently occurring words in the transcripts of the mothers' speech during the free play sessions, and video clips in which the mothers used those words were selected from the video footage. We selected six token utterances of each target word with only one of the target words occurring in each clip. The clips were roughly 40 seconds long, with 30 seconds of (silent) footage before and 10 seconds after the target word utterance. In some cases, the target word was used more than once within a 40-second window: in those cases, there was 30 seconds of footage before the first utterance and 10 seconds following the last utterance. As a result of these repetitions, the six token utterances for a given target word were spread over three to six separate video clips (depending on how many of the clips contained multiple token utterances).

Participants were told that they would see short videos of mothers interacting with their toddlers and that they would not be able to hear what the mothers and toddlers were saying because the soundtrack had been removed. Instead, they would hear a tone whenever the mothers used particular words, and their task was to guess what those words were. We told them that they would see six different instances in which the words were used and so they would have more than one opportunity to gather information about the word and to guess what it was. Finally, we told them they would see all the clips for a given word in succession and that they should provide a response at the end of each clip. Participants were instructed to provide their current conjecture at the end of each video clip; therefore, they provided between three and six guesses for each target word. No mention was made of the fact that some words were nouns and others were verbs, but some participants did ask what kinds of words they should consider. We simply told them they were the kinds of words mothers use when speaking to their toddlers.

We presented these video clips to three groups ($n = 24$) of undergraduate participants. The Western participants were native English speakers who had lived in Canada all their lives and whose parents were also native-born Canadians. The Eastern participants were Japanese students enrolled in an exchange program at the University of British Columbia. They were native Japanese speakers who had lived in Japan until coming to Canada 6 to 8 months previously and whose parents were native-born Japanese. The second-generation participants spoke English but had not necessarily acquired it as their first language: 12 of them reported that English was their first language and 12 indicated that they acquired their parents' language as their first language.[1] The second-generation participants were native-born Canadians, but their parents were born in Asia; thus, they had had significant exposure to both Eastern and Western cultures.

In analyzing the results, we looked at two different measures: first, the lexical categories of participants' responses (i.e., nouns vs. verbs) and second, the accuracy of their guesses. Recall that participants provided up to six responses for each target word: For both measures, we considered the full set of responses provided by participants. As a result, a participant could include far more than 16 words among their responses and could be credited with up to six accurate guesses for a single target word.

Lexical Categories

We began by looking at the lexical categories of the responses and compared the numbers of nouns and verbs provided by participants in each group. These numbers are illustrated in figure 20.1. If Westerners do pay particular attention to objects and other noun-relevant information, then they should be more likely to guess that the target word is a noun than a verb. If Easterners pay attention to relational and other verb-relevant information, they should be likely to include relatively more verbs than nouns among their guesses. Finally, second-generation participants, who have had exposure to both Eastern and Western cultures, should be expected to fall somewhere between those two patterns.

We first conducted a linear trend analysis to test for the general pattern of findings that should result from these predictions. We used a contrast model based

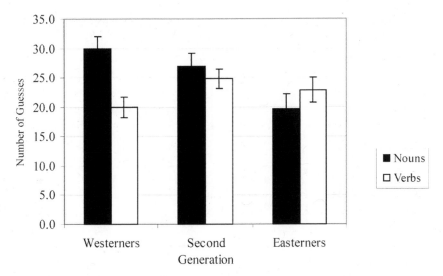

Figure 20.1. Mean numbers of nouns and verbs among participants' guesses.

on the expectation that the difference between the number of nouns and the number of verbs guessed would be greatest for Westerners, smaller for second-generation participants, and smallest for Easterners. This contrast was significant, $t(69) = 2.65$, $p = .005$, $\eta^2 = .092$, indicating that there were group differences among the numbers of nouns and verbs provided by participants and that these differences fell in the predicted direction.

We next tested the specific predictions for each group, comparing the numbers of noun versus verb guesses. As predicted, Westerners provided more noun guesses than verb guesses, $F(1, 69) = 8.37$, $p = .005$, $\eta^2 = .074$. This is consistent with the prediction that Westerners would be particularly attentive to noun-relevant information in the stimulus videos. Also as predicted, for the second-generation participants there were no significant differences between the numbers of noun and verb guesses, $F(1, 69) = .37$, $p = .545$, suggesting that they were equally attentive to both noun- and verb-relevant information. Easterners, like second-generation participants, provided similar numbers of noun and verb guesses, $F(1, 69) = .73$, $p = .394$. Apparently these participants were not particularly attentive to noun-relevant information, but neither were they disproportionately attentive to verb-relevant information.

The analyses based on the numbers of nouns and verbs among participants' responses indicate that participants from different cultural groups do pay attention to different aspects of the mother-toddler interactions depicted in the stimulus videos. The results further show that Westerners are attentive to those aspects of the scenes that are relevant to identifying nouns; second-generation and Eastern participants do not seem to direct any special attention to this noun-relevant

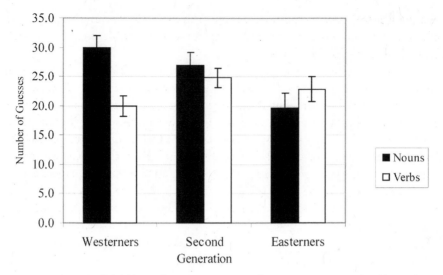

Figure 20.2. Mean numbers of accurate guesses for target nouns and verbs.

information. These group patterns should result in different levels of success with respect to correctly identifying the target words. We next looked at the accuracy of participants' responses to investigate this possibility.

Accuracy

We predicted that Westerners would be more accurate in identifying the target nouns and less so in identifying the target verbs, and that this noun advantage would be attenuated, if evident at all, among Easterners and second-generation participants.

To test this hypothesis, we tallied the numbers of accurate guesses for target nouns and verbs (see figure 20.2) made by each participant and submitted these data to a linear trend analysis to investigate the overall pattern of findings for all three groups. We used a contrast model based on the prediction that Westerners would correctly identify more nouns than verbs, and that this noun/verb difference would be smaller for second-generation participants and smallest for Easterners. This model was supported by a significant contrast, $t(69) = 2.21$, $p = .015$, $\eta^2 = .066$.

We next compared the accuracy of guesses for target nouns and verbs within each group. As predicted, Westerners did show a significant noun advantage: They were significantly more likely to be accurate on noun targets than on verb targets, $F(1, 69) = 32.17$, $p < .001$, $\eta^2 = .127$. This accuracy advantage for nouns was also significant for both the second-generation group, $F(1, 69) = 8.65$, $p = .004$, $\eta^2 = .034$, and the Eastern group, $F(1, 69) = 6.51$, $p = .013$, $\eta^2 = .026$; however, an inspection of effect sizes indicates that the noun advantage was substantially larger for Westerners than for either of the other two groups.

How can we integrate the results of the analyses based on the lexical categories of responses with those based on the accuracy of responses? Consider first the results for Westerners. These participants included many nouns and significantly fewer verbs among their responses, with the apparent result that they successfully identified more nouns than verbs. Now consider the second-generation and Eastern participants. These participants were less captured by the noun-relevant information, as evidenced by the fact that their guesses were more evenly distributed across the noun and verb categories. This more balanced pattern of guessing was associated with a more even distribution of *accurate* guesses: Compared to Westerners, second-generation and Eastern participants showed a significantly weaker noun advantage, as indexed by the accuracy of their guesses for noun and verb target words.

Perhaps, then, Westerners showed a stronger noun advantage in identifying target words because they were so attentive to noun-relevant information (and non-Westerners showed a weaker noun advantage because they were less captured by this information). To evaluate this possibility, we reexamined the accuracy scores, factoring out the effects derived from attending preferentially to noun- or verb-relevant information. Doing so allowed us to distinguish between two different factors that may produce a noun advantage in the simulated vocabulary learning task. One factor stems from the requirements of syntactic bootstrapping and should apply equally to all participants. Here we expect that the nonlinguistic information available in the simulated vocabulary learning task is more conducive to identifying nouns than verbs. In addition, we propose that a second factor, resulting from cultural differences, also plays a role in the identification of nouns and verbs. Unlike the first factor, this one should vary across participants. Here we expect that attending preferentially to noun-relevant information should result in a higher number of accurate guesses for nouns than for verbs. We argue that this second factor is responsible for the finding that Westerners showed a stronger noun advantage than did second-generation or Eastern participants. If we can compensate for the effect of this cultural factor, then the relatively stronger noun advantage among Westerners should disappear. All participants should still show some degree of noun advantage—as a result of the syntactic bootstrapping factor—but the advantage should be no stronger for Westerners than for the other two groups.

For each participant, we calculated proportion correct scores for both nouns and verbs: these scores are illustrated in figure 20.3. For nouns, these scores were calculated by dividing each participants' total number of noun target matches by their total number of noun guesses; similarly for verbs. The resulting numbers denote the proportion of responses from either lexical category that resulted in successful target matches. For example, a score of 1 (the highest possible score) would indicate that, for each noun (or verb) response the participant gave, a noun

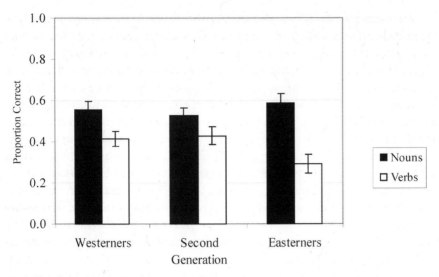

Figure 20.3. Proportion correct scores for target nouns and verbs.

(or verb) target match was successfully identified. A score closer to 0 (the lowest possible score) would indicate that few of the noun (or verb) responses resulted in target matches. Participants could achieve high or low scores regardless of how many nouns or verbs they included in their responses.

We then compared the proportion correct scores for nouns and verbs within each of the three cultural groups and found support for both factors. First, noun scores were still higher than verb scores; second, when we compensated for different attentional patterns, we found that the group differences largely disappeared. That is, proportion correct scores were higher for nouns than for verbs for all three groups (though the effect was marginal for second-generation participants), but the effect was no greater for Westerners, $F(1, 69) = 7.27$, $p = .009$, $\eta^2 = .034$, than for the other two groups: second-generation, $F(1, 69) = 3.46$, $p = .07$, $\eta^2 = .016$; Eastern, $F(1, 69) = 31.72$, $p < .001$, $\eta^2 = .146$. Though the group differences were attenuated in this analysis, there were still clear differences in accuracy on target nouns versus target verbs, indicating—as predicted by the syntactic bootstrapping hypothesis—that nouns are more easily identified than verbs in the simulated vocabulary learning task. That is, given that participants were attending appropriately to either noun- or verb-relevant information, if that nonlinguistic information were helpful then they should have a reasonably good chance of correctly identifying the target word. According to the requirements of syntactic bootstrapping, we would expect the noun-relevant information to be more helpful than any verb-relevant information. And that is, in fact, what we can conclude from the finding that noun proportion correct scores were higher than verb proportion correct scores.

We return now to our motivating question, how can we account for the gap between noun learning and verb learning in early lexical development? Consider first our account of the gap between noun identification and verb identification in the simulated vocabulary learning task. Participants from all three cultural groups were more successful in identifying target nouns than target verbs and we argue, following Gillette et al. (1999), that this is a result of the constraints imposed by the design of the task. In particular, the stimuli offer rich contextual information that provides good cues to identifying the referents of nouns but does not provide the linguistic information necessary for identifying the referents of verbs. We suggest, though, that this explanation does not account for the pattern of cross-cultural differences that we observed. Although the noun over verb advantage in the simulated vocabulary learning task was consistent across all three groups, this effect was particularly pronounced in the Western group. Based on η^2 calculations, the effect was four to five times larger for Westerners than for second-generation or Eastern participants. Westerners also appeared to be particularly attentive to noun-relevant information, as measured by the number of nouns and verbs among their responses. In the absence of any information about the kinds of words they should consider, Westerners assumed that nouns were likely candidates more frequently than they did so for verbs. When we factored out this discrepancy, the noun advantage was maintained but was no longer stronger for Westerners than it was for the non-Western groups. These findings suggest that, for Westerners, the noun advantage in the simulated vocabulary learning task can only be partially accounted for by syntactic bootstrapping. The fact that these participants were more attentive to aspects of the mother-toddler interactions that are labeled with nouns than to those that are labeled with verbs also contributed to the noun advantage Westerners showed in the simulated vocabulary learning task.

An important question to consider is whether the numbers of nouns and verbs among participants' responses really do provide an index of what they were attending to. For example, is it possible that Easterners and Westerners provided different types of responses, not because they attended to different aspects of the mother-toddler interactions, but because they speak languages that lexicalize those portions of the mother-toddler interactions differently? One could imagine scenarios for which two participants who speak different languages could attend to the same feature of a mother-toddler interaction but label it differently because their languages encode that feature differently. For example, both participants could attend to an event such as a child climbing onto a mother's lap. An English-speaking participant might label the manner portion of that action and guess that the target word for that scene was *climb*, while a Japanese speaking participant might label the path portion of the action and guess that the target word was *noboru* ("go up"). That is, speakers of different languages might come up with systematically different labels after attending to the same aspect of the same scene because their languages encode different features (i.e., path or manner) of the very same event. Notice, however, that in this example the differences stem from the fact that in some languages verbs tend to encode the path of an action while in others they tend to encode the manner. In either case, participants in the simulated vocabulary learning task would have guessed that the target word was a verb and we would have interpreted that (correctly in this example) as evidence that those participants were attending to verb-relevant information. The question is, could there be examples in which speakers of different languages come up with words from different lexical classes?

In theory, we think it unlikely that participants gave different types of responses because the same concept is lexicalized as a noun in English and a verb in Japanese (or any of the other languages spoken by non-Western participants). Though languages differ in the particular features of an action that they encode, all languages distinguish between nouns and verbs (e.g., Goldin-Meadow, Butcher, Mylander, & Dodge, 1994; Hawkins, 1988) and nouns and verbs lexicalize different types of concepts (Gentner, 1981). Thus, if two participants attend to the same aspect of a mother-toddler interaction, they should both have available to them—within the resources of their respective languages—a suitable noun or verb to label that portion of the interaction. It is, of course, possible to think of concepts that tend to be lexicalized as nouns in one language and as verbs in other languages. For example, a hungry English speaker might tell her office mate that she is "going out for sushi," using a noun (*sushi*) to describe what she is going out for. In contrast, a hungry Japanese speaker might tell her office mate that she is "going out for eating sushi" (*sushi o taberi ikimasu*), using a verb (*eating*) as well as a noun. These types of examples tend to be quite circumscribed, though: In most cases, concepts can be unambiguously lexicalized as either a noun or a verb. Certainly, the types of responses we were looking for and the types that we actually got fit into those unambiguous parameters.[2]

Ideally, we could conduct an empirical test of the question of whether language or attentional differences were responsible for the group differences observed in the simulated vocabulary learning task—perhaps by disentangling language and culture among our participants. For example, we could test Easterners and Westerners whose first language was English, or Westerners only whose first language was English or Japanese. Based on our proposal that attentional differences drove the group differences we observed in the simulated vocabulary learning task, we would expect to find group differences in the first case but not the second. In practice, we were only able to make a much weaker comparison within the second-generation group. Recall that half of the second-generation participants indicated that English was their first language while the other half told us they had acquired their parents' language as their first language. This is not an ideal comparison to make because even though they reported different first languages, most participants were bilingual. However, if language differences, rather than attentional differences, drove the observed effects then we might expect the English-first-language participants to respond more like Westerners and the remaining second-generation participants to respond more like Easterners. In fact, we found no such differences between these two subsets of second-generation participants.

If we can conclude, then, that Western participants were particularly attentive to noun-relevant information in the simulated vocabulary learning task, it may also be the case that Western children are particularly attentive to noun-relevant information in their own interactions with the world. If this is the case, then Western children should be expected to (and in fact do) acquire more nouns than verbs even after they have acquired the additional mechanisms required for learning verbs. In contrast, Eastern children should be expected to (and there is some evidence that they do) acquire similar numbers of nouns and verbs once they master the linguistic prerequisites for learning verbs.

In our attempts to illustrate how cultural differences may influence word learning, we have raised a number of questions. First, the data presented here support the plausibility of the proposal that cultural factors can influence the course of early noun and verb learning; however, we fully acknowledge the limitations of using data from an adult word identification task to address questions concerning word learning in young children. Further work is clearly required to determine whether the cultural differences observed among adults emerge soon enough to play a role in early lexical development. Gopnik and her colleagues (1996) have provided some evidence relevant to this question. They tested Western, English-learning toddlers and Eastern, Korean-learning toddlers on tasks that required children to make use of either their understanding of taxonomic categories (i.e., in an exhaustive sorting task) or their grasp of thematic relations between objects (i.e. to complete a means-ends task). The Western toddlers successfully solved the sorting task earlier than did the Eastern toddlers. This finding did not, however, reflect a general precocity among the Western toddlers; the Eastern toddlers solved the means-ends task earlier. Since taxonomic categories are labeled by nouns and thematic relations are captured by verbs, these findings suggest that—by 18 months—Western toddlers are better able to cope with noun-relevant information and Eastern toddlers with verb-relevant information. In support of this proposal, Gopnik and her colleagues also found that the Eastern toddlers acquired specific relational terms earlier than did Western toddlers, and that Western toddlers experienced a naming spurt earlier than did Eastern toddlers. It remains to be seen whether these early differences are related to the cultural differences observed among adults; however the Gopnik et al. (1996) studies provide a nice model for future work investigating the early emergence of cultural differences and their potential role in early word learning—without running into the methodological obstacles involved in looking for cross-linguistic differences in children's early vocabularies. In particular, their use of experimental tasks to address specific hypotheses about the course of early cognitive and linguistic differences among children acquiring different languages seems promising. The current work suggests that attention to different sources of information could play a role in early word learning; therefore, an experimental approach investigating attentional preferences in Eastern and Western toddlers could shed light on whether the current results are relevant to early word learning.

A second question raised by this work revolves around the source of the differences observed among the different groups of participants. The work reported here does not allow for precise considerations of just how a Westerner might come to attend preferentially to noun-relevant information or why an Easterner would not. One possibility is that the languages spoken by members of these cultures draw attention to different sources of information. Perhaps, as argued elsewhere (e.g., Choi & Gopnik, 1995; Gentner, 1982), nouns are more salient than verbs in English (e.g., because in a subject-verb-object language like English, noun frequently occur in the salient phrase-initial and phrase-final positions while verbs are buried in medial positions) and this might make the referents of nouns most salient to English speakers. On the other hand, nouns might be less salient in Japanese (e.g., because noun phrases are frequently elided) and so their referents might be less salient to Japanese speakers. On this account, we would again make the prediction discussed earlier that second-generation participants who acquired English as their first language should perform more like Westerners in the simulated vocabulary learning task, while those who acquired their parents' native language should perform more like Easterners. Given that there were no such differences, this leaves us with the possibility that other culturally linked factors are responsible for the group differences observed in the simulated vocabulary learning task. Further work is clearly required to investigate the nature of those factors.

A third question concerns the finding that, contrary to our predictions, Easterners did not show any reliable evidence of paying particular attention to verb-relevant information in the mother-toddler interactions presented in the simulated vocabulary learning task. In considering this point, it is important to point out that, because the mothers and toddlers in the stimulus videos were Western, these interactions were undoubtedly less familiar to Eastern than to Western or second-generation participants who would have had many more opportunities to observe Western mothers interacting with their toddlers. In follow-up work, we have found that when Eastern mother-toddler pairs are depicted, Eastern participants do show the predicted bias toward attending to verb-relevant information. These findings are in accordance with recent work by Snedeker, Li, and Yuan (2003) showing that adults in a similar task perform differently depending on whether stimuli are based on Eastern or Western mother-toddler interactions.

All considered, the evidence suggests that noun and verb acquisition differ as a function of at least three factors. First, nouns and verbs carry distinct learning requirements. Second, word learners themselves carry their own attentional biases that contribute to differences in noun versus verb learning. Third, the word learning context may vary across cultures in ways that carry different implications for noun versus verb learning. Together, these observations lead to the prediction that verb learning should be delayed relative to noun learning, but that the magnitude of this difference should vary as a function of cultural factors.

In considering the differences between learning nouns and learning verbs, we have taken seriously the notion that word learning is guided by a number of different interacting factors. We argue that cultural factors must contribute to this process, but do not deny the role of other critical sources of information, notably that verb learning requires access to linguistic knowledge that may not be available at the outset of word learning. We propose that cultural factors direct word learners' attention to particular types of information and that these attentional patterns hold important implications for the course of early noun and verb learning.

Acknowledgments This work was supported by an Operating Grant to D. Geoffrey Hall from the Natural Sciences and Engineering Research Council of Canada and by a Research Grant to Sandra R. Waxman from the National Institutes of Health.

Notes

1. The second-generation participants who reported that English was their first language may also have acquired their parents' native language, but they had acquired English from infancy (e.g., from English-educated parents) and felt more fluent in English than in any other language.

2. A small number of responses were actually ambiguous with respect to lexical category (e.g., *stick* could have been meant as a noun or a verb). These responses were not included in our analyses.

References

Au, T. K., Dapretto, M., & Song, Y. (1994). Input vs. constraints: Early word acquisition in Korean and English. *Journal of Memory and Language, 33,* 567–582.

Baldwin, D. A., Markman, E. M., Bill, B., Desjardins, R. N., Irwin, R. N., & Tidball, G. (1996). Infants' reliance on social criterion for establishing word-object relations. *Child Development, 67,* 3135–3153.

Bates, E., Marchman, V., Thal, D., Fenson, L., Dale, P., Reznick, J. S., et al. (1994). Developmental and stylistic variation in the composition of early vocabulary. *Journal of Child Language, 21,* 85–123.

Benedict, H. (1979). Early lexical development: comprehension and production. *Journal of Child Language, 6,* 183–200.

Bornstein, M. H., Cote, L. R., Maital, S., Painter, K., Park, S., Pascual, L., et al. (2004). Cross-linguistic analysis of vocabulary in young children: Spanish, Dutch, French, Hebrew, Italian, Korean, and American English. *Child Development, 75,* 1115–1139.

Choi, S., & Gopnik, A. (1995). Early acquisition of verbs in Korean: A cross-linguistic study. *Journal of Child Language, 22,* 497–529.

Choi, S., McDonough, L., Bowerman, M., & Mandler, J. M. (1999). Early sensitivity to language-specific spatial categories in English and Korean. *Cognitive Development, 14,* 241–268.

Clark, E. V. (1997). Conceptual perspective and lexical choice in acquisition. *Cognition, 64,* 1–37.

Fernald, A., & Morikawa, H. (1993). Common themes and cultural variations in Japanese and American mothers' speech to infants. *Child Development, 64,* 637–656.

Gentner, D. (1981). Some interesting differences between verbs and nouns. *Cognition and Brain Theory, 4,* 161–178.

Gentner, D. (1982). Why nouns are learned before verbs: Linguistic relativity versus natural partitioning. In S. Kuczaj (Ed.), *Language development: Language, cognition and culture* (pp. 301–334). Hillsdale, NJ: Erlbaum.

Gentner, D., & Boroditsky, L. (2001). Individuation, relativity, and early word learning. In M. Bowerman & S. C. Levinson (Eds.), *Language acquisition and conceptual development* (pp. 215–256). Cambridge: Cambridge University Press.

Gentner, D., & Boroditsky, L. (2004). *Nouns and verbs in early Navajo acquisition.* Paper presented at the International Conference on Infant Studies, Chicago.

Gillette, J., Gleitman, H., Gleitman, L., & Lederer, A. (1999). Human simulations of vocabulary learning. *Cognition, 73,* 135–176.

Gleitman, L. R. (1990). The structural sources of verb meaning. *Language Acquisition: A Journal of Developmental Linguistics, 1,* 3–55.

Gleitman, L. R., & Gleitman, H. (1992). A picture is worth a thousand words, but that's the problem: The role of syntax in vocabulary acquisition. *Current Directions in Psychological Science, 1,* 31–35.

Goldin-Meadow, S., Butcher, C., Mylander, C., & Dodge, M. (1994). Nouns and verbs in a self-styled gesture system: What's in a name? *Cognitive Psychology, 27,* 259–319.

Gopnik, A., & Choi, S. (1995). Names, relational words, and cognitive development in English and Korean speakers: Nouns are not always learned before verbs. In M. Tomasello & W. E. Merriman (Eds.), *Beyond names for things: Young children's acquisition of verbs* (pp. 63–80). Hillsdale, NJ: Erlbaum.

Gopnik, A., Choi. S., & Baumberger, T. (1996). Cross-linguistic differences in early semantic and cognitive development. *Cognitive Development, 11,* 197–227.

Hall, D. G., & Waxman, S. R. (Eds.). (2004). *Weaving a lexicon.* Cambridge, MA: MIT Press.

Hawkins, J. A. (1988). Explaining language universals. In J. A. Hawkins (Ed.), *Explaining language universals* (pp. 3–28). Oxford: Blackwell.

Hollich, G. J., Hirsh-Pasek, K., Golinkoff, R. M., Brand, R. J., Brown, E., Chung, H. L., et al. (2000). Breaking the language barrier: An emergentist coalition model for the origins of word learning. *Monographs of the Society for Research in Child Development, 65,* v–123.

Huttenlocher, J., & Smiley, P. (1987). Early word meanings: The case of object names. *Cognitive Psychology, 19,* 63–89.

Ji, L. J., Zhang, Z., & Nisbett, R. E. (2004). Is it culture, or is it language? Examination of language effects in cross-cultural research on categorization. *Journal of Personality and Social Psychology, 87,* 57–65.

Kim, M., McGregor, K. K., & Thompson, C. K. (2000). Early lexical development in English- and Korean-speaking children: Language-general and language-specific patterns. *Journal of Child Language, 27,* 225–254.

Landau, B., & Gleitman, L. R. (1985). *Language and experience: Evidence from the blind child.* Cambridge, MA: Harvard University Press.

Macnamara, J. (1972). Cognitive basis of language learning in infants. *Psychological Review, 79,* 1–13.

Markus, H. R., & Kitayama, S. (1991). Culture and the self: Implications for cognition, emotion, and motivation. *Psychological Review, 98,* 224–253.

Masuda, T., & Nisbett, R. E. (2001). Attending holistically versus analytically: Comparing the context sensitivity of Japanese and Americans. *Journal of Personality and Social Psychology, 81*, 922–934.

Naigles, L. (1990). Children use syntax to learn verb meanings. *Journal of Child Language, 17*, 357–374.

Naigles, L. (1996). The use of multiple frames in verb learning via syntactic bootstrapping. *Cognition, 58*, 221–251.

Naigles, L., & Hoff-Ginsberg, E. (1998). Why are some verbs learned before other verbs? Effects of input frequency and structure on children's early verb use. *Journal of Child Language, 25*, 95–120.

Nelson, K. (1973). Some evidence for the cognitive primacy of categorization and its functional basis. *Merrill-Palmer Quarterly, 19*, 21–39.

Nisbett, R. E., Peng, K., Choi, I., & Norenzayan, A. (2001). Culture and systems of thought: Holistic versus analytic cognition. *Psychological Review, 108*, 291–310.

Papafragou, A., Massey, C., & Gleitman, L. R. (2002). Shake, rattle, 'n' roll: The representation of motion in language and cognition. *Cognition, 84*, 189–219.

Pine, J. M., Lieven, E. V. M., & Rowland, C. (1996). Observational and checklist measures of vocabulary composition: What do they mean? *Journal of Child Language, 23*, 573–589.

Poulin-Dubois, D., & Forbes, J. N. (2002). Toddlers' attention to intentions-in-action in learning novel action words. *Developmental Psychology, 38*, 104–114.

Snedeker, J., Li, P., Yuan, S. (2003). Cross-cultural differences in the input to early word learning. In *Proceedings of the Twenty-fifth Annual Conference of the Cognitive Science Society*. Mahwah, NJ: Erlbaum.

Tardif, T. (1996). Nouns are not always learned before verbs: Evidence from Mandarin speakers' early vocabularies. *Developmental Psychology, 32*, 494–504.

Tardif, T., Gelman, S. A., & Xu, F. (1999). Putting the "noun bias" in context: A comparison of English and Mandarin. *Child Development, 70*, 620–635.

Tardif, T., Shatz, M., & Naigles, L. (1997). Caregiver speech and children's use of nouns versus verbs: A comparison of English, Italian, and Mandarin. *Journal of Child Language, 24*, 535–565.

Tomasello, M., & Barton, M. (1994). Learning words in nonostensive contexts. *Developmental Psychology, 30*, 639–650.

Tomasello, M., Kruger, A. C., & Ratner, H. H. (1993). Cultural learning. *Behavioral and Brain Sciences, 16*, 495–552.

Woodward, A. L., & Markman, E. M. (1998). Early word learning. In D. Kuhn & R. S. Siegler (Volume Eds.), W. Damon (Ed.), *Handbook of child psychology: Vol. 2. Cognition, perception, and language*. New York: John Wiley.

21   Why Verbs Are Hard to Learn

Dedre Gentner

Words do not all connect to the world in the same way. Some words basically point and refer to things in the world, while others organize the world into semantic systems and name according to the system. According to the natural partitions hypothesis, the noun class has the privilege of naming the highly cohesive bits of the world, whereas verbs and prepositions have the job of partitioning the leftovers—a diffuse set of largely relational components (Gentner, 1981, 1982; Gentner & Boroditsky, 2001). The contrast between concrete nouns and verbs is in part the contrast between local individuation and individuation as part of a semantic system. As Gentner (1982, p. 324) argued,

> There are in the experiential flow certain highly cohesive collections of percepts that are universally conceptualized as objects, and . . . these tend to be lexicalized as nouns across languages. Children learning language have already isolated these cohesive packages—the concrete objects and individuals—from their surroundings.

In other words, many concrete nouns refer to naturally individuated referents. In contrast, even fairly concrete verb meanings (such as those of motion verbs) make a selection from the available relational information, and just *which* information is selected varies across languages (Talmy, 1975, 1985). This brings us to Gentner's (1981, 1982) second theoretical claim made—namely, that verb meanings are more variable cross-linguistically than noun meanings:

> When we lexicalize the perceptual world, the assignment of relational terms is more variable crosslinguistically than that of nominal terms. . . . Predicates show a more variable mapping from concepts to words. . . . Thus, for verbs and other relational terms, children must discover how

their language combines and lexicalizes the elements of the perceptual field. (Gentner, 1982, pp. 323–325)

This claim—termed *relational relativity*—was inspired in large part by Talmy's (1975) seminal thesis research, which convincingly demonstrated that verb semantic structures vary substantially across languages. Talmy showed that languages differ in which semantic elements are incorporated into motion verbs: the path of the moving figure (as in Spanish), the manner of its motion (as in English), and/or the shape of the moving figure (as in Atsugewi). Since this time, further research has shown more examples of cross-linguistic variability in the semantics of relational terms: for example, Casad and Langacker (1985) on the semantics of spatial terms in Cora; Bowerman and Choi (2003; Choi & Bowerman, 1991) on verbs of support and containment in Korean versus English; Levinson (1996) and his colleagues on spatial terms in Mayan languages; and Slobin (1996) on motion verbs in English and Spanish.

Talmy did not himself claim that verbs are more variable in their semantics than nouns. But his findings for verbs offered a path toward understanding why children learn nouns before verbs. If verb meanings are linguistically shaped, then learning how verbs refer is embedded in language learning. In contrast, if at least some noun meanings are "given by the world," then these nouns can be learned before the infant has penetrated the semantic of her language. My hypothesis that names for concrete objects should be learnable very early was supported by two other lines of evidence. First was the finding by Spelke (1985, 1990) and Baillargeon (1987) that prelinguistic infants can form stable object concepts even during their first year of life, suggesting that objects can be individuated and parsed out from the perceptual flow purely on the basis of experience. The second line of support was Brent Berlin's anthropological work on biological categories, which suggested considerable cross-linguistic uniformity in naming, at least for some kinds of biological categories (Berlin, Breedlove, & Raven, 1973). Berlin and his colleagues asserted that generic categories (which Rosch, Mervis, Gray, Johnson, & Boynes-Braem, 1976, later called *basic level categories*) in biology tend to "carve nature at the joints" and that these categories are remarkably stable across cultures. Extrapolating from biological terms to other concrete nouns is of course a bit of a leap, but it suggests a generalization: that some noun referents are stable across cultures and languages.

Relational relativity combines the idea that verb meanings are cross-linguistically variable with the idea that some noun meanings are relatively stable across languages. It states that verb semantics varies more across languages than does noun semantics, at least for concrete nouns. Relational relativity is an outcome of a difference in word-to-world mapping transparency, which in turn stems from a deep difference in the way in which nouns and verbs connect to the world. For concrete nouns and proper nouns that name animate beings, the referents are naturally individuated out of the stream of perception. In contrast, there is no natural individuation for the referents of verbs. Verb meanings include only part of the available relational information, and just *which* information they include varies across languages (e.g., Bowerman & Choi, 2003; Casad & Langacker, 1985; Levinson, 1996; Slobin, 1996; Talmy, 1985). This theoretical framework implies that the mapping between word and referent is more transparent for concrete nouns than it is for verbs.

Acquisition

The assertion that concrete nouns have a more transparent mapping from language to the world than do verbs has important implications for acquisition: it implies that nouns will predominate over verbs in children's first vocabularies cross-linguistically:

> The natural partitions account has it that children learn concrete nouns early because, as object-reference terms, they have a particularly transparent semantic mapping to the perceptual-conceptual world. . . . Verbs and other predicate terms, however, have a less transparent relation to the perceptual world. (Gentner, 1982, p. 328)

The claim of the natural partitions hypothesis is that even a prelinguistic infant has already individuated many entities. Thus for many nouns, she or he has only to attach the noun to a referent that she or he has already isolated. This is not the case for relational terms such as verbs and prepositions; their referents are not simply "out there" in the experiential world, they are linguistically selected. To learn what a verb means, the child must discover which aspects of the situation enter into its meaning in her language (Gentner, 1982; Gentner & Boroditsky, 2001).

Of course, not all nouns are easily individuated. As Gentner (1982, p. 328) noted, these claims apply only to concrete nouns[1]—including proper nouns that name animate beings—and not to abstract and relational nouns (for further discussion of relational nouns, see Gentner, 2005; Gentner & Kurtz, 2005).

This view suggests that noun referential bindings are the natural starting point for language acquisition, and that these early-learned bindings may facilitate other aspects of language learning:

> Object-reference mappings may provide natural entry points into language—an initial set of fixed hooks with which children can bootstrap themselves into a position to learn the less transparent aspects of language. (Gentner, 1982, p. 329)

Noun-object bindings thus could provide a basis for working out the more variable aspects of language, including the binding of semantic relations to verb structures (see Fisher, 1996; Gleitman, 1990, for similar proposals).

The natural partitions/relational relativity (NP/RR) hypotheses makes two key predictions for acquisition: (1) there will be a universal early noun advantage in acquisition, and (2) possessing a stock of nouns will help children learn less transparent relational terms—notably verbs and prepositions. There is considerable support for the first prediction. Nouns predominate over verbs in early production and comprehension in English (Gentner, 1982; Goldin-Meadow, Seligman, & Gelman, 1976; Huttenlocher, 1974; Huttenlocher & Smiley, 1987; Macnamara, 1972; Nelson, 1973) and other languages (Au, Dapretto, & Song, 1994; Bornstein et al., 2004; Caselli et al., 1995; Gentner & Boroditsky, 2005; Kim, McGregor, & Thompson, 2000; Pae, 1993). Further, children appear to take novel words as names for objects (Landau, Smith, & Jones, 1998; Markman, 1989, 1990; Waxman, 1991; Waxman & Hall, 1993), even as early as 13 months of age (Waxman & Markow, 1995). Woodward and Markman's (1998) review of the evidence confirmed an early predominance of names for objects and individuals in early vocabulary and a later increase in the proportion of relational terms, consistent with the second prediction.

Further Predictions

Beyond these first two central predictions, four other predictions follow from the NP/RR hypothesis. Prediction 3 is that novel nouns should be learned more readily than novel verbs by young children. This prediction has been borne out in studies that controlled frequency and position in sentence (Schwartz & Leonard, 1980) as well as in studies that controlled phonology (Camarata & Leonard, 1986). A particularly relevant study was done by Childers and Tomasello (2002). They taught 2-year-olds new words—either nouns or verbs—or new actions to imitate. The children learned nouns far more rapidly than verbs, and actions more rapidly than either word class. This order belies the view that verbs should be learned early because children attend to dynamic events. An interest in dynamic events is not enough to learn verbs; the child must learn what to attend to. Another interesting finding was that the children learned better when presentation was distributed over several days than when an equal number of exposures was given on the same day. Childers and Tomasello (2002) note that this advantage of distributed over massed presentation has been found across a wide variety of learning studies, suggesting the operation of a general learning process.

Prediction 4 is that within the noun class, words for highly individuable entities, such as concrete objects and animate beings, will be learned especially early. I return to this prediction later. Prediction 5 is that even after verbs enter the vocabulary, children may take some time to fully learn their meanings. Indeed, Melissa Bowerman (1982) has found that children make semantic errors on verbs and other relational terms even quite late in language learning: for example, "I come it closer so it won't fall" (at 2 years, 9 months, while bringing the bowl closer to herself); "Want me to come it out?" (at 3 years, 9 months, referring to the broken end of a marker); "Don't dead him" (at 4 years, 10 months, as mother picks up a spider). Such errors suggest that children are still in the process of learning the semantic systems for verbs in their language.

Prediction 6 of the NP/RR hypothesis is that once the system of verb seman-tics has been mastered, it will influence the way in which new verbs are learned. That is, speakers of a given language should learn new verbs according to the se-mantic system in that language. Nagy and Gentner (1990) tested this claim by giving adults passages containing novel nouns or verb embedded in passages con-taining many rich contextual details that could have entered into the word's meaning. Later in the passage, the word was used again in a more neutral passage. After reading the passage, participants were given questions designed to reveal what they thought the words meant. The results showed that people were highly selective: they retained those features from the first context that were appropriate to whichever form class they had received.

Prediction 7 is that there should also be a noun advantage in second-language learning; this follows from the assumption that the lag in verb acquisition stems from lack of knowledge, not maturational factors. This prediction has been borne out in studies of second-language learning in English and other languages (Diet-rich, 1985; Källkvist, 1999). Further, second-language learners verbs make more errors for verbs than for nouns (Källkvist, 1999; Lennon, 1996).

Input-Level Explanations

Summarizing so far, the natural partitions (NP) hypothesis states that the map-ping between word and referent is highly transparent for some concrete nouns—those whose referents are readily individuated. The relational relativity claim implies further that there is no such preindividuated class of verbs. Their joint prediction, that nouns should predominate over verbs in children's first vocabu-laries across languages, has received considerable support in English and other languages.

However, before drawing the conclusion that the early noun advantage is a acquisitional universal, it is necessary to rule out the possibility that the noun ad-vantage results solely from specific characteristics of the input language. Gentner (1982) considered this possibility and presented cross-linguistic data that tested specific input factors, including word order, relative morphological transparency, and patterns of language teaching. Table 21.1 shows the "verb-friendliness" score for each of the six languages considered, along with the proportion of nouns in the early vocabulary. She concluded that, while linguistic input factors do influ-ence the degree of the noun advantage, they do not outweigh the semantic-conceptual advantage of nouns mapping to objects. However, the cross-linguistic vocabulary data in Gentner (1982) were admittedly rather spotty. They were mostly collected on the side by researchers whose main purpose was to collect other cross-linguistic data.

Fortunately, other researchers took up the issue, inspired (or infuriated) by this claim of a universal noun advantage in acquisition. These investigations focused on languages whose input properties seemed to favor verbs and which therefore

Table 21.1 Combined estimate of verb-friendly input factors

Language	Word Order	Verb-Final	Relative Morphological Complexity	Object-Reference Not Taught	Verb-Friendly Score	Proper Verbs
English	SVO		X		1	.17
German	SOV (some)	X		X	2	.14
Japanese	SOV	XX			2	.19
Mandarin	SVO		XX		2	.27
Turkish	SOV	XX		X	3	.21
Kaluli	SOV OSV	XX		XX	4	.26

X, Favors verbs.
The entries represent rough estimates of the degree of support for verb learning offered by the factor in question in the particular language verb.

Data from Gentner (1982).

seemed likely to show a verb advantage. On the basis of these studies, some researchers argued against the NP claim of a universal noun advantage. For example, Gopnik and Choi (1995) investigated early language use in Korean, which is verb-final and allows pro-drop, making the verb highly salient in speech to children (see also Choi & Gopnik, 1995). Based on the results of a questionnaire for parents concerning the language used by their young children, they concluded that the noun advantage does not appear in Korean.

Tardif (1996) investigated acquisition in Mandarin. Gentner (1982) had suggested that Mandarin might be more verb-friendly than English. This speculation was based on the fact that in Mandarin comes the closest of any language to having equal morphological complexity for verbs and nouns. In languages that use affixes and other morphological devices, the complexity and variability of the morphological system is greater for verbs than for nouns. For example, a child learning the verb *jump* will hear the forms *jump, jumps, jumped,* and *jumping,* whereas a child learning a noun such as *dog* will hear only *dog* and *dogs.* Thus, the difficulty in learning verb meanings in English could stem from having to trace the same verb root across different surface morphological forms. However, Mandarin has no morphology on *either* nouns or verbs, resulting in a level playing field, morphologically speaking. Gentner reasoned that if differential morphological complexity contributes to the noun advantage, then the noun advantage should be attenuated in Mandarin. This was not the case for the two Mandarin children included in Gentner's (1982) study. For both children, nominals (including proper nouns) were the dominant class (.65 and .59 mean proportions). This led Gentner to conclude that differences in morphological complexity could not by itself account for the noun advantage (see table 21.1).

Tardif (1996) found a very different result; she reported that Mandarin children at 2 years, 8 months had as many or more verbs as nouns. However, her later studies, using checklists,[2] have shown an early noun advantage in Mandarin (Tardif, 2002; Tardif, Gelman, & Xu, 1999). Other recent evidence also favors the claim of a universal noun advantage (Bornstein et al., 2004; Caselli et al., 1995). This evidence has shown early noun dominance even in verb-friendly languages such as Korean (Au et al., 1994; Kim et al., 2002; Pae, 1993) and Mandarin (Gelman & Tardif, 1998; Tardif et al., 1999; but see Tardif, Shatz, & Naigles, 1997).

In Korean, a comprehensive study was done by Pae (1993). She used a checklist adapted for Korean (as well as observational methods) to assess the vocabularies of 90 children of monolingual families living in Seoul between the ages of 12 and 23 months. She found a strong noun advantage throughout. At 51–100 words, the children's productive vocabularies contained 50–60% nouns and about 5% verbs. Indeed, as shown in figure 21.1, Pae found that the proportions of nouns and verbs in the productive vocabularies of Korean children were comparable to those found in English (though see Kim et al., 2000).

Imai et al.'s findings (chapter 17, this volume) that Mandarin-speaking children learn new nouns much more readily than new verbs—and even more strikingly, that Mandarin-speaking children learn new verbs less readily than Japanese- and English-speaking children—further undermine the suggestion of rapid verb learning in Mandarin. We discuss these findings further below.

Recent Findings Exploring Different Typologies

Our recent studies have explored a new typological arena, that of the richly morphologized American Indian languages. Our checklist studies have shown a noun advantage for both Navajo (Gentner & Boroditsky, 2001; 2005) and Tzeltal (Brown, Gentner, & Braun, 2005). The findings for Tzeltal are particularly interesting, as there is reason to believe that verb acquisition might be particularly rapid in Tzeltal (Brown, 1998; see de Leon, 1999, for similar claims concerning Tzotzil, a close neighbor). Tzeltal has rich morphology on both nouns and verbs, although (as is generally true), verbs take more inflections than nouns. It is a verb-object-subject language, and thus places the verb in the first position, a more salient position than in the English subject-verb-object order. Further, it allows noun-dropping, so that the child often hears a verb as the first or only element of a sentence. Further, many Tzeltal verbs—including those learned by children—are what Brown (1998) called *heavy verbs*—semantically specific verbs with rich, contextually specific meanings, incorporating many object properties. There are many different verbs for eating, carrying, and so on, depending on the shape, substance, position or orientation of the objects acted on. For example, instead of a general verb *to eat* as in English, Tzeltal has several different eat-verbs for eating different kinds of things: *we'*, eat tortilla or bread; *k'ux*, eat crunchy things; *lo'*, eat soft

Noun Proportion: Korean and English

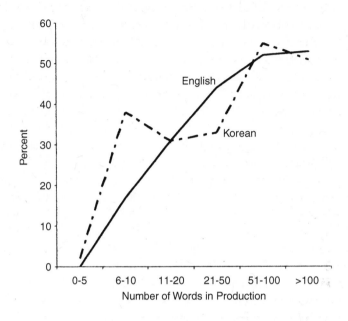

Verb Proportion: Korean and English

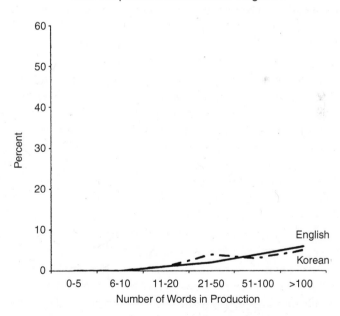

Figure 21.1. Proportions of nouns and verbs in early acquisition in Korean and English productive vocabularies (adapted from Pae, 1993).

things like bananas; and *ti*, eat meat, or bite. Because these verbs incorporate properties of their objects, acquiring their meaning does not require the same degree of abstraction from the situation as with more general verbs, such as English *eat*. Brown (1998) thus suggested that children could find them easier to acquire than English verbs, which require a greater degree of decontextualization. Consistent with this conjecture, de Leon (1999) reported rapid acquisition of verbs in a Tzotzil child, based on analyzing recorded transcripts.

To test this, we constructed a checklist for Tzeltal (see Brown et al., 2005). On the principle that it is better for a checklist to include too many words than too few, we began with an extremely broad list that included words from an English checklist (the MCDI for English toddlers; Fenson et al., 1993), a Korean checklist (Au et al., 1994), and a Navajo checklist (Gentner & Boroditsky, 2005). This extended list (in English gloss) was translated into Tzeltal by P. Brown. Brown also augmented and filtered the list, adding words that might possibly be heard by a Tzeltal child, and removing words that had no Tzeltal equivalent. This initial Tzeltal checklist was then read to women in the village, who were asked to say for each word whether a young child might know the word (either to say or to understand). The women also provided any other words that they thought a child might know instead of, or in addition to, the words on the initial list. This included child versions of words (the equivalent of "doggy" and "kitty cat").

We next administered the preliminary checklist to the grandmother of a Tzeltal child, eliciting comments such as "She doesn't say X, but she does say Y and Z." We added all such words Y and Z to the list (usually also retaining word X). Our goal was to create a maximally inclusive list. We tried to give the children every opportunity to display understanding of verbs; to this end we included more than one inflected form of the same verb when our informants considered both forms likely to be said by young children. This way a child who knew the verb in (for example) only the first-person form would not be mistakenly scored as not knowing the verb (as might occur if the verbs were only tested in one standard form). (Of course, it must be noted that this technique could result in overestimating the number of verbs children know, because different forms of the same verb are counted as separate verbs.)

The completed list contained 594 words—283 nouns, 207 verbs, and 104 other words. When we administered this list to five Tzeltal caretakers of young children, the results showed a uniform noun advantage across all the children. This can be seen in both the noun-verb ratio ($M = 1.34{:}1$, range $1.17{:}1–1.63{:}1$) and the proportion of nouns over the total productive vocabulary ($M = .57$, range .54–.62). All five children were reported to produce more nouns than verbs ($M = 174.6$, range 67–225 for nouns; $M = 132.6$, range 47–190 for verbs).

Words for animate beings (including relatives' names) are prominent in the early vocabularies, comprising about one third of children's nouns ($M = .30$, range .28–.33). This is consistent with Gentner and Boroditsky's (2002) claim that highly individuable entities will be lexicalized early (discussed further below).

Although the results show a clear noun advantage, they also reveal a comparatively large number of verbs; most studies have reported 10 or fewer verbs at the 50-word vocabulary level.[3] Assuming that our counts do not greatly overestimate the number of verbs acquired (as discussed above), these findings suggest that verb learning progresses relatively rapidly in Tzeltal. In this connection, it is reassuring that the noun-verb proportions are roughly consistent with those in Brown's (1998, table 1) report of a diary study of the vocabulary of a girl, Xan.[4] At 2 years 1 month years of age, she had 52 words: 20 verbs and 31 nouns (including proper nouns). This rapid verb learning may stem in part from the favorable word order. It is also consistent with Brown's (1998) conjecture that heavy verbs—with contextually rich semantics such as object incorporation—might be easier to acquire than semantically sparse (or more abstract) verbs. In summary, our findings suggest that Tzeltal children do indeed acquire verbs more rapidly than English children. However, even in this highly verb-friendly language, there is still a clear noun advantage. These findings strengthen the case for a universal early noun bias, and for individuability as a key factor in early word learning.

Studies of Teaching New Words

As Imai and colleagues point out (chapter 17, this volume), many of the methods used in assessing children's existing vocabularies have some difficulties (see also Gentner & Boroditsky, 2001; Pine, Lieven, & Rowland, 1996). Even if the obvious problems with using a few hours of transcript are avoided by adopting a checklist or journal method, it can be difficult to set up clear, objective criteria for classifying a given produced word into its appropriate form; and the fact that the child uses a given word in one context does not guarantee that she understands the full meaning of the word. This brings us to the second prediction of the NP hypothesis, namely, that early in learning, children should learn new nouns more readily than new verbs.

Childers and Tomasello (2002) investigated this question for English by teaching 2-year-olds either six novel nouns, six novel verbs, or six novel actions over a 2-week period. Children produced the nouns well before they produced the verbs (although comprehension was rapidly achieved for all three kinds of materials). Further, as noted above, (1) children learned the novel actions better than they learned either of the two word types, and (2) children learned both types of words better when exposures were distributed over four days than when they were massed in one day—a pattern typical of general learning processes.

The key question, of course, is whether this noun-dominance pattern in word learning will show up in languages whose input patterns are arguably more verb-friendly, such as Mandarin. Imai, Haryu, and Okada (2005) investigated this by showing a dynamic video scene of a person carrying out a novel action with a novel object and labeling it with either a novel noun or a novel verb. Then the children were asked to generalize the new word to a new scene, which either showed the same object in a new action (which would be correct for the noun, but not for the verb) or the same action with a new object (which had the reverse pattern). Japanese-speaking children correctly generalized the novel nouns by the age of 3 years. Verbs were more difficult. Japanese-speaking children correctly generalized verbs only at 5 years of age. Among Mandarin-speaking children, verbs were not correctly extended until 8 years of age (Imai et al., chapter 17, this volume). Chinese children, even as old as 3–5 years, tended to map the verb to the object rather than the action. It is striking that Mandarin-speaking children had more difficulty in mapping a novel verb to its meaning than did Japanese- or English-speaking children. Imai et al.'s results bear out the NP prediction of a universal noun advantage, even for a language that (at least on grounds of differential morphological complexity) could be classified as verb-friendly.[5]

Why Are Verbs Harder Than Nouns?

My conclusion from the above discussion is that there is a semantic-conceptual basis for the early noun bias (though other factors in the input also influence the degree of bias). It is now time to delve more deeply into the nature and causes of this advantage. At least four possible semantic-conceptual explanations have been proposed for why verbs lag behind nouns in early acquisition: (1) maturational limitations, (2) difficulty in detecting the conceptual components of verbs, (3) difficulty in learning which semantic components enter into verbs and how they combine, and (4) order of information. I consider each of these in turn.

Maturation

Perhaps some level of a maturationally linked cognitive capacity is required to learn verbs. Such a view would be consistent with Halford, Wilson, and Phillips's (1998) position that the ability to carry out relational processing is limited by maturational increases in processing capacity. Two lines of evidence argue against this view. First, as discussed above, second-language learners show the same pattern of rapid learning of nouns together with slow and errorful learning of verbs and prepositions (Dietrich, 1985; Källkvist, 1999; Lennon, 1996).

Second, research by Gillette, Gleitman, Gleitman, and Lederer (1999) demonstrates that maturation cannot be the whole explanation, for even adults show a noun advantage in mapping from language to the world. They showed adults silent videos of mothers talking to young children, with beeps marking the instances of a particular noun or verb, and asked them to guess the word uttered at the beeps. The participants identified about three times as many nouns as verbs. The fact that observational mapping was far more effective for nouns than for verbs, even for adults, shows that the noun advantage cannot be due to a maturational limitation that impedes the learning of verbs.

These findings are especially striking because unlike children acquiring language, the adults in these studies already knew the semantics of their verbs. Also, unlike children, they were told the form class—noun or verb—of the word they were seeking. These findings bear out the NP claim that there is greater difficulty in individuating verb referents than in individuating noun referents. Further, they demonstrate that maturational change is unlikely to be the explanation for the noun advantage.

Knowledge of Conceptual Components

Another possible reason that verbs might be slow in acquisition is that young children might lack knowledge of the conceptual and semantic components that enter into verbs. If children lack an understanding of the basic components of verb meanings, this could account for their slowness in learning verbs. This kind of explanation surely has a role to play; for example, a verb like *confiscate* or *divorce* can hardly be grasped without some understanding of the complex social relations they presuppose. And to take a more realistic example, Gentner (1975) investigated children's acquisition of verbs of possession and found that while semantically simple verbs *give* and *take* were enacted correctly by 3-year-olds, the verbs *buy* and *sell* were not correctly enacted until about 8 years of age. These verbs require some understanding of monetary transactions.

However, this kind of conceptual gap cannot explain the fact that children's understanding of motion verbs also lags behind their understanding of nouns (including many nouns that occur with considerable lower frequency). By a year of age, infants show considerable insight into simple events involving change of location or physical causation, yet motion verbs and causal verbs still lag behind nouns in their vocabulary acquisition. This underlines the point that there is more to verb learning than simply understanding conceptual relations in the world. As Gentner (1982, p. 326) put it:

> It is important to note that the Natural Partitions hypothesis does not assume that relations themselves are perceived later than objects . . . even those sparse relations that act as predicates over objects are, I suspect, *perceived* quite early. Movement, change, directionality, and so on, seem quite interesting to infants. . . . It is not perceiving relations but packaging and lexicalizing them that is difficult.

In other words, the problem is *mapping*: figuring out which constellations of the semantic components a given verb refers to (Gentner, 1982). Recent evidence bears out the supposition that understanding of the individual semantic components of motion verbs is present well before the knowledge of how to assemble those components into verbs. Event cognition appears to be highly developed even in infants (e.g., Baillargeon & Wang, 2002; Golinkoff & Kerr, 1978; Gordon, 2004).

Even some early insight into intentions and goals has been demonstrated (Baldwin et al., 1996; Tomasello & Barton, 1994; Woodward, 1999).

Hirsh-Pasek and Golinkoff and their students (Pruden, Hirsh-Pasek, Maguire, & Meyer, 2004) carried out studies that directly address whether and when infants can learn the semantic components that enter into motion verbs. They showed 7- to 9-, 10- to 12-, and 13- to 15-month-old infants a series of dynamic events that all had the same actor ("Starry," an animated character) and the same path, but had four different manners. Both groups of infants were able to align these events and abstract the common path. When subsequently given two test events in which Starry moved in a new manner, in a preferential looking task, the infants could differentiate a new path from the old (invariant) path by 10–12 months. By 13–15 months, the infants could also extract an invariant manner across four different paths.

Adding words to the preferential looking task appears to increase the likelihood that 7- to 9-month-olds will extract the invariant path across the four exemplars with varying manner. The repeated word may invite aligning and abstracting the path across the set of exemplars, consistent with Gentner and Namy's "words as invitations to compare" and with Brown's (1958) "words as invitations to form categories." Interestingly, even at this early stage there may be an influence of the language children are learning, at least among children with higher maternal reported vocabularies. In a set of studies that asked children to discriminate between manner and path changes in events with Starry as the protagonist, English-reared children more readily detected manner changes (Pulverman, Sootsman, Golinkoff, & Hirsh-Pasek, 2001, 2003; Maguire, Hirsh-Pasek, Golinkoff, & Imai, 2005). Thus it appears that infants can extract some of the separate manner and path components that enter into motion verbs.

However, a different story emerged when the semantic components were combined into words, as in a real verb-learning situation. Infants and toddlers were presented with scenes of several women, all performing the same action. When given this task nonverbally, 9- to 12-month-olds subsequently differentiated a new action from the familiar action (both performed by a new woman; Salkind, Sootsman, Golinkoff, Hirsh-Pasek, & Maguire, 2002). Yet, when the action was described by a novel verb, and the children were asked, "Where's she blicking? Find blicking," they failed to find the woman who was blicking. In fact, even 3-year-olds failed at this task (Maguire et al., 2001). When a set of relational components occurred across different actors, the presence of words no longer improved performance; instead, the reverse occurred. These results point up the gap between detecting particular facets of dynamic events and learning how to combine them into verb meanings.

This is a very instructive set of studies. It underscores the gap is between the ability to extract particular components of a verb's meaning in a focused task and the ability to select the right set of semantic components from the vast amount of potential relational information in the world. It also dramatizes an important methodological point. As Gentner and Namy (2004) point out, habituation and familiarization studies in which a series of highly alignable exemplars are presented represent an ideal learning situation. The ability to align the exemplars across such a series and abstract the common element does not entitle the researcher to conclude that the infant possesses that category. To draw such a conclusion, it must be shown that the infant can use the category in other situations. This kind of sequence of perfectly alignable exemplars should be seen as a boundary condition: it represents an existence proof that under ideal learning conditions the infant can derive the abstraction.

Golinkoff and Hirsh-Pasek's findings suggest that the ability to extract individual semantic components does not by itself solve the problem of verb learning. Childers and Tomasello's (2002) findings also argue against the idea that children's lag in learning verbs stems simply from a lack of knowledge of the semantic components. As discussed above, they found that when 2-year-olds were taught new nouns, new verbs, or new actions to imitate, they learned the action-imitation very quickly but learned the verbs slowly. Finally, Bauer and Dow (1994) have found that infants from 16 months to can remember and reproduce sequences of actions quite accurately after a delay. These findings suggest that children's difficulty with verbs does not stem solely from lack of understanding of events. They can readily grasp, retain, and correctly enact many events. Rather, what children lack is an understanding of how verbs map onto events and relations in the world.

Information Order

The "nouns before verbs" pattern in acquisition may be one instance of a very general pattern of order of learning. Learners of a new domain commonly show a *relational shift*: They focus on object properties before they are able to focus on relations—Gentner (1988; Gentner & Rattermann, 1991; Rattermann & Gentner, 1998). For example, 3-year-olds asked to choose the solution to an analogy task tend to choose an (incorrect) object match instead of the correct relational match. Gentner and Rattermann (1991) reviewed evidence that this shift is based on gains in knowledge, not simply on maturation; it occurs at different ages across different domains.

Early in their understanding of a given domain, children tend to focus on object matches, such as the match between a round red ball and a round red apple. With increasing knowledge, children come to make relational similarity matches (e.g., a ball rolling on a counter and a toy car rolling on the floor). For example, Gentner and Rattermann (1991) gave children a relational mapping task in which the object matches conflicted with the best relational match. The relation was a simple perceptual relation—same relative size and position. Even though children were shown the correct answer on each trial, 3-year-olds were at chance on this task; they had a strong tendency to make the (incorrect) object matches instead of the (correct) relational match. By 5 years of age, children succeeded at the relational mapping.

A relational shift was found at a later age in a more challenging causal picture mapping task. Gentner and Flusberg (2005) showed children two pictures—(1) a cat chasing a mouse and (2) a dog chasing a cat. The experimenter pointed to the cat in picture (1) and asked what it best matched in picture (2). Children aged 5–7 years strongly preferred the object match (cat to cat). When the experimenter emphasized the relation in the instructions (e.g., "Do you see this one that's chasing? What does it go with?"), the 7-year-olds, but not the 5-year-olds, chose the relational match (cat to dog).

These general learning patterns predict exactly the pattern found in children's word learning: earlier learning of object nouns than of relational terms such as verbs. Noun-object bindings can be learned locally, whereas learning a relation requires attending to the objects bound by the relation as well. A further parallel is that once a store of initial object matches are learned, they can facilitate the learning of verbs; a relation can more easily be inferred if its objects are clear.

Nouns and Names

Learning object nouns is relatively easy for children, but as noted above, it paves the way for learning less transparent relational words. But what exactly characterizes the easy object mappings? According to NP, it is ease of individuation that distinguishes the early easy mappings from word to world. This means that nouns with clearly individuable referents, such as concrete nouns and proper names of animate beings, are the privileged set. Recently, Gleitman and her colleagues have proposed an account of early word learning similar to the NP hypothesis, but differing in its characterization of the privileged, early-learned class of nouns (Gleitman, Cassidy, Nappa, Papafragou, & Trueswell, 2005; Kako, 2005). They suggest that the privileged referent class is basic level concrete categories, rather than highly individuable entities and categories as in the NP hypothesis.

These two positions overlap considerably. The members of concrete basic level categories are typically easily individuated. Also, basic-level category terms are highly likely to be used with children (Rosch et al., 1976). Thus basic level concrete object nouns should be acquired early on either account. However, one salient difference is that the NP hypothesis (but not the basic level categories hypothesis) extends to proper names for animate beings (see Kako, 2005). Animate beings are maximally individuable. Accordingly, the NP hypothesis predicts that in addition to basic-level terms like *dog*, proper names like *Mommy*, *Rover*, and *Auntie* should be highly frequent in early vocabularies.[6] Proper names for animate beings should be charter members of the privileged, easy-to-acquire class.[7]

What is the evidence on this point? Are names (including proper names) for animate beings learned especially early, as predicted by the NP hypothesis? Caselli et al. (1995) used the MacArthur checklist to assess the early vocabularies of 659

English-speaking and 195 Italian-speaking infants. Proper names for animate beings constituted two of the first five words produced on average in English (*Daddy* and *Mommy*) and three of the first five in Italian (*Mamma*, *Papa*, and *Nonna* [grandmother]). A fourth word, *bau-bau* (for dogs), also refers to animate beings. For the six children of six different languages whose early vocabularies are given in Gentner's (1982, table 5) corpus, names for animate beings (including both proper and common nouns) accounted for 33–100% of the first nominals.

There is some evidence that the proportion of animate nouns to total nouns drops as vocabulary size increases, as would be expected if animate beings are particularly easy to individuate. For example, a Kaluli girl at 1 year 8 months (with 16 recorded words) had as her first eight nominals seven names for people and one animal term. Thus, names for animate beings constituted 100% of her early nominals, with person names dominating. For Xiao-Jing, a Mandarin girl aged 1 year, 6 months with 37 recorded words, names for animate entities constituted 50% of the early nominals and 30% of her total vocabulary, and most of these were person names. An English girl (age 1 year, 2 months, vocabulary 39) and a German boy (age 1 year, 8 months, vocabulary 33) had 36% animates. But these children contrast with the Kaluli and Mandarin child: For these children, with their smaller extended families, animal names were as prominent as person names. The makeup of the early animates may differ cross-culturally. Children whose cultures emphasize extended sets of relatives, like the Kaluli and Mandarin child just discussed, tend to have large numbers of person names (proper names and kin terms); children who grow up in smaller families may learn a higher proportion of animal names. However, overall, proper names appear quite common in early vocabularies, consistent with the individuability account.

In sum, I have argued that words connect to the world in very different ways, that (concrete) nouns do so more transparently than verbs, and that verb meanings are more linguistically shaped than (concrete) noun meanings. Although many factors at all levels contribute to determining what is learned early by children, these semantic-conceptual factors are certainly among the core influences on how words connect to the world.

Notes

1. However, for brevity, I will use the term *noun* to refer to concrete nouns (and to proper nouns that refer to animate beings). I will use terms such as *abstract noun* and *relational noun* for other kinds of nouns.

2. Tardif (1996) initially reported that Mandarin at 2 years, 8 months had as many or more verbs than nouns. However, her vocabulary assessment was based on a transcription of the words spoken in 1 hour; vocabulary size was estimated at under 80 for children of this age, an improbably low estimate. In an extremely interesting study, Tardif, Gelman, and Xu (1999) showed that estimates from observational transcripts of both absolute and relative numbers of nouns and verbs are highly variable with

context, casting doubt on their value as vocabulary assessments. Further, using a check-list, they showed that Mandarin children aged 2 years, 2 months have twice as many nouns as verbs. The checklist also revealed a much higher (and more plausible) vocabulary count (over 300 words) than had been found using her earlier observational method. Thus it appeared that Mandarin children when tested with a checklist show a noun preponderance. Recently Tardif (2002) has reported corroborating findings: early Mandarin vocabularies show noun dominance, although subsequent verb learning is more rapid than in English.

3. For example, in Pae's (1993) detailed study of Korean acquisition, the results showed a mean of 2 verbs (and 17 nouns) at 21–50 words and a mean of 4 verbs (and 49 nouns) at 51–100 words, comparable to English.

4. Xan's vocabulary was assessed with a combination of transcripts and parental lists.

5. Of course, these results also call into question whether Mandarin is indeed a verb-friendly language. Gentner's (1982) original suggestion that Mandarin might be verb friendly was based on the fact that Mandarin has equal morphological complexity in nouns and verbs (i.e., none). But Imai et al.'s data call for a rethinking of this issue. Imai et al. suggest that the lack of *any* morphology on nouns and verbs in Mandarin may in fact make it more difficult for children to form separate syntactic classes of nouns and verbs. Of course, both ideas could be correct; it may be that (1) equal morphological complexity benefits verbs, but (2) having a morphological distinction between nouns and verbs also aids in verb learning. Unfortunately, to my knowledge there is no test language in which the number of inflections that can appear on nouns and verbs is equal but nonzero.

6. One implication of this point is that inclusion of proper names is essential in tests of the NP hypothesis. Many such studies have failed to include proper nouns (e.g., Tardif, 1996).

7. Comrie (1981, p. 179) notes that some languages treat proper names as being "higher in animacy" than common noun phrases: for example, "William Shakespeare" versus "the author of Hamlet."

References

Au, T. K., Dapretto, M., & Song, Y. K. (1994). Input vs. constraints: Early word acquisition in Korean and English. *Journal of Memory and Language, 33*(5), 567–582.

Baillargeon, R. (1987). Object permanence in 3.5- and 4.5-month-old infants. *Developmental Psychology, 23*, 655–664.

Baillargeon, R., & Wang, S. H. (2002). Event categorization in infancy. *Trends in Cognitive Sciences, 6*(2), 85–93.

Baldwin, D. A., Markman, E., Bill, B., Desjardins, R. N., Irwin, J. M., & Tidball, G. (1996). Infants' reliance on a social criterion for establishing word-object relations. *Child Development, 67*(6), 3135–3153.

Bauer, P. J., & Dow, G. A. (1994). Episodic memory in 16- and 20-month-old children: Specifics are generalized but not forgotten. *Developmental Psychology, 30*, 403–417.

Berlin, B., Breedlove, D. E., & Raven, P. H. (1973). General principles of classification and nomenclature in folk biology. *American Anthropologist, 75*, 214–242.

Bornstein, M. H., Cote, L. R., Maital, S., Painter, K., Park, S.-Y., Pascual, L., et al. (2004). Cross-linguistic analysis of vocabulary in young children: Spanish, Dutch, French, Hebrew, Italian, Korean, and American English. *Child Development, 75*(4), 1115–1139.

Bowerman, M. (1982). Reorganizational processes in lexical and syntactic development. In E. Wanner & L. R. Gleitman (Eds.), *Language acquisition: The state of the art* (pp. 319–346). New York: Cambridge University Press.

Bowerman, M., & Choi, S. (2003). Space under construction: Language-specific spatial categorization in first language acquisition. In D. Gentner & S. Goldin-Meadow (Eds.), *Language in mind: Advances in the study of language and cognition* (pp. 387–428). Cambridge, MA: MIT Press.

Brown, P. (1998). Children's first verbs in Tzeltal: Evidence for an early verb category. *Linguistics, 36*(4), 713–753.

Brown, P., Gentner, D., & Braun, K. (2005). *Early acquisition of nouns and verbs in Tzeltal.* Paper presented at the Tenth International Conference for the Study of Child Language, Berlin.

Brown, R. (1958). How shall a thing be called? *Psychological Review, 65*(1), 14–21.

Camarata, S., & Leonard, L. B. (1986). Young children pronounce object words more accurately than action words. *Journal of Child Language, 13*, 51–65.

Casad, E. H., & Langacker, R. W. (1985). "Inside" and "outside" in Cora grammar. *International Journal of American Linguistics, 51*, 247–281.

Caselli, M. C., Bates, E., Casadio, P., Fenson, J., Fenson, L., Sanderl, L., et al. (1995). A cross-linguistic study of early lexical development. *Cognitive Development, 10*, 159–199.

Childers, J. B., & Tomasello, M. (2002). Two-year-olds learn novel nouns, verbs, and conventional actions from massed or distributed exposures. *Developmental Psychology 38* (6), 967–978.

Choi, S., & Bowerman, M. (1991). Learning to express motion events in English and Korean: The influence of language-specific lexicalization patterns. *Cognition, 41*, 83–121.

Choi, S., & Gopnik, A. (1995). Early acquisition of verbs in Korean: A cross-linguistic study. *Journal of Child Language, 22*(3), 497–529.

Comrie, B. (1981). *Language universals and linguistic typology: Syntax and morphology.* Basil Blackwell: Oxford.

de Leon, L. (1999). *Why Tzotzil children prefer verbs over nouns.* Paper presented at the Fourth International Conference for the Study of Child Language. San Sebastian, Donostia, Spain.

Dietrich, R. (1985). *Nouns and verbs in the learner's lexicon.* Paper presented at the Workshop on European Second Language Acquisition Research, Linguistic Institute, Georgetown University.

Fenson, L. Dale, P., Reznick, Bates, E., Thal, D., Hartung, J., et al. (1993). *MacArthur Communicative Development Inventories: User's guide and technical manual.* San Diego, CA: Singular Publishing.

Fisher, C. (1996). Structural limits on verb mapping: The role of analogy in children's interpretations of sentences. *Cognitive Psychology, 31*, 41–81.

Gelman, S. A., & Tardif, T. (1998). Acquisition of nouns and verbs in Mandarin and English. In E. Clark (Ed.), *Proceedings of the 29th Annual Stanford Child Language Research Forum.* Stanford: CSLI.

Gentner, D. (1975). Evidence for the psychological reality of semantic components: The verbs of possession. In D. A. Norman, D. E. Rumelhart, & The LNR Research Group (Eds.), *Explorations in cognition* (pp. 211–246). San Francisco: Freeman.

Gentner, D. (1981). Some interesting differences between nouns and verbs. *Cognition and Brain Theory, 4*, 161–178.

Gentner, D. (1982). Why nouns are learned before verbs: Linguistic relativity versus natural partitioning. In S. A. Kuczaj (Ed.), *Language development: Vol. 2. Language, thought, and culture* (pp. 301–334). Hillsdale, NJ: Erlbaum.

Gentner, D. (1988). Metaphor as structure mapping: The relational shift. *Child Development, 59*, 47–59.

Gentner, D. (2003). Why we're so smart. In D. Gentner & S. Goldin-Meadow (Eds.), *Language in mind: Advances in the study of language and cognition* (pp. 195–236). Cambridge, MA: MIT Press.

Gentner, D. (2005). The development of relational category knowledge. In L. Gershkoff-Stowe & D. H. Rakison (Eds.), *Building object categories in developmental time* (pp. 245–275). Hillsdale, NJ: Erlbaum.

Gentner, D., & Boroditsky, L. (2001). Individuation, relativity and early word learning. In M. Bowerman & S. Levinson (Eds.), *Language acquisition and conceptual development* (pp. 215–256). Cambridge University Press.

Gentner, D., & Boroditsky, L. (2005, April). *Nouns and verbs in early Navajo acquisition.* Paper presented at the meeting of the Society for Research in Child Development, Atlanta, GA.

Gentner, D., & Flusberg, S. (2005). *The role of relational language in the development of analogical reasoning.* Manuscript in preparation

Gentner, D., & Kurtz, K. J. (2005). Relational categories. In W. K. Ahn, R. L. Goldstone, B.C. Love, A. B. Markman, & P. W. Wolff (Eds.), *Categorization inside and outside the laboratory: Essays in honor of Douglas L. Medin* (pp.151–175). Washington, DC: American Psychological Association.

Gentner, D., & Namy, L. (2004). The role of comparison in children's early word learning. In D. G. Hall & S. R. Waxman (Eds.), *Weaving a lexicon* (pp. 597–639). Cambridge, MA: MIT Press.

Gentner, D., & Rattermann, M. J. (1991). Language and the career of similarity. In S. A. Gelman & J. P. Brynes (Eds.), *Perspectives on thought and language: Interrelations in development* (pp. 225–277). London: Cambridge University Press.

Gillette, J., Gleitman, H., Gleitman, L., & Lederer, A. (1999). Human simulations of vocabulary learning. *Cognition, 73*(2), 135–176.

Gleitman, L. (1990). The structural sources of verb meanings. *Language Acquisition, 1*(1), 3–55.

Gleitman, L. R., Cassidy, K., Nappa, R., Papafragou, A., & Trueswell, J. C. (2005). Hard words. *Language Learning and Development, 1*(1), 23–64.

Goldin-Meadow, S., Seligman, M. E. P., & Gelman, R. (1976). Language in the two-year old. *Cognition, 4*, 189–202.

Golinkoff, R. M., & Kerr, J. L. (1978). Infants' perception of semantically defined action role changes in filmed events. *Merrill-Palmer Quarterly, 24*(1), 53–61.

Gopnik, A., & Choi, S. (1995). Names, relational words, and cognitive development in English and Korean speakers: Nouns are not always learned before verbs. In M. Tomasello & W. E. Merriman (Eds.), *Beyond names for things: Young children's acquisition of verbs* (pp. 63–80). Hillsdale, NJ: Erlbaum.

Gordon, P. (2004). The origins of argument structure in infant event representations. *Proceedings of the Annual Boston University Conference on Language Development, 28*, 189–198.

Halford, G. S., Wilson, W. H., & Phillips, S. (1998). Processing capacity defined by relational complexity: Implications for comparative, developmental, and cognitive psychology. *Behavioral and Brain Sciences, 21*, 803–864.

Huttenlocher, J. (1974). The origins of language comprehension. In R. L. Solso (Ed.), *Theories of cognitive psychology: The Loyola Symposium.* New York: Halsted Press, Winston-Wiley.

Huttenlocher, J., & Smiley, P. (1987). Early word meanings: The case of object names. *Cognitive Psychology, 19,* 63–89.

Imai, M., Haryu, E., & Okada, H. (2005). Mapping novel nouns and verbs onto dynamic action events: Are verb meanings easier to learn that noun meanings for Japanese children? *Child Development, 76,* 340–355.

Kako, E. T. (2005). Information sources for noun learning. *Cognitive Science, 29,* 223–260.

Källkvist, M. (1999). *Form-class and task-type effects in learner English: A study of advanced Swedish learners.* Lund, Sweden: Lund University Press.

Kim, M., McGregor, K. K., & Thompson, C. K. (2000). Early lexical development in English- and Korean-speaking children: Language-general and language-specific patterns. *Journal of Child Language, 27,* 225–254.

Landau, B., Smith, L., & Jones, S. (1998). Object shape, object function, and object name. *Journal of Memory & Language, 38,* 1–27.

Lennon, P. (1996). Getting "easy" verbs wrong at the advanced level. *International Review of Applied Linguistics in Language Teaching, 34,* 23–36.

Levinson, S. C. (1996). Relativity in spatial conception and description. In J. J. Gumperz & S. C. Levinson (Eds.), *Rethinking linguistic relativity* (pp. 177–202). Cambridge: Cambridge University Press.

Macnamara, J. (1972). Cognitive basis of language learning in infants. *Psychological Review, 79,* 1–13.

Maguire, M., Hennon, E., Hirsh-Pasek, K., Golinkoff, R. M., Slutzky, C., & Sootsman, J. (2001, November). *Mapping words to actions and events: How do 18-month-olds learn a verb?* Paper presented at Boston Child Language conference.

Maguire, M. J., Hirsh-Pasek, K., Golinkoff, R. M., & Imai, M. (2005). *What makes verb learning so difficult? Another perspective.* Paper presented at the meeting of the Society for Research in Child Development, Atlanta, GA.

Markman, E. M. (1989). *Categorization and naming in children: Problems of induction.* Cambridge, MA: MIT Press.

Markman, E. M. (1990). Constraints children place on word meanings. *Cognitive Science, 14,* 57–77.

Nagy, W., & Gentner, D. (1990). Semantic constraints on lexical categories. *Language and Cognitive Processes, 5,* 169–201.

Nelson, K. (1973). Structure and strategy in learning to talk. *Monographs of the Society for Research in Child Development, 38,* 1–136.

Pae, S. (1993). *Early vocabulary in Korean: Are nouns easier to learn than verbs?* Unpublished doctoral dissertation, University of Kansas, Lawrence.

Pine, J. M., Lieven, E. V. M., & Rowland, C. (1996). Observational and checklist measures of vocabulary composition: What do they mean? *Journal of Child Language, 23,* 573–590.

Pruden, S. M., Hirsh-Pasek, K., Maguire, M. J., & Meyer, M. A. (2004). Foundations of verb learning: Infants categorize path and manner in motion events. *Proceedings of the 28th Annual Boston University Conference on Language Development.*

Pulverman, R., Sootsman, J., Golinkoff, R. M., & Hirsh-Pasek, K. (2001). Infants nonlinguistic processing of motion events: One-year-old English speakers interested in manner. *Proceedings of the Stanford Language Conference.*

Pulverman, R., Sootsman, J. L., Golinkoff, R. M., & Hirsh-Pasek, K. (2003). The role of lexical knowledge in nonlinguistic event processing: English-speaking infants' attention to manner and path. *Proceedings of the 27th Annual Boston University Conference on Language Development*, 662–673.

Rattermann, M. J., & Gentner, D. (1998). More evidence for a relational shift in the development of analogy: Children's performance on a causal-mapping task. *Cognitive Development, 13*, 453–478.

Rosch, E., Mervis, C. B., Gray, W. D., Johnson, D. M., & Boyes-Braem, P. (1976). Basic objects in natural categories. *Cognitive Psychology, 8*, 382–439.

Salkind, S., Sootsman, J. L., Golinkoff, R. M., Hirsh-Pasek, K., & Maguire, M. J. (2002, April). *Lights, camera, action!: Infants and toddlers create action categories*. Paper presented at the International Conference on Infant Studies.

Schwartz, R. G., & Leonard, L. B. (1980). Words, objects, and actions in early lexical acquisition. *Child Language Development, 19*, 29–36.

Slobin, D. I. (1996). Two ways to travel: Verbs of motion in English and Spanish. In M. Shibatani & S. Thompson (Eds.), *Grammatical constructions: Their form and meaning* (pp. 195–220). Oxford: Clarendon Press.

Spelke, E. S. (1985). Perception of unity, persistence, and identity: Thoughts on infants' conception of objects. In R. Fox & J. Mehler (Eds.), *Neonate cognition: Beyond the booming, buzzing confusion* (pp. 89–114). Hillsdale, NJ: Erlbaum.

Spelke, E. S. (1990). Principles of object perception. *Cognitive Science, 14*, 29–56.

Talmy, L. (1975). Semantics and syntax of motion. In J. P. Kimball (Ed.), *Syntax and semantics* (Vol. 4, pp. 181–238). New York: Academic Press.

Talmy, L. (1985). Lexicalization patterns: Semantic structure in lexical forms. In T. Shopen (Ed.), *Language typology and syntactic description* (pp. 57–149). Boston: Cambridge University Press.

Tardif, T. (1996). Nouns are not always learned before verbs: Evidence from Mandarin speakers' early vocabularies. *Developmental Psychology, 32*(3), 492–504.

Tardif, T. (2002, April). *But are they really verbs*. Paper presented at the meeting of the Society for Child Development, Atlanta, GA.

Tardif, T., Gelman, S. A., & Xu, F. (1999). Putting the "noun bias" in context: A comparison of English and Mandarin. *Child Development, 70*(3), 620–635.

Tardif, T., Shatz, M., & Naigles, L. (1997). Caregiver speech and children's use of nouns versus verbs: A comparison of English, Italian, and Mandarin. *Journal of Child Language, 24*, 535–565.

Tomasello, M., & Barton, M. E. (1994). Learning words in nonostensive contexts. *Developmental Psychology, 30*(5), 639–650, p. 10

Waxman, S. R. (1991). Convergences between semantic and conceptual organization in the preschool years. In S. A. Gelman & J. P. Byrnes (Eds.), *Perspectives on language and thought: Interrelations in development* (pp. 107–145). Cambridge: Cambridge University Press.

Waxman, S. R., & Hall, D. G. (1993). The development of a linkage between count nouns and object categories: Evidence from fifteen- to twenty-month-old infants. *Child Development, 64*, 1224–1241.

Waxman, S. R., & Markow, D. B. (1995). Words as invitations to form categories: Evidence from 12- to 13-month-old infants. *Cognitive Psychology, 29*, 257–302.

Woodward, A. L. (1999). Infants' ability to distinguish between purposeful and nonpurposeful behaviors. *Infant Behavior & Development, 22*, 145–160.

Woodward, A. L., & Markman, E. M. (1998). Early word learning. In W. Damon (Series Ed.), D. Kuhn, & R. S. Siegler (Vol. Eds.), *Handbook of child psychology: Vol. 2. Cognition, perception and language* (5th ed., pp. 371–420). New York: Wiley.

Author Index

Subject Index